Honda
XL600/650V Transalp & XRV750 Africa Twin
Service and Repair Manual

by Matthew Coombs

(3919 - 336)

Models covered
XL600V Transalp. 583cc. 1987 to 1999
XL650V Transalp. 647cc. 2000 to 2002
XRV750 Africa Twin. 742cc. 1990 to 2002

© Haynes Publishing 2002

A book in the **Haynes Service and Repair Manual Series**

ISBN 1 85960 919 8

British Library Cataloguing in Publication Data
A catalogue record for this book is available from the British Library

ABCDE
FGHIJ
KLMNO
PQR

Printed in the USA

Haynes Publishing
Sparkford, Yeovil, Somerset, BA22 7JJ, England

Haynes North America, Inc
861 Lawrence Drive, Newbury Park, California 91320, USA

Editions Haynes S.A.
4, Rue de l'Abreuvoir, 92415 COURBEVOIE CEDEX, France

Haynes Publishing Nordiska AB
Box 1504, 751 45 UPPSALA, Sweden

Contents

Contents

REPAIRS AND OVERHAUL

Engine, transmission and associated systems

Chassis components

Electrical system

Wiring diagrams

REFERENCE

Index

The Birth of a Dream

by Julian Ryder

There is no better example of the Japanese post-war industrial miracle than Honda. Like other companies which have become household names, it started with one man's vision. In this case the man was the 40-year old Soichiro Honda who had sold his piston-ring manufacturing business to Toyota in 1945 and was happily spending the proceeds on prolonged parties for his friends.

However, the difficulties of getting around in the chaos of post-war Japan irked Honda, so when he came across a job lot of generator engines he realised that here was a way of getting people mobile again at low cost.

A 12 by 18-foot shack in Hamamatsu became his first bike factory, fitting the generator motors into pushbikes. Before long he'd used up all 500 generator motors and

started manufacturing his own engine, known as the 'chimney', either because of the elongated cylinder head or the smoky exhaust or perhaps both. The chimney made all of half a horsepower from its 50 cc engine but it was a major success and became the Honda A-type.

Less than two years after he'd set up in Hamamatsu, Soichiro Honda founded the Honda Motor Company in September 1948. By then, the A-type had been developed into the 90 cc B-type engine, which Mr Honda decided deserved its own chassis not a bicycle frame. Honda was about to become Japan's first post-war manufacturer of complete motorcycles. In August 1949 the first prototype was ready. With an output of three horsepower, the 98 cc D-type was still a simple two-stroke but it had a two-speed transmission and most importantly a pressed steel frame with telescopic forks and hard tail rear end. The frame was almost triangular in profile with the top rail going in a straight line from the massively braced steering head to the rear axle. Legend has it that after the D-type's first tests the entire workforce went for a drink to celebrate and try and think of a name for the bike. One man broke one of those silences you get when people are thinking, exclaiming 'This is like a dream!' 'That's it!' shouted Honda, and so the Honda Dream was christened.

'This is like a dream!' 'That's it' shouted Honda

Mr Honda was a brilliant, intuitive engineer and designer but he did not bother himself with the marketing side of his business. With hindsight, it is possible to see that employing Takeo Fujisawa who would both sort out the home market and plan the eventual expansion into overseas markets was a masterstroke. He arrived in October 1949 and in 1950 was made Sales Director. Another vital new name was Kiyoshi Kawashima, who along with Honda himself, designed the company's first four-stroke after Kawashima had told them that the four-stroke opposition to Honda's two-strokes sounded nicer and therefore sold better. The result of that statement was the overhead-valve 148 cc E-type which first ran in July 1951 just two months after the first drawings were made. Kawashima was made a director of the Honda Company at 34 years old.

The E-type was a massive success, over 32,000 were made in 1953 alone, a feat of mass-production that was astounding by the

Honda C70 and C90 OHV-engined models

standards of the day given the relative complexity of the machine. But Honda's lifelong pursuit of technical innovation sometimes distracted him from commercial reality. Fujisawa pointed out that they were in danger of ignoring their core business, the motorised bicycles that still formed Japan's main means of transport. In May 1952 the F-type Cub appeared, another two-stroke despite the top men's reservations. You could buy a complete machine or just the motor to attach to your own bicycle. The result was certainly distinctive, a white fuel tank with a circular profile went just below and behind the saddle on the left of the bike, and the motor with its horizontal cylinder and bright red cover just below the rear axle on the same side of the bike. This was the machine that turned Honda into the biggest bike maker in Japan with 70% of the market for bolt-on bicycle motors, the F-type was also the first Honda to be exported. Next came the machine that would turn Honda into the biggest motorcycle manufacturer in the world.

The C100 Super Cub was a typically audacious piece of Honda engineering and marketing. For the first time, but not the last, Honda invented a completely new type of motorcycle, although the term 'scooterette' was coined to describe the new bike which had many of the characteristics of a scooter but the large wheels, and therefore stability, of a motorcycle. The first one was sold in August 1958, fifteen years later over nine-million of them were on the roads of the world. If ever a machine can be said to have brought mobility to the masses it is the Super Cub. If you add

The CB250N Super Dream became a favorite with UK learner riders of the late seventies and early eighties

in the electric starter that was added for the C102 model of 1961, the design of the Super Cub has remained substantially unchanged ever since, testament to how right Honda got it first time. The Super Cub made Honda the world's biggest manufacturer after just two years of production.

Honda's export drive started in earnest in 1957 when Britain and Holland got their first bikes, America got just two bikes the next year. By 1962 Honda had half the American market with 65,000 sales. But Soichiro Honda had already travelled abroad to Europe and the USA, making a special

The GL1000 introduced in 1975, was the first in Honda's line of GoldWings

Carl Fogarty in action at the Suzuka 8 Hour on the RC45

An early CB750 Four

point of going to the Isle of Man TT, then the most important race in the GP calendar. He realised that no matter how advanced his products were, only racing success would convince overseas markets for whom 'Made in Japan' still meant cheap and nasty. It took five years from Soichiro Honda's first visit to the Island before his bikes were ready for the TT. In 1959 the factory entered five riders in the 125 class. They did not have a massive impact on the event being benevolently regarded as a curiosity, but sixth, seventh and eighth were good enough for the team prize. The bikes were off the pace but they were well engineered and very reliable.

The TT was the only time the West saw the Hondas in '59, but they came back for more the following year with the first of a generation of bikes which shaped the future of motorcycling – the double-overhead-cam four-cylinder 250. It was fast and reliable – it revved to 14,000 rpm – but didn't handle anywhere near as well as the opposition. However, Honda had now signed up non-Japanese riders to lead their challenge. The first win didn't come until 1962 (Aussie Tom Phillis in the Spanish 125 GP) and was followed up with a world-shaking performance at the TT. Twenty-one year old Mike Hailwood won both 125 and 250 cc TTs and Hondas filled the top five positions in both races. Soichiro Honda's master plan was starting to come to fruition, Hailwood and Honda won the 1961 250 cc World Championship. Next year Honda won three titles. The other Japanese factories fought back and inspired Honda to produce some of the most fascinating racers ever seen: the awesome six-cylinder 250, the five-cylinder 125, and the 500 four with which the immortal Hailwood battled Agostini and the MV Agusta.

When Honda pulled out of racing in '67 they had won sixteen rider's titles, eighteen manufacturer's titles, and 137 GPs, including 18 TTs, and introduced the concept of the modern works team to motorcycle racing. Sales success followed racing victory as Soichiro Honda had predicted, but only because the products advanced as rapidly as the racing machinery. The Hondas that came to Britain in the early '60s were incredibly sophisticated. They had overhead cams where the British bikes had pushrods, they had electric starters when the Brits relied on the kickstart, they had 12V electrics when even the biggest British bike used a 6V system. There seemed no end to the technical wizardry. It wasn't that the technology itself was so amazing but just like that first E-type, it was the fact that Honda could mass-produce it more reliably than the lower-tech competition that was so astonishing.

When in 1968 the first four-cylinder CB750 road bike arrived the world of motorcycling changed for ever, they even had to invent a new word for it, 'Superbike'. Honda raced again with the CB750 at Daytona and won the

World Endurance title with a prototype DOHC version that became the CB900 roadster. There was the six-cylinder CBX, the CX500T – the world's first turbocharged production bike, they invented the full-dress tourer with the GoldWing, and came back to GPs with the revolutionary oval-pistoned NR500 four-stroke, a much-misunderstood bike that was more a rolling experimental laboratory than a racer. Just to show their versatility Honda also came up with the weird CX500 shaft-drive V-twin, a rugged workhorse that powered a new industry, the courier companies that oiled the wheels of commerce in London and other big cities.

It was true, though, that Mr Honda was not keen on two-strokes – early motocross engines had to be explained away to him as lawnmower motors! However, in 1982 Honda raced the NS500, an agile three-cylinder lightweight against the big four-cylinder opposition in 500 GPs. The bike won in its first year and in '83 took the world title for Freddie Spencer. In four-stroke racing the V4 layout took over from the straight four, dominating TT, F1 and Endurance championships with the RVF750, the nearest thing ever built to a Formula 1 car on wheels. And when Superbike arrived Honda were ready with the RC30. On the roads the VFR V4 became an instant classic while the CBR600 invented another new class of bike on its way to becoming a best-seller. The V4 road bikes had problems to start with but the VFR750 sold world-wide over its lifetime while the VFR400 became a massive commercial success and cult bike in Japan. The original RC30 won the first two World Superbike Championships is 1988 and '89, but Honda had to wait until 1997 to win it again with the RC45, the last of the V4 roadsters. In Grands Prix, the NSR500 V4 two-stroke superseded the NS triple and became the benchmark racing machine of the '90s. Mick Doohan secured his place in history by winning five World Championships in consecutive years on it.

In yet another example of Honda inventing a new class of motorcycle, they came up with the astounding CBR900RR FireBlade, a bike with the punch of a 1000 cc motor in a package the size and weight of a 750. It became a cult bike as well as a best seller, and with judicious redesigns continues to give much more recent designs a run for their money.

When it became apparent that the high-tech V4 motor of the RC45 was too expensive to produce, Honda looked to a V-twin engine to power its flagship for the first time. Typically, the VTR1000 FireStorm was a much more rideable machine than its opposition and once accepted by the market formed the basis of the next generation of Superbike racer, the VTR-SP-1.

One of Mr Honda's mottos was that technology would solve the customers' problems, and no company has embraced cutting-edge technology more firmly than Honda. In fact Honda often developed new technology, especially in the fields of materials science and metallurgy. The embodiment of that was the NR750, a bike that was misunderstood nearly as much as the original NR500 racer. This limited-edition technological tour-de-force embodied many of Soichiro Honda's ideals. It used the latest techniques and materials in every component, from the oval piston, 32-valve V4 motor to the titanium coating on the windscreen, it was – as Mr Honda would have wanted – the best it could possibly be. A fitting memorial to the man who has shaped the motorcycle industry and motorcyles as we know them today.

The CX500 – Honda's first V-Twin and a favorite choice of dispatch riders

Honda Transalp & Africa Twin

When Honda announce that they have invented a new type of motorcycle, the world tends to think of the initials CB, VFR and NR. Imagine, then, the confusion the world's press felt on being confronted with the Transalp and being told that it was a 'Rally Tourer'. This was 1987 and the Paris-Dakar rally had already spawned knobbly-

The VFR400R was a cult bike in Japan and a popular grey import in the UK

The 1998 XL600V-W Transalp

tyred race-replicas like the Yamaha Ténéré, the bike that sold over 10,000 units in six months on Continental Europe.

But Honda, being Honda, didn't serve up a replica of their mighty NXR750 works desert racer, in fact the only thing the NXR and the Transalp XL600V had in common was the V-twin configuration of their engines. Just like the first VFR750, the first Transalp was decidedly understated, plain even. This was, of course, an attempt to get away from the already burgeoning obsession with sportsters

in several important markets by re-inventing the all-round motorcycle in a non-boring fashion.

To this end, they bored and stroked the VT500's motor and fitted it in a steel duplex-cradle frame with good quality suspension at both ends. The forks had an off-road friendly eight inches of movement and the rear shock over seven, but the rider got the sort of comprehensive instrumentation you only saw on a top-end road bike plus the sort of powerful brakes that are more of a

hindrance than help on dirt surfaces. The Transalp could be taken off road but no-one in their right mind would buy one for trail riding, however the plush suspension and comfortable power delivery worked perfectly on the sort of pot-holed, gravel strewn minor roads that characterise much of the rural parts of countries like France and Italy. Not that the Transalp was a slouch on good tarmac, Honda were confident enough to launch it alongside the new CBRs at the Suzuka Circuit where it was surefooted enough round the twisty bits to hang on to the fours without any dramas.

Contemporary tests show that the bike impressed and confused in equal measure but the Transalp while not fashionable did do what it was meant to and consequently sold steadily over the years. It's a measure of just how right it was that it has changed so little through its life.

For the first ten years of its life the XL600V Transalp didn't alter noticeably apart from the rear brake graduating from a drum to a disc in 1991. In 1997 production moved from Japan to Honda's Italian plant and you can recognise that year's V-V model by the twin front Brembo calipers replacing the Japanese Nissin units. That was just the prequel to the Transalp's only major modifications. The year 2000 XL650V-Y got a 650 cc motor in a totally new-look motor-cycle. The suspension and wheels stayed the same but bodywork, instrumentation, electrical systems and lights were all changed to bring the styling up to date. European concerns were also addressed with the fitting of Honda's HISS immobiliser and PAIR emission control system.

We had to wait until 1990 to find out why Honda had so underplayed the Paris-Dakar heritage of the Transalp, for that was when the Africa Twin was unleashed. This was a real race replica with stratospheric seat height, suspension with what seemed like endless travel, a giant fuel tank, twin trip meters and an aluminium chassis. Here was something that looked and rode like the bikes that thrashed across the Sahara every January. The motor was a bored and stroked version of the Transalp's V-twin. Note that there was an earlier version of the Africa Twin, the 1989 XRV650, although this was not imported into the UK.

Everyone agreed, here was a fantastic motorcycle, the suspension and brakes came in for special praise, one that you could ride all day two-up in comfort on anything from autobahns to dirt tracks. In typical Honda fashion the build quality was superb but there was just one problem: price. In markets like the UK the Africa Twin cost more than a CBR600 and it didn't matter how good the bike was, the punters wouldn't pay that much for a twin. It's their loss, the Africa Twin is a great motorcycle and has become a cult bike in countries like France and Germany where the Paris-Dakar Rally is a highlight of the sporting calendar.

The 1998 XRV750-W Africa Twin

Acknowledgements

Our thanks are due to Bransons Motorcycles of Yeovil and GT Motorcycles of Yeovil who supplied the machines featured in the illustrations throughout this manual. We would also like to thank NGK Spark Plugs (UK) Ltd for supplying the colour spark plug condition photo-graphs, the Avon Rubber Company for supplying information on tyre fitting and Draper Tools Ltd for some of the workshop tools shown.

Thanks are also due to Julian Ryder who wrote the introduction 'The Birth of a Dream' and to Honda (UK) Ltd who supplied model photographs.

About this Manual

The aim of this manual is to help you get the best value from your motorcycle. It can do so in several ways. It can help you decide what work must be done, even if you choose to have it done by a dealer; it provides information and procedures for routine maintenance and servicing; and it offers diagnostic and repair procedures to follow when trouble occurs.

We hope you use the manual to tackle the work yourself. For many simpler jobs, doing it yourself may be quicker than arranging an appointment to get the motorcycle into a dealer and making the trips to leave it and pick it up. More importantly, a lot of money can be saved by avoiding the expense the shop must pass on to you to cover its labour and overhead costs. An added benefit is the sense of satisfaction and accomplishment that you feel after doing the job yourself.

References to the left or right side of the motorcycle assume you are sitting on the seat, facing forward.

We take great pride in the accuracy of information given in this manual, but motorcycle manufacturers make alterations and design changes during the production run of a particular motorcycle of which they do not inform us. No liability can be accepted by the authors or publishers for loss, damage or injury caused by any errors in, or omissions from, the information given.

Model development

XL600V-H and V-J Transalp (1987 and 1988 model years)

The first Transalp was the XL600V-H introduced in 1987.

The Transalp has a 52° V-twin cylinder engine with chain drive to its single overhead camshafts which operate the two inlet and one exhaust valve per cylinder. The clutch is a conventional wet multi-plate unit and the gearbox is 5-speed. Drive from the gearbox output shaft is transmitted to the rear wheel by chain and sprockets. The cylinder heads have twin spark plugs.

The engine is mounted in a box-section steel cradle frame. Suspension is provided by conventional oil-damped telescopic forks at the front, and a box-section aluminium swingarm acting on a single shock absorber via a three-way linkage at the rear. The shock absorber is adjustable for spring pre-load. Braking is by a single disc and twin-piston sliding caliper at the front and by a drum brake at the rear.

The XL600V-H was available in white and metallic blue.

The XL600V-J model for 1988 was un-changed, though was also available in beige.

XL600V-K Transalp (1989 model year)

Apart from a new instrument cluster, modifications to the rear suspension linkage, and the inclusion of a sidestand switch in the starter safety circuit, the XL600V-K was unchanged from the H and J models.

Available in red and two shades of blue.

The V-K model remained on sale in the UK through to 1990. An XL600V-L model was available in Germany for the 1990 model year, but was basically unchanged from the V-K model.

XL600V-M Transalp (1991 model year)

The external oil pipe on the engine was removed, with the oil feed to the head now being housed internally. The front brake caliper was changed, though it remains a twin-piston sliding type, made by Nissin. The hose arrangement to the caliper was also modified. At the rear the drum brake was replaced by an hydraulic system using a single-piston sliding caliper, and the wheel was therefore changed to accommodate a disc instead of a drum.

Available in blue, green and silver.

XL600V-N and P (1992 and 1993) models were basically unchanged mechanically, but were available in green, blue and maroon.

XL600V-R Transalp (1994 and 1995 model years)

A different headlight was fitted and the fairing was slightly restyled to compliment it. A span adjuster was incorporated in the front brake lever. The front brake caliper was again changed, making pad renewal easier, though it remains a twin-piston sliding type, made by Nissin.

Available in blue, grey and black.

XL600V-T Transalp (1996 model year)

The front forks were modified, with a spacer being removed and a longer spring being fitted. There were also modifications to the air duct, which now incorporates a resonator chamber and sub-air filters.

The ignition system was modified, with the twin coils per cylinder being replaced with a single coil per cylinder, each coil feeding both spark plugs.

Available in blue, grey and red.

XL600V-V Transalp (1997 model year)

The front brake system was completely changed, with a twin disc system replacing the single disc. Brembo calipers replace the Nissin, but are still of the twin-piston sliding type. Production of the Transalp now shifted from Japan to Honda's factory in Italy.

The ignition system was modified, with the twin pulse generator coils being replaced with a single coil. Passenger grab-rails were added

Available in black, red and beige.

XL600V-W and X (1998 and 1999) models were unchanged, except for colours. V-W (1998) models were available in black, red and purple, and V-X (1999) models were available in red, green and blue.

XL650V-Y, V-1 and V-2 Transalp (2000 to 2002 model years)

A complete makeover sees the new Transalp with an increased engine size, up from 600cc to 650cc, by way of an increased bore.

Whilst the braking and suspension systems remain largely unchanged from the last of the XL600V models, with the exception of a new rear shock absorber that is now adjustable for compression damping, instrumentation, fairing, bodywork, seat (now lockable), turn signals, tail light and headlight are all new. UK models come fitted as standard with Honda's 'HISS' immobiliser system. A PAIR emission control system is also fitted as standard to reduce CO emissions.

Minor modifications were made to the transmission shafts and carburettors, and many components (fusebox, thermostat housing etc) were relocated. The coolant inlet pipe arrangement to the cylinders was modified, with the separate feed to each cylinder being replaced by a single feed to the front cylinder, and a link pipe being fitted between the cylinders.

V-Y (2000) models available in green, grey and red, and V-1/V-2 (2001/2) models available in silver, grey and blue.

XRV750-L Africa Twin (1990 model year)

The first Africa Twin was the XRV750-L introduced in 1990.

The Africa Twin has the same 52° V-twin cylinder engine as the Transalp, but with increased bore and stroke dimensions. It retains chain drive to its single overhead camshafts which operate the two inlet and one exhaust valve per cylinder. The clutch is a conventional wet multi-plate unit and the gearbox is 5-speed. Drive from the gearbox output shaft is transmitted to the rear wheel by chain and sprockets. The cylinder heads have twin spark plugs.

The engine is mounted in a box-section steel cradle frame. Suspension is provided by oil-damped, dual spring and air-assisted telescopic forks at the front, and a box-section aluminium swingarm acting on a single shock absorber via a three-way linkage at the rear. The shock absorber is adjustable for spring pre-load. Braking is hydraulic all-round, with twin discs and twin-piston sliding calipers at the front and a single disc and single-piston sliding caliper at the rear.

The fuel tank incorporates a low level sensor with a corresponding warning light, and the tank has twin taps. Fuel is supplied to the carburettors via an external pump and in-line filter.

The XRV750-L was available in two variations of white/blue.

The XRV750-M model for 1991 was unchanged mechanically, though was also available in white, black and blue.

XRV750-N Africa Twin (1992 model year)

Apart from a new instrument cluster and the addition of a digital trip meter mounted above it, the XRV750-N was unchanged from the L and M models.

Available in white, black and blue.

XRV750-P Africa Twin (1993 model year)

The Africa Twin was given a makeover for 1993, with a different fuel tank incorporating a single tap in place of the twin taps previously used, and losing the low fuel level sensor and warning circuit in place of a conventional tap providing a reserve facility. The air filter housing has been transferred from below the seat to under the front of the tank, thereby doing away with the air duct between the housing and the carburettors. The carburettors were changed, now being flat-slide instead of round-slide type. The front brake calipers were improved, making pad changes easier, though remain the twin-piston sliding type.

Other modifications include a modified rear shock absorber, different rear brake master cylinder, modified rear carrier, lockable seat, different side panels, a modified rotary as opposed to plunger-type sidestand switch, different coolant reservoir, relocated fusebox, and a restyled fairing.

The XRV750-P model was available in green, black and white.

XRV750-R and S (1994 and 1995) models were unchanged mechanically, but R models were available in black, white and blue, and S models in green, black and white.

XRV750-T Africa Twin (1996 model year)

The ignition system was modified, with the twin pulse generator coils being replaced by a single coil, and the twin HT coils per cylinder being replaced by a single coil per cylinder, each coil feeding both spark plugs. Otherwise, apart from minor modifications to the rear carrier, the model was unchanged.

Available in red, black and silver.

XRV750-V, W, X, Y, 1 and 2 Africa Twin (1997 to 2002 model years)

The Africa Twin has remained unchanged since 1996, with the exception of colour schemes.

V (1997) models were available in black, blue and silver.

W (1998) models were available in green, black and white.

X (1999) models were available in black, white and blue.

Y, 1 and 2 (2000 to 2002) models were available in black and blue/red.

Bike spec

Dimensions and weights – XL600V models

Overall length	2260 to 2270 mm (89.0 to 89.4 in)
Overall width	
H to P (1987 to 1993) models	865 mm (34.0 in)
R to X (1994 to 1999) models	905 mm (35.6 in)
Overall height	
H and J (1987 and 1988) models	1280 mm (50.4 in)
K to P (1989 to 1993) models	1310 mm (51.6 in)
R to X (1994 to 1999) models	1300 mm (51.2 in)
Wheelbase	1505 mm (59.3 in)
Seat height	850 mm (33.5 in)
Ground clearance – without centrestand fitted	
H and J (1987 and 1988) models	225 mm (8.9 in)
K and L (1989 and 1990) models	200 mm (7.9 in)
M to X (1991 to 1999) models	195 mm (7.7 in)
Weight (dry)*	
H to L (1987 to 1990) models	175 kg (386 lb)
M to R (1991 to 1995) models	183 kg (404 lb)
T to X (1996 to 1999) models	189 kg (417 lb)
Curb weight*	
H to L (1987 to 1990) models	194 kg (428 lb)
M to X (1991 to 1999) models	202 kg (445 lb)

*Add approximately 2 kg for Austrian and Swiss market models

Dimensions and weights – XL650V models

Overall length	2265 mm (89.2 in)
Overall width	865 mm (34.0 in)
Overall height	1280 mm (50.4 in)
Wheelbase	1505 mm (59.3 in)
Seat height	850 mm (33.5 in)
Ground clearance	225 mm (8.9 in)
Weight (dry)	175 kg (386 lb)
Curb weight	194 kg (428 lb)

Dimensions and weights – XRV750 models

Overall length	2315 to 2380 mm (91.1 to 93.7 in)
Overall width	
L to N (1990 to 1992) models	895 mm (35.2 in)
P models onwards (1993-on)	905 mm (35.6 in)
Overall height	
L to N (1990 to 1992) models	1420 mm (55.9 in)
P models onwards (1993-on)	1430 mm (56.3 in)
Wheelbase	1565 mm (61.6 in)
Seat height	
L to N (1990 to 1992) models	880 mm (34.6 in)
P to S (1993 to 1995) models	860 mm (33.9 in)
T models onwards (1996-on)	870 mm (34.3 in)
Ground clearance	
L to N (1990 to 1992) models	225 mm (8.9 in)
P models onwards (1993-on)	215 mm (8.5 in)
Weight (dry)	
L to N (1990 to 1992) models	210 kg (463 lb)
P models onwards (1993-on)	205 kg (452 lb)
Curb weight	
L to N (1990 to 1992) models	233 kg (514 lb)
P models onwards (1993-on)	229 kg (505 lb)

Engine

Type . . . .   Liquid-cooled six valve 52° V-twin
Capacity
   XL600V models . . . .   583 cc
   XL650V models . . . .   647 cc
   XRV750 models . . . .   742 cc
Bore and stroke
   XL600V models . . . .   75 x 66 mm
   XL650V models . . . .   79 x 66 mm
   XRV750 models . . . .   81 x 72 mm
Compression ratio
   XL600V and XL650V models . . . .   9.2 :1
   XRV750 models . . . .   9.0 :1
Camshafts . . . .   SOHC, chain-driven
Carburettors
   XL600V and XL650V models . . . .   2 x 34 mm Keihin CV type
   XRV750-L to S (1990 to 1995) models . . . .   2 x 36.5 mm Keihin CV type
   XRV750-T models onwards (1996-on) . . . .   2 x 36.0 mm Keihin CV type
Ignition system
   XL600V-H to R (1987 to 1995) and XRV750-L to S
     (1990 to 1995) models . . . .   CDI with electronic advance
   XL600V-T to X (1996 to 1999), XL650V and
     XRV750-T models onwards (1996-on) . . . .   Digital transistorised with electronic advance
Clutch . . . .   Wet multi-plate, cable-operated
Gearbox . . . .   5-speed constant mesh
Final drive . . . .   Chain and sprockets

Cycle parts

Frame type . . . .   Single downtube with double-loop cradle, rectangular section
Fuel tank capacity (including reserve)
   XL600V models . . . .   18.0 litres (3.96 Imp gal)
   XL650V models . . . .   19.6 litres (4.31 Imp gal)
   XRV750-L to N (1990 to 1992) models . . . .   24.0 litres (5.28 Imp gal)
   XRV750-P models onward (1993-on) . . . .   23.0 litres (5.06 Imp gal)
Front suspension
   XL600V and XL650V models . . . .   41 mm oil-damped telescopic forks, with 200 mm travel
   XRV750 models . . . .   43 mm oil-damped telescopic forks, with 220 mm travel, air-assisted on L to S (1990 to 1995) models
Rear suspension
   Type . . . .   Single shock absorber, rising rate linkage, Pro-Link box section aluminium swingarm
   Travel – XL600V and XL650V models . . . .   187 mm
   Travel – XRV750 models . . . .   210 mm
   Adjustment . . . .   Spring pre-load on all models. XL650V models also have compression damping adjustment
Wheels
   Front . . . .   21 inch spoke, aluminium rim
   Rear . . . .   17 inch spoke, aluminium rim
Tyres – XL600V and XL650V models
   Front 90/90-21 54S
   Rear 130/80-17 65S
Tyres – XRV750-L to N (1990 to 1992) models
   Front 90/90-21 54H
   Rear 130/90-17 65S
Tyres – XRV750-P models onward (1993-on)
   Front 90/90-21 54S
   Rear 140/80-R17 69H
Front brake
   XL600V-H to T (1987 to 1996) models . . . .   276 mm single disc with twin piston sliding caliper
   XL600V-V to X (1997 to 1999), XL650V and
     XRV750 models . . . .   276 mm twin discs with twin piston sliding calipers
Rear brake
   XL600V-H to L (1987 to 1990) models . . . .   130 mm single leading shoe drum
   XL600V-M to X (1991 to 1999) and XL650V models . . . . .   240 mm single disc with single piston sliding caliper
   XRV750 models . . . .   256 mm single disc with single piston sliding caliper

Performance data

Maximum power
XL600V models . . . . .46.5 bhp (34.7 kW) @ 7542 rpm
XL650V models . . . . .54 bhp (40 kW) @ 7500 rpm
XRV750 models . . . . .61 bhp (45.5 kW) @ 7500 rpm

Maximum torque
XL600V models . . . . .36.1 lbf ft (49 Nm) @ 5798 rpm
XL650V models . . . . .39 lbf ft (53 Nm) @ 5500 rpm
XRV750 models . . . . .45 lbf ft (61 Nm) @ 6000 rpm

Top speed
XL600/650V models . . . . .110 mph (177 kmh)
XRV750 models . . . . .112 mph (180 kmh)

Acceleration
XL600V models
   Time taken to cover a ¼ mile from a standing start . . .13.6 seconds
   Terminal speed after ¼ mile . . . . .94.7 mph (152 kmh)
XL650V models . . . . .not available
XRV750 models
   Time taken to cover a ¼ mile from a standing start . . .13.8 seconds
   Terminal speed after ¼ mile . . . . .93.6 mph (150 kmh)

Average fuel consumption
Miles per Imp gal, miles per litre, litres per 100 km
XL600V models . . . . .42 mpg, 9.2 mpl, 6.7 l/100 km
XL650V models . . . . .33 mpg, 7.3 mpl, 8.5 l/100 km
XRV750 models . . . . .36 mpg, 7.9 mpl, 7.8 l/100 km

Fuel tank range
Based on average fuel consumption rate
XL600V models . . . . .170 miles (273 km)
XL650V models . . . . .142 miles (228 km)
XRV750 models . . . . .180 to 190 miles (290 to 305 km)

XL600V power and torque curves

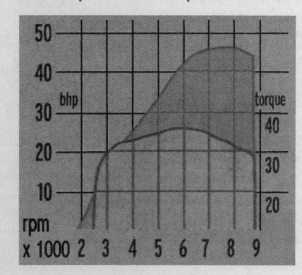

Performance data sourced from Motor Cycle News road test features. See the MCN website for up-to-date biking news.

MCN www.motorcyclenews.com

Identification numbers

Frame and engine numbers

The frame serial number is stamped into the right-hand side of the steering head. The engine number is stamped into the crankcase on the right-hand side of the engine. Both of these numbers should be recorded and kept in a safe place so they can be furnished to law enforcement officials in the event of a theft. There is also a colour code label on the top of the rear subframe (visible after removing the seat). The carburettors also have an ID number stamped into them.

The frame serial number, engine serial number, colour code and carburettor ID should also be kept in a handy place (such as with your driver's licence) so they are always available when purchasing or ordering parts for your machine.

Procedures in this manual identify bikes by model code and letter (e.g. XL600V-X) and by the production year (e.g. 1999). The model code or production year is printed on the colour code label.

Model codes and production years, together with their corresponding initial frame and engine numbers, are given below in two tables.

The frame number is stamped into the right-hand side of the steering head

The engine number is stamped into the crankcase on the right-hand side of the engine

The colour code label is on the rear subframe

All UK market models and Germany Type I full power models

XL600V and XL650V Transalp

Model	Year	Initial engine no.	Initial frame no.
XL600V-H	1987	PD06E-50	PD06-50
XL600V-J	1988	PD06E-51	PD06-51
XL600V-K	1989	PD06E-22	PD06-52
XL600V-L*	1990	PD06E-23	PD06-53
XL600V-M	1991	PD06E-24	PD06-54
XL600V-N	1992	PD06E-25	PD06-55
XL600V-P	1993	PD06E-26	PD06-56
XL600V-R	1994/5	PD06E-27	PD06-57
XL600V-T	1996	PD06E-28	PD06A-T
XL600V-V	1997	HM-PD06E-29	ZDCPD10A0-V
XL600V-W	1998	HM-PD06E-40	ZDCPD10A0-W
XL600V-X	1999	HM-PD06E-41	ZDCPD10A0-X
XL650V-Y	2000	HM-RD10E-20	ZDCRD10A0-Y
XL650V-1	2001	HM-RD10E-20	ZDCRD10A0-1
XL650V-2	2002	not available	

XL600V-L not available in the UK market

XRV750 Africa Twin

Model	Year	Initial engine no.	Initial frame no.
XRV750-L	1990	RD04E-20	RD04-20
XRV750-M	1991	RD04E-21	RD04-21
XRV750-N	1992	RD04E-22	RD04-22
XRV750-P	1993	RD04E-23	RD07-20
XRV750-R	1994	RD04E-24	RD07-21
XRV750-S	1995	RD04E-25	RD07-22
XRV750-T	1996	RD04E-26	JH2RD07A-T
XRV750-V	1997	RD04E-27	JH2RD07A-V
XRV750-W	1998	RD04E-28	JH2RD07A-W
XRV750-X	1999	RD04E-29	JH2RD07A-X
XRV750-Y	2000	RD04E-291	JH2RD07A-Y
XRV750-1	2001	not available	JH2RD07A-1
XRV750-2	2002	not available	

Germany Type II models (restricted power output)

XL600V and XL650V Transalp

Model	Year	Initial engine no.	Initial frame no.
XL600V-H	1987	PD06E-30	PD06-30
XL600V-J	1988	PD06E-31	PD06-31
XL600V-K	1989	PD06E-32	PD06-32
XL600V-M	1991	PD06E-34	PD06-34
XL600V-N	1992	PD06E-35	PD06-35
XL600V-P	1993	PD06E-36	PD06-36
XL600V-R	1994/5	PD06E-37	PD06-37
XL600V-T	1996	PD06E-61	PD06B-T
XL600V-V	1997	HM-PD06E-62	ZDCDP10B0-V
XL600V-W	1998	HM-PD06E-63	ZDCDP10B0-W
XL600V-X	1999	HM-PD06E-64	ZDCDP10B0-X
XL650V-Y	2000	HM-RD10E-30	ZDCRD10B0-Y
XL650V-1	2001	HM-RD10E-30	ZDCRD10B0-1
XL650V-2	2002	not available	

XRV750 Africa Twin

Model	Year	Initial engine no.	Initial frame no.
XRV750-L	1990	RD04E-30	RD04-30
XRV750-M	1991	RD04E-31	RD04-31
XRV750-N	1992	RD04E-32	RD04-32
XRV750-P	1993	RD04E-33	RD07-30
XRV750-R	1994	RD04E-34	RD07-31
XRV750-S	1995	RD04E-35	RD07-32
XRV750-T	1996	RD04E-36	JH2RD07B-T
XRV750-V	1997	RD04E-37	JH2RD07B-V
XRV750-W	1998	RD04E-38	JH2RD07B-W
XRV750-X	1999	RD04E-39	JH2RD07B-X
XRV750-Y	2000	RD04E-391	JH2RD07B-Y
XRV750-1	2001	not available	JH2RD07B-1
XRV750-2	2002	not available	

Buying spare parts

Once you have found all the identification numbers, record them for reference when buying parts. Since the manufacturers change specifications, parts and vendors (companies that manufacture various components on the machine), providing the ID numbers is the only way to be reasonably sure that you are buying the correct parts.

Whenever possible, take the worn part to the dealer so direct comparison with the new component can be made. Along the trail from the manufacturer to the parts shelf, there are numerous places that the part can end up with the wrong number or be listed incorrectly.

The two places to purchase new parts for your motorcycle – the franchised or main dealer and the parts/accessories store – differ in the type of parts they carry. While dealers can obtain every single genuine part for your motorcycle, the accessory store is usually limited to normal high wear items such as chains and sprockets, brake pads, spark plugs and cables, and to tune-up parts and various engine gaskets, etc. Rarely will an accessory outlet have major suspension components, camshafts, transmission gears, or engine cases.

Used parts can be obtained from breakers yards for roughly half the price of new ones, but you can't always be sure of what you're getting. Once again, take your worn part to the breaker for direct comparison, or when ordering by mail order make sure that you can return it if you are not happy.

Whether buying new, used or rebuilt parts, the best course is to deal directly with someone who specialises in your particular make.

Professional mechanics are trained in safe working procedures. However enthusiastic you may be about getting on with the job at hand, take the time to ensure that your safety is not put at risk. A moment's lack of attention can result in an accident, as can failure to observe simple precautions.

There will always be new ways of having accidents, and the following is not a comprehensive list of all dangers; it is intended rather to make you aware of the risks and to encourage a safe approach to all work you carry out on your bike.

Asbestos

● Certain friction, insulating, sealing and other products - such as brake pads, clutch linings, gaskets, etc. - contain asbestos. Extreme care must be taken to avoid inhalation of dust from such products since it is hazardous to health. If in doubt, assume that they do contain asbestos.

Fire

● Remember at all times that petrol is highly flammable. Never smoke or have any kind of naked flame around, when working on the vehicle. But the risk does not end there - a spark caused by an electrical short-circuit, by two metal surfaces contacting each other, by careless use of tools, or even by static electricity built up in your body under certain conditions, can ignite petrol vapour, which in a confined space is highly explosive. Never use petrol as a cleaning solvent. Use an approved safety solvent.

● Always disconnect the battery earth terminal before working on any part of the fuel or electrical system, and never risk spilling fuel on to a hot engine or exhaust.
● It is recommended that a fire extinguisher of a type suitable for fuel and electrical fires is kept handy in the garage or workplace at all times. Never try to extinguish a fuel or electrical fire with water.

Fumes

● Certain fumes are highly toxic and can quickly cause unconsciousness and even death if inhaled to any extent. Petrol vapour comes into this category, as do the vapours from certain solvents such as trichloro-ethylene. Any draining or pouring of such volatile fluids should be done in a well ventilated area.
● When using cleaning fluids and solvents, read the instructions carefully. Never use materials from unmarked containers - they may give off poisonous vapours.
● Never run the engine of a motor vehicle in an enclosed space such as a garage. Exhaust fumes contain carbon monoxide which is extremely poisonous; if you need to run the engine, always do so in the open air or at least have the rear of the vehicle outside the workplace.

The battery

● Never cause a spark, or allow a naked light near the vehicle's battery. It will normally be giving off a certain amount of hydrogen gas, which is highly explosive.

● Always disconnect the battery ground (earth) terminal before working on the fuel or electrical systems (except where noted).
● If possible, loosen the filler plugs or cover when charging the battery from an external source. Do not charge at an excessive rate or the battery may burst.
● Take care when topping up, cleaning or carrying the battery. The acid electrolyte, evenwhen diluted, is very corrosive and should not be allowed to contact the eyes or skin. Always wear rubber gloves and goggles or a face shield. If you ever need to prepare electrolyte yourself, always add the acid slowly to the water; never add the water to the acid.

Electricity

● When using an electric power tool, inspection light etc., always ensure that the appliance is correctly connected to its plug and that, where necessary, it is properly grounded (earthed). Do not use such appliances in damp conditions and, again, beware of creating a spark or applying excessive heat in the vicinity of fuel or fuel vapour. Also ensure that the appliances meet national safety standards.
● A severe electric shock can result from touching certain parts of the electrical system, such as the spark plug wires (HT leads), when the engine is running or being cranked, particularly if components are damp or the insulation is defective. Where an electronic ignition system is used, the secondary (HT) voltage is much higher and could prove fatal.

Remember...

✗ **Don't** start the engine without first ascertaining that the transmission is in neutral.
✗ **Don't** suddenly remove the pressure cap from a hot cooling system - cover it with a cloth and release the pressure gradually first, or you may get scalded by escaping coolant.
✗ **Don't** attempt to drain oil until you are sure it has cooled sufficiently to avoid scalding you.
✗ **Don't** grasp any part of the engine or exhaust system without first ascertaining that it is cool enough not to burn you.
✗ **Don't** allow brake fluid or antifreeze to contact the machine's paintwork or plastic components.
✗ **Don't** siphon toxic liquids such as fuel, hydraulic fluid or antifreeze by mouth, or allow them to remain on your skin.
✗ **Don't** inhale dust - it may be injurious to health (see Asbestos heading).
✗ **Don't** allow any spilled oil or grease to remain on the floor - wipe it up right away, before someone slips on it.
✗ **Don't** use ill-fitting spanners or other tools which may slip and cause injury.
✗ **Don't** lift a heavy component which may

be beyond your capability - get assistance.
✗ **Don't** rush to finish a job or take unverified short cuts.
✗ **Don't** allow children or animals in or around an unattended vehicle.
✗ **Don't** inflate a tyre above the recommended pressure. Apart from overstressing the carcass, in extreme cases the tyre may blow off forcibly.
✔ **Do** ensure that the machine is supported securely at all times. This is especially important when the machine is blocked up to aid wheel or fork removal.
✔ **Do** take care when attempting to loosen a stubborn nut or bolt. It is generally better to pull on a spanner, rather than push, so that if you slip, you fall away from the machine rather than onto it.
✔ **Do** wear eye protection when using power tools such as drill, sander, bench grinder etc.
✔ **Do** use a barrier cream on your hands prior to undertaking dirty jobs - it will protect your skin from infection as well as making the dirt easier to remove afterwards; but make sure your hands aren't left slippery. Note that long-term contact with used engine oil can be a health hazard.
✔ **Do** keep loose clothing (cuffs, ties etc. and long hair) well out of the way of moving

mechanical parts.
✔ **Do** remove rings, wristwatch etc., before working on the vehicle - especially the electrical system.
✔ **Do** keep your work area tidy - it is only too easy to fall over articles left lying around.
✔ **Do** exercise caution when compressing springs for removal or installation. Ensure that the tension is applied and released in a controlled manner, using suitable tools which preclude the possibility of the spring escaping violently.
✔ **Do** ensure that any lifting tackle used has a safe working load rating adequate for the job.
✔ **Do** get someone to check periodically that all is well, when working alone on the vehicle.
✔ **Do** carry out work in a logical sequence and check that everything is correctly assembled and tightened afterwards.
✔ **Do** remember that your vehicle's safety affects that of yourself and others. If in doubt on any point, get professional advice.
● If in spite of following these precautions, you are unfortunate enough to injure yourself, seek medical attention as soon as possible.

Note: *The daily (pre-ride) checks outlined in the owner's manual covers those items which should be inspected on a daily basis.*

Engine/transmission oil level check

Before you start:
✔ Take the motorcycle on a short run to allow it to reach normal operating temperature.

Caution: Do not run the engine in an enclosed space such as a garage or workshop.

✔ Stop the engine and support the motorcycle upright; use the centrestand if it has one. Allow it to stand undisturbed for a few minutes to allow the oil level to stabilise. Make sure the motorcycle is on level ground.

The correct oil
● Modern, high-revving engines place great demands on their oil. It is very important that the correct oil for your bike is used.
● Always top up with a good quality oil of the specified type and viscosity and do not overfill the engine.

Oil type	API grade SE, SF or SG
Oil viscosity*	SAE 10W40*

If you are using the motorcycle constantly in extreme conditions of heat or cold, other more suitable viscosity ranges may be used – refer to the viscosity table to select the oil best suited to your conditions.

Bike care:
● If you have to add oil frequently, check whether you have any oil leaks from the engine joints, seals and gaskets. If not, the engine could be burning oil, in which case there will be white smoke coming out of the exhaust – (see *Fault Finding*).

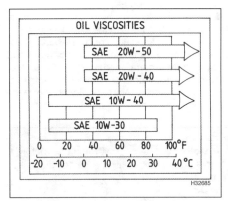
Oil viscosity table: select the oil best suited to your conditions

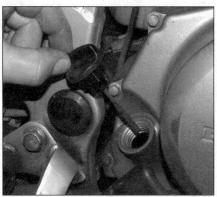
1 Unscrew the oil filler cap from the right-hand side crankcase cover. The dipstick is integral with the oil filler cap, and is used to check the engine oil level.

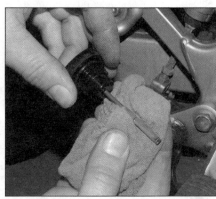
2 Using a clean rag or paper towel, wipe off all the oil from the dipstick.

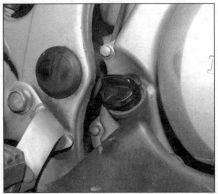
3 Insert the clean dipstick back into the engine, allowing it to rest on the bottom thread of the cap – do not screw it in.

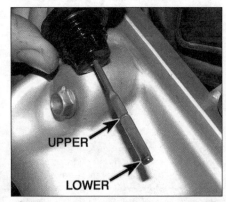
4 Remove the dipstick and observe the level of the oil, which should be somewhere in between the upper and lower level marks (arrowed).

5 If the level is below the lower mark, top the engine up with the recommended grade and type of oil, to bring the level up to the upper mark on the dipstick.

Coolant level check

⚠️ **Warning: DO NOT remove the radiator pressure cap to add coolant. Topping up is done via the coolant reservoir tank filler. DO NOT leave open containers of coolant about, as it is poisonous.**

Before you start:

✔ Make sure you have a supply of coolant available (a mixture of 50% distilled water and 50% corrosion inhibited ethylene glycol anti-freeze is needed).

✔ Always check the coolant level when the engine is at normal working temperature. Take the motorcycle on a short run to allow it to reach normal temperature.

Caution: Do not run the engine in an enclosed space such as a garage or workshop.

✔ Stop the engine and support the motorcycle upright; use the centrestand if it has one. Make sure the motorcycle is on level ground.

Bike care:

● Use only the specified coolant mixture. It is important that anti-freeze is used in the system all year round, and not just in the winter. Do not top the system up using only water, as the system will become too diluted.

● Do not overfill the reservoir tank. If the coolant is significantly above the UPPER level line at any time, the surplus should be siphoned or drained off to prevent the possibility of it being expelled out of the overflow hose.

● If the coolant level falls steadily, check the system for leaks (see Chapter 1). If no leaks are found and the level continues to fall, it is recommended that the machine is taken to a Honda dealer for a pressure test.

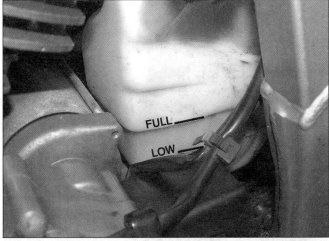

1 On XL600V and XL650V models the coolant reservoir is located on the left-hand side of the engine, between the rear cylinder and the frame. The coolant FULL and LOW level lines are on the front of the reservoir.

2 On XRV750 models the coolant reservoir is located behind the right-hand side panel. The coolant UPPER and LOWER level lines are visible by looking up at the back of it.

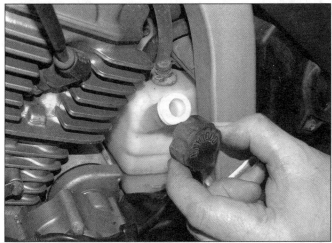

3 If the coolant level is not in between the level lines, remove the reservoir filler cap – where fitted on XL models, release the cap clamp by undoing the screw. On XRV models, remove the right-hand side panel to access the cap (see Chapter 8).

4 Top the coolant level up with the recommended coolant mixture, then fit the cap securely. Where fitted on XL models, secure the cap with its clamp. On XRV models, install the right-hand side panel (see Chapter 8).

Disc brake fluid level checks

All models are fitted with a front disc brake. Later XL600V models and all XL650V and XRV750 models are fitted with a rear disc brake.

> ⚠ *Warning: Brake hydraulic fluid can harm your eyes and damage painted surfaces, so use extreme caution when handling and pouring it and cover surrounding surfaces with rag. Do not use fluid that has been standing open for some time, as it is hygroscopic (absorbs moisture from the air) which can cause a dangerous loss of braking effectiveness.*

Before you start:

✔ The front master cylinder reservoir is integral with the master cylinder on the right-hand handlebar. The rear master cylinder reservoir is located under the side panel on the right-hand side.

✔ Make sure you have the correct hydraulic fluid. DOT 4 is recommended.

✔ Wrap a rag around the reservoir being worked on to ensure that any spillage does not come into contact with painted surfaces.

✔ Support the motorcycle upright on its centre-stand if fitted, or on an auxiliary stand, so that the reservoir being worked on is level – you may have to turn the handlebars to achieve this when working on the front reservoir.

Bike care:

● The fluid in the front and rear brake master cylinder reservoirs will drop slightly as the brake pads wear down (refer to Chapter 1, Section 3 to check the amount of wear in the pads if required).

● If either fluid reservoir requires repeated topping-up there could be an hydraulic leak somewhere in the system, which must be investigated immediately.

● Check for signs of fluid leakage from the hydraulic hoses and components – if found, rectify immediately (see Chapter 7).

● Check the operation of both brakes before taking the machine on the road; if there is evidence of air in the system (spongy feel to lever or pedal), it must be bled (see Chapter 7).

FRONT BRAKE FLUID LEVEL

1 The front brake fluid level, visible through the window in the reservoir body, must be above the LOWER level line (arrowed).

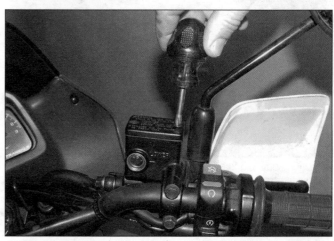

2 If the level is below the LOWER line, undo the two reservoir cover screws and remove the cover, diaphragm plate and diaphragm.

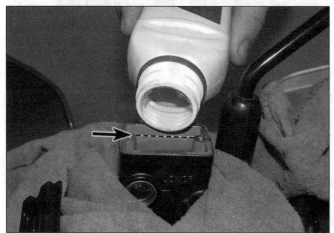

3 Top up with fluid of the recommended type until the level is up to the ridge along the inside of the front wall of the reservoir (arrowed). Do not overfill.

4 Ensure that the diaphragm is correctly seated before installing the plate and cover.

REAR BRAKE FLUID LEVEL

5 To view the rear brake fluid level, remove the right-hand side panel (see Chapter 8). The rear brake fluid level, visible through the reservoir body, must be above the LOWER level line.

6 If the level is below the LOWER level line, undo the two reservoir cover screws or unscrew the reservoir cap (according to model), and remove the diaphragm plate and diaphragm.

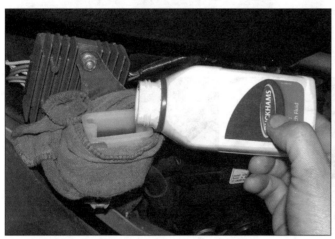

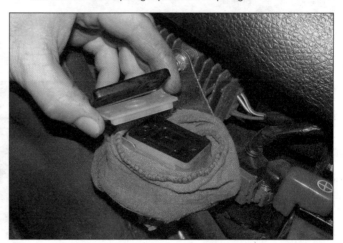

7 Top up with fluid of the recommended type until the level is up to the UPPER level line. Do not overfill.

8 Ensure that the diaphragm is correctly seated before installing the plate and cover or cap.

Drum brake checks

A rear drum brake is fitted to XL600V-H to L (1987 to 1990) models

Bike care:

✔ The amount of travel in the rear brake pedal before the brake takes effect will increase as the shoes wear down (refer to Chapter 1, Section 3 to check the amount of wear in the shoes if required).

✔ Check that the brake works effectively without binding when the pedal is released.

✔ Ensure that the rod linkage is properly lubricated (see Chapter 1).

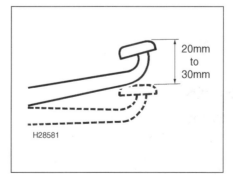

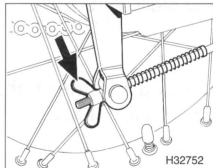

1 Measure the amount of free travel at the tip of the brake pedal from its rest position before the brake takes effect. There should be no more than 30 mm travel.

2 If the amount of travel exceeds 30 mm, turn the adjusting wingnut on the end of the brake rod in until the amount of travel is between 20 and 30 mm.

Tyre checks

The correct pressures:
● The tyres must be checked when **cold**, not immediately after riding. Note that low tyre pressures may cause the tyre to slip on the rim or come off. High tyre pressures will cause abnormal tread wear and unsafe handling.

● Use an accurate pressure gauge. Many forecourt gauges are wildly inaccurate. If you buy your own, spend as much as you can justify on a quality gauge.

● Proper air pressure will increase tyre life and provide maximum stability and ride comfort.

Tyre care:
● Check the tyres carefully for cuts, tears, embedded nails or other sharp objects and excessive wear. Operation of the motorcycle with excessively worn tyres is extremely hazardous, as traction and handling are directly affected.
● Check the condition of the tyre valve and ensure the dust cap is in place.
● Pick out any stones or nails which may have become embedded in the tyre tread. If left, they will eventually penetrate through the casing and cause a puncture.
● If tyre damage is apparent, or unexplained loss of pressure is experienced, seek the advice of a tyre fitting specialist without delay.

Tyre tread depth:
● At the time of writing UK law requires that tread depth must be at least 1 mm over 3/4 of the tread breadth all the way around the tyre, with no bald patches. Many riders, however, consider 2 mm tread depth minimum to be a safer limit. Honda recommend a minimum of 1.5 mm on the front and 2 mm on the rear.

● Many tyres now incorporate wear indicators in the tread. Identify the location marking on the tyre sidewall to locate the indicator bar and replace the tyre if the tread has worn down to the bar.

All XL600V and XL650V models, XRV750-L to N (1990 to 1992) models		
Loading	**Front**	**Rear**
Rider only	.29 psi (2.00 Bar)	29 psi (2.00 Bar)
Rider and passenger	.29 psi (2.00 Bar)	33 psi (2.25 Bar)
XRV750-P models onward (1993-on)		
Loading	**Front**	**Rear**
Rider only	.29 psi (2.00 Bar)	29 psi (2.00 Bar)
Rider and passenger	.29 psi (2.00 Bar)	36 psi (2.50 Bar)

1 Remove the dust cap from the valve and check the tyre pressures when **cold**. Do not forget to fit the cap after checking the pressure.

2 Measure tread depth at the centre of the tyre using a depth gauge.

3 Tyre tread wear indicator bar and its location marking (usually either an arrow, a triangle or the letters TWI) on the sidewall.

Suspension, steering and drive chain checks

Suspension and Steering:
● Check that the front and rear suspension operates smoothly without binding (see Chapter 1).

● Check that the suspension is adjusted as required, where applicable (see Chapter 6).
● Check that the steering moves smoothly from lock-to-lock.

Drive chain:
● Check that the chain isn't too loose or too tight, and adjust it if necessary (see Chapter 1).
● If the chain looks dry, lubricate it (see Chapter 1).

Legal and safety checks

Lighting and signalling:
● Take a minute to check that the headlight, tail light, brake light, licence plate light (where fitted), instrument lights and turn signals all work correctly.
● Check that the horn sounds when the button is pressed.
● A working speedometer, graduated in mph, is a statutory requirement in the UK.

Safety:
● Check that the throttle grip rotates smoothly when opened and snaps shut when released, in all steering positions. Also check for the correct amount of freeplay (see Chapter 1).
● Check that the engine shuts off when the kill switch is operated.
● Check that sidestand and centrestand (if fitted) return springs hold the stand(s) up securely when retracted.

Fuel:
● This may seem obvious, but check that you have enough fuel to complete your journey. If you notice signs of fuel leakage – rectify the cause immediately.
● Ensure you use the correct grade fuel – see Chapter 4 Specifications.

Chapter 1
Routine maintenance and servicing

Contents

Degrees of difficulty

Easy, suitable for novice with little experience 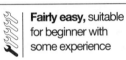	Fairly easy, suitable for beginner with some experience	Fairly difficult, suitable for competent DIY mechanic	Difficult, suitable for experienced DIY mechanic 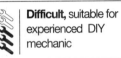	Very difficult, suitable for expert DIY or professional

Specifications

Engine

Engine idle speed
  XL600V models .... 1300 ± 100 rpm
  XL650V and XRV750 models .... 1200 ± 100 rpm
Spark plugs
  Type
    Standard .... NGK DPR8EA-9, or Denso X24EPR-U9
    Cold climate (below 5°C/41°F) .... NGK DPR7EA-9, or Denso X22EPR-U9
    Extended high speed riding .... NGK DPR9EA-9, or Denso X27EPR-U9
  Electrode gap .... 0.8 to 0.9 mm
Valve clearances (COLD engine)
  XL600V-H models
    Intake and exhaust valves .... 0.1 mm
  All other models
    Intake valves .... 0.13 to 0.17 mm
    Exhaust valves .... 0.18 to 0.22 mm
Carburettor synchronisation – max. difference between readings
  XL600V models .... 40 mm Hg
  XL650V models .... 20 mm Hg
  XRV750-L to N (1990 to 1992) models .... 30 mm Hg
  XRV750-P models onwards (1993-on) .... 20 mm Hg
Cylinder compression
  XL600V-H to P (1987 to 1993) models .... 157 to 185 psi (11.0 to 13.0 Bar)
  XL600V-R to X (1994 to 1999) models .... 164 to 192 psi (11.5 to 12.5 Bar)
  XL650V models .... 164 to 224 psi (11.5 to 15.5 Bar) @ 400 rpm
  XRV750 models .... 157 to 213 psi (11.0 to 15.0 Bar) @ 400 rpm
Oil pressure (at oil pressure switch, with engine warm)
  XL models .... 64 psi (4.5 Bar) @ 6000 rpm, oil @ 80°C
  XRV models .... 71 to 85 psi (5.0 to 6.0 Bar) @ 5000 rpm, oil @ 80°C

1

Cycle parts

Drive chain slack	35 to 45 mm
Throttle twistgrip freeplay	2 to 6 mm
Clutch lever freeplay	10 to 20 mm
Tyre pressures (cold)	see *Daily (pre-ride) checks*

Recommended lubricants and fluids

Engine/transmission oil type	API grade SE, SF or SG motor oil
Engine/transmission oil viscosity	SAE 10W40 (see also *Daily (pre-ride) checks*)
Engine/transmission oil capacity	
XL600V models	
Oil change	2.2 litres
Oil and filter change	2.4 litres
Following engine overhaul – dry engine, new filter	2.8 litres
XL650V models	
Oil change	2.4 litres
Oil and filter change	2.6 litres
Following engine overhaul – dry engine, new filter	3.0 litres
XRV750 models	
Oil change	2.4 litres
Oil and filter change	2.6 litres
Following engine overhaul – dry engine, new filter	3.2 litres
Coolant type	50% distilled water, 50% corrosion inhibited ethylene glycol anti-freeze
Coolant capacity	Approx. 2.0 litres
Brake fluid	DOT 4
Drive chain	SAE 80 or 90 gear oil or chain lubricant suitable for O-ring chains
Steering head bearings	multi-purpose grease
Swingarm pivot bearings	multi-purpose grease
Suspension linkage bearings	multi-purpose grease
Bearing seal lips	multi-purpose grease
Gearchange lever/rear brake pedal/footrest pivots	multi-purpose grease
Clutch lever pivot	multi-purpose grease
Sidestand and centrestand pivots	multi-purpose grease
Throttle grip	multi-purpose grease or dry film lubricant
Front brake lever pivot and piston tip	silicone grease
Cables	cable lubricant

Torque settings

Engine/transmission oil drain plug	
XL600V and XRV750 models	34 Nm
XL650V models	30 Nm
Engine/transmission oil filter	10 Nm
Fuel tap bowl (XL600V models)	4 Nm
Rear axle nut	
XL600V and XRV750 models	95 Nm
XL650V models	100 Nm
Rocker arm adjusting screw locknut	23 Nm
Spark plugs	14 Nm
Steering head bearing adjuster nut	
XL600V-H and J (1987 and 1988) models	4 to 6 Nm
XL600V-K to P (1989 to 1993) models	2.5 to 3.5 Nm
XL600V-R to X (1994 to 1999) models	5 Nm
XL650V models	5 Nm
XRV750 models	11 Nm
Steering stem nut	
XL600V-H to P (1987 to 1993) models	100 Nm
XL600V-R to X (1994 to 1999) models	105 Nm
XL650V models	105 Nm
XRV750-L to N (1990 to 1992) models	100 Nm
XRV750-P models onwards (1993-on)	128 Nm
Top yoke fork clamp bolts	27 Nm

Note: *The daily (pre-ride) checks outlined in the owner's manual covers those items which should be inspected on a daily basis. Always perform the pre-ride inspection at every maintenance interval (in addition to the procedures listed). The intervals listed below are the intervals recommended by the manufacturer for each particular operation during the model years covered in this manual. Your owner's manual may have different intervals for your model.*

Daily (pre-ride)

See 'Daily (pre-ride) checks' at the beginning of this manual.

After the initial 600 miles (1000 km)

Note: *This check is usually performed by a Honda dealer after the first 600 miles (1000 km) from new. Thereafter, maintenance is carried out according to the following intervals of the schedule.*

Every 600 miles (1000 km)

☐ Check, adjust and lubricate the drive chain (Section 1)

Every 4000 miles (6000 km) or 6 months (whichever comes sooner)

☐ Check and adjust the idle speed (Section 2)
☐ Check the brake shoes/pads (Section 3)
☐ Check the clutch (Section 4)
☐ Check the spark plugs (Section 5)
☐ Check the battery (Section 6)
☐ Check the condition of the wheels and tyres (Section 7)
☐ Check the air filter element (Section 8)
☐ Check the crankcase breather (Section 9)
☐ Check the fuel strainer (XL600V only) (Section 10)

Every 8000 miles (12,000 km) or 12 months (whichever comes sooner)

Carry out all the items under the 4000 mile (6000 km) check, plus the following
☐ Renew the spark plugs (Section 11)
☐ Lubricate the clutch/gearchange/brake lever/brake pedal/sidestand pivot, and the throttle, choke and clutch cables (Section 12)
☐ Renew the engine oil and filter (Section 13)
☐ Check the fuel system and hoses (Section 14)
☐ Check and adjust the throttle and choke cables (Section 15)
☐ Check and adjust the valve clearances (Section 16)
☐ Check and adjust the carburettor synchronisation (Section 17)
☐ Check the cooling system (Section 18)
☐ Check the brake system and brake light switch operation (Section 19)
☐ Check and adjust the headlight aim (Section 20)

Every 8000 miles (12,000 km) or 12 months (whichever comes sooner) (continued)

☐ Check the sidestand (Section 21)
☐ Check the suspension (Section 22)
☐ Check and adjust the steering head bearings (Section 23)
☐ Check the tightness of all nuts, bolts and fasteners (Section 24)
☐ Check the pulse secondary air injection (PAIR) system (XL650V only) (Section 25)

Every 12,000 miles (18,000 km) or 18 months (whichever comes first)

Carry out all the items under the 4000 mile (6000 km) check, plus the following
☐ Renew the air filter element (Section 26)

Every 12,000 miles (18,000 km) or two years (whichever comes first)

Carry out all the items under the 4000 mile (6000 km) check, plus the following
☐ Change the brake fluid (Section 27)

Every 24,000 miles (36,000 km) or two years (whichever comes sooner)

Carry out all the items under the 12,000 mile (18,000 km) and 8000 mile (12,000 km) checks, plus the following
☐ Change the coolant (Section 28)

Non-scheduled maintenance

☐ Check the cylinder compression (Section 29)
☐ Check the engine oil pressure (Section 30)
☐ Check the wheel bearings (Section 31)
☐ Re-grease the steering head bearings (Section 32)
☐ Re-grease the swingarm and suspension linkage bearings (Section 33)
☐ Renew the brake master cylinder and caliper seals (Section 34)
☐ Renew the brake hoses (Section 35)
☐ Renew the fuel hoses (Section 36)
☐ Change the front fork oil (Section 37)

Component locations – XL600V models

1 Steering head bearing adjuster
2 Clutch cable upper adjuster
3 Idle speed adjuster
4 Coolant reservoir filler cap
5 Air filter
6 Drive chain adjuster
7 Crankcase breather drain

8 Oil filter
9 Coolant drain plug
10 Oil drain plug
11 Fuel tap strainer
12 Rear brake fluid reservoir (V-M models onwards)
13 Battery

14 Rear brake light switch
15 Front brake fluid reservoir
16 Radiator pressure cap
17 Clutch cable lower adjuster
18 Oil level dipstick
19 Rear brake pedal height adjuster (V-M models onwards shown)

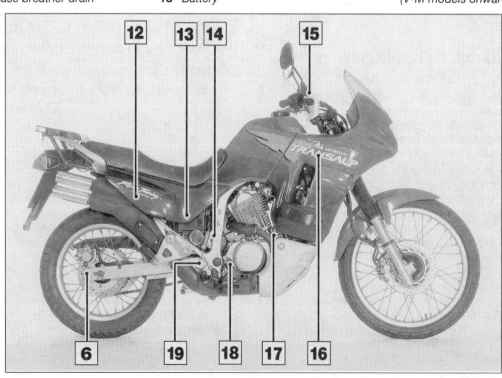

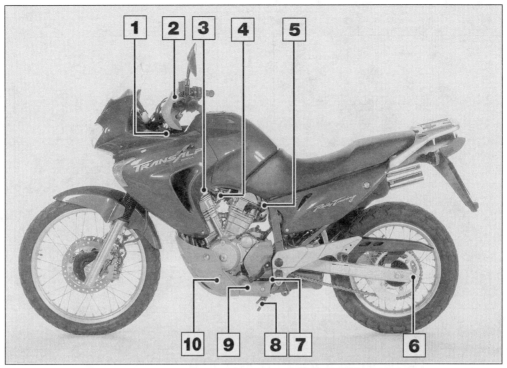

Component locations – XL650V models

1	Steering head bearing adjuster	**7**	Oil filter
2	Clutch cable upper adjuster	**8**	Crankcase breather drain
3	Fuel tap strainer	**9**	Coolant drain plug
4	Idle speed adjuster	**10**	Oil drain plug
5	Coolant reservoir filler cap	**11**	Rear brake fluid reservoir
6	Drive chain adjuster	**12**	Battery
		13	Rear brake light switch

14 Air filter
15 Front brake fluid reservoir
16 Radiator pressure cap
17 Clutch cable lower adjuster
18 Oil level dipstick
19 Rear brake pedal height adjuster

1

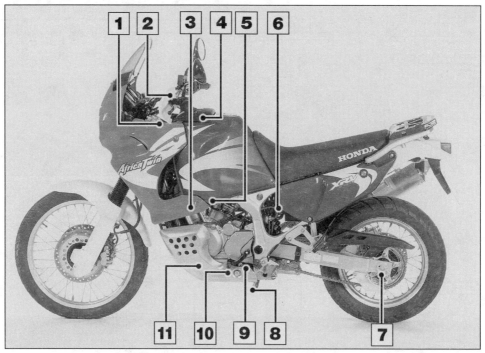

Component locations – XRV750 models

1 Steering head bearing adjuster
2 Clutch cable upper adjuster
3 Fuel tap strainers
  (L to N models)
4 Air filter
5 Idle speed adjuster
6 Fuel filter (in-line type)
7 Drive chain adjuster
8 Crankcase breather drain

9 Oil filter
10 Coolant drain plug
11 Oil drain plug
12 Coolant reservoir filler cap
13 Rear brake fluid reservoir (L to N
  models)
14 Battery
15 Rear brake fluid reservoir (P models
  onwards)

16 Rear brake light switch
17 Fuel tap strainer (P models
  onwards)
18 Front brake fluid reservoir
19 Radiator pressure cap
20 Clutch cable lower adjuster
21 Oil level dipstick
22 Rear brake pedal height
  adjuster

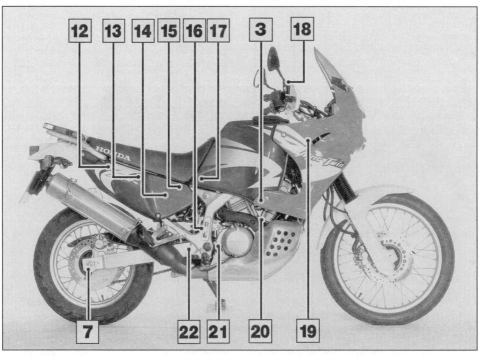

Introduction

1 This Chapter is designed to help the home mechanic maintain his/her motorcycle for safety, economy, long life and peak performance.

2 Deciding where to start or plug into the routine maintenance schedule depends on several factors. If your motorcycle has been maintained according to the warranty standards and has just come out of warranty, start routine maintenance as it coincides with the next mileage or calendar interval. If you have owned the machine for some time but have never performed any maintenance on it, start at the nearest interval and include some additional procedures to ensure that nothing important is overlooked. If you have just had a major engine overhaul, then start the maintenance routine from the beginning. If you have a used machine and have no knowledge of its history or maintenance record, combine all the checks into one large service initially and then settle into the specified maintenance schedule.

3 Before beginning any maintenance or repair, the machine should be cleaned thoroughly, especially around the oil filter, spark plugs, valve covers, body panels, carburettors, etc. Cleaning will help ensure that dirt does not contaminate the engine and will allow you to detect wear and damage that could otherwise easily go unnoticed.

4 Certain maintenance information is sometimes printed on labels attached to the motorcycle. If the information on the labels differs from that included here, use the information on the label.

Every 600 miles (1000 km)

1   Drive chain and sprockets –
      check, adjustment,
      cleaning and lubrication

Check

1 A neglected drive chain won't last long and will quickly damage the sprockets. Routine chain adjustment and lubrication isn't difficult and will ensure maximum chain and sprocket life.

2 To check the chain, place the bike on its sidestand and shift the transmission into neutral. Make sure the ignition switch is OFF.

3 Push up on the bottom run of the chain midway between the two sprockets and measure the amount of slack, then compare your measurement to that listed in this Chapter's Specifications **(see illustration)**. As the chain stretches with wear, adjustment will periodically be necessary (see below). Since the chain will rarely wear evenly, roll the bike forward so that another section of chain can be checked (having an assistant to do this makes the task a lot easier); do this several times to check the entire length of chain, and mark the tightest spot.

4 In some cases where lubrication has been neglected, corrosion and galling may cause the links to bind and kink, which effectively shortens the chain's length. Such links should be thoroughly cleaned and worked free. If the chain is tight between the sprockets, rusty or kinked, it's time to replace it with a new one. If you find a tight area, mark it with felt pen or paint, and repeat the measurement after the bike has been ridden. If the chain's still tight in the same area, it may be damaged or worn. Because a tight or kinked chain can damage the transmission bearings, it's a good idea to replace it with a new one.

5 Check the entire length of the chain for damaged rollers, loose links and pins, and missing O-rings, and replace it with a new one if damage is found. **Note:** *Never install a new chain on old sprockets, and never use the old chain if you install new sprockets – replace the chain and sprockets as a set.*

6 Remove the front sprocket cover (see Chapter 6). Check the teeth on the front sprocket and the rear sprocket for wear **(see illustration)**.

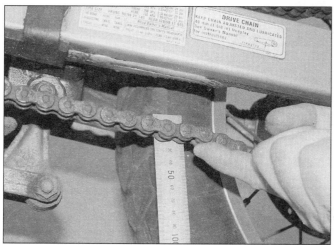

1.3 **Push up on the chain and measure the slack**

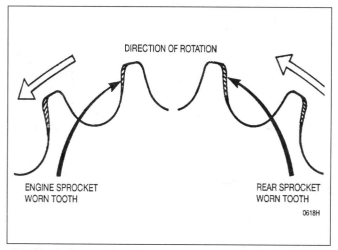

1.6 **Check the sprockets in the areas indicated to see if they are worn excessively**

1.9 Slacken the axle nut (arrowed)

1.10a Slacken the locknut (arrowed) . . .

1.10b . . . and turn the adjuster as required until the slack is correct

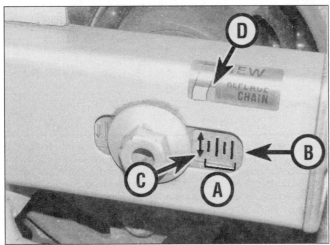

1.10c Make sure the alignment of the adjustment markers (A) in relation to the rear edge of the cutout (B) is the same on each side. Check the position of the arrow (C) in relation to the red zone (D)

1.10d On completion, counter-hold the adjuster and tighten the locknut against it

7 Inspect the drive chain slider on the front of the swingarm for excessive wear and damage. On some models there are wear limit lines marked on the front of the slider – replace it with a new one if it has worn down to the lines (see Chapter 6). If no lines are marked, renew the slider if it has worn to a thickness of 3 mm or less. Where fitted, similarly check the chain slipper near the rear sprocket, and renew it if it has worn to a thickness of 5 mm or less.

Adjustment

8 Move the bike so that the chain is positioned with the tightest point at the centre of its bottom run, then put it on the sidestand.
9 Slacken the rear axle nut **(see illustration)**.
10 On XL models, slacken the locknut on the adjuster on each end of the swingarm **(see illustration)**. Turn the adjuster nut on each side evenly until the amount of freeplay specified at the beginning of the Chapter is obtained at the centre of the bottom run of the chain **(see illustration)**. Following adjustment, check that each chain adjustment marker is in the same position in relation to the rear edge of the axle cutout in the swingarm **(see illustration)**. It is important the same index line on each adjuster aligns with the rear edge

of the cutout; if not, the rear wheel will be out of alignment with the front. If there is a discrepancy in the chain adjuster positions, adjust one of them so that its position is exactly the same as the other. Check the chain freeplay as described above and readjust if necessary. Also check the alignment of the wear decal on the left-hand

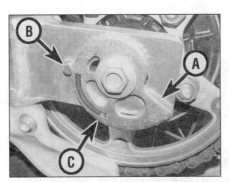

1.11 Adjust chain slack by turning the eccentric adjuster (A). Make sure the alignment of each adjuster in relation to the pin (B) is the same on each side. Renew the chain when the red zone (C) aligns with the pin (B)

adjustment marker with the arrow on the adjuster. When the arrow aligns with the red REPLACE CHAIN zone, the drive chain has stretched excessively and must be replaced with a new one. On completion, counter-hold the adjuster and tighten the locknut against it **(see illustration)**.
11 On XRV models, turn the eccentric adjuster on each side evenly until the amount of freeplay specified at the beginning of the Chapter is obtained at the centre of the bottom run of the chain **(see illustration)**. Following adjustment, check that each adjuster is in the same position in relation to the pin in the swingarm. It is important the same index line on each adjuster aligns with the pin; if not, the rear wheel will be out of alignment with the front. If there is a discrepancy in the chain adjuster positions, adjust one of them so that its position is exactly the same as the other. Check the chain freeplay as described above and readjust if necessary. Also check the alignment of the wear decal on the left-hand adjuster with the pin on the swingarm. When the red REPLACE CHAIN zone aligns with the pin, the drive chain has stretched excessively and must be replaced with a new one.

12 Counter-hold the axle head and tighten the axle nut to the torque setting specified at the beginning of the Chapter. Recheck the adjustment as above, then place the machine on its centrestand or an auxiliary stand and spin the wheel to make sure it runs freely.

Cleaning and lubrication

13 If required, wash the chain in paraffin (kerosene) or a suitable non-flammable or high flash-point solvent that will not damage the O-rings, using a soft brush to work any dirt out if necessary. Wipe the cleaner off the chain and allow it to dry, using compressed air if available. If the chain is excessively dirty it should be removed from the machine and allowed to soak in the paraffin or solvent (see Chapter 6). Note that if the motorcycle is ridden off-road, the chain should be cleaned and lubricated more often.
Caution: Don't use petrol (gasoline), an unsuitable solvent or other cleaning fluids which might damage the internal sealing properties of the chain. Don't use high-

1.14 Use only the correct lubricant and apply it as described

pressure water to clean the chain. The entire process shouldn't take longer than ten minutes, otherwise the O-rings could be damaged.
14 For routine lubrication, the best time to lubricate the chain is after the motorcycle has been ridden. When the chain is warm, the lubricant will penetrate the joints between the

sideplates better than when cold. **Note:** *Honda specifies SAE 80 to SAE 90 gear oil or an aerosol chain lube that it is suitable for O-ring or X-ring (sealed) chains; do not use any other chain lubricants – the solvents could damage the chain's sealing rings.* Apply the oil to the area where the sideplates overlap – not the middle of the rollers **(see illustration)**.

> **HAYNES HINT** *Apply the lubricant to the top of the lower chain run, so centrifugal force will work the oil into the chain when the bike is moving. After applying the lubricant, let it soak in a few minutes before wiping off any excess.*

> ⚠ *Warning: Take care not to get any lubricant on the tyres or brake system components. If any of the lubricant inadvertently contacts them, clean it off thoroughly using a suitable solvent or dedicated brake cleaner before riding the machine.*

Every 4000 miles (6000 km) or 6 months

2 Idle speed – 🔧
check and adjustment

1 The idle speed should be checked and adjusted before and after the carburettors are synchronised (balanced), after checking the valve clearances, and when it is obviously too high or too low. Before adjusting the idle speed turn the handlebars from side-to-side and check the idle speed does not change. If it does, the throttle cables may not be adjusted or routed correctly, or may be worn out. This is a dangerous condition that can cause loss of control of the bike. Be sure to correct this problem before proceeding.
2 The engine should be at normal operating temperature, which is usually reached after 10 to 15 minutes of stop-and-go riding. Place the

motorcycle on its sidestand, and make sure the transmission is in neutral.
3 The idle speed adjuster is a knurled knob located on the left-hand side of the carburettors **(see illustration)**. With the engine idling, adjust the speed by turning the adjuster until the idle speed listed in this Chapter's Specifications is obtained. Turn the screw clockwise to increase idle speed, and anti-clockwise to decrease it.
4 Snap the throttle open and shut a few times, then recheck the idle speed. If necessary, repeat the adjustment procedure.
5 If a smooth, steady idle can't be achieved, the fuel/air mixture may be incorrect (see Chapter 4) or the carburettors may need synchronising (see Section 17). Also check the intake manifold rubbers for cracks or a loose clamp which will cause an air leak, resulting in a weak mixture.

3 Brake shoes/pads – 🔧
wear check

Front brake – all models

1 Each brake pad has wear indicators in the form of cutouts in the top and bottom edges of the friction material; these cutouts should be visible by looking at the edges of the friction material from above or below the caliper body. On early XL600V models, a cast arrowhead in the top of the caliper body indicates where to view the pad material. The pads also have wear indicator grooves cut in the face of the friction material which will be visible by sighting along the disc surface to the side of the pad **(see illustration)**.
2 If the wear indicators aren't visible due to

2.3 Idle speed adjuster (arrowed)

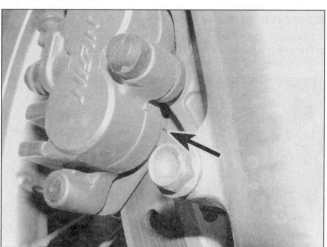

3.1 Brake pad wear indicator groove (arrowed)

1

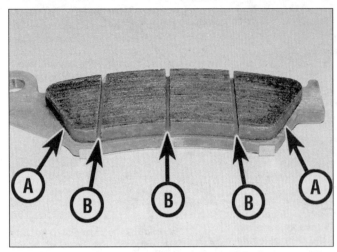

3.2 Front brake pad wear indicator cutouts (A) and grooves (B) – pad removed

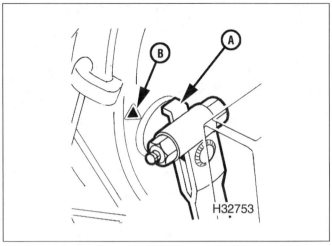

3.5 Rear brake shoe wear indicator pointer (A) and triangular reference mark on brake plate (B)

an accumulation of road dirt and brake dust, or there is any doubt as to how much friction material is left, the pads should be removed from the caliper for closer inspection **(see illustration)** as described in Chapter 7, Section 2.

3 If the friction material on any pad has worn down to expose the wear cutouts, or down level with the base of the grooves, the pads are worn and must be renewed, although it is advisable to renew the pads before they become this worn. **Note:** *Some after-market pads may use different wear indicators to those supplied as original equipment.*

4 Honda do not specify a minimum thickness for the brake pad friction material, but anything less than 1 mm should be considered worn. If the pads are excessively worn, check the brake disc(s) (see Chapter 7, Section 3). Note that the brake pads must be renewed as a pair. On models with twin front discs, both sets of pads in each front caliper should be renewed at the same time.

Rear brake

Rear drum brake – XL600V-H to L (1987 to 1990) models

5 The rear brake has a wear indicator to determine the amount of wear in the brake shoe friction material. The wear indicator is in the form of a pointer which moves with the brake arm when the pedal is applied. If, on full application of the brake pedal, the pointer aligns with the triangular reference mark on the brake plate the shoes are worn and must be replaced with new ones **(see illustration)**.

6 If you are in doubt as to the amount of friction material remaining, remove the brake plate and measure the thickness of the friction material on the shoes (see Chapter 7, Section 2). Honda specify a minimum thickness of 2 mm for the friction material. If the shoes are excessively worn they must be renewed as a pair.

7 If the shoes are renewed, also check the condition of the brake drum surface as described in Chapter 7, Section 3.

Rear disc brake – all models except the XL600V-H to L

8 Each brake pad has a wear indicator in the friction material which is in the form of a scribed line around the periphery. The wear indicators should be plainly visible by looking at the edges of the friction material from the rear edge of the pad from behind the caliper **(see illustration)**. If the indicators aren't visible due to an accumulation of road dirt and brake dust, or there is any doubt as to how much friction material is left, the pads should be removed from the caliper for closer

inspection **(see illustration)** as described in Chapter 7, Section 2.

9 If the friction material on either pad has worn down to the wear limit line, the pads are worn and must be renewed, although it is advisable to renew the pads before they become this worn. **Note:** *Some after-market pads may use different wear indicators to those supplied as original equipment.*

10 Honda do not specify a minimum thickness for the brake pad friction material, but anything less than 1 mm should be considered worn. If the pads are excessively worn, check the brake disc (see Chapter 7, Section 3).

11 The brake pads must be renewed as a pair.

4 Clutch – check and adjustment

1 Check that the clutch lever operates smoothly and easily.

2 If the clutch lever operation is heavy or stiff, remove the cable (see Chapter 2) and lubricate it (see Section 7). If the cable is still stiff, replace it with a new one. Install the lubricated or new cable (see Chapter 2).

3 With the cable operating smoothly, check that the clutch cable is correctly adjusted. Periodic adjustment is necessary to compensate for wear in the clutch plates and stretch of the cable. Check that the amount of freeplay in the cable, measured in terms of the amount of free movement at the clutch lever end, is within the specifications listed at the beginning of the Chapter.

4 If adjustment is required, pull back the rubber boot covering the adjuster at the lever end of the cable, then loosen the adjuster lockring and turn the adjuster in or out until the required amount of freeplay is obtained **(see illustrations)**. To increase freeplay, thread the adjuster into the lever bracket. To

3.8a View the rear brake pads (arrowed) from the rear of the caliper

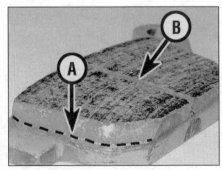

3.8b Brake pad wear indicator line (A) and groove (B)

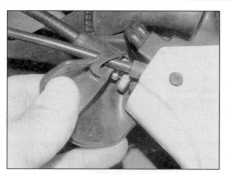

4.4a Pull back the rubber boot to access the adjuster

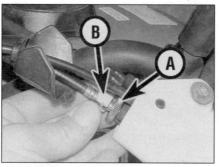

4.4b Slacken the lockring (A) and turn the adjuster (B) in or out as required

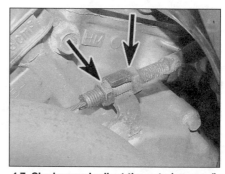

4.7 Slacken and adjust the nuts (arrowed) as described

reduce freeplay, thread the adjuster out of the bracket. Tighten the lockring securely.

5 When adjusting the cable make sure that the slots in the adjuster and lockring are not aligned with each other and the slot in the lever bracket – these slots are to allow removal of the cable, and if they are all aligned while the bike is in use the cable could jump out.

6 If all the adjustment has been taken up at the lever, reset the adjuster to give the maximum amount of freeplay (i.e. thread it all the way into the bracket), then set the correct amount of freeplay using the adjuster on the clutch end of cable. The adjuster (a threaded section in the cable with two locknuts) is set in a bracket on the clutch cover on the right-hand side of the engine. Access to it can be improved by removing either the belly-pan, the fairing side panel (XL600V and XRV750) or the fairing (XL650V), though this is not essential (just be careful not to let the spanner slip).

Caution: Take care not to burn your hands on the exhaust system if the engine has just been run.

7 Use the nuts on each end of the threaded section in the cable to adjust freeplay **(see illustration)**. To increase freeplay, slacken the front nut and tighten the rear nut until the freeplay is as specified, then tighten the front nut. To reduce freeplay, slacken the rear nut and tighten the front nut until the freeplay is as specified, then tighten the rear nut. Subsequent adjustments can now be made using the lever adjuster only.

5 Spark plugs – check and adjustment

1 Make sure your spark plug socket is the correct size before attempting to remove the plugs – a suitable one is supplied in the motorcycle's tool kit which is stored under the seat. Note that each cylinder has two spark plugs.

2 Access to the front cylinder spark plugs is best achieved after removing the fairing side panels (XL600V and XRV750) or the fairing (XL650V) as described in Chapter 8 **(see illustrations)**. While it is possible to access the plugs with the panels in situ, access is very restricted, making the task fiddly, and the panels can be easily damaged should a tool slip.

3 Access to the rear cylinder plug on the right-hand side is best achieved by either raising the rear of the fuel tank, or preferably by removing

the tank (see Chapter 4), although on XL600V models removing the right-hand side panel gives limited access **(see illustration)**. Access to the rear cylinder spark plug on the left-hand side is easy and unrestricted.

4 Work on one plug at a time. When working on the front cylinder left-hand plug and the rear cylinder right-hand plug, clean the area around the plug cap seal on the valve cover before removing the cap to prevent any dirt falling into the spark plug channel. When working on the front cylinder left-hand plug take great care not to damage the radiator fins **(see illustration 5.2b)**.

5 Pull the cap off the spark plug **(see illustration)**. Clean the area around the base of the plug to prevent any dirt falling into the engine. Using either the plug removing tool supplied in the bike's toolkit or a deep socket type wrench, unscrew and remove the plug from the cylinder head **(see illustration)**.

5.2a Front cylinder – right-hand plug

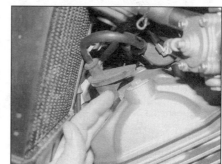

5.2b Front cylinder – left-hand plug

5.3 Rear cylinder – right-hand plug

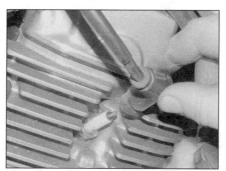

5.5a Pull the cap off the spark plug

5.5b If you are using the Honda tool, locate it onto the plug and use a ring spanner to turn it

1

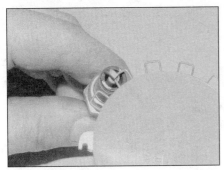

5.8a Using a wire type gauge to measure the spark plug electrode gap

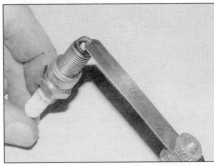

5.8b Using a feeler gauge to measure the spark plug electrode gap

5.8c Adjust the electrode gap by bending the side electrode only

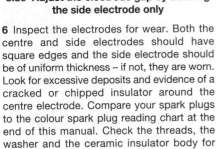

6 Inspect the electrodes for wear. Both the centre and side electrodes should have square edges and the side electrode should be of uniform thickness – if not, they are worn. Look for excessive deposits and evidence of a cracked or chipped insulator around the centre electrode. Compare your spark plugs to the colour spark plug reading chart at the end of this manual. Check the threads, the washer and the ceramic insulator body for cracks and other damage.

7 If the electrodes are not excessively worn, if no cracks or chips are visible in the insulator, and if the deposits can be easily removed with a wire brush, the plugs can be re-gapped and re-used. If in doubt concerning the condition of the plugs, replace them with new ones as the expense is minimal.

8 Before installing the plugs, make sure they are the correct type and heat range and check the gap between the electrodes **(see**

6.2 Make sure the level in each cell is between the UPPER and LOWER level lines

5.9 Fit the plug into the tool (the rubber insert should grip around the plug top) and thread it in by hand

illustrations). Compare the gap to that specified and adjust as necessary. If the gap must be adjusted, bend the side electrodes only and be very careful not to chip or crack the insulator nose **(see illustration)**. Make sure the washer is in place before installing each plug.

9 Fit the plug into the end of the tool, then use the tool to insert the plug **(see illustration)**. Since the cylinder head is made of aluminium, which is soft and easily damaged, thread the plug as far as possible into the head turning the tool by hand. Once the plug is finger-tight, the job can be finished with a spanner on the tool supplied or a socket drive **(see illustration 5.5b)**. If new plugs are being used, tighten them by 1/2 a turn after the washer has seated. If the old plugs are being reused, tighten them by 1/8 to 1/4 turn after they have seated, or if a torque wrench can be applied, tighten the spark

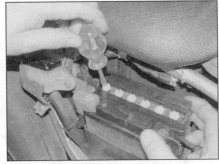

6.3a Remove the cell cap . . .

plugs to the torque setting specified at the beginning of the Chapter. Otherwise tighten them according the instructions on the box. Do not over-tighten them.

 HAYNES HiNT *You can slip a short length of hose over the end of the plug to use as a tool to thread it into place. The hose will grip the plug well enough to turn it, but will start to slip if the plug begins to cross-thread in the hole – this will prevent damaged threads.*

10 Fit the spark plug cap, making sure it locates correctly onto the plug **(see illustration 5.5a)**. Install all other components previously removed.

 HAYNES HiNT *Stripped plug threads in the cylinder head can be repaired with a Heli-Coil insert – see 'Tools and Workshop Tips' in the Reference section.*

6 Battery – check

Note: *The references made to the type of battery used in the different models assumes original spec equipment is installed. In the case of older models, it is possible that the standard battery has been replaced with a maintenance free (MF) battery at some point, in which case refer to the relevant text for the battery type, not the model of bike. The batteries are easy to distinguish – standard ones have removable caps (usually yellow) across the top, while MF batteries do not, and are usually marked MF on the front.*

Standard type batteries – XL600V and XRV750-L to N (1990 to 1992) models

Caution: *Be extremely careful when handling or working around the battery. The electrolyte is very caustic and an explosive gas (hydrogen) is given off when the battery is charging.*

1 Remove the right-hand side panel (see Chapter 8). Check that the terminals are clean and tight and that the casing is not damaged or leaking.

2 The electrolyte level is visible through the translucent battery case – it should be between the UPPER and LOWER level marks **(see illustration)**.

3 If the electrolyte is low, displace or remove the battery (see Chapter 9), then unscrew the cell caps and fill each cell to the upper level mark with distilled water **(see illustrations)**. Do not use tap water (except in an emergency), and do not overfill. The cell holes are quite small, so it may help to use a clean plastic squeeze bottle with a small spout to

6.3b . . . and top up the cell with distilled water

8.1a Undo the three screws . . .

8.1b . . . and withdraw the filter

add the water. Fit the battery cell caps, then install the battery (see Chapter 9).

4 See Chapter 9 for further details on batteries and other checks that can be made. If the machine is not in regular use, remove the battery and give it a refresher charge every month to six weeks (see Chapter 9).

Maintenance-free (MF) batteries – XL650V and XRV750-P models onwards (1993-on)

5 The above models are fitted with a sealed MF (maintenance free) battery. **Note:** *Do not attempt to remove the battery caps to check the electrolyte level or battery specific gravity. Removal will damage the caps, resulting in electrolyte leakage and battery damage.* All that should be done is to check that the terminals are clean and tight and that the casing is not damaged or leaking. See Chapter 9 for further details.

6 If the machine is not in regular use, remove the battery and give it a refresher charge every month to six weeks (see Chapter 9).

7 Wheels and tyres – general check

Tyres

1 Check the tyre condition and tread depth thoroughly – see *Daily (pre-ride) checks*.

Wheels

2 Visually check the spokes for damage, breakage and corrosion. A broken or bent spoke must be renewed immediately because the load taken by it will be transferred to adjacent spokes which may in turn fail.

3 Tap each spoke lightly with a screwdriver and note the sound produced. Properly tensioned spokes will make a sharp pinging sound, loose ones will produce a lower pitch and over-tight ones will be higher pitched. Unevenly tensioned spokes will promote rim misalignment. Spoke adjustment tools are available, but it is not just a case of slackening tight spokes and tightening loose ones as it is easy to create axial and radial runout in the rim by doing this. It is advisable to seek the help of a wheel building expert.

8 Air filter – check

Caution: If the machine is continually ridden in wet or dusty conditions, the air filter should be checked more frequently.

Air filter

1 On XL600V and XRV750-L to N (1990 to 1992) models, remove the left-hand side panel (see Chapter 8). Undo the screws securing the air filter in the housing and withdraw it **(see illustrations)**.

2 On XL650V models remove the fuel tank (see Chapter 4). Undo the screws securing the air filter housing cover and remove it **(see illustrations)**. Remove the filter from the housing, noting how it fits **(see illustration)**.

3 On XRV750-P models onwards (1993-on), undo the screws securing the air filter housing cover, noting which fit where, and remove the cover **(see illustrations)**. Withdraw the filter

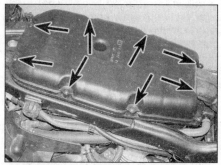

8.2a Undo the screws (arrowed) . . .

8.2b . . . then remove the cover . . .

8.2c . . . and lift out the filter

8.3a Undo the screws, noting which fits where . . .

8.3b . . . then remove the cover . . .

1

8.3c ... and withdraw the filter

8.4 Direct the air in the opposite direction of normal flow

from the housing, noting how it fits **(see illustration)**.

4 To clean the filter, tap it on a hard surface to dislodge any dirt and use compressed air to clear the element, directing the air in the opposite way to normal flow **(see illustration)**. Do not use any solvents or cleaning agents on the element as it is pre-treated with a dust adhesive. If the machine is constantly used in dirty or dusty conditions the filter should be replaced at more frequent intervals than specified. Check the element for tears and excessive oil contamination and replace it with a new one if necessary.

5 Install the filter in the housing, making sure

it is correctly seated, and secure it with its screws or cover. Install the side panel or fuel tank as required according to model.

Sub air-filter

Note: *There is no specific interval for cleaning the sub-air filter, but it should be inspected periodically to ensure the carburettor air vent system is clear.*

6 XL600V models have two sub-air filters, one on the back of each radiator – remove the fairing side panels to access them (see Chapter 8). XL650V models have one sub-air filter, mounted on the rear of the air filter housing.

7 On XL600V-T to X (1997 to 1999) models and XL650V models, remove the cover on the sub-air filter element housing(s), then remove the element and check for damage and excessive dirt or oil contamination and replace with new one(s) if necessary **(see illustrations)**.

1 Remove the plug from the end of the breather drain tube and allow it to drain into a suitable container **(see illustration)**. Check the condition of the tube, making sure it has

no cracks and splits. Replace the plug, making sure it is secure.

2 Drain the tube more regularly if the machine is regularly ridden at full throttle or in the rain, or at any time that an accumulation of deposits is noticed in the transparent tube.

10 Fuel strainer –
check (XL600V models)

⚠️ *Warning: Petrol (gasoline) is extremely flammable, so take extra precautions when you work on any part of the fuel system. Don't smoke or allow open flames or bare light bulbs near the work area, and don't work in a garage where a natural gas-type appliance is present. If you spill any fuel on your skin, rinse it off immediately with soap and water. When you perform any kind of work on the fuel system, wear safety glasses and have a fire extinguisher suitable for a Class B type fire (flammable liquids) on hand.*

1 Remove the left-hand fairing side panel (see Chapter 8). Turn the fuel tap OFF.

2 Unscrew the bowl on the underside of the fuel tap, noting the O-ring and being prepared to catch the residual fuel in a rag or suitable container **(see illustration)**. Remove the

8.7a Release the cover ...

8.7b ... and remove the element – XL600V shown

9.1 Remove the plug (arrowed) and allow any residue to drain

10.2a Unscrew the bowl using a spanner on the hex (arrowed) ...

10.2b . . . and remove the strainer

10.4a Install the strainer and fit a new O-ring . . .

10.4b . . . then thread the bowl onto the tap

strainer from the tap, noting how it fits (see illustration). Discard the O-ring and replace it with a new one.

3 Clean the bowl and the strainer using a non-flammable or high flash-point solvent.

Check the strainer for splits and other damage and replace it with a new one if necessary.

4 Fit the strainer into the tap, then install the bowl using a new O-ring and tighten it to the

torque setting specified at the beginning of the Chapter (see illustrations).

5 Turn the fuel tap ON and check for leaks around the rim of the bowl. Install the fairing side panel (see Chapter 8).

Every 8000 miles (12,000 km) or 12 months

Carry out all the items under the 4000 mile (6000 km) check, plus the following:

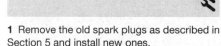

11 Spark plugs – renewal

1 Remove the old spark plugs as described in Section 5 and install new ones.

12 Stand(s), lever pivots and cables – lubrication

Note: *A centrestand is not fitted as standard on any of the models covered, but is available as an extra or aftermarket accessory.*

1 Since the controls, cables and various other components of a motorcycle are exposed to the elements, they should be lubricated periodically to ensure safe and trouble-free operation.

2 The footrests, clutch and brake levers, brake pedal (and on XL600V-H to L (1987 to 1990) models the linkage to the rear drum), gearchange lever and linkage, sidestand and centrestand (where fitted) pivots, should be lubricated frequently. In order for the lubricant to be applied where it will do the most good, the component should be disassembled. The lubricant recommended by Honda for each application is listed at the beginning of the Chapter. If chain or cable lubricant is being used, it can be applied to the pivot joint gaps and will usually work its way into the areas where friction occurs, so less disassembly of the component is needed (however it is always better to do so and clean off all dirt and old

lubricant first). If motor oil or light grease is being used, apply it sparingly as it may attract dirt (which could cause the controls to bind or wear at an accelerated rate). Note: *One of the best lubricants for the control lever pivots is a dry-film lubricant (available from many sources by different names).*

3 To lubricate the cables, disconnect the relevant cable at its upper end, then lubricate it with a pressure adapter and aerosol lubricant, or if one is not available, using the set-up shown (see illustrations). See Chapter 4 for the choke and throttle cable removal procedures, and Chapter 2 for the clutch cable.

13 Engine/transmission oil and filter – renewal

Warning: *Be careful when draining the oil, as the exhaust pipes, the engine, and the oil itself can cause severe burns.*

12.3a Lubricating a cable with a pressure lubricator. Make sure the tool seals around the inner cable

1 Consistent routine oil and filter changes are the single most important maintenance procedure you can perform on a motorcycle. The oil not only lubricates the internal parts of the engine, transmission and clutch, but it also acts as a coolant, a cleaner, a sealant, and a protectant. Because of these demands, the oil takes a terrific amount of abuse and should be replaced often with new oil of the recommended grade and type. Saving a little money on the difference in cost between a

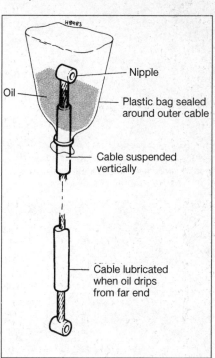

12.3b Lubricating a cable with a makeshift funnel and motor oil

1

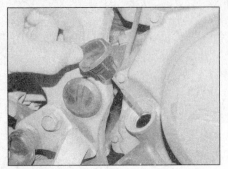

13.3 Unscrew the oil filler cap to act as a vent . . .

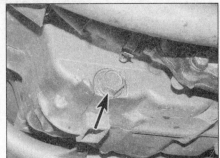

13.4a . . . then unscrew the oil drain plug (arrowed) . . .

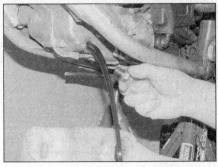

13.4b . . . and allow the oil to completely drain

good oil and a cheap oil won't pay off if the engine is damaged. The oil filter should be changed with every oil change.

2 Before changing the oil, warm up the engine so the oil will drain easily. Make sure the bike is on level ground. On models equipped with a centrestand, put the motorcycle on its sidestand instead. The oil drain plug is on the left-hand side of the engine so the angle created by using the sidestand will help the oil to drain. Remove the belly pan (see Chapter 8).

3 Position a clean drain tray below the engine. Unscrew the oil filler cap from the clutch cover to vent the crankcase and to act as a reminder that there is no oil in the engine **(see illustration)**.

4 Unscrew the oil drain plug from the left-hand side of the engine and allow the oil to flow into the drain tray **(see illustrations)**. Check the condition of the sealing washer on

the drain plug and replace it with a new one if it is damaged or worn – it is advisable to use a new one whatever the condition of the old one.

5 When the oil has completely drained, fit the plug to the sump, using a new sealing washer if necessary, and tighten it to the torque setting specified at the beginning of the Chapter **(see illustration)**. Avoid over-tightening, as it is quite easy to damage the threads in the sump.

6 Now place the drain tray below the oil filter, located on the back of the engine. Unscrew the oil filter using a filter socket (one can be obtained as a kit with the new filter from Honda dealers), a filter removing strap or a chain-wrench, and tip any residual oil into the drain tray **(see illustrations)**.

7 Smear clean engine oil onto the rubber seal on the new filter and thread it onto the engine **(see illustrations)**. Tighten it to the specified torque setting using the filter socket if

available **(see illustrations 13.6a and b)**, or tighten the filter as tight as possible by hand, or by the number of turns specified on the filter itself or its packaging. **Note:** *Do not use a strap or chain filter removing tool to tighten the filter as you will damage it.*

8 Refill the engine to the proper level using the recommended type and amount of oil (see *Daily (pre-ride) checks*). Install the filler cap **(see illustration 13.3)**. Start the engine and let it run for two or three minutes (make sure that the oil pressure light extinguishes after a few seconds). Shut it off, wait a few minutes, then check the oil level (see *Daily (pre-ride) checks*). If necessary, add more oil to bring the level to the upper mark on the dipstick. Check around the drain plug and the oil filter for leaks. A leak around the drain plug probably means a new washer is needed. A leak around the filter probably means it is not tight enough. Install the belly pan (see Chapter 8).

13.5 Install the drain plug, using a new sealing washer if necessary, and tighten it to the specified torque setting

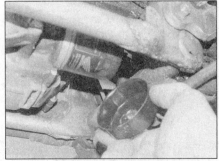

13.6a Unscrew the filter using a filter removing tool – the special socket shown . . .

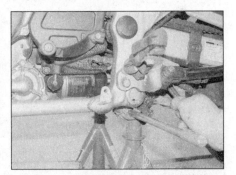

13.6b . . . with a socket extension is the easiest . . .

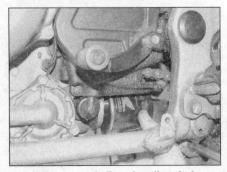

13.6c . . . and allow the oil to drain

13.7a Smear clean oil onto the seal . . .

13.7b . . . then install the filter and tighten it as described

HAYNES HiNT *Saving a little money on the difference between good and cheap oils won't pay off if the engine is damaged as a result.*

9 The old oil drained from the engine cannot be re-used and should be disposed of properly. Check with your local refuse disposal company, disposal facility or environmental agency to see whether they will accept the used oil for recycling. Don't pour used oil into drains or onto the ground.

HAYNES HiNT *Check the old oil carefully – if it is very metallic coloured, then the engine is experiencing wear from break-in (new engine) or from insufficient lubrication. If there are flakes or chips of metal in the oil, then something is drastically wrong internally and the engine will have to be disassembled for inspection and repair. If there are pieces of fibre-like material in the oil, the clutch is experiencing excessive wear and should be checked.*

14 Fuel system – check
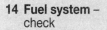

⚠ **Warning:** *Petrol (gasoline) is extremely flammable, so take extra precautions when you work on any part of the fuel system. Don't smoke or allow open flames or bare light bulbs near the work area, and don't work in a garage where a natural gas-type appliance is present. If you spill any fuel on your skin, rinse it off immediately with soap and water. When you perform any kind of work on the fuel system, wear safety glasses and have a fire extinguisher suitable for a Class B type fire (flammable liquids) on hand.*

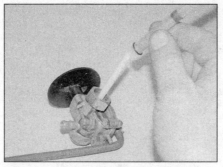

14.5a Remove the strainer from the tap . . .

Check

1 Check the tank, the fuel tap(s) and the fuel hoses for signs of leakage, deterioration or damage; in particular check that there is no leakage from the fuel hoses. Replace any hoses which are cracked or deteriorated with new ones. On XL models, similarly check the vacuum hose to the fuel tap.
2 If the fuel tap is leaking, tighten the mounting nut, bowl or any assembly screws according to your model and the source of the leak. Slacken all the screws a little first, then tighten them evenly and a little at a time to ensure the cover seats properly on the tap body. If leakage persists disassemble the tap (where possible), noting how the components fit (see Chapter 4).
3 Inspect and clean all components and rebuild the tap. On XL650V and XRV750 models, if leakage persists, replace the whole tap with a new one – individual components are not available. On XL600V models, if leakage persists, some components are available individually – consult your dealer.
4 If the carburettor gaskets are leaking, the carburettors should be disassembled and rebuilt using new gaskets and seals (see Chapter 4). On XL models, refer to Chapter 4 for checks on the operation of the vacuum diaphragm.

Filter cleaning

5 Cleaning or replacement of the fuel strainer and/or filter (XRV750 models only) is advised

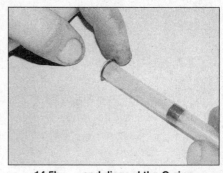

14.5b . . . and discard the O-ring

after a particularly high mileage has been covered. It is also necessary if fuel starvation is suspected, or if the filter looks clogged or dirty. Honda do not specify a replacement interval – fuel is so clean now that this may not always be necessary. Check the condition of the inside of your tank – if it is old and there is evidence of rust, remove, drain and clean the tank and tap (see Chapter 4), and fit a new filter afterwards.

Fuel strainer – all models

4 A fuel strainer is fitted in the tank and is held in place by the fuel tap. Remove the fuel tap (see Chapter 4).
5 Remove the gauze strainer and discard the O-ring **(see illustrations)**. Clean off all traces of dirt and fuel sediment. Check the gauze for holes. If any are found, a new strainer must be fitted.
6 Replace the O-ring with a new one, then fit the strainer onto the tap. Install the tap (see Chapter 4).

In-line fuel filter – XRV750 models

7 An in-line fuel filter is fitted in the hose from the fuel tap to the fuel pump. To replace the filter, raise the rear of the fuel tank, or remove it altogether for better access (see Chapter 4).
8 Release the clamp and detach the fuel hose from the tap **(see illustration)**. Have a rag handy to soak up any residual fuel, then release the clamp securing the fuel inlet hose to the fuel pump and detach the hose **(see illustration)**.

1

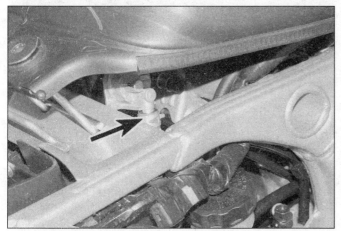

14.8a Release the clamp (arrowed) and detach the hose from the tap

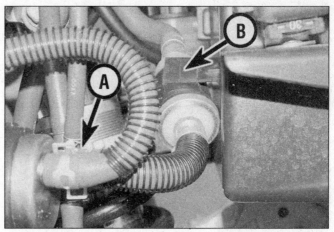

14.8b Release the clamp (A) and detach the hose from the pump, then free the filter from its holder (B) and remove it

15.3 Throttle cable freeplay is measured in terms of twistgrip rotation

Release the filter from its holder and remove it along with the hoses, then disconnect the hoses, noting which fits where, and discard the filter.

9 Fit the hoses to the unions on the new filter and secure them with the clamps (the hose from the fuel tap goes on the plain end, and the hose to the pump goes on the lipped end). Install the new filter so that its arrow points in the direction of fuel flow (i.e. towards the pump). Fit the hose to the inlet union on the pump and secure it with the clamp. Fit the hose to the fuel tap and secure it with the clamp, then lower the tank (see Chapter 4).

10 Start the engine and check that there are no leaks.

---

15 Throttle and choke cables – check and adjustment

Throttle cables

1 Make sure the throttle grip rotates smoothly and freely from fully closed to fully open with the front wheel turned at various angles. The grip should return automatically from fully open to fully closed when released.

2 If the throttle sticks, this is probably due to a

15.4a Pull back the rubber boot to access the adjuster

cable fault. Remove the cables (see Chapter 4) and lubricate them (see Section 12). Check that the inner cables slide freely and easily in the outer cables. If not, replace the cables with new ones. With the cables removed, make sure the throttle twistgrip rotates freely on the handlebar. Install the cables, making sure they are correctly routed. If this fails to improve the operation of the throttle, the cables must be replaced with new ones. Note that in very rare cases the fault could lie in the carburettors rather than the cables, necessitating their removal and inspection (see Chapter 4).

3 With the throttle operating smoothly, check for a small amount of freeplay in the cables, measured in terms of the amount of twistgrip rotation before the throttle opens, and compare the amount to that listed in this Chapter's Specifications **(see illustration)**. If it's incorrect, adjust the cables to correct it as follows.

4 Freeplay adjustments can be made using the adjuster in the accelerator cable where it leaves the throttle/switch housing on the handlebar. Pull the cable boot away from the housing **(see illustration)**. Loosen the locknut and turn the adjuster in or out as required until the specified amount of freeplay is obtained (see this Chapter's Specifications), then retighten the locknut **(see illustration)**.

5 If the adjuster has reached its limit of adjustment, reset it by turning it fully in so that the freeplay is at a maximum, then tighten the locknut and refit the boot. The cable must now be adjusted at the carburettor end. On XL600V models, remove the left-hand fairing side panel (see Chapter 8). On XL650V and XRV750 models, remove the fuel tank (see Chapter 4). The adjuster is on the lower cable in the bracket. Slacken the adjuster locknut, then screw the adjuster in or out as required, making sure the rear nut remains captive in the bracket, thereby threading itself along the adjuster as you turn it, until the specified amount of freeplay is obtained, then tighten the locknut **(see illustration)**. Subsequent adjustments can now be made at the throttle end. If the cable cannot be adjusted as specified, replace it with a new one (see Chapter 4).

⚠️ **Warning: Turn the handlebars all the way through their travel with the engine idling. Idle speed should not change. If it does, the cables may be routed incorrectly. Correct this condition before riding the bike.**

6 Check that the throttle twistgrip operates smoothly and snaps shut quickly when released.

Choke cable

7 If the choke does not operate smoothly this is probably due to a cable fault. Remove the cable (see Chapter 4) and lubricate it (see Section 12). Check that the inner cable slides freely and easily in the outer cable. If not, replace the cable with a new one. With the cable removed, make sure the choke lever is able to move freely. Install the cable, making sure it is correctly routed.

8 If this fails to improve the operation of the choke, the fault could lie in the choke plungers and their bores in the carburettors rather than the cable (see Chapter 4).

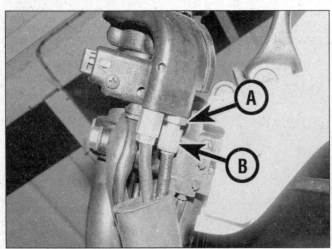

15.4b Throttle cable adjuster locknut (A) and adjuster (B) – throttle end

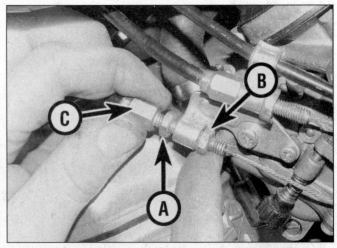

15.5 Slacken the locknut (A), then turn the adjuster (C) as required, keeping the rear (captive) nut (B) locked

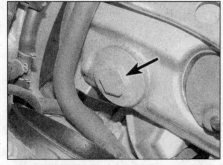

16.4 Remove the crankshaft end cap (A) and the timing inspection cap (B)

16.5a Unscrew the caps using a spanner on the hex (arrowed)

16.5b The covers are secured by two bolts (arrowed)

16 Valve clearances – check and adjustment

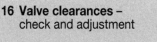
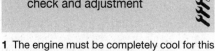

1 The engine must be completely cool for this maintenance procedure, so let the machine sit overnight before beginning.

2 Remove the fuel tank and the air duct on XL600V and XRV750-L to N (1990 to 1992) models. Remove the fuel tank and the air filter housing on XL650V and XRV750-P models onward (1993-on). Refer to Chapter 4 for details.

3 Either displace or remove the right-hand radiator (not necessary if working on rear cylinder only).

4 If the belly pan on your model obscures the alternator cover, remove it (see Chapter 8). Unscrew the crankshaft end cap and the timing mark inspection cap from the alternator cover (see illustration). Check the condition of the cap O-rings and discard them if they are damaged, deformed or deteriorated.

5 Remove the valve inspection caps/covers from each valve cover – the caps (above the exhaust valves) can be unscrewed using a suitable spanner or socket, while the covers (above the inlet valves) are secured by two bolts (see illustrations). Check the condition of the cap and cover O-rings and discard them

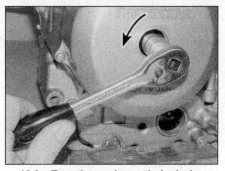

16.6a Turn the engine anti-clockwise using a socket on the timing rotor bolt . . .

if they are damaged, deformed or deteriorated. Unscrew the spark plugs to allow the engine to be turned over easier (see Section 5).

6 Starting with the front cylinder, rotate the engine anti-clockwise using a suitable socket on the alternator rotor bolt until the line next to the 'FT' mark on the flywheel aligns with the notch in the timing mark inspection hole (see illustrations). At this point make sure that the cylinder is at TDC (top dead centre) on the compression stroke (and not the exhaust stroke) by checking for some free movement between each rocker arm and the valve. There must be freeplay evident in all three rocker arms. If not, turn the engine anti-clockwise

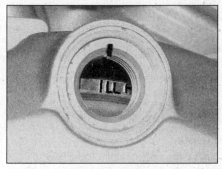

16.6b . . . until the line next to the FT mark aligns with the notch

through one full turn (360°) until the 'FT' mark again aligns with the notch. There should now be freeplay in all rocker arms indicating that the engine is correctly positioned.

7 Insert a feeler gauge of the correct thickness (see Specifications) between each rocker arm adjusting screw and valve and check that it is a firm sliding fit (see illustration). If it is either too loose or too tight, slacken the locknut and turn the adjusting screw in or out as required until a firm sliding fit is obtained, then tighten the locknut to the torque setting specified at the beginning of the Chapter, making sure the adjusting screw does not rotate as you do so (see illustration). Re-check the clearances,

1

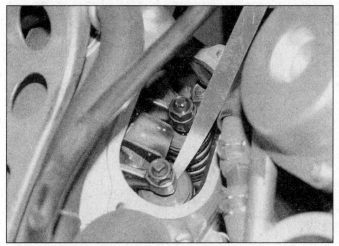

16.7a Insert the feeler gauge between the base of the adjusting screw and the top of the valve stem as shown

16.7b Slacken the locknut using an offset ring spanner and turn the adjusting screw using pliers

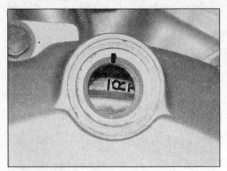

16.8 Turn the engine until the line next to the RT mark aligns with the notch

16.9a If necessary use new O-rings on the valve caps and covers . . .

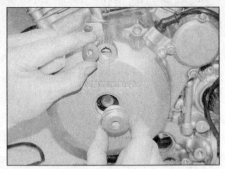

16.9b . . . and the inspection and end caps

not forgetting that on most models there is a difference between the inlet valve clearance and the exhaust valve clearance. On completion turn the engine anti-clockwise two full turns (720°), then align the marks so it is at TDC on the compression stroke as before and recheck the clearances.

8 Moving to the rear cylinder, rotate the engine anti-clockwise using a suitable socket on the alternator rotor bolt until the line next to the 'RT' mark on the flywheel aligns with the notch in the timing mark inspection hole **(see illustration)**. At this point make sure that the cylinder is at TDC (top dead centre) on the compression stroke (and not the exhaust stroke) by checking for some free movement between each rocker arm and the valve. There must be freeplay evident in all three rocker arms. If not, turn the engine anti-clockwise through one full turn (360°) until the 'RT' mark again aligns with the notch. There should now be freeplay in all rocker arms indicating that the engine is correctly positioned. Check and adjust the valve clearance as described in Step 7.

9 Install all disturbed components in a reverse of the removal sequence, referring to the relevant Chapters where necessary. Install the valve inspection caps and covers using new O-rings if necessary, and smear the O-rings with clean oil **(see illustration)**. Install the crankshaft and timing inspection caps using new O-rings if necessary, and smear the O-rings with clean oil **(see illustration)**. Apply a smear of molybdenum disulphide grease to the threads of the caps and tighten them securely.

17 Carburettors – synchronisation

> ⚠️ **Warning: Petrol (gasoline) is extremely flammable, so take extra precautions when you work on any part of the fuel system. Don't smoke or allow open flames or bare light bulbs near the work area, and don't work in a garage where a natural gas-type appliance is present. If you spill any fuel on your skin, rinse it off immediately with soap and water. When you perform any kind of work on the fuel system, wear safety glasses and have a fire extinguisher suitable for a Class B type fire (flammable liquids) on hand.**

> ⚠️ **Warning: Take great care not to burn your hand on the hot engine unit when accessing the gauge take-off points on the intake manifolds. Do not allow exhaust gases to build up in the work area; either perform the check outside or use an exhaust gas extraction system.**

1 Carburettor synchronisation is simply the process of adjusting the carburettors so they pass the same amount of fuel/air mixture to each cylinder. This is done by measuring the vacuum produced in each intake duct. Carburettors that are out of synchronisation will result in decreased fuel mileage, increased engine temperature, less than ideal throttle response and higher vibration levels.

2 To properly synchronise the carburettors,

you will need a set of vacuum gauges or calibrated tubes to indicate engine vacuum. The equipment used should be suitable for a twin cylinder engine and come complete with the necessary adapters and hoses to fit the take-off points. **Note:** *Because of the nature of the synchronisation procedure and the need for special instruments, most owners leave the task to a Honda dealer.*

3 Start the engine and let it run until it reaches normal operating temperature, then check that the idle speed is correctly set, and adjust it if necessary (see Section 2).

> ⚠️ **Warning: The engine and carburettors will be hot. With the restricted access to the screws, great care must be taken not to burn yourself while synchronising the carburettors.**

4 Remove the fuel tank (see Chapter 4).

5 On XL600V models, release the clamp and detach the fuel tap vacuum hose from the take-off point on the rear cylinder intake duct **(see illustration)**. Undo the blanking screw from the front cylinder intake duct and thread a suitable hose adapter in its place **(see illustrations)**.

6 On XL650V models, release the clamp and detach the fuel tap vacuum hose from the take-off point on the rear cylinder intake duct **(see illustration 17.5a)**. Release the clamp and detach the PAIR solenoid valve vacuum hose from the take-off point on the front cylinder intake duct **(see illustration)**.

7 On XRV750 models, undo the blanking screw from each cylinder intake duct and thread suitable hose adapters in their places **(see illustrations 17.5b and c)**.

17.5a Detach the fuel tap vacuum hose from the rear cylinder take-off point

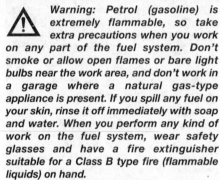

17.5b Undo the blanking screw (arrowed) . . .

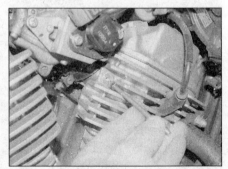

17.5c . . . and thread a suitable adapter in its place

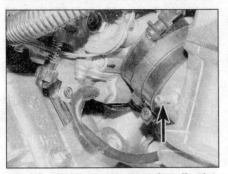

17.6 Front cylinder vacuum take-off point – XL650V models

17.8 Connect the gauge hoses to the vacuum take-off points

17.9 One way of setting up an auxiliary fuel supply

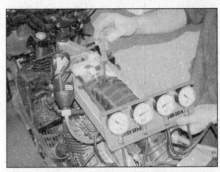

17.11 Adjusting carburettor synchronisation. Note how on XL models the adjustment screw is accessed via the hole in the air duct or filter housing

8 Connect the gauge hoses to the vacuum take-off points **(see illustration)**. Make sure they are a good fit because any air leaks will result in false readings.

9 Arrange a temporary fuel supply, either by using a small temporary tank (a two-stroke motorcycle oil tank works very well as it has an outlet union on its base to which a link hose can be attached. Similarly an old oil container with a nozzle type cap can be used **(see illustration)**, or by using extra long pipes to the now remote fuel tank, making sure on XL models the tank is sitting higher than the carburettors, or the fuel will not flow (XRV models have a fuel pump). On XRV750-P models onward (1993-on) the tank can be set in its normal place on the bike as the carburettor synchronisation screw is accessed from below the carburettors – on all other models this is not possible as the screw is accessed via a hole in the top of the air duct. On all XRV750 models, make sure that any auxiliary tank or hose is connected into the hose that normally attaches to the fuel tap so that the filter and pump are included in the supply system.

10 Start the engine. If using vacuum gauges fitted with damping adjustment, set this so that the needle flutter is just eliminated but so that they can still respond to small changes in pressure.

11 The vacuum readings for the cylinders should be the same, or at least within the maximum difference specified at the beginning of the Chapter. If the vacuum readings vary, adjust the carburettors by turning the synchronising screw situated in the throttle linkage between the carburettors until the readings are the same. On XRV750-P models onward (1993-on) the screw is accessed from below the carburettors – on all other models it is accessed using a long screwdriver inserted through the hole in the top of the air duct **(see illustration)**. **Note:** *Do not press hard on the screw whilst adjusting it, otherwise a false reading will be obtained.*

12 When the carburettors are synchronised, open and close the throttle quickly to settle the linkage, and recheck the gauge readings, readjusting if necessary.

13 When the adjustment is complete, recheck the vacuum readings, then adjust the idle speed by turning the throttle stop screw (see Section 2) until the idle speed listed in this Chapter's Specifications is obtained. Stop the engine.

14 Remove the vacuum gauges and the hose adapters, then replace the blanking screw(s) and/or attach the vacuum hose(s) to the take-off points as required by your model (see Step 5, 6 or 7). Install the fuel tank (see Chapter 4).

18 Cooling system – check

> ⚠ **Warning: The engine must be cool before beginning this procedure.**

1 Check the coolant level (see *Daily (pre-ride) checks*).

2 On XL600V and XRV750 models remove the fairing side panels, and on XL650V models remove the fairing (see Chapter 8). On all models remove the belly pan see Chapter 8).

3 Check the entire cooling system for evidence of leakage. Examine each rubber coolant hose along its entire length. Look for cracks, abrasions and other damage. Squeeze each hose at various points to see whether they are dried out or hard. They should feel firm, yet pliable, and return to their original shape when released. If necessary, replace them with new ones (see Chapter 3).

4 Check for evidence of leaks at each cooling system joint and around the pump on the left-hand side of the engine. Tighten the hose clips carefully to prevent future leaks. If the pump cover is leaking, check that the cover bolts are tight. If they are, replace the O-ring in the cover with a new one (see Chapter 3).

5 To prevent leakage of coolant from the cooling system to the lubrication system and vice versa, two seals are fitted on the pump shaft. On the bottom of the pump housing there is a drain hole **(see illustration)**. If either seal fails, the drain allows the coolant or oil to escape and prevents them mixing. If both seals fail the oil and coolant mix to form a white emulsion. The seal on the water pump side is of the mechanical type which bears on the rear face of the impeller. The second seal, which is mounted behind the mechanical seal

is of the normal feathered lip type. The oil seal is available separately, while the mechanical seal comes installed in the pump and is not available on its own. If on inspection the drain shows signs of oil leakage, remove the pump and replace the oil seal with a new one. If the drain shows signs of coolant leakage, or a coolant/oil mixture in the form of a white emulsion, remove the pump and replace it with a new one. Refer to Chapter 3 for details.

6 Check the radiator for leaks and other damage. Leaks in the radiator leave tell-tale scale deposits or coolant stains on the outside of the core below the leak. If leaks are noted, remove the radiator (see Chapter 3) and have it repaired or replace it with a new one.

Caution: Do not use a liquid leak stopping compound to try to repair leaks.

18.5 Check the pump drain hole (arrowed) for signs of leakage

1

18.8 Remove the pressure cap as described

7 Check the radiator fins for mud, dirt and insects, which may impede the flow of air through the radiator. If the fins are dirty, remove the radiator (see Chapter 3) and clean it using water or low pressure compressed air directed through the fins from the inner side. If the fins are bent or distorted, straighten them carefully with a screwdriver. If the air flow is restricted by bent or damaged fins over more than 20% of the surface area, replace the radiator with a new one.

8 Cover the pressure cap with a heavy cloth, then remove the cap from the radiator filler neck by turning it anti-clockwise until it reaches a stop **(see illustration)**. If you hear a hissing sound (indicating there is still pressure in the system), wait until it stops. Now press down on the cap and continue turning it until it can be removed. Check the condition of the coolant in the system. If it is rust-coloured or if accumulations of scale are visible, drain and flush the system and refill it with new coolant (see Section 28). Check the cap seal for cracks and other damage. If in doubt about the pressure cap's condition, have it tested by a Honda dealer or replace it with a new one.

9 Check the antifreeze content of the coolant with an antifreeze hydrometer. Sometimes coolant looks like it's in good condition, but might be too weak to offer adequate

protection. If the hydrometer indicates a weak mixture, drain, flush and refill the system (see Section 28).

10 Install the cap by turning it clockwise until it reaches the first stop then push down on it and continue turning until it can turn no further. Start the engine and let it reach normal operating temperature, then check for leaks again. As the coolant temperature increases, the electric fan (mounted on the back of the right-hand radiator) should come on automatically and the temperature should begin to drop. If it does not, refer to Chapter 3 and check the fan and fan circuit carefully.

11 If the coolant level is consistently low, and no evidence of leaks can be found, have the entire system pressure checked by a Honda dealer.

12 On XRV750 models, check the oil cooler (located below the left-hand radiator) and its hoses in a similar fashion to checking the radiator and its hoses **(see illustration)**. Refer to Chapter 2 for details of oil cooler and hose removal and installation if required.

19 Brake system – check

1 A routine general check of the brake system will ensure that any problems are discovered and remedied before the rider's safety is jeopardised.

2 Check the brake lever and pedal for loose connections, improper or rough action, excessive play, bends, and other damage. On XL600V-H to L (1987 to 1990) models, similarly check the linkage between the rear pedal and the rear wheel. Replace any damaged parts with new ones (see Chapter 7).

3 Make sure all brake component fasteners are tight. Check the brake shoes and/or pads for wear (see Section 3) and make sure the fluid level in the reservoirs is correct (see *Daily*

18.12 On XRV750 models check the oil cooler (arrowed) as well

(pre-ride) checks). Look for leaks at the hose and pipe connections and check for cracks in the hoses and pipes **(see illustration)**. If the lever or pedal is spongy, bleed the brakes (see Chapter 7).

4 Make sure the brake light operates when the front brake lever is pulled in. The front brake light switch, mounted on the underside of the master cylinder, is not adjustable. If it fails to operate properly, check it (see Chapter 7).

5 Make sure the brake light is activated just before the rear brake takes effect. If adjustment is necessary, hold the switch and turn the adjuster ring on the switch body until the brake light is activated when required **(see illustration)**. The switch is mounted on the inside of the frame, above the brake pedal and just ahead of the master cylinder. If the brake light comes on too late, turn the ring clockwise. If the brake light comes on too soon or is permanently on, turn the ring anti-clockwise. If the switch doesn't operate the brake light, check it (see Chapter 9).

6 On all except XL600V-H to P (1987 to 1993) models, the front brake lever has a span adjuster which alters the distance of the lever from the handlebar **(see illustration)**. Each setting is identified by a notch in the adjuster which aligns with the arrow on the lever. Turn

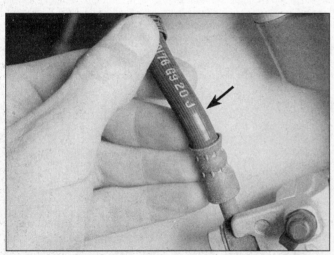

19.3 Flex the hoses and check for cracks, bulges and leaking fluid. Also check the pipes and all connections for leaks

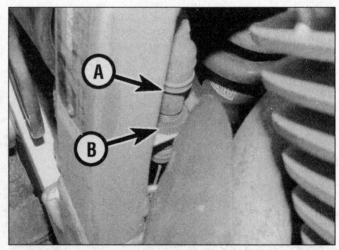

19.5 Hold the rear brake light switch body (A) and turn the adjuster ring (B) as required

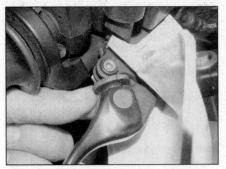

19.6 Adjusting the front brake lever span

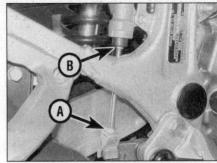

19.7a Slacken the locknut (A) and turn the pushrod using the hex (B) to adjust pedal height

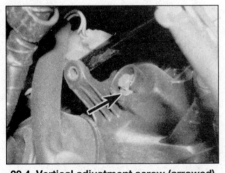

19.7b On some models the adjusting hex (B) is at the top of the pushrod. Locknut (A)

the adjuster ring until the setting which best suits the rider is obtained.

7 The height of the rear brake pedal can be adjusted to suit the rider's preference. On XL600V-H to L (1987 to 1990) models, slacken the locknut on the pedal stopper bolt in the footrest bracket, then turn the bolt until the pedal is at the desired height. After adjustment, make sure you adjust the amount of freeplay in the pedal before the brake takes effect (see *Daily (pre-ride) checks*). On all other models, slacken the clevis locknut, then turn the pushrod using a spanner on the hex (either on the base or at the top of the rod, according to model) until the pedal is at the desired height **(see illustrations)**. On completion tighten the locknut securely. On all models adjust the rear brake light switch after adjusting the pedal height (see Step 5).

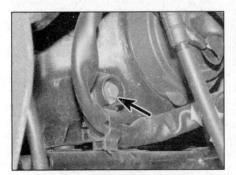

20.4 Vertical adjustment screw (arrowed)

20 Headlight aim – check and adjustment

Note: *An improperly adjusted headlight may cause problems for oncoming traffic or provide poor, unsafe illumination of the road ahead. Before adjusting the headlight aim, be sure to consult with local traffic laws and regulations – for UK models refer to MOT Test Checks in the Reference section.*

1 The headlight beam(s) can adjusted both horizontally and vertically. Before making any adjustment, check that the tyre pressures are correct and the suspension is adjusted as required. Make any adjustments to the headlight aim with the machine on level ground, with the fuel tank half full and with an assistant sitting on the seat. If the bike is usually ridden with a passenger on the back, have a second assistant to do this.

XL600V-H to P (1987 to 1993) models

2 Vertical adjustment is made by turning the adjuster screw below the headlight unit using a screwdriver inserted through the access hole in the fairing. Turn it clockwise to move the beam down, and anti-clockwise to move it up.

3 Horizontal adjustment is made by turning the adjuster screw on the left-hand side of the headlight, accessing it from inside the fairing.

Turn it clockwise to move the beam to the left, and anti-clockwise to move it to the right.

XL600V-R to X (1994 to 1999) models

4 Vertical adjustment is made by turning the adjuster screw on the top right-hand corner of the headlight **(see illustration)**. Turn it clockwise to move the beam up, and anti-clockwise to move it down.

5 Horizontal adjustment is made by turning the adjuster screw on the bottom left-hand corner of the headlight **(see illustration)**. Turn it clockwise to move the beam to the left, and anti-clockwise to move it to the right.

XL650V models

6 Vertical adjustment is made by turning the adjuster knob on the bottom left-hand corner of the headlight **(see illustration)**. Turn it clockwise to move the beam up, and anti-clockwise to move it down.

7 Horizontal adjustment is made by turning the adjuster screw on the bottom right-hand corner of the headlight **(see illustration 20.6)**. Turn it clockwise to move the beam to the right, and anti-clockwise to move it to the left.

XRV750 models

8 Vertical adjustment of the right-hand headlight unit is made by turning the wingnut on the bottom left-hand corner – turn it clockwise to move the beam down and anti-clockwise to move it up **(see illustration)**.

1

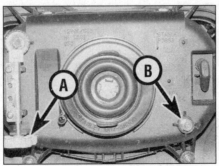

20.5 Horizontal adjustment screw (arrowed)

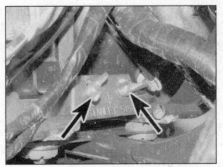

20.6 Vertical adjustment screw (A), horizontal adjustment screw (B)

20.8a Vertical adjustment wingnuts (arrowed)

20.8b Horizontal adjustment screws (arrowed)

Horizontal adjustment is made by turning the adjuster screw on the top right-hand corner of the unit – turn it clockwise to move the beam to the right and anti-clockwise to move it to the left **(see illustration)**.

9 Vertical adjustment of the left-hand headlight unit is made by turning the wingnut on the bottom right-hand corner – turn it clockwise to move the beam down and anti-clockwise to move it up **(see illustration 20.8a)**. Horizontal adjustment is made by turning the adjuster screw on the top left-hand corner of the unit – turn it clockwise to move the beam to the left and anti-clockwise to move it to the right **(see illustration 20.8b)**.

21 Sidestand – check

Note: All models are fitted with a sidestand as standard equipment. A centrestand is available as an optional extra.

1 Check the stand spring(s) for damage and distortion. The spring(s) must be capable of retracting the stand fully and holding it retracted when the motorcycle is in use. If a spring is sagged or broken it must be replaced with a new one.
2 Lubricate the stand pivots regularly (see Section 12).
3 Check the stand and its mount for bends and cracks. Stands can often be repaired by welding.
4 On all except XL600V-H and J (1987 and 1988) models, check the operation of the

sidestand switch by shifting the transmission into neutral, retracting the stand and starting the engine. Pull in the clutch lever and select a gear. Extend the sidestand. The engine should stop as the sidestand is extended. If the sidestand switch does not operate as described, check its circuit (see Chapter 9).

22 Suspension – check

1 The suspension components must be maintained in top operating condition to ensure rider safety. Loose, worn or damaged suspension parts decrease the motorcycle's stability and control.

Front suspension

2 While standing alongside the motorcycle, apply the front brake and push on the handlebars to compress the forks several times. See if they move up-and-down smoothly without binding. If binding is felt, the forks should be disassembled and inspected (see Chapter 6).
3 Lift the rubber gaiter off the top of each fork slider. Inspect the area around the dust seal for signs of oil leakage, then carefully lever up the seal using a flat-bladed screwdriver and inspect the area around the fork seal. If leakage is evident, the seals must be replaced with new ones (see Chapter 6). Seat the gaiter back into position after the check.
4 Check the tightness of all suspension nuts and bolts to be sure none have worked loose.

Rear suspension

5 Inspect the rear shock absorber for fluid leakage and tightness of its mountings. If leakage is found, the shock must be replaced with a new one (see Chapter 6).
6 With the aid of an assistant to support the bike, compress the rear suspension several times. It should move up and down freely without binding. If any binding is felt, the worn or faulty component must be identified and checked (see Chapter 6). The problem could be due to either the shock absorber, the suspension linkage components or the swingarm components.

7 Support the motorcycle on its centrestand if fitted, or on an auxiliary stand, so that the rear wheel is off the ground. Grab the swingarm and rock it from side to side – there should be no discernible movement at the rear **(see illustration)**. If there's a little movement or a slight clicking can be heard, inspect the tightness of all the swingarm and rear suspension mounting bolts and nuts, referring to the torque settings specified at the beginning of Chapter 6, and re-check for movement. Next, grasp the top of the rear wheel and pull it upwards – there should be no discernible freeplay before the shock absorber begins to compress **(see illustration)**. Any freeplay felt in either check indicates worn bearings or bushes (according to model) in the suspension linkage or swingarm, or worn shock absorber mountings. The worn components must be identified and replaced with new ones (see Chapter 6).
8 To make an accurate assessment of the swingarm bearings, remove the rear wheel (see Chapter 7) and the bolt securing the suspension linkage assembly to the swingarm (see Chapter 6).
9 Grasp the rear of the swingarm with one hand and place your other hand at the junction of the swingarm and the frame. Try to move the rear of the swingarm from side-to-side. Any wear (play) in the bearings should be felt as movement between the swingarm and the frame at the front. If there is any play the swingarm will be felt to move forward and backward at the front (not from side-to-side).
10 Next, move the swingarm up and down through its full travel. It should move freely, without any binding or rough spots. If there is any play in the swingarm or if it does not move freely, remove the bearings for inspection (see Chapter 6).
11 On XL600V-H and J (1987 and 1988) models the suspension linkage components, which have bushes as opposed to bearings, are equipped with grease nipples so that the bushes can be lubricated with fresh grease. Using a suitable grease gun, apply grease to each nipple. Note that the linkage should still be periodically be disassembled so that all the old grease can be cleaned out (see Section 33).

23 Steering head bearings – check and adjustment

1 Steering head bearings can become dented, rough or loose during normal use of the machine. In extreme cases, worn or loose steering head bearings can cause steering wobble – a condition that is potentially dangerous.

Check

2 Support the motorcycle on its centrestand if fitted, or on an auxiliary stand, so that the front wheel is off the ground.
3 Point the front wheel straight-ahead and

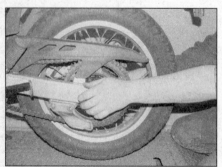

22.7a Checking for play in the swingarm bearings

22.7b Checking for play in the rear shock mountings and suspension linkage bearings

slowly move the handlebars from side-to-side. Any dents or roughness in the bearing races will be felt and the bars will not move smoothly and freely. Again point the wheel straight ahead, then tap the front of the wheel to one side. The wheel should 'fall' under its own weight to the limit of its lock, indicating that the bearings are not too tight. Check for similar movement to the other side. If the steering doesn't move freely through its entire lock, and it's not due to the resistance of cables or hoses, then the bearings should be adjusted as described below.

4 Next, grasp the bottom of the forks and gently pull and push them forward and backward **(see illustration)**. Any looseness or freeplay in the steering head bearings will be felt as front-to-rear movement of the forks. If play is felt, adjust the bearings as described below.

 Make sure you are not mistaking any movement between the bike and stand, or between the stand and the ground, for freeplay in the bearings. Do not pull and push the forks too hard – a gentle movement is all that is needed. Freeplay in the forks themselves due to worn bushes can also be misinterpreted as steering head bearing play – do not confuse the two.

Adjustment

5 As a precaution, remove the fuel tank (see Chapter 4). Though not actually necessary, this will prevent the possibility of damage should a tool slip.

6 Displace the handlebars from the top yoke (see Chapter 6). Support them so the brake master cylinder is upright to prevent the possibility of fluid leakage. There is no need to remove assemblies from the handlebars, or to disconnect any cables, hoses or wiring. Note that if you do not have a socket or torque wrench, and are using a spanner to slacken and tighten the steering stem nut, the handlebars can remain in place.

7 Slacken the fork clamp bolts in the top yoke **(see illustration)**.

23.4 Checking for play in the steering head bearings

8 Slacken the steering stem nut **(see illustration)**. If you have the Honda special tool for the adjuster nut, or a suitable equivalent (which can be made by cutting castellations into an old socket, or a peg spanner to which a torque wrench can be applied), or are using a C-spanner, release any cables and wiring from guides on the top yoke, and where if necessary (according to model) displace the fusebox, then unscrew and remove the steering stem nut and washer, then gently ease the top yoke up off the fork tubes and position it clear of the head bearings, using a rag to protect other components **(see illustration)**. Otherwise leave the yoke in position.

9 If you don't have the special tool or equivalent, use a drift located in one of the notches to slacken the adjuster nut slightly until pressure is just released, then tighten it until all freeplay is removed, yet the steering is able to move freely **(see illustration 23.8a)**. The object is to set the adjuster nut so that the bearings are under a very light loading, just enough to remove any freeplay, but not so much that the steering does not move freely from side to side as described in the check procedure above.

10 If the Honda tool or a suitable socket or peg spanner is being used, slacken the adjuster nut slightly until pressure is just released, then tighten it to the torque setting specified at the beginning of the Chapter, and this should give the correct loading. Turn the steering from lock-to-lock five times after tightening and recheck the adjustment or

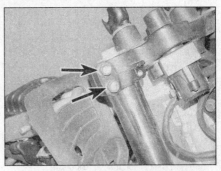

23.7 Slacken the fork clamp bolts (arrowed) on each side

torque setting. Do not rely on the torque setting alone and assume the loading to be correct – check the physical feel as described as well. If the bearings cannot be correctly adjusted, disassemble the steering head and check the bearings and races (see Chapter 6). If a C-spanner is being used, adjust according to the procedure in Step 9 **(see illustration)**. *Caution: Take great care not to apply excessive pressure because this will cause premature failure of the bearings.*

11 If displaced, fit the top yoke onto the steering stem, then install the washer and nut **(see illustration 23.8b and a)**.

12 Tighten the steering stem nut to the torque setting specified at the beginning of the Chapter. Now tighten both the fork clamp bolts to the specified torque **(see illustration 23.7)**.

13 Check the bearing adjustment as described above and re-adjust if necessary.

14 Install the handlebars if displaced (see Chapter 6), and the fuel tank (see Chapter 4).

24 Nuts and bolts – tightness check

1 Since vibration of the machine tends to loosen fasteners, all nuts, bolts, screws, etc. should be periodically checked for proper tightness.

2 Pay particular attention to the following:
Spark plugs
Engine oil drain plug and coolant drain plug

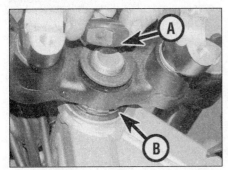

23.8a Slacken or unscrew the steering stem nut (A). The adjuster nut (B) is under the yoke

23.8b If required, gently ease the yoke up off the forks

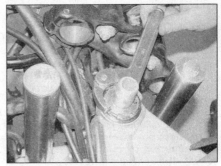

23.10 Adjust the bearings as described using either a C-spanner or a drift, or one of the special tools described

Lever and pedal bolts
Footrest and stand bolts
Engine mounting bolts
Shock absorber and suspension linkage
    bolts and swingarm pivot bolt
Handlebar clamp bolts
Front axle and axle holder nuts
Front fork clamp bolts (top and bottom yoke)
    and fork top bolts
Rear axle nut
Brake caliper and master cylinder mounting
    bolts
Brake hose banjo bolts and caliper bleed
    valves
Brake disc bolts
Exhaust system bolts/nuts

3 If a torque wrench is available, use it along with the torque specifications at the beginning of this and other Chapters.

25 Pulse secondary air injection (PAIR) system – check (XL650V models)

1 Remove the fuel tank and air filter housing (see Chapter 4), and the right-hand heat shield. Visually inspect the hoses between the reed valves on the valve covers and the PAIR control valve behind the right-hand radiator, and between the control valve and the air filter housing, for kinks and splits and any other damage or deterioration **(see illustration)**. Similarly check the vacuum hose between the control valve and its take-off point on the front cylinder intake duct. Make sure that all hoses are securely connected with a clamp on each end. Replace any hoses that are damaged or deteriorated.

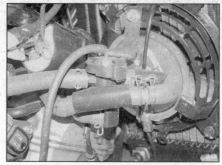

25.1 PAIR system control valve and hoses – XL650V models

2 See Chapter 4 for further information and tests on the system.

Every 12,000 miles (18,000 km) or 18 months

Carry out all the items under the 4000 mile (6000 km) check:

26 Air filter – renewal

Caution: If the machine is continually ridden in wet or dusty conditions, the filter should be replaced more frequently.

1 Refer to the procedure in Section 8 and replace the air filter with a new one.

Every 12,000 miles (18,000 km) or two years

27 Brake fluid – renewal

1 The brake fluid should be replaced at the prescribed interval or whenever a master cylinder or caliper overhaul is carried out. Refer to the brake bleeding section in Chapter 7, noting that all old fluid must be pumped from the fluid reservoir and hydraulic lines before filling with new fluid.

HAYNES HiNT *Old brake fluid is invariably much darker in colour than new fluid, making it easy to see when all old fluid has been expelled from the system.*

Every 24,000 miles (36,000 km) or two years

Carry out all the items under the 12,000 mile (18,000 km) and 8000 mile (12,000 km) checks, plus the following

28 Coolant – renewal

⚠ *Warning: Allow the engine to cool completely before performing this maintenance operation. Also, don't allow antifreeze to come into contact with your skin or the painted surfaces of the motorcycle. Rinse off spills immediately with plenty of water. Antifreeze is highly toxic if ingested. Never leave antifreeze lying around in an open container or in puddles on the floor; children and pets are attracted by its sweet smell and may drink it. Check with local authorities (councils) about disposing of antifreeze. Many communities have*

collection centres which will see that antifreeze is disposed of safely. Antifreeze is also combustible, so don't store it near open flames.

Draining

1 On XL600V and XRV750 models remove

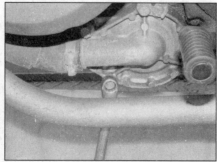

28.3a Unscrew the drain plug . . .

the fairing side panels, on XL650V models remove the fairing, and on all models remove the belly pan (see Chapter 8).
2 Cover the pressure cap with a heavy cloth and remove the cap from the top of the radiator by turning it anti-clockwise until it reaches a stop **(see illustration 18.8)**. If you hear a hissing sound (indicating there is still pressure in the system), wait until it stops. Now press down on the cap and continue turning the cap until it can be removed. Also remove the coolant reservoir cap.
3 Position a suitable container beneath the water pump on the left-hand side of the engine. Unscrew the drain plug and allow the coolant to completely drain from the system **(see illustrations)**. Retain the old sealing washer for use during flushing.
4 On XL650V and XRV750 models, place the container below the coolant reservoir (on XRV750 models remove the right-hand side panel to access it – see Chapter 8).

Disconnect the radiator overflow hose from the bottom of the reservoir and allow it to drain into the container. When the reservoir is empty, flush it out with clean water, then reconnect the hose.

5 On XL600V models, to drain and clean the reservoir you will either have to syphon out the coolant, or remove the reservoir and tip it out. Removing the reservoir involves removing the rear shock absorber (see Chapter 6).

Flushing

6 Flush the system with clean tap water by inserting a garden hose in the radiator filler neck. Allow the water to run through the system until it is clear and flows out cleanly. If the radiator is extremely corroded, remove it (see Chapter 3) and have it cleaned by a specialist.
7 Clean the drain hole in the water pump then install the drain plug using the old sealing washer.
8 Fill the cooling system with clean water mixed with a flushing compound. Make sure the flushing compound is compatible with aluminium components, and follow the manufacturer's instructions carefully. Fit the pressure cap and the reservoir cap.
9 Start the engine and allow it to reach normal operating temperature. Let it run for about ten minutes.
10 Stop the engine. Let it cool for a while, then cover the pressure cap with a heavy rag and turn it anti-clockwise to the first stop, releasing any pressure that may be present in the system. Once the hissing stops, push down on the cap and remove it completely.
11 Drain the system once again.

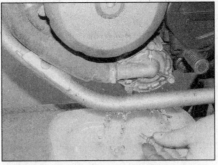

28.3b ... and allow the coolant to drain

12 Fill the system with clean water and repeat the procedure in Steps 6 to 11.

Refilling

13 Fit a new sealing washer onto the drain plug and tighten it securely.
14 Fill the system with the proper coolant mixture (see this Chapter's Specifications).
Note: *Pour the coolant in slowly to minimise the amount of air entering the system.*
15 When the system is full (all the way up to the base of the radiator filler neck), start the engine and allow it to idle for 2 to 3 minutes. Flick the throttle twistgrip part open 3 or 4 times, so that the engine speed rises to approximately 4000 – 5000 rpm, then stop the engine. This process will bleed any trapped air bubbles from the system.
16 If necessary, top up the coolant level to the base of the upper radiator filler neck and install the pressure cap. Also top up the

28.3c On XL650V models access the drain plug (arrowed) from underneath

coolant reservoir to the UPPER level mark (see *Daily (pre-ride) checks*).
17 Start the engine and allow it to reach normal operating temperature, then shut it off. Let the engine cool then remove the pressure cap as described in Step 2. Check that the coolant level is still up to the base of the upper radiator filler neck. If it's low, add the specified mixture until it reaches the base of the filler neck. Refit the cap.
18 Check the coolant level in the reservoir and top up if necessary.
19 Check the system for leaks. Install the fairing side panels or fairing as required, and the belly pan (see Chapter 8).
20 Do not dispose of the old coolant by pouring it down the drain. Instead pour it into a heavy plastic container, cap it tightly and take it into an authorised disposal site or service station – see **Warning** at the beginning of this Section.

Non-scheduled maintenance

29 Cylinder compression – check

1 Among other things, poor engine performance may be caused by leaking valves, incorrect valve clearances, a leaking head gasket, or worn pistons, rings and/or cylinder walls. A cylinder compression check will help pinpoint these conditions and can also indicate the presence of excessive carbon deposits in the cylinder heads.
2 The only tools required are a compression gauge and a spark plug wrench. A compression gauge with a threaded end for the spark plug hole is preferable to the type which requires hand pressure to maintain a tight seal. Depending on the outcome of the initial test, a squirt-type oil can may also be needed.
3 Make sure the valve clearances are correctly set (see Section 16) and that the cylinder head nuts are tightened to the correct torque setting (see Chapter 2).
4 Refer to *Fault Finding Equipment* in the Reference section for details of the

compression test. Refer to the specifications at the beginning of the Chapter for compression figures.

30 Engine oil pressure – check

1 The oil pressure warning light should come on when the ignition (main) switch is turned ON and extinguish a few seconds after the engine is started – this serves as a check that the warning light bulb is sound. If the oil pressure light comes on whilst the engine is running, low oil pressure is indicated – stop the engine immediately and carry out an oil level check (see *Daily (pre-ride) checks*).
2 An oil pressure check must be carried out if the warning light comes on when the engine is running yet the oil level is good (Step 1). It can also provide useful information about the condition of the engine's lubrication system.
3 To check the oil pressure, a suitable gauge and adapter (which screws into the crankcase) will be needed. Honda provide a gauge and adapter (part Nos. 07506-3000000

and 07510 4220100) for this purpose, or one can be obtained commercially. You will also need a container and some rags to catch and mop up any residual oil that gets lost in between removing the oil pressure switch and installing the gauge – on models fitted with a centrestand, place the bike on it, otherwise position the bike as upright as possible without it becoming unstable by placing a block under the sidestand, so that less oil gathers behind the switch to reduce spillage. Check the engine oil level after installing the gauge and replenish if necessary (see *Daily (pre-ride) checks*).
4 Warm the engine up to normal operating temperature then stop it.
5 Remove the oil pressure switch (see Chapter 9), and screw the adapter in its place. Connect the oil pressure gauge to the adapter.
6 Start the engine and briefly increase the engine speed to 6000 rpm whilst watching the gauge reading. The oil pressure should be similar to that given in the Specifications at the start of this Chapter.
7 If the pressure is significantly lower than the standard, either the pressure relief valve is stuck

1

31.2 Checking for play in the wheel bearings

open, the oil pump or its drive mechanism is faulty, the oil strainer or filter is blocked, or there is other engine damage. Also make sure the correct grade oil is being used. Begin diagnosis by checking the oil filter, strainer and relief valve, then the oil pump (see Chapter 2). If those items check out okay, chances are the bearing oil clearances are excessive and the engine needs to be overhauled.

8 If the pressure is too high, either an oil passage is clogged, the relief valve is stuck closed or the wrong grade of oil is being used.

9 Stop the engine. Refer to the oil pressure switch installation procedure in Chapter 9 and apply the sealant to the switch before removing the gauge. Unscrew the gauge and adapter from the crankcase and immediately install the oil pressure switch (see Chapter 9).

10 Check the oil level (see *Daily (pre-ride) checks*).

31 Wheel bearings – check

1 Wheel bearings will wear over a period of time and result in handling problems.

2 Support the motorcycle upright using the centrestand if fitted, or an auxiliary stand, and support it so that the wheel being checked is off the ground (remove the belly pan and anything else that could be damaged before placing a support under the engine). Check for any play in the bearings by pushing and pulling the wheel against the axle **(see illustration)**. Also spin the wheel and check that it rotates smoothly.

3 If any play is detected in the hub, or if the wheel does not rotate smoothly (and this is not due to brake or transmission drag), the wheel bearings must be removed and inspected for wear or damage (see Chapter 7).

32 Steering head bearings – re-greasing

1 Over a period of time the grease will harden or may be washed out of the bearings by incorrect use of jet washes.

2 Disassemble the steering head for re-greasing of the bearings. Refer to Chapter 6 for details.

33 Swingarm and suspension linkage bearings – re-greasing

1 Over a period of time the grease will harden or dirt will penetrate the bearings due to failed seals.

2 Remove the swingarm and suspension linkage as described in Chapter 6 for cleaning and re-greasing of the bearings. Note that XL600V-H and V-J models are equipped with two grease nipples in the rear suspension linkage components, enabling fresh grease to be applied periodically – see Section 22.

34 Brake caliper and master cylinder seals – renewal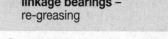

1 Brake seals will deteriorate over a period of time and lose their effectiveness, leading to sticking operation or fluid loss, or allowing the ingress of air and dirt. Refer to Chapter 7 and dismantle the components for seal renewal.

35 Brake hoses – renewal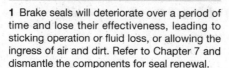

1 The hoses will in time deteriorate with age and should be renewed regardless of their apparent condition. Refer to Chapter 7 and disconnect the brake hoses from the master cylinders and calipers. Always replace the banjo union sealing washers with new ones.

2 Check the condition of the brake pipes, in particular looking for creases and dents, and renew them as necessary if damage is found.

36 Fuel hoses – renewal

Warning: Petrol (gasoline) is extremely flammable, so take extra precautions when you work on any part of the fuel system. Don't smoke or allow open flames or bare light bulbs near the work area, and don't work in a garage where a natural gas-type appliance is present. If you spill any fuel on your skin, rinse it off immediately with soap and water. When you perform any kind of work on the fuel system, wear safety glasses and have a fire extinguisher suitable for a Class B type fire (flammable liquids) on hand.

1 The fuel system hoses should be renewed at the first signs of cracking or hardening. This includes all the vent and drain hoses, and the vacuum hose(s).

2 Remove the fuel tank and the air duct or filter housing, according to model (see Chapter 4). Disconnect the fuel hoses between the fuel tank and the carburettors, noting the routing of each hose and where it connects (see Chapter 4 if required), and the vacuum hose(s) from the intake duct (s). It is advisable to make a sketch of the various hoses before removing them to ensure they are correctly installed.

3 Secure each new hose to its unions using new clamps. Run the engine and check that there are no leaks before taking the machine out on the road.

37 Front forks – oil change

1 Fork oil degrades over a period of time and loses its damping qualities. Refer to the fork oil change procedure in Chapter 6, Section 7. The forks do not need to be completely disassembled.

Chapter 2
Engine, clutch and transmission

Contents

Degrees of difficulty

| Easy, suitable for novice with little experience | | Fairly easy, suitable for beginner with some experience | | Fairly difficult, suitable for competent DIY mechanic | 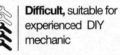 | Difficult, suitable for experienced DIY mechanic | | Very difficult, suitable for expert DIY or professional | |

Specifications

General

Capacity	
XL600V models	583 cc
XL650V models	647 cc
XRV750 models	742 cc
Bore	
XL600V models	75.0 mm
XL650V models	79.0 mm
XRV750 models	81.0 mm
Stroke	
XL600V and XL650V models	66.0 mm
XRV750 models	72.0 mm
Compression ratio	
XL600V and XL650V models	9.2 to 1
XRV750 models	9.0 to 1
Cylinder compression	
XL600V-H to P (1987 to 1993) models	157 to 185 psi (11.0 to 13.0 Bar)
XL600V-R to X (1994 to 1999) models	164 to 192 psi (11.5 to 12.5 Bar)
XL650V models	164 to 224 psi (11.5 to 15.5 Bar) @ 400 rpm
XRV750 models	157 to 213 psi (11.0 to 15.0 Bar) @ 400 rpm
Cooling system	Liquid cooled
Clutch	Wet multi-plate
Transmission	Five-speed constant mesh
Final drive	Chain and sprockets

Camshafts, rockers and cam chain – XL600V-H and J (1987 and 1988)

Cam chain tensioner projection (max) .... 6 mm
Camshafts
  Intake lobe height
    Standard .... 38.222 mm
    Service limit .... 38.00 mm
  Exhaust lobe height
    Standard .... 38.131 mm
    Service limit .... 37.90 mm
  Journal diameter
    Standard .... 21.959 to 21.980 mm
    Service limit .... 21.90 mm
  Camshaft bearing oil clearance
    Standard .... 0.141 to 0.220 mm
    Service limit .... 0.23 mm
  Camshaft runout
    Standard .... 0.03 mm
    Service limit .... 0.05 mm
Rockers
  Rocker shaft diameter
    Standard .... 11.966 to 11.984 mm
    Service limit .... 11.83 mm
  Rocker arm internal diameter
    Standard .... 12.000 to 12.018 mm
    Service limit .... 12.05 mm
  Rocker arm-to-shaft clearance
    Standard .... 0.016 to 0.052 mm
    Service limit .... 0.22 mm

Camshafts, rockers and cam chain – XL600V-K to X (1989 and 1999)

Cam chain tensioner projection (max) .... 6 mm
Camshafts
  Intake lobe height
    Standard .... 38.094 to 38.284 mm
    Service limit .... 38.074 mm
  Exhaust lobe height
    Standard .... 38.118 to 38.308 mm
    Service limit .... 38.098 mm
  Journal diameter
    Standard .... 21.959 to 21.980 mm
    Service limit .... 21.95 mm
  Camshaft bearing oil clearance
    Standard .... 0.050 to 0.111 mm
    Service limit .... 0.13 mm
  Camshaft runout
    Standard .... 0.03 mm
    Service limit .... 0.05 mm
Rockers
  Rocker shaft diameter
    Standard .... 11.966 to 11.984 mm
    Service limit .... 11.83 mm
  Rocker arm internal diameter
    Standard .... 12.000 to 12.018 mm
    Service limit .... 12.05 mm
  Rocker arm-to-shaft clearance
    Standard .... 0.016 to 0.052 mm
    Service limit .... 0.22 mm

Camshafts, rockers and cam chain – XL650V models

Cam chain tensioner projection (max) .... 6 mm
Camshafts
  Intake lobe height
    Standard .... 38.189 mm
    Service limit .... 38.17 mm
  Exhaust lobe height
    Standard .... 38.213 mm
    Service limit .... 38.19 mm

Camshafts, rockers and cam chain – XL650V models (continued)

Camshafts (continued)
  Journal diameter
    Standard . . . . 21.959 to 21.980 mm
    Service limit . . . . 21.95 mm
  Camshaft bearing oil clearance
    Standard . . . . 0.040 to 0.093 mm
    Service limit . . . . 0.13 mm
  Camshaft runout
    Standard . . . . 0.03 mm
    Service limit . . . . 0.05 mm
Rockers
  Rocker shaft diameter
    Standard . . . . 11.966 to 11.984 mm
    Service limit . . . . 11.96 mm
  Rocker arm internal diameter
    Standard . . . . 12.000 to 12.018 mm
    Service limit . . . . 12.03 mm
  Rocker arm-to-shaft clearance
    Standard . . . . 0.016 to 0.052 mm
    Service limit . . . . 0.07 mm

Camshafts, rockers and cam chain – XRV750 models

Cam chain tensioner projection (max) . . . . 6 mm
Camshafts
  Intake lobe height
    Standard . . . . 38.381 mm
    Service limit . . . . 38.10 mm
  Exhaust lobe height
    Standard . . . . 38.407 mm
    Service limit . . . . 38.20 mm
  Journal diameter
    Standard . . . . 21.959 to 21.980 mm
    Service limit . . . . 21.94 mm
  Camshaft bearing oil clearance
    Standard . . . . 0.050 to 0.111 mm
    Service limit . . . . 0.15 mm
  Camshaft runout
    Standard . . . . 0.03 mm
    Service limit . . . . 0.05 mm
Rockers
  Rocker shaft diameter
    Standard . . . . 11.966 to 11.984 mm
    Service limit . . . . 11.95 mm
  Rocker arm internal diameter
    Standard . . . . 12.000 to 12.018 mm
    Service limit . . . . 12.04 mm
  Rocker arm-to-shaft clearance
    Standard . . . . 0.016 to 0.052 mm
    Service limit . . . . 0.08 mm

Cylinder head

Warpage (max) . . . . 0.10 mm

Valves, guides and springs – XL600V-H to L (1987 to 1990) models

Intake valve
  Stem diameter
    Standard . . . . 5.475 to 5.490 mm
    Service limit . . . . 5.45 mm
  Guide bore diameter
    Standard . . . . 5.500 to 5.520 mm
    Service limit . . . . 5.56 mm
  Stem-to-guide clearance
    Standard . . . . 0.010 to 0.045 mm
    Service limit . . . . 0.10 mm
  Seat width
    Standard . . . . 0.9 to 1.1 mm
    Service limit . . . . 1.5 mm

2

Valves, guides and springs – XL600V-H to L (1987 to 1990) models (continued)

Intake valve (continued)

Spring free length – outer spring
- Standard . . . . 46.00 mm
- Service limit . . . . 44.30 mm

Spring free length – inner spring
- Standard . . . . 37.18 mm
- Service limit . . . . 35.58 mm
- Guide projection height (above cylinder head) . . . . 19.4 to 19.6 mm

Exhaust valve

Stem diameter
- Standard . . . . 6.565 to 6.570 mm
- Service limit . . . . 6.55 mm

Guide bore diameter
- Standard . . . . 6.600 to 6.620 mm
- Service limit . . . . 6.65 mm

Stem-to-guide clearance
- Standard . . . . 0.035 to 0.050 mm
- Service limit . . . . 0.11 mm

Seat width
- Standard . . . . 0.9 to 1.1 mm
- Service limit . . . . 1.5 mm

Spring free length – outer spring
- Standard . . . . 45.99 mm
- Service limit . . . . 44.29 mm

Spring free length – inner spring
- Standard . . . . 44.82 mm
- Service limit . . . . 43.32 mm
- Guide projection height (above cylinder head) . . . . 17.9 to 18.1 mm

Valve clearances . . . . see Chapter 1

Valves, guides and springs – XL600V-M to T (1991 to 1996) models

Intake valve

Stem diameter
- Standard . . . . 5.475 to 5.490 mm
- Service limit . . . . 5.46 mm

Guide bore diameter
- Standard . . . . 5.500 to 5.512 mm
- Service limit . . . . 5.55 mm

Stem-to-guide clearance
- Standard . . . . 0.010 to 0.037 mm
- Service limit . . . . 0.08 mm

Seat width
- Standard . . . . 0.9 to 1.1 mm
- Service limit . . . . 1.5 mm

Spring free length – outer spring
- Standard . . . . 42.14 mm
- Service limit . . . . 40.00 mm

Spring free length – inner spring
- Standard . . . . 38.11 mm
- Service limit . . . . 36.00 mm
- Guide projection height (above cylinder head) . . . . 19.4 to 19.6 mm

Exhaust valve

Stem diameter
- Standard . . . . 6.555 to 6.570 mm
- Service limit . . . . 6.54 mm

Guide bore diameter
- Standard . . . . 6.600 to 6.615 mm
- Service limit . . . . 6.69 mm

Stem-to-guide clearance
- Standard . . . . 0.030 to 0.060 mm
- Service limit . . . . 0.08 mm

Seat width
- Standard . . . . 0.9 to 1.1 mm
- Service limit . . . . 1.5 mm

Spring free length – outer spring
- Standard . . . . 42.83 mm
- Service limit . . . . 40.50 mm

Valves, guides and springs – XL600V-M to T (1991 to 1996) models (continued)
Exhaust valve (continued)
  Spring free length – inner spring
    Standard . . . . 38.81 mm
    Service limit . . . . 36.0 mm
  Guide projection height (above cylinder head) . . . . 17.9 to 18.1 mm
Valve clearances . . . . see Chapter 1

Valves, guides and springs – XL600V-V to X (1997 to 1999) models
Intake valve
  Stem diameter
    Standard . . . . 5.475 to 5.490 mm
    Service limit . . . . 5.45 mm
  Guide bore diameter
    Standard . . . . 5.500 to 5.520 mm
    Service limit . . . . 5.56 mm
  Stem-to-guide clearance
    Standard . . . . 0.010 to 0.045 mm
    Service limit . . . . 0.10 mm
  Seat width
    Standard . . . . 0.9 to 1.1 mm
    Service limit . . . . 1.5 mm
  Spring free length – outer spring
    Standard . . . . 42.14 mm
    Service limit . . . . 40.00 mm
  Spring free length – inner spring
    Standard . . . . 38.11 mm
    Service limit . . . . 36.00 mm
  Guide projection height (above cylinder head) . . . . 19.4 to 19.6 mm
Exhaust valve
  Stem diameter
    Standard . . . . 6.565 to 6.570 mm
    Service limit . . . . 6.55 mm
  Guide bore diameter
    Standard . . . . 6.600 to 6.620 mm
    Service limit . . . . 6.65 mm
  Stem-to-guide clearance
    Standard . . . . 0.035 to 0.050 mm
    Service limit . . . . 0.10 mm
  Seat width
    Standard . . . . 0.9 to 1.1 mm
    Service limit . . . . 1.5 mm
  Spring free length – outer spring
    Standard . . . . 42.83 mm
    Service limit . . . . 40.50 mm
  Spring free length – inner spring
    Standard . . . . 38.81 mm
    Service limit . . . . 36.0 mm
  Guide projection height (above cylinder head) . . . . 17.9 to 18.1 mm
Valve clearances . . . . see Chapter 1

Valves, guides and springs – XL650V models
Intake valve
  Stem diameter
    Standard . . . . 5.475 to 5.490 mm
    Service limit . . . . 5.47 mm
  Guide bore diameter
    Standard . . . . 5.500 to 5.512 mm
    Service limit . . . . 5.53 mm
  Stem-to-guide clearance
    Standard . . . . 0.010 to 0.037 mm
    Service limit . . . . 0.07 mm
  Seat width
    Standard . . . . 0.9 to 1.1 mm
    Service limit . . . . 1.5 mm
  Spring free length – outer spring
    Standard . . . . 42.14 mm
    Service limit . . . . 40.58 mm

2

Valves, guides and springs – XL650V models (continued)

Intake valve (continued)
  Spring free length – inner spring
    Standard . . . . 38.11 mm
    Service limit . . . . 36.47 mm
  Guide projection height (above cylinder head) . . . . 19.4 to 19.6 mm
Exhaust valve
  Stem diameter
    Standard . . . . 6.555 to 6.570 mm
    Service limit . . . . 6.55 mm
  Guide bore diameter
    Standard . . . . 6.600 to 6.615 mm
    Service limit . . . . 6.66 mm
  Stem-to-guide clearance
    Standard . . . . 0.030 to 0.060 mm
    Service limit . . . . 0.11 mm
  Seat width
    Standard . . . . 0.9 to 1.1 mm
    Service limit . . . . 1.5 mm
  Spring free length – outer spring
    Standard . . . . 42.83 mm
    Service limit . . . . 41.25 mm
  Spring free length – inner spring
    Standard . . . . 38.81 mm
    Service limit . . . . 37.51 mm
  Guide projection height (above cylinder head) . . . . 17.9 to 18.1 mm
Valve clearances . . . . see Chapter 1

Valves, guides and springs – XRV750 models

Intake valve
  Stem diameter
    Standard . . . . 5.475 to 5.490 mm
    Service limit . . . . 5.46 mm
  Guide bore diameter
    Standard . . . . 5.500 to 5.512 mm
    Service limit . . . . 5.55 mm
  Stem-to-guide clearance
    Standard . . . . 0.010 to 0.037 mm
    Service limit . . . . 0.08 mm
  Seat width
    Standard . . . . 0.9 to 1.1 mm
    Service limit . . . . 1.5 mm
  Spring free length – outer spring
    Standard . . . . 42.14 mm
    Service limit . . . . 40.00 mm
  Spring free length – inner spring
    Standard . . . . 38.11 mm
    Service limit . . . . 36.00 mm
  Guide projection height (above cylinder head) . . . . 19.4 to 19.6 mm
Exhaust valve
  Stem diameter
    Standard . . . . 6.555 to 6.570 mm
    Service limit . . . . 6.54 mm
  Guide bore diameter
    Standard . . . . 6.600 to 6.615 mm
    Service limit . . . . 6.69 mm
  Stem-to-guide clearance
    Standard . . . . 0.030 to 0.060 mm
    Service limit . . . . 0.12 mm
  Seat width
    Standard . . . . 0.9 to 1.1 mm
    Service limit . . . . 1.5 mm
  Spring free length – outer spring
    Standard . . . . 42.83 mm
    Service limit . . . . 40.50 mm
  Spring free length – inner spring
    Standard . . . . 38.81 mm
    Service limit . . . . 36.0 mm
  Guide projection height (above cylinder head) . . . . 17.9 to 18.1 mm
Valve clearances . . . . see Chapter 1

Cylinders – XL600V models
Bore diameter
   Standard . . . . 75.00 to 75.015 mm
   Wear limit . . . . 75.17 mm
Taper (max) . . . . 0.05 mm
Ovality (max) . . . . 0.05 mm
Warpage (max) . . . . 0.10 mm

Cylinders – XL650V models
Bore diameter
   Standard . . . . 79.00 to 79.015 mm
   Wear limit . . . . 79.05 mm
Taper (max) . . . . 0.05 mm
Ovality (max) . . . . 0.05 mm
Warpage (max) . . . . 0.10 mm

Cylinders – XRV750 models
Bore diameter
   Standard . . . . 81.00 to 81.015 mm
   Wear limit . . . . 81.15 mm
Taper (max) . . . . 0.05 mm
Ovality (max) . . . . 0.08 mm
Warpage (max) . . . . 0.05 mm

Pistons – XL600V models
Piston diameter (measured 10.0 mm up from skirt, at 90° to piston pin axis)
   Standard . . . . 74.965 to 74.990 mm
   Service limit . . . . 74.84 mm
   Oversizes . . . . +0.25 mm, +0.50 mm
Piston-to-bore clearance
   Standard . . . . 0.010 to 0.050 mm
   Service limit . . . . 0.32 mm
Piston pin diameter
   Standard . . . . 17.994 to 18.000 mm
   Service limit . . . . 17.80 mm
Piston pin bore
   Standard . . . . 18.002 to 18.008 mm
   Service limit . . . . 18.05 mm
Piston pin-to-bore clearance
   Standard . . . . 0.002 to 0.014 mm
   Service limit . . . . 0.025 mm
Connecting rod small-end internal diameter
   Standard . . . . 18.016 to 18.034 mm
   Service limit . . . . 18.09 mm
Piston pin-to-connecting rod small-end clearance
   Standard . . . . 0.016 to 0.040 mm
   Service limit . . . . 0.029 mm

Pistons – XL650V models
Piston diameter (measured 12.0 mm up from skirt, at 90° to piston pin axis)
   Standard . . . . 78.970 to 78.990 mm
   Service limit . . . . 78.92 mm
   Oversizes . . . . +0.25 mm, +0.50 mm
Piston-to-bore clearance
   Standard . . . . 0.010 to 0.035 mm
   Service limit . . . . 0.13 mm
Piston pin diameter
   Standard . . . . 19.994 to 20.000 mm
   Service limit . . . . 19.98 mm
Piston pin bore
   Standard . . . . 20.002 to 20.008 mm
   service limit . . . . 20.02 mm
Piston pin-to-bore clearance
   Standard . . . . 0.002 to 0.014 mm
   Service limit . . . . 0.03 mm
Connecting rod small-end internal diameter
   Standard . . . . 20.016 to 20.034 mm
   Service limit . . . . 20.04 mm

2

Pistons – XL650V models (continued)
Piston pin-to-connecting rod small-end clearance
    Standard .... 0.016 to 0.040 mm
    Service limit .... 0.06 mm

Pistons – XRV750 models
Piston diameter (measured 10.0 mm up from skirt, at 90° to piston pin axis)
    Standard .... 80.970 to 80.990 mm
    Service limit .... 80.85 mm
    Oversizes .... +0.25 mm, +0.50 mm
Piston-to-bore clearance
    Standard .... 0.010 to 0.045 mm
    Service limit .... 0.15 mm
Piston pin diameter
    Standard .... 19.994 to 20.000 mm
    Service limit .... 19.98 mm
Piston pin bore
    Standard .... 20.002 to 20.008 mm
    service limit .... 20.03 mm
Piston pin-to-bore clearance
    Standard .... 0.002 to 0.014 mm
    Service limit .... 0.04 mm
Connecting rod small-end internal diameter
    Standard .... 20.016 to 20.034 mm
    Service limit .... 20.05 mm
Piston pin-to-connecting rod small-end clearance
    Standard .... 0.016 to 0.040 mm
    Service limit .... 0.060 mm

Piston rings – XL600V models
Ring-to-groove clearance
  Top ring
    Standard .... 0.015 to 0.045 mm
    Service limit .... 0.10 mm
  2nd ring
    Standard .... 0.015 to 0.045 mm
    Service limit .... 0.10 mm
End gap (installed)
  Top ring
    Standard .... 0.10 to 0.30 mm
    Service limit .... 0.50 mm
  2nd ring
    Standard .... 0.10 to 0.30 mm
    Service limit .... 0.50 mm
  Oil ring
    Standard .... 0.20 to 0.70 mm
    Service limit .... 0.90 mm

Piston rings – XL650V models
Ring-to-groove clearance
  Top ring
    Standard .... 0.025 to 0.055 mm
    Service limit .... 0.11 mm
  2nd ring
    Standard .... 0.015 to 0.045 mm
    Service limit .... 0.10 mm
End gap (installed)
  Top ring
    Standard .... 0.20 to 0.35mm
    Service limit .... 0.7 mm
  2nd ring
    Standard .... 0.35 to 0.50 mm
    Service limit .... 0.7 mm
  Oil ring
    Standard .... 0.20 to 0.80 mm
    Service limit .... 1.0 mm

Piston rings – XRV750 models

Ring-to-groove clearance
  Top ring
    Standard .... 0.015 to 0.045 mm
    Service limit .... 0.08 mm
  2nd ring
    Standard .... 0.015 to 0.045 mm
    Service limit .... 0.08 mm
End gap (installed)
  Top ring
    Standard .... 0.20 to 0.35mm
    Service limit .... 0.7 mm
  2nd ring
    Standard .... 0.35 to 0.50 mm
    Service limit .... 0.7 mm
  Oil ring
    Standard .... 0.20 to 0.80 mm
    Service limit .... 1.0 mm

Clutch – XL600V models

Friction plate (see Section 17 for identification)
  Type A
    Quantity 6
    Thickness .... 2.92 to 3.08 mm
    Service limit .... 2.6 mm
  Type B
    Quantity 1
    Thickness .... 2.92 to 3.08 mm
    Service limit .... 2.6 mm
Plain plate
  Quantity 6
  Warpage (max) .... 0.3 mm
Springs
  Free length .... 39.0 mm
  Service limit .... 37.4 mm
Input shaft diameter at clutch housing guide
  Standard .... 21.967 to 21.980 mm
  Service limit .... 21.92 mm
Clutch housing guide
  Internal diameter
    Standard .... 21.991 to 22.016 mm
    Service limit .... 22.09 mm
  External diameter
    Standard .... 31.959 to 31.975 mm
    Service limit .... 31.92 mm
Clutch housing internal diameter
  Standard .... 32.000 to 32.025 mm
  Service limit .... 32.10 mm
Oil pump drive sprocket internal diameter
  Standard .... 32.000 to 32.025 mm
  Service limit .... 32.10 mm

Clutch – XL650V models

Friction plate (see Section 17 for identification)
  Type A
    Quantity 7
    Thickness .... 2.62 to 2.78 mm
    Service limit .... 2.3 mm
  Type B
    Quantity 1
    Thickness .... 2.92 to 3.08 mm
    Service limit .... 2.6 mm
Plain plate
  Quantity 7
  Warpage (max) .... 0.3 mm
Springs
  Free length .... 44.2 mm
  Service limit .... 42.2 mm

2

Clutch – XL650V models (continued)

Input shaft diameter at clutch housing guide
    Standard . . . . 21.967 to 21.980 mm
    Service limit . . . . 21.95 mm
Clutch housing guide
    Internal diameter
        Standard . . . . 21.991 to 22.016 mm
        Service limit . . . . 22.09 mm
    External diameter
        Standard . . . . 31.959 to 31.975 mm
        Service limit . . . . 31.92 mm
Oil pump drive sprocket internal diameter
    Standard . . . . 32.025 to 32.145 mm
    Service limit . . . . 32.15 mm

Clutch – XRV750 models

Friction plate
    Quantity 7
    Thickness . . . . 3.72 to 3.88 mm
    Service limit . . . . 3.6 mm
Plain plate
    Quantity 6
    Warpage (max) . . . . 0.15 mm
Springs
    Free length . . . . 41.2 mm
    Service limit . . . . 39.0 mm
Input shaft diameter at clutch housing guide
    Standard . . . . 24.967 to 24.980 mm
    Service limit . . . . 24.95 mm
Clutch housing guide
    Internal diameter
        Standard . . . . 24.991 to 25.016 mm
        Service limit . . . . 25.03 mm
    External diameter
        Standard . . . . 34.968 to 34.984 mm
        Service limit . . . . 34.96 mm
Oil pump drive sprocket internal diameter
    Standard . . . . 35.025 to 35.075 mm
    Service limit . . . . 35.10 mm

Starter clutch – XL600V models

Starter driven gear hub external diameter
    Standard . . . . 57.749 to 57.768 mm
    Service limit . . . . 57.60 mm

Starter clutch – XL650V models

Starter driven gear hub external diameter
    Standard . . . . 57.749 to 57.768 mm
    Service limit . . . . 57.73 mm
Starter driven gear hub internal diameter
    Standard . . . . 37.000 to 37.025 mm
    Service limit . . . . 37.10 mm

Starter clutch – XRV750 models

Starter driven gear hub external diameter
    Standard . . . . 57.749 to 57.768 mm
    Service limit . . . . 57.73 mm
Starter driven gear hub internal diameter
    Standard . . . . 40.000 to 40.021 mm
    Service limit . . . . 40.10 mm

Connecting rods – XL600V and XL650V models

Side clearance
    Standard . . . . 0.05 to 0.20 mm
    Service limit . . . . 0.30 mm
Bearing oil clearance
    Standard . . . . 0.028 to 0.052 mm
    Service limit . . . . 0.07 mm

Connecting rods – XL600V and XL650V models (continued)

Big-end internal diameter
    Size code 1 . . . .   43.000 to 43.008 mm
    Size code 2 . . . .   43.008 to 43.016 mm
Crankpin diameter
    Size code A . . . .   39.982 to 39.990 mm
    Size code B . . . .   39.974 to 39.983 mm
For connecting rod small-end specifications see under 'Pistons'

Connecting rods – XRV750 models

Side clearance
    Standard . . . .   0.15 to 0.30 mm
    Service limit . . . .   0.4 mm
Bearing oil clearance
    Standard . . . .   0.028 to 0.052 mm
    Service limit . . . .   0.10 mm
Big-end internal diameter
    Size code 1 . . . .   46.000 to 46.008 mm
    Size code 2 . . . .   46.008 to 46.016 mm
Crankpin diameter
    Size code A . . . .   42.982 to 42.990 mm
    Size code B . . . .   42.974 to 42.982 mm
For connecting rod small-end specifications see under 'Pistons'

Crankshaft and bearings – XL600V and XL650V models

Main bearing oil clearance
    Standard . . . .   0.025 to 0.041 mm
    Service limit . . . .   0.06 mm
Runout (max) . . . .   0.05 mm

Crankshaft and bearings – XRV750 models

Main bearing oil clearance
    Standard . . . .   0.025 to 0.041 mm
    Service limit . . . .   0.10 mm
Runout (max) . . . .   0.03 mm

Transmission – XL600V models

Gear ratios (No. of teeth)
  H to R (1987 to 1995) models
    Primary reduction . . . .   1.888 to 1 (68/36T)
    Final reduction . . . .   3.133 to 1 (47/15T)
    1st gear . . . .   2.571 to 1 (36/14T)
    2nd gear . . . .   1.777 to 1 (32/18T)
    3rd gear . . . .   1.380 to 1 (29/21T)
    4th gear . . . .   1.125 to 1 (27/24T)
    5th gear . . . .   0.961 to 1 (25/26T)
  T to X (1996 to 1999) models
    Primary reduction . . . .   1.888 to 1 (68/36T)
    Final reduction . . . .   3.133 to 1 (47/15T)
    1st gear . . . .   2.500 to 1 (35/14T)
    2nd gear . . . .   1.722 to 1 (31/18T)
    3rd gear . . . .   1.333 to 1 (28/21T)
    4th gear . . . .   1.111 to 1 (30/27T)
    5th gear . . . .   0.961 to 1 (25/26T)
Gear ID
  Input shaft 4th and 5th gears, output shaft 2nd and 3rd gears
    Standard . . . .   28.000 to 28.021 mm
    Service limit . . . .   28.04 mm
  Output shaft 1st gear
    Standard . . . .   24.000 to 24.021 mm
    Service limit . . . .   24.04 mm
Gear bushing OD
  Input shaft 4th and 5th gears, output shaft 2nd and 3rd gears
    Standard . . . .   27.959 to 27.980 mm
    Service limit . . . .   27.94 mm
  Output shaft 1st gear
    Standard . . . .   23.959 to 23.980 mm
    Service limit . . . .   23.94 mm

Transmission – XL600V models (continued)

Gear bushing ID
  Input shaft 4th gear, output shaft 2nd and 3rd gears
    Standard .... 25.000 to 25.021 mm
    Service limit .... 25.04 mm
  Output shaft 1st gear
    Standard .... 20.016 to 20.037 mm
    Service limit .... 20.06 mm
Gear-to-bushing clearance
  Standard .... 0.020 to 0.062 mm
  Service limit .... 0.10 mm
Input shaft OD at 4th gear bush point
  Standard .... 24.959 to 24.980 mm
  Service limit .... 24.90 mm
Output shaft OD
  1st gear bush point
    Standard .... 19.980 to 19.993 mm
    Service limit .... 19.92 mm
  2nd and 3rd gear bush point
    Standard .... 24.959 to 24.980 mm
    Service limit .... 24.90 mm
Shaft-to-bushing clearance
  Standard .... 0.005 to 0.047 mm
  Service limit .... 0.06 mm
Gear backlash
  1st gear
    Standard .... 0.089 to 0.170 mm
    Service limit .... 0.24 mm
  2nd, 3rd, 4th and 5th gears
    Standard .... 0.068 to 0.136 mm
    Service limit .... 0.18 mm

Transmission – XL650V models

Gear ratios (No. of teeth)
  Primary reduction .... 1.763 to 1 (67/38T)
  Final reduction .... 3.200 to 1
  1st gear .... 2.500 to 1 (35/14T)
  2nd gear .... 1.722 to 1 (31/18T)
  3rd gear .... 1.333 to 1 (28/21T)
  4th gear .... 1.111 to 1 (30/27T)
  5th gear .... 0.961 to 1 (25/26T)
Gear ID (input shaft 4th and 5th gears, output shaft 1st, 2nd and 3rd gears)
  Standard .... 28.000 to 28.021 mm
  Service limit .... 28.03 mm
Gear bush OD (input shaft 4th and 5th gears, output shaft 1st, 2nd and 3rd gears)
  Standard .... 27.959 to 27.980 mm
  Service limit .... 27.95 mm
Gear bush ID (input shaft 4th gear, output shaft 2nd and 3rd gears)
  Standard .... 25.000 to 25.021 mm
  Service limit .... 25.03 mm
Gear-to-bush clearance (input shaft 4th and 5th gears, output shaft 1st, 2nd and 3rd gears)
  Standard .... 0.020 to 0.062 mm
  Service limit .... 0.08 mm
Input shaft OD
  4th gear bushing point
    Standard .... 24.959 to 24.980 mm
    Service limit .... 24.95 mm
  Crankcase journal A
    Standard .... 19.980 to 19.993 mm
    Service limit .... 19.96 mm
  Crankcase journal B
    Standard .... 21.967 to 21.980 mm
    Service limit .... 21.94 mm
Output shaft OD
  2nd and 3rd gear bush point
    Standard .... 24.959 to 24.980 mm
    Service limit .... 24.95 mm

Transmission – XL650V models (continued)

Output shaft OD (continued)
  Crankcase journal A
    Standard . . . .   21.967 to 21.980 mm
    Service limit . . . .   21.94 mm
  Crankcase journal B
    Standard . . . .   21.967 to 21.980 mm
    Service limit . . . .   21.94 mm
Shaft-to-bushing clearance (input shaft 4th gear, output shaft 2nd and 3rd gears)
    Standard . . . .   0.020 to 0.062 mm
    Service limit . . . .   0.08 mm

Transmission – XRV750 models

Gear ratios (No. of teeth)
  L to N (1990 to 1992) models
    Primary reduction . . . .   1.763 to 1 (67/38T)
    Final reduction . . . .   2.875 to 1 (46/16T)
    1st gear . . . .   3.083 to 1 (37/12T)
    2nd gear . . . .   2.062 to 1 (33/16T)
    3rd gear . . . .   1.550 to 1 (31/20T)
    4th gear . . . .   1.272 to 1 (28/22T)
    5th gear . . . .   1.083 to 1 (26/24T)
  P models onwards (1993-on)
    Primary reduction . . . .   1.763 to 1 (67/38T)
    Final reduction . . . .   2.812 to 1 (45/16T)
    1st gear . . . .   3.083 to 1 (37/12T)
    2nd gear . . . .   2.062 to 1 (33/16T)
    3rd gear . . . .   1.550 to 1 (31/20T)
    4th gear . . . .   1.272 to 1 (28/22T)
    5th gear . . . .   1.083 to 1 (26/24T)
Gear ID
  Input shaft 3rd and 5th gears
    Standard . . . .   28.000 to 28.021 mm
    Service limit . . . .   28.04 mm
  Output shaft 1st, 2nd and 4th gears
    Standard . . . .   31.000 to 31.025 mm
    Service limit . . . .   31.05 mm
Gear bushing OD
  Input shaft 3rd and 5th gears
    Standard . . . .   27.959 to 27.980 mm
    Service limit . . . .   27.94 mm
  Output shaft 1st, 2nd and 4th gears
    Standard . . . .   30.950 to 30.975 mm
    Service limit . . . .   30.93 mm
Gear bushing ID
  Input shaft 3rd gear
    Standard . . . .   25.000 to 25.021 mm
    Service limit . . . .   25.04 mm
  Output shaft 2nd gear
    Standard . . . .   27.995 to 28.016 mm
    Service limit . . . .   28.04 mm
Gear-to-bushing clearance
  Input shaft 3rd and 5th gear
    Standard . . . .   0.020 to 0.062 mm
    Service limit . . . .   0.10 mm
  Output shaft 1st, 2nd and 4th gears
    Standard . . . .   0.025 to 0.075 mm
    Service limit . . . .   0.11 mm
Input shaft OD
  3rd gear bushing point
    Standard . . . .   24.972 to 24.993 mm
    Service limit . . . .   24.95 mm
  Crankcase journal A
    Standard . . . .   19.980 to 19.993 mm
    Service limit . . . .   19.96 mm
  Crankcase journal B
    Standard . . . .   24.980 to 24.993 mm
    Service limit . . . .   24.96 mm

Transmission – XRV750 models (continued)

Output shaft OD
  2nd gear bushing point
    Standard . . . . 27.967 to 27.980 mm
    Service limit . . . . 27.95 mm
  Crankcase journal A
    Standard . . . . 27.972 to 27.990 mm
    Service limit . . . . 27.95 mm
  Crankcase journal B
    Standard . . . . 19.980 to 19.993 mm
    Service limit . . . . 19.96 mm
Shaft-to-bushing clearance
  Input shaft 3rd gear
    Standard . . . . 0.007 to 0.049 mm
    Service limit . . . . 0.08 mm
  Output shaft 2nd gear
    Standard . . . . 0.015 to 0.049 mm
    Service limit . . . . 0.08 mm

Selector drum and forks – XL600V models

Selector fork end thickness
  Standard . . . . 5.93 to 6.00 mm
  Service limit . . . . 5.63 mm
Selector fork bore ID
  Standard . . . . 13.000 to 13.018 mm
  Service limit . . . . 13.04 mm
Selector fork shaft OD
  Standard . . . . 12.966 to 12.984 mm
  Service limit . . . . 12.90 mm
Selector drum OD at the left-hand journal
  Standard . . . . 13.966 to 13.984 mm
  Service limit . . . . 13.90 mm

Selector drum and forks – XL650V models

Selector fork end thickness
  Standard . . . . 5.93 to 6.00 mm
  Service limit . . . . 5.60 mm
Selector fork bore ID
  Standard . . . . 13.000 to 13.021 mm
  Service limit . . . . 13.04 mm
Selector fork shaft OD
  Standard . . . . 12.966 to 12.984 mm
  Service limit . . . . 12.90 mm
Selector drum OD at the left-hand journal
  Standard . . . . 11.966 to 11.984 mm
  Service limit . . . . 11.90 mm

Selector drum and forks – XRV750 models

Selector fork end thickness
  Standard . . . . 5.93 to 6.00 mm
  Service limit . . . . 5.90 mm
Selector fork bore ID
  Standard . . . . 13.000 to 13.021 mm
  Service limit . . . . 13.04 mm
Selector fork shaft OD
  Standard . . . . 12.966 to 12.984 mm
  Service limit . . . . 12.95 mm

Lubrication system

Oil type, viscosity and capacity . . . . see Chapter 1
Oil pressure (at oil pressure switch, with engine warm)
  XL models . . . . 64 psi (4.5 Bar) @ 6000 rpm, oil @ 80°C
  XRV models . . . . 71 to 85 psi (5.0 to 6.0 Bar) @ 5000 rpm, oil @ 80°C
Oil pump rotor tip-to-outer rotor clearance
  Standard . . . . 0.15 mm
  Service limit . . . . 0.20 mm
Oil pump outer rotor-to-body clearance
  Standard . . . . 0.15 to 0.22 mm
  Service limit . . . . 0.35 mm

Lubrication system (continued)

Oil pump rotor end float
Standard	0.02 to 0.07 mm
Service limit	0.10 mm

Torque settings

Engine mounting bolts – XL600V models
Upper front mounting brackets bolt nuts	27 Nm
Upper front mounting bolt nut	55 Nm
Lower front mounting bolt nut	55 Nm
Swingarm pivot/rear mounting bolt nut	110 Nm

Engine mounting bolts – XL650V models
Upper front mounting brackets bolt nuts	27 Nm
Upper front mounting bolt nut	55 Nm
Lower front mounting bolt nut	55 Nm
Swingarm pivot/rear mounting bolt nut	90 Nm

Engine mounting bolts – XRV750-L to N (1990 to 1992) models
Mounting bracket-to-frame bolts/nuts	33 Nm
Mounting bracket-to-engine 8 mm bolts/nuts	33 Nm
Mounting bracket-to-engine 10 mm bolts/nuts	55 Nm
Swingarm pivot/rear mounting bolt nut	110 Nm

Engine mounting bolts – XRV750-P models onwards (1993-on)
Lower frame section bolts/nuts	55 Nm
Cylinder head bracket-to-frame/engine bolts/nuts	53 Nm
Mounting bracket-to-frame bolts/nuts	32 Nm
Mounting bracket-to-engine 8 mm bolts/nuts	32 Nm
Mounting bracket-to-engine 10 mm bolts/nuts	53 Nm
10 mm engine mounting bolts/nuts	53 Nm
Swingarm pivot/rear mounting bolt nut	106 Nm

Oil cooler and distributor – XRV750 models
Cooler mounting bolts	12 Nm
Pipe union and retaining plate bolts	12 Nm
Pipe guide bolts	12 Nm

Valve cover bolts	10 Nm
Camshaft main holder bolts and nuts	23 Nm
Camshaft end holder bolts	10 Nm
Camshaft sprocket bolts	23 Nm
Cam chain tensioner mounting bolts	10 Nm

Cylinder head nuts/bolts
10 mm nuts – XL600V-H and J (1987 and 1988) models	43 Nm
10 mm nuts – all other models	47 Nm
8 mm nut/bolts	23 Nm
6 mm bolt	12 Nm

External oil pipe – XL600V-H to K (1987 to 1989) models
6 and/or 7 mm bolts	10 Nm
8 mm bolt	23 Nm

Clutch nut
XL600V-H and J (1987 and 1988) models	90 Nm
XL600V-K to X (1989 to 1999) models	128 Nm
XL650V models	128 Nm
XRV750 models	128 Nm

Clutch release plate bolts	12 Nm
Oil pump driven sprocket bolt	15 Nm
Clutch cover bolts	12 Nm
Gearchange selector drum cam plate bolt	12 Nm
Gearchange stopper arm bolt	12 Nm
Primary drive gear bolt	88 Nm

Starter clutch bolts
XL600V-H and J (1987 and 1988) models	23 Nm
All other models	30 Nm

Cylinder studs
8 mm stud	20 to 30 Nm
10 mm studs	30 to 50 Nm

Crankcase bolts
8 mm bolts	23 Nm
6 mm bolts	12 Nm

Connecting rod nuts
XL600V and XL650V models	34 Nm
XRV750 models	42 Nm

1 General information

The engine/transmission unit is a water-cooled 52° V-twin, fitted parallel with the frame. The engine has three valves per cylinder, two for the intake and one for the exhaust, operated by a single overhead camshaft via rocker arms. The camshafts are chain driven off the crankshaft.

The engine/transmission unit is constructed in aluminium alloy and the crankcase is divided vertically. The crankcase incorporates a wet sump, pressure fed lubrication system, and houses a chain driven oil pump. The one-piece forged crankshaft runs in two main bearings. The left-hand end of the crankshaft carries the alternator rotor. On XL600V and XL650V models the ignition timing rotor is on the right-hand end of the crankshaft. On XRV750 models the ignition timing triggers are incorporated in the alternator rotor.

The clutch is of the wet multi-plate type and is gear driven off the crankshaft. The transmission is of the five-speed constant mesh type. Final drive to the rear wheel is via a chain and sprockets.

2 Operations possible with the engine in the frame

The components and assemblies listed below can be removed without having to remove the engine/transmission assembly from the frame. If however, a number of areas require attention at the same time, removal of the engine is recommended.

Valve covers
Cam chain tensioners
Camshafts and rockers
Rear cylinder head (XL650V and XRV750)
Water pump
Ignition timing rotor and pulse generator coil(s)
Clutch
Gearchange mechanism
Starter motor
Alternator
Starter clutch and idle gear

3 Operations requiring engine removal

It is necessary to remove the engine/transmission assembly from the frame and separate the crankcase halves to gain access to the following components:

Cylinder heads (XL600V)
Front cylinder head (XL650V and XRV750)
Cylinder barrels, pistons and piston rings
Connecting rod big-ends and bearings
Crankshaft and bearings
Transmission shafts
Selector drum and forks
Oil pump

4 Major engine repair – general note

1 It is not always easy to determine when or if an engine should be completely overhauled, as a number of factors must be considered.
2 High mileage is not necessarily an indication that an overhaul is needed, while low mileage, on the other hand, does not preclude the need for an overhaul. Frequency of servicing is probably the single most important consideration. An engine that has regular and frequent oil and filter changes, as well as other required maintenance, will most likely give many miles of reliable service. Conversely, a neglected engine, or one which has not been run in properly, may require an overhaul very early in its life.
3 Exhaust smoke and excessive oil consumption are both indications that piston rings and/or valve guides are in need of attention, although make sure that the fault is not due to oil leakage.
4 If the engine is making obvious knocking or rumbling noises, the connecting rods and/or main bearings are probably at fault.
5 Loss of power, rough running, excessive valve train noise and high fuel consumption may also point to the need for an overhaul, especially if they are all present at the same time. If a complete tune-up does not remedy the situation, major mechanical work is the only solution.
6 An engine overhaul generally involves restoring the internal parts to the specifications of a new engine. The piston rings and main and connecting rod bearings are usually replaced and the cylinder walls honed or, if necessary, re-bored (oversize pistons are available), during a major overhaul. Generally the valve seats are re-ground, since they are usually in less than perfect condition at this point. The end result should be a like new engine that will give as many trouble-free miles as the original.
7 Before beginning the engine overhaul, read through the related procedures to familiarise yourself with the scope and requirements of the job. Overhauling an engine is not all that difficult, but it is time consuming. Plan on the motorcycle being tied up for a minimum of two weeks. Check on the availability of parts and make sure that any necessary special tools, equipment and supplies are obtained in advance.
8 Most work can be done with typical workshop hand tools, although a number of precision measuring tools are required for inspecting parts to determine if they must be renewed. Often a dealer will handle the inspection of parts and offer advice concerning reconditioning and renewal. As a

general rule, time is the primary cost of an overhaul so it does not pay to install worn or substandard parts.
9 As a final note, to ensure maximum life and minimum trouble from a rebuilt engine, everything must be assembled with care in a spotlessly clean environment.

5 Engine – removal and installation

Caution: The engine is very heavy. Engine removal and installation should be carried out with the aid of at least one assistant; personal injury or damage could occur if the engine falls or is dropped. A hydraulic or mechanical floor jack should be used to support and lower or raise the engine if available.

Removal

1 Position the bike on its centrestand if fitted or support it securely in an upright position using an auxiliary stand – do not use a stand which attaches to the swingarm pivots because the swingarm must be removed. Work can be made easier by raising the machine to a suitable working height on an hydraulic ramp or a suitable platform. Make sure the motorcycle is secure and will not topple over (also see *Tools and Workshop Tips* in the Reference section).
2 If the engine is dirty, particularly around its mountings, wash it thoroughly before starting any major dismantling work. This will make work much easier and rule out the possibility of caked on lumps of dirt falling into some vital component.
3 Remove the seat and the side panels (see Chapter 8). Disconnect the battery negative (–) lead (see Chapter 9).
4 Remove the fairing side panels (XL600V and XRV750) or fairing (XL650V), the stone guard and the belly pan (see Chapter 8).
5 Drain the engine oil and remove the oil filter (see Chapter 1).
6 Drain the coolant (see Chapter 1).
7 Remove the fuel tank (see Chapter 4).
8 Remove the carburettors (see Chapter 4). Plug the engine intake manifolds with clean rag. On XL650V models, remove the PAIR system control valve, detaching its hoses from the engine rather than the valve itself (see Chapter 4).
9 On XL models, remove the horn (see Chapter 9).
10 Remove the radiators along with their hoses (i.e. detach the hoses from the engine and water pump instead of the radiator) (see Chapter 3). Also detach and remove the hose(s) between the water pump and the inlet union(s) on the engine. On XRV750 models also remove the oil cooler (see Section 7).
11 Remove the front sprocket (see Chapter 6).
12 Remove the ignition HT coils (see Chapter 5).

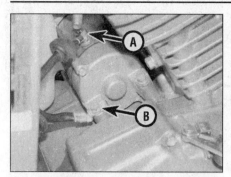

5.14 Detach the starter motor lead (A) and the earth lead (B)

5.17a Detach the neutral switch wiring connector . . .

5.17b . . . and the oil pressure switch wiring connector

13 Remove the exhaust system (Chapter 4).
14 Pull back the rubber boot covering the starter motor terminal, then unscrew the nut and detach the lead (see illustration). Also unscrew the relevant mounting bolt to release the earth cable.
15 Detach the clutch cable from the release arm on the clutch cover (see Section 19). Release the cable from any guides and secure it clear of the engine, noting its routing.
16 Trace the ignition pulse generator wiring and disconnect it at the connector – on XL models it exits from the front of the clutch cover on the right-hand side of the engine, and on XRV models from the alternator cover on the left-hand side. Coil the wiring between the cylinders so it does not impede engine removal.
17 Pull off the neutral switch wiring connector (see illustration). Pull back the rubber boot on the oil pressure switch, then undo the screw securing the wiring connector to the switch (see illustration). Free the wiring from any clips or guides and secure it clear of the engine, noting its routing. If you prefer to leave the wiring attached to the switches, trace it to its main connector and disconnect it, then feed the wiring back and coil it between the cylinders. Also check the routing of the sidestand switch wiring (from the switch to its connector) – if (as on some models) it is routed along with the neutral switch and oil pressure switch wires, then you need to free it from any clips and guides that attach it to the engine and position it clear. If

(as on most models) it is routed away from the engine along the frame tube, then you can leave it alone.
18 Trace the alternator wiring from the cover on the left-hand side of the engine and disconnect it at the connector, then coil the wiring in between the cylinders so that it does not impede engine removal. Note that on XL600V models you will have to unscrew the air filter housing bolts, noting the collars, and push the housing back to enable the wiring connector to pass between it and the frame (see illustration). On XL600V models, also unscrew the coolant reservoir bolts and displace it back so that it will be clear of the engine – there is no need to detach the hoses (see illustration).
19 On XL650V and XRV750 models, remove the rear brake pedal (see Chapter 7).
20 On XL600V and XRV750-L to N (1990 to 1992) models, unscrew the bolts securing the frame cross-member, noting which way round it fits, and the earth wires secured by one bolt (see illustration).
21 As the swingarm pivot bolt doubles as one of the engine mounting bolts, removing the swingarm means that it will not interfere with the process of manoeuvring the engine within the frame. The alternative is to displace the swingarm rearwards as far as possible after the bolt is removed. The engine and swingarm do not remain tight in the frame after the nut has been unscrewed and the amount of interference created is not that great, so base

your decision on the amount of assistance you have, the amount of time you have to carry out the extra work, and your experience as a mechanic. To remove the swingarm, refer to Chapter 6; otherwise follow the procedure below for your model for removing the swingarm pivot/engine mounting bolt.
22 At this point, position an hydraulic or mechanical jack under the engine with a block of wood between the jack head and sump. Make sure the jack is centrally positioned so the engine will not topple in any direction when the last mounting bolt is removed. Raise the jack to take the weight of the engine, but make sure it is not lifting the bike and taking the weight of that as well. The idea is to support the engine so that there is no pressure on any of the mounting bolts once they have been slackened, so they can be easily withdrawn. Note that it may be necessary to adjust the jack as some of the bolts are removed to relieve the stress transferred to the other bolts. Also place rags between the engine and frame to protect the paintwork as some contact between them is inevitable. After removing any mounting bolt, fit any spacer and/or bracket that go with the bolt back onto it, in the correct order and way round, then thread the nut onto the end of the bolt – this ensures that everything can be reassembled with ease later on, and that no brackets or spacers can be fitted the wrong way round or in the wrong place. In the case of through-bolts, also make a note of which side of the bike the bolt goes in from.

2

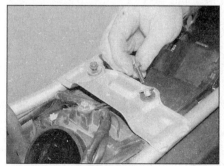

5.18a Note the collars fitted with air filter housing bolts

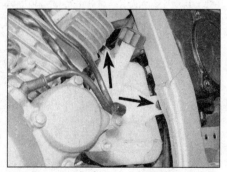

5.18b Coolant reservoir bolts (arrowed)

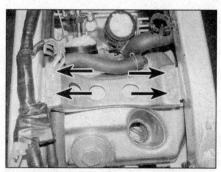

5.20 Unscrew the bolts (arrowed) and remove the frame piece, noting the earth wires – XL600V shown

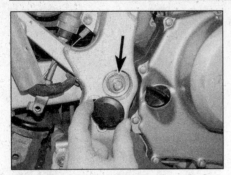

5.23a Remove the pivot cap, then slacken
the nut (arrowed)

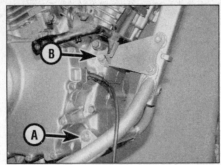

5.23b Lower front mounting bolt nut (A),
upper front mounting bolt nut (B)

5.24a Unscrew the bolts (arrowed) and
remove the support piece

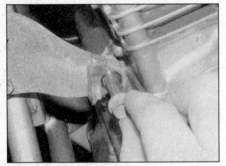

5.24b Withdraw the upper front mounting
bolt

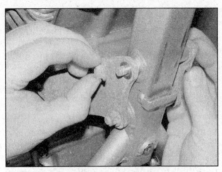

5.24c Unscrew the nuts and remove the
right-hand bracket . . .

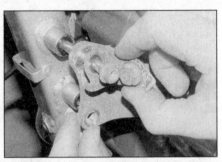

5.24d . . . then withdraw the bolts and
remove the left-hand piece, noting how all
components fit

XL600V models

23 If the swingarm has not been removed,
remove the cap from each end of the swingarm pivot/rear mounting bolt, then slacken the

5.25a Unscrew the nut . . .

nut (see illustration). Also slacken the lower
front mounting bolt nut (see illustration).
24 Unscrew the two bolts securing the fairing
side panel and belly pan support piece and
remove it, noting how it fits (see illustration).
Unscrew the nut on the upper front engine
mounting bolt (see illustration 5.23b) and
withdraw the bolt (see illustration). Unscrew
the nuts on the upper front mounting bracket
bolts, then withdraw the bolts and remove the
brackets, noting how they fit (see illustrations).
25 Check that the engine is properly
supported on the jack. If the swingarm has
not been removed, unscrew the nut on the
swingarm pivot/rear mounting bolt. Withdraw
the swingarm pivot/rear mounting bolt, then
push the swingarm back so that it is clear of
the engine (see illustrations).
26 Check that all wiring, cables and hoses
are well clear of the engine, that the engine is
still properly supported on the jack, and that

your assistant(s) is/are ready. Unscrew the nut
on the lower front mounting bolt, then
withdraw the bolt and remove the spacer that
fits between the right-hand frame bracket and
the engine (see illustrations). Move the back
of the engine to the right and disengage the
drive chain from around the transmission
output shaft and gearchange shaft (see
illustration). Lift the front of the engine so that
the front cylinder is raised, then tilt it to the
left, and manoeuvre the engine out from the
left-hand side, making sure the sump clears
the frame tube to avoid scratching it (see
illustration).

XL650V models

27 If the swingarm has not been removed,
remove the cap from each end of the
swingarm pivot/rear mounting bolt, then
slacken the nut. Also slacken the lower front
mounting bolt nut.

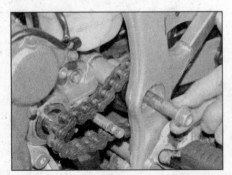

5.25b . . . and withdraw the swingarm
pivot/rear mounting bolt

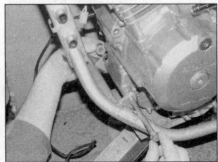

5.26a Unscrew the nut, withdraw the bolt
and remove the spacer

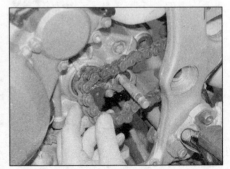

5.26b Disengage the drive chain from
around the shaft . . .

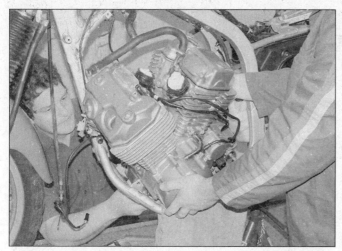

5.26c . . . and carefully manoeuvre the engine out of the frame

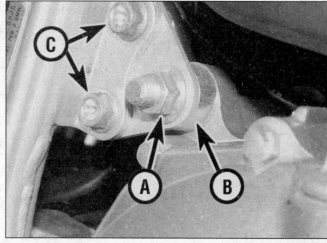

5.44a Unscrew the nut (A), noting the spacer (B). Bracket bolts (C)

28 Unscrew the two bolts securing the fairing side panel and belly pan support piece and remove it, noting how it fits. Unscrew the nut on the upper front engine mounting bolt, then withdraw the bolt and remove the spacers that fit between the brackets and the engine. Unscrew the nuts on the bracket bolts, then withdraw the bolts and remove the brackets, noting how they fit.

29 Check that the engine is properly supported on the jack. If the swingarm has not been removed, unscrew the nut on the swingarm pivot/rear mounting bolt. Withdraw the swingarm pivot/rear mounting bolt, then push the swingarm back so that it is clear of the engine.

30 Check that all wiring, cables and hoses are well clear of the engine, that the engine is still properly supported on the jack, and that your assistant(s) is/are ready. Unscrew the nut on the lower front mounting bolt, then withdraw the bolt and remove the spacer that fits between the right-hand frame bracket and the engine. Move the back of the engine to the right and disengage the drive chain from around the transmission output shaft and gearchange shaft. Lift the front of the engine so that the front cylinder is raised, then tilt it to the right, and manoeuvre the engine out from the right-hand side, making sure the sump clears the frame tube to avoid scratching it.

XRV750-L to N (1990 to 1992) models

31 If the swingarm has not been removed, remove the cap from each end of the swingarm pivot/rear mounting bolt, then slacken the nut.

32 Unscrew the two bolts securing the fairing side panel and fuel tank support piece and remove it, noting how it fits.

33 Unscrew the four bolts securing the front cylinder head bracket between the engine and frame and remove it, noting the spacer fitted with the outer bolt.

34 Unscrew the nut on the upper front engine mounting bolt, then withdraw the bolt and

remove the fairing support piece brackets, noting how they fit. Unscrew the nuts and withdraw the bolts securing the upper front brackets and remove them, noting how they fit.

35 Unscrew the nut on the lower front mounting bolt, then withdraw the bolt and remove the spacer that fits between the right-hand bracket and the engine. Unscrew the two bolts securing each lower front mounting bolt bracket and remove them, noting how they fit.

36 Check that the engine is properly supported on the jack. Unscrew the nut on the upper rear mounting bolt, then withdraw the bolt and remove the spacers that fit between the frame and the engine, noting which fits where. Unscrew the nuts and withdraw the bolts securing the upper rear mounting bolt bracket on the right-hand side and remove it, noting how it fits.

37 If the swingarm has not been removed, unscrew the nut on the swingarm pivot/rear mounting bolt. Withdraw the swingarm pivot/rear mounting bolt, then push the swingarm back so that it is clear of the engine.

38 Check that all wiring, cables and hoses are well clear of the engine, that the engine is still properly supported on the jack, and that your assistant(s) is/are ready. Move the back of the engine to the right and disengage the drive chain from around the transmission output shaft and gearchange shaft. Lift the front of the engine so that the front cylinder is raised, then tilt it to the right, and manoeuvre the engine out from the right-hand side, making sure the sump clears the frame tube to avoid scratching it.

XRV750-P models onward (1993-on)

39 If the swingarm has not been removed, remove the cap from each end of the swingarm pivot/rear mounting bolt, then slacken the nut.

40 Unscrew the four bolts securing the front cylinder head bracket between the engine and

frame and remove it, noting the spacers fitted with the lower bolts.

41 Unscrew the nut on the lower front mounting bolt, then withdraw the bolt and remove the spacer that fits between the right-hand bracket and the engine.

42 Unscrew the four bolts securing the lower frame section on the right-hand side and remove it, noting how it fits – the rear bolts have nuts which will have to be counter-held.

43 Unscrew the two bolts securing the lower front mounting bolt bracket on the left-hand side and remove it, noting how it fits.

44 Unscrew the nut on the upper rear mounting bolt, then withdraw the bolt and remove the spacers that fit between the frame and the engine, noting which fits where **(see illustrations)**. Unscrew the nuts and withdraw the bolts securing the upper rear mounting bolt bracket on the right-hand side and remove it, noting how it fits.

45 Check that the engine is properly supported on the jack. Unscrew the nut on the upper front engine mounting bolt and remove the guide, then withdraw the bolt and remove the spacer from between the bracket and engine. Unscrew the nuts and withdraw the bolts securing the upper front brackets, noting the sub-bracket, and remove them, noting how they fit.

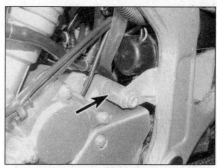

5.44b Withdraw the bolt, noting the spacer (arrowed)

2

46 If the swingarm has not been removed, unscrew the nut on the swingarm pivot/rear mounting bolt. Withdraw the swingarm pivot/rear mounting bolt, then push the swingarm back so that it is clear of the engine.

47 Check that all wiring, cables and hoses are well clear of the engine, that the engine is still properly supported on the jack, and that your assistant(s) is/are ready. Move the back of the engine to the right and disengage the drive chain from around the transmission output shaft and gearchange shaft. Lift the front of the engine so that the front cylinder is raised, then tilt it to the right, and manoeuvre the engine out from the right-hand side, making sure the sump clears the frame tube to avoid scratching it.

Installation

48 Installation is the reverse of removal, noting the following points:

● Make sure no wires, cables or hoses become trapped between the engine and the frame when installing the engine.

● If the swingarm has not been removed, do not forget to loop the drive chain around the transmission output shaft as you install the engine.

● Do not tighten any of the engine mounting bolts until they have all been installed. Make sure the spacers are correctly positioned.

● Tighten the engine mounting bolts and any other bolts to the torque settings specified at the beginning of the Chapter.

● Use new gaskets at all exhaust pipe connections.

● Make sure all wires, cables and hoses are correctly routed and connected, and secured by any clips or ties.

● Fit a new oil filter and refill the engine with oil (see Chapter 1).

● Refill the cooling system with coolant (see Chapter 1).

● Adjust the throttle and clutch cable freeplay (see Chapter 1).

---

6 Engine disassembly and reassembly – general information

Disassembly

1 Before disassembling the engine, thoroughly clean and degrease its external surfaces. This will prevent contamination of the engine internals, and will also make working a lot easier and cleaner. A high flash-point solvent, such as paraffin (kerosene) can be used, or better still, a proprietary engine degreaser. Use old paintbrushes and toothbrushes to work the solvent into the various recesses of the casings. Take care to exclude solvent or water from the electrical components and intake and exhaust ports.

 Warning: The use of petrol (gasoline) as a cleaning agent should be avoided because of the risk of fire.

7.3 Oil cooler mounting bolts (arrowed)

2 When clean and dry, position the engine on the workbench, leaving suitable clear area for working. Gather a selection of small containers, plastic bags and some labels so that parts can be grouped together in an easily identifiable manner. Also get some paper and a pen so that notes can be taken. You will also need a supply of clean rag, which should be as absorbent as possible.

3 Before commencing work, read through the appropriate section so that some idea of the necessary procedure can be gained. When removing components note that great force is seldom required, unless specified (checking the specified torque setting of the particular bolt being removed will indicate how tight it is, and therefore how much force should be needed). In many cases, a component's reluctance to be removed is indicative of an incorrect approach or removal method – if in any doubt, re-check with the text.

its crankcase. Alternatively place individual blocks under the crankcase as required to ensure the engine is stable.

4 When disassembling the engine, keep 'mated' parts together (including gears, cylinder bores, pistons, connecting rods, valves, etc. that have been in contact with each other during engine operation). These 'mated' parts must be reused or replaced as an assembly.

5 A complete engine/transmission disassembly should be done in the following general order with reference to the appropriate Sections.

Remove the valve covers
Remove the camshafts and cam chain tensioners

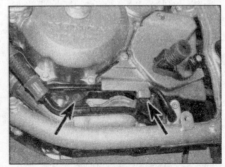

7.4a Unscrew the pipe retaining plate bolts (arrowed) . . .

Remove the cylinder heads
Remove the cylinder barrels
Remove the pistons
Remove the water pump (see Chapter 3)
Remove the pulse generator coils (see Chapter 5)
Remove the clutch
Remove the gearchange mechanism
Remove the primary drive gear
Remove the starter motor (see Chapter 9)
Remove the alternator rotor (see Chapter 9)
Remove the starter clutch and idle gear
Separate the crankcase halves
Remove the oil pump
Remove the crankshaft and the connecting rods
Remove the selector drum and forks
Remove the transmission shafts/gears

Reassembly

6 Reassembly is accomplished by reversing the general disassembly sequence.

---

7 Oil cooler and distributor – removal, inspection and installation (XRV750 models)

Note: *The oil cooler and distributor can be removed with the engine in the frame. If the engine has been removed, ignore the steps which do not apply.*

Oil cooler

Removal

1 The cooler is located on the front of the engine on the left-hand side. Remove the stone guard, and the belly pan (see Chapter 8). To prevent the possibility of damage should a tool slip, it is advisable to remove the left-hand fairing side panel as well (see Chapter 8).

2 Drain the engine oil (see Chapter 1). Keep the oil container handy to catch any residue oil from the cooler.

3 To remove the cooler without its feed and return pipes, unscrew the bolts securing the hose unions to the cooler and detach the hoses. Discard the O-rings as new ones must be used. Now unscrew the cooler mounting bolts, noting the collars, and remove the cooler **(see illustration)**.

4 To remove the cooler with its feed and return pipes, first remove the front sprocket cover (see Chapter 6). Unscrew the bolts securing the pipe retaining plate to the oil distributor on the crankcase and remove the plate, noting how it fits **(see illustration)**. Unscrew the pipe guide bolts, then carefully pull the pipe ends out of the distributor **(see illustration)**. Discard the O-rings as new ones must be used. Now unscrew the cooler mounting bolts, noting the collars, and remove the cooler and pipes **(see illustration 7.3)**.

5 To remove the pipes but leave the cooler in place, unscrew the bolts securing the hose unions to the cooler. Unscrew the bolts securing the pipe retaining plate to the oil distributor on the crankcase and remove the plate, noting how it fits **(see illustration 7.4a)**. Unscrew the pipe guide bolts, then carefully pull the pipe ends out of the distributor and off the cooler and remove them noting how they fit **(see illustration 7.4b)**. Discard the O-rings as new ones must be used.

Inspection

6 Check the cooler fins for mud, dirt and insects, which may impede the flow of air through the radiator. If the fins are dirty, clean the cooler using water or low pressure compressed air directed through the fins from the inner side of the radiator. If the fins are bent or distorted, straighten them carefully with a screwdriver. If the air flow is restricted by bent or damaged fins over more than 20% of the cooler's surface area, replace the cooler with a new one.

Installation

7 Installation is the reverse of removal, noting the following:
● Always use new O-rings on the pipe unions and smear them with clean oil.
● Check the condition of the cooler mounting grommets and replace them if they are damaged or deteriorated.
● Tighten the cooler mounting bolts, pipe union and retaining plate bolts, and pipe guide bolts to the torque settings specified at the beginning of the Chapter.
● Fill the engine with oil (see Chapter 1).

Oil distributor

Removal

22 Drain the engine oil and remove the filter (see Chapter 1).
23 Remove the front sprocket cover (see Chapter 6). Unscrew the bolts securing the pipe retaining plate to the oil distributor on the crankcase and remove the plate, noting how it fits **(see illustration 7.4a)**. Unscrew the pipe guide bolts, then carefully pull the pipe ends out of the distributor **(see illustration 7.4b)**. Discard the O-rings as new ones must be used.
24 Unscrew the distributor bolt and remove the distributor, noting how it fits. Discard the O-ring as a new one must be used. Note the

7.4b ... and the pipe guide bolts (arrowed)

locating dowel and remove it for safekeeping if it is loose – it could be in either the crankcase or the distributor.

Installation

25 Smear a new O-ring with clean oil and fit it into the groove in the distributor. Fit the dowel into the crankcase if it was removed.
26 Install the distributor, making sure it locates correctly on the dowel and the o-ring stays in place, and tighten the bolt to the torque setting specified at the beginning of the Chapter.
27 Fit the oil cooler pipes, using new O-rings, and tighten the pipe retaining plate bolts and pipe guide bolts to the torque settings specified at the beginning of the Chapter **(see illustrations 7.4a and b)**.
28 Fit a new oil filter and fill the engine with oil (see Chapter 1).

8 Valve covers – removal and installation

Note: *The valve covers can be removed with the engine in the frame. If the engine has been removed, ignore the steps which do not apply.*

Removal

1 Remove the carburettors (see Chapter 4).
2 Drain the coolant (see Chapter 1). If removing the front cylinder valve cover, either displace or remove the radiators (see Chapter 3).
3 On XL600V and XRV750-L to N (1990 to

8.4 Unscrew the bolt (arrowed) and withdraw the pipe from the head

1992) models, if removing the rear cylinder valve cover, unscrew the bolts securing the frame cross-member, noting which way round it fits and the earth wires secured by one bolt **(see illustration 5.20)**.
4 Unscrew the bolt securing the coolant outlet pipe to the cylinder head and remove the pipe **(see illustration)**. Discard the O-ring as a new one must be used. Detach any other hose(s) from the cover(s) according to the requirements of your model, noting which hose fits where.
5 Disconnect the spark plug leads from the plugs and secure them clear of the engine. Displace or remove the ignition HT coil(s) as required, according to your model and which cover is being removed (see Chapter 5).
6 Unscrew the valve cover bolts, noting the washers and the rubber seals **(see illustration)**. Remove the seals with the bolts if they are loose **(see illustration)**.
7 Lift the valve cover off the cylinder head **(see illustration)** If it is stuck, do not try to lever it off with a screwdriver. Tap it gently around the sides with a rubber hammer or block of wood to dislodge it. The rubber gasket is normally glued into the groove in the cover, and is best left there if it is reusable. If the gasket is in any way damaged, deformed or deteriorated, remove it and use a new one.
8 On XL650V models, note the dowels that link the PAIR system air passages between the valve cover and cylinder head and remove them for safekeeping if they are loose (which is unlikely), taking care not to drop them if they are not in the valve cover. Discard the seals as new ones must be used.

8.6a Valve cover bolts (arrowed)

8.6b Remove the rubber seals with the bolts if they are loose

8.7 Lift the cover off the cylinder head

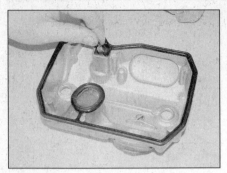

8.10 Use a new gasket if necessary and make sure it locates in the groove and stays there

8.12 Install the pipe using a new O-ring (arrowed)

Installation

9 On XL650V models, if removed, fit the PAIR system dowels, using new seals, into the valve cover or the cylinder head, whichever gives the tighter fit. If fitting them into the head, take care not to drop them.

10 Examine the valve cover gasket for signs of damage or deterioration and replace it with new one if necessary **(see illustration)**. If a new one is used, clean all traces of the old glue from the groove in the cover and clean it and the cylinder head mating surface with solvent. Fit the new gasket into the groove,

using a suitable glue, sealant or grease to hold it in place.

11 Position the valve cover on the cylinder head, making sure the gasket stays in place **(see illustration 8.7)**. If removed, fit the rubber seals into the cover, using new ones if required **(see illustration 8.6b)**. Install the cover bolts with the washers and tighten them to the specified torque setting.

12 Install the remaining components in the reverse order of removal. Use a new O-ring on the coolant outlet pipe and tighten the bolt securely **(see illustration)**.

9 Camshafts and rockers – removal, inspection and installation

Note: *The camshafts and rockers can be removed with the engine in the frame.*

Removal

1 Remove the valve covers (see Section 8).
2 If the belly pan on your model obscures the alternator cover, remove it (see Chapter 8). Unscrew the crankshaft end cap and the timing mark inspection cap from the alternator cover **(see illustration)**. Using a suitable socket on the alternator rotor bolt **(see illustration)**, rotate the engine anti-clockwise so that it is at TDC (Top Dead Centre) on the compression stroke of the cylinder being worked on. At TDC the line next to the 'FT' mark (if removing the front camshaft) or the 'RT' mark (if removing the rear camshaft) should align with the notch in the inspection hole **(see illustrations)**, the index lines on the camshaft sprocket should align with the top of the cylinder head mating surface and the TDC indicator notch on the sprocket end of the camshaft should be on the top **(see illustration)**, and both camshaft lobes should face down. If not, turn the engine anti-

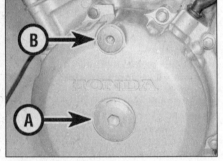

9.2a Remove the crankshaft end cap (A) and the timing inspection cap (B)

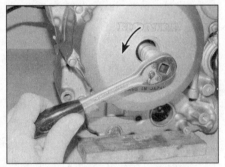

9.2b Turn the engine anti-clockwise using a socket on the timing rotor bolt . . .

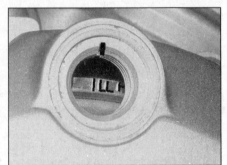

9.2c . . . until the line next to the FT mark . . .

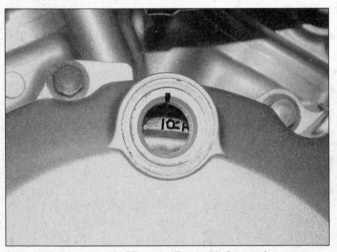

9.2d . . . or the RT mark aligns with the notch . . .

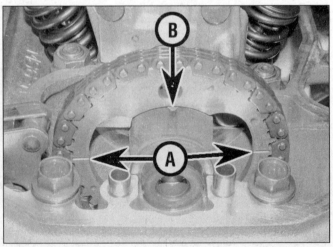

9.2e . . . and the index lines (A) are parallel with the head and the notch (B) faces up (camshaft holder shown removed for clarity)

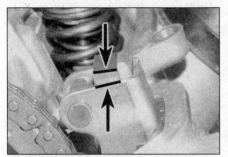

9.3a Measure the amount that the thick wedge projects above the tensioner unit as shown

9.3b Push the thick wedge down and pull the thin wedge out . . .

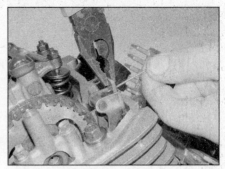

9.3c . . . and insert a pin in the hole . . .

9.3d . . . to secure it in place and so keep tension released

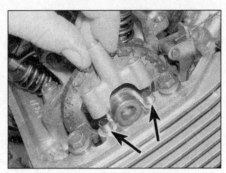

9.4 Remove the end camshaft holder and its dowels (arrowed) if loose

9.5 Turn the engine as described to access the sprocket bolts and unscrew them

clockwise through one full turn (360°) until the line next to the 'FT' or 'RT' mark again aligns with the notch – the marks should now all align as described indicating the engine is at TDC on compression.

3 At this point, measure the amount of projection of the thick wedge on the top of the cam chain tensioner **(see illustration)**. If the amount of projection exceeds the limit specified at the beginning of the Chapter, the cam chain must be replaced with a new one (see Section 10). Having taken the measurement, push the thick wedge down using a screwdriver and simultaneously pull the thin wedge straight up using a pair of

pliers and secure it in position using a 2 mm pin inserted through the hole in the wedge **(see illustrations)**.

4 Unscrew the two bolts securing the end camshaft holder adjacent to the cam chain sprocket and remove the holder, noting which way round it fits **(see illustration)**. Remove the two dowels if they are loose.

5 Rotate the engine 360° anti-clockwise to reveal the lower sprocket bolt and remove it, then return the engine to TDC on the compression stroke by rotating it another 360° anti-clockwise, and remove the other sprocket bolt **(see illustration)**. Use the socket on the alternator rotor bolt to stop the engine rotating

while unscrewing the sprocket bolts.

Caution: Do not rotate the camshaft after the cam chain has been disengaged as damage may occur if a valve contacts a piston. The crankshaft can be rotated as long as the valves are closed or if the camshaft has been removed.

6 Unscrew the bolts and the nuts securing the main camshaft holder **(see illustration)**. Slacken them evenly in a criss-cross pattern, then remove the holder along with the oil guide plate, noting any washers and how the assembly fits **(see illustrations)**. Retrieve the two dowels if they are loose. Mark each holder according to its cylinder (i.e. front or rear).

2

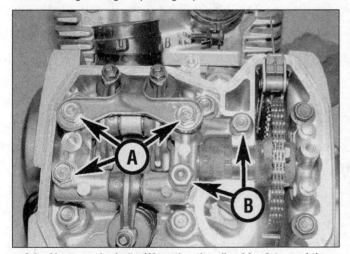

9.6a Unscrew the bolts (A), noting the oil guide plate, and the nut(s) (B) . . .

9.6b . . . noting the washers where fitted . . .

9.6c . . . and remove the holder, noting how it fits

9.7a Slip the sprocket off and remove the camshaft . . .

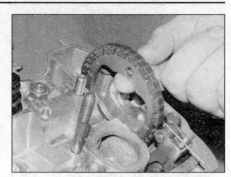

9.7b . . . then disengage the chain and remove the sprocket

7 Slip the sprocket off its boss on the camshaft **(see illustration)**. Remove the camshaft, then slip the cam chain off the sprocket and remove the sprocket **(see illustration)**. Tie the cam chain up to prevent it from dropping down into the crankcase, and do not allow it to go slack as it could bind between the crankshaft sprocket and the crankcase. Cover the top of the cylinder head with a rag to prevent anything falling into the engine. Mark each camshaft and sprocket according to its cylinder (i.e. front or rear). On most models the camshafts come with their cylinder identity already marked on the sprocket end of the shaft – 'F' for the front cylinder and 'R' for the rear, though on XL600V-H and J (1987 and 1988) models a thicker section in the camshaft is used to identify the front cylinder shaft. Check that the marks are visible and make your own if necessary). Note the 'IN' mark on the sprocket which must face inwards on installation.

8 If necessary, remove the rocker arm shafts from the camshaft holder, using a screwdriver to poke them out **(see illustration)**. If the shafts are difficult to remove, turn them using a screwdriver in the slot in the end then drift them out. Remove the rocker arms and their wave washers, noting how they fit **(see illustration)**. Mark each shaft and rocker arm according to its position (i.e. front or rear cylinder, intake or exhaust valve), and/or install each rocker arm back onto its shaft in its original position, along with its washers.

Inspection

Note: *Before renewing the camshafts or the cylinder head and camshaft holders because of damage, check with local machine shops specialising in motorcycle engineering work. In the case of the camshafts, it may be possible for cam lobes to be welded, reground and hardened, at a cost far lower than that of a new camshaft. If the bearing surfaces in the cylinder head are damaged, it may be possible for them to be bored out to accept bearing inserts. Due to the cost of a new cylinder head, it is recommended that all options be explored.*

9 Inspect the bearing surfaces of the camshaft holders and cylinder head and the corresponding journals on the camshafts. Look for score marks, deep scratches and evidence of spalling (a pitted appearance). Check the oil passages for clogging.

10 Check the camshaft lobes for heat discoloration (blue appearance), score marks, chipped areas, flat spots and spalling. Measure the height of each lobe with a micrometer and compare the results to the minimum height listed in this Chapter's Specifications **(see illustration)**. If damage is noted or wear is excessive, the camshaft must be replaced with a new one.

11 Check the amount of camshaft runout by supporting each end on V-blocks, and measuring any runout using a dial gauge. If the runout exceeds the specified limit the camshaft must be replaced with a new one.

 HAYNES HiNT *Refer to Tools and Workshop Tips in the Reference section for details of how to read a micrometer and dial gauge.*

12 Next, check the camshaft journal oil clearances. Clean the camshaft and the bearing surfaces in the cylinder head and camshaft holders with a clean lint-free cloth, then lay the camshaft in its correct location in the head with its lobes facing down (see Step 7) – there is no need to fit the sprockets or rocker arms (if removed).

13 Cut strips of Plastigauge and lay one piece on each bearing journal parallel with the camshaft centreline, making sure none is placed over the oil hole. Make sure the camshaft holder dowels are installed and fit the holders **(see illustrations 9.28a and 9.4)**. Ensuring the camshafts are not rotated at all, install the holder bolts and nuts with any washers and tighten them evenly and a little at a time in a criss-cross sequence to the torque settings specified at the beginning of the Chapter **(see illustration 9.6a)**.

14 Now unscrew the bolts and nuts evenly, a little at a time, in a criss-cross sequence and carefully lift off the holders, again making sure the camshaft is not rotated.

15 To determine the oil clearance, compare the crushed Plastigauge (at its widest point) on each journal to the scale printed on the Plastigauge container.

16 Compare the results to this Chapter's

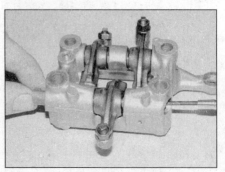

9.8a Withdraw the shafts . . .

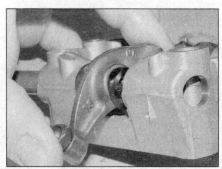

9.8b . . . and remove the rocker arms, noting the wave washers

9.10 Measure the height of each camshaft lobe with a micrometer

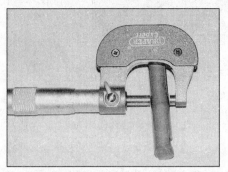

9.21a Measure the diameter of the shaft . . .

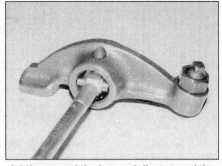

9.21b . . . and the internal diameter of the bore

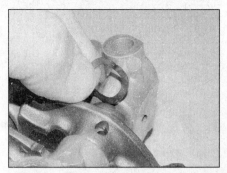

9.22a Locate the arms and fit the wave washers . . .

Specifications. If the oil clearance is greater than specified, measure the diameter of the camshaft bearing journal with a micrometer. If it is within specifications, replace the cylinder head and cam holders with new components. If the journal diameter is less than the specified limit, replace the camshaft with a new one and recheck the clearance. If the clearance is still too great, also replace the cylinder head and cam holders. Before replacing any worn parts with new ones, bear in mind the information in the **Note** preceding Step 9.

17 Except in cases of oil starvation, a cam chain wears very little. If a chain has stretched excessively, which makes it difficult to maintain proper tension, it must be replaced with a new one (see Section 10).

18 Check the sprocket for cracks and other damage, replacing it with a new one if necessary. Note that if a new sprocket is installed, a new cam chain must also be installed. If the sprockets are worn, the cam chain is also worn, and also the sprocket on the crankshaft (which can only be remedied by renewing the crankshaft). If wear this severe is apparent, the entire engine should be disassembled for inspection.

19 If available, blow through the oil passages in the rocker arms and camshaft holder with compressed air. Inspect the rocker arm contact points for pitting, spalling, score marks, cracks and rough spots. If the rocker arms are damaged they must be replaced along with the shafts as a set.

20 Check the condition of the wave washers

and replace them if they are damaged or deteriorated.

21 Measure the diameter of the rocker arm shafts in the area of contact with the rocker arms **(see illustration)**. Also measure the internal diameter of the rocker arm bores **(see illustration)**. Compare the measurements to the specifications listed at the beginning of the Chapter. If any components are worn beyond their limits, replace all the shafts and arms as a set.

Installation

22 If removed, apply a smear of molybdenum disulphide grease to the contact faces of each rocker arm, then install the arms and their wave washers into the camshaft holder, making sure they are returned to their original positions **(see illustration)**. The wave washers fit on the inside of the intake rocker arms, and on the left-hand side of the front cylinder exhaust rocker arm, and the right-hand side of the rear cylinder exhaust arm, adjacent to the triangular mark on the holder **(see illustration)**.

23 Apply a smear of molybdenum disulphide grease to the rocker arm shafts, then slide the shafts into the camshaft holder, making sure they are installed in their original positions, and that they pass through the rocker arms and wave washers **(see illustration)**. Position the shafts so that the grooves in the ends of the shafts are vertical and the holes in the shafts align with the bolt holes in the camshaft holder **(see illustration)**. Check that the arms move freely on the shafts.

24 If only the front camshaft has been removed, position the crankshaft at TDC on the compression stroke for the rear cylinder (see Step 2), then rotate the crankshaft anticlockwise 488° (at which point the 'FT' mark on the rotor will align with the notch in the inspection hole). This positions the front cylinder at TDC, and the front camshaft can be installed. If only the rear camshaft has been removed, position the crankshaft at TDC on the compression stroke for the front cylinder (see Step 2), then rotate the crankshaft anti-clockwise 232° (at which point the 'RT' mark on the rotor will align with the notch in the inspection hole). This positions the rear cylinder at TDC, and the rear camshaft can be installed. If both camshafts have been removed, install the front one first, with the crankshaft positioned so that the 'FT' mark on the rotor aligns with the notch in the inspection hole, then rotate the crankshaft anti-clockwise 232° (at which point the 'RT' mark on the rotor will align with the notch in the inspection hole). This positions the rear cylinder at TDC on the compression stroke, and the rear camshaft can be installed.

Caution: Keep the cam chains taut when rotating the crankshaft.

25 Check that the cam chain is engaged around the lower sprocket teeth on the crankshaft and that the crankshaft is positioned as described in Step 24. Apply a smear of molybdenum disulphide grease to the camshaft journals. Position the camshaft sprocket with the sprocket's 'IN' mark facing inwards, the index lines on the sprocket

2

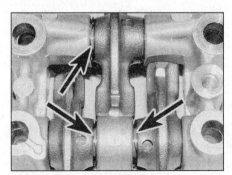

9.22b . . . making sure they are correctly positioned

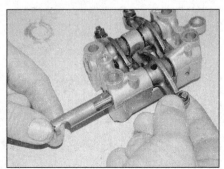

9.23a Slide the shaft in, aligning the arm as you do . . .

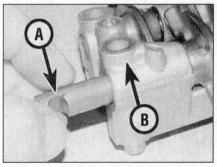

9.23b . . . and align the cutout in the shaft (A) with the bolt hole (B)

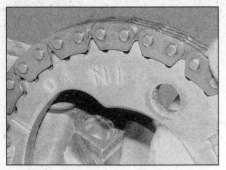

9.25a Make sure IN mark faces in

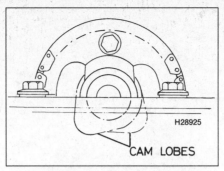

H28925

CAM LOBES

9.25b Position the camshaft so that its lobes point down as shown

9.25c Slip the chain around the sprocket if required

aligning with the cylinder head mating surface, and its mounting holes at top and bottom **(see illustration)**. Keeping the front run of the cam chain taut, engage the chain on the camshaft sprocket teeth **(see illustration 9.7b)**. Install the correct camshaft for the cylinder being worked on; the one with a thicker mid section (XL600V-H and J models) or marked 'F' (all other models) is for the front cylinder, the one without the thicker section or marked 'R' is for the rear cylinder. Fit the sprocket onto the camshaft and align the bolt holes **(see illustration 9.7a)**, and position it so that the TDC indicator notch on the sprocket end of the camshaft faces up **(see illustration 9.2e)** and the cam lobes face downwards **(see illustration)**. Install the top sprocket bolt finger-tight only **(see illustration 9.5)**. Check that the chain is tight at the front of the engine so that there is no slack between the crankshaft sprocket and the camshaft

9.27 Apply a locking compound to the sprocket bolts and tighten them to the specified torque

sprocket, and that all marks are still correctly aligned (see Step 2). If any slack is evident, move the chain around the sprocket so that the slack is taken up **(see illustration)**. Any slack in the chain must lie in the portion of the chain in the back of the cylinder so that it is then taken up by the tensioner.
26 Before proceeding further, check that everything aligns as described in Step 2. If it doesn't, the valve timing will be inaccurate and the valves will contact the piston when the engine is turned over.
27 Apply a suitable non-permanent thread locking compound to the camshaft sprocket bolt threads, then tighten the top bolt to the specified torque setting, using a socket on the alternator rotor bolt to stop the engine from rotating if necessary **(see illustration)**. Rotate the crankshaft anti-clockwise 360° to reveal the lower sprocket bolt and tighten that to the specified torque setting, then return the engine to TDC on the compression stroke for the cylinder being worked on by again rotating it anti-clockwise 360°.
28 If removed, install the main camshaft holder dowels into the cylinder head or holder **(see illustration)**, then install the holder, making sure it is the right way round and seats correctly **(see illustration 9.6c)**. Install the oil guide plate onto the holder with its guide facing the intake valves **(see illustration)**, then install the holder bolts and nuts with any washers, using new ones if necessary, and tighten them evenly and a little at a time in a criss-cross pattern to the torque setting specified at the beginning of the Chapter **(see illustration 9.6a)**.

29 Before proceeding further, again check that everything aligns as described in Step 2. If it doesn't, the valve timing will be inaccurate and the valves will contact the piston when the engine is turned over.
30 If removed, install the end camshaft holder dowels into the cylinder head **(see illustration 9.4)**. Install the holder, making sure its flat surface faces inwards and it seats correctly onto the dowels. Install the holder bolts and tighten them evenly to the specified torque setting.
31 With both holders tightened down, check that the valve timing marks still align (see Step 2). Check that each camshaft is free to rotate by turning it a few degrees in each direction using a suitable socket on the alternator rotor bolt. Lubricate the camshaft lobes with a mixture of engine oil and molybdenum disulphide grease.
32 Remove the 2 mm pin securing the thin wedge on the cam chain tensioner – the tensioner will automatically set itself **(see illustration 9.3c)**.
33 Rotate the engine anti-clockwise through 720° degrees and re-check that the valve timing for both cylinders is correct (see Step 2).
34 Check the valve clearances (Chapter 1) and adjust if necessary.
35 Install the crankshaft end and timing inspection caps using new O-rings if necessary, and smear the O-rings with clean oil **(see illustration)**. Apply a smear of molybdenum disulphide grease to the threads of the caps and tighten them securely.
36 Install the valve cover (see Section 8).
37 Check the engine oil level and top up if necessary (see Chapter 1).

9.28a Make sure the dowels (arrowed) are installed and the holder locates correctly

9.28b Fit the oil guide plate with the bolts

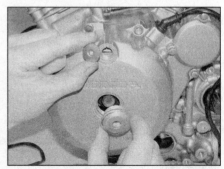

9.35 Smear the cap threads with grease and fit new O-rings if necessary

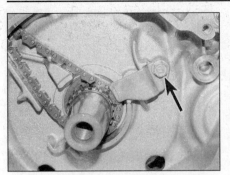

10.4a Unscrew the bolt (arrowed) and remove the plate

10.4b Slip the chain down the tunnel and off the shaft

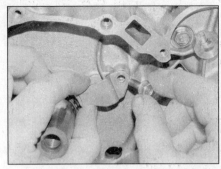

10.7 Apply a locking compound to the retainer plate bolt threads

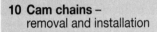

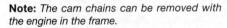

10 Cam chains – removal and installation

Note: *The cam chains can be removed with the engine in the frame.*

Front cylinder cam chain

Removal

1 Drain the engine oil (see Chapter 1).
2 Remove the alternator rotor (see Chapter 9).
3 Remove the camshaft (see Section 9). Remove the cam chain tensioner (see Section 11).
4 Unscrew the bolt securing the cam chain tensioner set plate to the crankcase and remove the plate, noting how it fits **(see illustration)**. Drop the cam chain down its tunnel and remove it from the end of the crankshaft **(see illustration)**. If difficulty is experienced in manoeuvring the chain past the cam chain guide blade, remove the cylinder head and lift the guide blade out of the crankcase.
5 Check the sprocket teeth on the crankshaft for wear and damage. The teeth are integral with the crankshaft, so if any significant wear or damage is found, the crankshaft must be replaced with a new one.

Installation

6 Hook the new cam chain onto a piece of wire and draw the chain up through its tunnel, making sure its bottom end engages around the sprocket on the crankshaft **(see**

illustration 10.4b). Secure the chain at the top to prevent it falling back down the tunnel.
7 If removed, install the cam chain guide blade and cylinder head. Install the cam chain tensioner set plate, then apply a suitable non-permanent thread-locking compound to its bolt and tighten it securely **(see illustration)**.
8 Install the cam chain tensioner (see Section 11).
9 Install the alternator/starter clutch assembly (see Section 21). Replenish the engine oil (see Chapter 1).

Rear cylinder cam chain

Removal

10 Drain the engine oil (see Chapter 1).
11 Remove the camshaft (see Section 9). Remove the cam chain tensioner (see Section 11).
12 On XL models, remove the ignition pulse generator coil(s) (see Chapter 5).
13 Remove the clutch and primary drive gear (see Section 18).
14 Drop the cam chain down its tunnel, then slide the sprocket towards the end of the shaft so that the chain clears the guide blade and remove it from the sprocket **(see illustration)**. Slide the cam chain sprocket off the end of the crankshaft, noting which way around it is fitted, and check it for wear or damage to both the outer teeth and the inner splines **(see illustration)**. If difficulty is experienced in manoeuvring the chain past the cam chain guide blade, remove the cylinder head and lift the guide blade out of the crankcase.

Installation

15 Align the extra wide spline on the crankshaft with that on the sprocket, then slide the sprocket part-way onto the crankshaft the same was around as noted on removal **(see illustration)**. Hook the new cam chain onto a piece of wire and draw the chain up through its tunnel, making sure its bottom end engages around the sprocket **(see illustration 10.14a)**. Slide the sprocket home and secure the chain at the top to prevent it falling back down the tunnel. If removed, install the cam chain guide blade and cylinder head.
16 Install the primary drive gear and clutch (see Section 18).
17 On XL models, install the ignition pulse generator coil(s) (see Chapter 5).
18 Install the cam chain tensioner (see Section 11) and the camshaft (see Section 9). Replenish the engine oil (see Chapter 1).

11 Cam chain tensioners and guide blades – removal, inspection and installation

Note: *The cam chain tensioners and guide blades can be removed with the engine in the frame.*

Cam chain tensioner

Removal

1 Remove the valve cover (see Section 8). The cam chain tensioner is located in the back of the cam chain tunnel. Note the position of

2

10.14a Slide the sprocket out and remove the chain . . .

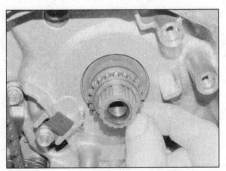

10.14b . . . then remove the sprocket

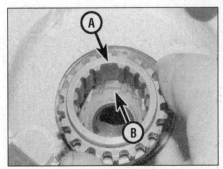

10.15 Align the wide spline on the sprocket (A) with that on the shaft (B)

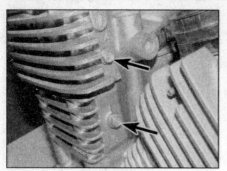

11.4a Unscrew the bolts (arrowed) . . .

11.4b . . . then withdraw the tensioner . . .

11.4c . . . and remove the rubber cushion, noting how it fits

the rubber cushion behind the top of the tensioner.

2 Follow Steps 2 to 5 in Section 9.

3 Slip the sprocket off its boss on the camshaft. **Note:** *Do not disengage the cam chain from the sprocket or the valve timing will have to be reset (see Section 9).* **Caution:** *Do not rotate either the camshaft or the crankshaft whilst the cam chain sprocket is displaced as damage could occur if a valve contacts a piston.*

4 Unscrew the two bolts securing the cam chain tensioner and withdraw it from the cylinder head **(see illustrations)**. Also remove the rubber cushion, noting which way up it fits **(see illustration)**.

Inspection

5 Examine the sliding surface of the tensioner for wear or damage, and replace it if necessary.

6 Check the tensioner spring for damage or a loss of tension, and replace it if necessary.

Installation

7 Fit the tensioner into the back of the cam chain tunnel in the cylinder head, making sure the base is correctly seated in its slot. Fit the rubber cushion with its widest end uppermost behind the top of the tensioner **(see illustration 11.4c)**. The top of the cushion sits flush with the top of the cylinder head. Make sure the sealing washers on the tensioner mounting bolts are in good condition, and replace them with new ones if necessary **(see illustration)**. Apply a suitable non permanent thread locking compound to the tensioner

bolts and tighten them to the torque setting specified at the beginning of the Chapter.

8 Mount the cam chain and sprocket onto the boss on the camshaft. Apply a suitable non-permanent thread locking compound to one camshaft sprocket bolt, then install it in the exposed hole at the top of the sprocket and tighten it to the specified torque setting, using a socket on the alternator bolt to stop the engine from rotating if necessary **(see illustrations 9.27)**. Rotate the crankshaft anti-clockwise 360° to reveal the other sprocket bolt hole, then threadlock the bolt and tighten it to the specified torque setting. Again rotate the crankshaft anti-clockwise 360° to bring it back to TDC on compression. Before proceeding further, check that everything aligns as described in Section 9, Step 2. If it doesn't, the valve timing will be inaccurate and the valves will contact the piston when the engine is turned over.

9 Follow Steps 30 to 35 in Section 9.

10 Install the valve cover (see Section 8).

11 Check the engine oil level and top up if necessary (see Chapter 1).

Cam chain guide blade

Removal

12 Remove the cylinder head (Section 12).

13 Lift the cam chain guide blade out of the front of the cam chain tunnel in the cylinder barrel, noting how it fits **(see illustration)**.

Inspection

14 Examine the sliding surface of the guide blade for wear or damage, and replace it if necessary.

Installation

15 Install the guide blade into the front of the cam chain tunnel, making sure its base locates correctly in its seat, and the lugs near the top seat correctly in their slots **(see illustration)**.

16 Install the cylinder head (see Section 12).

12 Cylinder heads – removal and installation

Caution: The engine must be completely cool before beginning this procedure or the cylinder heads may become warped.

Removal – front cylinder head

Note: *The engine must be removed from the frame to enable removal of the front cylinder head.*

1 Remove the engine from the frame (see Section 5).

2 Remove the valve cover (see Section 8).

3 Remove the spark plugs (see Chapter 1).

4 Remove the camshaft (see Section 9).

5 On XL600V-H to K (1987 to 1989) models, unscrew the bolts securing the external oil pipe and remove the pipe, noting how it fits and taking care not to bend it. Discard the sealing washers as new ones must be used.

6 Remove the cam chain tensioner (see Section 11).

7 The cylinder head is secured by four 10 mm nuts, one 8 mm nut (which on all except XL600V-H to K (1987 to 1989) models also

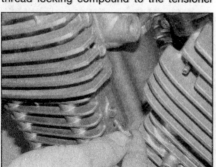

11.7 Use new sealing washers on the tensioner bolts if necessary

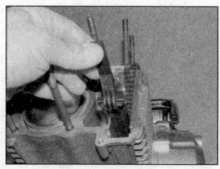

11.13 Draw the guide blade out of the tunnel

11.15 Make sure the lugs locate correctly in the cutouts (arrows)

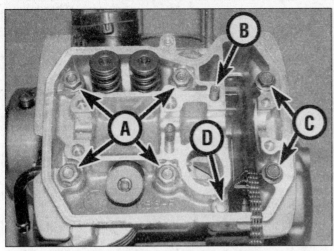

12.7 Cylinder head 10 mm nuts (A), 8 mm nut (B – see text), 8 mm bolts (C), 6 mm bolt (D)

12.8 Carefully lift the head up off the barrel

secures the main camshaft holder and has therefore already been removed), two 8 mm bolts and one 6 mm bolt **(see illustration)**. Slacken these evenly and a little at a time in a criss-cross pattern until they are all loose. Remove the nuts, bolts and washers. Take care not to drop any of the nuts or washers down the cam chain tunnel.

8 Hold the cam chain up and pull the cylinder head up off the barrel, then pass the cam chain down through the tunnel **(see illustration)**. Do not let the chain fall into the crankcase – secure it with a piece of wire or metal bar to prevent it from doing so. If it is stuck, tap around the base of the head with a soft-faced mallet to free it. Do not try to free the head by inserting a screwdriver between the head and cylinder barrel – you'll damage the sealing surfaces. Note that each head is marked 'F' or 'R' according to whether it is for the front or rear cylinder – the mark is located in the centre of the top of the head, between the valves.

9 Remove the old gasket **(see illustration 12.22)**.

10 If they are loose, remove the two dowels from the cylinder barrel studs **(see illustration 12.22)**. If either appears to be missing it is probably stuck in the underside of the cylinder head. If required, remove the cam chain guide blade from the front of the cam chain tunnel (see Section 11) **(see illustration 11.13)**.

11 Check the cylinder head gasket and the mating surfaces on the cylinder head and barrel for signs of leakage, which could indicate warpage. Refer to Section 14 and check the cylinder head for warpage.

Caution: If you do not plan to remove the cylinder barrel, take care not to break the gasket joint between the barrel and the crankcase when cleaning the top surface of the barrel or pulling out the dowels. If the joint is broken the barrel must be removed (see Section 15) and the gasket renewed, otherwise oil leaks may result.

12 Clean all traces of old gasket material from the cylinder head and barrel. If a scraper is used, take care not to scratch or gouge the soft aluminium. Be careful not to let any of the gasket material fall into the crankcase, the cylinder bore or the oil passages. Unless you are removing the cylinder barrel, cover it with a clean rag to prevent any debris falling into the engine.

Removal – rear cylinder head

Note: *On XL600V models the engine must be removed from the frame to enable removal of the rear cylinder head. On XL650V and XRV750 models removal of the rear cylinder head is possible with the engine in the frame.*

13 On XL600V, remove the engine from the frame (see Section 5).

14 On XL650V and XRV750 models, drain the coolant (see Chapter 1). Remove the carburettors and the rear cylinder exhaust pipe (see Chapter 4).

15 Remove the spark plugs (see Chapter 1).

16 Remove the camshaft (see Section 9).

17 Remove the cam chain tensioner (see Section 11).

18 On XL600V-H to K (1987 to 1989) models, unscrew the bolts securing the external oil pipe and remove the pipe, noting how it fits and taking care not to bend it. Discard the sealing washers as new ones must be used.

19 The remainder of the procedure is the same as for the front cylinder – follow Steps 7 to 12 above.

Installation – both heads

20 If removed, fit the cam chain guide blade into the front of the cam chain tunnel (see Section 11) **(see illustration 11.15)**.

21 If removed, fit the two dowels over the cylinder barrel studs and into the barrel **(see illustration 12.22)**. Lubricate the cylinder bores with new engine oil.

22 Ensure both cylinder head and barrel mating surfaces are clean, then lay the new head gasket in place on the cylinder barrel,

making sure it locates over the dowels **(see illustration)**. The gasket can only fit one way, so if the holes do not line up properly the gasket is upside down. Never re-use the old gasket.

23 Make sure you have the correct head for the cylinder being worked on – the front head is marked 'F' and the rear 'R', with the mark located in the centre of the top of the head, between the valves. Carefully lower the cylinder head over the studs and onto the barrel **(see illustration 12.8)**. It is helpful to have an assistant to pass the cam chain up through the tunnel and slip a piece of wire through it to prevent it falling back into the engine. Keep the chain taut to prevent it becoming disengaged from the crankshaft sprocket.

24 Install the 10 mm nuts with their washers, on XL600V-H to K (1987 to 1989) models the 8 mm nut with its washer, the 8 mm bolts with their washers and the 6 mm bolt; tighten them all finger-tight at this stage **(see illustration 12.7)**.

25 Now tighten the cylinder head nuts and bolts evenly and a little at a time in a criss-cross pattern to the torque settings specified at the beginning of the Chapter **(see illustration)**.

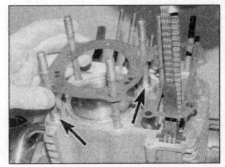

12.22 Install the dowels (arrowed) then lay the new gasket on the barrel

2

12.25 Tighten the nuts and bolts as described to the specified torque setting

26 Install all other components that have been removed in a reverse of the removal procedure, referring to the relevant sections where necessary. On XL600V-H to K (1987 to 1989) models blow through the external oil pipe and its bolts using compressed air if available, then install the pipe using new sealing washers and tighten its bolts to the specified torque setting.

27 If removed, install the engine as described in Section 5.

13 Valves/valve seats/ valve guides – servicing

1 Because of the complex nature of this job and the special tools and equipment required, most owners leave servicing of the valves, valve seats and valve guides to a professional.

14.5a Make sure the compressor locates correctly on the valve . . .

14.5b . . . and the spring retainer

However, you can make an initial assessment of whether the valves are seating correctly, and therefore sealing, by pouring a small amount of solvent into each of the valve ports. If the solvent leaks past any valve into the combustion chamber area the valve is not seating correctly and sealing.

2 You can also remove the valves from the cylinder head, clean the components, check them for wear to assess the extent of the work needed, and, unless a valve service is required, grind in the valves (see Section 14). The head can then be reassembled.

3 A dealer service department will remove the valves and springs, replace the valves and guides, recut the valve seats, check and replace the valve springs, spring retainers and collets (as necessary), replace the valve stem seals with new ones and reassemble the valve components.

4 After the valve service has been performed, the head will be in like-new condition. When the head is returned, be sure to clean it again very thoroughly before installation on the engine to remove any metal particles or abrasive grit that may still be present from the valve service operations. Use compressed air, if available, to blow out all the holes and passages.

14 Cylinder head and valves – disassembly, inspection and reassembly

1 As mentioned in the previous section, valve overhaul should be left to a Honda dealer. However, disassembly, cleaning and inspection of the valves and related components can be done (if the necessary special tools are available) by the home mechanic. This way no expense is incurred if the inspection reveals that overhaul is not required at this time.

2 To disassemble the valve components without the risk of damaging them, a valve spring compressor is absolutely essential. Make sure it is suitable for motorcycle work.

Disassembly

3 Before proceeding, arrange to label and store the valves along with their related

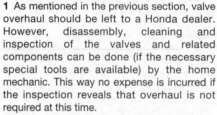

14.5c Remove the collets as described

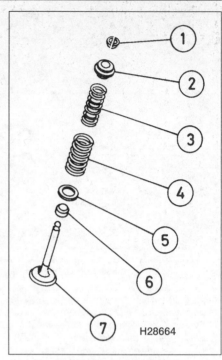

H28664

14.3 Valve components

1 Collets
2 Spring retainer
3 Inner spring
4 Outer spring
5 Spring seat
6 Stem seal
7 Valve

components in such a way that they can be returned to their original locations without getting mixed up **(see illustration)**. A good way to do this is to obtain a container which is divided into six compartments, and label each compartment with the location of a valve, i.e. left intake valve, right intake valve or exhaust valve. If a container is not available, use labelled plastic bags (an egg carton also does very well!).

4 Clean all traces of old gasket material from the cylinder head. If a scraper is used, take care not to scratch or gouge the soft aluminium.

 HAYNES HINT *Refer to Tools and Workshop Tips for details of gasket removal methods.*

5 Compress the valve spring on the first valve with a spring compressor, making sure it is correctly located onto each end of the valve assembly **(see illustrations)**. On the underside of the head make sure the plate on the compressor only contacts the valve and not the soft aluminium of the head – if the plate is too big for the valve, use a spacer between them. Do not compress the springs any more than is absolutely necessary. Remove the collets, using either needle-nose pliers, tweezers, a magnet or a screwdriver with a dab of grease on it **(see illustration)**. Carefully release the valve spring compressor and remove it. Remove the spring retainer,

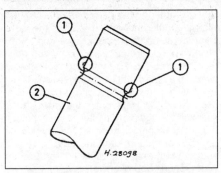

14.5d Remove any burrs (1) if the valve stem (2) won't pull through the guide

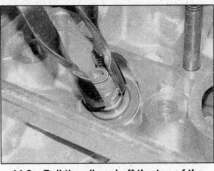

14.6a Pull the oil seal off the top of the guide . . .

14.6b . . . then remove the spring seat

noting which way up it fits (see illustration 14.28c). Remove the springs, noting that the closer wound coils are at the bottom (see illustrations 14.28a and 14.3). Press down on the top of the valve stem and draw the valve out from the underside of the head (see illustration 14.27b). If the valve binds in the guide (won't pull through), push it back into the head and deburr the area around the collet groove with a very fine file or whetstone (see illustration).

6 Once the valve has been removed and labelled, pull the valve stem oil seal off the top of the valve guide and discard it (the old seals should never be reused) (see illustration). Now remove the spring seat (see illustration). The seat is difficult to get hold of, so either use a small magnet or turn the head upside down and tip it out, taking care not to lose it.

7 Repeat the procedure for the remaining valves. Remember to keep the parts for each valve together and in order so they can be reinstalled in the same location.

8 Next, clean the cylinder head with solvent and dry it thoroughly. Compressed air will speed the drying process and ensure that all holes and recessed areas are reached.

9 Clean all of the valve springs, collets, retainers and spring seats with solvent and dry them thoroughly. Do the parts from one valve at a time so they don't get mixed up.

10 Scrape off any deposits that may have formed on the valve, then use a motorised wire brush to remove deposits from the valve heads and stems. Again, make sure the valves do not get mixed up.

Inspection

11 Inspect the head very carefully for cracks and other damage. If cracks are found, a new head will be required. Check the camshaft bearing surfaces for wear and evidence of seizure. Check the camshafts and holders for wear as well (see Section 9).

12 Using a precision straight-edge and a feeler gauge set to the warpage limit listed in the specifications at the beginning of the Chapter, check the head gasket mating surface for warpage. Refer to *Tools and Workshop Tips* in the Reference section for details of how to use the straight-edge.

13 Examine the valve seats in the

combustion chamber. If they are pitted, cracked or burned, the head will require work beyond the scope of the home mechanic. Measure the valve seat width and compare it to this Chapter's Specifications (see illustration). If it exceeds the service limit, or if it varies around its circumference, overhaul is required.

14 Measure the valve stem diameter (see illustration). Clean the valve guides using a guide reamer to remove any carbon build-up, then measure the inside diameters of the guides (at both ends and in the centre of the guide) with a small bore gauge, then measure the gauge with a micrometer (see illustration). Measure the guides at the ends and at the centre to determine if they are worn in a bell-mouth pattern (more wear at the ends). Subtract the stem diameter from the valve guide diameter to obtain the valve stem-to-guide clearance. If the stem-to-guide

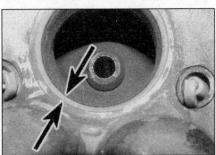

14.13 Measure the valve seat width with a ruler (or for greater precision use a Vernier caliper)

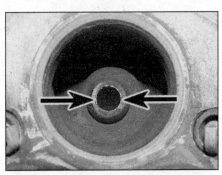

14.14b . . . then measure the guide bore using a small hole gauge and micrometer

clearance is greater than listed in this Chapter's Specifications, renew whichever components are worn beyond their specification limits. If the valve guide is within specifications, but is worn unevenly, it should be renewed.

15 Carefully inspect each valve face, stem and collet groove area for cracks, pits and burned spots (see illustration).

16 Rotate the valve and check for any obvious indication that it is bent, in which case it must be replaced with a new one. Check the end of the stem for pitting and excessive wear. The presence of any of the above conditions indicates the need for valve servicing. The stem end can be ground down, provided that the amount of stem above the collet groove after grinding is sufficient.

17 Check the end of each valve spring for wear and pitting. Measure the spring free lengths and compare them to the

14.14a Measure the valve stem diameter with a micrometer . . .

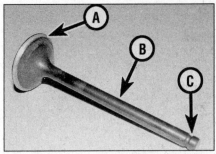

14.15 Check the valve face (A), stem (B) and collet groove (C) for signs of wear and damage

2

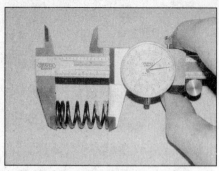

14.17a Measure the free length of the valve springs

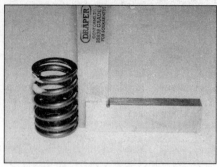

14.17b Check the valve springs for squareness

Specifications **(see illustration)**. If any spring is shorter than specified it has sagged and must be replaced with a new one. Also place the spring upright on a flat surface and check it for bend by placing a ruler against it, or alternatively lay it against a set square **(see illustration)**. If the bend in any spring is excessive, it must be replaced with a new one.

18 Check the spring seats, retainers and collets for obvious wear and cracks. Any questionable parts should not be reused, as extensive damage will occur in the event of failure during engine operation.

19 If the inspection indicates that no overhaul work is required, the valve components can be reinstalled in the head.

Reassembly

20 Unless a valve service has been performed, before installing the valves in the head they should be ground in (lapped) to ensure a positive seal between the valves and seats. This procedure requires coarse and fine valve grinding compound and a valve grinding tool (either hand-held or drill driven). If a grinding tool is not available, a piece of rubber or plastic hose can be slipped over the valve stem (after the valve has been installed in the guide) and used to turn the valve.

21 Apply a small amount of coarse grinding compound to the valve face, and some molybdenum disulphide oil (a 50/50 mixture of molybdenum disulphide grease and engine oil) to the valve stem, then slip the valve into the guide **(see illustrations)**. **Note:** *Make sure each valve is installed in its correct guide and be careful not to get any grinding compound on the valve stem.*

22 Attach the grinding tool (or hose) to the valve and rotate the tool between the palms of your hands. Use a back-and-forth motion (as though rubbing your hands together) rather than a circular motion (i.e. so that the valve rotates alternately clockwise and anti-clockwise rather than in one direction only) **(see illustration)**. If a motorised tool is being used, take note of the correct drive speed for it – if your drill runs too fast and is not variable, use a hand tool instead. Lift the valve off the seat and turn it at regular intervals to distribute the grinding compound properly. Continue the grinding procedure until the valve face and seat contact area is of uniform and correct width, and unbroken around the entire circumference **(see illustration and 14.13)**.

23 Carefully remove the valve from the guide and wipe off all traces of grinding compound, making sure none gets in the guide. Use solvent to clean the valve and wipe the seat area thoroughly with a solvent soaked cloth.

24 Repeat the procedure with fine valve grinding compound, then repeat the entire procedure for the remaining valves.

25 Working on one valve at a time, lay the spring seat in place in the cylinder head, making sure the shouldered side faces up **(see illustration)**.

26 Fit a new valve stem seal onto the guide, using a stem seal fitting tool or an appropriate size deep socket to push the seal over the end of the valve guide until it is felt to clip into place **(see illustrations)**. Don't twist or cock the seal, or it will not seal properly against the valve stem. Also, don't remove it again or it will be damaged.

27 Coat the valve stem with molybdenum disulphide oil (a 50/50 mixture of molybdenum

14.21a Apply the lapping compound very sparingly, in small dabs, to the valve face only

14.21b Lubricate the stem and insert the valve in the guide

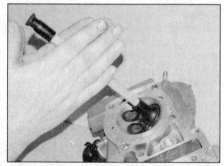

14.22a Rotate the valve grinding tool back and forth between the palms of your hands

14.22b The valve face and seat should show a uniform unbroken ring and the seat should be the specified width all the way round

14.25 Fit the spring seat, making sure it is the correct way up

14.26a Fit a new valve stem seal . . .

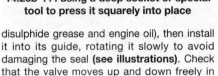

14.26b . . . using a deep socket or special tool to press it squarely into place

14.27a Lubricate the stem . . .

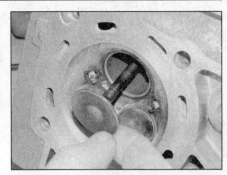

14.27b . . . and slide the valve into its correct location

disulphide grease and engine oil), then install it into its guide, rotating it slowly to avoid damaging the seal (see illustrations). Check that the valve moves up and down freely in the guide.

28 Next, install the inner and outer springs, with the closer-wound coils facing down into the cylinder head (see illustrations). Fit the spring retainer, with its shouldered side facing down so that it fits into the top of the springs (see illustration).

29 Compress the valve spring with a spring compressor, making sure it is correctly located onto each end of the valve assembly (see illustrations 14.5a and b). On the underside of the head make sure the plate on the compressor only contacts the valve and not the soft aluminium of the head – if the plate is too big for the valve, use a spacer between them. Do not compress the springs any more than is necessary to slip the collets into place. Apply a small amount of grease to the collets to help hold them in place (see illustration 14.5c). Locate each collet in turn into the groove in the valve stem, then carefully release the compressor, making sure the collets seat and lock as you do (see illustration). Check that the collets are securely locked in the retaining groove (see illustration).

30 Support the cylinder head on blocks so the valves can't contact the workbench top, then very gently tap the top of the valve stem with a brass drift. This will help seat the collets in the groove. If you don't have a brass drift, fit the shim into its recess in the top of the

valve spring retainer and use a soft-faced hammer and a piece of wood as an interface

> **HAYNES HiNT**
> Check for proper sealing of the valves by pouring a small amount of solvent into each of the valve ports. If the solvent leaks past any valve into the combustion chamber area the valve grinding operation on that valve should be repeated.

31 Repeat the procedure for the remaining valves. Remember to keep the parts for each valve together, and separate from the other valves, so they can be reinstalled in the same location. After the cylinder head and camshafts have been installed, check the valve clearances and adjust as required (see Chapter 1).

15 Cylinder barrels – removal, inspection and installation

Note: To remove the cylinder barrels the engine must be removed from the frame.

Removal

1 Remove the engine from the frame (see Section 5), then remove the cylinder head(s) (see Section 12) and the cam chain guide blade(s) (see Section 11).

2 On XL600V models, if required, unscrew the bolt securing the coolant inlet pipe to the cylinder and remove it. Discard the O-ring as a new one must be used.

3 On XL650V and XRV750 models, release one of the clips securing the coolant joint collar that connects between the two

14.28a Fit the inner valve spring . . .

14.28b . . . and the outer valve spring . . .

14.28c . . . then fit the spring retainer

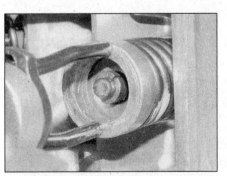

14.29a Make sure both collets lock into the groove as the compressor is released . . .

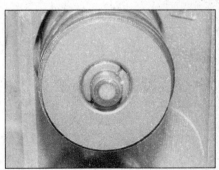

14.29b . . . and remain in place when it is removed

2

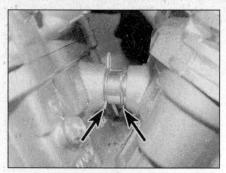

15.3 Remove one of the clips (arrowed) and slide the joint collar across

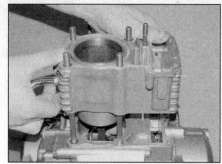

15.4 Lift the barrel up off the crankcase and remove it

cylinders **(see illustration)**. Slide the collar either forwards or backwards (depending on which clip was removed) so that it is detached from the stub on one or other of the cylinders. If required, unscrew the bolt securing the coolant inlet union to the front cylinder and remove it. Discard the O-ring as a new one must be used.

4 Let the cam chain drop down into its tunnel. Lift the cylinder up off the studs, taking care not to allow the connecting rod to knock against the side of the crankcase once the piston is free **(see illustration)**. If it is stuck, tap around its joint faces with a soft-faced mallet to free it from the crankcase. Don't attempt to free the cylinder by inserting a screwdriver between it and the crankcase – you'll damage the sealing surfaces. When the cylinder has been removed, stuff clean rags around the piston to prevent anything falling into the crankcase.

5 Note the location of the two dowels which will be either on the bottom of the cylinder or in the crankcase **(see illustration 15.19)**. Remove them if they are loose.

6 On XL650V and XRV750 models, remove the coolant joint collar from whichever barrel it is attached to, then remove the collar O-ring from the stub on each cylinder. Discard the O-rings as new ones must be used.

7 Remove the gasket and clean all traces of old gasket material from the cylinder and crankcase mating surfaces. If a scraper is used, take care not to scratch or gouge the soft aluminium. Don't let any gasket material fall into the crankcase or the oil passages.

Inspection

8 Do not attempt to separate the liner from the cylinder.

9 Check the cylinder bore walls carefully for scratches and score marks.

10 Using a precision straight-edge and a feeler gauge set to the warpage limit listed in the specifications at the beginning of the Chapter, check the top mating surface of the cylinder barrel for warpage. Refer to *Tools and Workshop Tips* in the Reference section for details of how to use the straight-edge. If warpage is excessive the cylinder must be replaced with a new one.

11 Using telescoping gauges and a micrometer (see *Tools and Workshop Tips*), check the dimensions of each cylinder bore to assess the amount of wear, taper and ovality. Measure near the top (but below the level of the top piston ring at TDC), centre and bottom (but above the level of the oil ring at BDC) of the bore, both parallel to and across the crankshaft axis **(see illustrations)**. Compare the results to the specifications at the beginning of the Chapter. If the cylinders are worn, oval or tapered beyond the service limit they can be rebored, and an oversize (+ 0.25 or +0.50) set of pistons and rings are available from Honda. Note that the person carrying out the rebore must be aware of the piston-to-bore clearance for the oversize piston (see Specifications).

12 If the precision measuring tools are not available, take the cylinders to a Honda dealer or specialist motorcycle repair shop for assessment and advice.

13 If the cylinder bores are in good condition

and the piston-to-bore clearance is within specifications (see Section 16), the bores should be honed (de-glazed). To perform this operation you will need the proper size flexible hone with fine stones, or a bottle-brush type hone, plenty of light oil or honing oil, some clean rags and an electric drill motor.

14 Hold the cylinder sideways (so that the bore is horizontal rather than vertical) in a vice with soft jaws or cushioned with wooden blocks. Mount the hone in the drill motor, compress the stones and insert the hone into the bore. Thoroughly lubricate the cylinder walls, then turn on the drill and move the hone up and down in the bore at a pace which produces a fine cross-hatch pattern on the cylinder wall with the lines intersecting at an angle of approximately 60°. Be sure to use plenty of lubricant and do not take off any more material than is necessary to produce the desired effect. Do not withdraw the hone from the cylinder while it is still turning. Switch off the drill and continue to move it up and down in the cylinder until it has stopped turning, then compress the stones and withdraw the hone. Wipe the oil from the cylinder and repeat the procedure on the other one. Remember, do not take too much material from the cylinder wall.

15 Wash the bores thoroughly with warm soapy water to remove all traces of the abrasive grit produced during the honing operation. Be sure to run a brush through the stud holes and flush them with running water. After rinsing, dry the cylinders thoroughly and apply a thin coat of light, rust-preventative oil to all machined surfaces.

16 If you do not have the equipment or desire to perform the honing operation, take the cylinders to a Honda dealer or specialist motorcycle repair shop.

Installation

17 On XL650V and XRV750 models, fit a new O-ring onto the coolant joint collar stub on each cylinder, then slide the collar as far as possible onto the stub of one of them.

18 Check that the mating surfaces of the cylinder and crankcase are free from oil or pieces of old gasket.

19 If removed, fit the dowels either over the studs and into the crankcase or into the barrel, and push them firmly home **(see illustration)**.

15.11a Use a bore gauge . . .

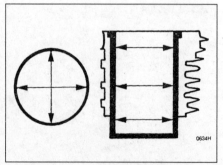

15.11b . . . and measure at the points shown

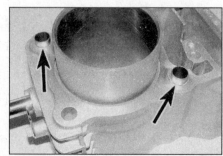

15.19 Install the two dowels (arrowed) either into the barrel or over the studs and into the crankcase

20 Remove the rags from around the piston, taking care not to let the connecting rod fall against the rim of the crankcase, and lay the new base gasket in place, locating it over the dowels (if they are in the crankcase) **(see illustration)**. The gasket can only fit one way, so if the holes do not line up properly the gasket is upside down. Never re-use the old gasket.

21 Space the piston rings gaps as described in Section 17. If required, fit a piston ring clamp onto the piston to ease its entry into the bore as the cylinder is lowered. This is not essential as there is a good lead-in, enabling the piston rings to be hand-fed into the bore. If possible, have an assistant support the cylinder while this is done.

22 Lubricate the cylinder bore, piston and piston rings with clean engine oil, then lower the barrel down over the studs until the piston crown fits into the bore **(see illustration)**.

23 Gently push the cylinder down, making sure the piston enters the bore squarely and does not get cocked sideways. If you are doing this without a piston ring clamp, carefully compress and feed each ring into the bore as the cylinder is lowered **(see illustration)**.

24 When the piston is correctly installed in the bore, press the cylinder down onto the base gasket, making sure the dowels locate. Hook the cam chain up the tunnel and secure it to prevent it dropping back down **(see illustration)**.

25 On XL600V models, if removed, fit a new O-ring onto the coolant inlet pipe, then fit it into the cylinder and secure it with the bolt.

26 On XL650V and XRV750 models, slide the coolant joint collar across and over the O-ring so that it is central on the stubs between the cylinders, then secure it in place with its clips **(see illustration 15.3)**. If removed, fit a new O-ring to the coolant inlet hose union and install the union onto the front of the front cylinder, tightening its bolts securely.

27 Install the cam chain guide blade(s) (see Section 11) and the cylinder head(s) (see Section 12).

16 Pistons –
removal, inspection and installation

Note: *The pistons can be removed with the engine in the frame.*

Removal

1 Remove the cylinder barrel(s) (see Section 15). Stuff clean rag into the crankcase aperture to support the connecting rod and to prevent anything falling in, such as the circlip.

2 Before removing the piston from the connecting rod, use a sharp scriber or felt marker pen to write the cylinder identity on the crown of each piston (or on the inside of the skirt if the piston is dirty and going to be cleaned). Each piston crown should already

be marked IN on the intake side of the cylinder, though the mark is likely to be invisible until the piston is cleaned **(see illustration)**.

3 Carefully prise out the circlip on one side of

the piston using needle-nose pliers or a small flat-bladed screwdriver inserted into the notch **(see illustration)**. Push the piston pin out from the other side to free the piston from the connecting rod **(see illustrations)**. Remove

15.20 Always use a new gasket

15.22 Carefully lower the barrel onto the piston . . .

15.23 . . . and feed the piston rings into the bore

15.24 Hook the cam chain out of the tunnel

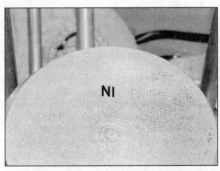
16.2 Note the "IN" mark on the piston which faces the intake side

16.3a Prise the piston pin circlip out from one side of the piston

16.3b Push the piston pin out from the other side . . .

16.3c . . . then withdraw it and remove the piston

2

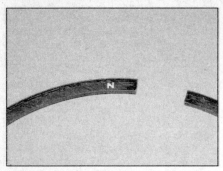

16.4 Note the marking on the top surface of the ring

16.10 Measure the piston ring-to-groove clearance with a feeler gauge

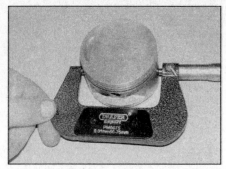

16.11 Measure the piston diameter with a micrometer

the other circlip and discard them as new ones must be used. When the piston has been removed, install its pin back into its barrel so that related parts do not get mixed up.

 If a piston pin is a tight fit in the piston bosses, soak a rag in boiling water then wring it out and wrap it around the piston – this will expand the alloy piston sufficiently to release its grip on the pin. If the piston pin is particularly stubborn, extract it using a drawbolt tool, but be careful to protect the piston's working surfaces.

Inspection

4 Using your thumbs or a piston ring removal and installation tool, carefully remove the rings from the pistons **(see illustrations 17.11, 10, and 8c, b and a)**. Do not nick or gouge the pistons in the process. Carefully note which way up each ring fits and in which groove as they must be installed in their original positions if being re-used. The upper surface of the top ring is marked with the letter R or N at one end, and the second (middle) ring is either marked RN or ●, or is unmarked **(see illustration)**. The top and middle rings can also be identified by their different profiles **(see illustration 17.12)**.
5 Scrape all traces of carbon from the tops of the pistons. A hand-held wire brush or a piece of fine emery cloth can be used once most of the deposits have been scraped away. Do not, under any circumstances, use a wire brush

mounted in a drill motor to remove deposits from the pistons; the piston material is soft and will be eroded away by the wire brush.
6 Use a piston ring groove cleaning tool to remove any carbon deposits from the ring grooves. If a tool is not available, a piece broken off an old ring will do the job. Be very careful to remove only the carbon deposits. Do not remove any metal and do not nick or gouge the sides of the ring grooves.
7 Once the deposits have been removed, clean the pistons with solvent and dry them thoroughly. If the identification previously marked on the piston is cleaned off, be sure to re-mark it with the correct identity. Make sure the oil return holes below the oil ring groove are clear.
8 Carefully inspect each piston for cracks around the skirt, at the pin bosses and at the ring lands. Normal piston wear appears as even, vertical wear on the thrust surfaces of the piston and slight looseness of the top ring in its groove. If the skirt is scored or scuffed, the engine may have been suffering from overheating and/or abnormal combustion, which caused excessively high operating temperatures. The oil pump should be checked thoroughly. Also check that the circlip grooves are not damaged.
9 A hole in the piston crown, an extreme to be sure, is an indication that abnormal combustion (pre-ignition) was occurring. Burned areas at the edge of the piston crown are usually evidence of spark knock (detonation). If any of the above problems exist, the causes must be corrected or the damage will occur again.

10 Measure the piston ring-to-groove clearance by laying each piston ring in its groove and slipping a feeler gauge in beside it **(see illustration)**. Make sure you have the correct ring for the groove (see Step 5). Check the clearance at three or four locations around the groove. If the clearance is greater than specified, renew both the piston and rings as a set. If new rings are being used, measure the clearance using the new rings. If the clearance is greater than that specified, the piston is worn and must be replaced with a new one.
11 Check the piston-to-bore clearance by measuring the bore (see Section 15) and the piston diameter. Make sure each piston is matched to its correct cylinder. Measure the piston 10.0 mm (XL600V and XRV750 models) or 12 mm (XL650V models) up from the bottom of the skirt and at 90° to the piston pin axis **(see illustration)**. Subtract the piston diameter from the bore diameter to obtain the clearance. If it is greater than the specified figure, and if not already done, check the cylinder for wear (see Section 15). If the cylinder is good but the piston is worn, replace it with a new one. If the cylinder is worn it can be rebored, and then oversize pistons and rings, available from Honda, can be fitted.
12 Apply clean engine oil to the piston pin, insert it into the piston and check for any freeplay between the two **(see illustration)**. Measure the pin external diameter and the pin bore in the piston **(see illustrations)**. Calculate the difference to obtain the piston pin-to-piston pin bore clearance. Compare

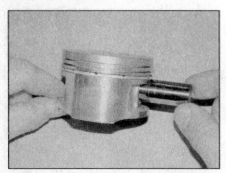

16.12a Slip the pin into the piston and check for freeplay between them

16.12b Measure the external diameter of the pin . . .

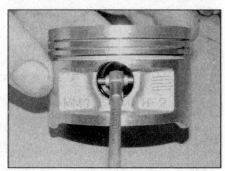

16.12c . . . and the internal diameter of the bore in the piston . . .

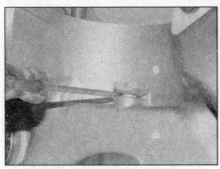

16.13a Prise out the oil jet

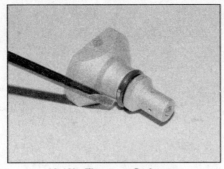

16.13b Fit a new O-ring . . .

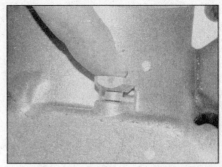

16.13c . . . and press the jet into place

the result to the specifications at the beginning of the Chapter. If the clearance is greater than specified, replace the components that are worn beyond their specified limits. If not already done (see Section 28), repeat the measurements between the pin and the connecting rod small-end (see illustration 28.6).

13 Prise the oil jets out of the crankcase using a small screwdriver, taking great care not to damage them or drop them into the crankcase – make sure your rag covers the hole completely (see illustration). Remove the O-rings and discard them (see illustration). Clean the jets with solvent and blow them through with compressed air if available. Fit new O-rings and press the jets back into the crankcase (see illustration).

Installation

14 Inspect and install the piston rings (see Section 17).

15 Lubricate the piston pin, the piston pin bore and the connecting rod small-end bore with molybdenum disulphide oil (a 50/50 mixture of molybdenum disulphide grease and clean engine oil).

16 When installing the pistons onto the connecting rods, make sure the IN mark on the piston crown faces the intake side of the cylinder (see illustration 16.2).

17 Install a *new* circlip in one side of the piston (do not re-use old circlips). Line up the piston on its correct connecting rod (see illustration 16.3c), and insert the piston pin from the other side (see illustration). Secure the pin with the other *new* circlip (see illustration). When installing the circlips, compress them only just enough to fit them in the piston, and make sure they are properly seated in their grooves with the open end away from the removal notch.

18 Install the cylinder barrel(s) (see Section 15).

17 Piston rings –
inspection and installation

1 It is good practice to renew the piston rings when an engine is being overhauled. Before installing the new rings, check the end gaps

16.17a Slide the pin through the piston and connecting rod . . .

with the rings installed in the bore, as follows.

2 Lay out the pistons and the new ring sets so the rings will be matched with the same piston and bore during the end gap measurement procedure and engine assembly.

3 To measure the installed ring end gap, insert the top ring into the top of the bore and square it up with the bore walls by pushing it in with the top of the piston (see illustration). The ring should be about 20 mm below the top edge of the bore. Slip a feeler gauge between the ends of the ring and compare the measurement to the specifications at the beginning of the Chapter (see illustration).

4 If the gap is larger or smaller than specified, double check to make sure that you have the correct rings before proceeding.

5 Excess end gap is not critical unless it exceeds the service limit. Again, double-check to make sure you have the correct rings

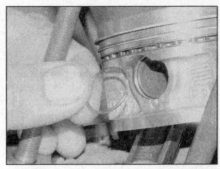

16.17b . . . and secure it with the circlip, locating the open end away from the notch in the piston

for your engine and check that the bore is not worn (see Section 15).

6 Repeat the procedure for each ring that will be installed in the bore. Remember to keep the rings, pistons and bores matched up.

7 Once the ring end gaps have been checked the rings can be installed on the pistons (see illustration 17.12).

8 Install the oil control ring (lowest on the piston) first. It is composed of three separate components, namely the expander and the upper and lower side rails. Slip the expander into the groove, making sure the ends don't overlap, then install the lower side rail (see illustrations). Do not use a piston ring installation tool on the side rails as they may be damaged. Instead, place one end of the side rail into the groove between the expander and the ring land. Hold it firmly in place and slide a finger around the piston while pushing

17.3a Fit the ring into the bore and square it up with the piston

17.3b Measuring piston ring end gap

2

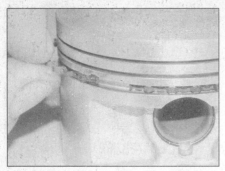

17.8a Install the oil ring expander in its groove . . .

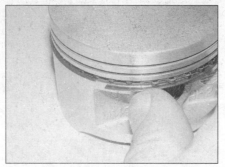

17.8b . . . then fit the lower side rail . . .

17.8c . . . and the upper side rail

the rail into the groove. Next, install the upper side rail in the same manner **(see illustration)**. Check that the ends of the expander have not overlapped.

9 After the three oil ring components have been installed, check to make sure that both the upper and lower side rails can be turned smoothly in the ring groove.

10 The upper surface of the top ring is marked with the letter R or N at one end, and the second (middle) ring is either marked RN or •, or is unmarked **(see illustration 16.4)**. The top and middle rings can also be identified by their different profiles **(see illustration 17.12)**. Install the second (middle) ring next. Make sure that the identification letter near the end gap is facing up, or if the ring is unmarked make sure the wider edge is at the bottom, as shown in the illustration of the profile **(see illustration 17.12)**. Fit the ring into the middle groove in the piston **(see**

illustration). Do not expand the ring any more than is necessary to slide it into place. To avoid breaking the ring, use a piston ring installation tool, or alternatively a feeler gauge blade can be used as shown.

11 Finally, install the top ring in the same manner into the top groove in the piston **(see illustration)**. Make sure the identification letter near the end gap is facing up.

12 Once the rings are correctly installed, check they move freely without snagging and stagger their end gaps as shown **(see illustration)**.

18 Clutch –
removal, inspection and installation

Note: The clutch can be removed with the engine in the frame. If the engine has already

17.10 Fit the middle ring into its groove . . .

17.11 . . . then fit the top ring

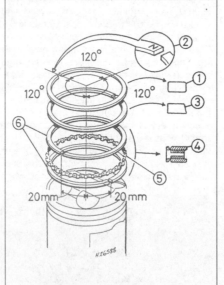

17.12 Arrange the ring end gaps like this

1 Top compression ring
2 Compression ring marking (see text)
3 Second compression ring
4 Oil ring complete
5 Expander ring
6 Side rails

been removed, ignore the preliminary steps which don't apply.

Removal

1 Drain the engine oil (see Chapter 1).

2 Remove the exhaust system (see Chapter 4).

3 On XL600V-H to K (1987 to 1989) models, unscrew the external oil pipe bolt from the clutch cover, and the pipe holder bolt (one of the cover bolts secures it). Discard the sealing washers as new ones must be used.

4 Working in a criss-cross pattern, slacken the clutch cover bolts, noting the clutch cable holder secured by one of the bolts **(see illustration and 18.35c)**. Fully unscrew the cable holder bolt first and detach the cable end from the lever on the crankcase cover **(see illustration 19.1c)**. Unscrew the remaining bolts and lift the cover away from the engine, being prepared to catch any residual oil. Note the release rod in the cover and remove it for safekeeping if required **(see illustration 18.34)**.

5 Remove the gasket and discard it. Note the positions of the two locating dowels fitted to the crankcase and remove them for safe-keeping if they are loose **(see illustration 18.35a)**. On XL600V-H, J and K (1987 to 1989) models, remove the oil orifice, noting which way round it fits, and discard its O-ring as a new one must be used.

6 Working in a criss-cross pattern, gradually slacken the clutch release plate bolts until spring pressure is released, then remove the bolts, plate and springs **(see illustrations)**.

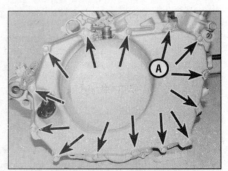

18.4 Clutch cover bolts (arrowed). Note the location of the cable bracket (A)

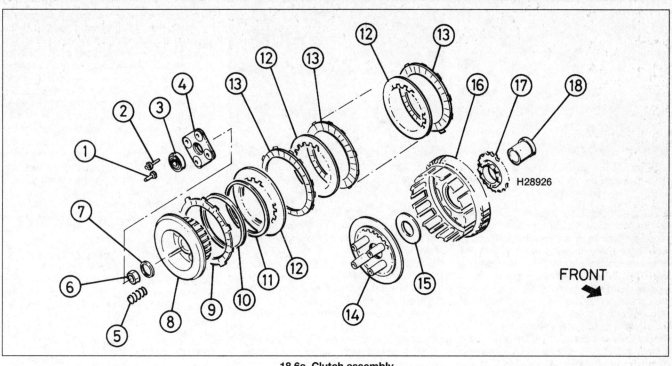

18.6a Clutch assembly

1	Release rod	6	Clutch nut	11	Anti-judder spring	15	Thrust washer
2	Release plate bolts	7	Washer	12	Plain plates	16	Clutch housing
3	Release bearing	8	Clutch centre	13	Friction plates –	17	Oil pump drive
4	Release plate	9	Friction plate – type B		type A		sprocket
5	Springs	10	Spring seat	14	Pressure plate	18	Clutch housing guide

7 Unstake the clutch nut from the notch in the shaft **(see illustration)**. To remove the clutch nut the transmission input shaft must be locked. This can be done in several ways. If the engine is in the frame, engage 5th gear and have an assistant hold the rear brake on hard with the rear tyre in firm contact with the ground. Alternatively, the Honda service tool (available from a dealer) can be used to stop the clutch centre from turning whilst the nut is slackened. If the engine has been removed from the frame (and the Honda tool is not available), a holding tool that bolts onto the rear sprocket (which can then be slipped onto the output shaft) can be easily made from two strips of steel bolted together (see *Tool Tip*). With the shaft locked, unscrew the clutch nut

and remove the washer(s) – XL600V-V to X and XL650V models have a spring washer and a plain washer, all other models have a plain washer only **(see illustration)**. Discard the nut as a new one must be used. Whilst the shaft is locked, and if you intend removing it, also slacken the oil pump driven sprocket bolt **(see illustration 18.12a)**.

TOOL TiP

A clutch centre holding tool can easily be made using two strips of steel bolted as shown, and with the ends drilled to accept bolts that can be threaded into the front sprocket. Thread a locknut up each bolt – these can then be tightened against the tool to secure the bolts after they have been threaded into the sprocket. Use an old sprocket if you have one.

18.7a Unstake the clutch nut . . .

18.6b Unscrew the bolts (arrowed) and remove the plate and springs

18.7b . . . then unscrew it as described in the text

2

18.8 Remove the clutch centre and plates as an assembly

8 Grasp the clutch centre with the complete set of clutch plates and the pressure plate and remove them as a pack (see illustration). Unless the plates are being replaced with new ones, keep them assembled in their original order on the clutch centre – positioning it upside down will prevent the plates slipping off. Otherwise, remove the pressure plate from the back of the clutch centre, then remove the friction and plain plates, noting how they fit. Finally remove the anti-judder spring and spring seat. Note that on XL models, there are two types of friction plate, identified as A and B (see illustration 18.6a). The outermost (type B) plate has a slightly larger internal diameter allowing it to fit over the anti-judder spring and

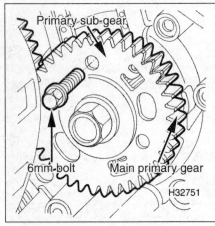

18.11 Align the gear teeth and insert a 6 mm bolt in the holes to lock them

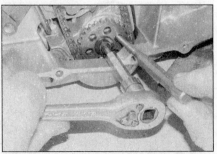

18.12b Use a rod through the sprocket and located against the crankcase to prevent the sprocket turning

18.10 Slide the clutch housing off the shaft

spring seat, and its tangs fit into the shallow slots in the clutch housing. Take care not to mix them up. On XRV models all the friction plates are the same.

9 Remove the thrust washer from the shaft (see illustration 18.28).

10 On XL models, slide the clutch housing off the shaft, noting that you may have to prevent the guide in the centre of the housing from sliding with it by pressing on its rim using a very small screwdriver (see illustration). If the guide slides with the housing, it brings the oil pump drive chain with it which could damage the chain.

11 On XRV750 models, to remove the clutch housing it is necessary to align the primary drive sub-gear teeth with the main gear teeth. To do this, first obtain a 6 mm bolt or rod to serve as a locking pin once the teeth are aligned. Locate a suitable screwdriver between the teeth and twist it to align them,

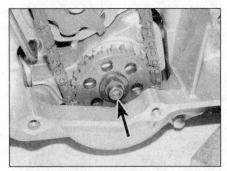

18.12a Oil pump driven sprocket bolt (arrowed)

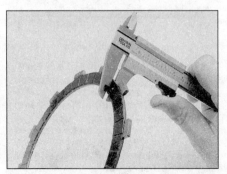

18.14 Measure the thickness of the friction plates

then insert the bolt or rod through the holes in the gears (see illustration). Slide the clutch housing off the shaft (see illustration 18.10). Keep the bolt or pin located in the primary drive gear until the housing has been installed.

12 If required, unscrew the oil pump driven sprocket bolt and remove the driven sprocket, the chain and the drive sprocket (see illustration and 18.25d, b and a). If the bolt wasn't slackened earlier (see Step 7), lock the sprocket by locating a rod between the one of the holes and the crankcase as shown to prevent it from turning (see illustration). On XL models, note the 'IN' mark on the back of the oil pump driven sprocket which must face inwards; on XRV models note the 'OUT' mark on the back of the sprocket which must face outwards.

13 Remove the clutch housing guide from the input shaft (see illustration 18.24). On XL models, note how the tabs on the oil pump drive sprocket locate in the slots in the back of the clutch housing. On XRV models, note how the pins on the oil pump drive sprocket locate in the holes in the back of the clutch housing.

Inspection

14 After an extended period of service the clutch friction plates will wear and promote clutch slip. Measure the thickness of each friction plate using a Vernier caliper (see illustration). If any plate has worn to or beyond the service limit given in the Specifications at the beginning of the Chapter, the friction plates must be replaced as a set. Also, if any of the plates smell burnt or are glazed, they must be replaced as a set.

15 The plain plates should not show any signs of excess heating (bluing). Check for warpage using a flat surface and feeler gauges (see illustration). If any plate exceeds the maximum amount of warpage, or shows signs of bluing, all plain plates must be renewed as a set.

16 Measure the free length of each clutch spring using a Vernier caliper (see illustration 14.17a). If any spring is below the service limit specified, renew all the springs as a set. Also check the anti-judder spring and spring seat for damage or distortion and replace them with new ones if necessary.

18.15 Check the plain plates for warpage

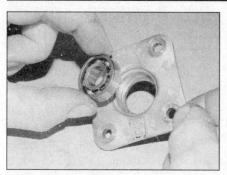

18.20 Check the release plate and bearing as described

18.21a Withdraw the shaft . . .

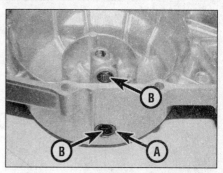

18.21b . . . and check the seal (A) and bearings (B)

17 Inspect the clutch assembly for burrs and indentations on the edges of the protruding tabs of the friction plates and/or slots in the edge of the housing with which they engage. Similarly check for wear between the inner tongues of the plain plates and the slots in the clutch centre. Wear of this nature will cause clutch drag and slow disengagement during gear changes as the plates will snag when the pressure plate is lifted. With care a small amount of wear can be corrected by dressing with a fine file, but if this is excessive the worn components should be renewed.

18 Using a Vernier caliper, measure the diameter of the output shaft where the clutch housing guide fits over it. Also measure the internal and external diameter of the housing guide and the internal diameter of the oil pump drive sprocket, and on XL600V models the internal diameter of the clutch housing where it fits over the guide. Compare the measurements to the Specifications at the beginning of the Chapter and replace any components that are worn beyond their service limit. Also check all the above components for signs of damage or scoring, and replace if necessary.

19 On XRV750 models, inspect the needle roller bearing in the clutch housing. If there are any signs of wear, pitting or other damage it must be renewed. The bearing is a press fit in the housing – refer to *Tools and Workshop Tips* in the Reference Section for details on bearing removal and installation. When removing the old bearing, note carefully at what depth it sits in the centre and install the new bearing so that it sits in exactly the same place.

20 Check the pressure plate and thrust washer for signs of roughness, wear or damage, and replace any parts as necessary. Check the clutch release plate for signs of damage. Check that the bearing outer race is a good fit in the centre of the plate, and that the inner race rotates freely without any rough spots **(see illustration)**. Renew the bearing if necessary.

21 Remove the release rod from the clutch cover (if not already done) **(see illustration 18.34)**. Check the release mechanism for a smooth action. If the action is stiff or rough, withdraw the shaft, noting the washer and

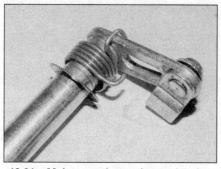

18.21c Make sure the washer and spring are correctly positioned . . .

18.21d . . . and the spring ends locate correctly

how the return spring ends locate, then clean and check the oil seal and the two needle bearings in the cover, replacing them with new ones if necessary **(see illustrations)**. The seal can be renewed by levering the old one out with a screwdriver and pressing the new one in. The needle bearings have to be drifted out – refer to *Tools and Workshop Tips* in the Reference Section for further information. Lubricate the bearings and shaft before installing the shaft. Make sure the washer is on the shaft and the return spring ends locate correctly **(see illustrations)**.

22 Check the teeth of the primary driven gear on the back of the clutch housing and the corresponding teeth of the primary drive gear on the crankshaft. Renew the clutch housing and/or primary drive gear if worn or chipped teeth are discovered (refer to Section 21 for the primary drive gear).

Installation

Note: *If the primary drive gear has been removed and not yet installed, do so before installing the clutch (see Section 21).*

23 Remove all traces of old gasket from the crankcase and clutch cover surfaces.

24 Smear the outside of the clutch housing guide with molybdenum disulphide oil (50% molybdenum grease and 50% engine oil), then slide the guide onto the input shaft **(see illustration)**.

25 Slide the oil pump drive sprocket onto the shaft, making sure the tabs or pins (according to model) face out, and slip the chain around the sprocket **(see illustrations)**. Engage the driven sprocket with the chain, on XL models making sure the 'IN' mark faces inwards and on XRV models making sure the 'OUT' mark faces outwards, then locate the sprocket on the oil pump, aligning the flats between

2

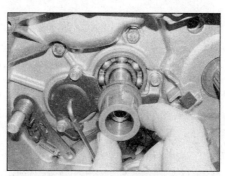

18.24 Slide the clutch housing guide onto the shaft . . .

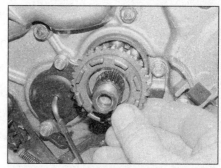

18.25a . . . then fit the drive sprocket with its tabs or pins facing out

18.25b Fit the chain around the sprocket . . .

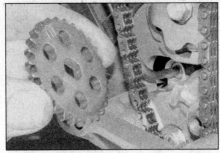

18.25c . . . then fit the driven sprocket into the chain, making sure it is the correct way round, . . .

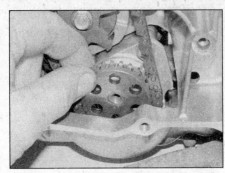

18.25d . . . and onto the shaft, aligning the flats

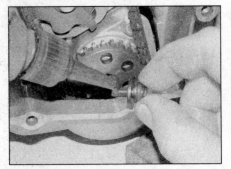

18.25e Apply a locking compound to the bolt . . .

18.25f . . . and tighten it to the specified torque, locking the sprocket as shown

the sub-gear and main gear teeth are aligned. If the bolt or rod was removed, fit it as described in Step 11.

27 Slide the clutch housing onto the housing guide on the input shaft, making sure the tabs or pins on the oil pump drive sprocket engage with the slots or holes in the rear of the housing (turn the sprocket with your finger while pressing on the housing until the tabs/pins are felt to locate and the housing moves in a bit further, then double-check by making sure the sprocket can't turn independently of the housing), and the teeth of the primary driven gear engage with those of the primary drive gear **(see illustrations)**.

28 Slide the thrust washer onto the shaft **(see illustration)**.

29 Place the clutch centre face down on the bench. Fit the anti-judder spring seat onto the clutch centre, followed by the anti-judder spring; making sure the outer rim is raised off the spring seat as shown **(see illustrations)**.

sprocket and shaft **(see illustrations)**. Apply a suitable non-permanent thread locking compound to the sprocket bolt **(see illustration)**. Fit the bolt with its washer and tighten it to the torque setting specified at the beginning of the chapter, locating a rod

through one of the holes and against the crankcase to prevent the sprocket turning **(see illustrations)**. Alternatively, tighten the bolt after tightening the clutch nut (see Step 32).

26 On XRV models, make sure the bolt or rod is still located in the primary drive gear so that

18.27a The tabs or pins on the sprocket must engage with the slots or holes on the back of the clutch housing

18.27b Slide the housing onto the guide, making sure it locates as described

18.28 Slide the thrust washer onto the shaft

18.29a Fit the spring seat . . .

18.29b . . . and the spring . . .

18.29c . . . making sure it is the correct way round

18.30a Locate the first friction plate over the anti-judder spring . . .

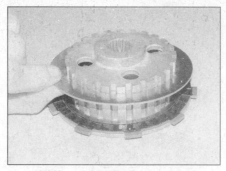

18.30b . . . then fit alternate plain plates . . .

18.30c . . . and friction plates . . .

18.30d . . . aligning them as shown

18.30e Fit the pressure plate into the centre, making sure it locates correctly

18.31a Slide the assembly onto the shaft . . .

30 Coat each clutch plate with engine oil, then build up the plates in the housing, starting with a friction plate (the type B plate with the wider ID on XL models), then a plain plate, then alternating friction plates (type A on XL models) and plain plates until all are installed **(see illustrations)**. Align the friction plate tabs as shown to make installation into the clutch housing easier – the outermost friction plate tabs locate into the shallow slots in the housing. Fit the pressure plate into the clutch centre, making sure it seats correctly with its protrusions locating in the slots in the centre **(see illustration)**.

31 Slide the clutch centre assembly onto the input shaft splines, feeding the friction plate tabs into the slots as you do, locating the outermost plate tabs into the shallow slots in the housing as shown **(see illustrations)**.

32 Fit the plain washer, and on XL600V-V to X and XL650V models the spring washer with the 'OUTSIDE' mark facing out, then fit a new clutch nut **(see illustrations)**. Using the method employed on removal to lock the input shaft (see Step 7), tighten the nut to the torque setting specified at the beginning of the Chapter **(see illustration)**. If you are using the home-made holding tool with the front sprocket, tilt the engine forward as shown so that the tool rests against the work surface and does not come up against the

2

18.31b . . . locating the outer plate tabs into the shallow slots

18.32a Fit the plain washer . . .

18.32b . . . and where fitted the spring washer . . .

18.32c . . . then fit the clutch nut . . .

18.32d . . . and tighten it to the specified torque

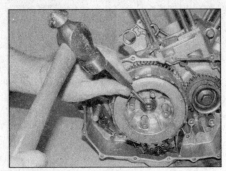

18.32e Stake the rim of the nut into the notch

18.33a Fit the springs . . .

18.33b . . . and the release plate, then tighten the bolts as described in the text

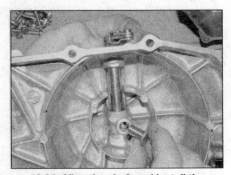

18.34 Align the shaft and install the release rod

18.35a Locate the new gasket onto the dowels (arrowed) . . .

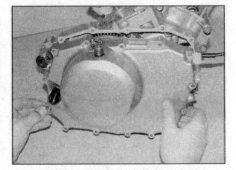

18.35b . . . then install the cover

gearchange shaft. Stake the rim of the nut into the indent in the end of the input shaft using a suitable punch (see illustration). Whilst the clutch is locked, and if not already done (see Step 25), also tighten the oil pump driven sprocket bolt to the specified torque setting, having first applied a suitable non-permanent thread locking compound to its threads. Note: Check that the clutch centre rotates freely after tightening the clutch nut.

33 Install the clutch springs, release plate and release plate bolts and tighten them evenly in a criss-cross sequence to the specified torque setting (see illustrations).

34 If removed, fit the release rod into the clutch cover, aligning the shaft so that the rod fits correctly (see illustration).

35 If removed, insert the dowels in the crankcase, then fit the new gasket, locating it over the dowels (see illustration). XL600V-H to K (1987 to 1989) models, fit a new O-ring

onto the oil orifice, then install the orifice into the crankcase with its smaller diameter hole facing out. Install the crankcase cover, making sure it locates correctly over the dowels (see illustration). Install all the clutch cover bolts except the one that also secures the clutch cable holder, and on XL600V-H to K (1987 to 1989) models the external oil pipe holder, and tighten them finger-tight. Connect the clutch cable end to the release arm (see illustration 19.1c), then locate the holder on the cover and secure it with its bolt (see illustration). Tighten the cover bolts evenly in a criss-cross sequence to the specified torque setting.

36 On XL600V-H to K (1987 to 1989) models, install the external oil pipe lower bolt, using new sealing washers, and the pipe holder bolt, and tighten them to the specified torque settings.

37 Install the exhaust system (see Chapter 4).

38 Refill the engine with oil (see Chapter 1).

39 Check the clutch lever freeplay and adjust if necessary (see Chapter 1).

19 Clutch cable – removal and installation

Caution: Take care not to burn your hands on the exhaust if the engine is hot.

Removal

1 Fully slacken the cable adjuster locknuts from the cable holder mounted to the right-hand side crankcase cover (see illustration). Access to it can be improved by removing either the belly-pan, the fairing side panel (XL600V and XRV750) or the fairing (XL650V), though this is not essential (just be careful not to let the spanner slip). Release the adjuster from the holder, noting how it fits and

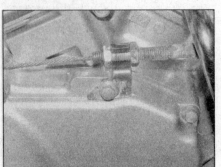

18.35c Clutch cable holder

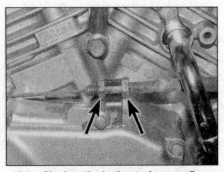

19.1a Slacken the locknuts (arrowed) . . .

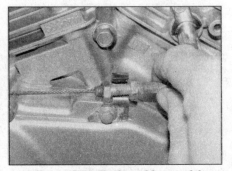

19.1b . . . then slip the cable out of the holder

19.1c . . . and free the end from the release arm

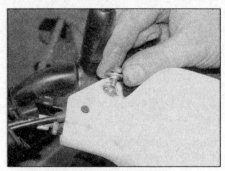

19.3a Unscrew the bolt . . .

19.3b . . . and the nut . . .

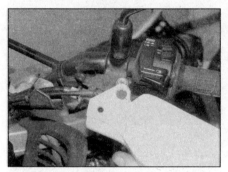

19.3c . . . and remove the handguard

19.4 Pull back the rubber cover, then slacken the lockring and thread the adjuster fully in

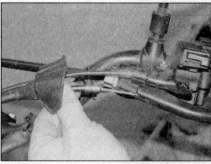

19.5a With the slots in the adjuster and lockwheel aligned, slip the cable out . . .

disconnect the cable end from the clutch release mechanism lever (see illustrations).
2 If necessary, unscrew the bolt securing the cable holder to the crankcase and remove the bracket (see illustration 18.35c).
3 Unscrew the bolt and remove the collar from the hand guard (see illustration). Counter-hold the screwhead and undo the nut on its bottom (see illustration). Remove the handguard (see illustration).
4 Pull back the rubber cover from the clutch adjuster at the handlebar end of the cable (see illustration). Fully slacken the lockring, then screw the adjuster fully in. This resets it to the beginning of its adjustment span.
5 Align the slots in the adjuster and lockwheel with that in the lever bracket, then pull the outer cable end from the socket in the adjuster and release the inner cable from the lever (see illustrations).
6 Take note of the exact routing of the cable

and any guides that hold it – incorrect installation could result in poor steering movement. Carefully withdraw the cable – if it gets stuck do not be tempted to pull it out using force as you will only damage something.

> **HAYNES HiNT**
> Before removing the cable from the bike, tape the lower end of the new cable to the upper end of the old cable. Slowly pull the lower end of the old cable out, guiding the new cable down into position. Using this method will ensure the cable is routed correctly.

Installation

7 Installation is the reverse of removal. Apply grease to the cable ends. Make sure the cable is correctly routed. Adjust the clutch cable (see Chapter 1).

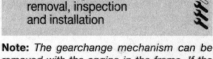
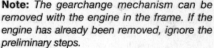

20 Gearchange mechanism – removal, inspection and installation

Note: The gearchange mechanism can be removed with the engine in the frame. If the engine has already been removed, ignore the preliminary steps.

Removal

1 Drain the engine oil (see Chapter 1).
2 Unscrew the gearchange lever pinch bolt and slide the lever off the shaft, noting the alignment of the punch mark on the shaft end with either the slit in the clamp or the punch mark on the lever, depending on your model (see illustration). Unscrew the bolts securing the front sprocket cover and remove it, and on XL650V and XRV750 models the drive chain guide plate, noting how it fits (see illustration).

2

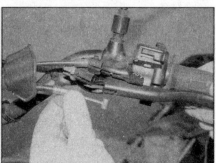

19.5b . . . and detach its end from the lever

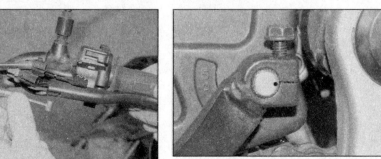

20.2a Note the alignment of the punch mark, then unscrew the bolt and remove the lever

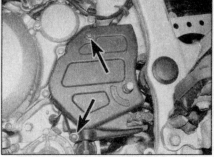

20.2b Sprocket cover bolts (arrowed)

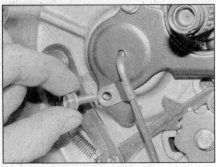

20.4a Unscrew the bolt . . .

20.4b . . . and remove the oil pipe

20.4c Unscrew the remaining bolts and remove the retainer plate

20.5 Lift the arm off the drum and withdraw the shaft

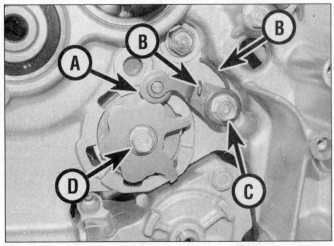

20.6 Note how the roller (A) and the spring ends (B) locate, then unscrew the bolt (C) and remove the arm. Cam plate bolt (D)

Wrap a single layer of thin insulating tape around the gearchange shaft splines to protect the oil seal lips as the shaft is removed.

3 Remove the clutch and the oil pump drive sprocket, chain and driven sprocket (see Section 18).

4 Unscrew the bolt securing the oil pipe **(see illustration)**. Carefully pull the oil pipe out of its sockets, noting that an O-ring retains it at the bottom **(see illustration)**. Discard the O-ring as a new one must be used. Unscrew the remaining bolts securing the transmission shaft bearing retainer plate and remove the plate, noting how it fits **(see illustration)**.

5 Note how the gearchange selector arm claw locates onto the pins in the selector drum cam plate, and how the gearchange shaft centralising spring ends locate **(see illustration 20.13c)**. Lift the selector arm claw off the selector drum and withdraw the gearchange shaft from the engine **(see illustration)**.

6 Note how the stopper arm spring ends locate and how the roller on the arm locates in the neutral detent on the selector drum cam, then unscrew the stopper arm bolt and remove the washer, the arm, the spring and the collar, noting how they fit **(see illustration)**.

7 If necessary, unscrew the bolt securing the cam plate to the selector drum and remove it, noting that there is a locating dowel that fits between them – it is advisable to place some rag in the bottom of the crankcase to catch the dowel should it drop out **(see illustration 20.6)**. Otherwise remove the dowel for safekeeping if it is loose. Also note the pins between the cam and the base plate and remove them if they are loose.

Inspection

8 Inspect the selector arm and the stopper arm return springs and the shaft centralising spring **(see illustrations)**. If they are fatigued, worn or damaged they must be replaced with new ones. Also check that the centralising spring locating pin in the crankcase is securely tightened. If it is loose, remove it and apply a non-permanent thread locking compound to its threads, then tighten it securely.

9 Check the gearchange shaft for straightness and damage to the splines. If the shaft is bent you can attempt to straighten it, but if the splines are damaged the shaft must be replaced with a new one. Also check the condition of the shaft oil seal in the left-hand side of the crankcase. If it is damaged, deteriorated or shows signs of leakage it must be replaced with a new one. Where fitted,

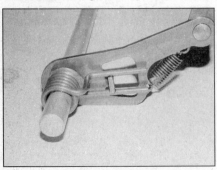

20.8a Check the selector arm assembly . . .

20.8b . . . and the stopper arm assembly as described

unscrew the bolt(s) securing the seal retainer plate and remove the plate, noting how it fits **(see illustration 23.3)**. Lever out the old seal with a screwdriver **(see illustration)**. Press or drive the new seal squarely into place, with its lip facing inward, using a seal driver or suitable socket **(see illustration)**. Fit the retainer plate where removed and tighten its bolt(s) securely.

10 Inspect the selector arm claw and the pins, and the stopper arm roller and the cam detents. If they are worn or damaged they must be replaced with new ones.

Installation

11 If removed, fit the pins into the cam base plate and push them through to the cam. Fit the locating dowel into the end of the selector drum. Install the cam plate, making sure the hole in the back of the base plate locates correctly on the dowel. Apply a suitable thread locking compound to the threads of the cam bolt and tighten it to the torque setting specified at the beginning of the Chapter.

12 Fit the stopper arm bolt with its washer through the stopper arm, the return spring and the collar, then apply a threadlock to the threads of the bolt **(see illustration 20.8b)**. Install the assembly onto the crankcase, making sure the spring ends locate correctly over the stopper arm and against the crankcase, and partially tighten the bolt **(see illustration)**. Lift the stopper arm using a screwdriver against the crankcase as a lever or a pair of pliers, then fully tighten the bolt, locating the roller onto the neutral detent in the cam as they become aligned **(see**

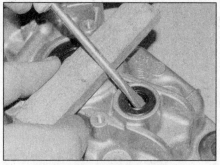

20.9a Lever out the old seal . . .

20.9b . . . and press or drive the new one into place

illustration). Tighten the bolt to the specified torque setting. Afterwards make sure the arm is free to move and is returned by the pressure of the spring.

13 Slide the gearchange shaft assembly into its hole in the engine, lifting the selector arm claw into position on the selector drum pins **(see illustrations)**. Ensure the centralising spring ends are correctly located on each side of the pins on the shaft and the crankcase **(see illustration)**.

14 Install the transmission shaft bearing retainer plate and secure it with the top bolts **(see illustration 20.4c)**. Fit a new O-ring onto the oil pipe **(see illustration)**. Locate the pipe in its sockets, pressing the bottom in until the O-ring is felt to locate **(see illustration 20.4b)**. Secure the pipe with the retainer plate bottom bolt **(see illustration 20.4a)**.

15 On XL650V and XRV750 models fit the drive chain guide plate. Install the front

sprocket cover and tighten its bolts **(see illustration 20.2b)**. Slide the gearchange lever onto the shaft, aligning the punch mark on the shaft end with that on the lever where there is one, or with the slit in the clamp if not **(see illustration 20.2a)**. Tighten the pinch bolt and check that the gearchange mechanism works correctly.

16 Install oil pump drive chain and sprockets and the clutch (see Section 18).

17 Replenish the engine with oil (see Chapter 1).

21 Primary drive gear – removal, inspection and installation

Note: *On XL models, the timing rotor is mounted on the right-hand end of the crankshaft along with the primary drive gear.*

20.12a Locate the stopper arm assembly on the crankcase . . .

20.12b . . . then position the arm on the cam and tighten the bolt

20.13a Slide the shaft into the crankcase . . .

20.13b . . . and locate the arm onto the drum

20.13c The installed assembly should be as shown

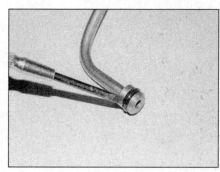

20.14 Fit a new O-ring onto the oil pipe

2

21.4a Unscrew the bolt (arrowed) . . .

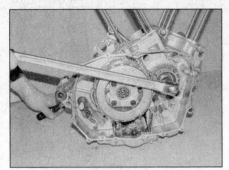

21.4b . . . locking the crankshaft as described . . .

21.4c . . . and on XL models remove the timing rotor

21.5 Slide the primary drive gear off the shaft

21.7 Slide the primary drive gear onto the shaft . . .

crankshaft, aligning the wide splines, and making sure on XL models the 'OUT' mark on the gear faces outwards, and on XRV models the thinner sub-gear is on the outside (see illustration).
8 On XL models install the timing rotor, aligning the wide splines (see illustration).
9 Install the bolt with its washer and tighten it finger-tight (see illustration 21.4c). Lock the crankshaft using the same method as on removal (see Step 3). With the crankshaft locked, tighten the primary drive gear bolt to the torque setting specified at the beginning of the Chapter (see illustration). Note that if you are using the alternator rotor bolt to counter-hold the crankshaft there should be no danger of it coming loose as it is set to a higher torque setting.
10 On XL models, install the ignition pulse generator coil(s) (see Chapter 5).
11 Install the clutch (see Section 18).

On XRV models, the ignition timing triggers are incorporated in the alternator rotor, so ignore references to the rotor when removing the primary drive gear.

Removal

1 Remove the clutch (see Section 18).
2 On XL models, remove the ignition pulse generator coil(s) (see Chapter 5).
3 To unscrew the primary drive gear bolt the crankshaft must be prevented from turning. To do this, either unscrew the crankshaft end cap from the alternator cover (see illustration 9.2a) and counter-hold the crankshaft using a socket on the alternator rotor bolt (there is no danger of the bolt coming undone as it has a left-hand thread, and no danger if it being overtightened as it has a higher torque setting than the primary drive gear bolt), or alternatively obtain the gear-jamming tool (part No. 07724-0010100), then refit the clutch

housing and locate the tool between the primary drive and driven gears at the top.
4 With the crankshaft locked, unscrew the primary drive gear bolt and remove the washer (see illustrations). On XL models remove the timing rotor, noting how it fits (see illustration).
5 Slide the primary drive gear off the end of the crankshaft, noting which way round it fits (see illustration).

Inspection

6 Check the teeth of the primary drive gear and the corresponding teeth of the primary driven gear on the back of the clutch housing. Renew the clutch housing and/or primary drive gear if worn or chipped teeth are discovered.

Installation

7 Slide the primary drive gear onto the

22 Starter clutch –
removal, inspection and installation

Note: *The starter clutch can be removed with the engine in the frame. If the engine has been removed, ignore the steps which do not apply.*

Check

1 The operation of the starter clutch can be checked while it is in situ. Remove the starter motor (see Chapter 9). Check that the starter drive gear is able to rotate freely anti-clockwise as you look at it via the starter motor aperture, but locks when rotated clockwise. If not, the starter clutch is faulty and should be removed for inspection.

Removal

2 Remove the alternator rotor – the starter clutch is mounted on the back of it (see Chapter 9). If the starter driven gear does not come away with the starter clutch, slide it off the crankshaft.

Inspection

3 With the alternator rotor face down on a workbench, check that the starter driven gear rotates freely in an anti-clockwise direction and locks against the rotor in a clockwise

21.8 . . . and on XL models the timing rotor

21.9 Tighten the bolt to the specified torque

22.3 Check that the starter driven gear rotates freely anti-clockwise

22.4a Withdraw the gear . . .

22.4b . . . and on XL models remove the thrust washer

direction **(see illustration)**. If it doesn't, the starter clutch should be dismantled for further investigation.

4 Withdraw the starter driven gear from the starter clutch **(see illustration)**. If the gear appears stuck, rotate it anti-clockwise as you withdraw it to free it from the starter clutch. On XL models, remove the thrust washer **(see illustration)**.

5 Check the condition of the sprags inside the clutch body and the corresponding surface on the driven gear hub **(see illustration)**. If they are damaged, marked or flattened at any point, they should be replaced with new ones. Measure the outside diameter of the hub and check that it has not worn beyond the service limit specified. To remove the sprag assembly, hold the rotor using a holding strap and unscrew the bolts inside the rotor **(see illustration)**. Remove the sprag housing from the rotor and the sprag assembly from the housing, noting how it fits. Install the new assembly in a reverse sequence. Apply clean engine oil to the sprags. Apply a suitable non-permanent thread locking compound to the bolts and tighten them to the torque setting specified at the beginning of the Chapter.

6 Slide the needle roller bearing off the crankshaft – you will have to remove the Woodruff key first if not already done **(see illustrations)**. Check the bearing and its corresponding surfaces in the starter driven gear hub and on the crankshaft. If the bearing surfaces show signs of excessive wear or the bearing itself is worn or damaged, they should be replaced with new ones. Measure the inside diameter of the hub and check that it has not worn beyond the service limit specified.

7 Check the teeth of the starter motor drive shaft, starter drive gear, idle/reduction gear and starter driven gear. Replace the gears and/or starter motor if worn or chipped teeth are discovered on related gears. Also check the starter drive gear and idle/reduction gear shafts for damage, and check that the gears are not a loose fit on the shaft. Replace the shafts with new ones if necessary.

Installation

8 Lubricate the needle roller bearing with

clean engine oil and slide it on the crankshaft **(see illustration 22.6b)**. Fit the Woodruff key **(see illustration 22.6a)**.

9 On XL models, install the thrust washer **(see illustration 22.4b)**. Lubricate the outside of the starter driven gear hub with clean engine oil, then fit the gear into the clutch, rotating it anti-clockwise as you do so to spread the sprags and allow the hub to enter **(see illustration 22.4a)**.

10 Install the alternator rotor (see Chapter 9).

23 Crankcase – separation and reassembly

Separation

1 To access the crankshaft and connecting rods, bearings, oil pump and transmission

components, the crankcase must be split into two parts.

2 To enable the crankcases to be separated, the engine must be removed from the frame (see Section 5) and the following assemblies removed:

Camshafts (Section 9)
Cam chain tensioners (Section 11)
Cylinder heads (Section 12)
Cylinder barrels (Section 15)
Water pump (Chapter 3)
Starter motor (Chapter 9)
Ignition pulse generator coils (Chapter 5)
Clutch (Section 18)
Gearchange mechanism (Section 20)
Primary drive gear (Section 21)
Alternator (Chapter 9)
Starter clutch (Section 22)
Cam chains (Section 10)

3 If required, unscrew the bolt(s) securing the oil seal retainer plate to the left-hand side of

22.5a Check the condition of the sprags and gear hub as described

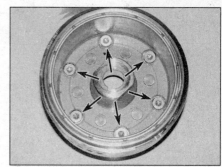

22.5b Sprag assembly bolts (arrowed)

22.6a Remove the Woodruff key . . .

22.6b . . . and slide the bearing off the shaft

23.3 Remove the oil seal retainer plate

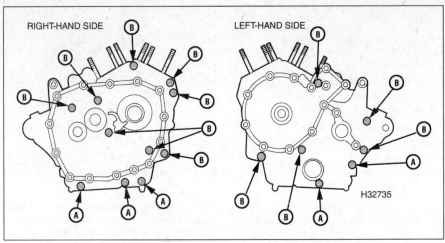

23.4 Crankcase 6 mm bolts (A) and 8 mm bolts (B)

the crankcase and remove the plate, noting how it fits **(see illustration)**.

4 Lay the engine on its right-hand side. Unscrew the 6 mm bolts in the left-hand side of the crankcase, followed by the 8 mm bolts **(see illustration)**. Slacken the bolts evenly and a little at a time in a criss-cross pattern until they are all loose, then remove the bolts. **Note:** *As each bolt is removed, store it in its relative position in a cardboard template of the crankcase halves. This will ensure all bolts are installed in the correct location on reassembly.*

5 Carefully turn the engine over onto its left-hand side and support it on wooden blocks so the end of the transmission output shaft is off the work surface. Unscrew the 6 mm bolts in the right-hand side of the crankcase, followed by the 8 mm bolts **(see illustration 23.4)**. Slacken the bolts evenly and a little at a time in a criss-cross pattern until they are all loose, then remove the bolts. Note the copper

sealing washer on the top 8 mm bolt in between the cylinders **(see illustration)**. **Note:** *As each bolt is removed, store it in its relative position in a cardboard template of the crankcase halves. This will ensure all bolts are installed in the correct location on reassembly.*

6 If the gear selector drum cam plate has not been removed (see Section 20), rotate it so that its outline shape matches the hole in the right-hand crankcase half, otherwise it will snag on the case when it is lifted **(see illustration)**. Carefully lift the right-hand crankcase half off the left-hand half, using a screwdriver in the leverage points and a soft hammer to tap around the joint and gently on the shaft ends to initially separate the halves if necessary **(see illustration)**. **Note:** *If the halves do not separate easily, make sure all fasteners have been removed. Do not try and separate the halves by levering against the crankcase mating surfaces as they are easily scored and will leak oil. Use only the special leverage point.* The right-hand side crankcase half will come away by itself, leaving the oil pump, crankshaft, transmission shafts, selector drum and selector forks in the left-hand crankcase half.

7 Remove the two locating dowels from the crankcase if they are loose (they could be in either crankcase half), noting their locations **(see illustration)**. If the oil pump and its pipe

are not being disturbed, remove the exposed O-ring from the oil pipe, noting which way up it fits, and discard it as a new one must be used. Check that the thrust washer is on the right-hand end of the transmission output shaft; if not, it is probably stuck to the bearing in the right-hand crankcase half.

Reassembly

8 Remove all traces of sealant from the crankcase mating surfaces. Support the left-hand half on wooden blocks so the end of the transmission output shaft is off the work surface.

9 Ensure that all components and their bearings are in place in the right and left-hand crankcase halves. If the oil pump and its pipe have not been removed, install a new O-ring, with its tapered side facing out, onto the exposed end of the pipe **(see illustration 23.7)**. Check that the thrust washer is installed on the right-hand end of the transmission output shaft.

10 Generously lubricate the transmission shafts, selector drum and forks, and the crankshaft, particularly around the bearings, with molybdenum disulphide oil (a mixture of 50% molybdenum disulphide grease and 50% engine oil), then use a rag soaked in high flash-point solvent to wipe over the gasket surfaces of both halves to remove all traces of oil.

23.5 Note the sealing washer (arrowed) with this bolt

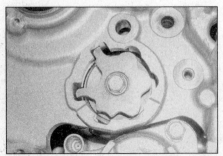

23.6a Rotate the selector drum cam plate until the arms match the holes in the crankcase

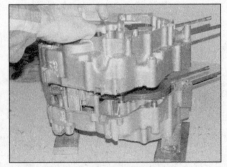

23.6b Lift the right-hand crankcase half off the left-hand half

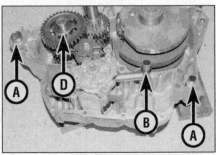

23.7 Remove the dowels (A) if loose, renew the O-ring (B), and note the thrust washer (C)

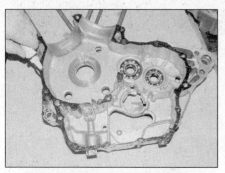

23.13 Apply a sealant to the mating surface of the right crankcase half

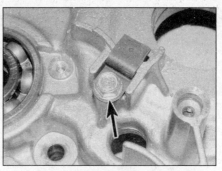

24.3 Unscrew the bolt (arrowed) and remove the plate

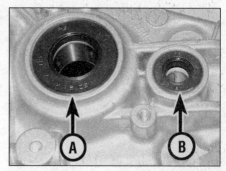

24.4a Check the transmission output shaft oil seal (A) and the gearchange shaft oil seal (B)

11 Install the two locating dowels in the left-hand crankcase half (see illustration 23.7).
12 If installed, make sure the selector drum cam plate is positioned as on removal to allow the right-hand crankcase half to fit over it (see illustration 23.6a). Also make sure that each connecting rod is positioned correctly for its cylinder.
13 Apply a small amount of suitable sealant to the mating surface of the right-hand crankcase half (see illustration).
Caution: Do not apply an excessive amount of sealant, as it will ooze out when the case halves are assembled and may obstruct oil passages.
14 Check again that all components are in position, then carefully fit the right-hand crankcase half onto the left-hand half (see illustration 23.6b). Make sure the dowels, oil pipe and shaft ends all locate correctly into the right-hand crankcase half. Note that it is easy for the oil pipe rim to contact the rim of its socket in the right-hand half and so prevent the crankcase seating. Insert a screwdriver into the gap between the crankcase halves and move the pipe slightly while applying light downward pressure on the crankcase – as soon as the pipe aligns with its socket the crankcase will lower onto it.
15 Check that the right-hand crankcase half is correctly seated. **Note:** *The crankcase halves should fit together without being forced. If the casings are not correctly seated, remove the right-hand half and investigate the problem. Do not attempt to pull them together using the bolts as the casing will crack and be ruined.*
16 Clean the threads of the right-hand crankcase bolts and insert them in their original locations (see illustration 23.4). Make sure the copper sealing washer is installed with the top 8 mm bolt in between the cylinders (see illustration 23.5). Secure all bolts hand-tight at first, then tighten the 8 mm bolts followed by the 6 mm bolts evenly and a little at a time in a criss-cross pattern to the torque settings specified at the beginning of the Chapter. When torquing the bolts, be sure to distinguish correctly between the 8 mm bolts and the 6 mm bolts.
17 Clean the threads of the left-hand crankcase bolts and install them in their

original locations (see illustration 23.4). Secure all bolts hand-tight at first, then tighten the 8 mm bolts followed by the 6 mm bolts evenly and a little at a time in a criss-cross pattern to the torque settings specified at the beginning of the Chapter. When torquing the bolts, be sure to distinguish correctly between the 8 mm bolts and the 6 mm bolts.
18 With all crankcase bolts tightened, check that the crankshaft and transmission shafts rotate smoothly and easily. Select each gear in turn and check the operation of the transmission in each gear, then select neutral and check that the shafts can turn freely and independently of each other. If there are any signs of undue stiffness, tight or rough spots, or of any other problem, the fault must be rectified before proceeding further.
19 Install all other removed assemblies in the reverse of the sequence given in Steps 2 and 3. Apply a suitable non-permanent thread-locking compound to the oil seal retainer plate bolts (see illustration 23.3).

24 Crankcase – inspection, servicing and renewal

Inspection and servicing

1 After the crankcases have been separated, remove the oil pump, and on XRV models the oil distributor, the crankshaft and connecting rods, transmission shafts, selector drum and forks, neutral switch and oil pressure switch, referring to the relevant Sections of this

Chapter, and to Chapter 9 for the neutral and oil pressure switches. Refer to Section 30 and to *Tools and Workshop Tips* in the Reference Section for checks and information on the transmission shaft bearings. Refer to Sections 26 and 27 and to *Tools and Workshop Tips* in the Reference Section for checks and information on the crankshaft main bearings.
2 If not already done (Section 16), prise the oil jets out of the crankcases using a small screwdriver (see illustration 16.13a) – take care not to damage them. Remove the O-rings and discard them (see illustration 16.13b). Clean the jets with solvent and blow them through with compressed air if available.
3 Unscrew the bolt securing the cam chain tensioner set plate to the right-hand crankcase half and remove the plate, noting how it fits (see illustration).
4 Unscrew the bolt(s) securing the oil seal retainer plate to the left-hand half of the crankcase and remove the plate, noting how it fits (see illustration 23.3). Check the condition of the oil seals and replace them with new ones if there are any signs of damage, deformation or oil leakage (see illustration). Lever out the old seal with a screwdriver, then press or drive the new seal in using a suitable socket or seal driver (see illustrations).
5 Remove all traces of old gasket sealant from the mating surfaces. Clean up minor damage to the surfaces with a fine sharpening stone or grindstone.
6 Clean the crankcases thoroughly with new solvent and dry them with compressed air. Blow out all oil passages with compressed air.

24.4b Lever out the old seal . . .

24.4c . . . and press or drive the new one into place

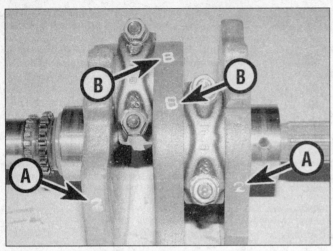

24.13a Main bearing journal size numbers (A), big-end bearing size letters (B)

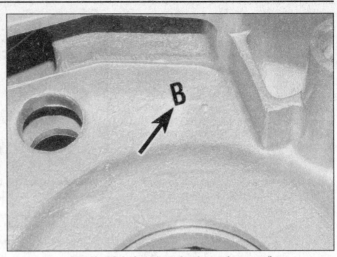

24.13b Main bearing size letter (arrowed)

Caution: *Be very careful not to nick or gouge the crankcase mating surfaces or oil leaks will result. Check both crankcase halves very carefully for cracks and other damage.*

7 Check that all the cylinder studs are tight in the crankcase halves. If any are loose, remove them, then clean their threads and apply a suitable non-permanent thread locking compound and tighten them to the torque setting specified at the beginning of the Chapter. When torquing the studs, be sure to distinguish correctly between the 8 mm stud and the 10 mm studs.

8 Small cracks or holes in aluminium castings can be repaired with an epoxy resin adhesive as a temporary measure. Permanent repairs can only be done by argon-arc welding, and only a specialist in this process is in a position to advise on the economy or practical aspect of such a repair. If any damage is found that can't be repaired, replace the crankcase halves as a set.

9 Damaged threads can be economically reclaimed using a diamond section wire insert, for example of the Heli-Coil type (though there are other makes), which is easily fitted after drilling and re-tapping the affected thread.

10 Sheared studs or screws can usually be removed with extractors, which consist of a tapered, left-hand thread screw of very hard

steel. These are inserted into a pre-drilled hole in the stud, and usually succeed in dislodging the most stubborn stud or screw. If a stud has sheared above its bore line, it can be removed using a conventional stud extractor which avoids the need for drilling.

HAYNES HINT *Refer to Tools and Workshop Tips for details of installing a thread insert and using screw extractors.*

11 Install all components and assemblies, referring to the Steps above and the relevant Sections of this and the other Chapters, before reassembling the crankcase halves. Fit new O-rings onto the oil jets **(see illustration 16.13b)** before installing them **(see illustration 16.13c).**

Crankcase renewal

12 If new crankcases are required, replacements are supplied on a selected fit according to the crankshaft main journal size – this is so that the crankcases are supplied with the correct size main bearings. Code numbers and letters stamped on the crankshaft and crankcase are used to identify the correct replacement.

13 Each crankshaft main bearing journal size

number is stamped on the outside crankshaft web adjacent to the journal, and will be either a 1 or a 2 **(see illustration)**. The corresponding main bearing size letter is stamped into the appropriate crankcase half adjacent to the bearing housing and will be either an A or a B **(see illustration)**. If the crankshaft journal size is coded 1, the corresponding crankcase main bearing must be coded A. If the crankshaft journal size is coded 2, the corresponding crankcase main bearing must be coded B.

25 Oil pump and pressure relief valve – removal, inspection and installation

Note: *To access the oil pump the engine must be removed from the frame and the crankcases separated.*

Removal

1 Separate the crankcase halves (Section 23).
2 Unscrew the bolt securing the pressure relief valve cover to the pump, then remove the cover from the end of the relief valve **(see illustrations)**. If required, withdraw the valve from the pump **(see illustration)**. Discard the valve O-ring as a new one must be used. Refer to Step 12 for relief valve checks.

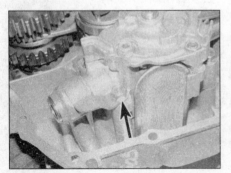

25.2a Unscrew the bolt (arrowed) . . .

25.2b . . . and remove the cover . . .

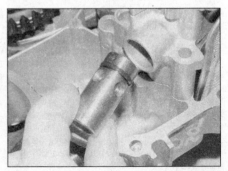

25.2c . . . and withdraw the pressure relief valve

25.3a Unscrew the bolts (arrowed) . . .

25.3b . . . and remove the pump assembly

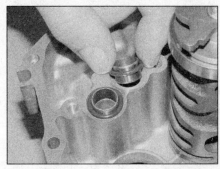

25.3c Remove the oil passage dowels . . .

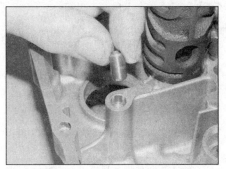

25.3d . . . and the pump dowel

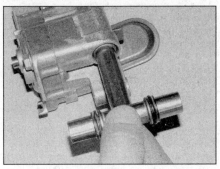

25.4 Remove the oil pipe and discard its O-rings

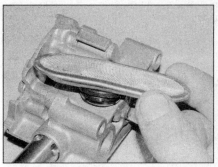

25.5 Remove the strainer, noting how it fits

3 Unscrew the remaining two bolts securing the pump assembly to the crankcase, then remove the pump along with its oil pipe **(see illustrations)**. Remove the two oil passage collars from the crankcase and discard their O-rings as new ones must be used **(see illustration)**. Remove the pump dowel if it is loose – it could be in either the pump or the crankcase **(see illustration)**.

Inspection

4 Remove the oil pipe from the pump and discard its O-rings as new ones must be used **(see illustration)**.
5 Remove the oil strainer from the pump, noting how it fits **(see illustration)**. Discard the seal as a new one must be used.
6 Unscrew the three bolts and separate the rotor housing from the pump body **(see illustration)**. Remove the dowels from either the housing or the body if they are loose **(see illustration)**.
7 Withdraw the pump drive shaft and remove the thrust washer and the drive pin, noting how it locates in the shaft and in the notches in the inner rotor. Remove the inner and outer rotors from the pump body. Note whether the punch mark on the outer rotor in or out of the housing so it can be installed the same way round. Clean all the components in solvent.
8 Inspect the pump body and rotors for scoring and wear **(see illustration)**. If any damage, scoring or uneven or excessive wear is evident, replace the pump with a new one (individual components are not available).
9 Measure the clearance between the inner

rotor tip and the outer rotor with a feeler gauge and compare it to the maximum clearance listed in the specifications at the beginning of the Chapter **(see illustration)**. If

25.6a Unscrew the bolts (arrowed) . . .

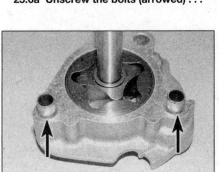

25.6c Remove the dowels (arrowed) if loose

the clearance measured is greater than the maximum listed, replace the pump with a new one.
10 Measure the clearance between the outer

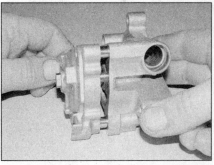

25.6b . . . and draw the rotor housing off the pump

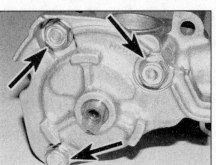

25.8 Scoring is evident on this pump rotor and in the housing

2

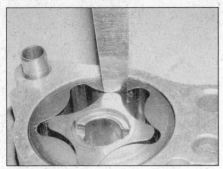

25.9 Measure the rotor tip clearance as shown

25.10 Measure the outer rotor to body clearance as shown

25.11 Measure the rotor end float as shown

rotor and the pump body with a feeler gauge and compare it to the maximum clearance listed in the specifications at the beginning of the Chapter **(see illustration)**. If the clearance measured is greater than the maximum listed, replace the pump with a new one.

25.12a Withdraw the relief valve from the pump

11 Lay a straightedge across the rotors and the pump body and, using a feeler gauge, measure the rotor end float (the gap between the rotors and the straightedge) **(see illustration)**. If the clearance measured is greater than the maximum listed, replace the pump with a new one.
12 If not already done, withdraw the relief valve from the pump **(see illustration)**. Discard its O-ring. Press down on the plunger and check that it moves freely in the body and returns under spring pressure **(see illustration)**. Remove the circlip from the end of the relief valve body and withdraw the washer, spring and valve plunger **(see illustrations)**. Clean all the components in solvent. Check that the plunger moves freely in the body and inspect it for wear or damage. If the valve is good, install the plunger into the body, followed by the spring and the washer, and secure them in place with the circlip **(see**

illustrations). Note that apart from the O-ring, none of the relief valve components are available separately. Fit a new O-ring onto the valve **(see illustration)**, and if required now, fit the valve into the pump **(see illustration 25.12a)**.
13 Check the pump drive chain and sprockets for wear or damage, and replace them as a set if necessary.
14 If the pump is good, make sure all the components are clean, then lubricate them with new engine oil. Fit the outer rotor into the housing with the punch mark facing the same way as noted on removal **(see illustration)**. Fit the inner rotor into the outer rotor so that its notches face out **(see illustration)**. Slide the thick-tabbed end of the shaft into the inner rotor, then fit the drive pin into the shaft **(see illustrations)**. Slide the shaft fully home so that the drive pin ends fit into the notches in the inner rotor **(see illustration)**. Fit the thrust

25.12b Check the plunger moves smoothly in the body

25.12c Remove the circlip . . .

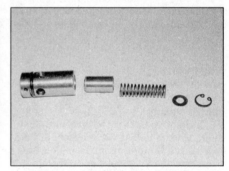

25.12d . . . and the washer, spring and plunger

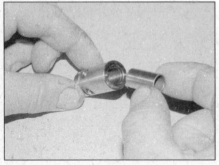

25.12e Insert the plunger . . .

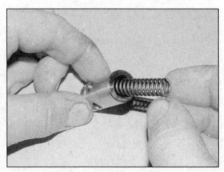

25.12f . . . and the spring . . .

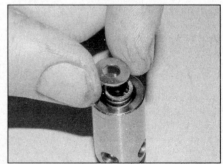

25.12g . . . then fit the washer and circlip

25.14a Install the outer rotor . . .

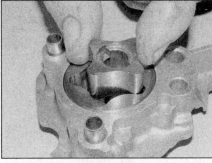

25.14b . . . followed by the inner rotor

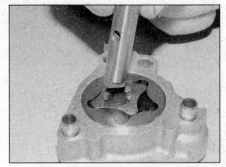

25.14c Insert the drive shaft . . .

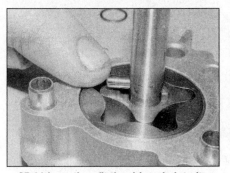

25.14d . . . then fit the drive pin into its hole . . .

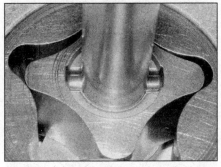

25.14e . . . and locate its ends in the inner rotor

25.14f Slide the thrust washer down the shaft

washer over the shaft and onto the inner rotor **(see illustration)**.
15 Fit the dowels into the pump body if they were removed **(see illustration 25.6c)**. Fit the

rotor housing, making sure the dowels locate correctly **(see illustration)**. Fit the three bolts into the pump body and tighten them securely **(see illustration)**.

16 Smear a new seal for the strainer with clean oil and fit it into the pump **(see illustration)**. Make sure the strainer is clean and free of any debris, then fit it into the seal, on models with an oval (as opposed to round) strainer making sure its rim locates correctly **(see illustrations)**.
17 Fit new O-rings, smeared with clean engine oil and with their tapered side facing out, to each end of the pump oil pipe, then fit the pipe into the pump **(see illustrations)**.

Installation

18 Fit the oil passage collars into the crankcase and fit new O-rings around them **(see illustration 25.3c)**. If removed, also fit the pump dowel **(see illustration 25.3d)**.
19 Before installing the pump, prime it by pouring oil into the outlet and turning the shaft

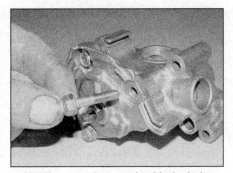

25.15a Slide the shaft through the pump and locate the rotor housing . . .

25.15b . . . and secure it with the bolts

25.16a Fit the seal . . .

25.16b . . . and the strainer . . .

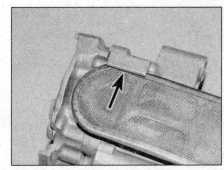

25.16c . . . making sure it locates correctly (arrow)

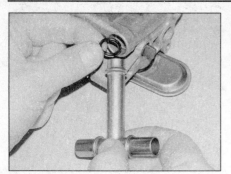

25.17a Fit new O-rings . . .

25.17b . . . making sure their tapered sides face out

by hand. This ensures that oil is being pumped as soon as the engine is turned over.
20 Install the pump with its oil pipe onto the crankcase, making sure the pump locates correctly onto the dowel and collars and the pipe is properly inserted into its hole **(see illustration 25.3b)**. Install the pump bolts and tighten them securely **(see illustration 25.3a)**.
21 If not already done, fit a new O-ring onto the pressure relief valve, then fit the valve into the pump **(see illustrations 25.12a and 25.2c)**. Fit the cover over the end of the valve and secure it with its bolt **(see illustrations 25.2b and a)**.

26 Main and connecting rod bearings – general information

1 Even though main and connecting rod bearings are generally replaced with new ones during the engine overhaul, the old bearings should be retained for close examination as they may reveal valuable information about the condition of the engine.
2 Bearing failure occurs mainly because of lack of lubrication, the presence of dirt or other foreign particles, overloading the engine and/or corrosion. Regardless of the cause of bearing failure, it must be corrected before the engine is reassembled to prevent it from happening again.
3 When examining the connecting rod bearings, remove them from the connecting rods and caps and lay them out on a clean surface in the same general position as their

location on the crankshaft journals. This will enable you to match any noted bearing problems with the corresponding crankshaft journal.
4 Dirt and other foreign particles get into the engine in a variety of ways. It may be left in the engine during assembly or it may pass through filters or breathers. It may get into the oil and from there into the bearings. Metal chips from machining operations and normal engine wear are often present. Abrasives are sometimes left in engine components after reconditioning operations, especially when parts are not thoroughly cleaned using the proper cleaning methods. Whatever the source, these foreign objects often end up imbedded in the soft bearing material and are easily recognised. Large particles will not imbed in the bearing and will score or gouge the bearing and journal. The best prevention for this cause of bearing failure is to clean all parts thoroughly and keep everything spotlessly clean during engine reassembly. Frequent and regular oil and filter changes are also recommended.
5 Lack of lubrication or lubrication breakdown has a number of interrelated causes. Excessive heat (which thins the oil), overloading (which squeezes the oil from the bearing face) and oil leakage or throw off (from excessive bearing clearances, worn oil pump or high engine speeds) all contribute to lubrication breakdown. Blocked oil passages will also starve a bearing and destroy it. When lack of lubrication is the cause of bearing failure, the bearing material is wiped or extruded from the steel backing of the

bearing. Temperatures may increase to the point where the steel backing and the journal turn blue from overheating.

 HAYNES HiNT *Refer to Tools and Workshop Tips for bearing fault finding.*

6 Riding habits can have a definite effect on bearing life. Full throttle low speed operation, or labouring the engine, puts very high loads on bearings, which tend to squeeze out the oil film. These loads cause the bearings to flex, which produces fine cracks in the bearing face (fatigue failure). Eventually the bearing material will loosen in pieces and tear away from the steel backing. Short trip riding leads to corrosion of bearings, as insufficient engine heat is produced to drive off the condensed water and corrosive gases produced. These products collect in the engine oil, forming acid and sludge. As the oil is carried to the engine bearings, the acid attacks and corrodes the bearing material.
7 Incorrect bearing installation during engine assembly will lead to bearing failure as well. Tight fitting bearings which leave insufficient bearing oil clearances result in oil starvation. Dirt or foreign particles trapped behind a bearing insert result in high spots on the bearing which lead to failure.
8 To avoid bearing problems, clean all parts thoroughly before reassembly, double check all bearing clearance measurements and lubricate the new bearings with clean engine oil during installation.

27 Crankshaft and main bearings – removal, inspection and installation

Removal

1 Separate the crankcase halves (refer to Section 23).
2 Lift the crankshaft out of the left-hand crankcase half **(see illustration)**. If it appears stuck, tap it gently using a soft-faced mallet.
3 If required, remove the connecting rods from the crankshaft (see Section 28).

Inspection

4 Clean the crankshaft with solvent, using a rifle-cleaning brush to scrub out the oil passages. If available, blow the crank dry with compressed air, and also blow through the oil passages. Check the cam chain sprockets for wear or damage. If any of the sprocket teeth on the left-hand end are excessively worn, chipped or broken, the crankshaft must be replaced with a new one.
5 Refer to Section 26 and examine the main bearings **(see illustration)**. If they are scored, badly scuffed or appear to have been seized, new bearings must be installed. Always replace the main bearings as a set. If they are

27.2 Lift the crankshaft out of the crankcase

27.5 Check the main bearings as described

27.9a Measure the diameter of the main journal . . .

27.9b . . . and the internal diameter of the main bearing

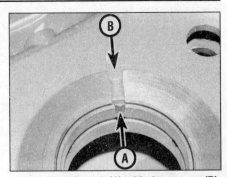

27.11 Align the tab (A) with the groove (B)

badly damaged, check the corresponding crankshaft journal. Evidence of extreme heat, such as discoloration, indicates that lubrication failure has occurred. Be sure to thoroughly check the oil pump and pressure relief valve as well as all oil holes and passages before reassembling the engine.

6 Inspect the crankshaft journals, paying particular attention where damaged bearings have been discovered. If the journals are scored or pitted in any way a new crankshaft will be required. Note that undersizes are not available, precluding the option of re-grinding the crankshaft.

7 Place the crankshaft on V-blocks and check the runout at the main bearing journals using a dial gauge. Compare the reading to the maximum specified at the beginning of the Chapter. If the runout exceeds the limit, the crankshaft must be replaced.

Oil clearance check

8 Whether new bearing shells are being fitted or the original ones are being re-used, the main bearing oil clearance should be checked prior to reassembly.

9 Using a Vernier caliper, measure the diameter of the crankshaft main bearing journals **(see illustration)**. Using a bore gauge and micrometer, measure the internal diameter of the main bearings **(see illustration)**. Calculate the difference between the two to determine the main bearing oil clearance and compare the results to the

specifications at the beginning of the Chapter. If the oil clearance exceeds the service limit, new main bearings must be selected and installed.

Main bearing selection

10 Replacement main bearings are supplied on a selected fit basis. Remove the old bearings from the crankcases (see below). Using a bore gauge and micrometer, measure the internal diameter of the bearing housing in each crankcase half and record them. Also note the crankshaft main journal size number, as marked on the crankshaft web adjacent to the journal **(see illustration 24.13a)**. To select the correct bearing for a particular journal and housing size, use the table below and cross-refer the journal size number (stamped on the crank web) with the housing size as measured to determine the colour code of the bearing required.

Main bearing replacement

11 Replacement of the main bearings requires the use of a hydraulic press in order to avoid damaging either the crankcase or the new bearings. It is therefore advised that replacement is undertaken by a Honda dealer or a suitably equipped specialist. Note that there is a tab on the main bearing which must align with the groove in the housing rim **(see illustration)**. Apply molybdenum disulphide oil (a mixture of 50% molybdenum disulphide grease and 50% engine oil) to the outside of the bearing to ease its entry into the housing.

Crankshaft selection

12 If a new crankshaft is required, the replacement is selected according to the crankcase main bearing size – this is so that the correct oil clearance is maintained. Code numbers and letters stamped on the crankshaft and crankcase are used to identify the correct replacement. Each crankshaft main bearing journal size number is stamped on the outside crankshaft web adjacent to the journal, and will be either a 1 or a 2 **(see illustration 24.13a)**. The corresponding main bearing size letter is stamped into the appropriate crankcase half adjacent to the bearing housing and will be either an A or a B **(see illustration 24.13b)**. If the main bearing size is coded A, the corresponding crankshaft journal must be coded 1. If the main bearing size is coded B, the corresponding crankshaft journal must be coded 2.

Installation

13 If removed, fit the connecting rods onto the crankshaft (see Section 28).

14 Apply molybdenum disulphide oil (a mixture of 50% molybdenum disulphide grease and 50% engine oil) to the main bearings **(see illustration)**. Carefully lower the tapered (alternator) end of the crankshaft into position in the left-hand crankcase **(see illustration 27.2)**.

15 Reassemble the crankcase halves (see Section 23).

2

XL models		
	Main bearing journal code	
Main bearing housing size	1 – (44.992 to 45.000 mm)	2 – (44.984 to 44.991 mm)
48.990 to 49.000 mm	C – Brown	B – Black
49.000 to 49.010 mm	B – Black	A – Blue
XRV models		
	Main bearing journal code	
Main bearing housing size	1 – (49.992 to 50.000 mm)	2 – (49.984 to 49.991 mm)
53.970 to 53.980 mm	C – Brown	B – Black
53.980 to 53.990 mm	B – Black	A – Blue

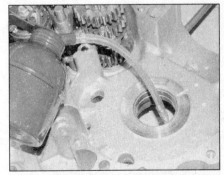

27.14 Lubricate the main bearings before installing the crankshaft

28.2 Measure the connecting rod side clearance

28 Connecting rods – removal, inspection and installation

Removal

1 Remove the crankshaft (see Section 27).
2 Before removing the rods from the crankshaft, measure the side clearance on each rod with a feeler gauge **(see illustration)**. If the clearance on any rod is greater than the service limit listed in this Chapter's Specifications, that rod will have to be replaced with a new one.
3 Using paint or a felt marker pen, mark the relevant cylinder identity on each connecting rod. Mark across the cap-to-connecting rod join to ensure that the cap is fitted the correct way around on reassembly. Do not obscure the existing markings on one of the connecting rod faces (mark the cylinder ID on the other side) –

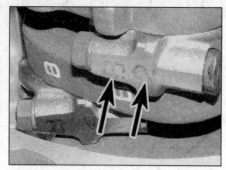

28.3 Note the rod's size and weight code markings (arrowed)

the number already marked is the connecting rod big-end size code, and the letter is the rod's weight code **(see illustration)**.
4 Unscrew the big-end cap nuts and separate the connecting rod, cap and both bearing shells from the crankpin **(see illustrations)**. Keep the rod, cap, nuts and (if they are to be re-used) the bearing shells together in their correct positions to ensure correct installation.

Inspection

5 Check the connecting rods for cracks and other obvious damage.
6 If not already done (see Section 16), apply clean engine oil to the piston pin, insert it into the connecting rod small-end and check for any freeplay between the two. Measure the pin OD **(see illustration 16.12b)** and the small-end bore ID and compare the measurements to the specifications at the beginning of the Chapter **(see illustration)**. Calculate the

difference between the measurements taken to obtain the piston pin-to-small end clearance and compare the result to the specifications. Replace components that are worn beyond the specified limits.
7 Refer to Section 26 and examine the connecting rod bearing shells. If they are scored, badly scuffed or appear to have seized, new shells must be installed. Always replace the shells in the connecting rods as a set. If they are badly damaged, check the corresponding crankpin. Evidence of extreme heat, such as discoloration, indicates that lubrication failure has occurred. Be sure to thoroughly check the oil pump and pressure relief valve as well as all oil holes and passages before reassembling the engine.
8 Have the rods checked for twist and bend by a Honda dealer if you are in doubt about their straightness.

Oil clearance check

9 Whether new bearing shells are being fitted or the original ones are being re-used, the connecting rod bearing oil clearance should be checked prior to reassembly.
10 Remove the bearing shells from the connecting rod and cap **(see illustration)**. Clean the backs of the shells and the bearing locations in both the rod and cap.
11 Press the bearing shells into their locations, ensuring that the tab on each shell engages the notch in the connecting rod/cap **(see illustrations)**. Make sure the bearings are fitted in the correct locations and take care not to touch any shell's bearing surface with your fingers.

28.4a Unscrew the connecting rod big end cap nuts (arrowed) . . .

28.4b . . . and separate the rod from the shaft

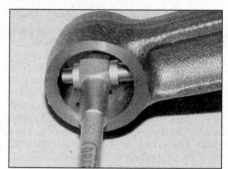

28.6 Measure the connecting rod small end internal diameter

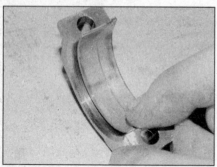

28.10 Remove the shells from the rod and cap

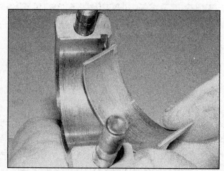

28.11a Fit the shell into its housing . . .

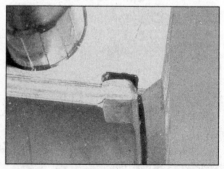

28.11b . . . making sure the tab locates in the notch

28.14 Measure the diameter of the crankpin to see if it is worn

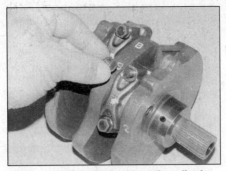

28.20a Lubricate the nuts as described . . .

28.20b . . . and tighten them to the specified torque setting

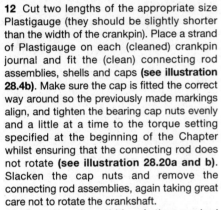

12 Cut two lengths of the appropriate size Plastigauge (they should be slightly shorter than the width of the crankpin). Place a strand of Plastigauge on each (cleaned) crankpin journal and fit the (clean) connecting rod assemblies, shells and caps **(see illustration 28.4b)**. Make sure the cap is fitted the correct way around so the previously made markings align, and tighten the bearing cap nuts evenly and a little at a time to the torque setting specified at the beginning of the Chapter whilst ensuring that the connecting rod does not rotate **(see illustration 28.20a and b)**. Slacken the cap nuts and remove the connecting rod assemblies, again taking great care not to rotate the crankshaft.

13 Compare the width of the crushed Plastigauge on each crankpin to the scale printed on the Plastigauge envelope to obtain the connecting rod bearing oil clearance.

14 If the clearance is not within the specified limits, the bearing shells may be the wrong grade (or excessively worn if the original shells are being re-used). Before deciding that different grade shells are needed, make sure that no dirt or oil was trapped between the bearing shells and the connecting rod or cap when the clearance was measured. If the clearance is excessive, even with new shells (of the correct size), measure the diameter of the crankpin and compare it to the specifications **(see illustration)**. If it is worn, the crankshaft should be replaced with a new one.

15 On completion carefully scrape away all traces of the Plastigauge material from the crankpin and bearing shells using a fingernail or other object which is unlikely to score the shells.

Bearing shell selection

16 Replacement bearing shells for the big-end bearings are supplied on a selected fit basis. Codes stamped on the crankshaft and rod are used to identify the correct replacement bearings. The crankpin journal size number is stamped on the crankshaft middle web adjacent to the crankpin and will be either an A or a B **(see illustration 24.12a)**. The connecting rod size code is marked on the flat face of the connecting rod and cap and will be either a 1 or a 2 **(see illustration 28.3)**.

17 A range of bearing shells is available. Select the correct bearing shells for a particular connecting rod in accordance with the table below. The bearings themselves are identified by a letter and a corresponding colour (see table below). The dimensions relating to the particular codes are given in the specifications at the beginning of the Chapter.

Connecting rod selection

18 If a connecting rod needs to be replaced, the weight of the replacement rod needs to be matched to the other rod being re-used. If both rods are being replaced, they need to be matched together. The connecting rod weight code is marked on the flat face of the connecting rod and cap and will be either an A, B, C or a D **(see illustration 28.3)**. Ideally each rod should have the same weight code as the other, but it is acceptable to be one letter different, e.g. A and B coded rods could be used together, but not A and C coded rods.

Installation

19 Clean the backs of the bearing shells and the bearing housings in both cap and rod. If new shells are being fitted, ensure that all traces of the protective grease are cleaned off using paraffin (kerosene). Wipe the shells, cap and rod dry with a clean lint free cloth. Fit the bearing shells in the connecting rods and caps, making sure the tab on each shell engages the notch in the connecting rod/cap **(see illustrations 28.10, 11a and b)**. Lubricate the shells with molybdenum disulphide oil (a 50/50 mixture of molybdenum disulphide grease and clean engine oil). Fit the connecting rod onto the crankpin and fit the cap onto the rod **(see illustration 28.4b)**. Make sure the cap is fitted the correct way around so the previously made markings align. Check to make sure that all components have been returned to their original locations using the marks made on disassembly.

20 Apply some clean oil to the threads and under the heads of the connecting rod nuts; if new rods are being fitted they should come supplied with new bolts and nuts. Fit the nuts and tighten them evenly and a little at a time to the torque setting specified at the beginning of the Chapter **(see illustrations)**.

21 Check that the rods rotate smoothly and freely on the crankpin. If there are any signs of roughness or tightness, remove the rods and re-check the bearing clearance.

22 Install the crankshaft (see Section 27).

29 Selector drum and forks – removal, inspection and installation

Note: *To access the selector drum and forks the engine must be removed from the frame and the crankcases separated.*

Removal

XL600V-H to R (1987 to 1995) models

1 Separate the crankcase halves (Section 23). Remove the crankshaft (see Section 27) – though not essential, working with it in place restricts access and makes the procedure fiddly.

2

XL models		
	Connecting rod code	
Crankpin journal code	**1 – (43.000 to 43.008 mm)**	**2 – (43.008 to 43.016 mm)**
A – (39.982 to 39.990 mm)	C – Brown	B – Black
B – (39.974 to 39.982 mm)	B – Black	A – Blue
XRV models		
	Connecting rod code	
Crankpin journal code	**1 – (46.000 to 46.008 mm)**	**2 – (46.008 to 46.016 mm)**
A – (42.982 to 42.990 mm)	F – Pink	E – Yellow
B – (42.974 to 42.982 mm)	E – Yellow	D – Green

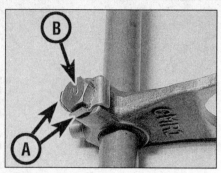

29.5 Bend back the lockwasher tabs (A) and remove the bolt (B)

29.7 Note the identification letter on each fork (arrow)

29.10 Measure the selector fork end thickness

2 The selector drum and forks must be removed along with the transmission shafts as a complete assembly. Note that each selector fork is marked for identification. The left-hand fork is marked with an 'L', the middle fork is marked with a 'C', and the right-hand fork is marked with an 'R', all of which must face the right-hand crankcase half **(see illustration 29.7)**. If no letters are visible, mark them yourself using a felt pen. The right and left-hand forks fit into the output shaft and the centre fork fits into the input shaft. At this point make a careful note of where each transmission shaft is positioned in relation to the selector drum and the fork assembly – the assembly must be removed an installed as one, and it is easy to get confused when assembling them together on the work bench before installation.

3 Grasp the input shaft and output shaft and the selector drum and forks and withdraw them from the crankcase as an assembly, noting their relative positions and how they fit together. Separate the selector drum, forks and transmission shafts, noting how the guide pin on each fork locates in its groove in the drum, and how each fork engages in the groove of its pinion.

4 Check whether the thrust washer on the left-hand end of each shaft is on the shaft or in the crankcase (probably lying loose on the bearing). Fit the washer onto the end of each shaft as a reminder for installation. Also note the thrust washer on the right-hand end of the output shaft.

5 If required, slide the outer forks off the shaft, then bend back the tabs on the centre

fork lockwasher, unscrew the bolt and remove the lockwasher, but note that unless you are performing the inspection process (see below) it is best to keep the forks assembled on the shaft in their correct order and way round **(see illustration)**.

All other models

6 Separate the crankcase halves (Section 23). Remove the crankshaft (see Section 27) – though not essential, working with it in place restricts access and makes the procedure fiddly.

7 Note that each selector fork is marked for identification. The left-hand fork is marked with an 'L', the middle fork is marked with a 'C', and the right-hand fork is marked with an 'R', all of which must face the right-hand crankcase half **(see illustration)**. If no letters are visible, mark them yourself using a felt pen. The right and left-hand forks fit into the output shaft and the centre fork fits into the input shaft.

8 Withdraw the selector fork shaft from the crankcase. Pivot each fork out of its track in the selector drum, then withdraw the selector drum from the crankcase **(see illustration 29.26b)**. Remove the selector forks, noting how they locate in the groove in their pinion **(see illustrations 29.5c, b and a)**. You may have to raise the bottom fork and its pinion so that the fork clears the crankcase land and can be removed. Once removed, slide the forks back onto the shaft in their correct order and way round.

Inspection

9 Inspect the selector forks for any signs of wear or damage, especially around the fork ends where they engage with the groove in the pinion. Check that each fork fits correctly in its pinion groove. Check closely to see if the forks are bent. If the forks are in any way damaged they must be replaced with new ones.

10 Measure the thickness of the fork ends and compare the readings to the Specifications **(see illustration)**. Replace the forks with new ones if they are worn beyond their specifications.

11 Check that the forks fit correctly on their shaft. They should move freely with a light fit but no appreciable freeplay. Measure the internal diameter of the fork bores and the corresponding diameter of the fork shaft **(see illustrations)**. Replace the forks and/or shaft with new ones if they are worn beyond their service limits. Check that the fork shaft holes in the casing are neither worn nor damaged.

12 Check the selector fork shaft for trueness by rolling it along a flat surface. A bent rod will cause difficulty in selecting gears and make the gearshift action heavy. Replace the shaft with a new one if it is bent.

13 Inspect the selector drum grooves and selector fork guide pins for signs of wear or damage. If either component shows signs of wear or damage the fork(s) and drum must be replaced with new ones.

14 Check that the selector drum bearing rotates freely and has no sign of freeplay between it and the casing **(see illustration)**.

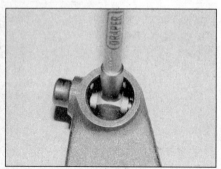

29.11a Measure the internal diameter of each fork bore . . .

29.11b . . . and the external diameter of its location on the shaft

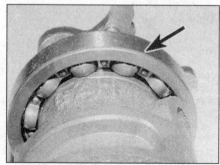

29.14a Check the bearing (arrowed)

To fit a new bearing, remove the selector drum cam plate by unscrewing the bolt in its centre **(see illustration)**. Note the locating pin in the end of the drum and remove it for safekeeping if required. Remove the old bearing and fit a new one (see *Tools and Workshop Tips* in the Reference Section if necessary). Install the selector drum cam, locating the pin in the cutout in the back of the cam plate. Apply a suitable non-permanent thread locking compound to the cam bolt and tighten it to the torque setting specified at the beginning of the Chapter.

15 On XL models, measure the diameter of the journal on the left-hand end of the drum and compare the measurement to the specifications **(see illustration)**. If it is worn beyond the service limit, replace the selector drum with a new one. Also check the drum journal hole in the crankcase for wear or damage.

Installation

XL600V-H to R (1987 to 1995) models

16 Slide the middle selector fork marked 'C' onto the fork shaft so that the 'C' faces the right-hand end of the shaft. Install the lockwasher and bolt, then tighten the bolt securely and bend back the tabs of the lockwasher to secure it in place **(see illustration 29.5)**.

17 Lubricate the selector fork shaft with molybdenum disulphide oil (a 50/50 mixture of molybdenum disulphide grease and clean engine oil). Slide the selector fork marked 'L' onto the left-hand end of the shaft so that the 'L' faces to the right-hand end. Slide the fork marked 'R' onto the right-hand end of the shaft so that the 'R' faces to the right-hand end.

18 The selector drum and forks must be installed along with the transmission shafts as a complete assembly. To achieve this without the entire assembly falling apart as it is installed, it is advisable to obtain some cable ties so the shafts and selector forks can be strapped together. Support the left-hand half of the crankcase on wooden blocks so the end of the transmission output shaft does not contact the work surface as it is installed.

19 Make sure that the thrust washer is

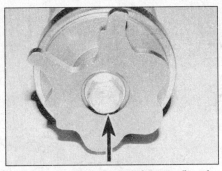

29.14b Unscrew the bolt (arrowed) and remove the cam plate

installed on the left-hand end of each shaft – apply a smear of grease to the inner face of each washer to make them stick to their adjacent pinions and so prevent them dropping off as the shafts are installed **(see illustrations 31.28b and 51d, and 30.17)**. Also make sure that the thrust washer is installed on the right-hand end of the output shaft **(see illustration 31.55d)**.

20 Lay the transmission input shaft and output shaft side by side on the bench so that the pinions for each gear mesh together **(see illustration 30.18)**. Make sure that the shafts are the correct way round, with the smallest pinion on the input shaft meshing with the largest pinion on the output shaft.

21 Fit the selector fork assembly onto the transmission shafts, locating each fork into the groove in its pinion, and making sure their identification marks are positioned as described in Step 2. Also make sure that the fork assembly is positioned correctly in relation to each shaft as noted on removal.

22 Engage the selector drum with the forks, locating their guide pins in the selector drum tracks, again making sure everything is correctly positioned – the right-hand end of the selector drum carries the bearing, so the selector fork marked 'R' must be engaged in the groove nearest the bearing, and at the same end of the assembly as the smallest pinion on the input shaft and the largest pinion on the output shaft. If you intend to use cable ties to hold the assembly together, fit them now.

23 Grasp the input shaft and output shaft

29.15 Measure the selector drum journal diameter

and the selector drum and forks and install them into the left-hand crankcase, making sure that both input shaft and output shaft ends engage in their bearings and the selector fork shaft end and the selector drum journal engage in their holes in the crankcase. Make sure the thrust washers do not drop off the ends of the shafts as they are installed. If cable ties were used, cut them and slip them out of position.

24 Install the crankshaft (see Section 27). Reassemble the crankcase halves (see Section 23).

All other models

25 Apply molybdenum disulphide oil (a 50/50 mixture of molybdenum disulphide grease and clean engine oil) to the selector fork ends. Install the selector fork marked 'L' first, with its letter facing up, and locate it in the groove of its pinion on the output shaft – you may have lift the pinion up the shaft a bit so that the fork clears the crankcase land **(see illustration)**. Next install the fork marked 'C' into the groove of its pinion on the input shaft, again with the letter facing up **(see illustration)**. Finally install the fork marked 'R', letter facing up, into the groove of its pinion on the output shaft **(see illustration)**. Position they forks so they will not get in the way of the selector drum when sliding it in.

26 Apply molybdenum disulphide oil (a 50/50 mixture of molybdenum disulphide grease and clean engine oil) to the journal on the left-hand end of the selector drum. Align the drum so that the neutral contact will be against the

2

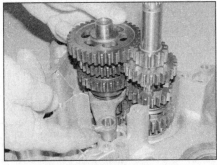

29.25a Locate the left-hand fork . . .

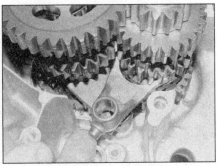

29.25b . . . the centre fork . . .

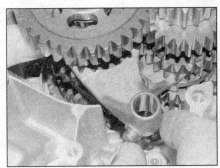

29.25c . . . and the right-hand fork in their pinions

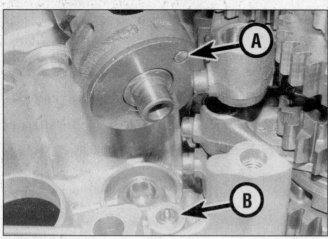

29.26a Align the drum so the neutral contact (A) will be against the neutral switch (B) . . .

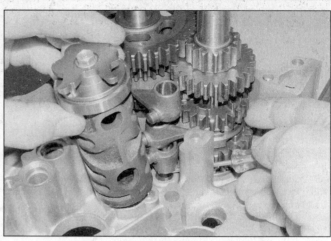

29.26b . . . then locate it in the crankcase

neutral switch and note the orientation of the cam in this position so that it can be returned to it later **(see illustration)**. Slide the drum into position in the crankcase, making sure the journal locates in its bore in the casing **(see illustration)**.

27 Locate the guide pin on the end of each fork into its groove in the selector drum – you may have to rotate the drum and/or move the forks and their pinions up to achieve this **(see illustration)**. Lubricate the selector fork shaft with molybdenum disulphide oil (a 50/50 mixture of molybdenum disulphide grease and clean engine oil) and slide it through each fork in turn, and into its bore in the crankcase **(see illustration 29.8a)**.

28 Install the crankshaft (see Section 27). Reassemble the crankcase halves (see Section 23).

30 Transmission shafts – removal and installation

Removal

XL600V-H to R (1987 to 1995) models

1 Separate the crankcase halves (Section 23). Remove the crankshaft (see Section 27) – though not essential, working with it in place

restricts access and makes the procedure fiddly.

2 The transmission shafts must be removed along with the selector drum and forks as a complete assembly. Note that each selector fork is marked for identification. The left-hand fork is marked with an 'L', the middle fork is marked with a 'C', and the right-hand fork is marked with an 'R', all of which must face the right-hand crankcase half **(see illustration 29.7)**. If no letters are visible, mark them yourself using a felt pen. The right and left-hand forks fit into the output shaft and the centre fork fits into the input shaft. At this point make a careful note of where each transmission shaft is positioned in relation to the selector drum and the fork assembly – the assembly must be removed an installed as one, and it is easy to get confused when assembling them together on the work bench before installation.

3 Grasp the input shaft and output shaft and the selector drum and forks and withdraw them from the crankcase as an assembly, noting their relative positions and how they fit together. Separate the selector drum, forks and transmission shafts, noting how the guide pin on each fork locates in its groove in the drum, and how each fork engages in the groove of its pinion.

4 Check whether the thrust washer on the left-hand end of each shaft is on the shaft or

in the crankcase (probably lying loose on the bearing). Fit the washer onto the end of each shaft as a reminder for installation. Also note the thrust washer on the right-hand end of the output shaft.

5 If necessary, the transmission shafts can be disassembled and inspected for wear or damage (see Section 31).

All other models

6 Separate the crankcase halves (Section 23). Remove the crankshaft (see Section 27) – though not essential, working with it in place restricts access and makes the procedure more fiddly.

7 Remove the selector drum and forks (see Section 29).

8 Grasp the input shaft and output shaft and withdraw them from the crankcase as an assembly, noting their relative positions and how they fit together **(see illustration)**. Separate the shafts. On XL600V models check whether the thrust washer on the left-hand end of each shaft, and on XL650V models the thrust washer on the left-hand end of the input shaft, is on the shaft or in the crankcase (probably lying loose on the bearing). Fit the washer onto the end of each shaft as a reminder for installation. On all models also note the thrust washer on the right-hand end of the output shaft.

9 If necessary, the transmission shafts can be disassembled and inspected for wear or damage (see Section 31).

Installation

XL600V-H to R (1987 to 1995) models

10 The transmission shafts must be installed along with the selector drum and forks as a complete assembly. To achieve this without the entire assembly falling apart as it is installed, it is advisable to obtain some cable ties so the shafts and selector forks can be strapped together. Support the left-hand half of the crankcase on wooden blocks so the end of the transmission output shaft does not contact the work surface as it is installed.

29.27 Pivot each fork so its guide pin locates in its track in the drum

30.8 Grasp the shafts and lift them out of the crankcase

30.17 Apply grease to each thrust washer to hold it in place

11 Make sure that the thrust washer is installed on the left-hand end of each shaft **(see illustrations 31.28b and 31.51d)**. Apply a smear of grease to the inner face of each washer to make them stick to their adjacent pinions and so prevent them dropping off as the shafts are installed **(see illustration 30.17)**. Also make sure that the thrust washer is installed on the right-hand end of the output shaft **(see illustration 31.55d)**.

12 Lay the input shaft and output shaft side by side on the bench so that the pinions for each gear mesh together **(see illustration 30.18)**. Make sure that the shafts are the correct way round, in which case the smallest pinion on the input shaft meshes with the largest pinion on the output shaft.

13 Fit the selector fork assembly onto the transmission shafts, locating each fork into the groove in its pinion, and making sure their identification marks are positioned as described in Step 2. Also make sure that the fork assembly is positioned correctly in relation to each shaft as noted on removal.

14 Engage the selector drum with the forks, locating their guide pins in the selector drum tracks, again making sure everything is correctly positioned – the right-hand end of the selector drum carries the bearing, so the selector fork marked 'R' must be engaged in the groove nearest the bearing, and at the same end of the assembly as the smallest pinion on the input shaft and the largest pinion on the output shaft. If you intend to use cable ties to hold the assembly together, fit them now.

15 Grasp the input shaft and output shaft and the selector drum and forks and install them into the left-hand crankcase, making sure that both input shaft and output shaft ends engage in their bearings and the selector fork shaft end and the selector drum journal engage in their holes in the crankcase. Make sure the thrust washers do not drop off the ends of the shafts as they are installed. If cable ties were used, cut them and slip them out of position.

16 Install the crankshaft (see Section 27). Reassemble the crankcase halves (see Section 23).

All other models

17 Support the left-hand half of the crankcase on wooden blocks so the end of the

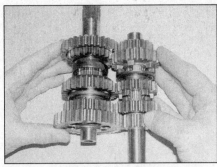

30.18 Position the shafts side by side so the relative pinions mesh

transmission output shaft does not contact the work surface as it is installed. On XL600V models make sure that the thrust washer is installed on the left-hand end of each shaft, and on XL650V models that one is installed on the left-hand end of the input shaft **(see illustrations 31.28b and 31.51d)**. Apply a smear of grease to the inner face of each washer to make them stick to their adjacent pinions and so prevent them dropping off as the shafts are installed **(see illustration)**. On all models make sure that the thrust washer is installed on the right-hand end of the output shaft **(see illustration 31.55d)**.

18 Lay the input shaft and output shaft side by side on the bench so that the pinions for each gear mesh together **(see illustration)**. Make sure that the shafts are the correct way round, in which case the smallest pinion on the input shaft meshes with the largest pinion on the output shaft.

19 Grasp the input shaft and output shaft and install them into the left-hand crankcase,

making sure that both ends engage in their bearings **(see illustration 30.8)**.
20 Install the selector drum and forks (see Section 29).
21 Install the crankshaft if removed (see Section 27). Join the crankcase halves (Section 23).

31 Transmission shafts – disassembly, inspection and reassembly

1 Remove the transmission shafts from the crankcase (see Section 30). Always disassemble the transmission shafts separately to avoid mixing up the components.

Input shaft disassembly

HAYNES HiNT *When disassembling the transmission shafts, place the parts on a long rod or thread a wire through them to keep them in order and facing the proper direction.*

Note: *When removing the circlips, do not expand the ends any further than is necessary as they are easily distorted. Also take care to keep them square as they twist easily. If in doubt about the condition of a circlip, replace it with a new one. It is advisable to use new ones as a matter of course.*

XL600V models

2 Remove the thrust washer from the left-hand end of the shaft, followed by the 2nd gear pinion **(see illustration and 31.28b and a)**.

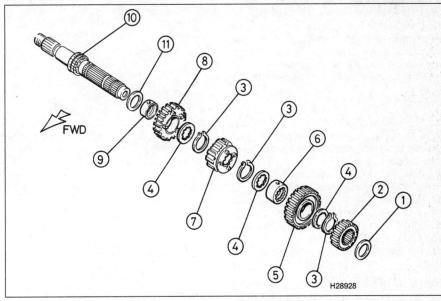

31.2 Transmission input shaft – XL600V

1	Thrust washer	5	5th gear pinion	8	4th gear pinion
2	2nd gear pinion	6	5th gear pinion bush	9	4th gear pinion bush
3	Circlip	7	3rd gear pinion	10	Input shaft with integral 1st gear pinion
4	Splined washer				

31.3 Carefully remove the circlip, taking care not to distort it

3 Remove the circlip from the shaft (see illustration). Slide the splined washer and the 5th gear pinion off the shaft, followed by the 5th gear splined bush and splined washer (see illustrations 31.27d, c, b and a).

4 Remove the circlip securing the 3rd gear pinion, then slide the pinion off the shaft (see illustrations 31.26b and a).

5 Remove the circlip securing the 4th gear pinion, then slide the splined washer and the pinion off the shaft, followed by the 4th gear bush and the thrust washer (see illustrations 31.25e, d, c, b and a).

6 The 1st gear pinion is integral with the shaft.

XL650V models

7 Remove the thrust washer from the left-hand end of the shaft, followed by the 2nd gear pinion (see illustration).

8 Slide the thrust washer off the shaft, followed by the 5th gear pinion, the 5th gear splined bush and the splined washer.

9 Remove the circlip securing the 4th gear pinion, then slide the pinion off the shaft.

10 Remove the circlip securing the 3rd gear pinion, then slide the splined washer and the pinion off the shaft, followed by the 3rd gear splined bush and the thrust washer.

11 The 1st gear pinion is integral with the shaft.

XRV750 models

12 Slide the 2nd gear pinion off the shaft, followed by the 5th gear pinion, the 5th gear splined bush and the splined washer (see illustration).

13 Remove the circlip securing the 4th gear pinion, then slide the pinion off the shaft.

14 Remove the circlip securing the 3rd gear pinion, then slide the splined washer and the pinion off the shaft, followed by the 3rd gear splined bush and the thrust washer.

15 The 1st gear pinion is integral with the shaft.

Input shaft inspection

16 Wash all of the components in clean solvent and dry them off.

17 Check the gear teeth for cracking chipping, pitting and other obvious wear or damage. Any pinion that is damaged as such must be renewed.

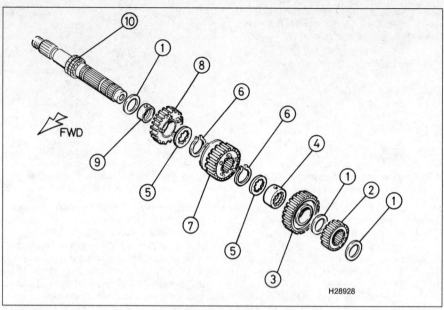

31.7 Transmission input shaft – XL650V

1	Thrust washer	5	Splined washer	9	3rd gear pinion bush
2	2nd gear pinion	6	Circlip	10	Input shaft with integral
3	5th gear pinion	7	4th gear pinion		1st gear pinion
4	5th gear pinion bush	8	3rd gear pinion		

18 Inspect the dogs and the dog holes in the gears for cracks, chips, and excessive wear especially in the form of rounded edges. Make sure mating gears engage properly. Renew the paired gears as a set if necessary.

19 Check for signs of scoring or blueing on the pinions, bushes and shaft. This could be caused by overheating due to inadequate lubrication. Check that all the oil holes and passages are clear. Renew any damaged pinions or bushes.

20 Check that each pinion moves freely on the shaft or bush but without undue freeplay. Check that each bush moves freely on the shaft but without undue freeplay. Measure the internal diameter of all gears which run on

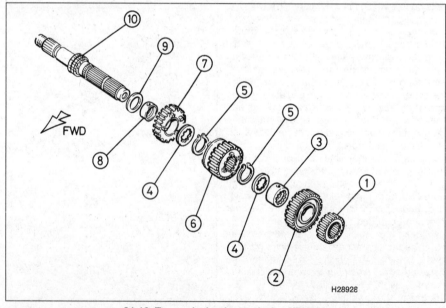

31.12 Transmission input shaft – XRV750

1	2nd gear pinion	5	Circlip	9	Thrust washer
2	5th gear pinion	6	4th gear pinion	10	Input shaft with integral
3	5th gear pinion bush	7	3rd gear pinion		1st gear pinion
4	Splined washer	8	3rd gear pinion bush		

bushes and the external diameter of the bushes which they run on **(see illustrations)**. If either component has worn to or beyond its service limit it must be replaced with a new one. Using the above measurements calculate the gear-to-bush clearance and compare the results to the specifications listed at the beginning of the Chapter. If the clearance exceeds the specified limit replace the relevant gear and bush as a pair. Also measure the internal diameters of the plain bushes and their corresponding shaft external diameter, and calculate the shaft-to-bush clearance **(see illustrations)**. The Specifications at the beginning of the Chapter list which components need to be measured.

21 The shaft is unlikely to sustain damage unless the engine has seized, placing an unusually high loading on the transmission, or the machine has covered a very high mileage. Check the surface of the shaft, especially where a pinion turns on it, and replace the shaft if it has scored or picked up, or if there are any cracks. Place the shaft on V-blocks and check the runout at the shaft centre using a dial gauge. Damage of any kind can only be cured by replacement.

22 Check the bearings for play or roughness, and that they are a tight fit in the crankcase **(see illustration)**. Renew any bearing that is worn. Refer to *Tools and Workshop Tips* in the reference Section for more information on bearing checks and removal and installation methods. Apply clean engine oil to the bearings.

23 Check the circlips and thrust washers and replace any that are bent or appear weakened or worn. It is a good idea to use new circlips as a matter of course.

Input shaft reassembly

XL600V models

24 During reassembly, apply molybdenum disulphide grease to the inside and outside of the bushes, and lubricate all the other components with engine oil. Make sure the oil holes in the shaft are aligned with those on the bush or pinion. When installing the circlips, do not expand the ends any further than is necessary. Install the stamped circlips and washers so that their chamfered side faces the pinion it secures **(see illustration 31.2)**.

31.20a **Measure the internal diameter of the gear . . .**

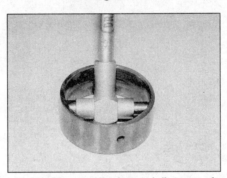
31.20c **Measure the internal diameter of the bush . . .**

25 Slide the thrust washer, 4th gear pinion bush and 4th gear pinion, with its dogs facing away from the integral 1st gear, onto the left-hand end of the shaft **(see illustrations)**. Slide the splined washer onto the shaft and fit the

31.22 **Check the transmission shaft bearings**

31.20b **. . . and the external diameter of its bush**

31.20d **. . . and the external diameter of the shaft**

circlip, making sure it locates correctly in its groove **(see illustrations)**.

26 Slide the 3rd gear pinion onto the shaft with its selector fork groove facing away from the 4th gear pinion, and secure it with the

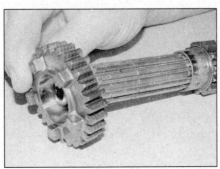
31.25a **Slide the thrust washer . . .**

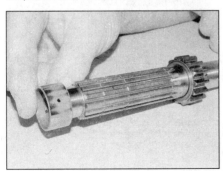
31.25b **. . . the 4th gear bush . . .**

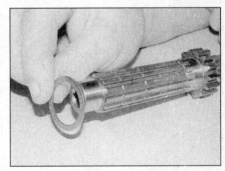
31.25c **. . . and the 4th gear pinion onto the shaft**

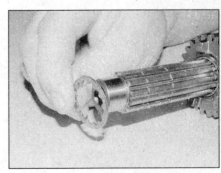
31.25d **Slide on the splined washer . . .**

2

31.25e . . . then fit the circlip . . .

31.25f . . . making sure it locates correctly

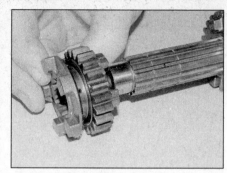

31.26a Slide the 3rd gear pinion onto the shaft . . .

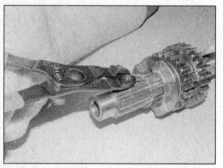

31.26b . . . then fit the circlip, making sure it locates in its groove

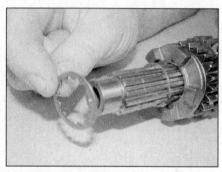

31.27a Slide the splined washer . . .

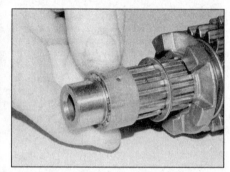

31.27b . . . the 5th gear splined bush . . .

circlip, making sure it locates correctly in its groove **(see illustrations)**.
27 Slide the splined washer, the 5th gear pinion splined bush, the 5th gear pinion with its

dogs facing the 3rd gear pinion, and the splined washer onto the shaft, then secure them in place with the circlip, making sure it locates correctly in its groove **(see illustrations)**.

28 Slide the 2nd gear pinion onto the shaft, followed by the thrust washer **(see illustrations)**.

31.27c . . . the 5th gear pinion . . .

31.27d . . . and the spline washer onto the shaft . . .

31.27e . . . then fit the circlip

31.27f . . . making sure it locates correctly

31.28a Slide the 2nd gear pinion onto the shaft . . .

31.28b . . . then fit the thrust washer

31.28c The assembled input shaft should look like this

XL650V models

29 During reassembly, apply molybdenum disulphide grease to the inside and outside of the bushes, and lubricate all the other components with engine oil. Make sure the oil holes in the shaft are aligned with those on the bush or pinion. When installing the circlips, do not expand the ends any further than is necessary. Install the stamped circlips and washers so that their chamfered side faces the pinion it secures (see illustration 31.7).
30 Slide the thrust washer, 3rd gear pinion bush and 3rd gear pinion, with its dogs facing away from the integral 1st gear, onto the left-hand end of the shaft. Slide the splined washer onto the shaft and fit the circlip, making sure it locates correctly in its groove.
31 Slide the 4th gear pinion onto the shaft with its selector fork groove facing the 3rd gear pinion, and secure it with the circlip, making sure it locates correctly in its groove.
32 Slide the splined washer, the 5th gear pinion splined bush, the 5th gear pinion with its dogs facing the 3rd gear pinion, and the thrust washer onto the shaft.
33 Slide the 2nd gear pinion onto the shaft, followed by the thrust washer.

XRV750 models

34 During reassembly, apply molybdenum disulphide grease to the inside and outside of the bushes, and lubricate all the other components with engine oil. Make sure the oil holes in the shaft are aligned with those on the bush or pinion. When installing the circlips, do not expand the ends any further than is necessary. Install the stamped circlips and washers so that their chamfered side faces the pinion it secures (see illustration 31.12).
35 Slide the thrust washer, 3rd gear pinion bush and 3rd gear pinion, with its dogs facing away from the integral 1st gear, onto the left-hand end of the shaft. Slide the splined washer onto the shaft and fit the circlip, making sure it locates correctly in its groove.
36 Slide the 4th gear pinion onto the shaft with its selector fork groove facing the 3rd gear pinion, and secure it with the circlip, making sure it locates correctly in its groove.
37 Slide the splined washer, the 5th gear splined bush, the 5th gear pinion with its dogs facing the 3rd gear pinion, and the 2nd gear pinion onto the shaft onto the shaft.

Output shaft disassembly

 HAYNES HINT When disassembling the transmission shafts, place the parts on a long rod or thread a wire through them to keep them in order and facing the proper direction.

XL600V models

38 Remove the thrust washer from the right-hand end of the shaft, then slide the 1st gear pinion, the 1st gear pinion bush and the thrust washer off the shaft (see illustration and 31.55d, c, b and a).
39 Slide the 4th gear pinion off the shaft (see illustration 31.54).
40 Remove the circlip securing the 3rd gear pinion, then slide the splined washer, the 3rd gear pinion, the 3rd gear pinion bush, and the thrust washer off the shaft (see illustration 31.53e, d, c, b and a).
41 Slide the 5th gear pinion off the wide section of the shaft (see illustration 31.52).
42 Remove the thrust washer from the left-hand end of the shaft, then slide the 2nd gear pinion, the 2nd gear pinion bush, and the thrust washer off the shaft (see illustrations 31.51d, c, b and a).

XL650V and XRV750 models

43 Slide the thrust washer off the shaft, followed by the 1st gear pinion, the 1st gear pinion bush, and the splined washer (see illustration overleaf).
44 Remove the circlip securing the 3rd gear pinion, then slide the pinion off the shaft.
45 Remove the circlip securing the 4th gear pinion, then slide the splined washer, the 4th gear pinion and the 4th gear pinion bush off the shaft.
46 Slide the tabbed lockwasher off the shaft, then turn the slotted splined washer to offset the splines and slide it off the shaft, noting how they fit together.
47 Slide the 5th gear pinion off the shaft.
48 Remove the circlip securing the 2nd gear pinion, then slide the splined washer, the pinion and its bush off the shaft.

Output shaft inspection

49 Refer to Steps 16 to 23 above.

Output shaft reassembly

XL600V models

50 During reassembly, apply molybdenum disulphide grease to the inside and outside of the bushes, and lubricate all the other parts with engine oil. Make sure the oil holes in the shaft are aligned with those on the bush or

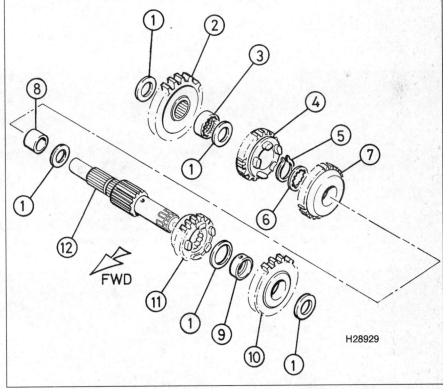

31.38 Transmission output shaft – XL600V

1 Thrust washer	5 Circlip	9 2nd gear pinion bush
2 1st gear pinion	6 Splined washer	10 2nd gear pinion
3 1st gear pinion bush	7 3rd gear pinion	11 5th gear pinion
4 4th gear pinion	8 3rd gear pinion bush	12 Output shaft

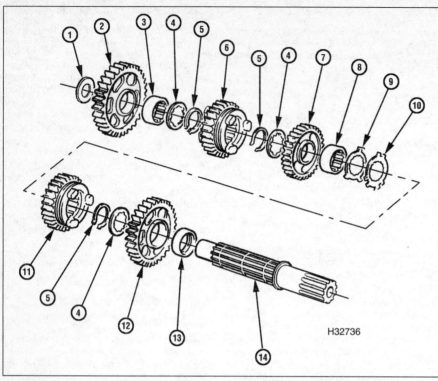

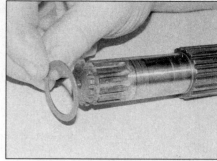

31.51a Slide the thrust washer . . .

pinion. When installing the circlips, do not expand the ends any further than is necessary. Install the stamped circlips and washers so that their chamfered side faces the pinion it secures **(see illustration 31.38)**.

51 Slide the thrust washer onto the left-hand end of the shaft, followed by the 2nd gear bush, the 2nd gear pinion and the thrust washer **(see illustrations)**.

52 From the right-hand end, slide the 5th gear pinion onto the wide section of the shaft with its selector fork groove facing away from the 2nd gear pinion **(see illustration)**.

53 Slide the thrust washer onto the right-hand end of the shaft, followed by the 3rd gear bush, the 3rd gear pinion with its dog holes facing out, and the splined washer, and secure them in place with the circlip, making sure it locates correctly in its groove **(see illustrations)**.

31.43 Transmission output shaft – XL650V and XRV750

1 Thrust washer	5 Circlip	10 Slotted splined washer
2 1st gear pinion	6 3rd gear pinion	11 5th gear pinion
3 1st gear pinion bush	7 4th gear pinion	12 2nd gear pinion
4 Splined washer	8 4th gear pinion bush	13 2nd gear pinion bush
	9 Tabbed lockwasher	14 Output shaft

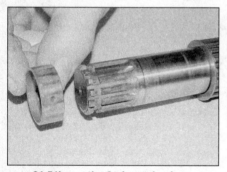

31.51b . . . the 2nd gear bush . . .

31.51c . . . the 2nd gear pinion . . .

31.51d . . . and the thrust washer onto the shaft

31.52 Slide the 5th gear pinion onto the wide section of the shaft

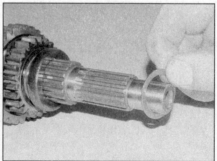

31.53a Slide the thrust washer . . .

31.53b . . . the 3rd gear bush . . .

31.53c . . . the 3rd gear pinion . . .

31.53d . . . and the splined washer onto the shaft . . .

31.53e . . . then fit the circlip

54 Slide the 4th gear pinion onto the shaft with its selector fork groove facing the 3rd gear pinion (see illustration).
55 Slide the thrust washer onto the shaft, followed by the 1st gear pinion bush, the 1st gear pinion and the thrust washer (see illustrations).

XL650V and XRV750 models

56 During reassembly, apply engine oil to the mating surfaces of the shaft, pinions and bushes. When installing the circlips, do not expand the ends any further than is necessary. Install the stamped circlips and washers so that their chamfered side faces the pinion it secures (see illustration 31.43).
57 Slide the 2nd gear pinion bush onto the shaft, followed by the 2nd gear pinion and the splined washer, then fit the circlip, making sure it locates correctly in its groove.
58 Slide the 5th gear pinion onto the shaft

with its selector fork groove facing away from the 2nd gear pinion.
59 Slide the slotted splined washer onto the shaft and locate it in its groove, then turn it in the groove so that the splines on the washer align with the splines on the shaft and secure the washer in the groove. Slide the lockwasher onto the shaft, so that the tabs on the lockwasher locate into the slots in the outer rim of the spline washer.
60 Slide the 4th gear pinion bush onto the shaft, followed by the 4th gear pinion with its dogs facing away from the 5th gear pinion, and the splined washer, then fit the circlip, making sure it locates correctly in its groove in the shaft.
61 Slide the 3rd gear pinion onto the shaft with its selector fork groove facing the 4th gear pinion, then fit the circlip, making sure it locates correctly in its groove.

62 Slide the splined washer onto the shaft, followed by the 1st gear pinion bush and the 1st gear pinion, then fit the thrust washer onto the end of the shaft.

32 Initial start-up after overhaul

1 Make sure the engine oil and coolant levels are correct (see *Daily (pre-ride) checks*). Make sure there is fuel in the tank.
2 Turn the engine kill switch to the ON position and shift the gearbox into neutral. Turn the ignition ON. Set the choke enough to encourage the bike to start, but not so much as to allow it to race.
3 Start the engine and allow it to run at a moderately fast idle until it reaches operating temperature.

31.53f . . . making sure it locates correctly

31.54 Slide the 4th gear pinion onto the shaft

31.55a Slide the thrust washer . . .

31.55b . . . the 1st gear pinion bush . . .

31.55c . . . and the 1st gear pinion onto the shaft . . .

31.55d . . . then fit the thrust washer

2

⚠ *Warning: If the oil pressure warning light doesn't go off, or it comes on while the engine is running, stop the engine immediately.*

4 Check carefully for oil and coolant leaks and make sure the transmission and controls, especially the brakes, function properly before road testing the machine. Refer to Section 33 for the recommended running-in procedure.

5 Upon completion of the road test, and after the engine has cooled down completely, recheck the valve clearances (see Chapter 1) and check the engine oil and coolant levels (see *Daily (pre-ride) checks*).

33 Recommended running-in procedure

1 Treat the machine gently for the first few miles to make sure oil has circulated throughout the engine and any new parts installed have started to seat.

2 Even greater care is necessary if new pistons/rings have been fitted or the cylinders rebored, and the bike will have to be run in as when new. This means greater use of the transmission and a restraining hand on the throttle until at least 600 miles (1000 km) have been covered. There's no point in keeping to any set speed limit – the main idea is to keep from labouring the engine and to gradually increase performance up to the 600 mile (1000 km) mark. Experience is the best guide, since it's easy to tell when an engine is running freely.

3 If a lubrication failure is suspected, stop the engine immediately and try to find the cause. If an engine is run without oil, even for a short period of time, severe damage will occur.

Chapter 3
Cooling system

Contents

Degrees of difficulty

Easy, suitable for novice with little experience	Fairly easy, suitable for beginner with some experience	Fairly difficult, suitable for competent DIY mechanic	Difficult, suitable for experienced DIY mechanic	Very difficult, suitable for expert DIY or professional 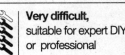

Specifications

Coolant
Mixture type and capacity . . . .   see Chapter 1

Cooling fan switch
Switch closes (fan ON) . . . .   98 to 102°C
Switch opens (fan OFF) . . . .   93 to 97°C

Coolant temperature sender
XL models
  Resistance @ 50°C . . . .   154 ohms
  Resistance @ 80°C . . . .   52 ohms
  Resistance @ 120°C . . . .   16 ohms
XRV models
  Resistance @ 50°C . . . .   130 to 180 ohms
  Resistance @ 100°C . . . .   25 to 30 ohms

Thermostat
Opening temperature . . . .   80 to 84°C
Fully open . . . .   95°C
Valve lift . . . .   8 mm (min)

Radiator
Cap valve opening pressure
  XL600V and XL650V models . . . .   13 to 18 psi (0.9 to 1.25 Bar)
  XRV750-L to N (1990 to 1992) models . . . .   14 to 18 psi (0.95 to 1.25 Bar)
  XRV750-P models onward (1993-on) . . . .   16 to 21 psi (1.1 to 1.4 Bar)

Torque settings
Coolant temperature sender . . . .   10 Nm
Cooling fan blade nut . . . .   3 Nm
Cooling fan motor nuts . . . .   5 Nm
Cooling fan switch . . . .   18 Nm
Radiator mounting bolts . . . .   10 Nm
Thermostat bolts . . . .   10 Nm

3

3.3a Fan wiring connector – XL600V

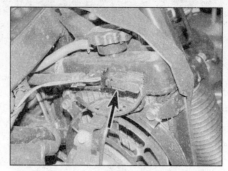

3.3b Fan wiring connector (arrowed) –
XL650V

3.3c Fan switch wiring connector
(arrowed)

1 General information

The cooling system uses a water/antifreeze coolant to carry away excess heat from the engine and maintain as constant a temperature as possible. Each cylinder is surrounded by a water jacket from which the heated coolant is circulated by thermo-syphonic action in conjunction with a water pump, which is driven by the oil pump. The hot coolant passes upwards to the thermostat and through to the radiator. The coolant then flows down across the core of the radiator, then to the water pump and back to the engine where the cycle is repeated.

A thermostat is fitted in the system to prevent the coolant flowing through the radiator when the engine is cold, therefore accelerating the speed at which the engine reaches normal operating temperature. A coolant temperature sender mounted in the thermostat housing transmits information to the temperature gauge on the instrument panel. A cooling fan is fitted to the back of the right-hand radiator to aid cooling in extreme conditions by drawing extra air through; a thermostatically-controlled switch fitted to the radiator triggers the operation of the fan motor.

The complete cooling system is partially sealed and pressurised, the pressure being controlled by a valve contained in the spring-loaded radiator cap. By pressurising the coolant the boiling point is raised, preventing premature boiling in adverse conditions. The overflow pipe from the system is connected to a reservoir into which excess coolant is expelled under pressure. The discharged coolant automatically returns to the radiator by the vacuum created when the engine cools.

⚠️ **Warning: Do not remove the pressure cap from the radiator when the engine is hot. Scalding hot coolant and steam may be blown out under pressure, which could cause serious injury. When the engine has cooled, place a thick rag, like a towel, over the pressure cap; slowly rotate the cap anti-clockwise to the first stop. This procedure allows any residual pressure to escape. When the steam has** stopped escaping, press down on the cap while turning it anti-clockwise and remove it.
Caution: Do not allow antifreeze to come in contact with your skin or painted surfaces of the motorcycle. Rinse off any spills immediately with plenty of water. Antifreeze is highly toxic if ingested. Never leave antifreeze lying around in an open container or in puddles on the floor; children and pets are attracted by its sweet smell and may drink it. Check with the local authorities about disposing of used antifreeze. Many communities will have collection centres which will see that antifreeze is disposed of safely.
Caution: At all times use the specified type of antifreeze, and always mix it with distilled water in the correct proportion. The antifreeze contains corrosion inhibitors which are essential to avoid damage to the cooling system. A lack of these inhibitors could lead to a build-up of corrosion which would block the coolant passages, resulting in overheating and severe engine damage. Distilled water must be used as opposed to tap water to avoid a build-up of scale which would also block the passages.

2 Radiator pressure cap – check

1 If problems such as overheating or loss of coolant occur, check the entire system as described in Chapter 1. The radiator cap opening pressure should be checked by a

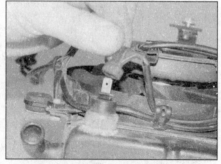

3.5 Disconnect the switch connector . . .

Honda dealer with the special tester required to do the job. If the cap is defective, replace it with a new one.

3 Cooling fan and fan switch – check and replacement

Cooling fan

Check

1 If the engine is overheating and the cooling fan isn't coming on, first check the cooling fan circuit fuse (see Chapter 9). If the fuse is good, check the fan switch as described below.
2 If the fan does not come on (and the fan switch is good), the fault lies in either the cooling fan motor or the relevant wiring. Test all the wiring and connections as described in Chapter 9, following the relevant Wiring Diagram. Disconnect the fan wiring connector and check that there is battery voltage at the black/blue or blue/black (according to model) wire terminal on the loom side of the connector with the ignition ON. If there is no voltage, check the wiring.
3 To test the cooling fan motor, on XL600V and XRV750 models remove the right-hand fairing side panel, and on XL650V models remove the fairing (see Chapter 8). Disconnect the fan wiring connector and the fan switch wiring connector **(see illustrations)**. Using a 12 volt battery and two jumper wires with suitable connectors, connect the battery positive (+) lead to the black/blue or blue/black (according to model) wire terminal on the fan side of the wiring connector, and the battery negative (–) lead to the fan switch wiring connector. Once connected the fan should operate. If it does not, and the wiring is all good, then the fan motor is faulty. Individual components are available for the fan assembly.

Replacement

⚠️ **Warning: The engine must be completely cool before carrying out this procedure.**
4 Remove the right-hand radiator (see Section 6).
5 Disconnect the wiring connector from the fan switch **(see illustration)**. Free the wiring from any clips.

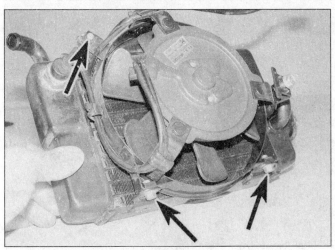

3.6 ... then undo the bolts (arrowed) and remove the fan assembly

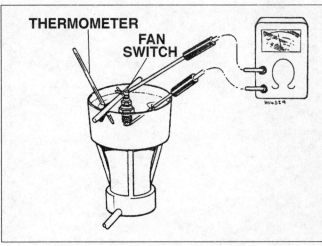

3.14 Cooling fan switch testing set-up

6 Undo the bolts securing the fan assembly to the radiator, noting that one of them also secures the earth (ground) wire **(see illustration)**.
7 Unscrew the fan blade nut and remove the blade, noting how it locates. Undo the nuts on the front of the fan motor securing it to the shroud and separate them.
8 Installation is the reverse of removal. Apply a suitable non-permanent thread locking compound the fan blade nut and tighten it to the torque setting specified at the beginning of the Chapter. Also tighten the fan motor nuts to the specified torque. Do not forget to attach the earth (ground) cable to the radiator when fitting the fan assembly bolts.
9 Install the radiator (see Section 6).

Cooling fan switch

Check

10 If the engine is overheating and the cooling fan isn't coming on, first check the cooling fan circuit fuse (see Chapter 9). If the fuse is blown, check the fan circuit for a short to earth (see the wiring diagrams at the end of this book).
11 If the fuse is good, on XL600V and XRV750 models remove the right-hand fairing side panel, and on XL650V models remove the fairing (see Chapter 8). Disconnect the wiring connector from the fan switch on the radiator **(see illustration 3.3b)**. Using a jumper wire if necessary, connect the wire to earth (ground). Turn the ignition switch ON. The fan should come on. If it does, the fan switch is defective and must be replaced with a new one. If it does not come on, check for battery voltage at the switch wiring connector with the ignition ON. If voltage is present, test the fan motor itself (see above). If there is no voltage, check the wiring and connectors for a fault or break.
12 If the fan is on the whole time, disconnect the wiring connector. The fan should stop. If it does, the switch is defective and must be replaced with a new one. If it doesn't, check

the wiring between the switch and the fan for a short to earth, and the fan itself.
13 If the fan works but is suspected of cutting in at the wrong temperature, a more comprehensive test of the switch can be made as follows.
14 Remove the switch (see Steps 16 and 17). Fill a small heatproof container with coolant and place it on a stove. Connect the positive (+) probe of an ohmmeter to the terminal of the switch and the negative (–) probe to the switch body, and using some wire or other support suspend the switch in the coolant so that just the sensing portion and the threads are submerged **(see illustration)**. Also place a thermometer capable of reading temperatures up to 110°C in the coolant so that its bulb is close to the switch. **Note:** *None of the components should be allowed to directly touch the container.*
15 Initially the ohmmeter reading should be very high indicating that the switch is open (OFF). Heat the coolant, stirring it gently.

⚠️ *Warning: This must be done very carefully to avoid the risk of personal injury.*
When the temperature reaches around 98 to 102°C the meter reading should drop to around zero ohms, indicating that the switch has closed (ON). Now turn the heat off. As the temperature falls below 93 to 97°C the meter reading should show infinite (very high) resistance, indicating that the switch has opened (OFF). If the meter readings obtained are different, or they are obtained at different temperatures, then the switch is faulty and must be replaced with a new one.

Replacement

⚠️ *Warning: The engine must be completely cool before carrying out this procedure.*
16 Drain the cooling system (see Chapter 1).
17 Disconnect the wiring connector from the fan switch on the right-hand radiator **(see illustration 3.3b)**. Unscrew the switch

and withdraw it from the radiator. Discard the O-ring as a new one must be used.
18 Install the switch using a new O-ring and some suitable sealant on the upper portion of the threads, and tighten it to the torque setting specified at the beginning of the Chapter. Take care not to overtighten the switch as the radiator could be damaged.
19 Reconnect the switch wiring and refill the cooling system (see Chapter 1).

4 Coolant temperature gauge and sender – check and replacement

Coolant temperature gauge

Check

1 The circuit consists of the sender mounted in the thermostat housing and the gauge assembly mounted in the instrument cluster. If the system malfunctions first check the fuse.
2 If the gauge is not working, remove the fuel tank (see Chapter 4) and access the sender according the appropriate model. Note that on XL600V and XRV750 models, you may be able to access the sender from the side **(see illustration)**. Otherwise access it from the top as follows:

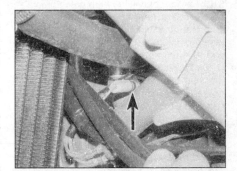

4.2a Coolant temperature sender (arrowed) – XRV model shown

3

4.2b Remove the trim panel . . .

4.2c . . . to access the thermostat housing and temperature sender (arrowed)

● On XL600V and XRV750-L to N (1990 to 1992) models move aside the boot containing the wiring connectors as required.
● On XRV750-P models onward (1993-on) remove the air filter housing (see Chapter 4), then disconnect all the wiring connectors in the bracket above the thermostat housing and draw the connectors out of the bracket.
● On XL650V models remove the left-hand trim panel to access the sender **(see illustrations)**.
3 Disconnect the wiring connector from the sender and turn the ignition switch ON **(see illustration 4.2a or c)**. The temperature gauge needle should be on the 'C' on the gauge. Using a jumper wire attached to the wiring connector terminal, earth the sender wire on the engine – the needle should swing immediately over to the 'H' on the gauge. If the needle moves as described above, the gauge is proven good, and the sender could be faulty – check it as described below (steps 8 to 12).
Caution: Do not earth the wire for any longer than is necessary to take the reading, or the gauge may be damaged.
4 If the needle movement is still faulty, or if it does not move at all, the fault lies in the wiring or the gauge itself. Remove the fairing (see Chapter 8) and disconnect the instrument cluster wiring connector(s).
5 Check for continuity in the green/blue wire between the temperature sender and the temperature gauge wiring connector. If there is no continuity, locate the break in the wire and repair it or replace it with a new one. Also check for battery voltage at the sender end of the wire with the ignition ON. If voltage is present, the gauge is faulty and must be replaced with a new one (see Chapter 9).
6 If no voltage is present, check for battery voltage between the black (+) and green or green/black (–) (according to model – refer to the *Wiring Diagrams* at the end of Chapter 9) wire terminals on the instrument cluster wiring connector(s) with the ignition ON. If voltage is present, replace the gauge with a new one

(see Chapter 9). If there is no voltage, check the black and green or green/black wires for continuity between the fusebox and earth (ground) respectively, referring to the *Wiring Diagrams* at the end of Chapter 9.

Replacement
7 See Chapter 9.

Coolant temperature sender

Check
8 If the gauge is not working in normal use but the above checks have proven it to be good, access the sender as described in Step 2.
9 Drain the cooling system (see Chapter 1).
10 Remove the sender (see Steps 13 and 14 below).
11 Fill a small heatproof container with coolant and place it on a stove. Using an ohmmeter, connect the positive (+) probe of the meter to the terminal on the sender, and the negative (–) probe to the body of the sender. Using some wire or other support suspend the sender in the coolant so that just the sensing head and the threads are submerged, with the head a minimum of 40 mm above the bottom of the container. Also place a thermometer capable of reading temperatures up to 130°C in the water so that its bulb is close to the sender **(see illustration 3.14)**. **Note:** *None of the components should be allowed to directly touch the container.*
12 Begin to heat the coolant, stirring it gently.

⚠ *Warning: This must be done very carefully to avoid the risk of personal injury.*

Refer to the Specifications at the beginning of the Chapter and check the temperatures at which resistance readings should be taken for your model. When the temperature reaches the first checkpoint, turn the heat down and maintain the temperature steady for three minutes. The meter reading should be as specified at the beginning of the Chapter. Turn the heat on again. When the temperature reaches the next checkpoint, again turn the

heat down and maintain it for three minutes. The meter reading should again be as specified at the beginning of the Chapter. Take a third reading if required according to you model. If the meter readings obtained are different by a margin of 10% or more, then the sender is faulty and must be replaced with a new one.

Replacement

⚠ *Warning: The engine must be completely cool before carrying out this procedure.*

13 The sender is mounted in the thermostat housing. Access the sender as described in Step 2.
14 Disconnect the sender wiring connector. Unscrew the sender and remove it from the thermostat housing.
15 Apply a smear of sealant to the threads of the new sender, making sure none gets on the head. Install the sender and tighten it to the torque setting specified at the beginning of the Chapter. Connect the sender wiring.
16 Install the fuel tank and any other removed parts according to your model and method (see Chapter 4). Refill the cooling system (see Chapter 1).

---

5 Thermostat and housing – removal, check and installation

Removal

Note: *The complete thermostat housing can be removed without removing the thermostat itself.*

⚠ *Warning: The engine must be completely cool before carrying out this procedure.*

1 The thermostat is automatic in operation and should give many years service without requiring attention. In the event of a failure, the valve will probably jam open, in which case the engine will take much longer than

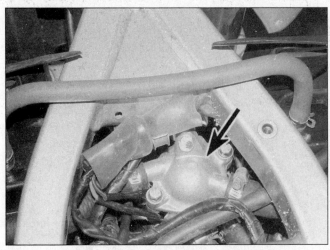

5.3a On XL600V models move the wiring connector boot aside to access the thermostat housing (arrowed)

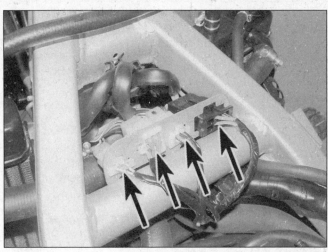

5.3b On XRV750 models disconnect and withdraw the wiring connectors (arrowed) . . .

normal to warm up. Conversely, if the valve jams shut, the coolant will be unable to circulate and the engine will overheat. Neither condition is acceptable, and the fault must be investigated promptly.

XL600V and XRV750 models

2 Drain the cooling system (see Chapter 1). Remove the fuel tank (see Chapter 4).

3 On XL600V and XRV750-L to N (1990 to 1992 models) move aside the boot containing the wiring connectors as required (see illustration). On XRV750-P models onward (1993-on) remove the air filter housing (see Chapter 4), then disconnect all the wiring

5.3c . . . to access the thermostat housing (arrowed)

connectors in the bracket above the thermostat housing and draw them out of the bracket (see illustrations).

4 To remove the thermostat, slacken the clamps securing the coolant hoses to the thermostat cover and detach the hoses (see illustration). Unscrew the bolt securing the cover to the frame. Unscrew the two bolts securing the cover to the housing and separate it from the housing (see illustration). Discard the O-ring as a new one must be used. Withdraw the thermostat, noting the orientation of the bleed hole and how it fits (see illustration).

5 To remove the thermostat housing, disconnect the coolant temperature sender wiring connector (see illustration 4.2a). Slacken the clamps securing all the hoses to the cover and housing and detach them, noting which fits where (see illustration 5.4a). Unscrew the bolt securing the cover to the frame and remove the housing.

XL650V models

6 Drain the cooling system (see Chapter 1). Remove the fuel tank (see Chapter 4). Remove the left-hand trim panel to access the thermostat housing (see illustrations 4.2b and c).

7 To remove the thermostat, disconnect the coolant temperature sender wiring connector

(see illustration 4.2c). Unscrew the two bolts securing the cover to the housing, noting how they also secure it to the mounting bracket and separate the cover and housing. Discard the O-ring as a new one must be used. Withdraw the thermostat, noting how it fits.

8 To remove the thermostat housing, disconnect the coolant temperature sender wiring connector (see illustration 4.2c). Slacken the clamps securing all the hoses to the cover and housing and detach them, noting which fits where. Unscrew the bolt securing the housing bracket to the frame and remove the housing along with the bracket.

Check

9 Examine the thermostat visually before carrying out the test. If it remains in the open position at room temperature, it should be replaced with a new one.

10 Suspend the thermostat by a piece of wire in a container of cold water. Place a thermometer capable of reading temperatures up to 110°C in the water so that the bulb is close to the thermostat (see illustration). Heat the water, noting the temperature when the thermostat opens, and compare the result with the Specifications given at the beginning of the Chapter. Also check the amount the valve opens after it has been heated for a few

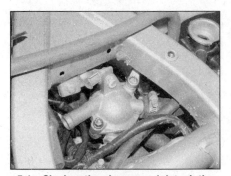

5.4a Slacken the clamps and detach the hoses, then unscrew the bolts . . .

5.4b . . . remove the cover . . .

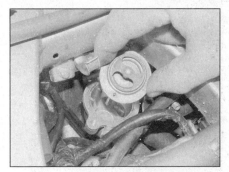

5.4c . . . and lift out the thermostat

3

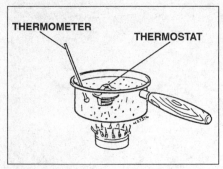

5.10 Thermostat testing set-up

minutes and compare the measurement to the Specifications. If the readings obtained differ from those given, the thermostat is faulty and must be replaced with a new one.

11 In the event of thermostat failure, as an emergency measure only, it can be removed and the machine used without it (this is better than leaving a permanently closed thermostat in, but if it is permanently open, you might as well leave it in). **Note:** *Take care when starting the engine from cold as it will take much longer than usual to warm up.* Ensure that a new unit is installed as soon as possible.

Installation

12 Installation is the reverse of removal, noting the following:

● Fit the thermostat with the bleed hole orientated as noted on removal, and make sure it locates correctly in the groove in the housing **(see illustration 5.4c)**.

● Fit a new O-ring into the groove in the cover, using a dab of grease to keep it in place if required **(see illustration)**. Tighten the cover and mounting bolts securely.
● Make sure all hoses are pushed fully onto their unions and secured by the clamps.
● Do not forget to connect the temperature sender wiring connector **(see illustration 4.2a or c)**.
● Refill the cooling system (see Chapter 1).

6 Radiators –
removal and installation

Removal

> ⚠ **Warning: The engine must be completely cool before carrying out this procedure.**

Note: *If the radiators are being removed as part of the engine removal procedure, detach the hoses from their unions on the engine rather than on the radiators and remove the radiators with the hoses attached to it. Note the routing of the hoses.*

1 Drain the cooling system (see Chapter 1).
2 Remove the fuel tank (see Chapter 4). On XL650V models remove the trim panel **(see illustration 4.2b)**.
3 When removing the right-hand radiator, disconnect the fan wiring connector **(see illustration 3.3a or b)**.
4 Slacken the clamps securing all the hoses to the radiator and detach them, noting which fits where **(see illustrations)**.

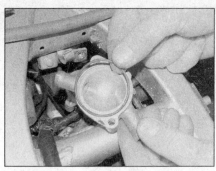

5.12 Fit a new O-ring onto the cover

5 Support the radiator and unscrew its mounting bolts, then remove the radiator, noting how it fits **(see illustrations)**. On XRV750 models, you will have to move a small rubber flap aside to access the bolts, and if required (for example if you are removing the engine) release the front stone guard from its mounts and remove it, noting how it fits **(see illustration)**. Note the arrangement of the collars and rubber grommets in the radiator mounts.

6 If necessary, remove the cooling fan and its switch from the radiator (see Section 3). Remove the shroud/protective grill from the front of the radiator. Check the radiator for signs of damage and clear any dirt or debris that might obstruct air flow and inhibit cooling. If the radiator fins are badly damaged or broken the radiator must be replaced with a new one. Also check the rubber mounting grommets, and renew them if necessary **(see illustration)**.

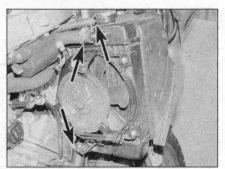

6.4a Detach the hoses (arrowed) from the right-hand radiator . . .

6.4b . . . and the left-hand radiator – XL600V shown

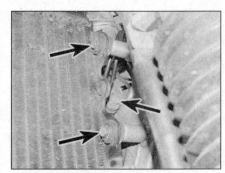

6.5a Unscrew the bolts (arrowed) . . .

6.5b . . . and remove the radiator

6.5c On XRV750 models move the rubber flap aside to access the bolts

6.6 Check the condition of the rubber grommets

Installation

7 Installation is the reverse of removal, noting the following.

● Make sure the collars and washers are correctly installed with the mounting bolts.

● Make sure that the fan wiring is correctly connected.

● Ensure the coolant hoses are in good condition (see Chapter 1), and are securely retained by their clamps, using new ones if necessary.

● On completion refill the cooling system as described in Chapter 1.

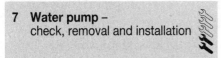

7 Water pump – check, removal and installation

Check

1 The water pump is located on the lower left-hand side of the engine. Visually check the area around the pump for signs of leakage.

2 To prevent leakage of water from the cooling system to the lubrication system and vice versa, two seals are fitted on the pump shaft. On the bottom of the pump housing there is also a drain hole **(see illustration)**. If either seal fails, the drain allows the coolant or oil to escape and prevents them mixing. You will have to remove the belly pan to see the drain hole (see Chapter 8).

3 The seal on the water pump side is of the mechanical type which bears on the rear face of the impeller. The second seal, which is mounted behind the mechanical seal, is of the normal feathered lip type. If on inspection the drain shows signs of leakage, remove the pump and replace it with a new one – it comes as an assembly.

7.2 Check the drain hole (arrowed) for signs of leakage

Removal

4 Drain the coolant and the engine oil (see Chapter 1). On XRV750 models, detach the oil cooler hoses from the oil distributor (see Chapter 2).

5 To remove the pump cover for inspection of the impeller, on XL models slacken the clamp securing the coolant hose to the cover and detach the hose **(see illustration)**. On XRV models unscrew the bolt securing the pipe to the cover and detach the pipe. Discard its O-ring.

6 Unscrew the four bolts and remove the cover, noting any wiring guide **(see illustration)**. Remove the O-ring from the cover or pump and discard it as a new one must be used. Note the locating dowels and remove them if they are loose.

7 Wiggle the water pump impeller back-and-forth and in-and-out. If there is excessive movement, replace the pump with a new one. Also check for corrosion or a build-up of scale in the pump body and clean or replace the pump as necessary. If you now need to remove the pump body, carefully draw it from the crankcase, noting how it fits **(see**

illustration). It may be necessary to lever it out to overcome the O-ring on the pump body. Remove the O-ring from the rear of the pump body and discard it as a new one must be used **(see illustration 7.10a)**.

8 To remove the pump assembly as a whole, on XL models slacken the clamps securing the coolant hoses to the pump cover and body and detach the hoses, noting which fits where **(see illustration 7.5)**. On XRV750 models, unscrew the bolt securing the pipe to the cover and detach the pipe, then slacken the clamp securing the coolant hose to the body and detach the hose. Discard the pipe O-ring.

9 Unscrew the two pump mounting bolts and carefully draw the pump from the crankcase, noting how it fits **(see illustration 7.6)**. It may be necessary to lever it out to overcome the O-ring on the pump body. Remove the O-ring from the rear of the pump body and discard it as a new one must be used **(see illustration 7.10a)**.

Installation

10 Installation is the reverse of removal.

7.5 Slacken the clamp (arrowed) and detach the cover hose

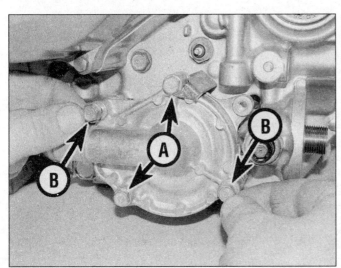

7.6 Water pump cover bolts (A and B) and mounting bolts (B)

7.7 Draw the pump out of the engine

3

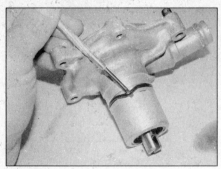

7.10a Fit a new O-ring onto the pump body . . .

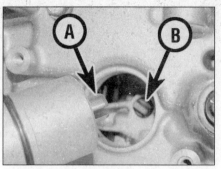

7.10b . . . then install the pump, aligning the slot in the shaft (A) with the tab on the oil pump shaft (B)

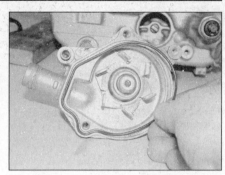

7.11 Fit a new O-ring then install the cover

Apply a smear of grease to the new pump body O-ring and fit it into the groove in the body **(see illustration)**. Slide the pump into the crankcase, aligning the slot in the impeller shaft with the tab on the oil pump shaft **(see illustration)**. Fit the coolant hose onto the pump body and secure it with the clamp. If the cover was not removed, install the mounting bolts and tighten them securely.

11 Smear the new cover O-ring with grease and fit it into its groove in the pump, then fit the cover onto the pump **(see illustration)**. Install the bolts and tighten them securely.

12 On XL models, fit the coolant hose onto the pump cover and secure it with the clamp **(see illustration 7.5)**. On XRV models, fit the pipe into the cover using a new O-ring and tighten the bolt securely.

13 Use a new sealing washer on the drain bolt. Refill the cooling system (see Chapter 1).

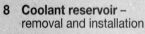
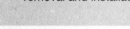

8 Coolant reservoir – removal and installation

Removal

XL600V models

1 The coolant reservoir is located behind the engine on the left-hand side. Remove the rear shock absorber to access it (see Chapter 8).

2 Note how the reservoir is located and how the various hoses and cables are routed around it before removing it. Detach the

hoses, noting which fits where. Unscrew the mounting bolts and remove the reservoir, then drain it into a suitable container.

XL650V models

3 The coolant reservoir is located behind the engine. Remove the side panels (see Chapter 8), the battery and its box (see Chapter 9), and the rear cylinder ignition coil (see Chapter 5).

4 Place a suitable container for catching the coolant below the reservoir. Remove the reservoir cap. Detach the radiator overflow hose from the bottom of the reservoir and allow it to drain into the container.

5 Detach the breather hose from the top of the reservoir. Unscrew the reservoir mounting bolt and manoeuvre the reservoir out, noting how the peg on the bottom locates in the grommet.

XRV750 models

6 Remove the right-hand side panel (see Chapter 8).

7 Place a suitable container for catching the coolant below the reservoir. Remove the reservoir cap. Detach the radiator overflow hose from the bottom of the reservoir and allow it to drain into the container **(see illustration)**.

8 Detach the breather hose from the top of the reservoir. Unscrew the reservoir mounting bolts and remove the reservoir.

Installation

9 Installation is the reverse of removal. On completion refill the reservoir (see *Daily (pre-ride) checks*).

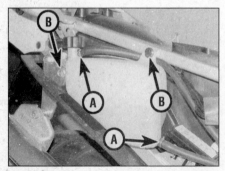

8.7 Reservoir hoses (A) and mounting bolts (B)

9.4 Coolant inlet union (arrowed) – XL600V

9 Coolant hoses and unions – removal and installation

Removal

1 Before removing a hose, drain the coolant (see Chapter 1).

2 Use a screwdriver to slacken the larger-bore hose clamps, then slide them back along the hose and clear of the union spigot. The smaller-bore hoses are secured by spring clamps which can be expanded by squeezing their ears together with pliers.

Caution: The radiator unions are fragile. Do not use excessive force when attempting to remove the hoses.

3 If a hose proves stubborn, release it by rotating it on its union before working it off. If all else fails, cut the hose with a sharp knife. Whilst this means replacing the hose, it is preferable to buying a new radiator.

4 The inlet and outlet unions to the cylinders and cylinder heads can be removed by unscrewing their bolt(s) **(see illustration)**. If a union is removed, its O-ring must be replaced with a new one.

Installation

5 Slide the clamps onto the hose and then work the hose on to its union.

> **HAYNES HiNT** *If the hose is difficult to push on its union, soften it by soaking it in very hot water, or alternatively a little soapy water on the union can be used as a lubricant.*

6 Rotate the hose on its unions to settle it in position before sliding the clamps into place and tightening them securely.

7 If an inlet or outlet union to the engine has been removed, install it using a new O-ring, smeared with a dab of grease to hold it in place if necessary. Install the union and tighten the bolt(s) securely.

Chapter 4
Fuel and exhaust systems

Contents

Degrees of difficulty

Easy, suitable for novice with little experience	Fairly easy, suitable for beginner with some experience	Fairly difficult, suitable for competent DIY mechanic	Difficult, suitable for experienced DIY mechanic	Very difficult, suitable for expert DIY or professional

Specifications

Fuel
Grade . . . . Unleaded, minimum 91 RON (Research Octane Number)
Fuel tank capacity
  XL600V models . . . . 18 litres
  XL650V models . . . . 19.6 litres
  XRV750-L to N (1990 to 1992) models . . . . 24 litres
  XRV750-P models onward (1993-on) . . . . 23 litres
Fuel tank reserve capacity
  XL600V models . . . . 3.5 litres
  XL650V models . . . . 3.8 litres
  XRV750-L to N (1990 to 1992) models . . . . warning light system
  XRV750-P models onward (1993-on) . . . . 5.1 litres

Carburettor adjustments
Pilot screw setting (turns out)
  XL600V-H and J (1987 and 1988) models . . . . 2 ½
  XL600V-K to P (1989 to 1993) models . . . . 2 ¼
  XL600V-R to T (1994 to 1996) models . . . . 1 ¾
  XL600V-V to X (1997 to 1999) models . . . . 2 ¼
  XL650V models 3
  XRV750-L to N (1990 to 1992) models . . . . 2 ¼
  XRV750-P to S (1993 to 1995) models . . . . 2 ½
  XRV750-T models onward (1996-on) . . . . 2 ⅜
Float height
  XL600V, XL650V, XRV750-L to N (1990 to 1992) models . . . . 7.0 mm
  XRV750-P models onward (1993-on) . . . . 13.7 mm
Idle speed . . . . see Chapter 1
Synchronisation vacuum range . . . . see Chapter 1

4

Jet sizes
Pilot jet
XL600V and XL650V models 38
XRV750-L to N (1990 to 1992) models 42
XRV750-P models onward (1993-on) 40
Main jet
XL600V-H to R (1987 to 1995) models
Front cylinder 128
Rear cylinder 130
XL600V-T (1996) models
Front cylinder 118
Rear cylinder 120
XL600V-V to X (1997 to 1999) models
Front cylinder 115
Rear cylinder 118
XL650V models
Front cylinder 132
Rear cylinder 132
XRV750-L to N (1990 to 1992) models
Front cylinder 118
Rear cylinder 122
XRV750-P to S (1993 to 1995) models
Front cylinder 118
Rear cylinder 120
XRV750-T models onwards (1996-on)
Front cylinder 115
Rear cylinder 115

Fuel gauge sender unit – XL650V models
Sender unit resistance
Full position .... 9.3 ohms
Empty position .... 92.3 ohms

Torque settings
Exhaust system
Downpipe nuts .... 27 Nm
Clamp bolts .... 21 Nm
Fuel level sender unit nuts – XL650V models .... 7 Nm
Fuel level sensor – XRV750-L to N (1990 to 1992) models .... 23 Nm
Fuel tap nut
XL600V models .... 40 Nm
XL650V models .... 27 Nm
XRV750-L to N (1990 to 1992) models .... 23 Nm
XRV750-P models onward (1993-on) .... 34 Nm

1 General information and precautions

General information
The fuel system consists of the fuel tank, the fuel tap(s) and strainer(s), the carburettors, fuel hoses and control cables, and on XRV750 models the fuel pump and in-line filter.

XL600V models
The fuel tap is semi-automatic in that it has both a manually operated valve and a vacuum operated valve, and has an integral strainer inside the fuel tank. The manual valve need only be closed (FUEL OFF) when the fuel tank is removed. With the manual valve open (ON or RES), the automatic valve is opened by a vacuum acting on a diaphragm, the vacuum being created when the engine is turned. If the manual valve is closed, the diaphragm valve will not bypass it when the engine is turned. The reserve (RES) position on the fuel tap allows a few miles to be covered after the main tank has run out, and serves as a low fuel level warning.

The carburettors are Keihin CV types. For cold starting, a choke lever mounted on the left-hand handlebar and connected by a cable, controls an enrichment circuit in each carburettor. Air is drawn into the carburettors via an air filter housed under the seat.

The exhaust system is a two-into-one design.

XL650V models
The fuel tap has an automatic vacuum operated valve with an integral strainer inside the fuel tank. The valve is opened by a vacuum acting on a diaphragm, the vacuum being created when the engine is turned. There is no manual facility on the tap. There is also no reserve facility, but a level sensor inside the tank transmits to a fuel gauge in the instrument cluster.

The carburettors are Keihin CV types. For cold starting, a choke lever mounted on the left-hand handlebar and connected by a cable, controls an enrichment circuit in each carburettor. Air is drawn into the carburettors via an air filter housed under the fuel tank.

The exhaust system is a two-into-one design.

XRV750 models
The XRV750-L to N (1990 to 1992) models have two fuel taps, and P models onwards (1993-on) have one tap. Each tap is of the gravity feed type with an integral strainer inside the fuel tank.

The taps have a manually operated valve which need only be closed (OFF) when the fuel tank is removed. When the manual valve is open, fuel flow is created by a pump which is controlled by a relay that actuates the pump circuit when the engine is turned. If the manual valve is closed, fuel will not flow when the engine is turned.

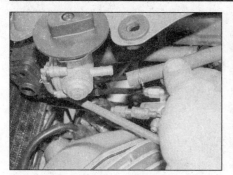

2.3a Detach the fuel hose . . .

2.3b . . . and the vacuum hose (arrowed)

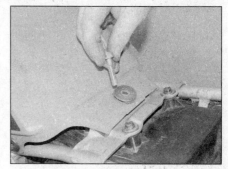

2.4 Unscrew the mounting bolt . . .

XRV750-L to N (1990 to 1992) models have no manual reserve facility, but a level sensor inside the tank transmits to a low fuel warning light in the instrument cluster. On later models the reserve (RES) position on the fuel tap allows a few miles to be covered after the main tank has run out, and serves as a low fuel level warning.

The carburettors are Keihin CV types. For cold starting, a choke lever mounted on the left-hand handlebar and connected by a cable, controls an enrichment circuit in each carburettor. Air is drawn into the carburettors via an air filter housed under the seat on XRV750-L to N (1990 to 1992) models, and in front of the fuel tank on XRV750-P models onwards (1993-on).

The exhaust system is a two-into-one design.

Precautions

⚠️ *Warning: Petrol (gasoline) is extremely flammable, so take extra precautions when you work on any part of the fuel system. Don't smoke or allow open flames or bare light bulbs near the work area, and don't work in a garage where a natural gas-type appliance is present. If you spill any fuel on your skin, rinse it off immediately with soap and water. When you perform any kind of work on the fuel system, wear safety glasses and have a fire extinguisher suitable for a class B type fire (flammable liquids) on hand.*

Always perform service procedures in a well-ventilated area to prevent a build-up of fumes.

Never work in a building containing a gas appliance with a pilot light, or any other form of naked flame. Ensure that there are no naked light bulbs or any sources of flame or sparks nearby.

Do not smoke (or allow anyone else to smoke) while in the vicinity of petrol or of components containing it. Remember the possible presence of vapour from these sources and move well clear before smoking.

Check all electrical equipment belonging to the house, garage or workshop where work is being undertaken (see the Safety First! section of this manual). Remember that certain

electrical appliances such as drills, cutters etc create sparks in the normal course of operation and must not be used near petrol or any component containing it. Again, remember the possible presence of fumes before using electrical equipment.

Always mop up any spilt fuel and safely dispose of the rag used.

Any stored fuel that is drained off during servicing work must be kept in sealed containers that are suitable for holding petrol, and clearly marked as such; the containers themselves should be kept in a safe place. Note that this last point applies equally to the fuel tank if it is removed from the machine; also remember to keep its cap closed at all times.

Note that the fuel system consists of the fuel tank and tap, with its cap and related hoses.

Read the Safety first! section of this manual carefully before starting work.

2 Fuel tank and tap – removal and installation 🔧

⚠️ *Warning: Refer to the precautions given in Section 1 before starting work.*
Caution: The fuel tanks on these machines are quite large, which means if they are full they will be heavy. It is advisable therefore to only remove the tank when it is at least half empty. If the tank is full it is best to

2.5 . . . and carefully remove the tank

drain it before removal. The best way to do this is to obtain a commercially available syphoning tool and a jerry can. Alternatively attach a suitable hose to the tap and feed its open end into a jerry can. On XL models you will have to apply a vacuum to the tap before it can be drained, otherwise the fuel will not flow out.

Fuel tank

Removal – XL600V models

1 Make sure the fuel tap is turned to the OFF position. Make sure the fuel cap is secure.
2 Remove the seat and the fairing side panels (see Chapter 8).
3 Release the fuel hose clamp and detach the hose from the tap (see illustration). Release the vacuum hose clamp and detach the hose from the tap (see illustration).
4 Unscrew and remove the fuel tank mounting bolt (see illustration).
5 Remove the tank by carefully drawing it back and away from the bike (see illustration). Take care not to lose the mounting rubbers from the rear of the tank, and from between the sides of the tank and the frame, noting how they fit.
6 Check the tank mounting rubbers for damage or deterioration and replace them with new ones if necessary (see illustration).

Removal – XL650V models

7 Make sure the fuel cap is secure.
8 Remove the seat and the fairing (see Chapter 8).

4

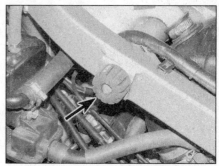

2.6 Check the mounting rubbers (arrow) for damage and deterioration

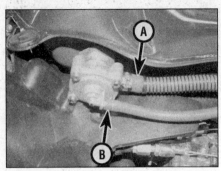

2.9 Detach the fuel hose (A) and the vacuum hose (B)

2.10 Unscrew the bolt (arrowed), then raise the tank at the rear

2.11a Disconnect the wiring connector (arrowed) . . .

2.11b . . . and draw it out from under the frame rail

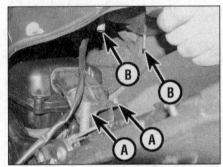

2.11c Detach the overflow and breather hoses (A) from their unions (B)

2.12 Carefully remove the tank

9 Release the fuel hose clamp and detach the hose from the tap (see illustration). Release the vacuum hose clamp and detach the hose from the tap.
10 Unscrew and remove the fuel tank

2.17a Undo the screws . . .

mounting bolt (see illustration).
11 Raise the tank at the rear and support it using a block of wood if required. Disconnect the fuel level sensor wiring connector, then carefully draw the wiring under the frame tube, noting its routing (see illustrations). Also disconnect the overflow and breather hoses from their unions on the tank, noting which fits where (see illustration).
12 Remove the tank by carefully drawing it back and away from the bike (see illustration). Take care not to lose the mounting rubbers from the rear of the tank, and from between the sides of the tank and the frame, noting how they fit.
13 Check the tank mounting rubbers for damage or deterioration and replace them with new ones if necessary.

Removal – XRV750 models

14 Make sure the fuel tap is turned to the

OFF position. Make sure the fuel cap is secure.
15 Remove the seat and the fairing side panels (see Chapter 8).
16 On L to N (1990 to 1992) models, disconnect the fuel level sensor wiring connector, located below the tank on the left-hand side.
17 On P models onward (1993-on), undo the screws securing the air filter housing cover, noting which fit where, and remove it (see illustrations). Also undo the screw in the centre of the fuel tap knob and remove the knob (see illustrations). Unscrew and remove the fuel tank mounting bolts (see illustration). Remove the tank prop from under the seat, then raise the tank at the rear and insert the prop between the tank and its bracket, using the bolt holes in each as anchors for the support (see illustrations).

2.17b . . . and remove the cover

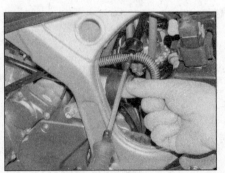

2.17c Undo the screw . . .

2.17d . . . and remove the knob

2.17e Unscrew the mounting bolts

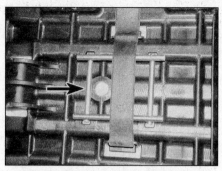

2.17f Remove the prop (arrowed) from under the seat . . .

2.17g . . . then raise the back of the tank . . .

2.17h . . . and locate the prop between it and the bracket

2.18a Detach the fuel hose (arrowed) . . .

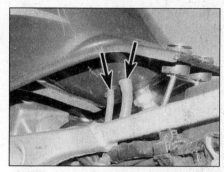

2.18b . . . and the breather and overflow hoses (arrowed) – later model type shown

18 Release the fuel hose clamp and detach the hose from the tap – remember that on L to N (1990 to 1992) models there are two fuel taps (see illustration). On P models onwards

2.21 Take care not to dislodge the rubbers (arrow) as you locate the tank

(1993-on), also disconnect the overflow and breather hoses from their unions on the tank, noting which fits where (see illustration).
19 Remove the tank by carefully drawing it back and away from the bike. Take care not to lose the mounting rubbers from the rear of the tank, and from between the sides of the tank and the frame, noting how they fit.
20 Check the mounting rubbers for damage or deterioration and replace them with new ones if necessary.

Installation – all models

21 Installation is the reverse of removal, noting the following:
● If removed, install the tank mounting rubbers (see illustration 2.6). Make sure the rubbers remain in place when installing the tank (see illustration).

● Check that the tank is properly seated and is not pinching any control cables or wires.
● Make sure the fuel hose is fully pushed onto its union on the tap and secure it with its clamp.
● Turn the fuel tap to the ON or RES position and check that there is no sign of fuel leakage. Start the engine and check again that there is no sign of fuel leakage, then shut if off.

Fuel tap

Removal

22 The tap should not be removed unnecessarily.
23 Remove the fuel tank as described above.
24 Unscrew the nut securing the tap to the tank and withdraw the tap assembly, noting its orientation (see illustrations).

4

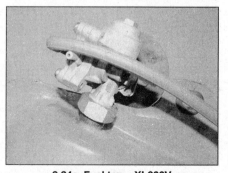

2.24a Fuel tap – XL600V

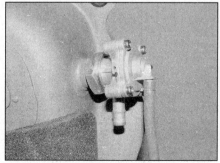

2.24b Fuel tap – XL650V

2.24c Fuel tap – XRV750-P models onwards

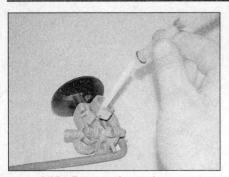

2.25a Remove the strainer . . .

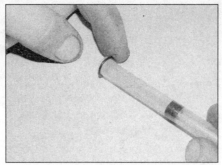

2.25b . . . and discard its O-ring

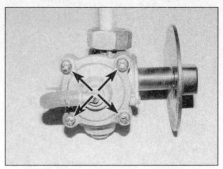

2.26 Fuel tap cover screws (arrowed)

Inspection

25 Remove the strainer **(see illustration)**. Discard the O-ring **(see illustration)**. Clean the strainer to remove all traces of dirt and fuel sediment. Check the gauze for holes. If any are found, a new strainer should be fitted. Fit the strainer using a new O-ring.

26 On XL models, if the tap is faulty, it can be disassembled and inspected. The most likely problem is a hole or split in the diaphragm. Before removing and dismantling the tap, check that there are no splits or cracks in the vacuum hose. If in doubt, attach a spare hose to the vacuum union on the tap and apply a vacuum to the hose. If fuel does not flow through the tap (make sure it is turned ON), or if fuel flows when there is no vacuum applied, undo the cover screws and remove the spring and diaphragm, noting how they fit **(see illustration)**. Hold the diaphragm up to a light

to check for splits or holes. On XL600V models, a new cover assembly including the spring and diaphragm is available. On XL650V models a new tap must be installed.

Installation

27 Installation is the reverse of removal. Make sure the tap is pointing the correct way **(see illustration 2.24a, b or c)**. Tighten the nut securely – if the correct tools are available tighten it to the torque setting specified at the beginning of the Chapter.

---

3 Fuel tank – cleaning and repair

1 All repairs to the fuel tank should be carried out by a professional who has experience in this critical and potentially dangerous work.

Even after cleaning and flushing of the fuel system, explosive fumes can remain and ignite during repair of the tank.
2 If the fuel tank is removed from the bike, it should not be placed in an area where sparks or open flames could ignite the fumes coming out of the tank. Be especially careful inside garages where a natural gas-type appliance is located, because the pilot light could cause an explosion.

---

4 Air filter/duct housing– removal and installation

Air duct housing – XL600V and XRV750-L to N (1990 to 1992) models

Removal

1 Remove the fuel tank (see Section 2).
2 Slacken the clamp screws securing the air duct housing to the air filter housing joint piece and the carburettor intakes **(see illustrations)**. On XL600V-T to X (1997 to 1999) models, unscrew the bolt securing the resonator tank to the frame **(see illustration)**. Remove the air duct, noting how it fits **(see illustration)**. If required, slacken the clamp screw securing the joint piece to the air filter housing and remove it, noting how it locates **(see illustration)**.

Installation

3 Installation is the reverse of removal. Locate

4.2a Slacken the joint piece clamp screw (arrowed) . . .

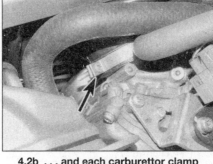

4.2b . . . and each carburettor clamp screw (arrow)

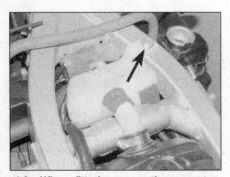

4.2c Where fitted, unscrew the resonator tank bolt (arrowed)

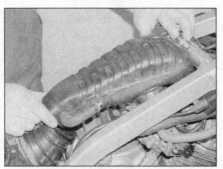

4.2d Lift the duct housing up off the carburettors

4.2e Slacken the clamp screw (arrowed) and remove the joint piece if required

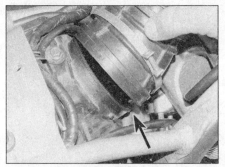

4.3a Make sure the tab locates correctly (arrow)

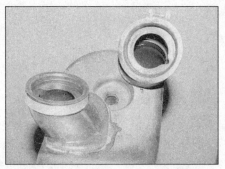

4.3b Make sure the ducts are correctly positioned

4.5a Detach the hose (arrowed) from its union

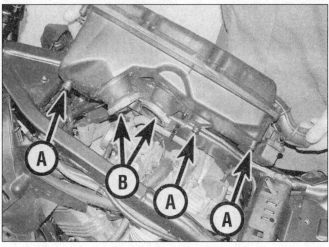

4.5b Hose unions (A), clamps (B)

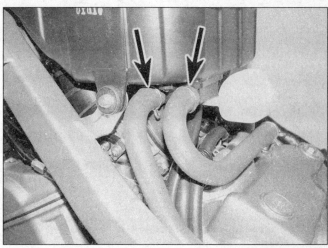

4.9 Detach the hoses (arrowed) from their unions

the tab on the air filter housing in the slot in the joint piece (see illustration). Make sure the intake ducts to the carburettors are correctly orientated (see illustration). Tighten all clamps screws securely.

Air filter housing – XL650V and XRV750-P models onwards (1993-on)

Removal – XL650V models

4 Remove the fuel tank (see Section 2).
5 Release the clamp securing the hose to the sub-air cleaner and detach it (see illustration). Also detach the PAIR system, crankcase breather and drain hoses from the front, middle and back of the housing – if you find them difficult to access do this as they become accessible after lifting the housing off the carburettors (see illustration).
6 Slacken the clamp screws securing the air filter housing to the carburettor intakes (see illustration 4.5b).
7 Unscrew the bolt securing the front of the air filter housing to the frame, then carefully lift the housing up off the carburettors, noting how it fits (see illustration 4.5b).

Removal – XRV750 models

8 Remove the fuel tank (see Section 2).

9 Release the clamps and detach the crankcase breather and drain hoses from the housing (see illustration).
10 Slacken the clamp screws securing the air filter housing to the carburettor intakes (see illustration).
11 Unscrew the bolts securing the front and sides of the air filter housing to the frame, then carefully lift the housing up off the carburettors, noting how it fits (see illustrations).

Installation – all models

12 Installation is the reverse of removal. Make sure all the hoses are correctly installed and secured by their clamps.

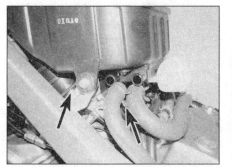

4.10 Slacken the clamp screws (arrowed)

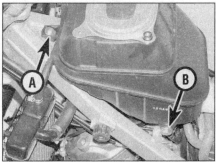

4.11a Unscrew the bolt at the front (A) and the bolt on each side (B) . . .

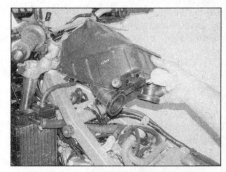

4.11b . . . and remove the housing

5.1a Pilot screw (arrowed) –
XL model carburettor

5.1b Pilot screw (arrowed) –
XRV model carburettor

5 Air/fuel mixture adjustment – general information

Adjustment

1 If the engine runs extremely rough at idle or continually stalls, and if a carburettor overhaul does not cure the problem (and it definitely is a carburation problem – see Section 6), the pilot screws may require adjustment. It is worth noting at this point that unless you have the experience to carry this out it is best to entrust the task to a motorcycle dealer, tuner or fuel systems specialist. The front cylinder's pilot screw is accessible from the right-hand side of the carburettor assembly and the rear cylinder's pilot screw is accessible from the left **(see illustrations)**. Make sure the carburettors are synchronised before adjusting the pilot screws (see Chapter 1).

2 Before adjusting the pilot screws, warm the engine up to normal working temperature. Screw in the pilot screw on both carburettors until they seat lightly, then back them out to the number of turns specified (see this Chapter's Specifications). This is the base position for adjustment.

3 Start the engine and reset the idle speed to the correct level (see Chapter 1). Working on one carburettor at a time, turn the pilot screw by a small amount either side of this position to find the point at which the highest consistent idle speed is obtained. When you've reached this position, reset the idle speed to the specified amount (see Chapter 1). Repeat on the other carburettor.

Caution: The catalytic converter fitted in the exhaust system of XL650V models may be damaged if the air/fuel mixture is maladjusted.

Restrictions

4 Due to the increased emphasis on controlling exhaust emissions in certain world markets,

regulations have been formulated which prevent adjustment of the air/fuel mixture. On such models the pilot screw positions are pre-set at the factory and in some cases have a limiter cap fitted to prevent tampering. Where adjustment is possible, it can only be made in conjunction with an exhaust gas analyser to ensure that the machine does not exceed the emissions regulations.

6 Carburettor overhaul – general information

1 Poor engine performance, hesitation, hard starting, stalling, flooding and backfiring are all signs that major carburettor maintenance may be required.

2 Keep in mind that many so-called carburettor problems are really not carburettor problems at all, but mechanical problems within the engine or ignition system or other electrical malfunctions. Try to establish for certain that the carburettors are in need of maintenance before beginning a major overhaul.

3 Check the fuel tap and strainer, the fuel and vacuum hoses, the intake manifold joint clamps, the air filter, the ignition system, the spark plugs, valve clearance and carburettor synchronisation before assuming that a carburettor overhaul is required.

4 Most carburettor problems are caused by dirt particles, varnish and other deposits which build up in and block the fuel and air passages. Also, in time, gaskets and O-rings shrink or deteriorate and cause fuel and air leaks which lead to poor performance.

5 When overhauling the carburettors, disassemble them completely and clean the parts thoroughly with a carburettor cleaning solvent and dry them with filtered, unlubricated compressed air. Blow through the fuel and air passages with compressed air to force out any dirt that may have been loosened but not removed by the solvent.

Once the cleaning process is complete, reassemble the carburettor using new gaskets and O-rings.

6 Before disassembling the carburettors, make sure you have all necessary O-rings and other parts, some carburettor cleaner, a supply of clean rags, some means of blowing out the carburettor passages and a clean place to work. It is recommended that only one carburettor be overhauled at a time to avoid mixing up parts.

7 Carburettors – removal and installation

⚠️ *Warning: Refer to the precautions given in Section 1 before starting work.*

Removal

1 Remove the fuel tank (see Section 2).

2 Remove the air filter/duct housing, according to model (see Section 4). On XL models, also remove the rear cylinder ignition HT coil (see Chapter 5).

3 Undo the two screws securing the throttle cable holder to the carburettors and detach the cable ends from the carburettors, noting which fits where **(see illustration)**.

7.3 Undo the screws (arrowed) and detach the bracket from the carburettors

7.4a Unscrew the nut (arrowed) . . .

7.4b . . . and withdraw the choke plunger

7.5a Detach the vent hoses (arrowed) –
XL models

7.5b Detach the air vent hose –
XRV models

7.6a Disconnect the throttle position
sensor wiring connector

7.6b Trace the wiring from the heater
(arrow) and disconnect it at the connector

4 Undo the nut securing the choke plunger in each carburettor and draw the plungers out **(see illustrations)**.
5 Detach the air vent hoses from their unions,

noting what fits where **(see illustrations)**.
6 On XL600V-T to X (1997 to 1999) models, XL650V models, and XRV750-T models onwards (1996-on), disconnect the throttle

position sensor wiring connector **(see illustration)**. On UK XL650V models, disconnect each carburettor heater wiring connector **(see illustration)**.
7 On XRV750-L to N (1990 to 1992) models, release the idle speed adjuster from its holder. On all XRV750 models, release the clamp and detach the fuel supply hose from its union **(see illustration)**. Also detach the overflow/drain hoses **(see illustration)**.
8 Slacken the clamps securing the carburettors to the cylinder head inlet rubbers, then ease the carburettors off, noting how they fit, and manoeuvre them out of the frame as shown **(see illustrations)**. **Note:** *Keep the carburettors as upright as possible to prevent fuel spillage from the float chambers and the possibility of the piston diaphragms being damaged.*

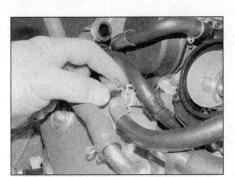

7.7a Disconnect the fuel hose . . .

7.7b . . . and the overflow/drain hoses

7.8a Slacken the clamp screw (arrowed)
on each side . . .

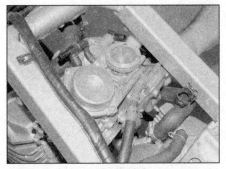

7.8b . . . then lift the carburettors out of
the intakes . . .

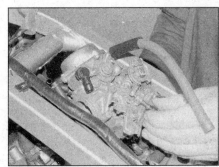

7.8c . . . and remove them as shown

4

7.9a Carburettor drain screw (arrowed) – XL models

7.9b Carburettor drain screw (arrowed) – XRV models

7.11 Make sure the carburettors engage fully in the ducts

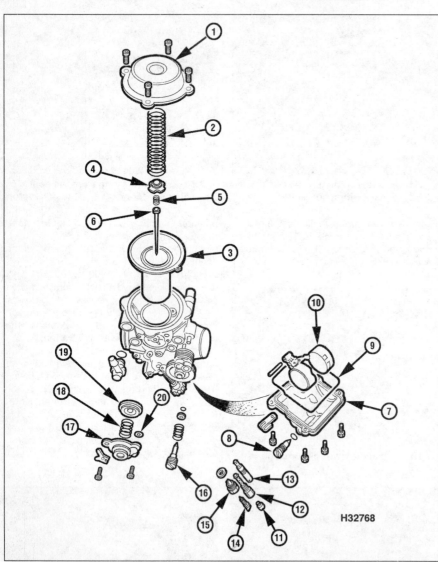

8.1a Carburettor components – XL models and XRV750-L to N (1990 to 1992) models

1 Top cover	8 Drain screw	15 Float needle valve
2 Spring	9 Rubber seal	seat
3 Piston/diaphragm	10 Float and float pin	16 Pilot screw
4 Needle holder	11 Main jet	17 Air cut-off valve cover
5 Spring	12 Needle jet	18 Spring
6 Jet needle	13 Pilot jet	19 Diaphragm
7 Float chamber	14 Float needle valve	20 O-ring

9 Place a suitable container below the float chambers, then slacken the drain screws and drain all the fuel from the carburettors **(see illustrations)**. Once all the fuel has been drained, tighten the drain screws securely.

10 If necessary, release the clamps securing the inlet rubbers to the cylinder heads and remove them, noting how they fit.

Installation

11 Installation is the reverse of removal, noting the following.

● Check for cracks or splits in the cylinder head inlet rubbers. If they have been removed from the cylinder head, make sure they are installed with the slotted tab on the adapter aligning with the raised lip on the underside of the cylinder head stub .

● Make sure the carburettors are fully engaged with the cylinder head inlet rubbers and the clamps are securely tightened **(see illustration)**.

● Make sure all hoses are correctly routed and connected and secured, and are not trapped or kinked.

● Check the operation of the choke and throttle cables and adjust them as necessary (see Chapter 1).

● Check idle speed and carburettor synchronisation; adjust as necessary (see Chapter 1).

8 Carburettors – disassembly, cleaning and inspection

⚠ **Warning: Refer to the precautions given in Section 1 before starting work.**

Disassembly

1 Remove the carburettors (see Section 7). **Note:** *Do not separate the carburettors unless absolutely necessary; each carburettor can be dismantled sufficiently for all normal cleaning and adjustments while in place on the mounting brackets. Dismantle the carburettors separately to avoid interchanging parts* **(see illustrations)**.

2 Unscrew and remove the top cover retaining screws **(see illustration)**. Lift off the cover and remove the spring from inside the piston.

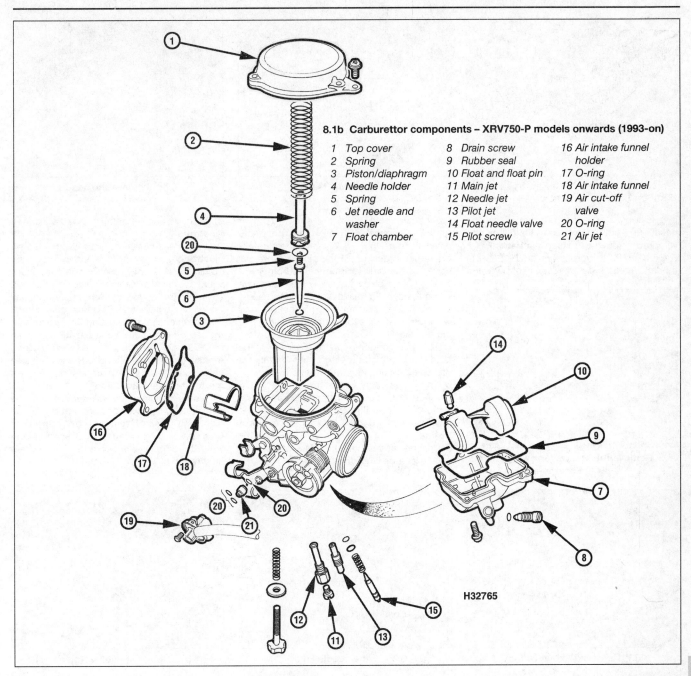

8.1b Carburettor components – XRV750-P models onwards (1993-on)

1 Top cover	8 Drain screw	16 Air intake funnel
2 Spring	9 Rubber seal	holder
3 Piston/diaphragm	10 Float and float pin	17 O-ring
4 Needle holder	11 Main jet	18 Air intake funnel
5 Spring	12 Needle jet	19 Air cut-off
6 Jet needle and	13 Pilot jet	valve
washer	14 Float needle valve	20 O-ring
7 Float chamber	15 Pilot screw	21 Air jet

H32765

3 Carefully peel the diaphragm away from its sealing groove in the carburettor and withdraw the diaphragm and piston assembly. **Caution:** *Do not use a sharp instrument to displace the diaphragm as it is easily damaged*. Note how the tab on the diaphragm fits in the recess in the carburettor body.

4 On XL models and XRV750-L to N (1990 to 1992) models, push down on the jet needle retainer using either a Phillips screwdriver or a suitable socket and rotate it until its tabs are released from the protrusions inside the piston **(see illustration)**. Remove the retainer, noting the spring on its underside – it should stay in place, but take care not to lose it and remove it

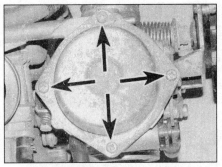

8.2 Undo the screws (arrowed) and remove the cover and spring

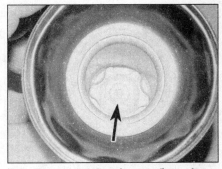

8.4a Turn the retainer (arrowed) to release its tabs . . .

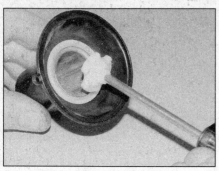

8.4b ... then withdraw it ...

8.4c ... noting its spring

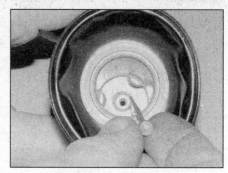

8.4d Remove the needle

if it is loose (see illustrations). Push the needle up from the bottom of the piston and withdraw it from the top (see illustration).

5 On XRV750-P models onwards (1993-on) models, thread a 4 mm screw into the top of

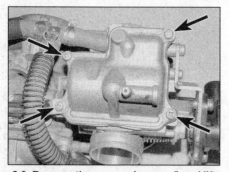

8.6 Remove the screws (arrowed) and lift off the chamber

the needle holder (one of the top cover retaining screws is ideal), then grasp the screw head using a pair of pliers and carefully draw the holder out of the piston. Note the spring in the base of the needle holder – it should stay in place, but take care not to lose it and remove it if it is loose. Push the needle up from the bottom of the piston and withdraw it from the top. Note the washer that fits between the needle head and the piston. Check the condition of the O-ring on the holder and replace it with a new one if it is damaged, deformed or deteriorated.

6 Undo the screws securing the float chamber to the base of the carburettor and remove it (see illustration). Remove the rubber seal and discard it as a new one must be fitted.

7 Unscrew and remove the main jet from the needle jet (see illustration).

8 Unscrew and remove the needle jet (see illustration).

9 Unscrew and remove the pilot jet (see illustration).

10 Using a pair of thin-nose pliers, carefully withdraw the float pivot pin (see illustration). If necessary, displace the pin using a small punch or a nail. Remove the float and unhook the float needle valve, noting how it fits onto the tab on the float (see illustration). On XL models and XRV750-L to N (1990 to1992) models unscrew and remove the float needle valve seat, taking care not to damage its gauze filter (see illustration).

11 The pilot screw can be removed from the carburettor, but note that its setting will be disturbed (see Haynes Hint opposite). Unscrew and remove the pilot screw along with its spring, washer and O-ring (see illustration 5.1a or b).

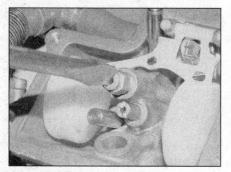

8.7 Remove the main jet ...

8.8 ... the needle jet ...

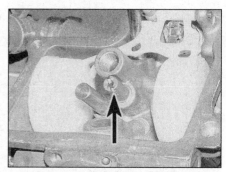

8.9 ... and the pilot jet (arrowed)

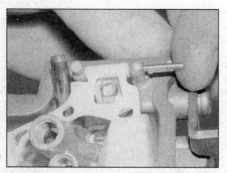

8.10a Displace the float pivot pin ...

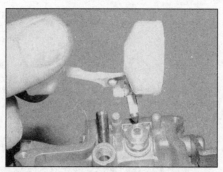

8.10b ... and remove the float assembly

8.10c Float needle valve seat (arrowed)

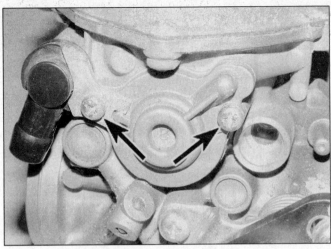

8.12a Undo the screws (arrowed) . . .

8.12b . . . then release the cover and remove the spring and diaphragm. Also remove the O-ring (arrowed)

To record the pilot screw's current setting, turn the screw in until it seats lightly, counting the number of turns necessary to achieve this, then fully unscrew it. On installation, the screw is simply backed out the number of turns you've recorded.

12 On XL models and XRV750-L to N (1990 to 1992) models, remove the two screws securing the air cut-off valve cover and its plate, noting that it is under spring pressure **(see illustration)**. Carefully release the cover and remove the spring and cut-off valve diaphragm, noting how they fit **(see illustration)**. Also remove the O-ring.

13 On XRV750-P models onwards (1993-on), detach the hose from the union on the air cut-off valve, then remove the screw and draw the valve out of the carburettor. Remove the air jet. Discard the O-rings as new ones must be used.

14 On XL600V-T to X (1997 to 1999) models, XL650V models, and XRV750-T models onwards (1996-on), do not remove the throttle position sensor unnecessarily. If you do need to remove it, refer to Chapter 5.

15 On XRV750-P models onwards (1993-on), undo the screws securing the air intake funnel assembly and remove it, noting how it fits. Separate the funnel from its holder if required by twisting it to free the tabs, noting how it fits. Discard the O-ring if it is in any way damaged, deformed or deteriorated.

Cleaning

Caution: Use only a petroleum based solvent for carburettor cleaning. Don't use caustic cleaners.

16 Submerge the metal components in the solvent following the product manufacturer's instructions.

17 After the carburettor has soaked long enough for the cleaner to loosen and dissolve most of the varnish and other deposits, use a nylon-bristled brush to remove the stubborn deposits. Rinse it again, then dry it with compressed air.

18 Use a jet of compressed air to blow out all of the fuel and air passages in the main and upper body, not forgetting the air jets in the carburettor intake.

Caution: Never clean the jets or passages with a piece of wire or a drill bit, as they will be enlarged, causing the fuel and air metering rates to be upset.

Inspection

19 Inspect the choke plunger assembly for wear and damage **(see illustration 7.4b)**.

20 If removed from the carburettor, check the tapered portion of the pilot screw and the spring and O-ring for wear or damage. Replace them with new ones if necessary.

21 Check the carburettor body, float chamber and top cover for cracks, distorted sealing surfaces and other damage. If any defects are found, replace the faulty component, although replacement of the entire carburettor will probably be necessary (check with a Honda dealer on the availability of separate components).

22 Check the piston diaphragm for splits, holes and general deterioration. Holding it up to a light will help to reveal problems of this nature.

23 Insert the piston in the carburettor body and check that it moves up-and-down smoothly. Check the surface of the piston for wear. If it's worn excessively or doesn't move smoothly in the guide, renew the components as necessary.

24 Check the jet needle for straightness by rolling it on a flat surface such as a piece of glass. Replace it with a new one if it's bent or if the tip is worn.

25 Check the tip of the float needle valve and the valve seat. If either has grooves or scratches in it, or is in any way worn, they should be renewed as a set. Gently push down on the rod on the top of the needle valve then release it – if it doesn't spring back, replace the valve with a new one.

26 Operate the throttle shaft to make sure the throttle butterfly valve opens and closes smoothly. If it doesn't, cleaning the throttle linkage may help. Otherwise, replace the carburettor with a new one.

27 Check the float for damage. This will usually be apparent by the presence of fuel inside the float. If the float is damaged, it must be replaced with a new one.

28 On XL models and XRV750-L to N (1990 to 1992) models, check the air cut-off valve diaphragm for splits, holes and general deterioration. Holding it up to a light will help to reveal problems of this nature. Also check the spring for deformation and weakness and replace it with a new one if necessary.

29 On XRV750-P models onwards (1993-on), to check the air cut-off valve, apply a vacuum to the union on the valve cover. With the vacuum applied, air should not be able to flow between the ports in the valve. With no vacuum applied, air should be able to flow. If the valve does not behave as described, replace it with a new one.

9 Carburettors – separation and joining

Warning: Refer to the precautions given in Section 1 before proceeding

Separation

1 The carburettors do not need to be separated for normal overhaul. If you need to separate them (to replace a carburettor body, for example), refer to the following procedure **(see illustrations overleaf)**.

2 Remove the carburettors from the machine (see Section 7). Mark the body of each

4

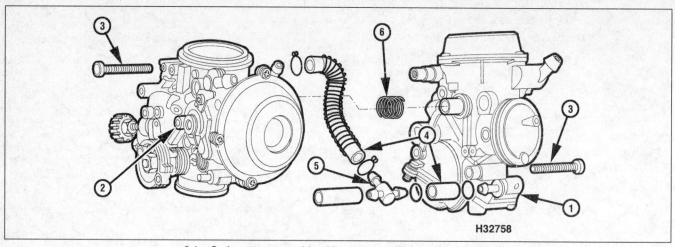

9.1a Carburettor assembly – XL models and early XRV models

1 *Front cylinder carburettor*
2 *Rear cylinder carburettor*
3 *Joining screws*
4 *Fuel hose*
5 *Fuel hose union*
6 *Throttle return spring*

carburettor with its cylinder location to ensure that it is positioned correctly on reassembly.

3 Make a note of how the throttle return spring, linkage assembly and carburettor synchronisation spring are arranged to ensure that they are fitted correctly on reassembly **(see illustrations)**. Also note the arrangement of the various hoses and their unions **(see illustration)**. On XRV750-P models onwards (1993-on), remove the split pin and washers from the arm between the carburettors at the front, noting the order of the washers.

4 Undo the two screws (XL models and XRV750-L to N (1990 to 1992) models) or bolts (XRV750-P models onwards (1993-on)) securing the carburettors together and carefully separate them **(see illustration)**. On XL models and XRV750-L to N (1990 to 1992) models retrieve the synchronisation spring.

Joining

5 Assembly is the reverse of the disassembly procedure, noting the following.

● Obtain a new seal and O-ring set for your model and use all the parts contained **(see illustration 9.1a or b)**.

● Make sure the fuel and air hoses and elbows are correctly and securely inserted into the carburettors **(see illustrations 9.4 and 9.3c and b)**.

9.1b Carburettor assembly – later XRV models

1 *Front cylinder carburettor*
2 *Rear cylinder carburettor*
3 *Joining bolts*
4 *Fuel hoses*
5 *Split pin*
6 *Washer*
7 *Plastic washer*
8 *Washer*
9 *O-ring*

9.3a Note the linkage and return spring arrangement . . .

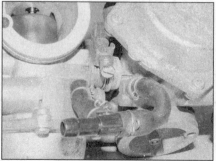

9.3b . . . the synchronisation screw and spring arrangement . . .

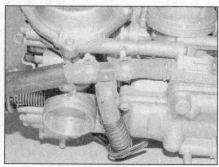

9.3c . . . and the arrangement of the hoses and their unions . . .

9.4 ... then undo the joining screws or bolts (arrow) – XL600V type carburettor shown

● On XL models and XRV750-L to N (1990 to 1992) models install the synchronisation spring after the carburettors are joined together. Make sure it is correctly and squarely seated (see illustration 9.3b).
● Check the operation of the throttle linkage ensuring that it operates smoothly and returns quickly under spring pressure.
● Install the carburettors (see Section 7) and check carburettor synchronisation and idle speed (see Chapter 1).

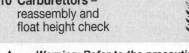

10 Carburettors – reassembly and float height check

⚠ Warning: Refer to the precautions given in Section 1 before proceeding.

Note: When reassembling the carburettors, be sure to use the new O-rings, seals and other parts supplied in the rebuild kit. Do not overtighten the carburettor jets and screws as they are easily damaged.

1 On XL models and XRV750-L to N (1990 to1992) models, fit a new air cut-off valve O-ring, making sure its flat side faces against the carburettor (see illustration and 8.1a). Fit the air cut-off valve diaphragm, making sure the pointed centre fits into the passage and it is properly seated (see illustration). Fit the spring between the cover and the diaphragm (see illustration), then locate the cover and tighten its screws securely, not forgetting the hose union retainer plate where fitted (see illustration 8.12a).
2 On XRV750-P models onwards (1993-on), fit the air jet and air cut-off valve, using new O-rings, and secure the assembly with its screws (see illustration 8.1b). Connect the hose onto the union on the air cut-off valve.

3 Install the pilot screw (if removed) along with its spring, washer and O-ring, turning it in until it seats lightly (see illustration 5.1a or b). Now turn the screw out the number of turns previously recorded, or as specified at the beginning of the Chapter.
4 On XL models and XRV750-L to N (1990 to1992) models, install the float needle valve seat with its washer, making sure the filter is attached (see illustration).
5 Hook the float needle valve onto the float tab (see illustration). Position the float assembly in the carburettor and install the pin, making sure it is secure (see illustrations 8.10b and a).
6 Screw the pilot jet into the body of the carburettor (see illustration).
7 Screw the needle jet into the body of the carburettor (see illustration). Screw the main jet into the end of the needle jet (see illustration).

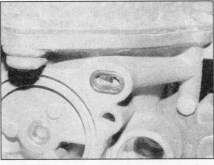

10.1a Fit the O-ring, making sure the flat side is on the inside

10.1b Locate the diaphragm ...

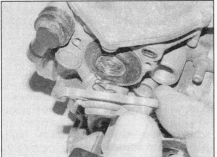

10.1c ... then fit the spring and cover

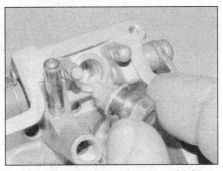

10.4 Fit the needle valve seat with its washer

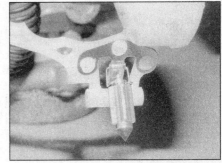

10.5 Hook the valve onto its tab

4

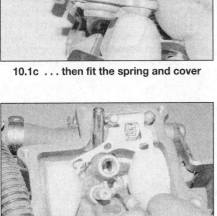

10.6 Install the pilot jet ...

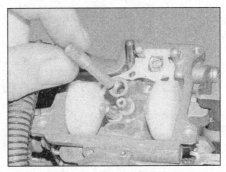

10.7a ... the needle jet. . .

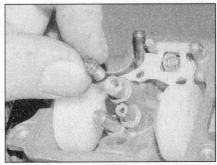

10.7b ... and the main jet

10.8 Measuring the float height

10.9 Fit a new O-ring into the groove and install the float chamber

10.10 Insert the retainer, locating the spring on the top of the needle, then press down and turn to secure its tabs

8 To check the float height, hold the carburettor so the float hangs down, then tilt it back until the needle valve is just seated, but not so far that the needle's spring-loaded tip is compressed. Measure the distance between the base of the carburettor body and the bottom of the float with an accurate ruler **(see illustration)**. The correct setting should be as given in the Specifications at the beginning of the Chapter. If the float height is incorrect, on brass floats it can be adjusted by carefully bending the float tab a little at a time until the correct height is obtained **(see illustration 10.5)**; on plastic floats an incorrect float height can only be corrected by renewing the float.

9 With the float height checked, fit a new seal into the groove in the float chamber, then fit the chamber onto the carburettor and secure it with the screws **(see illustration)**.

10 On XL models and XRV750-L to N (1990

to 1992) models, carefully fit the jet needle into the piston **(see illustration 8.4d)**. Check that the spring is fitted to the retainer and is secure **(see illustration 8.4c)**. Insert the retainer and push down on the spring using a Phillips screwdriver or suitable socket and rotate it until its tabs lock under the protrusions in the piston **(see illustration and 8.4a)**.

11 On XRV750-P models onwards (1993-on), fit the washer underneath the jet needle head. Fit the needle into the piston, making sure the washer does not fall off. Fit a new O-ring into the groove in the needle holder and smear it with oil. Check that the spring is in the base of the needle holder, or install it if removed. Align the tabs on the holder with the slots in the piston and insert the holder, pushing it down until the O-ring is felt to locate in its groove. Remove the screw used on removal from the holder, if not already done.

12 Turn the diaphragm inside out so that its

rim faces down. Insert the piston/diaphragm assembly into the carburettor, ensuring the needle is correctly aligned with the needle jet **(see illustration)**. Keep a finger on the bottom of the piston to keep it raised (inserting your finger via the air intake) so the diaphragm stays inside out – this will prevent the rim popping out of the groove. Align the loop on the diaphragm rim with its groove in the carburettor body, then press the diaphragm outer edge into its groove, making sure it is correctly seated **(see illustration)**.

13 Keeping the piston raised, fit the spring, locating it over the needle holder **(see illustration)**. Fit the top cover onto the carburettor, locating the top of the spring inside the raised section in the cover **(see illustration)**. Align the protrusion on the cover with the loop on the diaphragm **(see illustration)**. Make sure the diaphragm rim stays seated in its groove and does not get pinched by the cover, then install the cover screws and tighten them securely. You can now let the piston drop. Check that the piston moves up and down smoothly.

14 On XRV750-P models onwards (1993-on), fit new air intake funnel O-rings into the groove in the intake side of each carburettor. Fit the air funnel into the holder and rotate it so that its tabs are locked in place. Align the cutouts in the air funnel with the corresponding raised lands on the intake bore, and fit the pins on the holder into the holes in the carburettor body. Tighten the four screws securely.

15 If removed, install the throttle position sensor (See Chapter 5).

16 Install the carburettors (see Section 7).

10.12a Fit the piston into the carburettor . . .

10.12b . . . then press the diaphragm rim into the groove, making sure the loop (arrowed) locates correctly

10.13a Insert the spring . . .

10.13b . . . then fit the cover . . .

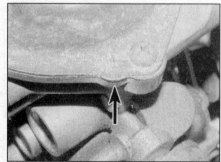

10.13c . . . making sure the protrusion (arrowed) aligns with the loop

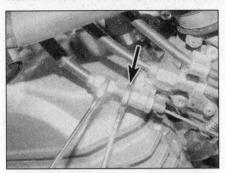

11.2a Counter-hold the adjuster, then slacken the locknut (arrowed) and thread it up . . .

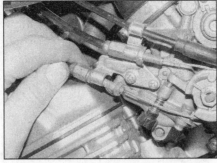

11.2b . . . and slip the cable out of the bracket

11.3a Slacken the locknut and slip the cable out of the bracket

11 Throttle cables –
removal and installation

> **Warning: Refer to the precautions given in Section 1 before proceeding.**

Removal

1 Remove the fuel tank (see Section 2). Mark each cable according to its position at each end.

2 Slacken the lower (opening) cable locknut and thread it up the adjuster a little, then slide the adjuster along until the captive nut clears the small lug on the bracket and slip it out of the bracket **(see illustration)**.

3 Slacken the upper (closing) cable locknut and slip the adjuster out of the bracket **(see illustration)**. Detach the inner cable ends from the carburettor **(see illustration)**.

4 Pull back the rubber cover from the throttle housing on the handlebars **(see illustration)**. Slacken the locknut on the opening cable adjuster and the holder on the closing cable. Undo the two throttle pulley housing screws and separate the two halves **(see illustration)**. Remove the cable guide, noting how it fits **(see illustration)**. Detach the cable nipples from the pulley, then unscrew the adjuster and the holder and remove the cables from the housing, noting how they fit **(see illustrations)**. Mark each cable to ensure it is connected correctly on installation.

5 Remove the cables from the machine noting their correct routing.

Installation

6 Install the cables making sure they are correctly routed. The cables must not interfere with any other component and should not be kinked or bent sharply.

7 Fit the cables into the throttle pulley housing, making sure each is installed into its correct position, and thread the adjuster and holder into the housing **(see illustration 11.4e)**. Lubricate the cable nipples with multi-purpose grease and fit them into the throttle pulley **(see illustration 11.4d)**. Fit the cable guide into the housing **(see illustration 11.4c)**.

8 Fit the two halves of the housing onto the handlebar, making sure the top mating surfaces align with the punch mark in the handlebar, and install the screws, tightening them securely **(see illustrations)**.

9 Lubricate the cable lower ends with multi-

11.3b Detach the cable ends from the throttle cam

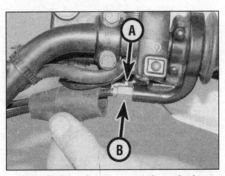

11.4a Pull back the cover, then slacken the locknut (A) and holder (B)

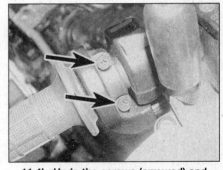

11.4b Undo the screws (arrowed) and separate the halves

4

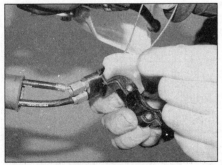

11.4c Remove the guide . . .

11.4d . . . then detach the cable ends from the pulley . . .

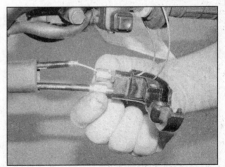

11.4e . . . and thread the adjuster and holder out of the housing

11.8a Assemble the housing . . .

11.8b . . . aligning the mating surfaces with the punch mark (arrowed)

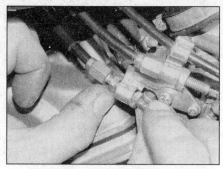

11.9 Fit the cable into the bracket

purpose grease and attach them to the throttle cam on the carburettor **(see illustration 11.3b)**. Fit the upper (closing) cable into the mounting bracket and tighten the locknut against it **(see illustration 11.3a)**. Fit the lower (opening) cable into the bracket and draw the captive nut against the lug on the bracket **(see illustration)**. Tighten the locknut against the bracket **(see illustration 11.2a)**.

10 Operate the throttle to check that it opens and closes freely.

11 Check the amount of freeplay in the throttle cables and adjust if necessary (Chapter 1). Turn the handlebars back and forth to make they don't cause the steering to bind.

12 Install the fuel tank (see Section 2).

13 Start the engine and check that the idle speed does not rise as the handlebars are turned. If it does, the throttle cables are routed incorrectly. Correct the problem before riding the motorcycle.

12 Choke cable – removal and installation

Removal

1 Remove the fuel tank (see Section 2).

2 Unscrew each choke plunger assembly nut from the carburettors and withdraw the plunger assembly from each carburettor body **(see illustrations 7.4a and b)**. Compress the spring and detach the cable end from the choke plunger, noting how it fits. Withdraw the cable from the assembly. If the carburettor is not being disassembled for cleaning, it is advisable to reinstall the choke plunger assembly into the carburettor to avoid losing any of the components.

3 Unscrew the bolt and remove the collar from the hand guard on the left-hand side

(see illustration). Counter-hold the screw-head and undo the nut on its bottom **(see illustration)**. Remove the handguard **(see illustration)**.

4 Pull back the rubber cover on the choke cable **(see illustration)**. Undo the screw securing the lever, then detach the lever, noting the wave washer and plate beneath it **(see illustration)**. Draw the cable end out of the lever bracket, then slip the inner cable out using the slot and detach the nipple from the lever.

5 Remove the cable from the machine noting its correct routing.

Installation

6 Install the cable making sure it is correctly routed. The cable must not interfere with any other component and should not be kinked or bent sharply.

7 Lubricate the upper cable nipple with multi-purpose grease. Fit the cable end into the lever, then slip the inner cable into the bracket and fit the outer cable end into its socket. Mount the lever on the bracket, making sure the plate and wave washer are fitted, and install the screw. Fit the handguard, then thread the locknut onto the bottom of the screw. Fit the top bolt with its collar.

8 Pass the lower end of each inner cable through its plunger assembly nut and spring, then attach the nipple to the plunger, making sure it is secure. Install each plunger assembly into the carburettor body and tighten its nut securely.

9 Fit the cable in its guide. Check the operation of the choke cable as described in Chapter 1.

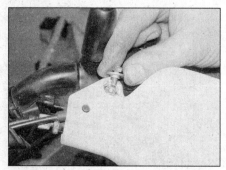

12.3a Unscrew the bolt and remove the collar

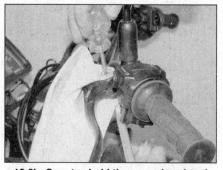

12.3b Counter-hold the screwhead and undo the nut on the bottom . . .

12.3c . . . and remove the handguard

12.4a Pull back the cover (arrowed) . . .

12.4b . . . then undo the screw (arrowed), lift off the lever and detach the cable

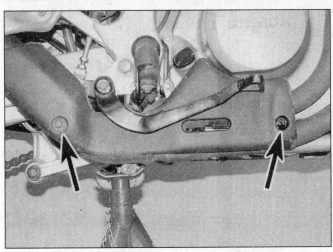

13.1a Unscrew the bolts (arrowed) . . .

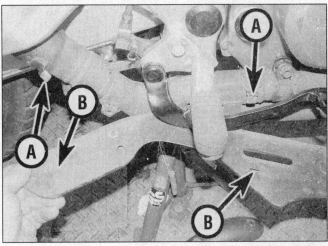

13.1b . . . and remove the heatshield, noting how the tabs (A) locate in the slots (B) – XL600V shown

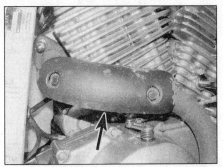

13.1c On XL models, also remove the rear downpipe shield (arrowed) if required

13 Exhaust system –
removal and installation

Warning: If the engine has been running the exhaust system will be very hot. Allow the system to cool before carrying out any work.

Removal

1 Remove the right-hand side panel, the belly-pan, on XL600V and XRV750 models the right-hand fairing side panel, and on XL650V models the fairing (see Chapter 8). Remove the heat shield, noting how it fits **(see illustrations)**.

2 Slacken the silencer clamp bolts, then unscrew the silencer mounting bolts and remove the silencer, noting how it fits **(see illustrations)**. On XL models note the collar fitted with the front mounting bolt.

3 On XL650V models, slacken the front downpipe clamp bolt **(see illustration)**. On all models unscrew the front downpipe flange retaining nuts from the cylinder head studs **(see illustrations)**. Draw the flange off the studs, then twist the pipe so it is clear of the engine and remove it.

4 Unscrew the rear downpipe flange retaining

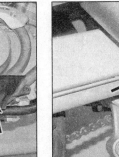

13.1d The shield on the XL650V is secured by three bolts (arrowed)

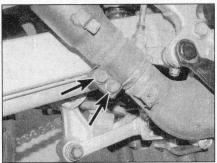

13.2a On XL models, slacken the clamp bolts (arrowed) . . .

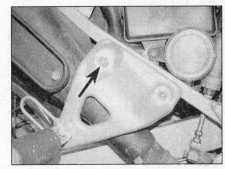

13.2b . . . then unscrew the front bolt (arrowed) . . .

13.2c . . . and the rear bolt (arrowed) . . .

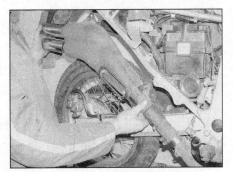

13.2d . . . and remove the silencer

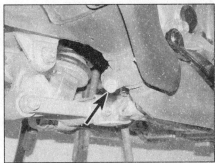

13.2e On XRV models, slacken the clamp bolt (arrowed) . . .

13.2f . . . then unscrew the mounting bolts (arrowed) and remove the silencer

13.3a Slacken the clamp bolt (arrowed)

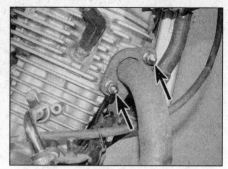

13.3b Front downpipe flange nuts (arrowed) – XL models

13.3c Front downpipe flange nuts (arrowed) – XRV models

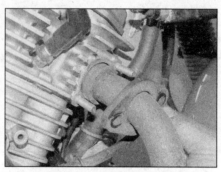

13.3d Draw the flange off the studs . . .

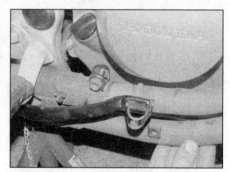

13.3e . . . and remove the pipe

nuts from the cylinder head studs. Slacken the rear downpipe clamp bolt, then twist the pipe so it is clear of the engine and remove it **(see illustrations)**.

5 Remove the gasket from each cylinder head, noting that the rear gasket is a smaller diameter than that of the front, and discard them as new ones must be fitted **(see illustration)**.

6 On XL650V models, if required, unscrew the collector box mounting bolts and remove the box, noting how it fits **(see illustration)**.

7 Check the condition of the sealing rings between the components and replace them with new ones if they are damaged or deformed **(see illustrations)**. Honda recommend always

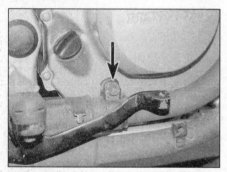

13.4a Slacken the clamp bolt (arrowed) . . .

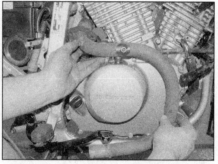

13.4b . . . and remove the downpipe

13.5 Remove the gasket from each head

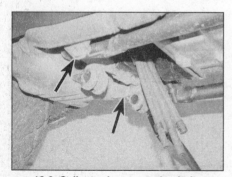

13.6 Collector box mounting bolts (arrowed) – XL650V

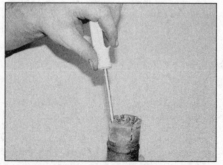

13.7a Dig out the old sealing ring . . .

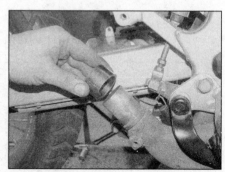

13.7b . . . and fit a new one

13.8 Fit a new gasket into each head

15.2a Fuel pump (arrowed)

using new ones, but they can be difficult to remove, and unless they are damaged they are re-usable. It is too easy to damage a new one trying to install it to make it worthwhile destroying a good one that is already installed.

Installation

8 Installation is the reverse of removal, noting the following:
● Use a new gasket in each cylinder head port (see illustration). Replace any damaged, deformed or deteriorated mounting rubbers with new ones.
● Use a new sealing ring between each component if required, bearing in mind the information in Step 7 above (see illustration 13.7b).
● Apply a smear of copper grease to all bolts to prevent them from seizing up.
● Leave all fasteners loose until the entire system has been installed, making alignment of the various sections easier. Tighten the silencer mounting last.
● Tighten the downpipe nuts to the torque

setting specified at the beginning of the Chapter.
● Run the engine and check the system for leaks.

14 Catalytic converter – general information (XL650V models)

1 A catalytic converter is incorporated in the exhaust system to minimise the level of exhaust pollutants released into the atmosphere. It is of the open-loop type, with no feedback to the ignition or fueling systems.
2 The catalyst is automatic in operation and requires no maintenance. The following precautions should, however, be observed.
● DO NOT use leaded or lead replacement petrol (gasoline) – the additives will coat the precious metals, reducing their converting efficiency and will eventually destroy the catalytic converter.
● Always keep the ignition and fuel systems

well-maintained in accordance with the manufacturer's schedule – if the fuel/air mixture is suspected of being incorrect have it checked on an exhaust gas analyser.
● DO NOT use fuel or engine oil additives – these may contain substances harmful to the catalytic converter.
● DO NOT continue to use the bike if the engine burns oil to the extent of leaving a visible trail of blue smoke.
● Remember that the catalytic converter is FRAGILE – take care not to strike the exhaust system with tools during servicing work.

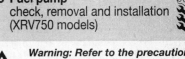

15 Fuel pump – check, removal and installation (XRV750 models)

⚠ Warning: Refer to the precautions given in Section 1 before starting work.

Check

1 The fuel pump is controlled through a cut-off relay, so that it runs whenever the ignition is switched ON and the ignition is operative (i.e., only when the engine is turning over). As soon as the ignition is killed, the relay cuts off the fuel pump's electrical supply (so that there is no risk of fuel being sprayed out under pressure in the event of an accident).
2 The fuel pump is mounted below the rear of the fuel tank – remove the left-hand side panel to access it (see Chapter 8) (see illustration). On L to N (1990 to 1992) models the relay is mounted below the instrument cluster – remove the fairing to access it (see Chapter 8) (see illustration). On P models onwards (1993-on) the relay is mounted on the rear sub-frame on the left-hand side – remove the left-hand side panel to access it (see Chapter 8) (see illustration).
3 It should be possible to hear or feel the fuel pump running whenever the engine is turning over – either place your ear close beside the pump or feel it with your fingertips. If you can't hear or feel anything, check the circuit fuse (see Chapter 9). If the fuse is good, check the pump and relay for loose or corroded connections or physical damage and rectify as necessary. If all is good so far, perform the following checks:

4

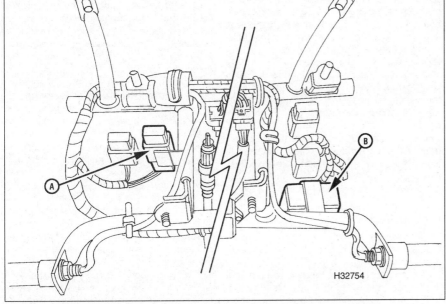

15.2b Fuel cut-off relay (A), fuel warning light circuit checker (B) – XRV750-L to N models

15.2c Fuel cut-off relay (arrowed) – XRV750-P models onward

4 Disconnect the relay wiring connector **(see illustration 15.2c)**. Connect the positive (+) probe of a voltmeter to the black/red wire terminal on the loom side of the wiring connector and the negative (–) probe to earth. With the ignition switch ON there should be battery voltage present. If there is no voltage, check the black/red wire for faults, referring to the *Wiring Diagrams* at the end of Chapter 9.

5 If battery voltage was present, check for continuity in the black/blue wire between the relay connector and the pump connector, and then between the green wire in the pump connector and earth (ground). If there is no continuity there is a fault in the black/blue or green wire. If there is continuity, check for continuity in the blue/yellow or black/yellow wire (according to model) between the relay and the ignition control unit. If there is none, trace the fault and repair the wire. If all is good, short between the black/red and black/blue wire terminals in the relay wiring connector (thereby effectively by-passing it). Now check for battery voltage at the fuel pump wiring connector black/blue wire with the ignition ON. If there is voltage, the relay is faulty and must be replaced with a new one.

6 If the pump still does not work, trace the wiring from the pump and disconnect it at the 2-pin wiring connector – remove the seat and raise the rear of the fuel tank to access it (see Chapter 8 and Section 2), but be prepared to remove the fuel tank if access to the connector is too restricted with it in place. Using a fully charged 12 volt battery and two insulated jumper wires, connect the positive (+) terminal of the battery to the pump's black/blue terminal, and the negative (–) terminal of the battery to the pump's green terminal. The pump should operate. If the pump does not operate it must be replaced with a new one. If the pump works, check for battery voltage at the black/blue terminal on the supply side of the connector with the ignition ON. If there is no voltage, check the wiring.

7 If the pump operates but is thought to be delivering an insufficient amount of fuel, first check that all fuel hoses are in good condition and not pinched or trapped. Check that the in-line filter, the strainer in the fuel tank and the fuel delivery hoses are not blocked.

8 The fuel pump's output can be checked as follows: make sure the ignition switch is OFF. If it was removed, install the fuel tank in the raised position (see Section 2).

9 Release the clamp securing the fuel supply hose to the three-way union on the carburettors, being prepared to catch any residual fuel **(see illustration 7.7a)**. Place the end into a graduated beaker suitable for holding about 1/4 litre of petrol.

10 Disconnect the relay wiring connector **(see illustration 15.2c)**. Using a short length of insulated jumper wire, connect between the black/red and the black/blue wire terminals of the connector.

11 Set the kill switch to RUN, then turn the

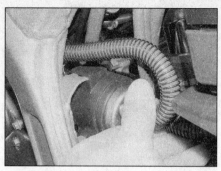

15.14 Draw the pump off its mounting lug and remove it

ignition switch ON and let fuel flow from the pump into the beaker for 5 seconds, then switch the ignition OFF.

12 Measure the amount of fuel that has flowed into the beaker, then multiply that amount by 12 to determine the fuel pump flow rate per minute. The minimum flow rate required is 900 cc per minute. If the flow rate recorded is below this, then the fuel pump must be replaced with a new one.

Removal

13 Make sure the ignition is switched OFF.

14 The fuel pump is mounted below the rear of the fuel tank – remove the left-hand side panel to access it (see Chapter 8) **(see illustration)**. Trace the wiring from the pump and disconnect it at the black 2-pin wiring connector – remove the seat and raise the rear of the fuel tank to access it (see Chapter 8 and Section 2), but be prepared to remove the fuel tank if access to the connector is too restricted with it in place. Free the wiring from any clips or ties and feed it back to the pump, noting its routing. Make a note or sketch of which fuel hose fits on which union on the pump as an aid to installation. Using a rag to mop up any spilled fuel, disconnect the two hoses from the pump. Displace the pump from its mount and either disconnect the drain hose from the underside or remove the pump with it attached, noting its routing.

15 On L to N (1990 to 1992) models the relay is mounted below the instrument cluster – remove the fairing to access it (see Chapter 8) **(see illustration 15.2b)**. On P models onwards (1993-on) the relay is mounted on the rear sub-frame on the left-hand side – remove the left-hand side panel to access it (see Chapter 8) **(see illustration 15.2c)**. Disconnect the relay wiring connector and remove the relay from its mounting.

Installation

16 Installation is the reverse of removal. Make sure the fuel hoses are correctly and securely fitted to the pump – the hose from the in-line filter attaches to the union marked INLET; the hose to the carburettors attaches to the other union. Start the engine and check carefully that there are no leaks at the pipe connections.

16 Fuel level indicator circuit – check and replacement

XRV750-L to N (1990 to 1992) models

Check – warning light circuit

1 XRV750-L to N (1990 to 1992) models are fitted with a fuel warning light circuit checker **(see illustration 15.2b)**. When the ignition is switched ON, both low fuel warning lights (one red, one orange) should come on for a few seconds, then extinguish. If they do not, first check the fuses, then check the bulbs (see Chapter 9). If they are good, check the fuel sensor and its circuit (see below).

2 If all is good so far, disconnect the wiring connector from the circuit checker, located below the instrument cluster on the right-hand side. With the ignition switch ON, check for battery voltage between the black (+) and green/white (–) wire terminals on the connector. There should be battery voltage. If not, check the wiring and connectors for faults, referring to the *Wiring Diagrams* at the beginning of the Chapter. If there is voltage, the checker is faulty and must be replaced with a new one.

Check – fuel sensor circuit

3 The circuit consists of the fuel level sensor mounted in the fuel tank and the low fuel warning light mounted in the instrument panel. If the system malfunctions first check that the bulb and fuses are good (see Chapter 9).

4 Remove the left-hand fairing side panel (see Chapter 8). Disconnect the fuel level sensor wiring connector, located below the tank on the left-hand side. Also disconnect the wiring connector from the circuit checker, located below the instrument cluster. Using an insulated jumper wire, short between the orange/white and green wire terminals on the loom side of the sensor wiring connector. Turn the ignition switch ON. If the orange warning light comes on, check the orange/white and green wires between the connector and the sensor itself in the tank for loose or broken connections. If the wiring is good, replace the sensor with a new one. If the orange warning light does not come on, check wiring between the connector and the instrument cluster for loose or broken connections.

5 Now short between the grey/black and green wire terminals on the loom side of the sensor wiring connector. Turn the ignition switch ON. If the red warning light comes on, check the grey/black and green wires between the connector and the sensor itself in the tank for loose or broken connections. If the wiring is good, replace the sensor with a new one. If the orange warning light does not come on, check wiring between the connector and the instrument cluster for loose or broken connections.

Replacement

6 See Chapter 9 for replacement of the warning light bulb.

7 To replace either sensor, remove the fuel tank and drain it (see Section 2). Disconnect the wiring connectors from the sensor.

8 Unscrew the sensor and draw it out of the tank. Discard the O-ring. Fit a new O-ring onto the sensor. Apply a smear of suitable sealant to the upper portion of the sensor threads, then screw it into the tank and tighten it to the torque setting specified at the beginning of the Chapter.

9 Install the tank (see Section 2), and check carefully for leaks before using the bike.

XL650V models

Check

10 The circuit consists of the fuel level sender unit mounted in the fuel tank and the gauge mounted in the instrument panel. If the system malfunctions first check that the fuses are good, then check the power input to the instrument cluster (see Chapter 9, Sections 5 and 16).

11 Remove the fuel gauge sender unit (see below). Connect an ohmmeter across the sender unit wire terminals then check the resistance reading whilst moving the float arm slowly from the full to empty position and back again. Compare the readings obtained to those given in the Specifications. Not only should the full and empty readings be as specified but the value should change evenly and progressively as the float arm is moved. If not the sender unit is faulty and should be renewed.

12 If the sender unit functions correctly, connect it to the wiring connector then switch the ignition ON. Move the float arm up and down again and check that the operation of the gauge corresponds to the movement of the arm. If the gauge does not function correctly, switch off the ignition and remove the fairing (see Chapter 8).

13 Disconnect the wiring connectors from the instrument cluster and fuel gauge sender unit. Use an ohmmeter to check for continuity in the grey/black and green/black wires between the cluster and sender unit, using the relevant *Wiring Diagram* at the end of Chapter 9 to make sure you have the correct instrument cluster connector. Also check for continuity to earth (ground) in the green/black wire. If continuity (zero resistance) is not present, repair/replace the wiring harness. If continuity exists, then the gauge is probably faulty.

Replacement

14 See Chapter 9 for replacement of the fuel gauge.

15 To replace the sender unit, remove the fuel tank and drain it (see Section 2).

16 Unscrew the nuts securing the sender and carefully manoeuvre it out of the tank, taking

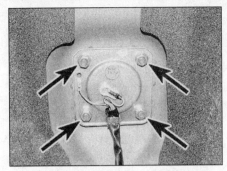

16.16 Fuel level sender mounting nuts (arrowed)

care not to bend the float arm **(see illustration)**. Discard the O-ring.

17 Fit a new O-ring onto the sensor and install it in the tank. Tighten the nuts evenly and a little at a time to the torque setting specified at the beginning of the Chapter.

18 Install the tank (see Section 2), and check carefully for leaks before using the bike.

---

17 Pulse secondary air (PAIR) system – XL650V models

General information

1 To reduce the amount of unburned hydrocarbons released in the exhaust gases, a pulse secondary air (PAIR) system is fitted. The system consists of the control valve (mounted behind the right-hand radiator), the reed valves (fitted in the valve covers) and the hoses linking them **(see illustration)**. The control valve is linked by hose to the front cylinder intake duct and actuated by the vacuum created therein.

2 Under certain operating conditions, the vacuum in the front cylinder intake duct opens up the PAIR control valve which then allows filtered air to be drawn through the reed valves and cylinder head passages and into the exhaust ports. The air mixes with the exhaust gases, causing any unburned particles of the fuel in the mixture to be burnt in the exhaust port/pipes. This process changes a considerable amount of

hydrocarbons and carbon monoxide into relatively harmless carbon dioxide and water. The reed valves in the valve cover are fitted to prevent the flow of exhaust gases back up the cylinder head passages and into the air filter housing.

Testing

Control valve

3 Remove the valve from the motorcycle (see below).

4 Check the operation of the control valve by blowing through the air filter housing hose union; air should flow freely through the reed valve hose unions. Now apply a vacuum to the vacuum hose union and repeat the check; no air should now flow through the valve if it is functioning correctly.

Reed valves

5 Disconnect the reed valve hoses from the control valve (see below).

6 Check each valve by blowing and sucking on the hose end. Air should flow through the hose only when blown down it and not when sucked back up. If this is not the case the reed valve is faulty.

Component renewal

Control valve

7 Remove the fairing (see Chapter 8).

8 Disconnect the vacuum hose from the top of the valve **(see illustration 17.1)**.

9 Release the clamps securing the reed valve hoses and the air filter hose and disconnect them, then remove the control valve from the motorcycle.

10 Installation is the reverse of removal.

Reed valves

11 Remove the fuel tank and the air filter housing (see Sections 2 and 4).

12 To remove either valve, first release the clamp and detach the air hose from its union **(see illustration)**. Unscrew the bolts securing the reed valve cover and remove the cover. Remove the reed valve and the base plate, noting which way around they are fitted.

13 Installation is the reverse of removal. Clean off any carbon deposits and make sure the reed valve components are correctly fitted.

4

17.1 PAIR system control valve – XL650V models

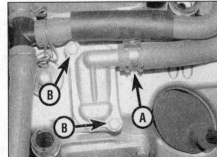

17.12 Release the clamp (A) and detach the hose, then unscrew the cover bolts (B)

Chapter 5
Ignition system

Contents

Degrees of difficulty

Easy, suitable for novice with little experience	Fairly easy, suitable for beginner with some experience	Fairly difficult, suitable for competent DIY mechanic 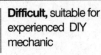	Difficult, suitable for experienced DIY mechanic	Very difficult, suitable for expert DIY or professional

Specifications

General information

Firing order	Front (232°), Rear (488°)
Spark plugs	see Chapter 1

Ignition timing

XL600V-H to T (1987 to 1996) models

At idle	10° BTDC
Full advance	30° BTDC @ 4500 rpm

XL600V-V to X (1997 to 1999) models

At idle	10° BTDC
Full advance	30° BTDC @ 5000 rpm

XL650V models

At idle	10° BTDC
Full advance	32° BTDC @ 6000 rpm

XRV750 models

At idle	10° BTDC
Full advance	28° BTDC @ 4500 rpm

Pulse generator coil

Resistance

XL600V models	360 to 540 ohms at 20°C
XRV750-L to S (1990 to 1995) models	180 to 280 ohms at 20°C

Minimum peak voltage

XL650V and XRV750-T onwards (1996-on) – see text	0.7 volts

Ignition HT coils

XL600V-H to S (1987 to 1995) models, XRV750-L to S (1990 to 1995) models

Primary winding resistance	0.1 to 0.2 ohms at 20°C
Secondary winding resistance	
With plug cap	7.4 to 10.8 K-ohms at 20°C
Without plug cap	3.6 to 4.5 K-ohms at 20°C
Plug cap resistance	approx. 5 K-ohms

XL600V-T to X (1997 to 1999) models, XL650V models, XRV750 T models onwards (1996-on)

Primary winding resistance	2.2 to 2.6 ohms at 20°C
Secondary winding resistance	
With plug cap	30 to 36 K-ohms at 20°C
Without plug cap	25 to 30 K-ohms at 20°C
Plug cap resistance	approx. 5 K-ohms
Minimum peak voltage	100 volts

Throttle position sensor

Note: This is only fitted on XL600V-T to X (1997 to 1999) models, XL650V models, and XRV750-T models onwards (1996-on)

Resistance	4 to 6 K-ohms at 20°C
Input voltage (see text)	4.7 to 5.3 volts

5

1 General information

All models are fitted with an electronic ignition system, which due to its lack of mechanical parts is totally maintenance free.

The system comprises the timing rotor, pulse generator coil(s), ignition control unit, ignition HT coils, and on XL600V-T to X (1997 to 1999) models, XL650V models, and XRV750-T models onward (1996-on) a throttle position sensor. Refer to the wiring diagrams at the end of Chapter 9 for details.

On XL models an ignition timing rotor, which is on the right-hand end of the crankshaft, has triggers which magnetically actuate the pulse generator coil(s) as the crankshaft rotates. The pulse generator coil sends a signal to the ignition control unit which then supplies the ignition HT coils with the power necessary to produce a spark at the plugs. On XRV models the system is basically the same except the triggers for the pulse generator are incorporated in the alternator rotor, which is on the left-hand end of the crankshaft. The system incorporates an electronic advance system.

The throttle position sensor (where fitted) supplies the control unit with information on throttle position and rate of opening or closing.

XL600V-H to R (1987 to 1995) models and XRV750-L to S (1990 to 1995) models have one coil for each spark plug, therefore two coils per cylinder. XL600V-T to X (1997 to 1999) models, XL650V models and XRV750 T models onward (1996-on) have one twin-lead coil per pair of plugs, therefore one coil per cylinder.

The system incorporates a safety interlock circuit which will cut the ignition if the sidestand is extended whilst the engine is running and in gear, or if a gear is selected whilst the engine is running and the sidestand is down. It also prevents the engine from being started if the sidestand is down and the engine is in gear. The engine can be started with the sidestand up when it is in gear as long as the clutch lever is pulled in.

XL650V models have an immobiliser system which will not allow the engine to be started unless the correct key is used. The immobiliser system has its own fault-diagnosis function. Refer to Section 8 for further details.

Because of their nature, the individual ignition system components can be checked but not repaired. If ignition system troubles occur, and the faulty component can be isolated, the only cure for the problem is to replace the part with a new one. Keep in mind that most electrical parts, once purchased, cannot be returned. To avoid unnecessary expense, make very sure the faulty component has been positively identified before buying a replacement part.

Note that there is no provision for adjusting the ignition timing on these models.

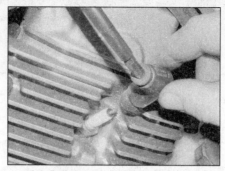

2.2 Pull the cap off the spark plug

2 Ignition system –
check

⚠ *Warning: The energy levels in electronic systems can be very high. On no account should the ignition be switched on whilst the plugs or plug caps are being held. Shocks from the HT circuit can be most unpleasant. Secondly, it is vital that the engine is not turned over or run with any of the plug caps removed, and that the plugs are soundly earthed (grounded) when the system is checked for sparking. The ignition system components can be seriously damaged if the HT circuit becomes isolated.*

1 As no means of adjustment is available, any failure of the system can be traced to failure of a system component or a simple wiring fault. Of the two possibilities, the latter is by far the most likely. In the event of failure, check the system in a logical fashion, as described below.

2 Working on one HT lead at a time, disconnect the lead from its spark plug – to access them refer to Chapter 1, Section 5

TOOL TiP

A simple spark gap testing tool can be made from a block of wood, a large alligator clip and two nails, one of which is fashioned so that a spark plug cap or bare HT lead end can be connected to its end. Make sure the gap between the two nail ends is the same as specified

(see illustration). Connect the lead to a spare spark plug that is known to be good and lay the plug against the cylinder head with the threads contacting it. If necessary, hold the spark plug with an insulated tool.

⚠ *Warning: Do not remove any of the spark plugs from the engine to perform this check – atomised fuel being pumped out of the open spark plug hole could ignite, causing severe injury! Make sure the plugs are securely held against the engine – if they are not earthed when the engine is turned over, the ignition control unit could be damaged.*

3 Having observed the above precautions, check that the kill switch is in the RUN position and the transmission is in neutral, then turn the ignition switch ON and turn the engine over on the starter motor. If the system is in good condition a regular, fat blue spark should be evident at the plug electrode. If the spark appears thin or yellowish, or is non-existent, further investigation will be necessary. Turn the ignition OFF and repeat the check for each lead.

4 The ignition system must be able to produce a spark which is capable of jumping a particular size gap. Honda do not provide a specification, but a healthy system should produce a spark capable of jumping at least 6 mm. A simple testing tool can be made to test the minimum gap across which the spark will jump (see **Tool Tip**). Alternatively spark testing tools are available, some of which are adjustable to set the spark gap distance.

5 Connect one of the spark plug HT leads from one coil to the protruding electrode on the test tool, and clip the tool to a good earth (ground) on the engine or frame. Check that the kill switch is in the RUN position, turn the ignition switch ON and turn the engine over on the starter motor. If the system is in good condition a regular, fat blue spark should be seen to jump the gap between the nail ends. Repeat the test for the other lead(s) and coil. If the test results are good the entire ignition system can be considered good. If the spark appears thin or yellowish, or is non-existent, further investigation will be necessary.

6 Ignition faults can be divided into two categories, namely those where the ignition system has failed completely, and those which are due to a partial failure. The likely faults are listed below, starting with the most probable source of failure. Work through the list systematically, referring to the subsequent sections for full details of the necessary checks and tests. **Note:** *Before checking the following items ensure that the battery is fully charged and that all fuses are in good condition.*

● Loose, corroded or damaged wiring connections, broken or shorted wiring between any of the component parts of the ignition system (see Chapter 9).

● Faulty HT lead or spark plug cap, faulty spark plug, dirty, worn or corroded plug electrodes, or incorrect gap between electrodes.

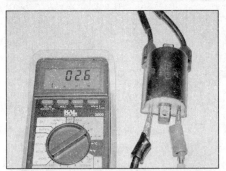

3.4 To test the HT coil primary resistance, connect the multimeter leads between the primary circuit terminals

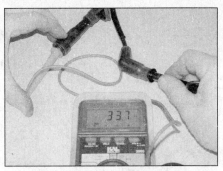

3.7 To test the HT coil secondary resistance, connect the multimeter leads between the spark plug sockets

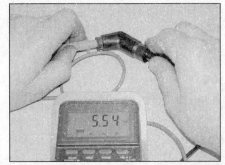

3.8 Measuring spark plug cap resistance

● Faulty ignition (main) switch or engine kill switch (see Chapter 9).
● Faulty neutral, clutch or sidestand switch (see Chapter 9).
● Faulty pulse generator coil or damaged trigger on timing or alternator rotor (according to model).
● Faulty ignition HT coil(s).
● Faulty throttle position sensor (if fitted).
● Faulty ignition control unit.

7 If the above checks don't reveal the cause of the problem, have the ignition system tested by a Honda dealer.

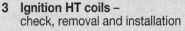

3 Ignition HT coils – check, removal and installation

Check

1 Remove the fuel tank (see Chapter 4). Check the coils visually for loose or damaged terminals, cracks and other damage.
2 Remove the seat (see Chapter 8). Disconnect the battery negative (–) lead.
3 Remove the coil being tested (see Steps 16 to 18).

Primary windings check – all models

4 Set an ohmmeter or multimeter to the ohms x 1 scale and measure the resistance between the primary circuit terminals on the coil **(see illustration)**. This will give a resistance reading of the primary windings of the coil and should be consistent with the value given in the Specifications at the beginning of the Chapter.

Secondary windings check – all models

5 To check the condition of the secondary windings, set the meter to the K-ohm scale.
6 On XL600V-H to R (1987 to 1995) models and XRV750-L to S (1990 to 1995) models, connect one meter probe to the spark plug cap and the other probe to the green primary circuit terminal on the coil.
7 On XL600V-T to X (1997 to 1999) models, XL650V models and XRV750-T models onward (1996-on), connect one meter probe to one spark plug cap and the other probe to

the other cap **(see illustration)**.
8 If, on all models, the reading obtained is not within the range shown in the Specifications, unscrew the cap(s) from the end of the HT lead(s) and repeat the measurement. If the reading is now as specified, then the cap(s) could be faulty. To test the cap(s), measure the resistance, which should be around 5 K-ohms **(see illustration)**.
9 If the caps are good, separate the lead from the coil by unscrewing its retainer, and check the lead for continuity (zero resistance). If there is no continuity (i.e. a very high resistance), the lead is faulty. With the lead(s) detached, recheck the coil. If the coil reading is still outside the specified range, it is likely that the coil is defective.
10 It is advisable to confirm your findings with a Honda dealer before buying a new coil. Note that on later models the following peak voltage test can be made to confirm the coil's condition.

Peak voltage test – XL600V-T to X (1997 to 1999) models, XL650V models and XRV750 T models onwards (1996-on)

11 Honda specify their own Imrie diagnostic tester (model 625), or the peak voltage adapter (Pt. No. 07HGJ-0020100) with an aftermarket digital multimeter having an impedance of 10 M-ohm/DCV minimum, for the peak voltage test. If this equipment is available, install and reconnect the coils as described in Steps 19 to 21.

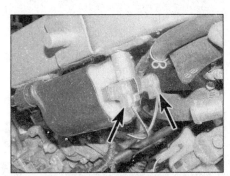

3.17 Disconnect the primary wiring connectors (arrowed)

12 Connect the positive (+) lead of the voltmeter and peak voltage adapter arrangement to the blue/yellow (front cylinder coil) or yellow/blue (rear cylinder coil) wire terminal on the coil, with the wiring connector still securely connected, and connect the negative (–) lead to a suitable earth (ground) point.
13 Check that the kill switch is in the RUN position and the transmission is in neutral, then turn the ignition switch ON. Note the initial voltage reading on the meter, then turn the engine over on the starter motor and note the ignition coil peak voltage reading on the meter. Once both readings have been noted, turn the ignition switch off and disconnect the meter.
14 If the initial voltage reading is not as expected or the peak voltage readings are lower than the specified minimum (see Specifications) then a fault is present somewhere else in the ignition system circuit (see Section 2); note that the peak voltage readings for each coil can be different but each one must exceed the specified minimum.
15 If the initial and peak voltage readings are as specified and the plug does not spark, then the ignition HT coil, HT lead or plug cap are faulty (the plug caps and leads are available separately). In order to determine conclusively that an ignition coil is defective, it should be tested by a Honda dealer. If the coil is confirmed to be faulty, it must be renewed; the coil is a sealed unit and cannot therefore be repaired.

Removal

16 Remove the fuel tank (see Chapter 4). Mark the locations of all wires and leads before disconnecting them. The coils can now be removed. Note the spacers fitted on the coil mounting.
17 Disconnect the primary circuit wiring connectors from the coils **(see illustration)**. Pull the caps off the spark plugs **(see illustration 2.2)**.
18 Unscrew the bolts/nuts securing the coil or its mounting bracket (according to model), noting the spacers, and remove the coil, noting how it fits **(see illustrations)**.

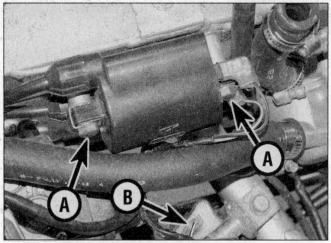

3.18a Rear cylinder HT coil mounting bolts (A), front cylinder coil (B) – XL600V single coil per cylinder models

3.18b Front cylinder HT coil (arrowed) – XL650V

3.18c Rear cylinder HT coil (arrowed) – XL650V

3.18d Front cylinder HT coil (arrowed) – XRV single coil per cylinder models

3.18e Rear cylinder HT coil (arrowed) – XRV single coil per cylinder models

3.20 Note the markings as described and make sure all leads are correctly connected

Installation

19 Installation is the reverse of removal.
20 On models with two coils per cylinder, note that each coil is marked according to the spark plug it feeds, e.g. a coil marked FR-R is for the front cylinder right-hand spark plug. On models with one coil per cylinder, note that each HT lead is marked according to the spark plug it feeds, e.g. a lead marked FR-R is for the front cylinder right-hand spark plug **(see illustration)**.
21 Make sure the wiring connectors and HT leads are securely connected – on single HT lead coils, the black/blue (front) and black/

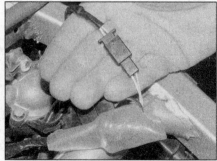

4.2a Pulse generator coil wiring connector – XL600V

yellow (rear) primary circuit wire connectors are for the black terminals on the coils, the green wire connectors are for the green terminals. On twin HT lead coils, the black/white wire connectors are for the black terminals, and the blue/yellow (front) or yellow/blue (rear) wire connectors are for the green terminals.

4 Pulse generator coil(s) – check, removal and installation

Check

1 On XL and XRV750-L to N (1990 to 1992) models, remove the fuel tank (see Chapter 4). On XRV750-P models onwards (1993-on) remove the left-hand side panel. On XL650V remove the left-hand heat shield **(see illustration)**.
2 Trace the wiring back from the coil(s), mounted in the clutch cover on the right-hand side of the engine on XL models and in the alternator cover on the left-hand side on XRV models, to its wiring connector and disconnect it **(see illustrations)**. Perform the following check(s).
3 Using an ohmmeter check for continuity between each of the connector terminals on the coil side of the connector and earth

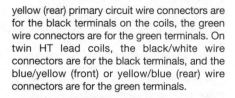

4.1 Remove the heat shield

**4.2b Pulse generator coil wiring connector
– XL650V**

**4.2c Pulse generator coil wiring connector
– XRV750**

**4.6 Measuring pulse generator coil
resistance**

(ground). If there is continuity between any of the connector terminals and earth (ground) then the pulse generator coil is faulty.

XL600V-H to T (1987 to 1996) models

4 To check the front cylinder coil, measure the resistance between the blue wire terminal and the white wire terminal with the blue collar. To check the rear cylinder coil, measure the resistance between the yellow wire terminal and the white wire terminal with the yellow collar.

5 If either reading is different to that specified at the beginning of the chapter, first check the connector and the wiring between the connector and the coil itself (see below to access it). If the wiring is good, replace the coil with a new one.

XL600V-V to X (1997 to 1999) models

6 Measure the resistance between the terminals in the wiring connector **(see illustration)**.

7 If the reading is different to that specified at the beginning of the chapter, first check the connector and the wiring between the connector and the coil itself (see below to access it). If the wiring is good, replace the coil with a new one.

XRV750-L to S (1990 to 1995) models

8 To check the front cylinder coil, measure the resistance between the blue/yellow wire terminal and the green/white wire terminal. To check the rear cylinder coil, measure the resistance between the white/yellow wire terminal and the green/white wire terminal.

9 If either reading is different to that specified at the beginning of the chapter, first check the connector and the wiring between the connector and the coil itself (see below to access it). If the wiring is good, replace the coil with a new one.

XL650V and XRV750-T models onward (1996-on) models

10 Honda specify their own Imrie diagnostic tester (model 625), or the peak voltage adapter (Pt. No. 07HGJ-0020100) with an aftermarket digital multimeter having an impedance of 10 M-ohm/DCV minimum, for a complete test.

11 If this equipment is available, connect the positive (+) lead of the voltmeter and peak voltage adapter arrangement to the white/yellow terminal of the pulse generator coil connector and the negative (–) lead to the yellow terminal of the connector. Turn the engine over on the starter motor and note the voltage reading obtained. If this reading is below the specified minimum, the pulse generator coil is faulty.

12 If the pulse generator coil functions correctly then the fault must be in the wiring harness or the ignition control unit (ICU). Check the wiring between the loom side of the connector and the ICU connector for continuity, and check the connectors themselves for loose or broken terminals. If the wiring is good the ICU could be faulty (see Section 5).

Removal

13 Remove the fuel tank (see Chapter 4) and the belly pan (see Chapter 8), and on XRV750-P models onward (1993-on) the left-hand side panel (see Chapter 8). On XL650V remove the left-hand heat shield **(see illustration 4.1)**.

14 Trace the wiring back from the coil(s), mounted behind the clutch cover on the right-hand side of the engine on XL models and in the alternator cover on the left-hand side on XRV models, to its wiring connector and disconnect it **(see illustration 4.2a, b or c)**. Release the wiring from any clips and ties and feed it through to the cover, noting its routing.

15 On XL models, refer to Chapter 2 and remove the clutch cover.

16 On XRV models, unscrew the pulse generator cover bolts and remove the cover **(see illustration)**. Discard the O-ring as a new one must be used.

17 Undo the coil mounting bolts, then free the wiring grommet from the cover and remove the coil(s) **(see illustrations)**.

Installation

18 Remove all traces of sealant from the wiring grommet and its cutout and apply a smear of fresh sealant to the grommet.

19 Locate the grommet and coil(s) and tighten the bolts securely **(see illustration 4.17b and a)**.

20 On XL models, refer to Chapter 2 and install the clutch cover.

21 On XRV models install the cover using a new O-ring.

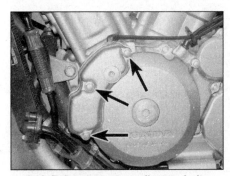

**4.16 Pulse generator coil cover bolts
(arrowed) – XRV models**

4.17a Unscrew the bolts (arrowed) . . .

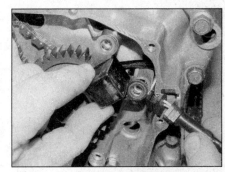

**4.17b . . . then free the wiring grommet and
remove the coil – XL single coil model shown**

5

5.3a Ignition control unit (arrowed) – XL600V

5.3b Ignition control unit (arrowed) – XL650V

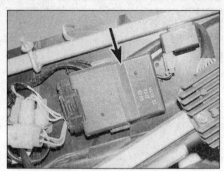

5.3c Ignition control unit (arrowed) – XRV750

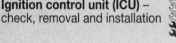

5 Ignition control unit (ICU) – check, removal and installation

Check

1 If the tests shown in the preceding Sections have failed to isolate the cause of an ignition fault, it is possible that the ignition control unit is faulty. No details are available with which the unit can be tested on home workshop equipment. Take the machine to a Honda dealer for testing.

Removal

2 Remove the seat, and on XL650V and XRV750 models the left-hand side panel (see Chapter 8). Note that XL600V-H to R (1987 to 1995) models there are two control units, one for each cylinder.
3 Disconnect the wiring connector(s) and remove the unit (see illustrations).

Installation

4 Installation is the reverse of removal. Make sure the wiring connector(s) is/are correctly and securely connected.

6 Ignition timing – general information and check

General information

1 Since no provision exists for adjusting the

ignition timing and since no component is subject to mechanical wear, there is no need for regular checks; only if investigating a fault such as a loss of power or a misfire, should the ignition timing be checked.
2 The ignition timing is checked dynamically (engine running) using a stroboscopic lamp. The inexpensive neon lamps should be adequate in theory, but in practice may produce a pulse of such low intensity that the timing mark remains indistinct. If possible, one of the more precise xenon tube lamps should be used, powered by an external source of the appropriate voltage. **Note:** *Do not use the machine's own battery as an incorrect reading may result from stray impulses within the machine's electrical system.*

Check

3 Warm the engine up to normal operating temperature then stop it.
4 If the belly pan on your model obscures the alternator cover, remove it (see Chapter 8). Unscrew the timing mark inspection cap from the alternator cover (see illustration). Check the condition of the cap O-ring and discard it if it is damaged, deformed or deteriorated.
5 The timing mark on the rotor is an 'F' which indicates the firing point at idle speed (note that each cylinder has its own 'F' mark, that for the front cylinder being adjacent to the 'FT' mark, that for the rear cylinder being adjacent to the 'RT' mark) (see illustration). The static timing mark with which this should align is a notch in the top of the inspection hole.

6.4 Unscrew the timing inspection cap (arrowed)

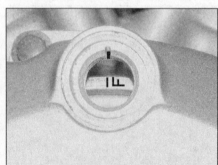

6.5 'F' mark and static timing mark

HAYNES HiNT *The rotor timing mark can be highlighted with white paint to make it more visible under the stroboscope light.*

6 Connect the timing light to the relevant HT lead as described in the manufacturer's instructions.
7 Start the engine and aim the light at the static timing mark.
8 With the machine idling at the specified speed, the timing mark should align with the static timing mark ('F' or 'R').
9 Slowly increase the engine speed whilst observing the timing mark. The timing mark should move anti-clockwise, increasing in relation to the engine speed until it reaches the full advance mark (no identification letter).
10 As already stated, there is no means of adjustment of the ignition timing on these machines. If the ignition timing is incorrect, or suspected of being incorrect, one of the ignition system components is at fault, and the system must be tested as described in the preceding Sections of this Chapter.
11 Install the timing inspection cap using a new O-ring if necessary, and smear the O-ring with clean oil. Apply a smear of molybdenum disulphide grease to the threads of the cap and tighten it securely.

7 Throttle position sensor – check and replacement

Note: *The throttle position sensor is fitted to XL600V-T to X (1997 to 1999) models, XL650V models, and XRV750-T models onwards (1996-on).*

Check

1 The throttle position sensor (TPS) is mounted on the right-hand side of the front cylinder carburettor and is keyed to the throttle shaft. The sensor provides the ignition control unit with information on throttle position and rate of opening or closing.
2 Remove the fuel tank (see Chapter 4). Disconnect the sensor's wiring connector (see illustration 7.6a in Chapter 4).

3 Connect the probes of an ohmmeter between the green/black and yellow/black terminals on the sensor and measure the resistance. Compare the reading to the value specified at the beginning of the Chapter.

4 Now connect the probes between the yellow/black and red/yellow terminals on the sensor. Slowly open the throttle from fully closed to fully open and back to fully closed. Check that the resistance increases as the throttle is opened and decreases as it is closed.

5 To check the input voltage to the sensor, connect the positive (+) lead of a voltmeter to the green/black wire terminal on the connector and the negative (–) lead to the yellow/black wire terminal. Turn the ignition switch ON and check that a voltage of 4.7 to 5.3 volts is present. If it isn't, there is a fault in the wiring or the ignition control unit.

6 If the throttle position sensor functions correctly then the fault must be in the wiring harness or the ignition control unit (ICU). Check the wiring between the TPS connector and the ICU connector for continuity, and check the connectors themselves for loose or broken terminals. If the wiring is good the ICU could be faulty (see Section 5).

Replacement

Note: *The sensor is not available separately from the carburettor bodies on XL600 and 650 models, and is only available as a unit with its mounting bracket on XRV750 models. Do not disturb it unnecessarily.*

7 Remove the carburettors (see Chapter 4). The throttle sensor is mounted on the right-hand end of the carburettor assembly **(see illustration)**.

8 Undo the three screws which retain the sensor mounting bracket to the carburettor body – do not disturb the screws which secure the sensor to its bracket.

9 Install the sensor, locating the tab on the throttle shaft in the cutouts on the inside of the sensor, and tighten the screws securely.

---

8 Immobiliser system (HISS) – XL650V models

General information

1 Honda's HISS (Honda Ignition Security System) immobiliser is fitted to XL650V models as an anti-theft device. The system will only allow the machine to be started if the correct registered key is used to turn the ignition ON. The system consists of a transponder which is part of the ignition key, a receiver which is fitted around the ignition switch, and the ignition control unit (ICU).

2 When the ignition is switched ON, the ICU sends power through the receiver to the transponder. The transponder sends a coded signal back through the receiver to the ICU. If the signal sent by the transponder matches the signal stored in the ICU memory, the immobiliser indicator light in the tachometer (marked by a key symbol) comes on for two seconds, then goes out, and the ICU allows the engine to be started. If the key code signal is not recognised, or if there is a fault in the system, the indicator light stays on. If the light stays on, refer to the fault diagnosis and troubleshooting Sections below. Likewise if the light does not come on at all.

3 The ICU can store the codes for up to four registered keys. They keys should be kept separately (i.e. not on the same key-ring) as the proximity of another key to the one being used in the switch can lead to the signal from it being jammed, and the bike will not start. The key has a built in transponder which can be damaged if the key is dropped or knocked, gets too hot, is too close to a magnetic object, or is submerged in water for too long. If all the keys are lost, the ICU must be replaced with a new one, so always make sure you have at least one spare key. If a new key is obtained, it must be registered into the system before the bike can be started.

Key registration procedure

To register a new key

Note: *To do this you will need the Honda special tools (Part Nos. 07XMZ-MBW0100, 07YMZ-MCB0100 or 07XMZ-MBW0101, and 07YMZ-0010100) which are a wiring loom and adapter that plug into the ignition pulse generator wiring connector. If this tool is not available, registration must be carried at a Honda dealer with the special tool.*

4 Obtain a new key from a Honda dealer, then have it cut to match the original key.

5 Remove the fuel tank (see Chapter 4), then disconnect the 2-pin ignition pulse generator wiring connector. Connect the special tool wiring connector to the ICU side of the connector, then connect the red coloured clip of the tool to the battery positive (+ve) terminal and the green coloured clip to the battery negative (-ve) terminal.

6 Turn the ignition switch ON using your original key. The immobiliser indicator light should come on and stay on (if it starts to flash after ten seconds, then there is a fault in the system, which will have gone into fault diagnosis mode, and the pattern of the

7.7 Throttle position sensor (arrowed)

flashes it emits should be matched with the fault code (see below)). Now disconnect the red clip from the battery positive terminal and leave it disconnected for at least two seconds, then reconnect it. The indicator should now come on for two seconds, then begin to flash repeatedly four times. This indicates that the system is in registration mode. At this point the registrations of all keys except the one in the switch will have been cancelled, so if you have another spare apart from the new one you want to register, this will also have to registered.

7 Turn the ignition OFF and remove the original key, placing it well away from the receiver.

8 Insert the new key into the switch and turn it ON. The indicator should now come on for two seconds, then begin to flash repeatedly four times. This indicates that the system has registered the new key. Turn the ignition OFF and remove the key.

9 To register any other spare keys that will have been cancelled, repeat Steps 7 and 8. Up to four keys can be registered.

10 On completion turn the ignition OFF, then remove the special tool and reconnect the ignition pulse generator wiring connector. Now turn the ignition ON using any of the registered keys to return the system to normal mode.

11 Check that all registered keys can start the motorcycle.

To register new keys with a new ignition switch

Note: *To do this you will need the Honda special tool (Part No. 07XMZ-MBW0100) which is a wiring loom adapter that plugs into the ignition pulse generator wiring connector. If this tool is not available, registration must be carried at a Honda dealer with the special tool.*

12 Obtain a new switch and two (or more if you want) new keys (which I presume come with the switch).

13 Remove the faulty switch (see Chapter 9), but retain the receiver to fit with the new switch.

14 Remove the fuel tank (see Chapter 4), then disconnect the 2-pin ignition pulse generator wiring connector. Connect the special tool wiring connector to the ICU side of the connector, then connect the red coloured clip of the tool to the battery positive (+) terminal and the green coloured clip to the battery negative (–) terminal.

15 Place one of the original registered keys for the faulty switch next to the receiver.

16 Connect the new ignition switch to its connector in the wiring loom, but keep it away from the receiver. Turn the new switch ON with one of the new keys. The immobiliser indicator light should come on and stay on, which means the ICU recognises the old key that is next to the receiver (if it starts to flash after ten seconds, then there is a fault in the system, which will have gone into fault diagnosis mode, and the pattern of the

5

flashes it emits should be matched with the fault code (see below). Now disconnect the red clip from the battery positive terminal and leave it disconnected for at least two seconds, then reconnect it. The indicator should now come on for two seconds, then begin to flash repeatedly four times. This indicates that the system is in registration mode. At this point the registrations of all keys except the one near the receiver will have been cancelled.

17 Turn the ignition OFF and remove the new key.

18 Install the new ignition switch, then fit the receiver onto it (see Chapter 9).

19 Insert the new key into the switch and turn it ON. The indicator should now come on for two seconds, then begin to flash repeatedly four times. This indicates that the system has registered the new key. Turn the ignition OFF and disconnect the red clip of the special tool from the battery positive terminal.

20 Turn the ignition ON using the newly registered key. The indicator light should come on for two seconds, then go off.

21 Turn the ignition OFF and reconnect the red clip to the battery positive terminal.

22 Turn the ignition ON using the newly registered key. The indicator light should come on and stay on. Now disconnect the red clip from the battery positive terminal and leave it disconnected for at least two seconds, then reconnect it. The indicator should now come on for two seconds, then begin to flash repeatedly four times. This indicates that the system is in registration mode. At this point the registrations of all old keys (for the faulty switch) are cancelled.

23 Turn the ignition OFF and remove the key, placing it well away from the receiver.

24 Insert the second new unregistered key and turn the ignition ON. The indicator should now come on for about two seconds, then begin to flash repeatedly four times. This indicates that the system has registered the second new key. Turn the ignition OFF and remove the key.

25 To register any other new spare keys, repeat Steps 23 and 24. Up to four keys can be registered.

26 On completion turn the ignition OFF, then remove the special tool and reconnect the ignition pulse generator wiring connector. Now turn the ignition ON using any of the registered keys to return the system to normal mode.

27 Check that all newly registered keys can start the motorcycle.

To register new keys with a new ICU

28 Obtain a new ICU along with two (or more if you want) new keys. Install the ICU (see Section 5). Have the keys cut to match the original key for your ignition switch.

29 Insert a new key into the switch and turn it ON. The indicator should now come on for two seconds, then begin to flash repeatedly four times. This indicates that the system has registered the new key. If the indicator stays on for ten seconds then starts to flash, then there is a fault in the system, which will have gone into fault diagnosis, and the pattern of the flashes it emits should be matched with the fault code (see below)).

30 Turn the ignition OFF and remove the key.

31 Insert the second new key and turn the ignition ON. The indicator should now come on for two seconds, then begin to flash repeatedly four times. This indicates that the system has registered the second new key.

32 Turn the ignition OFF and remove the key.

33 The new ICU will only register two new keys at this stage. If you have a third key that you want to register, refer to Steps 4 to 10 to register it, noting that you will need the special tool mentioned therein.

34 Check that both newly registered keys can start the motorcycle.

Fault diagnosis

Note: *To enter the fault diagnosis mode of the system you will need the Honda special tools (Part Nos. 07XMZ-MBW0100, 07YMZ-MCB0100 or 07XMZ-MBW0101, and 07YMZ-0010100) which are a wiring loom adapter that* plugs into the ignition pulse generator wiring connector. If this tool is not available, fault diagnosis must be carried at a Honda dealer with the special tool.

35 There are two fault diagnosis modes, one for if there is a fault during normal use, and one for a fault that occurs when registering a new key. Make sure you refer to the correct table below when matching the fault code pattern.

36 If the indicator light has come on and stayed on during normal use, remove the fuel tank (see Chapter 4). Disconnect the 2-pin ignition pulse generator wiring connector. Connect the special tool wiring connector to the ICU side of the connector, then connect the red coloured clip of the tool to the battery positive (+) terminal and the green coloured clip to the battery negative (–) terminal.

37 Turn the ignition switch ON. The indicator light in the tachometer will come on for ten seconds, then start to flash. This means it has entered diagnostic mode, and the pattern of the flashes indicates the fault that has occurred. The pattern repeats continuously. Match the pattern with the fault codes shown below, making sure you refer to the relevant table. If the indicator stays on after ten seconds and does not flash, then there is no fault logged in the system.

Troubleshooting procedure

Indicator light does not come on when ignition switched ON

38 Check the fuses (see Chapter 9).

39 If the fuses are good, check whether the neutral and oil pressure warning lights have come on.

40 If the lights have not come on, remove the fairing (see Chapter 8). Disconnect the instrument cluster wiring connectors. Using a voltmeter, connect the positive (+) probe to the black wire terminal on the loom side of the 6-pin connector and the negative (–) probe to the green wire terminal on the loom side of the 9-pin connector. With the ignition ON there should be battery voltage. If voltage is

Table 1: If fault is indicated during normal use

Flash pattern	Fault	Solution
Two short, one long, one short	Faulty ICU	Install new ICU
Two short, two long	Faulty receiver or wiring	Follow Troubleshooting procedure below
One long, three short	Signal jammed by other key	Place other key well away from receiver
One long, two short, one long	Signal jammed by other key	Place other key well away from receiver

Table 2: If fault is indicated during key registration

Flash pattern	Fault	Solution
One short, one long, one short, one long	Key already registered	Use a new or cancelled key
Two short, two long	Faulty receiver or wiring	Follow Troubleshooting procedure below
One short, one long, two short	Key already registered on old ICU	Use a new key

present, the indicator unit is faulty and must be replaced with a new one (see Chapter 9). If there is no voltage, check for continuity in the wiring, referring to the *Wiring Diagrams* at the end of Chapter 9. The green wire goes to earth (ground).

41 If the lights have come on, remove the left-hand side panel (see Chapter 8). Disconnect the ICU 22-pin wiring connector. Using a voltmeter, connect the positive (+ve) probe to the white/red wire terminal on the loom side of the indicator connector and the negative (-ve) probe to earth (ground). Turn the ignition ON – there should be battery voltage.

42 If there was no voltage, using a voltmeter, connect the positive (+) probe to the white/red wire terminal on the loom side of the indicator connector and the negative (–) probe to the green wire terminal on the loom side of the instrument cluster connector. Turn the ignition ON – there should be no voltage for two seconds, then there should be battery voltage. If there is no voltage after two seconds, check for continuity in the wiring, referring to the *Wiring Diagrams* at the end of Chapter 9. The green wire goes to earth (ground). If no voltage is present, the indicator unit is faulty and must be replaced with a new one (see Chapter 9). If there is voltage, check for continuity in the white/red wire between the indicator unit and the ICU.

43 If there is voltage in Step 41, disconnect the ICU wiring connector. Using a voltmeter, connect the positive (+) probe to the black/white wire terminal on the loom side of the ICU connector and the negative (–) probe to earth (ground). Turn the ignition ON – there should be battery voltage. If there is no voltage, check for continuity in the black/white wire, referring to the *Wiring Diagrams* at the end of Chapter 9. If voltage is present, check for continuity to earth (ground)

in the green wire. If the wiring is good, check the ICU connector for loose, damaged or corroded terminals. If the connector is good, then the ICU could be faulty, and should be checked by a Honda dealer.

Indicator light stays on when ignition switched ON

44 Check that none of the other registered keys are close to the receiver. If they are, remove them and try the ignition again.

45 Turn the ignition ON with a spare key and check the indicator light, which should come on for two seconds, then go out. If it does, the first key is faulty. If it doesn't, perform the fault diagnosis procedure described above. If a fault code is displayed, use the appropriate table to determine the fault and the solution.

46 If no fault code is displayed, or the system does not go into fault diagnosis mode, remove the seat (see Chapter 8). Disconnect the ICU 22-pin black wiring connector. Using a voltmeter, connect the positive (+) probe to the white/red wire terminal on the loom side of the indicator connector and the negative (–) probe to earth (ground). Turn the ignition ON – there should be battery voltage. If there is no voltage, check for continuity in the white/red wire between the ICU and the indicator unit.

47 If there is voltage, check for continuity in the yellow and white/yellow wires between the ICU and the ignition pulse generator, referring to the *Wiring Diagrams* at the end of Chapter 9. If there is no continuity, trace the fault and repair or replace the wiring as necessary. If there is continuity, the ICU could be faulty and should be taken to a Honda dealer for assessment.

Fault code indicated by flash pattern

48 If the 'two short, two long' flash pattern has been indicated during the fault diagnosis procedure, remove the fairing (see Chapter 8).

Trace the wiring from the receiver on the ignition switch and disconnect it at the connector. Using a voltmeter, connect the positive (+) probe to the yellow/red wire terminal on the loom side of the receiver connector and the negative (–) probe to earth (ground). Turn the ignition ON – there should be approximately 5 volts present. If there is no voltage, check for continuity in the yellow/red wire between the ICU and the receiver, and repair or replace the wiring if there is no continuity.

49 If there is 5 volts present, check for continuity to earth (ground) in the green/orange wire, and repair or replace the wiring if there is no continuity.

50 If the wiring is good, using a voltmeter, connect the positive (+) probe to the pink wire terminal on the loom side of the receiver connector and the negative (–) probe to earth (ground). Turn the ignition ON – there should be approximately 5 volts present. If there is, the receiver is faulty.

51 If there is no voltage, check for continuity in the orange/blue and pink wires between ICU and the receiver, and repair or replace the wiring if there is no continuity between the connectors, or if there is continuity in either to earth (ground). If the wiring is good, the receiver is faulty.

Replacement

52 To replace the receiver, remove the fairing (see Chapter 8). Trace the wiring from the receiver on the ignition switch and disconnect it at the connector. Undo the screws securing the receiver around the ignition switch and remove the receiver, noting how it fits. If you don't have the correct tools to easily access the screws, follow the procedure for removing the top yoke in the ignition switch replacement Section in Chapter 9.

53 To replace the ICU, see Section 5.

Chapter 6
Frame, suspension and final drive

Contents

Degrees of difficulty

Easy, suitable for novice with little experience	**Fairly easy,** suitable for beginner with some experience	**Fairly difficult,** suitable for competent DIY mechanic	**Difficult,** suitable for experienced DIY mechanic	**Very difficult,** suitable for expert DIY or professional

Specifications

Front forks

Fork oil type	5 W fork oil
Fork oil capacity	
XL600V models	549 cc
XL650V models	542 cc
XRV750-L to N (1990 to 1992) models	635 cc
XRV750-P models onward (1993-on)	648 cc
Fork oil level*	
XL600V models	125 mm
XL650V models	141 mm
XRV750-L to N (1990 to 1992) models	118 mm
XRV750-P models onward (1993-on)	106 mm
Fork air pressure – XRV750-L to S (1990 to 1995) models	0 to 5.7 psi (0 to 0.4 Bar)
Fork spring free length	
XL600V-H to R (1987 to 1995) models	
Standard	571.5 mm
Service limit	565.5 mm
XL600V-T to X (1996 to 1999) models	
Standard	612 mm
Service limit	605 mm
XL650V models	
Standard	599.4 mm
Service limit	589.2 mm
XRV750-L to N (1990 to 1992) models	
Upper spring	
Standard	52.2 to 55.2 mm
Service limit	49.6 mm
Lower spring	
Standard	575.7 to 578.7 mm
Service limit	546.9 mm

Front forks (continued)

Fork spring free length (continued)
  XRV750-P models onward (1993-on)
    Upper spring
      Standard .... 68.3 mm
      Service limit .... 66.9 mm
    Lower spring
      Standard .... 564.1 mm
      Service limit .... 552.8 mm
Fork tube runout limit .... 0.2 mm
Oil level is measured from the top of the tube with the fork spring removed and the leg fully compressed.

Rear shock absorber

Spring free length
  XL600V-H and J (1987 and 1988) models
    Standard .... 259.5 mm
    Service limit .... 256.5 mm
  XL600V-K to X (1989 to 1999) models
    Standard .... 268.5 mm
    Service limit .... 265.5 mm
  XL650V models .... Not available
  XRV750-L to N (1990 to 1992) models
    Standard .... 238.0 to 241.0 mm
    Service limit .... 233.0 mm
  XRV750-P models onwards (1993-on)
    Standard .... 245.5 mm
    Service limit .... 240.6 mm
Spring installed length
  XL600V-H and J (1987 and 1988) models
    Standard .... 254.8 mm
    Maximum .... 258.5 mm
    Minimum .... 249.8 mm
  XL600V-K to X (1989 to 1999) models
    Standard .... 262.9 mm
    Maximum .... 266.5 mm
    Minimum .... 257.8 mm
  XL650V models
    Standard .... 193.9 mm
    Maximum and minimum .... Not available
  XRV750-L to N (1990 to 1992) models
    Standard .... 230.5 mm
    Maximum .... 235.5 mm
    Minimum .... 222.5 mm
  XRV750-P models onward (1993-on)
    Standard .... 242.7 mm
    Maximum and minimum .... Not available

Rear suspension linkage – XL600V-H and J models

Suspension linkage arm bush ID
  Shock absorber pivot
    Standard .... 15.103 to 15.158 mm
    Service limit .... 15.188 mm
  Swingarm pivot
    Standard .... 18.099 to 18.159 mm
    Service limit .... 18.195 mm
  Linkage rod pivot
    Standard .... 15.103 to 15.158 mm
    Service limit .... 15.188 mm
Suspension linkage arm collar OD
  Shock absorber pivot
    Standard .... 15.040 to 15.055 mm
    Service limit .... 15.010 mm
  Swingarm pivot
    Standard .... 17.947 to 17.980 mm
    Service limit .... 17.911 mm
  Linkage rod pivot
    Standard .... 15.040 to 15.055 mm
    Service limit .... 15.010 mm

Rear suspension linkage – XL600V-H and J models (continued)

Suspension linkage rod bush ID at shock absorber pivot
   Standard . . . . 17.103 to 17.153 mm
   Service limit . . . . 17.187 mm
Suspension linkage rod collar OD at shock absorber pivot
   Standard . . . . 16.966 to 16.984 mm
   Service limit . . . . 16.932 mm

Final drive

Drive chain slack and lubricant . . . . see Chapter 1

Drive chain	Type	Length
XL600V-H to R (1987 to 1995) models	DID 525V8-LE or RK 525SMO-LE	118 links
XL600V-T to W (1996 to 1998) models	DID 525HV8 or RK 525SMOZ5	118 links
XL600V-X (1999) models	DID 525H-LJF4 or RK 525SMOZ5-JFZ	120 links
XL650V models	DID 525HV or RK 525ROZ1	110 links
XRV750-L to N (1990 to 1992) models	DID 525V8-LE or RK 525SMO-Z3XLE	124 links
XRV750-P to T (1993 to 1996) models	DID 525V8 or RK 525SMO-Z4	124 links
XRV750-V models onwards (1997-on)	DID 525V8 or RK 525SMO-Z5	124 links

Joining link pin projection from side plate (unstaked)
   DID type chain . . . . 1.15 to 1.55 mm
   RK type chain . . . . 1.20 to 1.40 mm
Joining link staked ends diameter
   DID type chain . . . . 5.50 to 5.80 mm
   RK type chain . . . . 5.55 to 5.85 mm
Sprocket sizes
   Front (engine) sprocket
      XL600V and XL650V models 15T
      XRV750 models 16T
   Rear (wheel) sprocket
      XL600V models 47T
      XL650V models 48T
      XRV750-L to N (1990 to 1992) models 46T
      XRV750-P models onward (1993-on) 45T

Torque settings

Front brake master cylinder clamp bolts . . . . 12 Nm
Front fork clamp bolts in bottom yoke . . . . 33 Nm
Front fork clamp bolts in top yoke . . . . 27 Nm
Front fork damper rod bolt . . . . 20 Nm
Front fork top bolt . . . . 23 Nm
Front sprocket retainer plate bolts . . . . 10 Nm
Handlebar holder clamp bolts . . . . 26 Nm
Rear sprocket nuts
   XL600V and XL650V models . . . . 45 Nm
   XRV750-L to N (1990 to 1992) models . . . . 46 Nm
   XRV750-P models onward (1993-on) . . . . 98 Nm
Shock absorber mounting bolt nuts . . . . 44 Nm
Sidestand pivot bolt . . . . 10 Nm
Sidestand pivot bolt nut
   XL600V and XRV750 models . . . . 40 Nm
   XL650V models . . . . 30 Nm
Steering head bearing adjuster nut (see text)
   XL600V-H and J (1987 and 1988) models . . . . 4 to 6 Nm
   XL600V-K to P (1989 to 1993) models . . . . 2.5 to 3.5 Nm
   XL600V-R to X (1994 to 1999) models . . . . 5 Nm
   XL650V models . . . . 5 Nm
   XRV750 models . . . . 11 Nm
Steering stem nut
   XL600V-H to P (1987 to 1993) models . . . . 100 Nm
   XL600V-R to X (1994 to 1999) models . . . . 105 Nm
   XL650V models . . . . 105 Nm
   XRV750-L to N (1990 to 1992) models . . . . 100 Nm
   XRV750-P models onward (1993-on) . . . . 128 Nm
Swingarm pivot bolt nut
   XL600V models . . . . 110 Nm
   XL650V models . . . . 90 Nm
   XRV750-L to N (1990 to 1992) models . . . . 110 Nm
   XRV750-P models onward (1993-on) . . . . 106 Nm

6

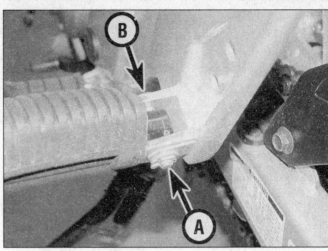

3.1a Remove the split pin and washer (A) and withdraw the pivot pin (B), noting the return spring ends (C) – front footrest, XL600V shown

3.1b Remove the split pin and washer (A) and withdraw the pivot pin (B) – rear footrest, XL650V shown

1 General information

All models have a box-section steel cradle frame.

Front suspension is by a pair of oil-damped telescopic forks, with air assistance on XRV750-L to S (1990 to 1995) models. The forks have a conventional type damper, and are not adjustable.

At the rear, a box-section aluminium swing-arm acts on a single shock absorber via a three-way linkage. The shock absorber is adjustable for spring pre-load on all models, and for compression damping on XL650V models.

The drive to the rear wheel is by chain and sprockets.

2 Frame – inspection and repair

1 The frame should not require attention unless accident damage has occurred. In most cases, frame replacement is the only satisfactory remedy for such damage. A few frame specialists have the jigs and other equipment necessary for straightening the frame to the required standard of accuracy, but even then there is no simple way of assessing to what extent the frame may have been over stressed.

2 After the machine has accumulated a lot of miles, the frame should be examined closely for signs of cracking or splitting at the welded joints. Loose engine mount bolts can cause ovaling or fracturing of the mounting tabs. Minor damage can often be repaired by welding, depending on the extent and nature of the damage.

3 Remember that a frame which is out of alignment will cause handling problems. If misalignment is suspected as the result of an accident, it will be necessary to strip the machine completely so the frame can be thoroughly checked.

3 Footrests, brake pedal and gearchange lever – removal and installation

Footrests

1 Remove the split pin and washer from the bottom of the footrest pivot pin, then withdraw the pivot pin and remove the foot-rest (see illustrations). On the front footrests, note the fitting of the return spring ends.

2 The footrest rubbers can be separated from the footrest and renewed if required.

3 Installation is the reverse of removal.

Brake pedal

Removal

4 Unhook the brake pedal return spring and the brake light switch spring from the hook on the pedal (see illustration).

5 Mark the alignment between the brake pedal arm on the inside and the pedal itself so it can be installed in the same position – there should be a punch mark on the pedal shaft which aligns with the slit in the arm, but it may be difficult to see. Unscrew the pinch bolt on the brake pedal arm on the inside of the frame (see illustration). If you can't access it because of its position, on XL600V-H to K (1987 to 1989) models fully unscrew the adjusting wingnut on the end of the brake rod, and on all other models remove the split pin from the clevis pin securing the brake pedal to the master cylinder pushrod, then remove the clevis pin and separate the pedal from the pushrod (see illustrations). Rotate the pedal until the bolt can be accessed (see

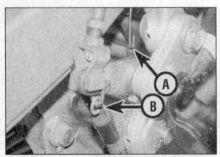

3.4 Unhook the brake light switch spring (A) and the pedal return spring (B) – XL600V shown

3.5a Brake pedal arm pinch bolt (arrowed) – XL650V

3.5b Remove the split pin . . .

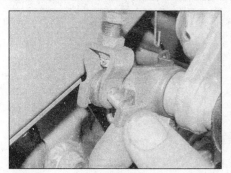

3.5c . . . and withdraw the clevis pin

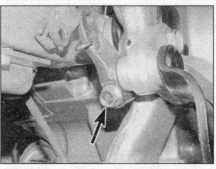

3.5d Brake pedal arm pinch bolt (arrowed) – XL600V

illustration). If access is still not possible (it varies between models), unscrew the footrest bracket bolts and displace the bracket.

6 Draw the pedal out of the arm and footrest bracket and remove the arm and pedal (see illustration 3.5). Depending on the height setting of the pedal, you may have to remove the footrest (see above) to prevent the pedal hitting it as you draw it out.

Installation

7 Installation is the reverse of removal, noting the following:
● Make sure the splines on the pedal shaft and those in the brake pedal arm are in good condition. If they are worn or damaged (i.e. flattened), there is a danger that the pedal could slip round in the arm, making the brake ineffective. Replace them with new ones if necessary, or if you are in doubt.
● Apply some grease to the brake pedal pivot. Make sure the pedal and arm are correctly aligned (see Step 5).
● Use a new split pin on the clevis pin securing the brake pedal to the master cylinder pushrod (see illustration 3.5b).
● Tighten the footrest bracket mounting bolts securely.
● Check the operation of the rear brake light switch (see Chapter 1).

Gearchange lever

8 Before removing the lever, note the alignment of the punch mark on the gearchange shaft end with either the punch mark on the lever or with the slit in the lever clamp (according to model) (see illustration). If no marks are visible make your own so that the lever can be installed in the correct position straight away.
9 Unscrew the pinch bolt and slide the lever off the shaft.
10 Installation is the reverse of removal.

4 Sidestand – removal and installation

Sidestand

1 The sidestand is attached to a bracket on the frame. Springs anchored between them ensure the stand is held in the retracted or extended position. Support the bike on the centrestand.
2 On models with a rotary type sidestand switch (i.e. XL600V-R to X, XL650V and XRV750-P onwards) displace the sidestand switch (see Chapter 9). There is no need to

disconnect its wiring connector or remove it completely, just let it hang from its wiring.
3 Unhook the stand springs. Unscrew the nut from the pivot bolt, then unscrew the bolt and remove the stand (see illustration).
4 On installation apply grease to the pivot bolt shank. Install the bolt and tighten it to the torque setting specified at the beginning of the Chapter securely, then install and tighten the nut to the specified torque (see illustration 4.3). Reconnect the springs and check that they hold the stand securely up when not in use – an accident is almost certain to occur if the stand extends while the machine is in motion.
5 Where applicable, install the sidestand switch. Check the operation of the switch (see Chapter 1).

Centrestand

Note: The centrestand is not standard equipment, but is available as an optional extra on certain models.

XRV750-L to N (1990 to 1992) models and XL600V-K to V-X (1988 to 1999) models

6 Support the motorcycle on its sidestand.
7 Disconnect the two return springs from their lug on the centrestand.
8 Straighten the split pin at the end of the centrestand pivot shaft, then pull the split pin out and remove the washer. Support the stand and withdraw its pivot shaft.
9 On installation, apply grease to the outside surface of the pivot shaft and the inside surfaces of the stand lugs and frame lugs. Fit the components in the reverse order of dismantling and fit a new split pin to secure the pivot shaft. Check that the return springs hold the stand fully retracted.

XRV750-P models onwards (1993-on)

10 Support the motorcycle on its sidestand.
11 Disconnect the two return springs from their lugs on the centrestand.

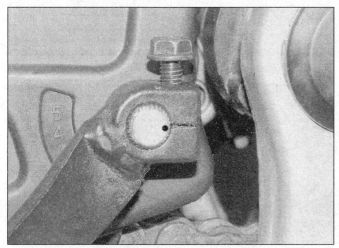

3.8 Note the alignment of the punch mark, then unscrew the bolt and remove the lever

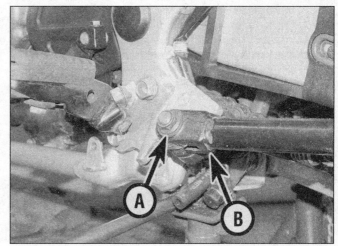

4.3 Unscrew the nut (A), then unscrew the pivot bolt (B)

12 Each pivot lug of the stand is secured to the frame by a short pivot sleeve; straighten and remove the split pins, remove the washers and withdraw the pivot sleeves to free the stand from the frame.

13 On installation, apply grease to the outside surfaces of the pivot sleeves and the inside surfaces of the stand lugs and frame lugs. Fit the components in the reverse order of dismantling and fit new split pins to secure the pivot sleeves. Check that the return springs hold the stand fully retracted.

5 Handlebars and levers –
removal and installation

Handlebars

Removal

Note: *The handlebars can be displaced from the top yoke without having to remove the individual assemblies from them – follow Steps 8 and 9 only.*

1 Remove the rear view mirrors (see Chapter 8).

2 Disconnect the wires from the brake light switch **(see illustration)**. Unscrew the two front brake master cylinder assembly clamp bolts and position the assembly clear of the handlebar, making sure no strain is placed on the hydraulic hose or pipe **(see illustration)**. Keep the master cylinder reservoir upright to prevent possible fluid leakage.

3 Disconnect the wires from the clutch switch

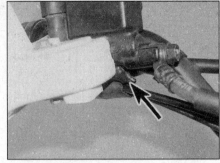

5.2a Disconnect the wiring connectors (arrowed)

5.2b Unscrew the master cylinder clamp bolts (arrowed) and displace the assembly

(see illustration). Unscrew the two clutch lever assembly clamp bolts and position it clear of the handlebar.

4 Unscrew the handlebar switch screws and free the switches from the handlebar **(see illustrations)**. Release the ties securing the wiring to the handlebars.

5 Refer to Chapter 4, Section 11, and detach the throttle cables from the twistgrip.

6 Unscrew the right handlebar end-weight retaining screw, then remove the weight from the end of the handlebar and slide the throttle twistgrip off the end. If required, unscrew the left handlebar end-weight retaining screw, then remove the weight from the end of the handlebar and slide off the grip. If the grip has been glued on, you will probably have to slit it with a knife to remove it.

7 If the handlebar holders are being removed from the top yoke, slacken the nuts securing them on the underside of the yoke now.

8 If the handlebars are just being displaced and the front brake master cylinder assembly is still attached, unscrew the bolt securing the brake hose clamp to the top yoke and the bolts securing the pipe clamps to the bottom yoke – this will allow more movement in the handlebars and prevent stress on the hose and pipes **(see illustration)**.

9 Unscrew the handlebar holder clamp bolts, and remove the clamps and the handlebars **(see illustrations)**.

10 If required, unscrew the nuts and remove the washers on the handlebar holders, then draw them out of the top yoke. Check the condition of the rubber bushes in the top yoke and replace them with new ones if they are damaged or deteriorated.

Installation

11 Installation is the reverse of removal, noting the following.

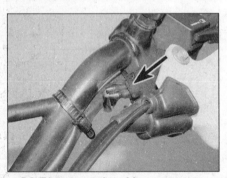

5.3 Disconnect the wiring connectors (arrowed)

5.4a Right-hand switch screws (arrowed)

5.4b . . . and left-hand switch screws (arrowed)

5.8 Unscrew the bolt (arrowed) and displace the brake pipe holder from the top yoke

5.9a Unscrew the holder bolts (arrowed) . . .

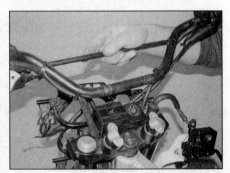

5.9b . . . and remove the handlebars

5.11a Align the punch mark (arrowed) with the clamp mating surfaces

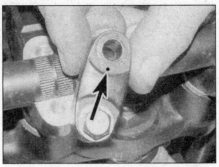

5.11b Fit the holder with its punch mark (arrowed) at the front

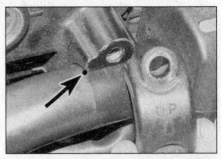

5.11c Align the punch mark (arrowed) with the clamp mating surfaces, and fit the clamp with the UP mark facing up

● If removed, tighten the handlebar holder nuts after the handlebars are installed.
● Align the punch mark on the back of the handlebar with the mating surfaces of the left handlebar holder and clamp (see illustration). Fit the handlebar clamps with the punch mark at the front, and tighten the front clamp bolts first, then the rear, to the specified torque setting (see illustration).
● Apply some grease to the throttle twistgrip section of the handlebar.
● Make sure the front brake master cylinder assembly clamp is installed with the UP mark facing up, and with the clamp mating surfaces aligned with the punch mark on the top of the handlebar (see illustration). Tighten the master cylinder clamp bolts to the specified torque setting, tightening the top bolt first.
● Align the clutch lever assembly clamp mating surfaces with the punch mark on the back of the handlebar, and tighten the front bolt before the rear bolt.
● Make sure the pin in the lower half of each switch housing locates in its hole in the handlebar. Tighten the front housing screw first, then the rear.
● Align the throttle cable housing half mating surfaces with the punch mark on the handlebar.
● When installing the handlebar end-weights, align the boss with the groove on the inner weight inside the handlebar. Use some non-permanent thread locking compound on the screws. If new grips are being fitted, secure them using a suitable adhesive.
● Check the throttle cable adjustment as described in Chapter 1.
● Do not forget to reconnect the front brake light switch and clutch switch wiring connectors.

Handlebar levers

Front brake lever

12 Unscrew the nut and remove the collar on the underside of the handguard (see illustration). Unscrew the pivot bolt and remove the handguard, then remove the lever (see illustrations).
13 Installation is the reverse of removal. Apply grease to the pivot bolt shaft and the contact areas between the lever and its bracket.

Clutch lever

14 Pull the rubber boot off the clutch cable

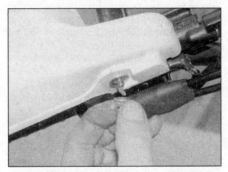

5.12a Unscrew the nut and remove the collar

adjuster. Slacken the adjuster lockring and thread the adjuster fully into the bracket to provide maximum freeplay in the cable (see illustration).
15 Unscrew the bolt and remove the collar

5.12c . . . and the lever

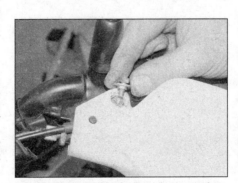

5.15a Unscrew the bolt and remove the collar

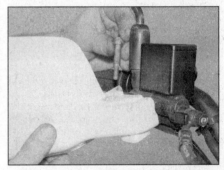

5.12b Unscrew the pivot bolt and remove the handguard . . .

from the hand guard (see illustration). Counter-hold the screwhead and undo the nut on its bottom (see illustration). Remove the handguard (see illustration).
16 Unscrew the pivot bolt and washer and

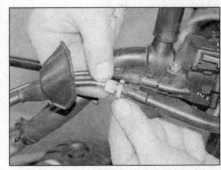

5.14 Pull back the boot, then slacken the lockring and thread the adjuster in

5.15b Counter-hold the screwhead and undo the nut on the bottom . . .

6

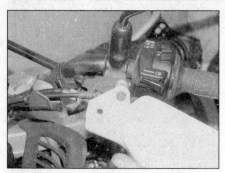

5.15c ... and remove the handguard

5.16 Undo the screw (arrowed), lift off the choke lever, slide out the clutch lever and detach the cable

Slackening the fork clamp bolts in the top yoke before slackening the fork top bolts releases pressure on the top bolt. This makes it much easier to remove and helps to preserve the threads.

remove the choke lever and the clutch lever, detaching the cable nipples as you do so (see illustration). Note the wave washer between the choke lever and the lever plate. Remove the plate from the lever bracket if required, noting how it fits.

17 Installation is the reverse of removal. Apply grease to the pivot bolt shaft and the contact areas between the lever and its bracket, and to the cable nipples. Adjust the clutch cable freeplay (see Chapter 1).

6 Forks –
removal and installation

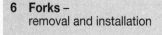

Removal

Caution: Although not strictly necessary, before removing the forks it is

recommended that the fairing and fairing panels are removed (see Chapter 8). This will prevent accidental damage to the paintwork.

1 Remove the front mudguard (see Chapter 8).
2 Remove the front wheel (see Chapter 7). Tie the front brake calipers and hoses back so that they are out of the way.
3 Release the speedometer cable and any wiring from the fork, noting its routing.
4 Working on one fork at a time, slacken the fork clamp bolts in the top yoke (see illustration). If the fork is to be disassembled, or if the fork oil is being changed, it is advisable to slacken the fork top bolt at this stage (see illustration). On XRV750-L to S (1990 to 1995) models, first remove the air valve cap, then depress the valve to release any air under pressure. Note the amount of protrusion of the fork above the top yoke.

5 Slacken the fork clamp bolts in the bottom yoke, and remove the fork by twisting it and pulling it downwards (see illustrations).

If the fork legs are seized in the yokes, spray the area with penetrating oil and allow time for it to soak in before trying again.

Installation

6 Remove all traces of corrosion from the fork tube and the yokes. Slide the fork up through the bottom yoke and into the top yoke, making sure it passes through the cable tie(s) and all cables, hoses and wiring are routed on the correct side of the fork (see illustration 6.5b).
7 Set the top of the fork tube (not the top of the fork top bolt) flush with the top surface of the top yoke (see illustration). Make sure it is the same on both sides.
8 Tighten the fork clamp bolts in the bottom yoke to the torque setting specified at the beginning of the Chapter (see illustration 6.5a). If the fork has been dismantled or if the fork oil was changed, tighten the fork top bolt to the specified torque setting (see illustration). Now

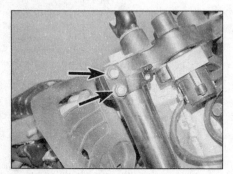

6.4a Slacken the fork clamp bolts (arrowed) in the top yoke ...

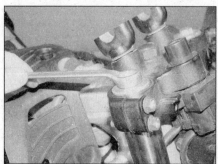

6.4b ... and if required the fork top bolt

6.5a Bottom yoke fork clamp bolts (arrowed)

6.5b Draw the fork down and out of the yokes

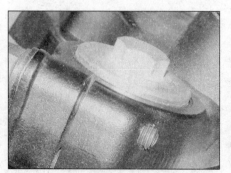

6.7 Set the fork height as shown, making sure it is the same on both sides

6.8 Tighten the fork top bolt to the specified torque setting

6.9 Push the gaiter up against the yoke and tighten the clamp screw (arrowed)

tighten the fork clamp bolts in the top yoke to the specified torque **(see illustration 6.4a)**.

9 If the forks were disassembled, push the gaiter up the fork tube until contacts the underside of the bottom yoke, then tighten its clamp screw **(see illustration)**.

10 Install the front wheel (see Chapter 7), and the front mudguard (see Chapter 8). Make sure the speedometer cable is properly routed and secure in it s guides.

11 Check the operation of the front forks and brakes before taking the machine out on the road.

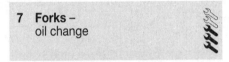

7 Forks –
oil change

XL600V-H to V-R (1987 to 1995) and XRV750-L to S (1990 to 1995) models

Note: The forks fitted to early models are equipped with an oil drain bolt at the lower rear face of each fork slider, enabling the oil to be changed without removing the forks from the motorcycle.

1 Position a container below each fork leg drain bolt and have ready a piece of card or similar to direct oil away from the tyre during draining. Remove the drain bolt from the fork slider and, with the bike off its stand, pump the forks to expel the fork oil into the container.

2 On completion of draining, refit the drain bolts with their sealing washers, and tighten them securely. Renew the washers if necessary.

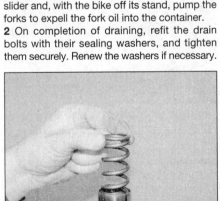

7.12 Remove the spring

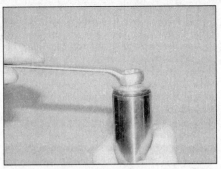

7.10 Thread the top bolt out of the tube

3 Displace the handlebars from the top yoke as described in Section 5. Unscrew the top bolt from the top of each fork **(see illustration 7.10)**.

⚠ *Warning: The fork spring is pressing on the fork top bolt with considerable pressure. Unscrew the bolt very carefully, keeping a downward pressure on it and release it slowly as it is likely to spring clear. It is advisable to wear some form of eye and face protection when carrying out this operation.*

4 On XL600 models, withdraw the spacer, spring seat and the spring from the tube. On XRV750 models, withdraw the upper spring, spring seat and lower spring from the tube. Note which way up the spring fits.

5 Working on one fork at a time, slowly pour in the specified quantity of the specified grade of fork oil and pump the fork at least ten times to distribute it evenly **(see illustration 7.14)**. When both forks have been filled, fully compress the front end so that the fork tubes are fully compressed into the sliders, then measure the oil level. Check that the level is the same in each fork and that it is as specified at the beginning of the Chapter.

6 Extend the forks, then install the spring with its closer-spaced coils at the bottom. On XL600 models now install the spring seat and the spacer. On XRV750 models install the spring seat and the upper spring.

7 Fit a new O-ring to each fork top bolt and thread the bolts into the top of the fork tubes **(see illustration 7.16)**. Screw each top bolt carefully into its fork tube making sure it is not cross-threaded, then tighten it to the specified torque setting.

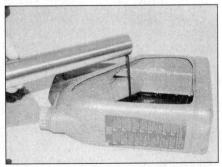

7.13 Invert the fork over a container and pump the tube to expel the oil

⚠ *Warning: It will be necessary to compress the spring by pressing it down using the top bolt to engage the threads of the top bolt with the fork tube. This is a potentially dangerous operation and should be performed with care, using an assistant if necessary. Wipe off any excess oil before starting to prevent the possibility of slipping.*

8 Install the handlebars (see Section 5).

XL600V-T models onward (1996-on), XL650V models and XRV750-T (1996-on) models onward

9 Remove the forks (see Section 6). Always work on the fork legs separately to avoid interchanging parts and thus causing an accelerated rate of wear **(see illustration 8.1a or b)**.

10 If the fork top bolt was not slackened with the fork in situ, carefully clamp the fork tube in a vice equipped with soft jaws, taking care not to overtighten or score its surface, and slacken the top bolt **(see illustration)**.

11 Unscrew the fork top bolt from the top of the fork tube.

⚠ *Warning: The fork spring is pressing on the fork top bolt with considerable pressure. Unscrew the bolt very carefully, keeping a downward pressure on it and release it slowly as it is likely to spring clear. It is advisable to wear some form of eye and face protection when carrying out this operation.*

12 Slide the fork tube down into the slider. On XL600 and 650 models, withdraw the spring from the tube **(see illustration)**. On XRV750 models, withdraw the upper spring, spring seat and lower spring from the tube. Note which way up the spring fits.

13 Invert the fork over a suitable container and pump the fork tube vigorously to expel as much oil as possible **(see illustration)**. Support the fork upside down in the container for a while to allow as much oil as possible to drain, and pump the fork again.

14 Slowly pour in the specified quantity of the specified grade of fork oil and pump the fork at least ten times to distribute it evenly **(see illustration)**. Fully compress the fork tube into the slider and measure the oil level, and make any adjustment by adding more or

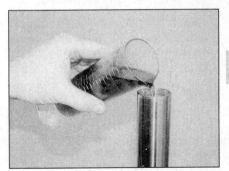

7.14 Pour the oil into the top of the tube

6

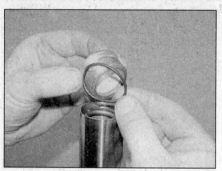

7.16 Fit the top bolt using a new O-ring

tipping some out until the oil is at the level specified at the beginning of the Chapter.

15 Clamp the slider in a soft-jawed vice using the brake caliper mounting lugs, taking care not to overtighten and damage them. Pull the fork tube out of the slider as far as possible then install the spring with its closer-spaced coils at the bottom **(see illustration 7.12)**. On XRV750 models, now install the spring seat and the upper spring.

16 Fit a new O-ring to the fork top bolt and thread the bolt into the top of the fork tube **(see illustration)**.

 Warning: It will be necessary to compress the spring by pressing it down using the top bolt to engage the threads of the top bolt with the fork tube. This is a potentially dangerous operation and should be performed with care, using an assistant if necessary. Wipe off any excess oil before starting to prevent the possibility of slipping.

Keep the fork tube fully extended whilst pressing on the spring. Screw the top bolt carefully into the fork tube making sure it is not cross-threaded. **Note:** *The top bolt can be tightened to the specified torque setting at this stage if the tube is held between the padded jaws of a vice, but do not risk distorting the tube by doing so. A better method is to tighten the top bolt when the fork has been installed in the bike and is securely held in the bottom yoke (see illustration 6.8).*

TOOL TiP *Use a ratchet-type tool when installing the fork top bolt. This makes it unnecessary to remove the tool from the bolt whilst threading it in making it easier to maintain a downward pressure on the spring.*

9 Install the forks (see Section 6).

8 Forks –
disassembly, inspection and reassembly

Disassembly

1 Remove the forks (see Section 6). Always dismantle the fork legs separately to avoid interchanging parts and thus causing an accelerated rate of wear. Store all components in separate, clearly marked containers **(see illustrations)**.

2 Slacken the gaiter clamp screw(s) and slide the gaiter off the top of the fork, noting how its bottom end locates around the top of the fork slider **(see illustration)**.

3 Before dismantling the fork, it is advisable to slacken the damper rod bolt now as there is less chance of the damper rotating with it (due to the pressure of the spring). Compress the fork tube in the slider so that the spring exerts maximum pressure on the damper head, then have an assistant slacken the bolt in the base of the fork slider **(see illustration)**.

4 If the fork top bolt was not slackened with the fork in situ, carefully clamp the fork tube in

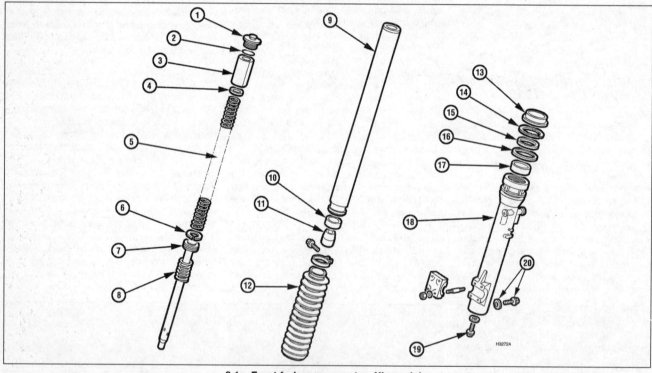

8.1a Front fork components – XL models

1 Top bolt	*7 Damper rod*	*15 Oil seal*
2 O-ring	*8 Rebound spring*	*16 Washer*
3 Spacer – H to R (1987 to 1995) models	*9 Fork tube*	*17 Top bush*
4 Spring seat – H to R (1987 to 1995) models	*10 Bottom bush*	*18 Slider*
	11 Damper rod seat	*19 Damper rod bolt and sealing washer*
5 Spring	*12 Gaiter*	*20 Oil drain bolt and sealing washer – H to R (1987 to 1995) models*
6 Piston ring	*13 Dust seal*	
	14 Retaining clip	

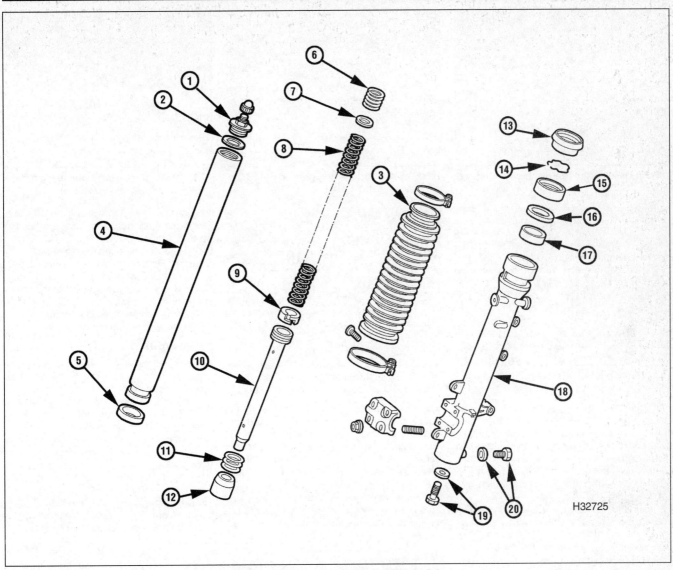

8.1b Front fork components – XRV models

1	Top bolt	7	Spring seat
2	O-ring	8	Lower spring
3	Gaiter	9	Piston ring
4	Fork tube	10	Damper rod
5	Bottom bush	11	Rebound spring
6	Upper spring	12	Damper rod seat

13	Dust seal
14	Retaining clip
15	Oil seal
16	Washer
17	Top bush
18	Slider

19 Damper rod bolt and
    sealing washer
20 Oil drain bolt and sealing
    washer – L to S
    (1990 to 1995) models

a vice equipped with soft jaws, taking care not to overtighten or score its surface, and slacken the top bolt **(see illustration 7.10)**.
5 Unscrew the fork top bolt from the top of the fork tube.

⚠ *Warning: The fork spring is pressing on the fork top bolt with considerable pressure. Unscrew the bolt very carefully, keeping a downward pressure on it and release it slowly as it is likely to spring clear. It is advisable to wear some form of eye and face protection when carrying out this operation.*

6 Slide the fork tube down into the slider. On XL600V-H to R (1987 to 1995) models,

8.2 Remove the gaiter

8.3 Slacken the damper rod bolt

6

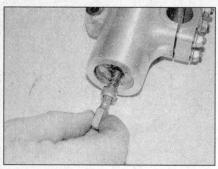

8.8a Unscrew and remove the damper rod bolt . . .

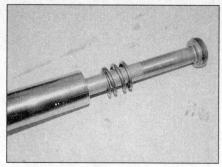

8.8b . . . then tip the damper rod out of the fork

8.9 Prise out the dust seal using a flat bladed screwdriver

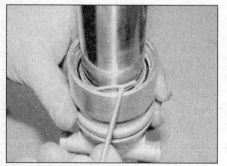

8.10 Prise out the retaining clip using a flat bladed screwdriver

8.11a To separate the fork tube from the slider, pull them apart firmly several times . . .

12 With the tube removed, slide off the oil seal, washer and top bush, noting which way up they fit **(see illustration 8.11b)**. Discard the oil seal as a new one must be used. **Caution: Do not remove the bottom bush from the tube unless it is to be replaced.**

13 Tip the damper rod seat out of the slider – you may have to push it from the bottom via the damper bolt hole **(see illustration)**. Discard the O-ring as a new one must be used.

Inspection

14 Clean all parts in solvent and blow them dry with compressed air, if available. Check the fork tube for score marks, scratches, flaking of the chrome finish and excessive or abnormal wear. Look for dents in the tube and replace the tube in both forks if any are found. Check the fork seal seat for nicks, gouges and scratches. If damage is evident, leaks will occur. Also check the oil seal washer for damage or distortion and replace it if necessary.

15 Check the fork tube for runout using V-blocks and a dial gauge. If the amount of runout exceeds the service limit specified, the tube should be replaced.

⚠ *Warning: If the tube is bent or exceeds the runout limit, it should not be straightened; replace it with a new one.*

16 Check the springs (the main spring, the rebound spring on the damper rod, and on XRV750 the upper spring) for cracks and other damage **(see illustration)**. Measure the main spring free length and compare the measure-

withdraw the spacer, spring seat and the spring from the tube. On XL600V-T to X (1996 to 1999) models and XL650V models, withdraw the spring from the tube **(see illustration 7.12)**. On XRV750 models, withdraw the upper spring, spring seat and lower spring from the tube. Note which way up the spring fits.

7 Invert the fork over a suitable container and pump the fork tube vigorously to expel as much oil as possible **(see illustration 7.13)**. Support the fork upside down in the container for a while to allow as much oil as possible to drain, and pump the fork again.

8 Remove the previously slackened damper rod bolt and its copper sealing washer from the bottom of the slider **(see illustration)**. Discard the sealing washer as a new one must be used on reassembly. Invert the fork and tip the damper rod out of the top of the tube.

9 Carefully prise out the dust seal from the

top of the slider to gain access to the oil seal retaining clip **(see illustration)**. Discard the dust seal as a new one must be used.

10 Carefully remove the retaining clip, taking care not to scratch the surface of the tube **(see illustration)**. It is advisable to compress the fork beforehand because then any accidental damage to the tube will be away from its main point of contact with the seal.

11 To separate the tube from the slider it is necessary to displace the oil seal and top bush. The bottom bush does not pass through the top bush, and this can be used to good effect. Push the tube gently inwards until it stops against the damper seat. Take care not to do this forcibly or the seat may be damaged. Now pull the tube sharply outwards until the bottom bush strikes the top bush **(see illustration)**. Repeat this operation until the top bush and seal are tapped out of the slider **(see illustration)**.

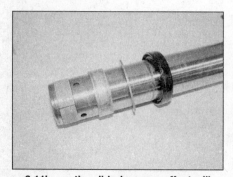

8.11b . . . the slide-hammer effect will displace the oil seal and bush

8.13 Remove the damper rod seat from the slider

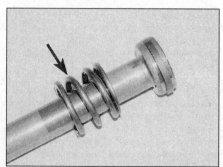

8.16 Check the compression spring(s) and rebound spring (arrowed)

8.17a This bush is worn

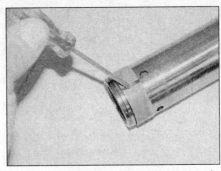

8.17b Carefully lever the ends apart and slide the bush off

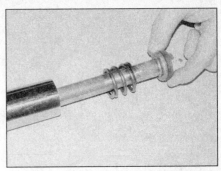

8.19a Slide the damper rod into the tube . . .

ment to the Specifications at the beginning of the Chapter. If it is defective or sagged below the service limit, replace the main springs in both forks with new ones. Never replace only one spring.

17 Examine the working surfaces of the two bushes; if worn or scuffed they must be replaced with new ones – they are worn if the grey Teflon coating has rubbed off to reveal the copper surface (see illustration). To remove the bottom bush from the fork tube, prise it apart at the slit using a flat-bladed screwdriver and slide it off. Make sure the new one seats properly (see illustration).

18 Check the damper rod and its piston ring for damage and wear, and replace them with new ones if necessary (see illustration 8.16). Do not remove the ring from the top of the rod unless it is being renewed.

Reassembly

19 If removed, fit the piston ring into the groove in the damper rod head, then slide the rebound spring onto the rod (see illustration 8.16). Insert the damper rod into the fork tube and slide it into place so that it projects fully from the bottom of the tube (see illustration). Fit the seat onto the bottom of the damper, then push the seat and rod up into the tube (see illustrations).

20 Oil the fork tube and bottom bush with the specified fork oil and insert the assembly into the slider (see illustration). Fit a new copper sealing washer onto the damper rod bolt and apply a few drops of a suitable non-permanent thread locking compound, then install the bolt into the bottom of the slider (see illustration). Tighten the bolt to the

specified torque setting (see illustration). If the damper rod rotates inside the tube, temporarily install the fork spring(s), spacer where fitted, and top bolt (see Steps 27 and 28) and compress the fork to hold the damper rod. Alternatively, a long metal bar or length of wood doweling (such as a broom handle) pressed hard into the damper rod head quite often suffices. Otherwise, wait until the fork is fully reassembled before tightening the bolt.

21 Push the fork tube fully into the slider, then oil the top bush and slide it down over the tube (see illustration). Press the bush squarely into its recess in the slider as far as possible, then install the oil seal washer with its flat side facing up (see illustration). Use either the Honda service tool (Pt. Nos. 07947-KA50100 and 07947-KF00100 (XL models) or 07947-KA40200 (XRV models)) or a suitable

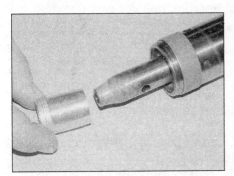

8.19b . . . so that it projects from the bottom, then fit the seat . . .

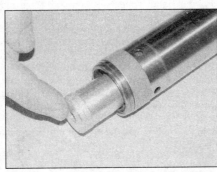

8.19c . . . and push the assembly into the tube

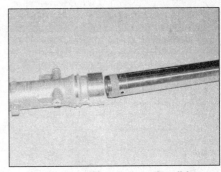

8.20a Slide the tube into the slider

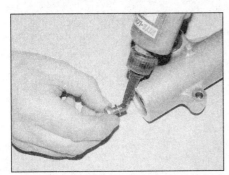

8.20b . . . then fit the bolt using threadlock and a new sealing washer . . .

8.20c . . . and tighten it to the specified torque

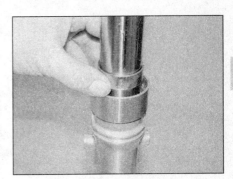

8.21a Install the top bush . . .

6

8.21b . . . followed by the washer

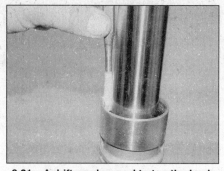

8.21c A drift can be used to tap the bush into place

8.23 Smear the oil seal with clean fork oil then slide it down the tube. Press it into the top of the slider with your fingers, then drive it in as described

piece of tubing to tap the bush fully into place; the tubing must be slightly larger in diameter than the fork tube and slightly smaller in diameter than the bush recess in the slider. Take care not to scratch the fork tube during this operation; wind insulating tape around the exposed length of tube, and push the tube fully into the slider so that any accidental scratching is confined to the area which is normally above the oil seal. A drift or punch can be used, but this does not help the bush enter squarely, and the angle narrows as the bush gets deeper and makes it more difficult to make a good contact with a hammer **(see illustration)**. If using a drift or punch, wrap tape around it to prevent it scratching the tube.

HAYNES HINT | *If a new bush is being installed, place the old bush on top of the new one to protect it when driving it into place.*

22 Remove the washer to check the bush is seated fully and squarely in its recess in the slider, then wipe the recess clean. Refit the washer.
23 Smear the seal's lips with fork oil and slide it over the tube so that its markings face

upwards **(see illustration)**. Press the seal into the slider, then drive it fully into place as described in Step 21 until the retaining clip groove is visible above it **(see illustration)**.

HAYNES HINT | *Place the old oil seal on top of the new one to protect it when driving it into place.*

24 Once the seal is correctly seated, fit the retaining clip, making sure it is correctly located in its groove **(see illustration)**.
25 Lubricate the lips of the new dust seal then slide it down the fork tube and press it into position **(see illustration)**.
26 Slowly pour in the specified quantity of the specified grade of fork oil and pump the fork at least ten times to distribute it evenly **(see illustration 7.14)**. Fully compress the fork tube and damper rod into the slider and measure the oil level, and make any adjustment by adding more or tipping some out until it is at the level specified at the beginning of the Chapter.
27 Clamp the slider in a soft-jawed vice using the brake caliper mounting lugs, taking care not to overtighten and damage them. Pull the fork tube out of the slider as far as possible

then install the spring with its closer-spaced coils at the bottom **(see illustration 7.12)**. On XL600V-H to R (1987 to 1995) models, now install the spring seat and the spacer. On XRV750 models, now install the spring seat and the upper spring.
28 Fit a new O-ring to the fork top bolt and thread the bolt into the top of the fork tube **(see illustration 7.16)**.

⚠ *Warning: It will be necessary to compress the spring by pressing it down using the top bolt to engage the threads of the top bolt with the fork tube. This is a potentially dangerous operation and should be performed with care, using an assistant if necessary. Wipe off any excess oil before starting to prevent the possibility of slipping.*

Keep the fork tube fully extended whilst pressing on the spring. Screw the top bolt carefully into the fork tube making sure it is not cross-threaded. **Note:** *The top bolt can be tightened to the specified torque setting at this stage if the tube is held between the padded jaws of a vice, but do not risk distorting the tube by doing so. A better method is to tighten the top bolt when the fork*

8.24 Install the retaining clip . . .

8.25 . . . followed by the dust seal

has been installed in the bike and is securely held in the bottom yoke.

> **HAYNES HINT** *Use a ratchet-type tool when installing the fork top bolt. This makes it unnecessary to remove the tool from the bolt whilst threading it in making it easier to maintain a downward pressure on the spring.*

29 If the damper rod bolt requires tightening (see Step 20), clamp the fork slider between the padded jaws of a vice and have an assistant compress the tube into the slider so that maximum spring pressure is placed on the damper rod head – tighten the damper rod bolt to the specified torque setting.
30 Fit the gaiter onto the fork, locating its bottom rim onto the top of the fork slider **(see illustration)**. Rotate the gaiter so that the breather holes are facing the back of the fork **(see illustration)**. On XRV750 models tighten the lower clamp.
31 Install the forks (see Section 6).

9 Steering stem – removal and installation

Removal

1 Remove the fuel tank (see Chapter 4). On XL600V and XRV750 models remove the

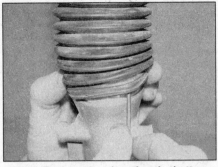
8.30a Fit the gaiter, locating the bottom onto the top of the slider . . .

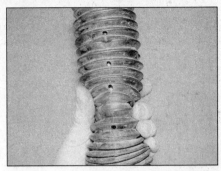
8.30b . . . and making sure the breather holes face the back

fairing side panels, and on XL650V models remove the fairing (see Chapter 8). This will prevent the possibility of damage should a tool slip. Also remove the front forks (see Section 6) and displace the handlebars (see Section 5). Note how the brake pipe arrangement routes round the back of the right-hand fork. If required as a precaution, you can unscrew the brake master cylinder assembly clamp bolts and detach it from the handlebars, then remove the entire front brake system from the bike. Unscrew the bolts securing the shield to the bottom yoke and remove it, noting how it fits.
2 If the top yoke is being removed from the bike rather than just being displaced, trace the wiring from the ignition switch, and where fitted the HISS immobiliser receiver, and disconnect it/them at the connector(s).
3 Unscrew the steering stem nut and remove the washer **(see illustration)**. Lift the top yoke

up off the steering stem and position it clear, using a rag to protect the tank or other components if it is only being displaced **(see illustration)**.
4 Supporting the bottom yoke, unscrew the adjuster nut using either a C-spanner, a peg-spanner or socket, or a drift located in one of the notches **(see illustration)**. Remove the adjuster nut and the grease seal from the steering stem **(see illustration)**. Check the condition of the grease seal and discard it if it is damaged.
5 Gently lower the bottom yoke and steering stem out of the frame **(see illustration)**. Take care not to strain or knock the brake hoses.
6 Remove the inner race and bearing from the top of the steering head **(see illustrations)**. Remove the bearing from the base of the steering stem **(see illustration)**. Remove all traces of old grease from the bearings and races and check them for wear

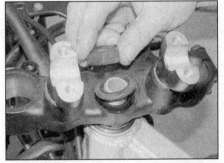
9.3a Unscrew the nut and remove the washer . . .

9.3b . . . and lift off the top yoke

9.4a Unscrew and remove the adjuster nut . . .

9.4b . . . and the grease seal

9.5 Draw the bottom yoke/steering stem out of the steering head

9.6a Remove the inner race . . .

6

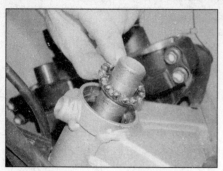

9.6b . . . and the upper bearing

9.6c Remove the lower bearing from the steering stem

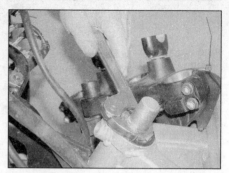

9.10 Tighten the adjuster nut as described

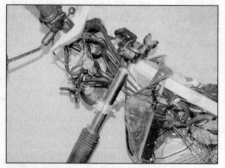

9.11a Slide the left-hand fork up through the yokes . . .

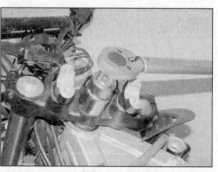

9.11b . . . and tighten the steering stem nut to the specified torque

or damage as described in Section 10. **Note:** *Do not attempt to remove the races from the steering head or the steering stem unless they are to be replaced with new ones.*

Installation

7 Smear a liberal quantity of multi-purpose grease onto the bearing races, and work some grease well into both the upper and lower bearings. Also smear the grease seal lip, using a new seal if necessary. Fit the lower bearing onto the steering stem **(see illustration 9.6c)**.

8 Carefully lift the steering stem/bottom yoke up through the steering head **(see illustration 9.5)**. Fit the upper bearing and its inner race into the top of the steering head **(see illustrations 9.6b and a)**. Fit install the grease seal **(see illustration 9.4b)**. Apply some clean engine oil to the adjuster nut and thread the nut on the steering stem **(see illustration 9.4a)**.

9 If the correct tools are available, tighten the adjuster nut to the torque setting specified at the beginning of the Chapter, then turn the steering stem through its full lock at least five times and re-tighten the adjuster nut to the specified setting. Ensure that the steering stem is able to move freely from lock to lock following adjustment – if necessary reset the bearing adjustment as described in Chapter 1.

10 If the correct tools are not available, tighten the nut using a C-spanner or drift so that bearing play is eliminated, but the steering stem is able to move freely from lock to lock – refer to the procedure in Chapter 1

for details, but note that setting the bearings is a lot easier and more accurate after the forks and wheel are installed as their leverage and inertia need to be taken into account **(see illustration)**. To do it that way, make sure the nut is tight enough to hold the steering stem in the head without any play, then install the forks and wheel, then refer to the procedure in Chapter 1.

Caution: Take great care not to apply excessive pressure because this will cause premature failure of the bearings.

11 When the bearings are correctly adjusted, fit the top yoke onto the steering stem **(see illustration 9.3b)**, then install the washer and the steering stem nut and tighten it finger-tight **(see illustration 9.3a)**. Temporarily install the left-hand fork to align the top and bottom yokes, and secure it by tightening the bottom yoke clamp bolt only **(see illustration)**. Now tighten the steering stem nut to the torque

10.4a Drive the bearing races out with a brass drift . . .

setting specified at the beginning of the Chapter **(see illustration)**.

12 Install the remaining components in a reverse of the removal procedure, referring to the relevant Sections or Chapters, and to the torque settings specified at the beginning of the Chapter. Note that you must install the handlebars and secure the brake hose and pipe clamp bolts on the yokes before installing the forks – if the forks are installed first it is impossible to route the brake pipes around them.

13 Carry out a check of the steering head bearing freeplay as described in Chapter 1, and if necessary re-adjust.

10 Steering head bearings – inspection and replacement

Inspection

1 Remove the steering stem (see Section 9).
2 Remove all traces of old grease from the bearings and races and check them for wear or damage.
3 The outer races should be polished and free from indentations. Inspect the bearing rollers (early models) or balls (later models) for signs of wear, damage or discoloration, and examine their retaining cage for signs of cracks or splits. If there are any signs of wear on any of the above components both upper and lower bearing assemblies must be renewed as a set. Only remove the outer races in the steering head and the lower bearing inner race on the steering stem if they need to be renewed – do not re-use them once they have been removed.

Replacement

4 The outer races are an interference fit in the steering head and can be tapped from position with a suitable drift **(see illustrations)**. Tap firmly and evenly around each race to ensure that it is driven out squarely. It may prove advantageous to curve the end of the drift slightly to improve access.
5 Alternatively, the races can be removed using a slide-hammer type bearing extractor; these can often be hired from tool shops.

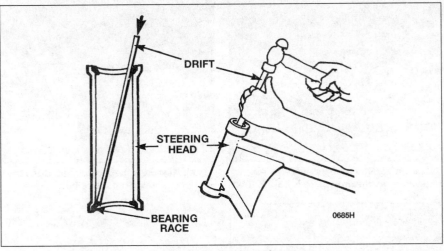

10.4b . . . locating it as shown

6 The new outer races can be pressed into the head using a drawbolt arrangement **(see illustration)**, or by using a large diameter tubular drift. Ensure that the drawbolt washer or drift (as applicable) bears only on the outer edge of the race and does not contact the working surface. Alternatively, have the races installed by a Honda dealer equipped with the bearing race installation tools.

 Installation of new bearing outer races is made much easier if the races are left overnight in the freezer. This causes them to contract slightly making them a looser fit. Alternatively, use a freeze spray.

7 The lower bearing inner race should only be removed from the steering stem if a new one is being fitted **(see illustration)**. To remove the race, use two screwdrivers placed on opposite sides to work it free, using blocks of wood to improve leverage and protect the yoke, or tap under it using a cold chisel. If the steering stem is placed on its side on a hard surface, thread a suitable nut onto the top to prevent the threads being damaged. If the race is firmly in place it will be necessary to use a puller **(see illustration)**.

8 Remove the dust seal from the bottom of the stem and replace it with a new one. Smear the new one with grease.
9 Fit the new lower race onto the steering stem. A length of tubing with an internal diameter slightly larger than the steering stem will be needed to tap the new race into position **(see illustration)**.
10 Install the steering stem (see Section 9).

11 Rear shock absorber –
removed, inspection and installation

⚠ *Warning: Do not attempt to disassemble this shock absorber. It is nitrogen-charged under high pressure. Improper disassembly could result in serious injury. Instead, take the shock to a dealer service department with the proper equipment to do the job.*

Removal

1 Support the motorcycle on its centrestand

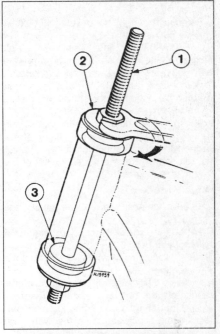

10.6 Drawbolt arrangement for fitting steering stem bearing races

1 *Long bolt or threaded bar*
2 *Thick washer*
3 *Guide for lower race*

if fitted, or on an auxiliary stand that does not take the weight through any part of the rear suspension, or by using a hoist. Position a support under the rear wheel or swingarm so that it does not drop when the shock absorber is removed, but also making sure that the weight of the machine is off the rear suspension so that the shock is not compressed.
2 Make a note of which side the bolts go in from, and make a note of which way round the shock absorber fits (i.e. on XL650V and XRV750 models note which side the reservoir is on).

10.7a Remove the lower bearing inner race . . .

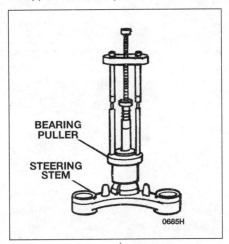

10.7b . . . using a puller if necessary

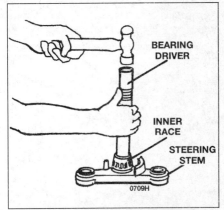

10.9 Drive the new race on using a suitable bearing driver or a length of pipe that bears only against the inner edge of the race

6

XL600V models

3 Remove the right-hand side panel (see Chapter 8).

4 Unscrew the nut and withdraw the bolt securing the linkage rods to the linkage arm, then swing the rods down **(see illustration)**. Unscrew the nut and withdraw the bolt securing the bottom of the shock absorber to the linkage arm **(see illustration)**.

5 Unscrew the nut on the shock absorber upper mounting bolt **(see illustration)**. Support the shock absorber, then withdraw the bolt and manoeuvre the shock out of the bottom **(see illustrations)**.

XL650V models

6 Remove the seat and the side panels (see Chapter 8).

7 Undo the screws securing the mud deflector just behind the shock absorber and remove it. Unscrew the nut and withdraw the bolt securing the bottom of the shock absorber to the linkage arm **(see illustration)**.

8 Unscrew the nut on the shock absorber upper mounting bolt **(see illustration)**. Support the shock absorber, then withdraw the bolt and manoeuvre the shock out of the left-hand side of the bike.

XRV750 models

9 Remove the side panels (see Chapter 8).

10 Displace the fuel pump from its mount – there is no need to detach the hoses or disconnect the wiring connector **(see illustration)**.

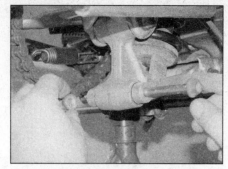

11.4a On XL600V models unscrew the nut and withdraw the linkage rods-to-arm bolt

11.4b Unscrew the nut and withdraw the lower mounting bolt

11.5a Unscrew the nut on the bolt (arrowed) . . .

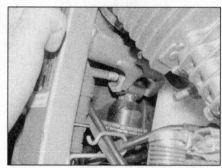

11.5b . . . then withdraw the bolt . . .

Slacken the reservoir clamp screw and draw the reservoir out of the clamp **(see illustration)**.

11 Unscrew the nut and withdraw the bolt securing the linkage rods to the linkage arm,

11.5c . . . and remove the shock absorber from the bottom

11.7 On XL650V models unscrew the nut (arrowed) and withdraw the lower mounting bolt

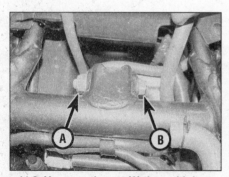

11.8 Unscrew the nut (A) then withdraw the bolt (B)

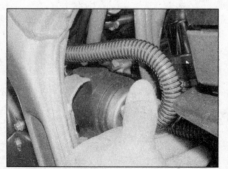

11.10a On XRV750 models displace the fuel pump from its mount

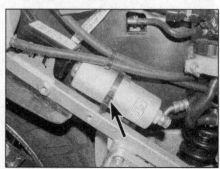

11.10b Slacken the clamp screw (arrowed) and draw the reservoir out

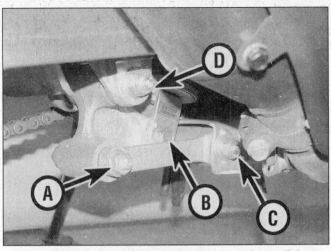

11.11 Linkage rods-to-arm bolt (A), shock absorber-to-linkage arm bolt (B), linkage rods-to-frame bolt (C), linkage arm-to-swingarm bolt (D)

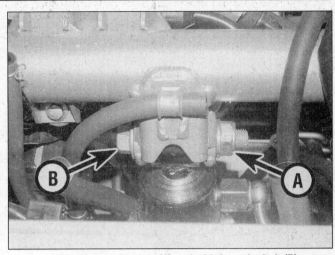

11.12 Unscrew the nut (A) and withdraw the bolt (B)

then swing the rods down **(see illustration)**. Unscrew the nut and withdraw the bolt securing the bottom of the shock absorber to the linkage arm.

12 Unscrew the nut on the shock absorber upper mounting bolt **(see illustration)**. Support the shock absorber, then withdraw the bolt and manoeuvre the shock out of the bottom.

Inspection

13 Inspect the shock absorber for obvious physical damage and the coil spring for looseness, cracks or signs of fatigue.

14 Inspect the damper rod for signs of bending, pitting and oil leakage.

15 Inspect the pivot hardware at the top and bottom of the shock for wear or damage. On XL600V models the top bush is available – remove the old one and install the new one using a press or drawbolt arrangement (see *Tools and Workshop Tips* in the Reference Section for further information). On XL650V models remove the collars and seals to access the needle bearings in the top pivot. Remove the old one and install the new one using a press or drawbolt arrangement (see *Tools and Workshop Tips* in the Reference Section for further information).

16 If the shock absorber on XL600V models is in any way damaged or worn, it can be disassembled and the damaged or worn components replaced **(see illustration)**. Disassembly of the shock absorber requires the use of a spring compressor.

17 With this in place on the spring, unscrew the adjuster locknut using a suitable C-spanner and thread it all the way up the threads and off the shock absorber. Now mark the position of the adjuster so it can be installed in the same place, then unscrew and remove it in the same way. Draw the spring off the shock and release the compressor.

18 Measure the free length of the spring and replace it with a new one if it is below the minimum specified length. If required, slacken the locknut on the lower mount, then thread the mount and the stopper plate off the rod, noting how the pin on the plate locates against the cutout in the mount. Remove the spring guide and seat, and if required the locknut and rubber damper, noting how they all fit.

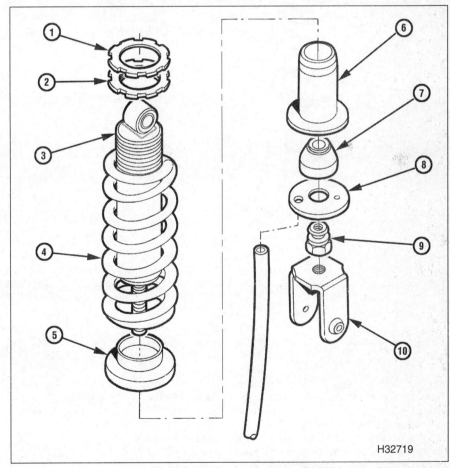

11.16 Shock absorber components – XL600V

1 Locknut	4 Spring	6 Spring guide	8 Stopper plate
2 Adjuster nut	5 Spring	7 Rubber	9 Locknut
3 Damper unit	seat	damper	10 Lower mount

H32719

6

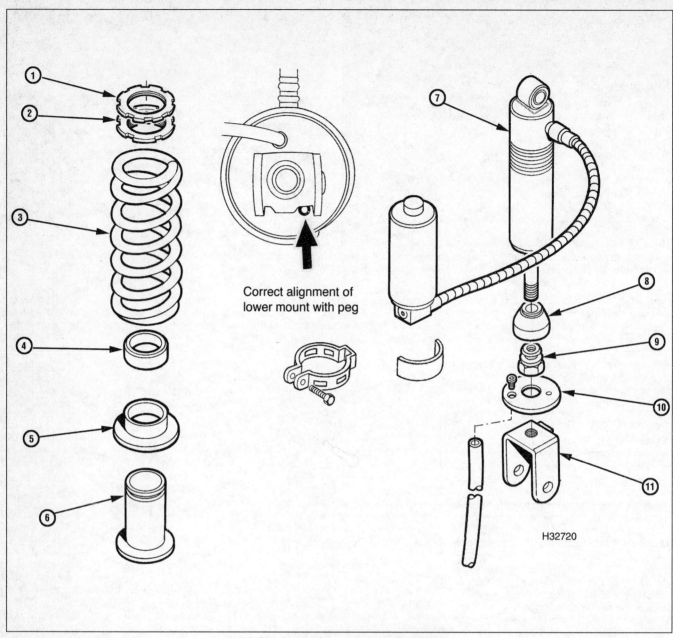

Correct alignment of
lower mount with peg

H32720

11.20 Shock absorber components – XRV750

1 Locknut	4 Seal	7 Damper unit	10 Stopper plate
2 Adjuster nut	5 Spring seat	8 Rubber damper	11 Lower mount
3 Spring	6 Spring guide	9 Locknut	

19 On XL650V models individual components are not available for the shock absorber, so if it is worn or damaged it must be replaced with a new one.

20 On XRV750-L to N (1990 to 1992) the shock absorber can be disassembled and components renewed in the same way as for the XL600V (see Step 8) **(see illustration)**. On all other XRV750 models individual components are not available.

21 Honda advise that the pressurised nitrogen gas should be released before discarding the shock absorber. Take the shock absorber to a Honda dealer for disposal - **do not** attempt gas dispersal yourself.

Installation

22 Installation is the reverse of removal, noting the following:

● Apply multi-purpose grease to the shock absorber and linkage plate pivot points.

● On XL600V and XRV750-L to N (1990 to 1992) models install the shock absorber with the breather tube facing the front.

● On XL650V models make sure the reservoir is on the left-hand side.

● On XRV750-P models onward (1993-on) make sure the reservoir hose is on the left, and on the right on all other XRV models.

● Do not tighten the nuts until both bolts (or all components if the suspension linkage has been removed as well) are in position, then tighten them to the torque setting specified at the beginning of the Chapter.

12 Rear suspension linkage – removal, inspection and installation

Removal

1 Support the motorcycle on its centrestand if fitted, or on an auxiliary stand that does not take the weight through any part of the rear suspension, or by using a hoist. Position a support under the rear wheel or swingarm so that it does not drop when the shock absorber is removed, but also making sure that the weight of the machine is off the rear suspension so that the shock is not compressed. Make a note of which side the bolts go in from.

2 On XL600V models unscrew the bolts securing the brake hose channel to the underside of the swingarm on the right-hand side and displace it **(see illustration)**.

3 On XL650V models unscrew the bolt securing the chain guide to the frame on the left-hand side and remove it, noting how it fits.

4 On XRV750-L to N (1990 to 1992) models unscrew the bolt securing the drain hose guide to the frame on the left-hand side and remove it, noting how it fits.

5 Unscrew the nuts and withdraw the bolts securing the linkage components to each other, the shock absorber, the swingarm and the frame, noting which way round and how they fit **(see illustrations 11.4a and b, 12.5a, b and c, and 11.11)**. It is best to mark the top or side of the linkage arm and rod so that it can be installed the same way round. On XL600V and XRV750 models they may already be marked, but whether the marks are visible is another matter.

Inspection

6 Withdraw the spacers from the linkage arm and swingarm, noting any difference in sizes, then lever out the grease seals **(see illustrations)**. Thoroughly clean all components, removing all traces of dirt, corrosion and grease.

7 Inspect all components closely, looking for obvious signs of wear such as heavy scoring, or for damage such as cracks or distortion.

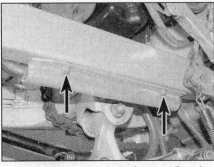

12.2 Unscrew the bolts (arrowed) and displace the hose guard

12.5b . . . and remove the linkage components

12.5a Unscrew the nuts, withdraw the bolts . . .

12.5c Suspension linkage assembly bolts (arrowed) – XL650V

Slip each spacer back into its bush or bearing and check that there is not an excessive amount of freeplay between the two components. Renew any components as required.

8 On XL600V-H and J (1987 and 1988) models check the condition of the bushes in the linkage arm and rod. Measure the internal diameter of the bush sleeve and the external diameter of the spacer that fits in it and renew any components that are worn beyond the service limit specified at the beginning of the Chapter.

9 On all other models check the condition of the needle roller bearings **(see illustration)**. Refer to *Tools and Workshop Tips* (Section 5) in the Reference section for more information on bearings.

10 Worn bushes or bearings can be drifted out of their bores, but note that removal will destroy them; new bearings should be obtained before work commences. The new bushes or bearings should be pressed or drawn into their bores rather than driven into position. In the absence of a press, a suitable drawbolt tool can be made up as described in *Tools and Workshop Tips* in the Reference section. Set them centrally in their bores.

11 Check the condition of the grease seals and renew them if they are damaged, deformed or deteriorated. Lubricate the needle bearings, spacers and seals with multi-purpose grease **(see illustration)**.

12 Press the seals squarely into place **(see illustration)**. Install the spacers **(see illustration 12.6a)**.

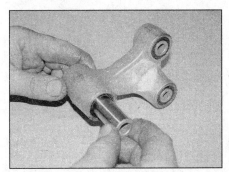

12.6a Withdraw the spacers . . .

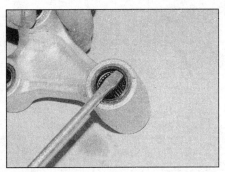

12.6b . . . and lever out the grease seals

12.9 Check the needle bearings for wear and damage

6

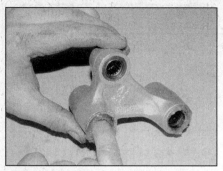

12.11 Smear the bearings with grease

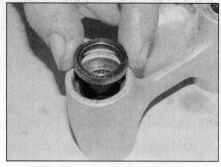

12.12a Press the grease seals in . . .

12.12b . . . using a hammer and piece of wood if necessary

Installation

13 Installation is the reverse of removal. Apply multi-purpose grease to the bearings, spacers and bolts. Where marked, install the linkage arm with the arrow before the FR or FRONT mark pointing to the front, and the linkage rod with the marked side facing up **(see illustration)**. Install the bolts and nuts finger-tight only until all components are in position, then counter-hold the bolts and tighten the nuts securely.

13 Suspension – adjustments

Front forks

1 On XRV750-L to S (1990 to 1995) models only, the forks are air-assisted and the air pressure can be varied within the specified range (see Specifications). The air valve is incorporated in the top bolt of each fork.

2 To check the air pressure use a gauge which is suitable for reading low pressures; do not use a tyre pressure gauge. Gauges and hand-operated pumps are available for suspension system use.

3 Ensure that all weight is off the front suspension when the air pressure is checked. Place the motorcycle on an auxiliary stand so that the front wheel is off the ground. Take care not to increase air pressure beyond the range – excess pressure will damage the fork oil seals – and ensure that the pressure in both forks is equal.

Rear shock absorber

Spring pre-load – all models

4 Slacken the adjuster lockring using a suitable C-spanner **(see illustration)**. Now thread the adjuster up or down as required, again using the C-spanner – thread it up to decrease pre-load or lower the ride height, and down to increase pre-load or raise the ride height.

5 Make sure you stay within the adjustment limits as defined by the installed length of the spring according to the Specifications at the beginning of the Chapter. Tighten the locknut securely against the adjuster on completion.

Compression damping – XL650V models

6 Adjustment is made using a flat bladed screwdriver via the aperture in the left-hand side panel (remove the side panel for

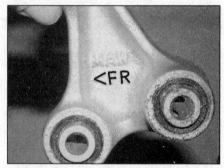

12.13 Make sure any directional arrows point forwards

improved access – see Chapter 8) **(see illustration)**. Turn the adjuster clockwise to increase damping for a firmer ride, and turn it anti-clockwise to reduce damping for a softer ride.

7 To set the damping at the standard (factory set) amount, turn the adjuster clockwise until it lightly seats (do not force it), then turn it anti-clockwise approximately one full turn until the punch marks on the adjuster and the reservoir body are aligned – remove the side panel (see Chapter 8) to make the punch marks easier to see.

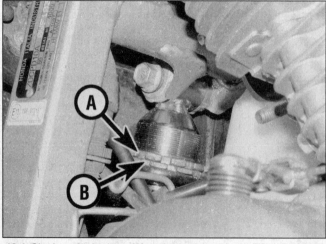

13.4 Slacken the locknut (A) and turn the adjuster (B) as required

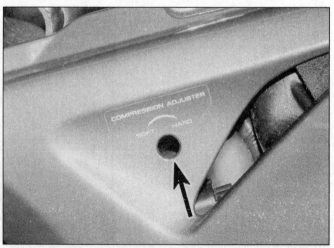

13.6 On XL650V models, adjust compression damping via the aperture (arrowed)

14.2a Unscrew the brake hose guide bolts (arrowed) . . .

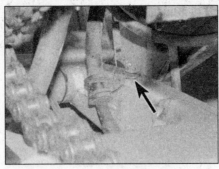

14.2b . . . even the hidden ones – XL600V shown

14.2c On XL650V models release the hose from its guides

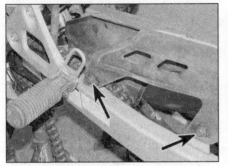

14.3a Chainguard bolts (arrowed) – XL600V

14.3b Chainguard bolts (arrowed) – XRV750

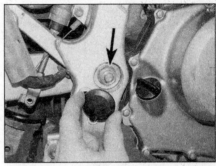

14.5a Remove the swingarm pivot cap to access the pivot bolt head and nut (arrowed)

14 Swingarm –
removal and installation

Removal

1 Remove the rear wheel (see Chapter 7).
2 Unscrew the bolt(s) securing each rear brake hose guide to the swingarm **(see illustrations)**, or release the hose from its guides, according to model **(see illustration)**. Note the routing of the brake hose around the swingarm as an aid to installation. Displace the rear brake caliper and bracket assembly from the swingarm (there is no need to disconnect the brake hose), noting how it locates and how the hose routes, and tie it to the frame, making sure no strain is placed on the hoses **(see illustration)**.
3 Unscrew the bolts securing the chain guard to the swingarm and remove the guard, noting how it locates **(see illustrations)**.
4 Support the swingarm, then unscrew the nut and withdraw the bolt securing the suspension linkage arm to the swingarm **(see illustration 12.5a, 12.5c or 11.11)**.
5 Remove the swingarm pivot caps. Unscrew the nut on the right-hand end of the swingarm pivot bolt and remove the washer (if fitted) **(see illustration)**. Support the swingarm then withdraw the pivot bolt from the left-hand side **(see illustration)**. Manoeuvre the swingarm clear of the shock absorber and out of the frame **(see illustration)**.

6 Remove the chain slider from the swingarm if necessary, noting how it fits **(see illustration)**. If it is badly worn or damaged (see Chapter 1, Section 1), it should be

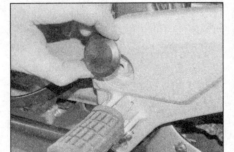

14.5b Swingarm pivot cap – XL650V

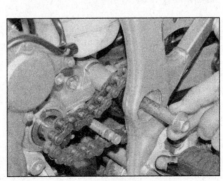

14.5d . . . withdraw the bolt . . .

replaced with a new one. Inspect all pivot components for wear or damage as described in Section 15.

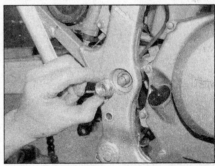

14.5c Unscrew the nut . . .

14.5e . . . and remove the swingarm

6

14.6 Remove the chain slider (arrowed) if required

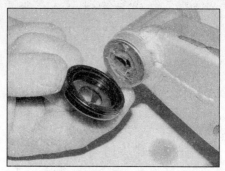

14.7a Remove the dust cap . . .

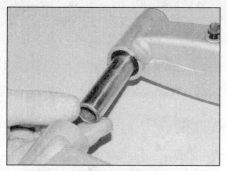

14.7b . . . and withdraw the spacer – XL600V shown

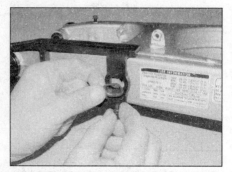

14.8 Do not forget the collar(s), where fitted

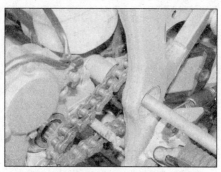

14.9 Slide the pivot bolt through the swingarm

14.10 Tighten the pivot bolt nut to the specified torque

Installation

7 Remove the dust cap and/or collar (where fitted according to model) from each swingarm pivot, then withdraw the spacers, noting what fits where **(see illustrations)**. Clean off all old grease, then lubricate the grease seals, bearings, collars, spacers and the pivot bolt with multi-purpose grease. Insert the spacers, then fit the collars and/or caps according to model.

8 If removed, install the chain slider, making sure it locates correctly, then fit the collar(s) and tighten the screw(s) securely **(see illustration)**.

9 Offer up the swingarm and have an assistant hold it in place **(see illustration 14.5e)**. Make sure the drive chain is looped over the front of the swingarm and the brake hose is correctly routed as noted on removal. Slide the pivot bolt through from the left-hand side and push it all the way through **(see illustration)**.

10 Fit the washer (where removed) and the nut **(see illustration 14.5c)**. Counter-hold the head of the pivot bolt and tighten the nut to the specified torque setting **(see illustration)**.

11 Align the swingarm with the suspension linkage arm, then install the bolt and tighten the nut securely **(see illustration 12.5a, 12.5c or 11.11)**. Fit the pivot caps.

12 Install the chain guard, making sure it locates correctly, and tighten the bolts securely **(see illustration 16.14, 14.3a and 14.3b)**.

13 Fit the rear brake caliper and bracket assembly onto the swingarm, making sure it locates correctly and the hose is correctly routed **(see illustrations)**. Fit the brake hose guides and tighten their bolts securely **(see illustrations 14.2a, b and c)**.

14 Install the rear wheel (see Chapter 7).

15 Check and adjust the drive chain slack (see Chapter 1). Check the operation of the rear suspension and brake before taking the machine on the road.

15 Swingarm – inspection, bearing check and replacement

Inspection

1 Remove the swingarm (see Section 14). Remove the chain adjusters if required, noting how they fit, especially the UP mark on XL models **(see illustration)**.

2 Thoroughly clean the swingarm, removing all traces of dirt, corrosion and grease.

3 Inspect the swingarm closely, looking for

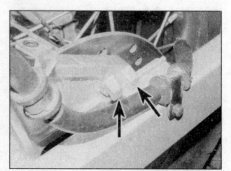

14.13a Make sure the brake caliper locates correctly (arrows) – XL600V

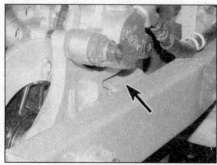

14.13b Make sure the brake caliper locates correctly (arrow) – XL650V

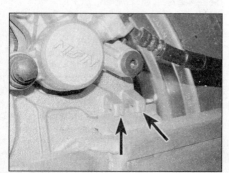

14.13c Make sure the brake caliper locates correctly (arrows) – XRV750

obvious signs of wear such as heavy scoring, and cracks or distortion due to accident damage. Any damaged or worn component must be replaced.

4 Check the swingarm pivot bolt for straightness by rolling it on a flat surface such as a piece of plate glass (first wipe off all old grease and remove any corrosion using wire wool). If the pivot bolt is bent, renew it.

Bearing check and replacement

5 Remove the dust cap and/or collar (where fitted according to model) from each swingarm pivot, then withdraw the spacers, noting what fits where **(see illustrations 14.7a and b)**. Lever out the grease seals **(see illustration)**. Clean off all old grease.

6 Refer to *Tools and Workshop Tips (Section 5)* in the Reference section and check the bearings – both caged ball bearings and needle bearings are fitted. XL600V models have two needle bearings in each pivot. XL650V models have two caged ball bearings separated by a spacer and secured by a circlip in the right-hand pivot and a needle bearing in the left-hand pivot. XRV750 models have two needle bearings in the right-hand pivot and a needle bearing and two caged ball bearings separated by a spacer and secured by a circlip in the left-hand pivot.

7 Clean the bearings and inspect them for wear or damage **(see illustration)**. If they do not run smoothly and freely or if there is excessive freeplay, they must be replaced with new ones – refer to the Reference Section for removal and installation methods.

8 The caged ball bearing(s) are held by a circlip and separated by a spacer. The needle bearing(s) must be renewed if removed – they cannot be reused. Measure the depth in the pivot that each bearing is set at and set the new bearings to the same depth.

9 Check the condition of the grease seals and replace them with new ones if they are damaged, deformed or deteriorated **(see illustration)**.

10 Lubricate the grease seals, bearings, collars and spacers with multi-purpose grease. Insert the spacers, then fit the collars and/or caps according to model **(see illustrations 14.7b and a)**.

---

16 Drive chain –
removing, cleaning and installation

Note: *The original equipment drive chain fitted to XL600-H to R (1987 to 1995) models and XRV750-L to N (1990 to 1992) models is an endless chain, which means it doesn't have a split link and therefore cannot be split. Removal requires the removal of the swingarm. However it is quite possible that the endless chains have been replaced by staked-link chains as fitted to all other models, so make sure you identify the type of chain you have and select the relevant procedure. Such*

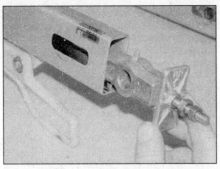

15.1 Note how and which way round the chain adjusters fit – XL type shown

chains can be recognised by the master link side plate's identification marks (and usually its different colour), as well as by the staked ends of the link's two pins which look as if they have been deeply centre-punched, instead of peened over as with all the other pins. The original equipment drive chain fitted to all other models has a staked -type master (joining) link which can be disassembled using either Honda service tool, Pt. No. 07HMH-MR10103, or one of several commercially-available drive chain cutting/staking tools.

⚠ **Warning: NEVER install a drive chain which uses a clip-type master (split) link.**

Endless chains

Removal

1 Remove the rear wheel (see Chapter 7), and the swingarm (see Section 14).

2 If the sprockets are also being renewed, remove the front sprocket (see Section 17), then remove the chain. Otherwise, remove the front sprocket cover (see Section 17) and slip the chain off the sprocket and remove it from the bike.

Cleaning

3 Soak the chain in kerosene (paraffin) for approximately five or six minutes, then clean it using a soft brush.

Caution: Don't use gasoline (petrol), solvent or other cleaning fluids which might damage its internal sealing properties. Don't use high-pressure water. Remove the chain, wipe it off, then blow dry it with compressed air immediately.

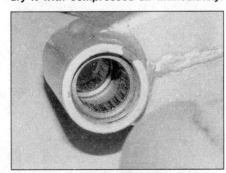

15.7 . . . and check the bearings

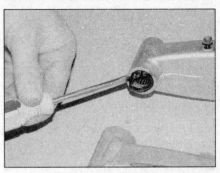

15.5 Lever out the seals . . .

The entire process shouldn't take longer than ten minutes – if it does, the O-rings in the chain rollers could be damaged.

Installation

4 Installation is the reverse of removal. On completion adjust and lubricate the chain following the procedures described in Section 1.

Staked-link chains

Removal

⚠ **Warning: NEVER install a drive chain which uses a clip-type master (split) link. Use ONLY the correct service tools to secure the staked-type of master link – if you do not have access to such tools, have the chain replaced by a dealer service department or bike repair shop to be sure of having it securely installed.**

5 Locate the joining link in a suitable position to work on by rotating the back wheel. Slacken the drive chain as described in Chapter 1.

6 Unscrew the bolts securing the chain guard to the swingarm and remove the guard, noting how it locates **(see illustrations 14.3a and b)**.

7 Remove the front sprocket cover (see Section 17).

8 Split the chain at the joining link using the chain cutter, following carefully the manufacturer's operating instructions (see also Section 8 in *Tools and Workshop Tips* in the Reference Section). Remove the chain from the bike, noting its routing around the swingarm.

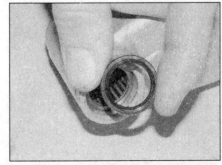

15.9 Use new grease seals if necessary

6

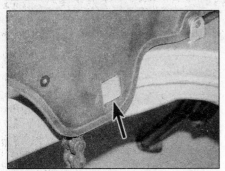

16.14 Make sure the chainguard locates correctly (arrow) – XL600V type shown

Cleaning

9 Refer to Step 3.

Installation

⚠️ *Warning: NEVER install a drive chain which uses a clip-type master (split) link. If you do not have access to a chain riveting tool, have the chain fitted by a dealer service department.*

10 Fit the drive chain around the swingarm and sprockets, leaving the two ends in a convenient position to work on.

11 Refer to Section 8 in *Tools and Workshop Tips* in the Reference Section. Install the new joining link from the inside with the four O-rings correctly located between the link plate and side plate. Install the new side plate with its identification marks facing out. Measure the amount that the joining link pins project from the side plate and check they are within the measurements specified at the

beginning of the Chapter. Stake the new link using the drive chain cutting/staking tool, following carefully the instructions of both the chain manufacturer and the tool manufacturer. DO NOT re-use old joining link components.

12 After staking, check the joining link and staking for any signs of cracking. If there is any evidence of cracking, the joining link, O-rings and side plate must be replaced. Measure the diameter of the staked ends in two directions and check that it is evenly staked and within the measurements specified at the beginning of the Chapter.

13 Install the sprocket cover (see Section 17).

14 Install the chain guard, making sure it locates correctly, and tighten the bolts securely **(see illustration and 14.3a and b)**.

15 On completion, adjust and lubricate the chain following the procedures described in Chapter 1.

17 Sprockets – check and replacement

Check

1 Unscrew the gearchange lever pinch bolt and slide the lever off the shaft, noting the alignment of the punch mark on the gearchange shaft end with either the punch mark on the lever or with the slit in the lever clamp (according to model) **(see illustration 3.8)**. If no marks are visible make your own so that the lever can be installed in the correct position straight away.

2 Unscrew the bolts securing the front sprocket cover and remove the cover, and on XL650V and XRV750 models the drive chain guide plate **(see illustration)**.

3 Check the wear pattern on both sprockets (see Chapter 1, Section 1). If the sprocket teeth are worn excessively, replace the chain and both sprockets as a set. Whenever the sprockets are inspected, the drive chain should be inspected also (see Chapter 1). If you are renewing the chain, renew the sprockets as well.

4 Adjust and lubricate the chain following the procedures described in Chapter 1.

Replacement

Front sprocket

> **HAYNES HiNT** *Keep your old front sprocket as it can be used along with a holding tool to lock the transmission input shaft should you ever need to remove the clutch (see Chapter 2).*

5 Unscrew the gearchange lever pinch bolt and slide the lever off the shaft, noting the alignment of the punch mark on the gearchange shaft end with either the punch mark on the lever or with the slit in the lever clamp (according to model) **(see illustration 3.8)**. If no marks are visible make your own so that the lever can be installed in the correct position straight away.

6 Unscrew the bolts securing the front sprocket cover and remove the cover, and on XL650V and XRV750 models the drive chain guide plate.

7 Have an assistant apply the rear brake. Unscrew the sprocket retainer plate bolts, then rotate the plate in its groove in the shaft so that the splines are misaligned, and slide the plate off the shaft **(see illustration)**.

8 Slacken the drive chain as described in Chapter 1.

9 Slide the sprocket and chain off the shaft and slip the sprocket out of the chain **(see illustrations)**.

10 Engage the new sprocket with the chain, making sure the marked side is facing out, and slide it on the shaft **(see illustrations 17.9b and a)**. Take up the slack in the chain.

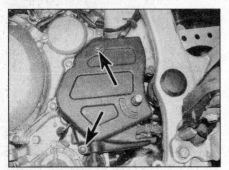

17.2 Unscrew the bolts (arrowed) and remove the cover

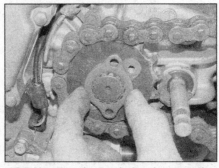

17.7 Unscrew the two bolts, then turn the plate as described and draw it off the shaft

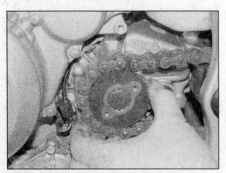

17.9a Draw the sprocket off the shaft . . .

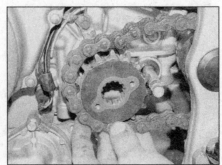

17.9b . . . and disengage it from the chain

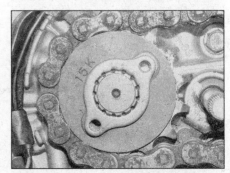

17.11a Fit and align the retainer plate . . .

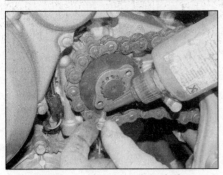

17.11b . . . then install the bolts

17.12 Install the sprocket cover

**17.14 Rear sprocket bolts (arrowed) –
XL600V shown**

11 Slide the sprocket retainer onto the shaft and align it with the groove across the shaft splines **(see illustration 17.7)**, then turn the plate so its splines align with those on the shaft, thereby locking it on the shaft, and so the bolt holes align **(see illustration)**. Apply a non-permanent threadlock to the bolts and tighten them to the specified torque setting, using the rear brake to prevent the sprocket turning **(see illustration)**.
12 On XL650V and XRV750 models fit the guide plate. Fit the sprocket cover and tighten its bolts **(see illustration)**. Slide the gearchange lever onto the shaft, aligning it as noted on removal, and tighten the pinch bolt securely **(see illustration 3.8)**. Adjust and lubricate the chain following the procedures described in Chapter 1.

Rear sprocket

13 Remove the rear wheel (see Chapter 7).
14 On XL models, unscrew the nuts and bolts securing the sprocket to the hub assembly, and remove the washers **(see illustration)**. Remove the sprocket, noting which way round it fits. Fit the sprocket onto the hub with the stamped mark facing out. Lubricate the threads of the bolts with oil.

Install the bolts and the nuts with their washers, and tighten the nuts evenly and in a criss-cross sequence to the torque setting specified at the beginning of the Chapter.
15 On XRV models, unscrew the nuts securing the sprocket to the hub assembly. Remove the sprocket, noting which way round it fits. Check that the studs are tight in the hub – if any are loose, remove them all using the correct tools, then clean their threads, apply a suitable thread-locking compound, then fit them back into the hub and tighten them securely. Fit the sprocket onto the hub with the stamped mark facing out. Lubricate the threads and seats of the nuts with oil. Install the nuts and tighten them evenly and in a criss-cross sequence to the torque setting specified at the beginning of the Chapter.
16 Install the rear wheel (see Chapter 7).

**18 Rear sprocket coupling/rubber dampers –
check and replacement**

1 Remove the rear wheel (see Chapter 7).

Caution: Do not lay the wheel down on the disc as it could become warped. Lay the wheel on wooden blocks so that the disc is off the ground.

2 Lift the sprocket coupling away from the wheel leaving the rubber dampers in position **(see illustration)**. Note the spacer inside the coupling – it should be a tight fit but remove it if it is likely to drop out. Check the coupling for cracks or any obvious signs of damage. Also check the sprocket studs for wear or damage.
3 Lift the rubber damper segments from the wheel and check them for cracks, hardening and general deterioration **(see illustration)**. Renew them as a set if necessary.
4 Check the condition of the hub O-ring and replace it with a new one if it is damaged, deformed or deteriorated **(see illustration)**.
5 Checking and replacement procedures for the sprocket coupling bearing are described in Chapter 7.
6 Installation is the reverse of removal. Make sure the spacer is still correctly installed in the coupling, or install it if it was removed.
7 Install the rear wheel (see Chapter 7).

18.2 Lift the sprocket coupling out of the wheel

18.3 Check the rubber dampers . . .

18.4 . . . and the O-ring

6

Chapter 7
Brakes, wheels and tyres

Contents

Degrees of difficulty

Easy, suitable for novice with little experience	**Fairly easy,** suitable for beginner with some experience	**Fairly difficult,** suitable for competent DIY mechanic 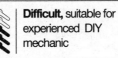	**Difficult,** suitable for experienced DIY mechanic	**Very difficult,** suitable for expert DIY or professional

Specifications

Brakes – XL600V-H to L (1987 to 1990) models

Brake fluid type . . . . DOT 4
Front caliper bore ID
   Standard . . . . 30.230 to 30.280 mm
   Service limit . . . . 30.29 mm
Front caliper piston OD
   Standard . . . . 30.148 to 30.199 mm
   Service limit . . . . 30.14 mm
Front master cylinder bore ID
   Standard . . . . 12.700 to 12.743 mm
   Service limit . . . . 12.76 mm
Front master cylinder piston OD
   Standard . . . . 12.657 to 12.684 mm
   Service limit . . . . 12.65 mm
Front disc thickness
   Standard . . . . 4.5 mm
   Service limit . . . . 3.5 mm
Front disc maximum runout . . . . 0.3 mm
Rear brake shoe lining thickness . . . . 2 mm minimum
Rear drum ID
   Standard . . . . 130 mm
   Service limit . . . . 131 mm

7

Brakes – XL600V-M to P (1991 to 1993) models

Brake fluid type	DOT 4
Front caliper bore ID	
Standard	30.230 to 30.280 mm
Service limit	30.29 mm
Front caliper piston OD	
Standard	30.148 to 30.199 mm
Service limit	30.14 mm
Front master cylinder bore ID	
Standard	11.000 to 11.040 mm
Service limit	11.05 mm
Front master cylinder piston OD	
Standard	10.850 to 10.910 mm
Service limit	10.84 mm
Rear caliper bore ID	
Standard	38.180 to 38.230 mm
Service limit	38.24 mm
Rear caliper piston OD	
Standard	38.115 to 38.148 mm
Service limit	38.11 mm
Rear master cylinder bore ID	
Standard	14.000 to 14.043 mm
Service limit	14.05 mm
Rear master cylinder piston OD	
Standard	13.957 to 13.984 mm
Service limit	13.95 mm
Disc thickness (front and rear)	
Standard	4.8 to 5.2 mm
Service limit	4.0 mm
Disc maximum runout	0.3 mm

Brakes – XL600V-R to T (1994 to 1996) models

Brake fluid type	DOT 4
Front caliper bore ID	
Standard	27.000 to 27.050 mm
Service limit	26.99 mm
Front caliper piston OD	
Standard	26.935 to 26.968 mm
Service limit	26.97 mm
Front master cylinder bore ID	
Standard	11.000 to 11.043 mm
Service limit	11.05 mm
Front master cylinder piston OD	
Standard	10.957 to 10.984 mm
Service limit	10.95 mm
Rear caliper bore ID	
Standard	38.180 to 38.230 mm
Service limit	38.24 mm
Rear caliper piston OD	
Standard	38.115 to 38.148 mm
Service limit	38.11 mm
Rear master cylinder bore ID	
Standard	14.000 to 14.043 mm
Service limit	14.05 mm
Rear master cylinder piston OD	
Standard	13.957 to 13.984 mm
Service limit	13.95 mm
Disc thickness (front and rear)	
Standard	4.8 to 5.2 mm
Service limit	4.0 mm
Disc maximum runout	0.3 mm

Brakes – XL600V-V to X (1997 to 1999) models

Brake fluid type	DOT 4
Front caliper bore ID	
Standard	30.230 to 30.280 mm
Service limit	30.29 mm

Brakes – XL600V-V to X (1997 to 1999) models (continued)

Front caliper piston OD
  Standard .... 30.148 to 30.199 mm
  Service limit .... 30.14 mm
Front master cylinder bore ID
  Standard .... 12.700 to 12.743 mm
  Service limit .... 12.76 mm
Front master cylinder piston OD
  Standard .... 12.657 to 12.684 mm
  Service limit .... 12.65 mm
Front disc thickness
  Standard .... 4.5 mm
  Service limit .... 3.5 mm
Front disc maximum runout .... 0.3 mm
Rear caliper bore ID
  Standard .... 38.180 to 38.230 mm
  Service limit .... 38.24 mm
Rear caliper piston OD
  Standard .... 38.115 to 38.148 mm
  Service limit .... 38.11 mm
Rear master cylinder bore ID
  Standard .... 14.000 to 14.043 mm
  Service limit .... 14.05 mm
Rear master cylinder piston OD
  Standard .... 13.957 to 13.984 mm
  Service limit .... 13.95 mm
Rear disc thickness
  Standard .... 4.8 to 5.2 mm
  Service limit .... 4.0 mm
Rear disc maximum runout .... 0.3 mm

Brakes – XL650V models

Brake fluid type .... DOT 4
Front caliper bore ID
  Upper bore
    Standard .... Not available
    Service limit .... 32.040 mm
  Lower bore
    Standard .... Not available
    Service limit .... 30.040 mm
Front caliper piston OD
  Upper piston
    Standard .... Not available
    Service limit .... 31.910 mm
  Lower piston
    Standard .... Not available
    Service limit .... 29.910 mm
Front master cylinder bore ID
  Standard .... Not available
  Service limit .... 13.043 mm
Front master cylinder piston OD
  Standard .... Not available
  Service limit .... 12.955 mm
Front disc thickness
  Standard .... 4.5 mm
  Service limit .... 3.5 mm
Front disc maximum runout .... 0.3 mm
Rear caliper bore ID
  Standard .... 38.180 to 38.230 mm
  Service limit .... 38.24 mm
Rear caliper piston OD
  Standard .... 38.003 to 38.148 mm
  Service limit .... 38.09 mm
Rear master cylinder bore ID
  Standard .... 14.000 to 14.043 mm
  Service limit .... 14.055 mm
Rear master cylinder piston OD
  Standard .... 13.957 to 13.984 mm
  Service limit .... 13.945 mm

7

Brakes – XL650V models (continued)

Rear disc thickness
    Standard .... 5.0 mm
    Service limit .... 4.0 mm
Rear disc maximum runout .... 0.25 mm

Brakes – XRV750 models

Brake fluid type .... DOT 4
Front caliper bore ID
    Standard .... 27.000 to 27.050 mm
    Service limit .... 27.06 mm
Front caliper piston OD
    Standard .... 26.968 to 26.935 mm
    Service limit .... 26.92 mm
Front master cylinder bore ID
    Standard .... 12.700 to 12.743 mm
    Service limit .... 12.75 mm
Front master cylinder piston OD
    Standard .... 12.657 to 12.684 mm
    Service limit .... 12.64 mm
Front disc thickness
    Standard .... 4.5 mm
    Service limit .... 3.5 mm
Front disc maximum runout .... 0.3 mm
Rear caliper bore ID
    Standard .... 38.180 to 38.230 mm
    Service limit .... 38.24 mm
Rear caliper piston OD
    Standard .... 38.115 to 38.148 mm
    Service limit .... 38.11 mm
Rear master cylinder bore ID
    Standard .... 14.000 to 14.043 mm
    Service limit .... 14.05 mm
Rear master cylinder piston OD
    Standard .... 13.957 to 13.984 mm
    Service limit .... 13.95 mm
Rear disc thickness
    Standard .... 5.0 mm
    Service limit .... 4.0 mm
Rear disc maximum runout .... 0.25 mm

Wheels

Maximum wheel runout (front and rear)
    Axial (side-to-side) .... 2.0 mm
    Radial (out-of-round) .... 2.0 mm
Maximum axle runout (front and rear) .... 0.20 mm

Tyres

Tyre pressures .... see *Daily (pre-ride)* checks
Tyre sizes*
    XL models
        Front 90/90-21 54S
        Rear 130/80-17 65S
    XRV750-L to N (1990 to 1992) models
        Front 90/90-21 54H
        Rear 130/90-17 65S
    XRV750-P models onwards (1993-on)
        Front 90/90-21 54S
        Rear 140/80-R17 69H
*Refer to the owners handbook or the tyre information label on the swingarm for approved tyre brands.

Torque settings

Brake caliper bleed valves .... 6 Nm
Brake disc bolts .... 42 Nm
Brake hose banjo bolts .... 34 Nm
Front axle .... 64 Nm
Front axle clamp nuts .... 12 Nm
Front brake master cylinder clamp bolts .... 12 Nm
Rear axle nut .... 90 Nm
Rear brake master cylinder bolts .... 12 Nm

1 General information

All models covered in this manual are fitted with spoked wheels designed for tubed tyres only.

All models have hydraulically operated disc brakes on the front. The XL600V-H to T (1987 to 1996) models use a single disc and all other models have twin discs.

The rear brake is either a drum type (XL600V-H to L (1987 to 1990) models) or an hydraulically operated disc brake (all other models).

Caution: Hydraulic disc brake components rarely require disassembly. Do not disassemble components unless absolutely necessary. If an hydraulic brake line is loosened, the entire system must be disassembled, drained, cleaned and then properly filled and bled upon reassembly. Do not use solvents on internal brake components. Solvents will cause the seals to swell and distort. Use only clean brake fluid or denatured alcohol for cleaning. Use care when working with brake fluid as it can injure your eyes and it will damage painted surfaces and plastic parts.

2 Brake pads and shoes – replacement

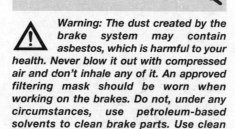

⚠️ *Warning: The dust created by the brake system may contain asbestos, which is harmful to your health. Never blow it out with compressed air and don't inhale any of it. An approved filtering mask should be worn when working on the brakes. Do not, under any circumstances, use petroleum-based solvents to clean brake parts. Use clean brake fluid, brake cleaner or denatured alcohol only.*

Note: *On models with twin front disc brakes, always renew both sets of pads in the front calipers at the same time.*

Front brake pads – XL600V-H to P (1987 to 1993) models and XRV750-L to N (1990 to 1992) models

1 On XRV models, remove the fork guards (see Chapter 8).
2 To allow for the increased friction material thickness of new pads, push the brake caliper against the disc so that the piston is forced back into the caliper **(see illustration 2.31)**. It may be necessary to remove the

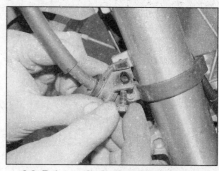

2.3 Release the brake hose from the clamp

master cylinder reservoir cover and diaphragm and siphon out some fluid. If the pistons are difficult to push back, attach a length of clear hose to the bleed valve and place the open end in a suitable container, then open the valve and try again. Take great care not to draw any air into the system. If in doubt, bleed the brakes afterwards (see Section 10).
3 Unscrew the bolt securing the brake hose in the clamp on the front fork and release it, noting how it fits **(see illustration)**.
4 On XL600V-H to L (1987 to 1990) models, unscrew the pad pin retainer bolt and remove the retainer, noting how it fits **(see illustration)**. On XL600V-M to P (1991 to

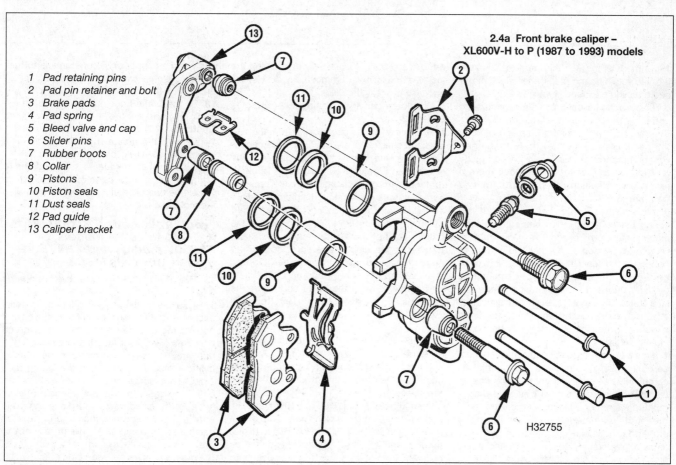

2.4a Front brake caliper – XL600V-H to P (1987 to 1993) models

1 Pad retaining pins
2 Pad pin retainer and bolt
3 Brake pads
4 Pad spring
5 Bleed valve and cap
6 Slider pins
7 Rubber boots
8 Collar
9 Pistons
10 Piston seals
11 Dust seals
12 Pad guide
13 Caliper bracket

H32755

7

2.4b Front brake caliper – XRV750-L to N (1990 to 1992) models

1   Pad pin plug – 2 off
2   Pad retaining pin – 2 off
3   Brake pads
4   Pad spring
5   Caliper body
6   Bleed valve and cap
7   Pistons seals
8   Dust seals
9   Pistons
10 Slider pins
11 Rubber boots
12 Caliper bracket
13 Pad guide

FRONT

H.22500

1993) models and XRV750 models, unscrew the pad retaining pin plugs, then slacken the pad retaining pins **(see illustration)**.

5 Unscrew the caliper bracket mounting bolts and slide the caliper assembly off the disc. Remove the pad retaining pins and remove the pads, noting how they fit. Note the pad spring in the top of caliper and the pad guide on the caliper bracket and remove them if required for cleaning or replacement, noting how they fit.

6 Inspect the surface of each pad for contamination and check whether the friction material has worn beyond its service limit (see Chapter 1, Section 3). If either pad is worn to or beyond the service limit, is fouled with oil or grease, or is heavily scored or damaged by dirt and debris the pads must be renewed (see **Note**). Note that it is extremely difficult to effectively degrease the friction material; if the pads are contaminated in any way new ones must be fitted.

7 If the pads are in good condition clean them carefully, using a fine wire brush which is completely free of oil and grease to remove all traces of road dirt and corrosion. Using a pointed instrument, clean out the grooves in the friction material and dig out any embedded particles of foreign matter. Any areas of glazing may be removed using emery cloth. Spray with a dedicated brake cleaner to

remove any dust. It is also worth spraying the inside of the caliper to remove any dust there, and also to spray the discs.

8 Check the condition of the brake disc (see Section 3).

9 Remove all traces of corrosion from the pad pins and check they are not bent or damaged. Smear the pins, the backs of the pads and the leading and trailing edges of the backing material with copper-based grease, making sure that none gets on the friction material.

10 Make sure that the pad spring and pad guide are correctly fitted. Fit the pads into the caliper so that the friction material of each pad faces the disc. Make sure the leading edges locate correctly against the guide on the bracket. Press the pads up against the pad spring to align the holes and insert the pad pins. On XL600V-M to P (1991 to 1993) models and XRV750, tighten the pins finger-tight.

11 Slide the caliper onto the disc making sure the pads locate on each side. Apply a suitable non-permanent thread-locking compound to the mounting bolts and tighten them securely.

12 On XL600V-H to L (1987 to 1990) models, fit the retainer onto the pins and secure it with its bolt. On XL600V-M to P (1991 to 1993) models and XRV750, tighten the pad pins securely, then fit the plugs – it is advisable to

apply some copper or silicone grease to their threads. Where twin discs are fitted, renew the pads in the other caliper.

13 Fit the brake hose into its clamp on the front fork and secure it with the bolt **(see illustration 2.3)**.

14 Top up the master cylinder reservoir if necessary (see *Daily (pre-ride) checks*).

15 Operate the brake lever several times to bring the pads into contact with the disc. Check the operation of the brake before riding the motorcycle.

Front brake pads – XL600V-R to X (1994 to 1999) models, XL650V models and XRV750-P models onwards (1993-on)

16 On XRV models, remove the fork guards (see Chapter 8).

17 To allow for the increased friction material thickness of new pads, push the brake caliper against the disc so that the piston is forced back into the caliper **(see illustration 2.31)**. It may be necessary to remove the master cylinder reservoir cover and diaphragm and siphon out some fluid. If the pistons are difficult to push back, attach a length of clear hose to the bleed valve and place the open end in a suitable container, then open the valve and try again. Take great care not to draw any air into the system. If in doubt, bleed the brakes afterwards (see Section 9).

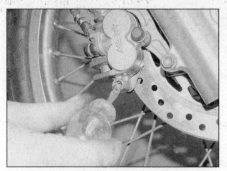

2.18a Unscrew the brake pad retaining pin plug . . .

2.18b . . . then unscrew the retaining pin

2.18c . . . and draw the pads out of the caliper

18 Unscrew the pad retaining pin plug, then unscrew the pad retaining pin **(see illustrations)**. Withdraw the pin and slide the pads down out of the caliper **(see illustrations)**.

19 Refer to Steps 5, 6, 7 and 8 above.
20 If fitted, make sure the shim on the back of each pad is correctly located **(see illustration)**. Fit the pads into the caliper so

that the friction material of each pad faces the disc, making sure the leading edges locate correctly against the guide **(see illustrations)**. Press the pads up against the pad spring to

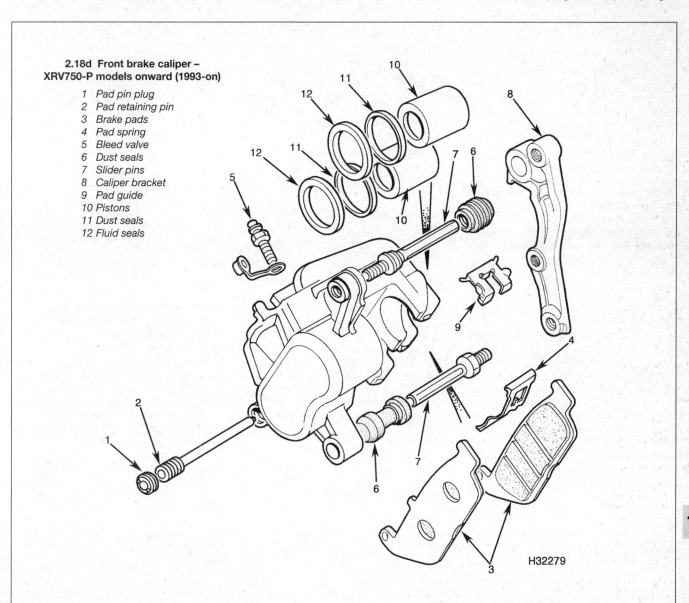

2.18d Front brake caliper – XRV750-P models onward (1993-on)

1 Pad pin plug
2 Pad retaining pin
3 Brake pads
4 Pad spring
5 Bleed valve
6 Dust seals
7 Slider pins
8 Caliper bracket
9 Pad guide
10 Pistons
11 Dust seals
12 Fluid seals

H32279

7

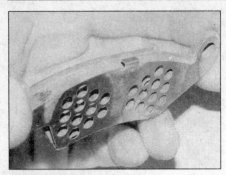

2.20a Make sure the shim is correctly fitted

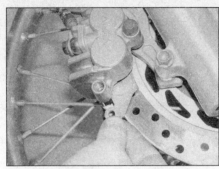

2.20b Slide the pads up into the caliper . . .

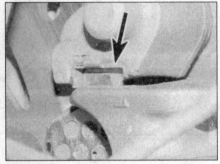

2.20c . . . making sure they locate correctly (arrow)

2.20d Press the pad up against the spring and insert the retaining pin

align the holes and insert the pad pin, then tighten it securely **(see illustration)**. Install the pad pin plug – it is advisable to apply some copper or silicone grease to its threads **(see illustration 2.18a)**. Repeat the pad renewal procedure on the other caliper.

21 Top up the master cylinder reservoir if necessary (see *Daily (pre-ride) checks*).

22 Operate the brake lever several times to bring the pads into contact with the disc. Check the operation of the brake before riding the motorcycle.

Rear brake shoes – XL600V-H to L (1987 to 1990) models

23 Remove the rear wheel (see Section 14).

24 Lift the brake plate out of the drum in the wheel hub **(see illustration)**.

25 Note which way round the shoes fit and how they locate against the actuating cam and the spindle they pivot on. Grasp each shoe and 'fold' them up towards each other – when they are almost vertical the springs will relax and the shoes can be lifted of the cam and the spindle. Remove the springs.

26 Check the brake shoe linings for wear, damage and signs of contamination from road dirt or water. If the linings are visibly defective, renew the shoes. Measure the thickness of the lining material (just the lining material, not the metal backing) and renew the shoes if the linings have worn down to or below the minimum thickness (see Specifications) at any point.

27 Check the ends of the shoes where they contact the brake cam and pivot posts and renew the shoes if there are signs of wear. Check the lugs on the shoes where the springs locate. Also check that the springs are not stretched and that their ends are not deformed.

28 Clean all old grease from the flats of the operating cam and around the spindle, then apply a smear of fresh copper grease to these areas ensuring that none gets on the lining material.

29 Fit the springs into the shoes and hold the shoes 'folded' together so that the springs are under a slight tension and will not drop out. Pull the ends of the shoes apart slightly and locate them against the actuating cam and the spindle, then fold the shoes flat onto the brake plate so that the springs become tensioned and effectively pull the ends of the shoes against the cam and spindle. Operate the cam and check that the shoes pivot correctly.

30 Fit the brake plate assembly into the drum in the rear wheel hub. Install the wheel (see Section 14).

Rear brake pads – XL600V-M to X (1991 to 1999) models, XL650V models and XRV750 models

31 To allow for the increased friction material thickness of new pads, push the brake caliper against the disc so that the piston is forced back into the caliper **(see illustration)**. It may

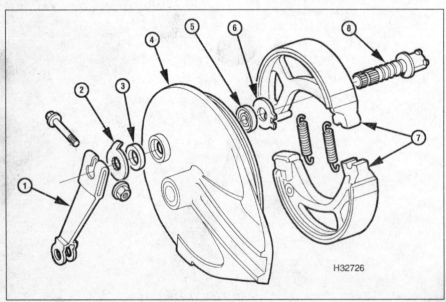

2.24 Drum brake components – XL600V-H to L (1987 to 1990) models

1 *Brake arm*	3 *Grease seal*	5 *Grease seal*	7 *Brake shoes*
2 *Indicator plate*	4 *Brake plate*	6 *Thrust plate*	8 *Actuating cam*

H32726

2.31 Push the caliper against the disc to force the piston in

be necessary to remove the master cylinder reservoir cover and diaphragm and siphon out some fluid. If the pistons are difficult to push back, attach a length of clear hose to the bleed valve and place the open end in a suitable container, then open the valve and try again. Take great care not to draw any air into the system. If in doubt, bleed the brakes afterwards (see Section 10).

32 Unscrew the pad retaining pin plug, then slacken the pad retaining pin **(see illustrations)**. On XL600V models unscrew the bolt securing the brake hose clamp to the caliper bracket **(see illustration)**.

33 Unscrew the caliper rear mounting bolt/slider pin **(see illustration)**. Pivot the back of the caliper up off the disc then unscrew the pad retaining pin and remove the pads, noting how they fit **(see illustration)**. Note the pad spring in the top of caliper and the pad guide on the caliper bracket and remove them if required for cleaning or replacement, noting how they fit.

34 Refer to Steps 6, 7 and 8 above.

35 Install the pads so that the friction material of each pad will face the disc and insert the pad pin, tightening it finger tight **(see illustration)**. Pivot the caliper down onto the disc while keeping the pads held in position, locating the leading edges correctly against the guide on the bracket **(see illustration)**. Apply a suitable non-permanent thread locking compound to the rear mounting bolt/slider pin and tighten it securely **(see illustration)**. Now tighten the pad pin securely. Install the pad pin plug – it is advisable to apply some copper or silicone grease to its threads **(see illustration 2.32a)**.

36 Top up the master cylinder reservoir if necessary (see *Daily (pre-ride) checks*).

37 Operate the brake lever several times to bring the pads into contact with the disc. Check the operation of the brake before riding the motorcycle.

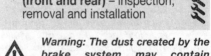

3 Brake drum and discs (front and rear) – inspection, removal and installation

⚠️ *Warning: The dust created by the brake system may contain asbestos, which is harmful to your health. Never blow it out with compressed air and don't inhale any of it. An approved filtering mask should be worn when working on the brakes. Do not, under any circumstances, use petroleum-based solvents to clean brake parts. Use clean brake fluid, brake cleaner or denatured alcohol only.*

Rear brake drum – XL600V-H to L (1987 to 1990) models

Removal

1 Remove the rear wheel (see Section 14).

2 Lift the brake plate out of the drum in the wheel hub (see illustration 2.24).

2.32a Unscrew the plug . . .

2.32c Remove the brake hose clamp bolt

Inspection

3 Visually inspect the surface of the drum for score marks, cracks and other damage. Light scratches are normal after use and won't affect brake operation, but deep grooves,

2.33b . . . then pivot the caliper up, withdraw the retaining pin and remove the pads

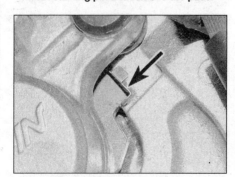

2.35b Make sure the pads locate correctly (arrow)

2.32b . . . then slacken the retaining pin (arrowed)

2.33a Unscrew the bolt (arrowed) . . .

cracks and heavy score marks will reduce braking efficiency and accelerate shoe wear. If the drum is in bad condition the wheel hub must be replaced with a new one.

4 Measure the internal diameter of the drum.

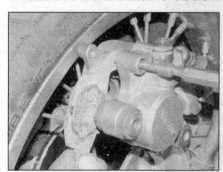

2.35a Locate the pads and insert the retaining pin

2.35c Install the bolt and tighten it securely

7

3.8 Checking disc runout

If it has worn beyond the service limit specified at the beginning of the Chapter the wheel hub must be replaced with a new one.

5 If the hub needs to be renewed, obtain the new one then take the whole wheel to a specialist wheel builder who will have the correct equipment for rebuilding spoked wheels. Although it is not that difficult to actually rebuild, it is tricky to set up so that it is all correctly aligned, tensioned and balanced.

Installation

6 Fit the brake plate assembly into the drum in the rear wheel hub. Install the wheel (see Section 14).

Brake discs – front and rear

Note: *Honda recommend using new disc mounting bolts when the old ones are removed. This is because the bolts are pre-treated with a locking compound. It is possible, however, to clean up the old bolts and reinstall them using a suitable non-permanent thread locking compound that is commercially available.*

Inspection

7 Visually inspect the surface of the disc for score marks and other damage. Light scratches are normal after use and won't affect brake operation, but deep grooves and heavy score marks will reduce braking efficiency and accelerate pad wear. If a disc is badly grooved it must be machined or replaced with a new one.

8 To check disc runout, position the bike on its centrestand if fitted or on an auxiliary stand so that the wheel being checked is off the ground.

3.9b Checking disc thickness

3.9a The minimum thickness is marked on each disc

Mount a dial gauge to a fork leg or on the swingarm, according to wheel, with the plunger on the gauge touching the surface of the disc about 10 mm (1/2 in) from the outer edge **(see illustration)**. Rotate the wheel and watch the indicator needle, comparing the reading with the limit listed in the Specifications at the beginning of the Chapter. If the runout is greater than the service limit, check the wheel bearings for play (see Chapter 1). If the bearings are worn, replace them with new ones (see Section 15) and repeat this check. It is also worth removing the disc (see below) and checking for built-up corrosion (see Step 12) as this will cause runout. If the runout is still excessive, it will have to be replaced with a new one, although machining by an engineer may be possible.

9 The disc must not be machined or allowed to wear down to a thickness less than the service limit as listed in this Chapter's Specifications and as marked on the disc itself **(see illustration)**. Check the thickness of the disc using a micrometer **(see illustration)**. If the thickness of the disc is less than the service limit, it must be replaced with a new one.

Removal

Note: *Always renew the brake pads if fitting new discs. On models with twin front discs, always renew both front brake discs at the same time.*

10 Remove the wheel (see Section 13 or 14).

11 Mark the relationship of the disc to the wheel, so it can be installed in the same position. Unscrew the disc retaining bolts,

3.11 Disc mounting bolts (arrowed) – XL600V rear disc shown

loosening them a little at a time in a criss-cross pattern to avoid distorting the disc, then remove the disc from the wheel **(see illustration)**. On the front wheel also remove the hub cover if required, noting how it fits.

Installation

12 Before installing the disc, make sure there is no dirt or corrosion where the disc seats on the hub, particularly right in the angle of the seat, as this will not allow the disc to sit flat when it is bolted down and it will appear to be warped when checked or when using the brake.

13 If removed, fit the hub cover onto the front wheel, making sure it locates correctly and, on XRV750 models, is on the correct side (the one with the larger internal diameter fits on the right-hand side). Install the disc on the wheel, making sure the directional arrow is on the outside and pointing in the direction of normal (i.e. forward) rotation. Also note any R or L marking on twin front disc models that denotes on which side of the wheel it must be mounted. Align the previously applied matchmarks (if you're reinstalling the original disc).

14 Install the disc mounting bolts, either using new ones or cleaning and applying a suitable non-permanent thread locking compound to the threads of the old ones (see **Note** above), and tighten them evenly in a criss-cross pattern to the torque setting specified at the beginning of the Chapter **(see illustration 3.11)**. Clean off all grease from the brake disc(s) using acetone or brake system cleaner. If a new brake disc has been installed, remove any protective coating from its working surfaces.

15 Install the wheel (see Section 13 or 14).

16 Operate the brake lever and pedal several times to bring the pads into contact with the disc. Check the operation of the brakes carefully before riding the bike.

| 4 | Front brake caliper(s) – removal, overhaul and installation | |

⚠️ *Warning: If a caliper indicates the need for an overhaul (usually due to leaking fluid or sticky operation), all old brake fluid should be flushed from the system. Also, the dust created by the brake system may contain asbestos, which is harmful to your health. Never blow it out with compressed air and don't inhale any of it. An approved filtering mask should be worn when working on the brakes. Do not, under any circumstances, use petroleum-based solvents to clean brake parts. Use clean brake fluid, brake cleaner or denatured alcohol only.*

Removal

1 If the caliper is just being displaced and not completely removed or overhauled, do not disconnect the brake hose. If the caliper is being completely removed or overhauled, remove the brake hose banjo bolt and detach

the hose, noting the alignment with the caliper **(see illustration)**. Plug the hose end or wrap a plastic bag tightly around to minimise fluid loss and prevent dirt entering the system. Discard the sealing washers as new ones must be used on installation. **Note:** *If you are planning to overhaul the caliper and don't have a source of compressed air to blow out the piston, just loosen the banjo bolt at this stage and retighten it lightly. The bike's hydraulic system can then be used to force the piston out of the body once the pads have been removed. Disconnect the hose once the piston have been sufficiently displaced.*

2 On XRV models, remove the fork guards (see Chapter 8). On all models, unscrew the bolt securing the brake hose in the clamp on the front fork and release it, noting how it fits **(see illustration 2.3)**.

3 If the caliper is being overhauled, remove the brake pads (see Section 2). On XL600V-H to P (1987 to 1993) models and XRV750-L to N (1990 to 1992) models this involves removing the calipers, so ignore Step 4.

4 Unscrew the caliper bracket mounting bolts and slide the caliper assembly off the disc **(see illustration)**.

Overhaul

Refer to illustrations 2.4a, 2.4b and 2.18d for exploded views of the caliper

5 Separate the caliper from the bracket by sliding them apart **(see illustration)**. If required, remove the pad spring from the caliper and the guide from the bracket, noting how they fit **(see illustrations)**.

6 Clean the exterior of the caliper with denatured alcohol or brake system cleaner.

7 Remove the pistons from the caliper body, either by pumping them out by operating the brake pedal, or by using compressed air. If the compressed air method is used, place a wad of rag over the pistons to act as a cushion, then use compressed air directed into the fluid inlet to force the pistons out of the body. Use only low pressure to ease the pistons out, and make sure they are displaced at the same time. If the air pressure is too high and a pistons are forced out, the caliper and/or pistons may be damaged.

⚠️ **Warning:** *Never place your fingers in front of the piston in an attempt to catch or protect it when applying compressed air, as serious injury could result. Place the caliper piston side down on a bench, with the rag between them, and let the air lift the caliper off the piston.*

Caution: Do not try to remove the pistons by levering them out, or by using pliers or any other grips.

8 Using a wooden or plastic tool, remove the dust seals from the caliper bore. Discard them as new ones must be used on installation. If a metal tool is being used, take great care not to damage the caliper bores.

9 Remove and discard the piston seals in the same way.

4.1 Brake hose banjo bolt (arrowed)

10 Clean the pistons and bores with denatured alcohol, clean brake fluid or brake system cleaner. If compressed air is available, use it to dry the parts thoroughly (make sure it's filtered and unlubricated).

Caution: Do not, under any circumstances, use a petroleum-based solvent to clean brake parts.

11 Inspect the caliper bores and pistons for signs of corrosion, nicks and burrs and loss of plating. If surface defects are present, the caliper and/or pistons must be replaced with new ones. If the necessary measuring equipment is available, compare the dimensions of the pistons and bores to those given in the Specifications Section of this Chapter, replacing any component that is worn beyond its service limit. If the caliper is in bad shape the master cylinder should also be checked.

12 Remove the slider pin rubber boots from the caliper and the bracket **(see illustration)**. Clean off all traces of corrosion and hardened

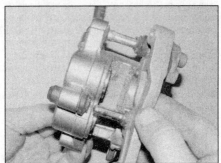
4.5a Separate the caliper and bracket . . .

4.5c . . . and the pad guide (arrowed) – late model XL600V shown

4.4 Unscrew the bolts (arrowed) and slide the caliper off the disc

grease from the boots and pins. Renew the rubber boots if they are damaged, deformed or deteriorated. Apply a smear of silicone based grease to the boots and slider pins. Fit the boots into their bores.

13 Lubricate the new piston seals with clean brake fluid and fit them in their grooves in the caliper bores. Note that on XL650V models different sizes of bore and piston are used (see Specifications), and care must therefore be taken to ensure that the correct size seals are fitted to the correct bores. The same applies when fitting the new dust seals and pistons.

14 Lubricate the new dust seals with clean brake fluid and fit them in their grooves in the caliper bore.

15 Lubricate the pistons with clean brake fluid and fit them closed-end first into the caliper bores. Using your thumbs, push the pistons all the way in, making sure they enter the bore squarely.

4.5b . . . and remove the pad spring (arrowed) . . .

4.12 Remove the rubber boots (arrowed)

7

4.19 Slide the caliper onto the disc and install the bolts

5.1a Brake hose banjo bolt (arrowed) – XL600V

5.1b Brake hose banjo bolt (arrowed) – XL650V and XRV750

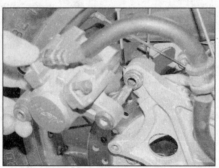

5.2 Slide the caliper off the bracket

16 Make sure that the pad spring and pad guide are correctly fitted (see illustrations 4.5b and c). Slide the caliper and bracket together (see illustration 4.5a).

Installation

17 If the caliper has not been overhauled, separate the caliper from the bracket by sliding them apart (see illustration 4.5a). Remove the slider pin rubber boots from the caliper and the bracket (see illustration 4.12). Clean off all traces of corrosion and hardened grease from the boots and pins. Renew the rubber boots if they are damaged, deformed or deteriorated. Apply a smear of silicone based grease to the boots and slider pins. Fit the boots into their bores. Make sure that the pad spring and pad guide are correctly fitted (see illustrations 4.5b and c).

18 If the caliper has been overhauled, install the brake pads (see Section 2).

19 Slide the caliper onto the disc making sure the pads locate on each side (see illustration). Apply a suitable non-permanent thread-locking compound to the mounting bolts and tighten them securely.

20 If detached, connect the brake hose to the caliper, using new sealing washers on each side of the fitting. Align the hose as noted on removal (see illustration 4.1). Tighten the banjo bolt to the torque setting specified at the beginning of the Chapter.

21 Fit the brake hose into its clamp on the front fork and secure it with the bolt.

22 Fill the master cylinder reservoir with DOT 4 brake fluid (see Daily (pre-ride) checks) and bleed the hydraulic system as described in Section 10.

23 Check for leaks and thoroughly test the operation of the brake before riding the motorcycle.

5 Rear brake caliper – removal, overhaul and installation

⚠ *Warning: If a caliper indicates the need for an overhaul (usually due to leaking fluid or sticky operation), all old brake fluid should be flushed from the system. Also, the dust created by the brake system may contain asbestos, which is harmful to your health. Never blow it out with compressed air and don't inhale any of it. An approved filtering mask should be worn when working on the brakes. Do not, under any circumstances, use petroleum-based solvents to clean brake parts. Use clean brake fluid, brake cleaner or denatured alcohol only.*

Removal

1 If the caliper is just being displaced and not completely removed or overhauled, do not disconnect the brake hose. If the caliper is being completely removed or overhauled, remove the brake hose banjo bolt and detach the hose, noting the alignment with the caliper (see illustrations). Plug the hose end or wrap a plastic bag tightly around to minimise fluid loss and prevent dirt entering the system. Discard the sealing washers as new ones must be used on installation. Note: *If you are planning to overhaul the caliper and don't have a source of compressed air to blow out the piston, just loosen the banjo bolt at this stage and retighten it lightly. The bike's hydraulic system can then be used to force the piston out of the body once the pads have been removed. Disconnect the hose once the piston have been sufficiently displaced.*

2 If the caliper is being overhauled, remove the brake pads (see Section 2), then slide the caliper off the bracket, noting how it fits (see illustration).

3 If the caliper is just being displaced, on XL600V models unscrew the bolt securing the brake hose clamp to the caliper bracket (see illustration 2.32c). Unscrew the caliper rear mounting bolt/slider pin, then pivot the caliper up off the disc and slide it off the bracket, noting how it fits (see illustration 2.35c and 5.2).

Overhaul

4 If required, remove the pad spring from the caliper and the guide from the bracket, noting how they fit (see illustrations).

5 Clean the exterior of the caliper with denatured alcohol or brake system cleaner (see illustration).

6 Remove the piston from the caliper body, either by pumping it out by operating the brake pedal, or by using compressed air. If the compressed air method is used, place a wad of rag over the piston to act as a cushion, then use compressed air directed into the fluid inlet to force the piston out of the body. Use only low pressure to ease the piston out.

5.4a Remove the pad spring (arrowed) . . .

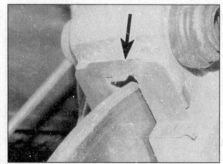

5.4b . . . and the pad guide (arrowed)

If the air pressure is too high and the piston is forced out, the caliper and/or piston may be damaged.

⚠️ **Warning: Never place your fingers in front of the piston in an attempt to catch or protect it when applying compressed air, as serious injury could result. Place the caliper piston side down on a bench, with the rag between them, and let the air lift the caliper off the piston.**
Caution: Do not try to remove the piston by levering it out, or by using pliers or any other grips.

7 Using a wooden or plastic tool, remove the dust seal from the caliper bore. Discard it as a new one must be used on installation. If a metal tool is being used, take great care not to damage the caliper bore.

8 Remove and discard the piston seal in the same way.

9 Clean the piston and bore with denatured alcohol, clean brake fluid or brake system cleaner. If compressed air is available, use it to dry the parts thoroughly (make sure it's filtered and unlubricated).

Caution: Do not, under any circumstances, use a petroleum-based solvent to clean brake parts.

10 Inspect the caliper bore and piston for signs of corrosion, nicks and burrs and loss of plating. If surface defects are present, the caliper and/or piston must be replaced with new ones. If the necessary measuring equipment is available, compare the dimensions of the piston and bore to those given in the Specifications Section of this Chapter, replacing any component that is worn beyond its service limit. If the caliper is in bad shape the master cylinder should also be checked.

11 Remove the collar from the rear slider pin rubber boot and remove the boots from the caliper and the bracket **(see illustrations)**. Clean off all traces of corrosion and hardened grease from the collar, boots and pins. Renew the rubber boots if they are damaged, deformed or deteriorated. Apply a smear of silicone based grease to the collar, boots and slider pins. Fit the boots into their bores, then fit the collar into the rear boot **(see illustrations 5.11b and a)**.

12 Lubricate the new piston seal with clean brake fluid and fit it in its groove in the caliper bore.

13 Lubricate the new dust seal with clean brake fluid and fit it in its groove in the caliper bore.

14 Lubricate the piston with clean brake fluid and fit it closed-end first into the caliper bore. Using your thumbs, push the piston all the way in, making sure it enters the bore squarely.

Installation

15 If the caliper has not been overhauled, remove the collar from the rear slider pin rubber boot and remove the boots from the caliper and the bracket **(see illustrations 5.11a and b)**. Clean off all traces of corrosion

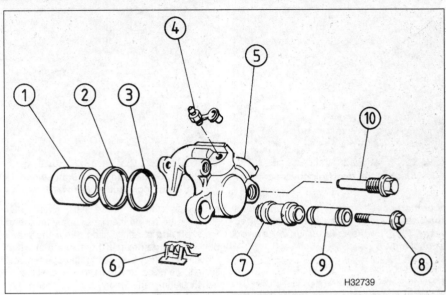

5.5 Rear brake caliper assembly

1 Piston
2 Dust seal
3 Piston seal
4 Bleed valve
5 Caliper
6 Pad spring
7 Boot
8 Mounting bolt/slider pin
9 Collar
10 Slider pin

and hardened grease from the collar, boots and pins. Renew the rubber boots if they are damaged, deformed or deteriorated. Apply a smear of silicone based grease to the collar, boots and slider pins. Fit the boots into their bores, then fit the collar into the rear boot **(see illustrations 5.11b and a)**.

16 Make sure that the pad spring and pad guide are correctly fitted **(see illustrations 5.4a and b)**. Slide the caliper into the bracket **(see illustration 5.2)**.

17 If removed, install the brake pads (see Section 2). If the pads are already installed, pivot the caliper down onto the disc while keeping the pads held in position, locating the leading edges correctly against the guide on the bracket **(see illustration 2.35b)**. Apply a suitable non-permanent thread locking compound to the rear mounting bolt/slider pin and tighten it securely **(see illustration 2.35c)**.

18 If detached, connect the brake hose to the caliper, using new sealing washers on each side of the fitting. Align the hose as noted on removal **(see illustration 5.1a or b)**.

Tighten the banjo bolt to the torque setting specified at the beginning of the Chapter.

19 Fill the master cylinder reservoir with DOT 4 brake fluid (see *Daily (pre-ride) checks*) and bleed the hydraulic system as described in Section 10.

20 Check for leaks and thoroughly test the operation of the brake before riding the motorcycle.

6 Rear brake plate assembly – removal, overhaul and installation (drum brake)

Note: *This procedure applies only to XL600V-H to L (1987 to 1990) models.*

⚠️ **Warning: The dust created by the brake system may contain asbestos, which is harmful to your health. Never blow it out with compressed air and don't inhale any of it. An approved filtering mask should be worn when working on the brakes. Do not, under any**

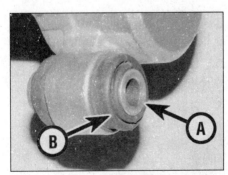

5.11a Withdraw the collar (A) and remove the caliper boot (B) . . .

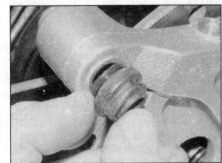

5.11b . . . and the bracket boot

7

7.4 Slacken the reservoir cover screws

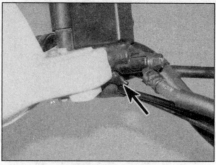

7.5 Disconnect the brake light switch wiring connectors (arrowed)

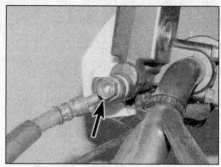

7.6 Brake hose banjo bolt (arrowed)

circumstances, use petroleum-based solvents to clean brake parts. Use clean brake fluid, brake cleaner or denatured alcohol only.

Removal

1 Remove the rear wheel (see Section 14).
2 Lift the brake plate out of the drum in the wheel hub. Remove the brake shoes (see Section 2) **(see illustration 2.24)**.

Inspection

3 Visually inspect the surface of the brake plate for distortion, cracks and other damage, and replace it with a new one if necessary.
4 Check the operation of the actuating cam. If there are any signs of roughness or stiffness, disassemble the plate assembly as follows.
5 Unscrew the nut and withdraw the bolt securing the arm on the end of the actuating shaft and slide the arm off. Note the alignment of the indicator plate then slide that off the shaft. Withdraw the shaft. Remove the thrust plate, noting how it locates.
6 Clean all components in solvent. Check the condition of the splines on the shaft and arm and replace them with new ones if the splines are worn or deformed. Remove the grease seals from the plate and clean the bore. Fit new grease seals if the old ones are deformed, damaged or deteriorated – if there is evidence of dirt and water ingress in the bore and on the shaft then renew them whatever they look like. Check the cam on the inner end of the shaft for wear.
7 Grease the lips of the seals and press them into place. Apply grease to the thrust plate

and place it on the brake plate, locating its slot over the pin on the plate. Apply grease to the shaft and carefully slide it into the brake plate, making sure the thrust plate stays in place, and taking care not to damage the seal lips – it is a good idea to wrap a single layer of thin insulating tape around the shaft splines to prevent damage. Slide the indicator plate onto the shaft with its pointer facing in, and aligning its tab with the cutout on the shaft. Slide the arm onto the shaft, aligning the punch mark on the end of the shaft with that on the outside of the arm. Fit the bolt and secure it with the nut.

Installation

8 Install the brake shoes (see Section 2). Fit the plate assembly into the drum in the rear wheel hub.
9 Install the wheel (see Section 14).

7 Front brake master cylinder – removal, overhaul and installation

1 If the master cylinder is leaking fluid, or if the lever does not produce a firm feel when the brake is applied, and bleeding the brakes does not help (see Section 10), and the hydraulic hoses and unions are all in good condition, then master cylinder overhaul is recommended.
2 Before disassembling the master cylinder, read through the entire procedure and make sure that you have the correct rebuild kit. Also, you will need some new DOT 4 brake

fluid, some clean rags and internal circlip pliers. **Note:** *To prevent damage to the paint from spilled brake fluid, always cover the fuel tank when working on the master cylinder.*
Caution: Disassembly, overhaul and reassembly of the brake master cylinder must be done in a spotlessly clean work area to avoid contamination and possible failure of the brake hydraulic system components.

Removal

Note: *If the master cylinder is being displaced from the handlebar and not being removed completely or overhauled, follow Steps 5 and 7 only.*

3 Remove the rear view mirror (see Chapter 8). Remove the front brake lever (see Chapter 6).
4 Loosen, but do not remove, the screws holding the reservoir cover in place **(see illustration)**.
5 Disconnect the electrical connectors from the brake light switch **(see illustration)**.
6 On XL600V-M to X (1991 to 1999) models and XL650V models, unscrew the brake hose banjo bolt and separate the hose from the master cylinder, noting its alignment **(see illustration)**. Discard the two sealing washers as they must be replaced with new ones. Wrap the end of the hose in a clean rag and suspend it in an upright position or bend it down and place the open end in a clean container. The objective is to prevent excessive loss of brake fluid, fluid spills and system contamination.
7 On XL600V-H to L (1987 to 1990) models and XRV750 models, counter-hold the hose nut, then unscrew the locknut and separate the hose from the hose joint in the master cylinder **(see illustration)**. Wrap the end of the hose in a clean rag and suspend it in an upright position or bend it down and place the open end in a clean container. The objective is to prevent excessive loss of brake fluid, fluid spills and system contamination. If required, unscrew the hose joint and remove it from the master cylinder. Discard the sealing washer as a new one must be used.
8 Unscrew the master cylinder clamp bolts, then lift the master cylinder and reservoir away from the handlebar, noting how the top mating surfaces of the clamp align with the punch mark on the top of the handlebar **(see illustration)**.

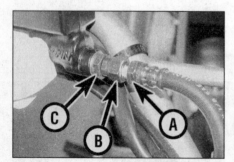

7.7 Counter-hold the hose nut (A), then unscrew the locknut (B) and separate the hose from the hose joint (C)

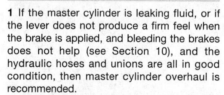

7.8 Front master cylinder clamp bolts (arrowed)

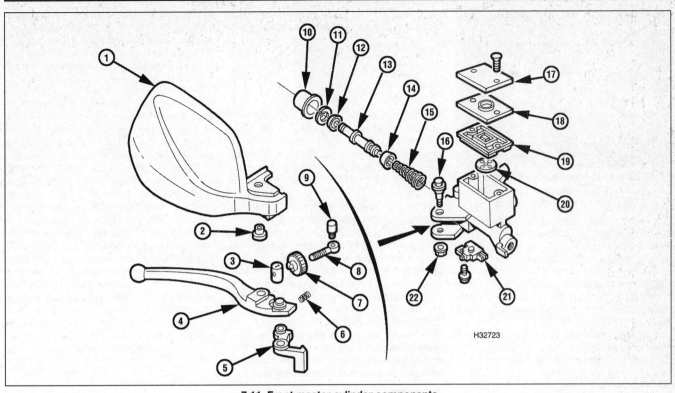

7.11 Front master cylinder components

1 Hand guard	7 Adjuster wheel	13 Piston	18 Plate
2 Collar	8 Adjuster thread	14 Cup	19 Diaphragm
3 Trunnion	9 Pivot	15 Spring	20 Separator
4 Brake lever	10 Rubber boot	16 Lever pivot	21 Brake light
5 Span adjuster	11 Circlip	bolt	switch
6 Spring	12 Seal	17 Reservoir cover	22 Nut

Caution: Do not tip the master cylinder upside down or brake fluid will run out.

9 Remove the reservoir cover, diaphragm plate and rubber diaphragm. Drain the brake fluid from the reservoir into a suitable container. Wipe any remaining fluid out of the reservoir with a clean rag.

10 If required undo the brake light switch screw and remove the switch, noting how it fits.

Overhaul

11 Carefully remove the dust boot from the end of the master cylinder and from around the piston, noting how it locates **(see illustration)**.

12 Push the piston in and, using circlip pliers, remove the circlip from its groove in the master cylinder and slide out the piston assembly and the spring, noting how they fit. If they are difficult to remove, apply low pressure compressed air to the fluid outlet. Lay the parts out in order as you remove them to prevent confusion during reassembly.

13 Clean all parts with clean brake fluid or denatured alcohol. If compressed air is available, use it to dry the parts thoroughly (make sure it's filtered and unlubricated).

Caution: Do not, under any circumstances,

use a petroleum-based solvent to clean brake parts.

14 Check the master cylinder bore for corrosion, scratches, nicks and score marks. If the necessary measuring equipment is available, compare the dimensions of the piston and bore to those given in the Specifications Section of this Chapter. If damage or wear is evident, the master cylinder must be replaced with a new one. If the master cylinder is in poor condition, then the calipers should be checked as well. Check that the fluid inlet and outlet ports in the master cylinder are clear.

15 The dust boot, circlip, piston, seal, cup and spring are included in the rebuild kit. Use all of the new parts, regardless of the apparent condition of the old ones. If the seal and cup are not already on the piston, fit them according to the layout of the old one.

16 Lubricate the cup, seal and piston with clean brake fluid.

17 Fit the spring into the piston so that its narrow end points out, then fit the piston into the master cylinder, making sure it is the correct way round and that it locates correctly against the spring. Make sure the lips on the cup and seal do not turn inside out when they enter the bore. Depress the piston and install

the new circlip, making sure that it locates in the groove in the master cylinder.

18 Apply some silicone grease to the inside of the rubber dust boot, then install it, making sure it is seated properly in the groove in the master cylinder and around the piston.

19 Inspect the reservoir rubber diaphragm and renew it if it is damaged or deteriorated.

Installation

20 Locate the brake light switch on the underside of the master cylinder and secure it with the screw.

21 Attach the master cylinder to the handlebar and fit the clamp with its UP mark facing up **(see illustration)**. Align the top mating surfaces of the clamp with the punch mark on the top of the handlebar, then tighten the top bolt first, then the bottom bolt to the torque setting specified at the beginning of the Chapter.

22 On XL600V-M to X (1991 to 1999) models and XL650V models, connect the brake hose to the master cylinder, using new sealing washers on each side of the union, and aligning the hose as noted on removal **(see illustration 7.6)**. Tighten the banjo bolt to the torque setting specified at the beginning of the Chapter.

7

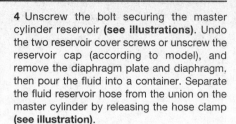

7.21 Align the clamp mating surfaces with the punch mark (arrowed), and fit the clamp with the UP mark facing up

23 On XL600V-H to L (1987 to 1990) models and XRV750 models, if removed thread the hose joint into the master cylinder using a new sealing washer and tighten it securely. Fit the brake hose onto the hose joint and tighten the locknut onto the hose, counter-holding the hose nut to prevent the hose twisting **(see illustration 7.7)**. Do not overtighten the locknut.

24 Connect the brake light switch wiring **(see illustration 7.5)**.

25 Install the brake lever (see Chapter 6) and the rear view mirror (see Chapter 8).

26 Fill the fluid reservoir with new DOT 4 brake fluid as described in *Daily (pre-ride) checks*. Refer to Section 10 of this Chapter and bleed the air from the system.

27 Fit the rubber diaphragm, making sure it is correctly seated, the diaphragm plate and the cover or cap onto the reservoir.

28 Check the operation of the front brake and brake light before riding the motorcycle.

8 Rear brake master cylinder – removal, overhaul and installation

1 If the master cylinder is leaking fluid, or if the lever does not produce a firm feel when the brake is applied, and bleeding the brakes does not help (see Section 10), and the hydraulic hoses and unions are all in good condition, then master cylinder overhaul is recommended.

2 Before disassembling the master cylinder, read through the entire procedure and make sure that you have the correct rebuild kit. Also, you will need some new DOT 4 brake fluid, some clean rags and internal circlip pliers. **Note:** *To prevent damage to the paint from spilled brake fluid, always cover the surrounding components when working on the master cylinder.*

Caution: Disassembly, overhaul and reassembly of the brake master cylinder must be done in a spotlessly clean work area to avoid contamination and possible failure of the brake hydraulic system components.

Removal

3 Remove the right-hand side panel (see Chapter 8). On XRV750-L to N (1990 to 1992) models, unscrew the bolts securing the right-hand passenger footrest bracket and remove it, noting how it fits.

4 Unscrew the bolt securing the master cylinder reservoir **(see illustrations)**. Undo the two reservoir cover screws or unscrew the reservoir cap (according to model), and remove the diaphragm plate and diaphragm, then pour the fluid into a container. Separate the fluid reservoir hose from the union on the master cylinder by releasing the hose clamp **(see illustration)**.

5 Unscrew the brake hose banjo bolt and separate the hose from the master cylinder, noting its alignment **(see illustration)**. Discard the sealing washers as they must be replaced with new ones. Wrap the end of the hose in a clean rag and suspend it in an upright position, or bend it down carefully and place the open end in a clean container. The objective is to prevent excessive loss of brake fluid, fluid spills and system contamination.

6 Remove the split pin from the clevis pin securing the brake pedal to the master cylinder pushrod, then remove the clevis pin and separate the pedal from the pushrod **(see illustrations)**.

7 Unscrew the two bolts securing the master cylinder to the bracket and remove the master cylinder **(see illustration 8.4c)**.

Overhaul

8 If required, and where it is not secured by a roll pin, mark the position of the clevis locknut on the pushrod, then slacken the locknut and thread the clevis and its base nut off the pushrod **(see illustration)**. If a roll pin is fitted, it will have to be drifted out.

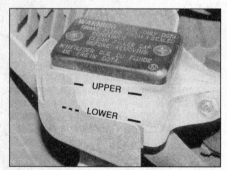

8.4a Master cylinder reservoir – XL600V

8.4b Master cylinder reservoir – XRV750

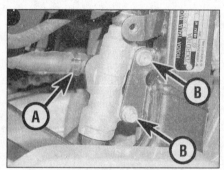

8.4c Reservoir hose clamp (A), master cylinder mounting bolts (B)

8.5 Brake hose banjo bolt (arrowed)

8.6a Remove the split pin . . .

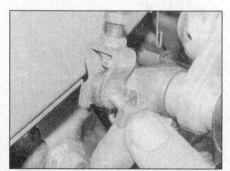

8.6b . . . then withdraw the clevis pin

9 Dislodge the rubber dust boot from the base of the master cylinder and from around the pushrod, noting how it locates, and slide it up the pushrod.

10 Push the pushrod in and, using circlip pliers, remove the circlip from its groove in the master cylinder and slide out the piston assembly and the spring, noting how they fit. If they are difficult to remove, apply low pressure compressed air to the fluid outlet. Lay the parts out in the proper order to prevent confusion during reassembly.

11 If required, remove the screw securing the fluid reservoir hose union and detach it from the master cylinder. Discard the O-ring as a new one must be used. Inspect the reservoir hose for cracks or splits and replace with a new one if necessary.

12 Clean all of the parts with clean brake fluid or denatured alcohol.

Caution: Do not, under any circumstances, use a petroleum-based solvent to clean brake parts. If compressed air is available, use it to dry the parts thoroughly (make sure it's filtered and unlubricated).

13 Check the master cylinder bore for corrosion, scratches, nicks and score marks. If the necessary measuring equipment is available, compare the dimensions of the piston and bore to those given in the Specifications Section of this Chapter. If damage or wear is evident, the master cylinder must be replaced with a new one. If the master cylinder is in poor condition, then the caliper should be checked as well.

14 The dust boot, circlip, piston, seal, cup and spring are included in the rebuild kit. Use all of the new parts, regardless of the apparent condition of the old ones. If the seal is not already on the piston, fit it according to the layout of the old one. Slide the new boot onto the pushrod, making sure it is the correct way round.

15 Fit the cup over the end of the spring so that its inner raised section fits into the outer coil on the spring. Lubricate the cup, seal and piston with clean brake fluid.

16 Install the spring in the master cylinder with the cup facing out, then fit the piston into the master cylinder, making sure it is the correct way round. Make sure the lips on the cup and seal do not turn inside out when they enter the bore.

17 Apply some silicone grease to the end of the pushrod and fit it into the master cylinder. Depress the pushrod, then install the new circlip, making sure it is properly seated in the groove.

18 Install the rubber dust boot, making sure it is seated properly in the groove in the master cylinder and around the pushrod.

19 If removed, fit a new O-ring to the fluid reservoir hose union, then fit the union onto the master cylinder and secure it with its screw.

20 If removed, thread the clevis locknut and the clevis onto the master cylinder pushrod end. Set the clevis position as noted on

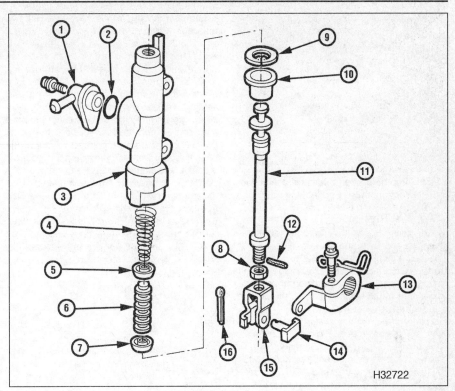

8.8 Rear master cylinder components

1 Reservoir hose union	6 Piston	11 Pushrod
2 O-ring	7 Seal	12 Roll pin
3 Master cylinder	8 Nut	13 Brake pedal arm
4 Spring	9 Circlip	14 Clevis pin
5 Cup	10 Rubber boot	15 Clevis
		16 Split pin

removal. Honda specify the distance between the eye in the clevis and the lower mounting bolt hole should be 100 mm. Tighten the clevis locknut securely against the clevis.

21 Where the clevis is retained by a roll pin, secure it in position with a new pin.

Installation

22 Fit the master cylinder onto the footrest bracket and tighten its mounting bolts to the torque setting specified at the beginning of the Chapter **(see illustration 8.4c)**.

23 Align the brake pedal with the master cylinder pushrod clevis, then slide in the clevis pin and secure it using a new split pin **(see illustrations 8.6b and a)**.

24 Connect the brake hose to the master cylinder, using new sealing washers on each side of the union. Align the hose as noted on removal and tighten the banjo bolt to the specified torque setting **(see illustration 8.5)**.

25 Fit the fluid reservoir on its mount and secure it with its bolt **(see illustration 8.4a or b)**. Ensure that the hose is correctly routed then connect it to the union on the master cylinder and secure it with the clamp **(see illustration 8.4c)**. Check that the hose is secure and clamped at the reservoir end as well. If the clamps have weakened, use new ones.

26 Fill the fluid reservoir with new DOT 4 brake fluid (see *Daily (pre-ride) checks*) and bleed the system following the procedure in Section 10.

27 Check the operation of the brake and brake light carefully before riding the motorcycle.

28 On XRV750-L to N (1990 to 1992) models, install the right-hand passenger footrest bracket and tighten its bolts securely. Install the right-hand side panel (see Chapter 8).

9 Brake hoses and unions – inspection and replacement

Inspection

1 Brake hose and pipe condition should be checked regularly (see Chapter 1).

2 Twist and flex the rubber hoses while looking for cracks, bulges and seeping fluid **(see illustration)**. Check extra carefully around the areas where the hoses connect with the banjo fittings, as these are common areas for hose failure.

3 Inspect the metal brake pipes and the banjo union fittings connected to the brake hoses. If the fittings are rusted, scratched or cracked, replace them with new ones.

7

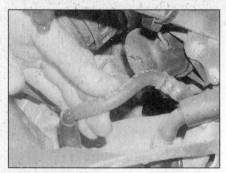

9.2 Flex the brake hoses and check for cracks, bulges and leaking fluid

Replacement

4 The brake hoses have banjo union fittings on each end, with the exception of the front master cylinder hose on XL600V-H to L (1987 to 1990) models and XRV750 models which has a hose joint piece, and the brake pipes have joint nuts securing them in their unions **(see illustrations 7.6 and 7.7)**. Cover the surrounding area with plenty of rags and unscrew the banjo bolt or joint nut at each end of the hose or pipe, noting its alignment. On the front master cylinder hose on XL600V-H to L (1987 to 1990) models and XRV750 models, counter-hold the hose nut and unscrew the locknut and separate the hose from the hose joint in the caliper **(see illustration 7.7)**. If required, unscrew the hose joint from the master cylinder. Free the hoses/pipes from any clips or guides and remove them. Discard the sealing washers as new ones must be used.

5 Position the new hose, making sure it isn't twisted or otherwise strained, and abut the tab on the hose union with the lug on the component casting, where present. Otherwise align the hose or pipe as noted on removal. Install the hose banjo bolts using new sealing washers on both sides of the unions. Tighten the banjo bolts to the torque setting specified at the beginning of this Chapter.

6 Locate the end of the new pipe into its union and tighten the nut securely, but not overtight.

7 On the front master cylinder hose on XL600V-H to L (1987 to 1990) models and XRV750 models, if removed, thread the joint piece into the master cylinder using a new sealing washer and tighten it securely **(see illustration 7.7)**. Fit the hose against the hose joint and tighten the locknut onto the hose, counter-holding the hose nut to prevent the hose twisting. Do not overtighten the locknut.

8 Make sure the hoses and pipes are correctly aligned and routed clear of all moving components. Flush the old brake fluid from the system, refill with new DOT 4 brake fluid (see *Daily (pre-ride) checks*) and bleed the air from the system (see Section 10). Check the operation of the brakes carefully before riding the motorcycle.

10 Brake system –
bleeding and fluid renewal

Bleeding

Note: *Honda recommend using a commercially available vacuum-type brake bleeding tool (see illustration). If bleeding the system using the conventional method does not work sufficiently well, it is advisable to obtain a bleeder and repeat the procedure detailed below, following the manufacturers instructions for using the tool. If the tool is not available, take the machine to a Honda dealer.*

1 Bleeding the brakes is simply the process of removing all the air bubbles from the brake fluid reservoirs, the hoses and the brake calipers. Bleeding is necessary whenever a brake system hydraulic connection is loosened, when a component or hose is replaced, or when the master cylinder or caliper is overhauled. Leaks in the system may also allow air to enter, but leaking brake

10. NOTE Bleeding the brakes using a commercial vacuum-operated bleeding tool

fluid will reveal their presence and warn you of the need for repair.

2 To bleed the brakes, you will need some new DOT 4 brake fluid, a length of clear vinyl or plastic tubing, a small container partially filled with clean brake fluid, some rags and a ring spanner to fit the brake caliper bleed valves.

3 Cover the fuel tank, fairing panels, front mudguard and other painted components to prevent damage in the event that brake fluid is spilled.

4 Remove the reservoir cover or cap, diaphragm plate and diaphragm (see Daily (pre-ride) checks) and slowly pump the brake lever or pedal a few times, until no air bubbles can be seen floating up from the holes in the bottom of the reservoir. Doing this bleeds the air from the master cylinder end of the line. Loosely refit the reservoir cover.

5 Pull the dust cap off the bleed valve **(see illustration)**. Attach one end of the clear vinyl or plastic tubing to the bleed valve and submerge the other end in the brake fluid in the container **(see illustration)**.

6 Remove the reservoir cap or cover and check the fluid level. Do not allow the fluid level to drop below the lower mark during the bleeding process.

10.5a Brake caliper bleed valve (arrowed)

10.5b To bleed the brakes, you need a spanner, a short section of clear tubing, and a clear container half-filled with brake fluid

7 Carefully pump the brake lever or pedal three or four times and hold it in (front) or down (rear) while opening the caliper bleed valve. When the valve is opened, brake fluid will flow out of the caliper into the clear tubing and the lever will move toward the handlebar or the pedal will move down.

8 Retighten the bleed valve, then release the brake lever or pedal gradually. Repeat the process until no air bubbles are visible in the brake fluid leaving the caliper and the lever or pedal is firm when applied. On completion, disconnect the bleeding equipment, then tighten the bleed valve to the torque setting specified at the beginning of the chapter and install the dust cap. On models with twin front disc brakes repeat the procedure on the other caliper.

9 Install the diaphragm, plate and cover or cap assembly, wipe up any spilled brake fluid and check the entire system for leaks.

 If it's not possible to produce a firm feel to the lever or pedal the fluid my be aerated. Let the brake fluid in the system stabilise for a few hours and then repeat the procedure when the tiny bubbles in the system have settled out. Also check to make sure that there are no 'high-spots' in the brake hose in which an air bubble can become trapped – this will occur most often in an incorrectly mounted hose union, but can also arise through bleeding the brakes while some of the brake system components are at such an angle to encourage this. Reversing the angle or displacing and moving the offending component around will normally dislodge any trapped air.

Renewing the fluid

10 Changing the brake fluid is a similar process to bleeding the brakes and requires the same materials plus a suitable tool for siphoning the fluid out of the hydraulic reservoir. Also ensure that the container is large enough to take all the old fluid when it is flushed out of the system.

11 Follow Steps 3 and 5, then remove the reservoir cap, diaphragm plate and diaphragm and siphon the old fluid out of the reservoir. Fill the reservoir with new brake fluid, then follow Step 7.

12 Retighten the bleed valve, then release the brake lever or pedal gradually. Keep the reservoir topped-up with new fluid to above the LOWER level at all times or air may enter the system and greatly increase the length of the task. Repeat the process until new fluid can be seen emerging from the bleed valve.

 Old brake fluid is invariably much darker in colour than new fluid, making it easy to see when all old fluid has been expelled from the system.

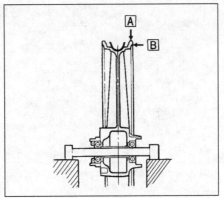

11.2 Check the wheel for radial (out-of-round) runout (A) and axial (side-to-side) runout (B)

13 Disconnect the hose, then tighten the bleed valve to the specified torque setting and install the dust cap.

14 Top-up the reservoir, install the diaphragm, plate and cover or cap, and wipe up any spilled brake fluid. Check the entire system for fluid leaks.

15 Check the operation of the brakes before riding the motorcycle.

11 Wheels – inspection and repair

1 Position the motorcycle on its centrestand if fitted or on an auxiliary stand. When checking the front wheel, support the bike so that it is raised off the ground. Clean the wheels thoroughly to remove mud and dirt that may interfere with the inspection procedure or mask defects. Make a general check of the wheels (see Chapter 1) and tyres (see *Daily (pre-ride) checks*).

2 To check axial (side-to-side) runout, attach a dial gauge to the fork slider or the swingarm and position its stem against the side of the rim **(see illustration)**. Spin the wheel slowly and check the amount of runout at the rim. To accurately check radial (out of round) runout with the dial gauge, remove the wheel from the machine, and the tyre from the wheel. With the axle clamped in a vice and the dial gauge positioned on the top of the rim, rotate the wheel and check the runout.

3 An easier, though slightly less accurate,

method is to attach a stiff wire pointer to the fork slider or the swingarm and position the end a fraction of an inch from the wheel (where the wheel and tyre join). If the wheel is true, the distance from the pointer to the rim will be constant as the wheel is rotated. **Note:** *If wheel runout is excessive, check the wheel bearings and axle very carefully before replacing.*

4 Visually inspect the wheels for cracks, flat spots on the rim, and other damage. Look very closely for dents in the area where the tyre bead contacts the rim.

5 If damage is evident, or if runout in either direction is excessive, the wheel will have to be rebuilt by a professional wheel builder who will replace the damaged components with new ones, then make sure the wheel is properly aligned, tensioned and balanced.

12 Wheels – alignment check

1 Misalignment of the wheels, which may be due to a cocked rear wheel or a bent frame or fork yokes, can cause strange and possibly serious handling problems. If the frame or yokes are at fault, repair by a frame specialist or replacement with new parts are the only alternatives.

2 To check the alignment you will need an assistant, a length of string or a perfectly straight piece of wood and a ruler. A plumb bob or other suitable weight will also be required.

3 Place the bike on the centrestand (where fitted) or an auxiliary stand. Measure the width of both tyres at their widest points. Subtract the smaller measurement from the larger measurement, then divide the difference by two. The result is the amount of offset that should exist between the front and rear tyres on both sides.

4 If a string is used, have your assistant hold one end of it about halfway between the floor and the rear axle, touching the rear sidewall of the tyre.

5 Run the other end of the string forward and pull it tight so that it is roughly parallel to the floor **(see illustration)**. Slowly bring the string into contact with the front sidewall of the rear tyre, then turn the front wheel until it is parallel with the string. Measure the distance from the front tyre sidewall to the string.

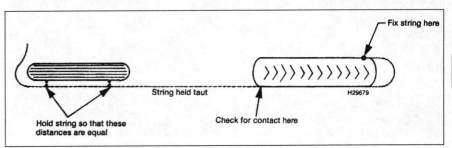

12.5 Wheel alignment check using string

7

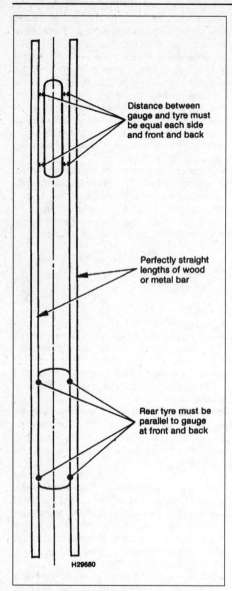

Distance between gauge and tyre must be equal each side and front and back

Perfectly straight lengths of wood or metal bar

Rear tyre must be parallel to gauge at front and back

H29680

12.7 Wheel alignment check using a straight edge

6 Repeat the procedure on the other side of the motorcycle. The distance from the front tyre sidewall to the string should be equal on both sides.

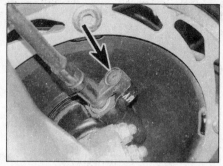

13.3 Undo the screw (arrowed) and detach the cable

7 As previously mentioned, a perfectly straight length of wood or metal bar may be substituted for the string (see illustration). The procedure is the same.
8 If the distance between the string and tyre is greater on one side, or if the rear wheel appears to be cocked, refer to Chapter 1 and check that the chain adjuster markings are in the same position on each side of the swingarm.
9 If the front-to-back alignment is correct, the wheels still may be out of alignment vertically.
10 Using a plumb bob, or other suitable weight, and a length of string, check the rear wheel to make sure it is vertical. To do this, hold the string against the tyre upper sidewall and allow the weight to settle just off the floor. When the string touches both the upper and lower tyre sidewalls and is perfectly straight, the wheel is vertical. If it is not, place thin spacers under one leg of the stand until it is.
11 Once the rear wheel is vertical, check the front wheel in the same manner. If both wheels are not perfectly vertical, the frame and/or major suspension components are bent.

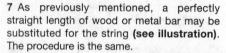

13 Front wheel –
removal and installation

Removal

1 Position the motorcycle on its centrestand if fitted or on an auxiliary stand and support it

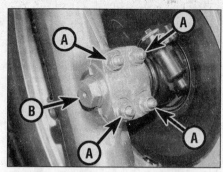

13.4 Slacken the axle clamp nuts (A), then unscrew the axle (B)

so that the front wheel is off the ground. Always make sure the motorcycle is properly supported.
2 Displace the brake calipers (see Section 4). Support the calipers with a cable tie or a bungee cord so that no strain is placed on the hydraulic hoses. There is no need to disconnect the hoses from the calipers. **Note:** *Do not operate the front brake lever with the calipers removed.*
3 Undo the screw securing the speedometer cable in the drive housing on the right-hand side of the wheel and detach the cable, noting how it locates (see illustration).
4 Slacken the axle clamp nuts on the bottom of the right-hand fork, then unscrew the axle (see illustration).
5 Support the wheel, then withdraw the axle from the right-hand side, using a drift to tap it out if necessary, and carefully lower the wheel (see illustration).
6 Remove the speedometer drive housing from the right-hand side of the wheel, noting how it fits, and the spacer from the left-hand side, noting which way round it fits (see illustrations).
Caution: Don't lay the wheel down and allow it to rest on a disc – the disc could become warped. Set the wheel on wood blocks so the disc doesn't support the weight of the wheel.
7 Check the axle for straightness by rolling it on a flat surface such as a piece of plate glass (first wipe off all old grease and remove any corrosion using fine emery cloth). If the equipment is available, place the axle in

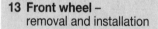

13.6a Remove the speedometer drive housing . . .

13.6b . . . and the spacer

13.5 Withdraw the axle and remove the wheel

V-blocks and measure the runout using a dial gauge. If the axle is bent or the runout exceeds the limit specified, replace it with a new one.

8 Check the condition of the grease seals and wheel bearings (see Section 15).

Installation

9 Apply a smear of grease to the inside of the speedometer drive housing and the wheel spacer, and also to the outside where they fit into the wheel. Fit the drive housing into the right-hand side of the wheel, locating its slots over the drive plate tabs, and the spacer into the left-hand side, with its shouldered end facing out (see illustrations 13.6a and b).

10 Manoeuvre the wheel into position between the fork sliders with the speedometer drive on the right-hand side. Apply a thin coat of grease to the axle.

11 Lift the wheel into place, making sure the drive housing and spacer remain in position. Slide the axle in from the right-hand side (see illustration 13.5) and thread it into place. Rotate the speedometer drive housing so that its lug butts up against the back of the stopper on the front fork (see illustration), then tighten the axle to the torque setting specified at the beginning of the Chapter (see illustration). Check that the wheel spins freely.

12 Lower the front wheel to the ground, then install the brake calipers (see Section 4).

13 Apply the front brake a few times to bring the pads back into contact with the discs. Move the motorcycle off its stand, apply the front brake and pump the front forks a few times to settle all components in position.

14 Now tighten the axle clamp nuts on the bottom of the right-hand fork to the specified torque setting, tightening the upper ones first, then the lower ones (see illustration 13.4). Note that if the clamp face was removed it must be fitted with the UP mark pointing up (see illustration).

15 Fit the speedometer cable into the drive housing, making sure it engages correctly, and secure it with its screw (see illustrations).

16 Check for correct operation of the brakes before riding the motorcycle.

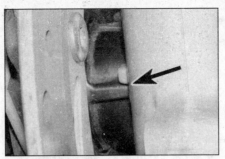

13.11a Butt the speedometer drive housing against the back of the lug (arrowed)

14 Rear wheel – removal and installation

XL600V-H and V-L models (1987 to 1990)

Removal

1 Position the motorcycle on its centrestand if fitted or on an auxiliary stand and support it so that the rear wheel is off the ground. Always make sure the motorcycle is properly supported.

2 Fully unscrew the adjusting wingnut on the end of the brake rod, then pivot the arm rearwards and off the rod. Take care not to lose the spring that locates between the arm and the but on the rod.

3 Slacken the rear axle nut.

4 Slacken the locknut on the adjuster on each end of the swingarm, then turn the adjuster nut out on each side to provide some slack in the chain. Move the rear wheel forwards in the swingarm to create the slack.

5 Unscrew the axle nut and remove the washer, noting how it locates.

6 Support the wheel, then withdraw the axle from the left-hand side and lower the wheel to the ground. Disengage the chain from the sprocket and remove the wheel from the swingarm. If the axle is difficult to withdraw, drive it through, making sure you don't damage the threads.

Caution: Do not lay the wheel down and allow it to rest on the sprocket – it could

13.11b Tighten the axle to the specified torque

become warped. Set the wheel on wood blocks so the sprocket doesn't support the weight of the wheel.

7 Remove the spacer from the left-hand side of the wheel.

8 Check the axle for straightness by rolling it on a flat surface such as a piece of plate glass (if the axle is corroded, first remove the corrosion with fine emery cloth). If the equipment is available, place the axle in V-blocks and check the runout using a dial gauge. If the axle is bent or the runout exceeds the limit specified at the beginning of the Chapter, replace it with a new one.

9 Check the condition of the grease seals and wheel bearings (see Section 15).

Installation

10 Apply a smear of grease to the inside of the wheel spacer, and also to the outside it fits into the wheel. Fit the spacer into the left-hand side.

11 Manoeuvre the wheel so that it is in between the ends of the swingarm. Apply a thin coat of grease to the axle. Make sure the brake plate is correctly fitted into the drum and that the sprocket carrier is correctly fitted in the hub.

12 Engage the drive chain with the sprocket and lift the wheel into position. Make sure the spacer remains correctly in place, and that the slot in the brake plate locates over the lug on the swingarm to prevent it turning.

13 Install the axle from the left, making sure it passes through the chain adjusters. Check that everything is correctly aligned.

14 Fit the washer, making sure its squared

13.14 Make sure the UP mark faces up

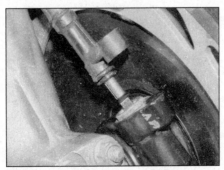

13.15a Make sure the drive tab locates in the slot in the cable end . . .

13.15b . . . then secure the cable with the screw

7

14.20a Axle nut (arrowed) – XL models

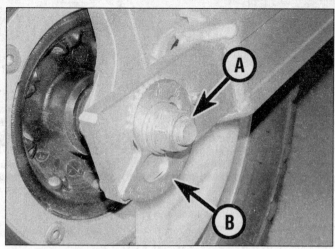

14.20b Axle nut (A) and eccentric adjuster (B) – XRV models

edge locates correctly under the swingarm, then fit the nut.

15 Make sure the spring is located on the brake rod, then pivot the brake arm rearwards and slide it onto the rod.

16 Now check and adjust the drive chain slack (see Chapter 1). On completion tighten the axle nut to the torque setting specified at the beginning of the Chapter, counter-holding the axle head on the other side of the wheel to prevent it turning if necessary.

17 Operate the brake pedal several times to bring the shoes into contact with the drum. Check the operation of the rear brake carefully before riding the bike.

14.21a Slacken the locknut (arrowed) . . .

XL600V-M models onward (1991-on), XL650V and XRV750 models

Removal

18 Position the motorcycle on its centrestand if fitted or on an auxiliary stand and support it so that the rear wheel is off the ground. Always make sure the motorcycle is properly supported.

19 On all XL600V models, remove the brake caliper rear bolt and pivot it up (see Section 5).

20 Slacken the rear axle nut (see illustrations).

21 On XL models, slacken the locknut on the adjuster on each end of the swingarm, then turn the adjuster nut out on each side to provide some slack in the chain (see illustrations). On XRV models, turn the eccentric adjuster on each side to provide some slack in the chain (see illustration 14.20b). Move the rear wheel forwards in the swingarm to create the slack.

22 Unscrew the axle nut and remove the washer, on XL models noting how it locates (see illustration 14.20a). On XRV models remove the right-hand adjuster from the end of the axle (see illustration 14.20b).

23 Support the wheel, then withdraw the axle from the left-hand side and lower the wheel to the ground (see illustration). Disengage the chain from the sprocket and remove the wheel from the swingarm (see illustration). If the axle is difficult to withdraw, drift it through, making sure you don't damage the threads. On XRV750 retrieve the left-hand chain adjuster from the axle or the floor.

24 Note how the rear brake caliper bracket locates against the swingarm, and support it so that it will not fall off. If required, displace it from the swingarm, noting how it fits, and tie it up, making sure no strain is placed on the hose.

Caution: Do not lay the wheel down and allow it to rest on the disc or the sprocket – they could become warped. Set the wheel on wood blocks so the disc or the sprocket doesn't support the weight of the wheel. Do not operate the brake pedal with the wheel removed.

25 Remove the spacer from each side of the wheel for safekeeping, noting which fits where (see illustrations).

26 Check the axle for straightness by rolling it on a flat surface such as a piece of plate glass (if the axle is corroded, first remove the corrosion with fine emery cloth). If the equipment is available, place the axle in V-blocks and check the runout using a dial gauge. If the axle is bent or the runout exceeds the limit specified at the beginning of the Chapter, replace it with a new one.

14.21b . . . then turn the adjuster out to provide slack

14.23a Withdraw the axle . . .

14.23b . . . then lower the wheel to the ground and disengage the chain

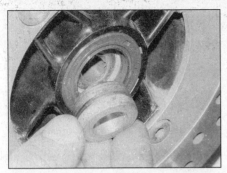

14.25a Remove the spacer from the right-hand side . . .

14.25b . . . and from the left-hand side, noting which fits where

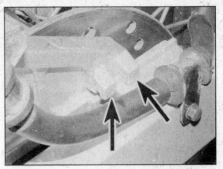

14.28a Make sure the brake caliper locates correctly (arrows) – XL600V

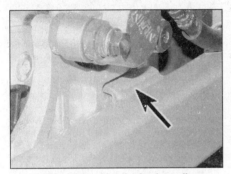

14.28b Make sure the brake caliper locates correctly (arrow) – XL650V

14.28c Make sure the brake caliper locates correctly (arrows) – XRV750

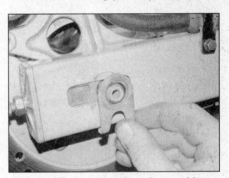

14.32a Fit the shaped washer, making sure it locates correctly . . .

27 Check the condition of the grease seals and wheel bearings (see Section 15).

Installation

28 Apply a smear of grease to the inside of the wheel spacers, and also to the outside where they fit into the wheel. Fit the short spacer into the right-hand side of the wheel and the long spacer into the left-hand side **(see illustrations 14.25a and b)**. If displaced, fit the brake caliper bracket onto the swingarm, making sure it locates correctly **(see illustrations)**.

29 Manoeuvre the wheel so that it is in between the ends of the swingarm. Apply a thin coat of grease to the axle. Make sure the brake caliper bracket is still correctly positioned against the swingarm and the sprocket carrier is correctly fitted in the hub.

30 Engage the drive chain with the sprocket and lift the wheel into position **(see illustration 14.23b)**. Make sure the spacers and caliper bracket and sprocket carrier remain correctly in place and that the brake disc fits squarely into the caliper, with the pads positioned correctly each side of the disc.

31 On XRV750 models fit the left-hand chain adjuster onto the axle, making sure it is the correct way round. On all models install the axle from the left, on XL models making sure it passes through the chain adjusters **(see illustration 14.23a)**. Check that everything is correctly aligned.

32 On XL models, fit the washer, making sure its squared edge locates correctly under the swingarm, then fit the nut **(see illustrations)**. On XRV models fit the right-hand adjuster onto the end of the axle, making sure it is the

correct way round, then fit the washer and nut **(see illustration 14.20b)**.

33 Now check and adjust the drive chain slack (see Chapter 1). On completion tighten the axle nut to the torque setting specified at the beginning of the Chapter, counter-holding the axle head on the other side of the wheel to prevent it turning if necessary.

34 Operate the brake pedal several times to bring the pads into contact with the disc. Check the operation of the rear brake carefully before riding the bike.

15 Wheel bearings – removal, inspection and installation

Front wheel bearings

Note: *Always replace the wheel bearings in pairs. Never replace the bearings individually. Avoid using a high pressure cleaner on the wheel bearing area.*

1 Remove the wheel, and if not already done remove the speedometer drive housing and spacer from it (see Section 13).

2 Set the wheel on blocks so as not to allow the weight to rest on the brake disc.

3 Prise out the seal on the left-hand side of the wheel using a flat-bladed screwdriver, taking care not to damage the rim of the hub, then turn the wheel over and remove the seal from the right-hand side **(see illustration)**. Discard the seals as new ones should be used. Remove the speedometer drive plate

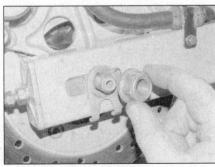

14.32b . . . then fit the nut

15.3a Lever out the grease seal on each side

7

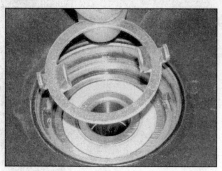

15.3b Remove the speedometer drive plate, noting how it fits

15.4a Knock out the bearings using a drift . . .

Refer to Tools and Workshop Tips (Section 5) for more information about bearings.

7 Hold the outer race of the bearing and rotate the inner race – if the bearing doesn't turn smoothly, has rough spots or is noisy, replace it with a new one.

8 If the bearing is good and can be re-used, wash it in solvent once again and dry it, then pack the bearing with grease if it is of the unsealed type.

9 Thoroughly clean the hub area of the wheel. Install the left-hand bearing into the recess in the hub, with the marked or sealed side facing outwards. Using the old bearing (if new ones are being fitted), a bearing driver or a socket large enough to contact the outer race of the bearing, drive it in until it's completely seated (see illustration).

10 Turn the wheel over and install the bearing spacer. Drive the other bearing into place as described above.

11 Fit the speedometer drive plate into the right-hand side of the wheel, locating the tabs in the cutouts in the hub (see illustration 15.3b). Apply a smear of grease to the lips of the seals, then press them into the wheel (see illustration). Gently drive them into place if necessary using a seal or bearing driver, a suitable socket or a piece of wood (see illustration).

12 Clean off all grease from the brake discs using acetone or brake system cleaner then install the wheel (see Section 13).

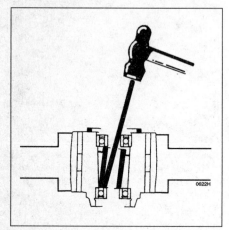

15.4b . . . locating it as shown

from the right-hand side of the wheel, noting how it locates (see illustration).

4 Using a metal rod (preferably a brass drift punch) inserted through the centre of the upper bearing, tap evenly around the inner race of the lower bearing to drive it from the hub (see illustrations). The bearing spacer will also come out.

5 Lay the wheel on its other side so that the remaining bearing faces down. Remove the seal and drive the bearing out of the wheel using the same technique as above.

6 If the bearings are of the unsealed type or are only sealed on one side, clean them with a high flash-point solvent (one which won't leave any residue) and blow them dry with compressed air (don't let the bearings spin as you dry them). Apply a few drops of oil to the bearing. Note: If the bearing is sealed on both sides don't attempt to clean it.

Rear wheel bearings

13 Remove the rear wheel, and if not already done remove the spacers from it (see Section 14). Lift the sprocket coupling out of the left-hand side of the wheel, noting how it fits (see illustration). On XL600V-H to L (1987 to 1990) models, lift the brake plate assembly out of the right-hand side of the wheel, noting how it fits.

14 Set the wheel on blocks so as not to allow the weight of the wheel to rest on the brake disc.

15 On all except XL600V-H to L (1987 to 1990) models, lever out the grease seal on the right-hand side of the wheel using a flat-bladed screwdriver, taking care not to damage the rim of the hub (see illustration).

15.9 A socket can be used to drive in the bearing

15.11a Fit the grease seal and press it into place . . .

15.11b . . . or use a socket to drive it in if necessary

15.13 Lift the sprocket coupling out of the wheel

15.15 Lever out the grease seal

15.17 Drive the bearings out as described

15.20 A socket can be used to drive in the bearing

15.21 Check the O-ring and fit a new one if necessary

Discard the seal as a new one should be used.

16 Using a metal rod (preferably a brass drift punch) inserted through the centre of the right-hand bearing, tap evenly around the inner race of the left-hand bearing to drive it from the hub **(see illustrations 15.4a and b)**. The bearing spacer will also come out.

17 Lay the wheel on its other side so that the remaining bearing faces down. Drive the bearing out of the wheel using the same technique as above **(see illustration)**.

18 Refer to Steps 6 to 8 above and check the bearings.

19 Thoroughly clean the hub area of the wheel. First install the right-hand bearing into its recess in the hub, with the marked or sealed side facing outwards. Using the old bearing (if new ones are being fitted), a bearing driver or a socket large enough to

contact the outer race of the bearing, drive it in squarely until it's completely seated **(see illustration 15.9)**.

20 Turn the wheel over and install the bearing spacer. Drive the left-hand side bearing into place as described above **(see illustration)**.

21 Check the condition of the hub O-ring and renew it if it is damaged, deformed or deteriorated **(see illustration)**.

22 On all except XL600V-H to L (1987 to 1990) models, apply a smear of grease to the lips of the new grease seal, and press it into the right-hand side of the wheel, using a seal or bearing driver, a suitable socket or a piece of wood to drive it into place if necessary **(see illustration)**.

23 Clean off all grease from the brake disc using acetone or brake system cleaner. Fit the sprocket coupling assembly onto the wheel **(see illustration 15.13)**. On XL600V-H to L

(1987 to 1990) models, fit the brake plate assembly into the wheel. Install the wheel (see Section 14).

Sprocket coupling bearing

24 Remove the rear wheel, and if not already done remove the spacer(s) from it (see Section 14). Lift the sprocket coupling out of the wheel, noting how it fits **(see illustration 15.13)**.

25 Using a flat-bladed screwdriver, lever out the grease seal from the outside of the coupling **(see illustration)**.

26 Remove the spacer from the inside of the coupling bearing, noting which way round it fits. The spacer could be a tight fit and may have to be driven out from the outside using a suitable socket or piece of tubing **(see illustration)**. Support the coupling on blocks of wood to do this.

27 Support the coupling on blocks of wood and drive the bearing out from the inside using a bearing driver or socket **(see illustration)**.

28 Refer to Steps 6 to 8 above and check the bearing.

29 Thoroughly clean the bearing recess then install the bearing into the coupling, with the marked or sealed side facing out. Using the old bearing (if a new one is being fitted), a bearing driver or a socket large enough to contact the outer race of the bearing, drive it in until it is completely seated **(see illustration)**.

30 Fit the spacer into the inside of the coupling, making sure it is the correct way round and fits squarely into the bearing. Drive

15.22 Fit the grease seal and press or tap it into place

15.25 Lever out the grease seal

15.26 Drive out the spacer...

15.27 ...then drive out the bearing

15.29 Drive in the new bearing

7

15.30 Support the bearing on a socket when driving in the spacer

15.32a Press or drive the seal into the coupling

15.32b Using a piece of wood as shown automatically sets the seal flush

it into place if it is tight, supporting the bearing inner race on a suitable socket as you do to prevent it from being damaged or driven out at the same time **(see illustration)**.
31 Check the condition of the hub O-ring and replace it with a new one if it is damaged, deformed or deteriorated **(see illustration 15.21)**.
32 Apply a smear of grease to the lips of the new seal, and press it into the coupling, using a seal or bearing driver, a suitable socket or a flat piece of wood to drive it into place if necessary **(see illustration)**. As the seal sits flush with the top surface of their housing, using a piece of wood as shown will automatically set it flush without the risk of setting it too deep and having to lever it out again **(see illustration)**.
33 Check the sprocket coupling/rubber dampers (see Chapter 6).

34 Clean off all grease from the brake disc using acetone or brake system cleaner. Fit the sprocket coupling into the wheel **(see illustration 15.13)**, then install the wheel (see Section 14).

16 Tyres –
general information and fitting

General information

1 The wheels fitted to all models are designed to take tubed tyres only. Tyre sizes are given in the Specifications at the beginning of this chapter.
2 Refer to the *Daily (pre-ride) checks* listed at the beginning of this manual for tyre maintenance.

Fitting new tyres

3 When selecting new tyres, refer to the tyre information label on the swingarm and the tyre options listed in the owners handbook. Ensure that front and rear tyre types are compatible, the correct size and correct speed rating; if necessary seek advice from a Honda dealer or tyre fitting specialist **(see illustration)**.
4 It is recommended that tyres are fitted by a motorcycle tyre specialist rather than attempted in the home workshop. A specialist will be equipped with the correct tools and levers, protectors for the rim, will have compressed air, and will be able to balance the wheels after tyre fitting. While the tyre is being fitted it is worth asking for an alignment check and spoke tension check.

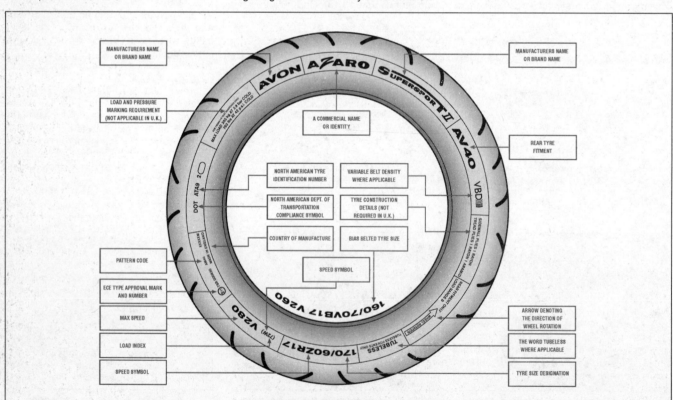

16.3 Common tyre sidewall markings

Chapter 8
Bodywork

Contents

Degrees of difficulty

Easy, suitable for novice with little experience	**Fairly easy,** suitable for beginner with some experience	**Fairly difficult,** suitable for competent DIY mechanic	**Difficult,** suitable for experienced DIY mechanic	**Very difficult,** suitable for expert DIY or professional

---

1 General information

This Chapter covers the procedures necessary to remove and install the body parts. Since many service and repair operations on these motorcycles require the removal of body parts, the procedures are grouped here and referred to from other Chapters.

In the case of damage to the body parts, it is usually necessary to remove the broken component and replace it with a new (or used) one. The material that the body panels are composed of doesn't lend itself to conventional repair techniques. There are however some shops that specialise in 'plastic welding', so it may be worthwhile seeking the advice of one of these specialists before consigning an expensive component to the bin.

When attempting to remove any body panel, first study it closely, noting any fasteners and associated fittings, to be sure of returning everything to its correct place on installation. In some cases the aid of an assistant will be required when removing panels, to help avoid the risk of damage to paintwork. Once the evident fasteners have been removed, try to withdraw the panel as described but DO NOT FORCE IT – if it will not release, check that all fasteners have been removed and try again. Where a panel engages another by means of tabs, be careful not to break the tab or its mating slot or to damage the paintwork. Remember that a few moments of patience at this stage will save you a lot of money in replacing broken fairing panels!

When installing a body panel, first study it closely, noting any fasteners and associated fittings removed with it, to be sure of returning everything to its correct place. Check that all fasteners are in good condition, including all trim nuts or clips and damping/rubber mounts; any of these must be replaced if faulty before the panel is reassembled. Check also that all mounting brackets are straight and repair or replace them if necessary before attempting to install the panel. Where assistance was required to remove a panel, make sure your assistant is on hand to install it. Tighten the fasteners securely, but be careful not to overtighten any of them or the panel may break (not always immediately) due to the uneven stress.

Where trim clips are used, to release them unscrew the centre of the clip, then pull the body of the clip out of the panel. When installing them, fit the body of the clip onto the panel then push the centre fully into the body. As they are made of plastic, the threads easily become worn and the centres may not unscrew, in which case lever the centre out of the body using a small screwdriver.

 Note that a small amount of lubricant (liquid soap or similar) applied to the mounting rubber grommets of the seat cowling will assist the lugs to engage without the need for undue pressure.

8

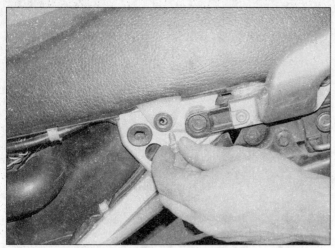

2.2a Unscrew the bolt on each side . . .

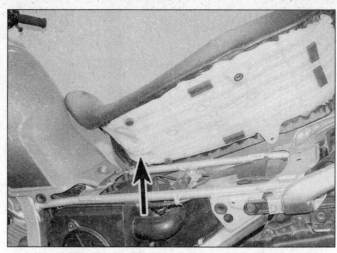

2.2b . . . then remove the seat, noting how the tab (arrowed) locates under the tank bracket

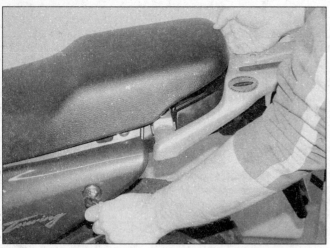

2.3a Unlock the seat, lift it up at the rear and draw it back . . .

2.3b . . . noting where the tabs locate (arrows)

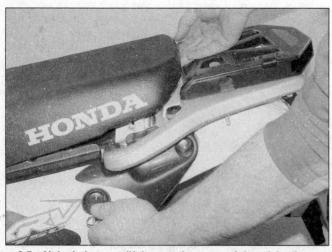

2.5a Unlock the seat, lift it up at the rear and draw it back . . .

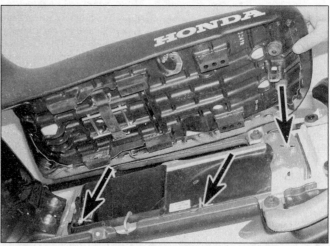

2.5b . . . noting where the tabs locate (arrows)

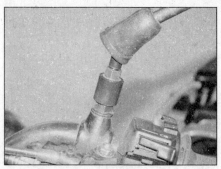

3.1 Pull up the rubber cover to access the mount

2 Seat – removal and installation

Removal

XL600V models

1 Remove the side panels (see Section 4).
2 Unscrew the two bolts (one on each side) securing the seat and remove it, noting how the tab at the front locates under the fuel tank bracket (see illustrations).

XL650V models

3 Insert the ignition key into the seat lock located in the left-hand side panel and turn it clockwise to unlock the seat (see illustration). Remove the seat by drawing it back and up, noting how it locates (see illustration).

XRV750 models

4 On L to N (1990 to 1992) models, remove the side panels (see Section 4). Unscrew the two bolts (one on each side) securing the seat and remove it, noting how the tab at the front locates under the fuel tank bracket.

5 On P models onwards (1993-on), insert the ignition key into the seat lock located in the left-hand side panel and turn it clockwise to unlock the seat (see illustration). Remove the seat by drawing it back and up, noting how it locates (see illustration).

Installation

6 Installation is the reverse of removal. Make sure the hooks and tabs locate correctly.

3 Rear view mirrors – removal and installation

Removal

1 The mirrors simply screw into the handlebar mounting – pull up the rubber cover, then either unscrew the mirror using the hex at the base of the stem, or slacken the bottom locknut and then unscrew the mirror, according to model (see illustration).

Installation

2 Installation is the reverse of removal. The position of the mirror can be adjusted by slackening the upper locknut, moving the mirror as required, then retightening the nut.

4 Fairing and body panels – removal and installation (XL600V models)

Note: All models have some rubber collars with captive threaded inserts that the screws thread into that fit into the panels at various places. Where the collar fits through both the panels it joins, it has to be removed before the panels can be separated. Where the head of the collar sits between the two panels it joins, and therefore only actually passes through the

4.2 Undo the four screws and remove the panel

lower of the two, it can remain in place. Take care not to lose them, and remove them for safekeeping if necessary. Check the rubber for damage, deformation and deterioration and replace the collars with new ones if necessary. Do not overtighten the screws or the collars could be damaged.

Cockpit trim panel(s)

1 On H and J (1987 and 1988) models, there is a panel on each side, each secured by three screws. Undo the screws and remove the panel, noting how it fits.
2 On K to X (1989 to 1999) models, there is a single panel surrounding the instrument cluster secured by four screws. Undo the screws and remove the panel, noting how its tabs locate in the fairing side panels (see illustration).
3 Installation is the reverse of removal.

Fairing side panels

4 Undo the three screws securing the panel (see illustration). Carefully draw the panel off the tank to release the pegs from the grommets, then release it from the cockpit trim panel and lift it to release the lower grommet from the peg on the bracket at the bottom (see illustrations).

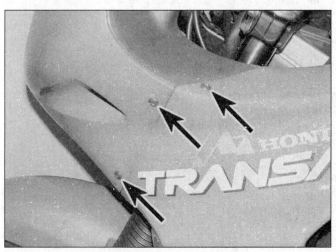

4.4a Undo the screws (arrowed) . . .

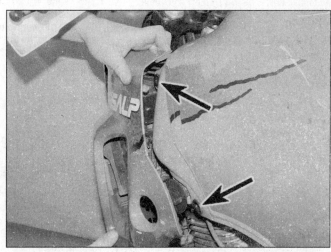

4.4b . . . then release the pegs from the grommets (arrowed)

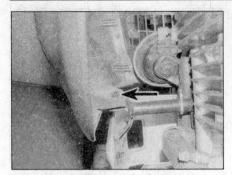

4.4c Lift the panel off the peg (arrowed) . . .

4.5 . . . and remove the bulbholder or disconnect the connector

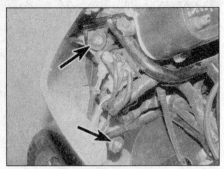

4.9 Unscrew the two bolts (arrowed) on each side

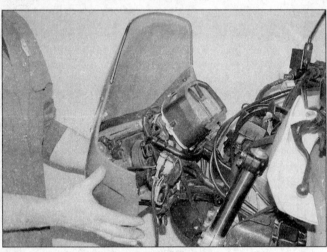

4.10a Draw the fairing forward . . .

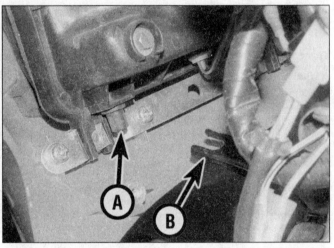

4.10b . . . noting how the peg (A) locates in the bracket (B) . . .

5 Either disconnect the turn signal wiring connector as it becomes accessible, or release the bulbholder from the turn signal by twisting it anti-clockwise **(see illustration)**.
6 Installation is the reverse of removal.

Fairing

7 Remove the cockpit trim panel(s) (see above).

8 Undo the two screws securing the fairing on each side to the fairing side panels **(see illustration 4.4a)**.
9 Support the fairing, then unscrew the four bolts securing it to the bracket **(see illustration)**.
10 Draw the fairing forward, noting how the pegs locate in the bracket, and disconnect the headlight and sidelight wiring connectors as

they become accessible **(see illustrations)**.
11 Installation is the reverse of removal.

Windshield

12 Undo the screws securing the windshield to the fairing and remove the rubber collars, then carefully remove the windshield, noting how it fits **(see illustration)**.
13 Installation is the reverse of removal.

4.10c . . . and disconnect the headlight wiring connector . . .

4.10d . . . and the sidelight wiring connector

4.12 Windshield screws (arrowed)

4.14a Unscrew the bolt . . .

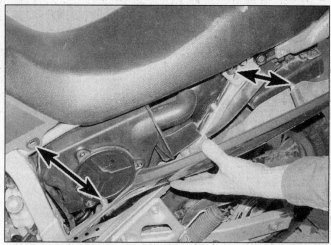

4.14b . . . and release the pegs from the grommets (arrowed)

4.16 Removing the belly pan

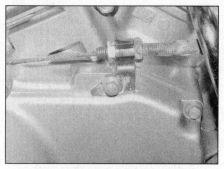

4.18a Unscrew the cable holder bolt . . .

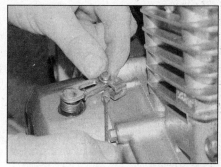

4.18b . . . and release the cable end from the arm

Side panels

14 Unscrew the single bolt on the bottom of the panel, then carefully draw the panel away to release the pegs from the grommets (see illustrations).
15 Installation is the reverse of removal.

Belly pan

16 Undo the three screws and the two bolts and remove the belly pan (see illustration).
17 Installation is the reverse of removal. Replace the rubbers with new ones if they are

damaged, deformed or deteriorated. Make sure the collars are fitted in the rubbers.

Stone guard

18 Unscrew the bolt securing the clutch cable holder to the clutch cover, then detach the cable end from the release arm, noting how it fits (see illustrations). Draw the cable out of the guard, noting its routing.
19 Unscrew the two bolts in the middle, then lift the guard to release the tab on the bottom from the hook on the frame (see illustration).
20 Installation is the reverse of removal.

5 Fairing and body panels – removal and installation (XL650V models)

Cockpit trim panel

1 Remove the top windshield screw on each side (see below). Unscrew the lower fairing bolt on each side (see illustration).
2 Release and withdraw the trim clip on each side securing the trim panel to the fairing inner panels (see illustration).

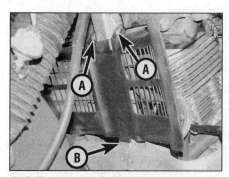

4.19 Unscrew the bolts (A) and release the tab (B)

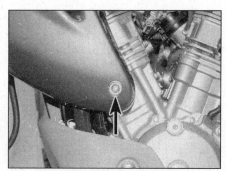

5.1 Unscrew the fairing bolt (arrowed) on each side

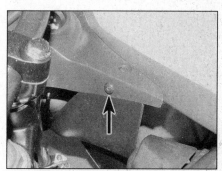

5.2 Release the trim clip (arrowed) on each side

8

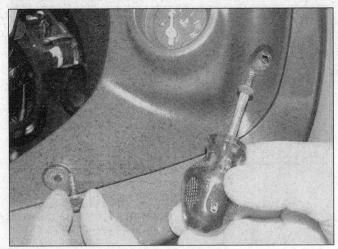

5.3a Undo the screws on each side

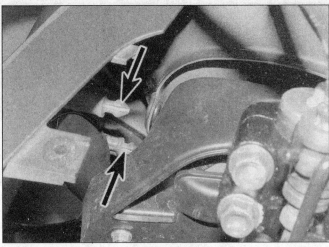

5.3b Pull the sides off the tank to release the pegs (arrowed) from the grommets

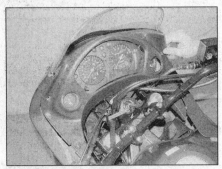

5.3c Manoeuvre the trim panel off the instrument cluster and out of the fairing

3 Undo the two screws on each side, noting which fits where (see illustration). Carefully pull the fairing away from the tank on each side to release the pegs from the grommets (see illustration). Remove the panel, noting how it fits (see illustration).

4 Installation is the reverse of removal. The self tapping screws fit in the upper holes, and the normal screws in the lower holes (see illustration 5.3a).

Fairing

5 Remove the windshield, the cockpit trim panel, and the stone guard (see below and above).

6 Either disconnect the turn signal wiring connectors, or release each bulbholder from the turn signals by twisting them anti-clockwise (see illustration).

7 Unscrew the two bolts on the top (see illustration) and the bolt on each side at the bottom (see illustration 5.1).

8 Draw the fairing forwards, noting how the lugs locate in the grommets in the bracket, then disconnect the headlight and sidelight wiring connectors as they become accessible (see illustrations).

9 Installation is the reverse of removal.

5.6 Either disconnect the wiring connector (arrowed), or release the bulbholder

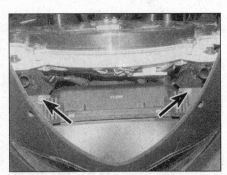

5.7 Unscrew the two bolts (arrowed)

5.8a Draw the fairing forward . . .

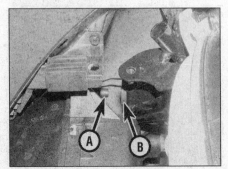

5.8b . . . noting how the peg (A) locates in the grommet (B) . . .

5.8c . . . and disconnect the headlight wiring connector . . .

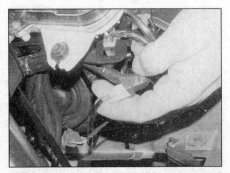

5.8d . . . and the sidelight wiring connector

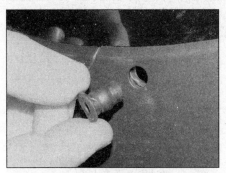

5.10a Undo the screws and remove the rubber collars . . .

5.10b . . . then remove the windshield

5.14a Undo the screws (arrowed) . . .

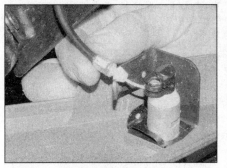

5.14b . . . then release the outer cable from the bracket . . .

5.14c . . . and the inner cable end from the lever

5.19a Remove the trim clips, then release the tabs . . .

Windshield

10 Undo the screws securing the windshield to the fairing and remove the washers and rubber collars (see illustration). Carefully lift

5.19b . . . and remove the stone guard

the windshield out, noting how its tabs on the bottom at the front locate (see illustration).
11 Installation is the reverse of removal. Make sure it locates properly.

Side panels

12 Remove the seat (see Section 2).
13 To remove the right-hand panel, undo the three screws and remove it (see illustration 5.14a).
14 To remove the left-hand panel, undo the three screws securing the side panel, then draw the panel away and release the seat lock cable from the bracket and the lever (see illustrations).
15 Installation is the reverse of removal.

Belly pan

16 Undo the five screws and the bolt and remove the belly pan.

17 Installation is the reverse of removal. Replace the rubbers with new ones if they are damaged, deformed or deteriorated. Make sure the collars are fitted in the rubbers.

Stone guard

18 Release and withdraw the two trim clips on each side.
19 Manoeuvre the panel to release the side tabs from the fairing and the centre tabs on the top from the frame (see illustrations).
20 Installation is the reverse of removal.

Luggage rack and tail light cover

21 Remove the seat (see Section 2) and the side panels (see above).
22 Unscrew the four bolts securing the rack, noting the collars, and remove the rack, noting how it fits (see illustrations).

5.22b . . . noting the collars . . .

5.22c . . . and remove the rack . . .

5.22a Unscrew the bolts . . .

8

23 Lift the tail light cover off the rear sub-frame **(see illustration)**. Note the collars in the cover and remove them for safekeeping if they are loose.
24 Installation is the reverse of removal. Make sure the all the collars are fitted in the tail light cover and with the rack bolts.

6 Fairing and body panels – removal and installation (XRV750 models)

Cockpit trim panel(s) – L to N (1990 to 1992) models only

1 There is a panel on each side, each secured by three screws, with the rearmost screws having washers and nuts on the underside of the panel. Undo the screws, counter holding the nuts and taking care not to lose them or the washers when removing the rear screws, and remove the panel, noting how it fits.

Fairing side panels

2 On L to N (1990 to 1992) models, undo the three screws securing the panel to the fairing and the trim panel, then release the quick-release screws by turning them 1/4 turn anti-

5.23 . . . and the tail light cover

clockwise, and remove the panel, noting how it fits.
3 On P models onward (1993-on), undo the three screws securing the panel to the fairing, the two screws securing the panel to the fuel tank, and the single screw securing the panel to the stone guard, and remove the panel, noting how it fits **(see illustrations)**.
4 Installation is the reverse of removal.

Fairing

5 On L to N (1990 to 1992) models, undo the two screws securing the fairing on each side to

the fairing side panels. Support the fairing, then unscrew the four nuts securing it to the bracket and draw it forwards off the headlight assembly.
6 On P models onward (1993-on), remove the fairing side panels (see above). Undo the rearmost windshield screw on each side **(see illustration)**. Unscrew the bolt on each side at the bottom **(see illustration)**. Support the fairing and remove the central screw at the front, then draw the fairing forwards off the headlight assembly **(see illustration)**.
7 Installation is the reverse of removal.

Windshield

8 Undo the screws securing the windshield to the fairing and remove the washers, then carefully remove the windshield, noting how it fits **(see illustration)**.
9 Installation is the reverse of removal. Make sure the cutout on each side locates correctly between the fairing and bracket.

Side panels

10 On L to N (1990 to 1992) models, undo the two screws, then carefully draw the panel away to release the pegs from the grommets.
11 On P models onward (1993-on), undo the two screws, then carefully draw the panel

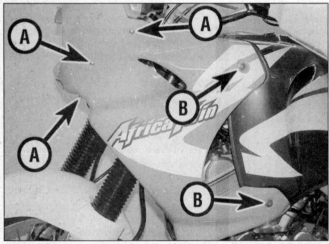

6.3a Undo the fairing screws (A), the fuel tank screws (B) . . .

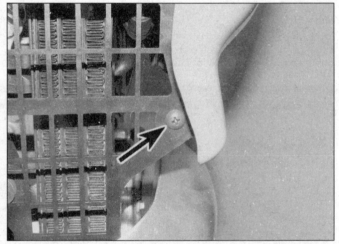

6.3b . . . and the stone guard screw (arrowed) . . .

6.3c . . . and remove the panel

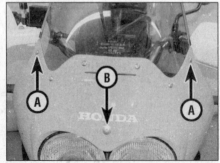

6.6a Undo the windshield screws (A), and the front screw (B) . . .

6.6b . . . and the bolt (arrowed) on each side . . .

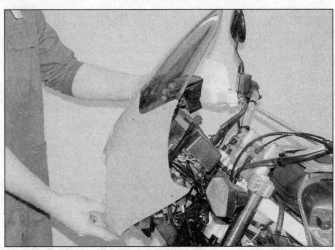

6.6c . . . and draw the fairing off the headlight

6.8 Windshield screws (arrowed)

6.11a Undo the screws (arrowed) . . .

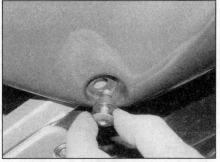

6.11b . . . noting the collars and rubbers . . .

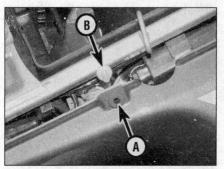

6.11c . . . then free the grommet (A) from the peg (B)

away to release the peg from the grommet (**see illustrations**).

12 Installation is the reverse of removal.

Belly pan

13 Undo the four bolts and remove the belly pan (**see illustrations**).

14 Installation is the reverse of removal. Replace the rubbers with new ones if they are damaged, deformed or deteriorated. Make sure the collars are fitted in the rubbers.

Stone guard

15 On L to N (1990 to 1992) models, remove the horn (see Chapter 9). Unscrew the bolt securing the clutch cable holder to the clutch cover, then detach the cable end from the release arm, noting how it fits. Draw the cable out of the guard, noting its routing. Unscrew the two bolts in the middle and the screw on each side, then lift the guard to release the tab on the bottom from the hook on the frame. If you have trouble manoeuvring the guard out, you will have to remove one of the fairing side panels.

16 On P models onward (1993-on), remove the horn (see Chapter 9). Undo the screw on each side (**see illustration 6.3b**), then release the hooks from the lugs at the top and lift the guard to release the tab on the bottom from the hook on the frame (**see illustrations**).

6.13a Unscrew the two bolts at the front (arrowed) . . .

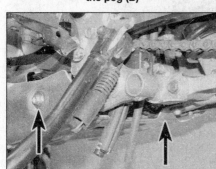

6.13b . . . the two bolts at the back (arrowed) . . .

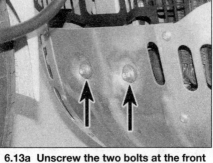

6.13c . . . and remove the belly pan

6.16a Release the hooks at the top . . .

8

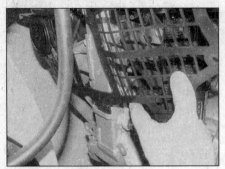

6.16b . . . and the tab at the bottom, and remove the guard

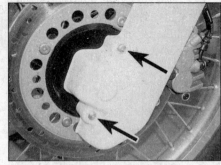

6.18 Fork guard bottom bolts (arrowed)

17 Installation is the reverse of removal.

Fork guards

18 Release the speedometer cable from its guide on the right-hand guard. Unscrew the two bolts on the bottom of the guard, and the bolt at the top, then release the guard from the mudguard, noting how its tabs locate and taking care not to break them **(see illustration)**.
19 Installation is the reverse of removal.

Luggage rack and tail light cover

20 Remove the seat (see Section 2) and the side panels (see above).
21 On L to N (1990 to 1992) models, carefully prise the caps off the luggage rack bolts.

Unscrew the six bolts and remove the collars and the rack. Unscrew the four bolts securing the rack base and remove the base and the tail light cover, noting how they fit.
22 On P models onward (1993-on), disconnect the tail light wiring connector. Where fitted, carefully prise the caps off the luggage rack carrier bolts, then unscrew the six bolts and remove the carrier and rack, noting the collars. Unscrew the bolt on each side of the tail light cover and remove the cover/mudguard/tail light assembly. If required, unscrew the nuts and withdraw the bolts securing the rear mudguard to the tail light cover and separate them. If required, carefully prise the caps off the bolts securing the luggage rack to the carrier, then unscrew

the bolts and separate them, noting the collars. Separate the tail light from the mudguard if required.
23 Installation is the reverse of removal. Make sure the all the collars are fitted in the tail light cover and with the rack bolts.

7 Front mudguard – removal and installation

Removal

1 On XL models, release the speedometer cable from its guide on the right-hand side **(see illustration)**. Unscrew the four bolts securing the mudguard to the fork sliders, noting how one of the bolts secures the speedometer cable guide on some models, and remove the mudguard, noting how it fits **(see illustration)**. Also remove the mudguard bridge, noting how it fits **(see illustration)**.
2 On XRV models, remove the fork guards (see Section 4). Unscrew the two front bolts securing the mudguard to the fork sliders and remove the mudguard, noting how it fits. Also remove the mudguard bridge, noting the arrow mark which must point forwards on installation.

Installation

3 Installation is the reverse of removal.

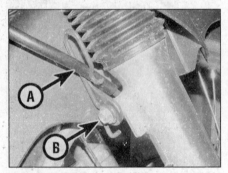

7.1a Release the cable (A) from the guide, then unscrew the rear bolt (B) on each side . . .

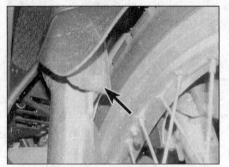

7.1b . . . and the front bolt (arrowed) on each side and remove the guard . . .

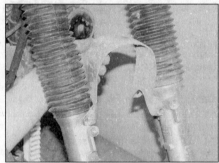

7.1c . . . and the bridge

Chapter 9
Electrical system

Contents

Degrees of difficulty

Easy, suitable for novice with little experience	Fairly easy, suitable for beginner with some experience	Fairly difficult, suitable for competent DIY mechanic	Difficult, suitable for experienced DIY mechanic	Very difficult, suitable for expert DIY or professional

Specifications

Battery
Capacity
  XL600V models . . . . 12 V, 12 Ah
  XL650V models . . . . 12 V, 10 Ah
  XRV750 models . . . . 12 V, 12 Ah
Voltage
  Fully charged . . . . 13.0 to 13.2 V
  Uncharged . . . . below 12.3 V
Specific gravity
  Fully charged 1.280
  Uncharged . . . . below 1.240
Charging rate
  XL600V models
    Normal . . . . 1.2 A for 5 to 10 hrs
    Quick . . . . 4.0 A for 1.0 hr
  XL650V models
    Normal . . . . 0.9 A for 5 to 10 hrs
    Quick . . . . 4.0 A for 1.0 hr
  XRV750 models
    Normal . . . . 1.2 A for 5 to 10 hrs
    Quick . . . . 4.0 A for 1.0 hr
Current leakage . . . . 0.1 mA (max)

Alternator

Stator coil resistance .... 0.1 to 1.0 ohms
Output
  XL600V-H and J (1987 and 1988) models .... 310 W @ 5000 rpm
  XL600V-K to P (1989 to 1993) models .... 350 W @ 5000 rpm
  XL600V-R to X (1994 to 1999) models .... 310 W @ 5000 rpm
  XL650V models
    UK models .... 368 W @ 5000 rpm
    European models .... 310 W @ 5000 rpm
  XRV750 models .... 360 W @ 5000 rpm

Regulator/rectifier

Regulated voltage output
  XL600V models .... 13.5 to 15.5 V @ 5000 rpm
  XL650V models .... 14.0 to 15.0 V @ 5000 rpm
  XRV750 models .... 14.0 to 15.0 V @ 5000 rpm

Starter motor

Brush length
  Standard
    XL models .... 12.0 to 13.0 mm
    XRV models .... 10.0 mm
  Service limit (min) .... 6.5 mm

Fuses

Main 30A
Others
  XL600V models
    UK models .... 10A x 3, 15A x 1
    German models .... 10A x 4, 15A x 1
  XL650V models .... 10A x 4, 15A x 1
  XRV750-L and M (1990 and 1991) models .... 10A x 2, 20A x 2
  XRV750-N (1992) models .... 5A x 1, 10A x 2, 20A x 3
  XRV750-P to S (1993 to 1995) models .... 10A x 3, 15A x 1, 20A x 1 (x 2 for Germany)
  XRV750-T models onwards (1996-on) .... 10A x 3, 15A x 1, 20A x 1

Bulbs

Headlight .... 60/55 W halogen
Sidelight
  XL600V models .... 4.0 W
  XL650V models .... 5.0 W
  XRV750 models .... 4.0 W
License plate light (where fitted) .... 5.0 W
Brake/tail light .... 21/5 W
Turn signal lights .... 21 W
Instrument lights
  XL600V-H and J (1987 and 1988) models .... 1.7 W x 3
  XL600V-K to X (1989 to 1999) models .... 3.4 W x 3, 3.0 W x 1
  XL650V models .... 1.7 W x 3
  XRV750-L and M (1990 and 1991) models .... 1.7 W x 3
  XRV750-N models onward (1992-on) .... 1.7 W x 3, 2.0 W x 1
Turn signal indicator light
  XL600V models .... 3.4 W
  XL650V models .... 3.4 W
  XRV750-L and M (1990 and 1991) models .... 3.4 W
  XRV750-N models onward (1992-on) .... 3.0 W
High beam indicator light
  XL600V-H and J (1987 and 1988) models .... 1.7 W
  XL600V-K to X (1989 to 1999) models .... 3.0 W
  XL650V models .... 1.7 W
  XRV750 models .... 1.7 W
Neutral indicator light
  XL600V-H and J (1987 and 1988) models .... 3.4 W
  XL600V-K to X (1989 to 1999) models .... 3.0 W
  XL650V models .... 3.4 W
  XRV750-L and M (1990 and 1991) models .... 3.4 W
  XRV750-N models onward (1992-on) .... 3.0 W

Bulbs (continued)

Oil pressure indicator light

XL600V-H and J (1987 and 1988) models	3.4 W
XL600V-K to X (1989 to 1999) models	1.7 W
XL650V models	1.7 W
XRV750-L and M (1990 and 1991) models	3.4 W
XRV750-N models onward (1992-on)	3.0 W

Sidestand indicator light

XL600V-K to X (1989 to 1999) models	1.7 W
XL650V models	1.7 W
XRV750-L and M (1990 and 1991) models	3.4 W
XRV750-N models onward (1992-on)	3.0 W
Immobiliser indicator light (XL650V)	3.4 W

Torque settings

Alternator rotor bolt (left-hand thread)

XL600V-H and J (1987 and 1988) models	110 Nm
All other models	128 Nm
Alternator stator bolts	12 Nm
Neutral switch	12 Nm
Oil pressure switch	12 Nm

1 General information

All models have a 12-volt electrical system charged by a three-phase alternator with a separate regulator/rectifier.

The regulator maintains the charging system output within the specified range to prevent overcharging, and the rectifier converts the ac (alternating current) output of the alternator to dc (direct current) to power the lights and other components and to charge the battery. The alternator rotor is mounted on the left-hand end of the crankshaft.

The starter motor is mounted on the top of the crankcase behind the cylinders on the left-hand side. The starting system includes the motor, the battery, the relay and the various wires and switches, and a starter safety interlock system. On XL600V-H and J (1987 and 1988) models without a sidestand switch, if the engine kill switch is in the RUN position and the ignition (main) switch is ON, the interlock system prevents the engine from being started if the engine is in gear unless the clutch lever is pulled in. On all other models, if the engine kill switch is in the RUN position and the ignition (main) switch is ON, the system prevents the engine from being started if the sidestand is down and the engine is in gear – the engine can be started with the sidestand up when it is in gear as long as the clutch lever is pulled in.

Note: *Keep in mind that electrical parts, once*

purchased, often cannot be returned. To avoid unnecessary expense, make very sure the faulty component has been positively identified before buying a replacement part.

2 Electrical system – fault finding

⚠ *Warning: To prevent the risk of short circuits, the ignition (main) switch must always be OFF and the battery negative (–) terminal should be disconnected before any of the bike's other electrical components are disturbed. Don't forget to reconnect the terminal securely once work is finished or if battery power is needed for circuit testing.*

1 A typical electrical circuit consists of an electrical component, the switches, relays, etc. related to that component and the wiring and connectors that link the component to the battery and the frame. To aid in locating a problem in any electrical circuit, and to guide you with the wiring colour codes and connectors, refer to the *Wiring Diagrams* at the end of this Chapter.

2 Before tackling any troublesome electrical circuit, first study the wiring diagram (see end of Chapter) thoroughly to get a complete picture of what makes up that individual circuit. Trouble spots, for instance, can often be narrowed down by noting if other components related to that circuit are operating properly or not. If several components or circuits fail at one time, chances are the fault lies in the fuse or earth

(ground) connection, as several circuits often are routed through the same fuse and earth (ground) connections.

3 Electrical problems often stem from simple causes, such as loose or corroded connections or a blown fuse. Prior to any electrical fault finding, always visually check the condition of the fuse, wires and connections in the problem circuit. Intermittent failures can be especially frustrating, since you can't always duplicate the failure when it's convenient to test. In such situations, a good practice is to clean all connections in the affected circuit, whether or not they appear to be good. All of the connections and wires should also be wiggled to check for looseness which can cause intermittent failure.

4 If testing instruments are going to be utilised, use the wiring diagram to plan where you will make the necessary connections in order to accurately pinpoint the trouble spot.

5 The basic tools needed for electrical fault finding include a battery and bulb test circuit or a continuity tester, a test light, and a jumper wire. A multimeter capable of reading volts, ohms and amps is a very useful alternative and performs the functions of all of the above, and is necessary for performing more extensive tests and checks where specific voltage, current or resistance values are needed.

 HAYNES HiNT *Refer to Fault Finding Equipment in the Reference section for details of how to use electrical test equipment.*

9

3 On XL models and XRV750-L to N (1990 to 1992) models, remove the fairing (see Chapter 8). On XRV750-P models onward (1993-on), remove the air filter housing (see Chapter 4). Trace the wiring from the relevant switch and disconnect it at the connector.

4 Check for continuity between the terminals of the switch connector with the switch in the various positions (i.e. switch off – no continuity, switch on – continuity) – see the *wiring diagrams* at the end of this Chapter. Continuity should exist between the terminals connected by a solid line on the diagram when the switch is in the indicated position.

5 If the continuity check indicates a problem exists, refer to Section 21, displace the switch housing and spray the switch contacts with electrical contact cleaner (there is no need to remove the switch completely). If they are accessible, the contacts can be scraped clean with a knife or polished with crocus cloth. If switch components are damaged or broken, it will be obvious when the switch is disassembled.

21 Handlebar switches –
removal and installation

Removal

1 If the switch is to be removed from the bike, rather than just displaced from the handlebar, on XL models and XRV750-L to N (1990 to 1992) models, remove the fairing (see Chapter 8). On XRV750-P models onward (1993-on), remove the air filter housing (see Chapter 4). Trace the wiring from the relevant switch and disconnect it at the connector. Work back along the harness, freeing it from any clips and ties, noting its correct routing.

2 Disconnect the two wires from the brake light switch (if removing the right-hand switch) or the clutch switch (if removing the left-hand switch) **(see illustration 14.2 or 24.2)**.

3 Undo the handlebar switch screws and free the switch from the handlebar by separating the halves **(see illustration)**.

Installation

4 Installation is the reverse of removal. Make sure the locating pin in the switch housing locates in the hole in the handlebar.

22 Neutral switch –
check, removal and installation
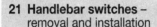

Check

1 Before checking the electrical circuit, check the bulb (see Section 17) and fuse (see Section 5).

2 The switch is located in the left-hand side of the transmission casing below the front sprocket cover. You should be able to access it without removing anything, but if required remove the belly pan (see Chapter 8), and for best access the front sprocket cover (see Chapter 6). Detach the wiring connector from the switch **(see illustration)**. Make sure the transmission is in neutral.

3 With the connector disconnected and the ignition switch ON, the neutral light should be out. If not, the wire between the connector and instrument cluster must be earthed (grounded) at some point.

4 If you removed the sprocket cover, temporarily slide the gearchange lever back onto the shaft. Check for continuity between the switch terminal and the crankcase. With the transmission in neutral, there should be continuity. With the transmission in gear, there should be no continuity. If the tests prove otherwise, then the switch is faulty.

5 If the continuity tests prove the switch is good, check for voltage at the wire terminal with the ignition switch ON. If there's no voltage present, check the wire between the switch, the instrument cluster and fusebox (see the *wiring diagrams* at the end of this Chapter).

Removal

6 The switch is located in the left-hand side of the transmission casing below the front sprocket cover. You should be able to access it without removing anything, but if required remove the belly pan (see Chapter 8), and for best access the front sprocket cover (see Chapter 6).

7 Detach the wiring connector from the switch **(see illustration 22.2)**.

8 Unscrew the switch and withdraw it from the crankcase **(see illustration)**. Discard the sealing washer as a new one should be used.

Installation

9 Install the switch using a new washer and tighten it to the torque setting specified at the beginning of the Chapter.

10 Connect the wiring connector and check the operation of the neutral light **(see illustration 22.2)**.

11 Install the sprocket cover (see Chapter 6) and belly pan (see Chapter 8) if required.

22.2 Disconnect the wiring connector from the switch

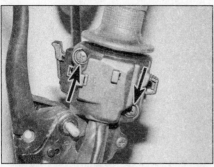

21.3 Handlebar switch screws (arrowed) – left-hand switch shown

23 Sidestand switch –
check and replacement

1 The sidestand switch is mounted either on the frame next to the sidestand, or on the back of the sidestand, depending on whether it is a plunger type or a rotary type.

2 XL600V-K to P (1989 to 1993) models and XRV750-L to N (1990 to 1992) are fitted with a plunger type switch, while all other models have a rotary type switch. XL600V and XRV750 models have a warning light in the instrument cluster to show when the sidestand is down.

3 The switch is part of the safety circuit which prevents or stops the engine running if the transmission is in gear whilst the sidestand is down, and prevents the engine from starting if the transmission is in gear unless the sidestand is up, and unless the clutch is pulled in.

Check

4 Before checking the electrical circuit, check the fuse (see Section 5), and on XL and XRV models the warning bulb (see Section 17).

5 Trace the wiring back from the switch and disconnect at the wiring connector – remove the seat and/or left-hand side panel to access it (see Chapter 8). Check the operation of the switch using an ohmmeter or continuity test light as follows, according to model:

6 On XL600V-K to P (1989 to 1993) models and XRV750-L to N (1990 to 1992) models, connect the meter between the light

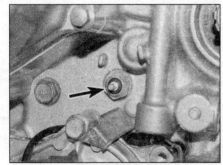

22.8 Neutral switch (arrowed)

23.13 Sidestand switch mounting bolt (arrowed)

green/yellow and green wire terminals on the switch side of the connector – with the sidestand up there should be continuity (zero resistance) between the terminals, and with the stand down there should be no continuity (infinite resistance). Now connect the meter between the pink and green wire terminals on the switch side of the connector – with the sidestand up there should be no continuity (infinite resistance) between the terminals, and with the stand down there should be continuity (zero resistance).

7 On XL600V-R to X (1994 to 1999) models and XRV750-P models onward (1993-on), connect the meter between the green/white and green wire terminals on the switch side of the connector – with the sidestand up there should be continuity (zero resistance) between the terminals, and with the stand down there should be no continuity (infinite resistance). Now connect the meter between the yellow/black and green wire terminals on the switch side of the connector – with the sidestand up there should be no continuity (infinite resistance) between the terminals, and with the stand down there should be continuity (zero resistance).

8 On XL650V models connect the meter between the green/white and green wire terminals on the switch side of the connector – with the sidestand up there should be continuity (zero resistance) between the terminals, and with the stand down there should be no continuity (infinite resistance).

9 If the switch does not perform as expected, it is faulty and must be replaced with a new one.

10 If the switch is good, check the wiring and connectors between the various components in the starter safety circuit using a continuity tester (see the *wiring diagrams* at the end of this book). Also check for voltage at the green/white wire terminal on the loom side of the connector with the ignition ON – there should be battery voltage. Repair or renew the wiring as required.

Replacement

11 The sidestand switch is mounted either on the frame next to the sidestand, or on the back of the sidestand, depending on whether it is a plunger type switch or a rotary type. Trace the wiring back from the switch and disconnect at the wiring connector – remove the seat and/or left-hand side panel to access it (see Chapter 8). Work back along the switch wiring, freeing it from any clips and ties, noting its correct routing.

12 On XL600V-K to P (1989 to 1993) models and XRV750-L to N (1990 to 1992) models, unscrew the switch cover bolts and remove the cover, then unscrew the remaining switch bolt and remove the switch, noting how it fits. Fit the new switch onto the bracket, making sure the plunger locates correctly against the sidestand. Secure the switch and its cover with the bolts and tighten them securely.

13 On XL600V-R to X (1994 to 1999) models, XL650V models and XRV750-P models onwards (1993-on), unscrew the switch bolt and remove the switch from the stand, noting how it fits **(see illustration)**. Fit the new switch onto the sidestand making sure the pin locates in the hole in the sidestand, and the lug on the stand bracket locates into the cutout in the switch body. Secure the switch with its bolt and tighten it to securely.

14 Make sure the wiring is correctly routed up to the connector and retained by any clips and ties.

15 Reconnect the wiring connector and check the operation of the switch.

16 Install the seat and/or left-hand side panel as required (see Chapter 8).

24 Clutch switch – check and replacement

Check

1 The clutch switch is mounted in the clutch lever bracket. The switch is part of the starter safety interlock system (see Section 1). The switch isn't adjustable.

2 To check the switch, disconnect the wiring connectors from it **(see illustration)**. Connect the probes of an ohmmeter or a continuity tester to the two switch terminals. With the clutch lever pulled in, there should be continuity (zero resistance). With the clutch lever out, there should be no continuity (infinite resistance).

3 If the switch is good, check the other

components in the starter circuit as described in the relevant sections of this Chapter. If all components are good, check the wiring between the various components (see the *wiring diagrams* at the end of this book).

Replacement

4 The clutch switch is mounted on the clutch lever bracket.

5 Disconnect the wiring connectors from the switch **(see illustration 24.2)**. Remove the single screw securing the switch to the bracket and remove the switch, noting how it fits **(see illustration)**.

6 Installation is the reverse of removal. Install the switch with the small catch at the bottom and press it in until the catch is felt to locate.

25 Diode(s) – check and replacement

1 The diode(s) is/are part of the starter safety interlock system (see Section 1). A diode is a small block that allows current flow in one direction only, and plugs into a connector either in the fusebox or in the wiring loom, depending on the model application. Refer to the relevant *Wiring Diagrams* at the end of the Chapter for details.

2 There is usually a diode in the clutch switch circuit, housed in the fusebox, one for the sidestand switch circuit that plugs into the loom (and can usually be identified by the fact that it has black insulating tape wrapped round it, and is usually located under the seat or behind one of the side panels) **(see illustrations opposite)**, and one for the neutral switch circuit that is integral with the ignition control unit. Twin terminal diode blocks contain one diode, and triple terminal diode blocks contain two diodes. Using the *Wiring Diagrams*, identify which is/are the input terminal(s) and which is the output terminal – the input(s) have the line which leads to the flat side of the triangle on the symbol, and the output comes from the line across the point of the triangle.

3 To test a twin terminal diode, connect the positive (+) probe of an ohmmeter or continuity tester to the input terminal on the

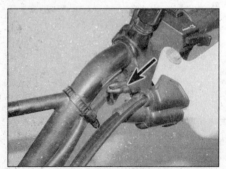

24.2 Clutch switch wiring connectors (arrowed)

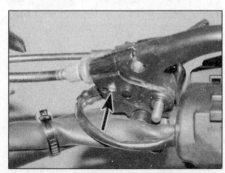

24.5 Clutch switch screw (arrowed)

25.2a Diode (arrowed) –
XL600V

25.2b Diode (arrowed) –
XL650V

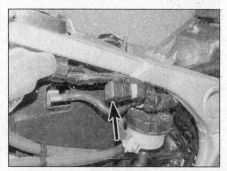

25.2c Diode (arrowed) –
XRV750

diode and the negative (–) probe to the output terminal. There should be continuity. Now reverse the probes. There should be no continuity. If it doesn't behave as stated, replace the diode with a new one.

4 To test a triple terminal diode, connect the positive (+) probe of an ohmmeter or continuity tester to one of the input terminals on the diode and the negative (–) probe to the output terminal. There should be continuity. Now reverse the probes. There should be no continuity. Repeat the tests between the other input terminal and the output terminal. The same results should be achieved. If it doesn't behave as stated, replace the diode with a new one.

5 On XRV750-L to S (1990 to1995) models, it is possible to test the neutral switch diode in the ignition control unit (ICU). Remove the seat (see Chapter 8) and disconnect the white 2-pin connector from the ICU. Connect the positive

(+) probe of an ohmmeter or continuity tester to one of the light green/red wire terminals on the ICU and the negative (–) probe to the other light green/red wire terminals. Now reverse the probes. There should be continuity in one direction and no continuity in the other.

6 If a diode is faulty, pull it out of its socket and replace it with a new one. If the neutral switch diode on XRV750-L to S (1990 to1995) models is faulty, replace the ICU with a new one.

7 If the diodes are good, check the other components in the starter circuit as described in the relevant sections of this Chapter. If all components are good, check the wiring between the various components (see the *wiring diagrams* at the end of this book).

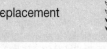

26 Horn –
check and replacement

Check

1 The horn is mounted below the left-hand radiator on XL models and the right-hand radiator on XRV models **(see illustrations)**. On XL models, remove the stone guard (see Chapter 8), and for best access the left-hand fairing side panel (XL600V) or the fairing (XL650V) (see Chapter 8). On XRV models you should be able to get at the horn from the front quite easily, but remove the left-hand side panel if required (see Chapter 8).

2 Unplug the wiring connectors from the horn **(see illustration)**. Using two jumper wires, apply battery voltage directly to the terminals

on the horn. If the horn sounds, check the switch (see Section 21). Also check for voltage at the light green wire connector with the ignition ON and the horn button pressed. If voltage is present, check the green wire for continuity to earth. If no voltage was present, check the light green wire for continuity between the horn and the switch, and in the black/brown or white/green (according to model) wire from the switch to the fusebox, and then to the ignition switch (see the *wiring diagrams* at the end of this Chapter). With the ignition switch ON, there should be voltage at the black/brown or white/green wire to the horn button in the left-hand switch gear.

3 If the horn doesn't sound, replace it with a new one.

Replacement

4 The horn is mounted below the left-hand radiator on XL models and the right-hand radiator on XRV models **(see illustration 26.1a, b or c)**. On XL models, remove the stone guard, and for best access the left-hand fairing side panel (XL600V) or the fairing (XL650V) (see Chapter 8). On XRV models you should be able to get at the horn from the front quite easily, but remove the left-hand side panel if required (see Chapter 8).

5 Unplug the wiring connectors from the horn **(see illustration 26.2)**. Unscrew the nut securing the horn and remove it from the bike.

6 Install the horn and tighten the nut securely. Connect the wiring to the horn. Check that it works, then install the stone guard, fairing side panel or fairing as required according to model and your procedure (see Chapter 8).

26.1a Horn –
XL600V

26.1b Horn –
XL650V

26.1c Horn –
XRV750

26.2 Disconnect the wiring connectors

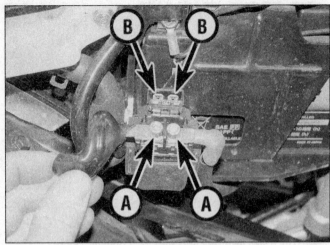
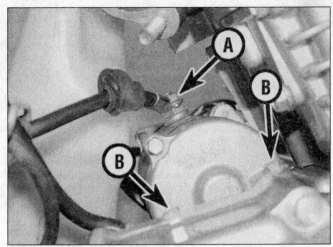

27.3 Starter relay battery and starter motor leads (A) and wiring connector terminals (B)

28.3 Pull back the terminal cover then unscrew the nut (A) and detach the lead. Starter mounting bolts (B)

27 Starter relay – check and replacement

Check

1 If the starter circuit is faulty, first check the fuse (see Section 5).
2 The starter relay is behind the right-hand side panel on XL models and XRV750-L to N (1990 to 1992) models, and behind the left-hand side panel on all other XRV models **(see illustration 5.2a, 3.7 or 5.2b)**. Remove the panel for access (see Chapter 8).
3 Lift the rubber terminal cover and unscrew the bolt securing the starter motor lead **(see illustration)**; position the lead away from the relay terminal. With the ignition switch ON, the engine kill switch in the RUN position, and the transmission in neutral, press the starter switch. The relay should be heard to click.
4 If the relay doesn't click, switch off the ignition and remove the relay as described below; test it as follows.
5 Set a multimeter to the ohms x 1 scale and connect it across the relay's starter motor and battery lead terminals **(see illustration 27.3)**. There should be no continuity. Using a fully-charged 12 volt battery and two insulated jumper wires, connect the positive (+) terminal of the battery to the yellow/red wire terminal of the relay, and the negative (–) terminal to the green/red wire terminal of the relay. At this point the relay should be heard to click and the multimeter read 0 ohms (continuity). If this is the case the relay is proved good. If the relay does not click when battery voltage is applied and indicates no continuity (infinite resistance) across its terminals, it is faulty and must be replaced with a new one.
6 If the relay is good, check for continuity in the main lead from the battery to the relay. Also check that the terminals and connectors at each end of the lead are tight and

corrosion-free. Next check for battery voltage at the yellow/red wire when the starter button is pressed. If there is no voltage, check the wiring between the relay wiring connector and the starter button. If voltage is present, check that there is continuity to earth in the green/red wire with the transmission in neutral, the clutch lever pulled in and the sidestand up (note that there will be a very slight resistance due to the diode). If there is no continuity, check the other components in the starter circuit as described in the relevant sections of this Chapter. If all components are good, check the wiring between the various components (see the *wiring diagrams* at the end of this book).

Replacement

7 The starter relay is behind the right-hand side panel on XL models and XRV750-L to N (1990 to 1992) models, and behind the left-hand side panel on all other XRV models **(see illustration 5.2a, 3.7 or 5.2b)**. Remove the panel for access (see Chapter 8).
8 Disconnect the battery terminals, remembering to disconnect the negative (–) terminal first.
9 Disconnect the relay wiring connector, then lift the insulating cover and unscrew the bolts

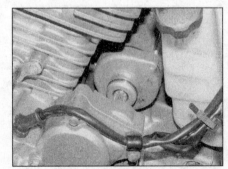

28.4 Slide the starter motor out of the crankcase

securing the starter motor and battery leads to the relay and detach the leads **(see illustration 27.3)**. Remove the relay with its rubber sleeve from its mounting lug on the frame. If the relay is being replaced with a new one, remove the main fuse from the relay, and remove the relay from its sleeve.
10 Installation is the reverse of removal. Make sure the terminal bolts are securely tightened. Do not forget to fit the main fuse into the relay, if removed. Connect the negative (–) lead last when reconnecting the battery.

28 Starter motor – removal and installation

Removal

1 Disconnect the battery negative (–) lead (see Section 3). The starter motor is mounted on the crankcase behind the cylinders on the left-hand side.
2 Remove the rear cylinder exhaust downpipe (see Chapter 4).
3 Peel back the rubber terminal cover on the starter motor **(see illustration)**. Unscrew the nut securing the starter lead to the motor and detach the lead.
4 Unscrew the two bolts securing the starter motor to the crankcase, noting the earth lead secured by one of the bolts **(see illustration 28.3)**. Slide the starter motor out and remove it **(see illustration)**
5 Remove the O-ring on the end of the starter motor and discard it as a new one must be used.

Installation

6 Fit a new O-ring onto the end of the starter motor, making sure it is seated in its groove **(see illustration)**. Apply a smear of engine oil to the O-ring to aid installation.

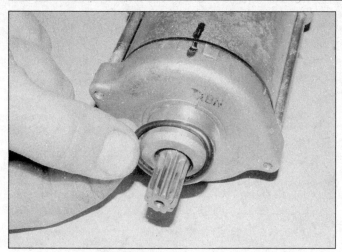

28.6 Fit a new O-ring and lubricate it

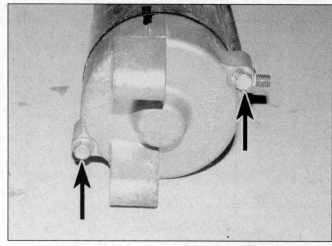

29.3a Unscrew and remove the two bolts (arrowed) . . .

7 Manoeuvre the motor into position and slide it into the crankcase **(see illustration 28.4)**. Ensure that the starter motor teeth mesh correctly with those of the starter drive gear. Install the mounting bolts, not forgetting to secure the earth lead, and tighten them securely **(see illustration 28.3)**.

8 Connect the starter lead to the motor and secure it with the nut **(see illustration 28.3)**. Fit the rubber cover over the terminal.

9 Install the rear cylinder exhaust downpipe (see Chapter 4).

10 Connect the battery negative (–) lead.

29 Starter motor –
disassembly, inspection and reassembly

Disassembly

1 Remove the starter motor (see Section 28).

2 Note the alignment marks between the main housing and the front and rear covers, or make your own if they aren't clear.

3 Unscrew the two long bolts, on XL600-H and J (1987 and 1988) models noting the

washers, then remove the front cover from the motor along with its sealing ring **(see illustrations)**. Discard the sealing ring as a new one must be used. Remove the tabbed washer from the cover and, except on XL600-H and J (1987 and 1988) models, slide the insulating washer and shim(s) from the front end of the armature, noting the number of shims and their correct fitted order **(see illustrations)**.

4 Remove the rear cover from the motor along with its sealing ring **(see illustration)**. Discard the sealing ring as a new one must be used. Remove the shim(s) from the rear end of the armature noting how many and their correct fitted positions **(see illustration)**.

5 Withdraw the armature from the front of the main housing **(see illustration)**.

6 At this stage check for continuity between the terminal bolt and the brush with insulation. There should be continuity (zero resistance). Check for continuity between the terminal bolt and the housing. There should be no continuity (infinite resistance). Also check for continuity between the brush with uninsulated wire and the brushplate. There should be continuity (zero resistance). If there is no continuity when there should be or vice versa,

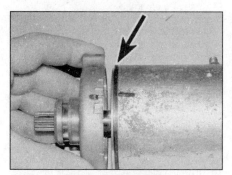

29.3b . . . then remove the front cover and sealing ring (arrowed)

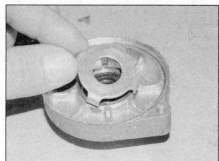

29.3c Remove the tabbed washer . . .

29.3d . . . and the shims (arrowed)

29.4a Remove the rear cover and its sealing ring (arrowed) . . .

29.4b . . . and remove the shims (arrowed)

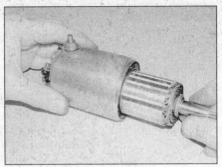

29.5 Withdraw the armature

29.7a Unscrew the nut and remove the large and small insulating washers and the O-ring

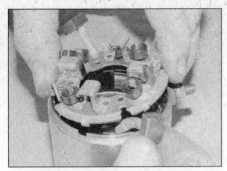

29.7b Remove the brushplate assembly . . .

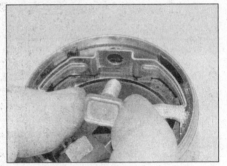

29.7c . . . the terminal bolt . . .

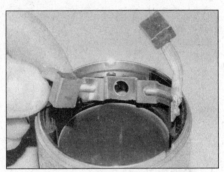

29.7d . . . the brush piece . . .

29.7e . . . the insulator . . .

identify the faulty component and replace it with a new one.

7 Noting the correct fitted location of each component, unscrew the nut from the terminal bolt and remove the plain washer, the one large and two small insulating washers and the rubber O-ring (see illustration). Slide the insulated brushes out of their holders (see illustration 29.16a). Make an alignment mark between the brushplate and the housing to aid installation – it is easy to install the plate in the wrong position without knowing it. Remove the brushplate assembly, noting how it locates and how the insulated brush wires are routed (see illustration). Withdraw the terminal bolt from the main housing, noting how it locates, then remove the brush piece, the insulator and the holder (see illustrations).

8 Slide the brushplate brushes out of their holders.

Inspection

9 The parts of the starter motor that are most likely to require attention are the brushes. Measure the length of each brush and compare the results to the Specifications at the beginning of the Chapter (see illustration). If the brushes are worn beyond the service limit, replace the brushplate assembly and brush piece with new ones. If the brushes are not worn excessively, nor cracked, chipped, or otherwise damaged, they may be re-used.

10 Inspect the commutator bars on the armature for scoring, scratches and discoloration. The commutator can be cleaned and polished with crocus cloth, but

do not use sandpaper or emery paper. After cleaning, wipe away any residue with a cloth soaked in electrical system cleaner or denatured alcohol.

11 Using an ohmmeter or a continuity tester, check for continuity between the commutator bars (see illustration). Continuity should exist between each bar and all of the others. Also, check for continuity between the commutator bars and the armature shaft. There should be no continuity (infinite resistance) between the commutator and the shaft. If the checks indicate otherwise, the armature is defective.

12 Check the starter pinion gear for worn, cracked, chipped and broken teeth. If the gear is damaged or worn, replace the starter motor.

13 Inspect the end covers for signs of cracks or wear. Check the needle bearing in the front

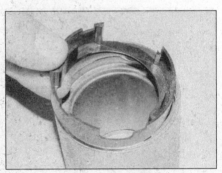

29.7f . . . and the holder

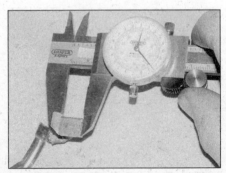

29.9 Measure the length of each brush

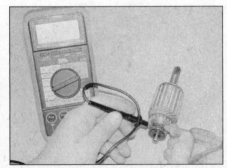

29.11 Continuity should exist between the commutator bars

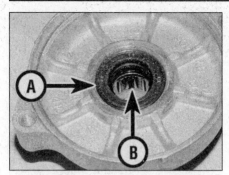

29.13 Check the seal (A) and needle bearing (B) in the front cover

29.15 Slide each brush into its housing and place the spring end onto its outer end

29.16a Slide each brush into its housing . . .

29.16b . . . and place the spring end onto its outer end

29.17 Locate the spring ends onto the brushes

29.18 Fit a new sealing ring onto the rear of the housing

cover and the bush in the rear cover for wear and damage (see illustration). Inspect the magnets in the main housing and the housing itself for cracks.

14 Inspect the insulating washers, O-ring, sealing rings and front cover oil seal for signs of damage deformation and deterioration and renew if necessary.

Reassembly

15 Slide the brushplate brushes back into position in their housings and locate the brush spring ends onto the outer ends of the brushes so that the brushes are held retracted and will not interfere when the armature is slid through (see illustration).

16 Fit the holder, insulator and the brush piece into the main housing (see illustrations 29.7f, e, and d), then insert the terminal bolt through them and the housing (see illustration 29.7c). Slide the rubber O-ring and small insulating washers onto the terminal bolt, followed by the large insulating washer and the plain washer (see illustration 29.7a). Fit the nut onto the terminal bolt and tighten it securely. Fit the brushplate onto the housing, making sure it is aligned as marked on removal and its tab is correctly located in the housing slot and that the insulated brush wires are routed through the cutouts in the plate (see illustration 29.7b). Slide the insulated brushes into their housings, then locate the spring ends onto the outer ends of the brushes (see illustrations).

17 Insert the armature into the front of the main housing, taking care as the magnets within the housing will want to forcefully pull it

in (see illustration 29.5). With the armature installed, place each brush spring end against the end of its brush so that the brush is pressed against the commutator bars (see illustration).

18 Fit the shims onto the rear of the armature shaft (see illustration 29.4b). Apply a smear of grease to the end of the shaft. Fit the sealing ring onto the rear of the housing (see illustration). Fit the rear cover, aligning the marks made on removal (see illustration 29.4a).

19 Apply a smear of grease to the front cover oil seal lip. Fit the toothed washer into the cover so that its teeth are correctly located with the cover ribs (see illustration 29.3c).

20 Except on XL600-H and J (1987 and 1988) models, slide the shim(s) onto the front end of the armature shaft then fit the insulating washer (see illustration 29.3d). Fit the sealing ring onto the front of the housing (see illustration). Slide the front cover into

position, aligning the marks made on removal (see illustration 29.3b).

21 Check the marks made on removal are correctly aligned then fit the long bolts, on XL600-H and J (1987 and 1988) models not forgetting the washers, and tighten them securely (see illustration).

22 Install the starter motor (see Section 28).

30 Charging system testing – general information and precautions

1 If the performance of the charging system is suspect, the system as a whole should be checked first, followed by testing of the individual components. **Note:** *Before beginning the checks, make sure the battery is fully charged and that all system connections are clean and tight.*

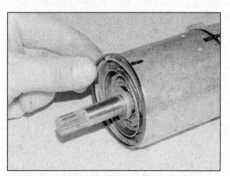

29.20 Fit a new sealing ring onto the front of the housing

29.21 Fit the long bolts and tighten them securely

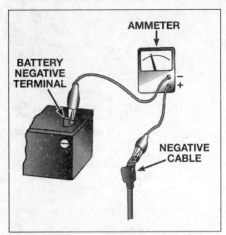

31.3 Checking the charging system leakage rate – connect the meter as shown

2 Checking the output of the charging system and the performance of the various components within the charging system requires the use of a multimeter (with voltage, current and resistance checking facilities).

3 When making the checks, follow the procedures carefully to prevent incorrect connections or short circuits, as irreparable damage to electrical system components may result if short circuits occur.

4 If a multimeter is not available, the job of checking the charging system should be left to a Honda dealer.

31 Charging system – leakage and output test

1 If the charging system of the machine is thought to be faulty, perform the following checks.

Leakage test

Caution: Always connect an ammeter in series, never in parallel with the battery, otherwise it will be damaged. Do not turn the ignition ON or operate the starter motor when the ammeter is connected – a sudden surge in current will blow the meter's fuse.

2 Turn the ignition switch OFF and

disconnect the lead from the battery negative (–) terminal (see Section 3).

3 Set the multimeter to the Amps function and connect its negative (–) probe to the battery negative (–) terminal, and positive (+) probe to the disconnected negative (–) lead **(see illustration)**. Always set the meter to a high amps range initially and then bring it down to the mA (milli Amps) range; if there is a high current flow in the circuit it may blow the meter's fuse.

4 If the current leakage indicated exceeds the amount specified at the beginning of the Chapter, there is probably a short circuit in the wiring. Use the wiring diagrams at the end of this book and systematically disconnect individual electrical components until the source is identified.

> **HAYNES HiNT** *If an alarm system has been fitted, note that its current draw should be taken into account when measuring current leakage.*

5 Disconnect the meter and connect the negative (–) lead to the battery, tightening it securely.

Output test

6 Start the engine and warm it up to normal operating temperature.

7 To check the voltage output, allow the engine to idle and connect a multimeter set to the 0-20 volts DC scale (voltmeter) across the terminals of the battery (positive (+) lead to battery positive (+) terminal, negative (–) lead to battery negative (–) terminal). Slowly increase the engine speed to 5000 rpm and note the reading obtained. The regulated voltage should be as specified at the beginning of the Chapter. If the voltage is outside these limits, check the alternator and the regulator (see Sections 32 and 33).

> **HAYNES HiNT** *Clues to a faulty regulator are constantly blowing bulbs, with brightness varying considerably with engine speed, and battery overheating.*

32 Alternator – check, removal and installation

Check

1 Trace the wiring back from the alternator cover on the left-hand side of the engine and disconnect it the wiring connector containing the three yellow wires – on XL600V models, remove the seat, on XL650V and XRV750-P models onwards (1993-on) remove the left-hand side panel, and on XRV750-L to N (1990 to 1992) models remove the right-hand side panel to access the connector **(see illustrations)**. Check the connector terminals for corrosion and security.

2 Using a multimeter set to the ohms x 1 (ohmmeter) scale measure the resistance between each of the yellow wires on the alternator side of the connector, taking a total of three readings, then check for continuity between each terminal and ground (earth). If the stator coil windings are in good condition the three readings should be within the range shown In the Specifications at the start of this Chapter, and there should be no continuity (infinite resistance) between any of the terminals and ground (earth). If not, the alternator stator coil assembly is at fault and should be replaced with a new one. Note: *Before condemning the stator coils, check the fault is not due to damaged wiring between the connector and the coils.*

Removal

Note: *The alternator rotor bolt has left-hand threads. This means it has to be slackened and tightened in the OPPOSITE direction to normal bolts. Turn the bolt clockwise to unscrew it, and anti-clockwise to tighten it.*

3 On XL600V and XRV750 models remove the left-hand fairing side panel, and on XL650V models remove the fairing – although they do not actually restrict access on any model, if they're not there they can't be damaged should a tool slip when loosening and tightening the alternator rotor bolt. On all models remove the belly pan (see Chapter 8) and the front sprocket cover (see Chapter 6).

4 Either drain the engine oil (see Chapter 1), or

32.1a Alternator wiring connector (arrowed) – XL600V

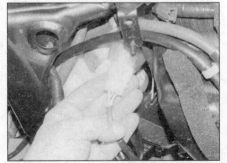

32.1b Alternator wiring connector – XL650V

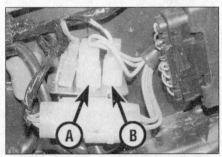

32.1c Alternator wiring connector (A), pulse generator wiring connector (B) – XRV750

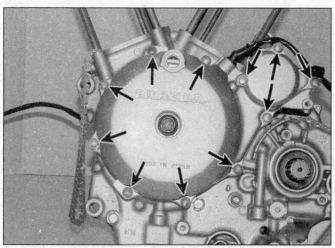

32.6 Alternator cover bolts (arrowed)

32.7 Withdraw the shafts (arrowed) and remove the gears

place a container under the engine to catch the oil that will come out when the alternator cover is removed. If your model has a centrestand place the bike on it so that it is level – this minimises oil loss. If your model does not have a centrestand and you do not have an auxiliary stand it is best to drain the oil.

5 Trace the wiring back from the alternator cover on the left-hand side of the engine and disconnect it the wiring connector containing the three yellow wires – on XL600V models, remove the seat, on XL650V and XRV750-P models onward (1993-on) remove the left-hand side panel, and on XRV750-L to N (1990 to 1992) models remove the right-hand side panel to access the connector **(see illustration 32.1a, b or c)**. Release the wiring from any clips or ties. On XRV750 models also disconnect the pulse generator coil wiring connector – on L to N (1990 to 1992) models you will have to remove the fuel tank to access it (see Chapter 4), on all other models it is on the right of the alternator connector **(see illustration 32.1c)**.

6 Working in a criss-cross pattern, evenly slacken the alternator cover bolts **(see illustration)**. Lift the cover away from the engine, noting that it will be restrained by the force of the rotor magnets, and be prepared to catch any residual oil. Remove the gasket and discard it. Remove the dowels from either the cover or the crankcase if it is loose.

7 Withdraw the starter drive gear shaft from the crankcase and remove the gear, noting which way round it fits **(see illustration)**. Withdraw the idle/reduction gear shaft from the crankcase and remove the gear, noting which way round it fits.

8 To remove the rotor bolt it is necessary to stop the rotor from turning. The best way is to use a commercially available rotor strap **(see illustration)**. If one is not available, try placing the transmission in gear and having an assistant apply the rear brake hard. Unscrew the bolt, remembering that it has left-hand threads (see **Note** above), and noting that it is very tight. Note the washer fitted with the bolt.

9 To remove the rotor from the shaft it is necessary to use a rotor puller. Thread the rotor puller into the centre of the rotor and turn it until the rotor is displaced from the shaft, holding the rotor to prevent the engine turning. Remove the Woodruff key from its slot in the crankcase if it is loose, and if required slide the needle bearing off the shaft **(see illustrations)**. Separate the starter clutch from the rotor if required (see Chapter 2).

10 To remove the stator from the cover, unscrew the bolts securing the stator, and the bolt securing the wiring clamp, then remove the assembly, noting how the rubber wiring grommet fits **(see illustration)**.

Installation

11 Fit the stator into the cover, aligning the rubber wiring grommet with the groove **(see illustration 32.10)**. Apply a suitable non-permanent thread locking compound to the stator bolt threads. Install the bolts and tighten them to the torque setting specified at the beginning of the Chapter. Apply a suitable sealant to the wiring grommet, then press it into the cut-out in the cover. Secure the wiring with its clamp and tighten the bolt securely.

12 If separated, fit the starter clutch onto the back of the rotor (see Chapter 2). Apply some oil to the needle bearing and slide it onto the end of the crankshaft **(see illustration 32.9b)**.

32.8 Using a rotor strap to hold the rotor while unscrewing the bolt

32.9b . . . and slide the bearing off the shaft

32.9a Remove the Woodruff key if it is loose . . .

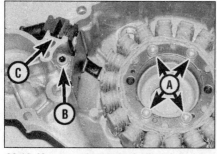

32.10 Unscrew the stator bolts (A) and the wiring clamp bolt (B) and free the grommet (C)

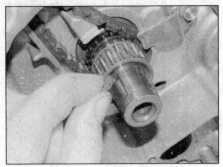

32.13 Fit the Woodruff key into its slot

32.14a Install the bolt with its washer . . .

32.14b . . . and tighten it to the specified torque

13 Clean the tapered end of the crankshaft and the corresponding mating surface on the inside of the rotor with a suitable solvent. Fit the Woodruff key into its slot in the crankshaft if removed **(see illustration)**. Make sure that no metal objects have attached themselves to the magnet on the inside of the rotor. Slide the rotor onto the shaft, making sure the groove on the inside of the rotor is aligned with and fits over the Woodruff key. Make sure the Woodruff key does not become dislodged when installing the rotor.

14 Apply some clean oil to the rotor bolt threads and the underside of the head. Install the rotor bolt with its washer, making sure the slightly raised centre of the washer is facing the bolt, and tighten it to the torque setting specified at the beginning of the Chapter, using the method employed on removal to prevent the rotor from turning, and not forgetting it has left-hand threads **(see illustrations)**.

15 Lubricate the idle/reduction gear shaft with clean engine oil. Position the gear in the crankcase, making sure the smaller pinion faces inwards and its teeth mesh correctly with the teeth of the starter driven gear, then slide the shaft into the gear **(see illustration)**. Lubricate the starter drive gear shaft with clean engine oil. Position the gear in the crankcase, making sure the OUT mark faces outwards and its teeth mesh correctly with the teeth of the idle/reduction gear and the starter motor shaft, then slide the shaft into the gear **(see illustration)**.

16 Fit the dowels into the crankcase if removed. Install the alternator cover using a new gasket, making sure they locate onto the dowels, and that the bores in the cover locate onto the idle/reduction and starter drive gear shafts **(see illustrations)**. Tighten the cover bolts evenly in a criss-cross sequence.

17 Reconnect the wiring at the connector(s)

and secure it with any clips or ties previously released **(see illustration 32.1a, b or c)**.

18 Fill the engine with oil, or top it up to the correct level, according to you removal method (see Chapter 1). Install the front sprocket cover, belly pan and any other components also removed.

33 Regulator/rectifier – check and replacement

Check

1 On XL600V models and XRV750-L to N (1990 to 1992) models remove the right-hand side panel **(see illustration)**. On XL650V and XRV750-P models onwards (1993-on) remove the left-hand side panel **(see illustrations)**. Either trace the wiring from the regulator/

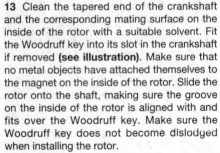

32.15a Install the idle/reduction gear . . .

32.15b . . . and the starter drive gear

32.16a Locate the new gasket onto the dowels (arrowed) . . .

32.16b . . . then install the cover . . .

32.16c . . . making sure the gear shafts locate in their bores (arrows)

33.1a Regulator/rectifier (arrowed) – XL600V

rectifier and disconnect it at the connectors, or disconnect the connector from the regulator/rectifier, according to model. Check the connectors for loose, damaged or corroded terminals.

2 Set the multimeter to the 0-20 dc volts setting. Connect the meter positive (+) probe to the red/white wire terminal (use either terminal where there are two, and check both) on the loom side of the connector and the negative (–) probe to a suitable ground (earth) and check for voltage. Full battery voltage should be present at all times (i.e. with the ignition OFF). On XL600V-H to K (1987 to 1989) models and XRV750-L and M (1990 and 1991) models, perform a similar check for battery voltage at the black wire terminal, this time with the ignition ON.

3 Switch the multimeter to the resistance (ohms) scale. Check for continuity between the green wire terminal on the loom side of the connector and ground (earth). There should be continuity.

4 On XRV750 models, set the multimeter to the K-ohms (ohmmeter) scale and measure the resistance between each of the terminals as indicated by the table for your model **(see illustrations)**. The readings should be within the range shown. Honda provide no such figures for XL models, but you could use the XRV figures as a guide for checking the internal circuitry. Usually a fault is identifiable by the absence or presence of infinite or zero resistance when there should in fact be a measurable amount.

5 If the above checks do not provide the expected results check the wiring and connectors between the battery, regulator/rectifier and alternator for shorts, breaks, and loose or corroded terminals (see the *wiring diagrams* at the end of this book).

6 If the wiring checks out, the regulator/rectifier unit is probably faulty. Take it to a Honda dealer for confirmation of its condition before replacing it with a new one. Alternatively obtain a known good one to use as a substitute, then check whether the fault has been corrected.

Replacement

7 On XL600V models and XRV750-L to N (1990 to 1992) models remove the right-hand side panel **(see illustration 33.1a)**. On XL650V and XRV750-P models onwards (1993-on) remove the left-hand side panel **(see illustrations 33.1b or c)**. Either trace the wiring from the regulator/rectifier and disconnect it at the connectors, or disconnect the connector from the regulator/rectifier, according to model. Free the wiring from any clips or ties and feed it back to the regulator/rectifier.

8 Unscrew the two nuts or bolts securing the regulator/rectifier, noting any earth wires, and on XL600 models the rear brake master cylinder reservoir, secured by them, and remove the regulator/rectifier.

9 Installation is the reverse of removal.

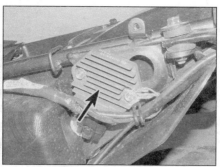

33.1b Regulator/rectifier (arrowed) – XL650V

33.1c Regulator/rectifier (arrowed) – XRV750-P models onward (1993-on)

+ Probe / – Probe	Black	Red/white	Yellow	Yellow	Yellow	Green
Black		20 to 100 kΩ	15 to 80 kΩ	15 to 80 kΩ	15 to 80 kΩ	10 to 50 kΩ
Red/white	∞		∞	∞	∞	∞
Yellow	∞	0.5 to 10 kΩ		∞	∞	∞
Yellow	∞	0.5 to 10 kΩ	∞		∞	∞
Yellow	∞	0.5 to 10 kΩ	∞	∞		∞
Green	1 to 20 kΩ	1 to 20 kΩ	0.5 to 10 kΩ	0.5 to 10 kΩ	0.5 to 10 kΩ	

33.4a Regulator/rectifier test details – XRV750-L to N (1990 to 1992) models

∞ Infinity   kΩ K-ohms

+ Probe / – Probe	Red/white	Yellow	Yellow	Yellow	Green
Red/white		∞	∞	∞	∞
Yellow	500 Ω to 10 kΩ		∞	∞	∞
Yellow	500 Ω to 10 kΩ	∞		∞	∞
Yellow	500 Ω to 10 kΩ	∞	∞		∞
Green	700 Ω to 15 kΩ	500 Ω to 10 kΩ	500 Ω to 10 kΩ	500 Ω to 10 kΩ	

33.4a Regulator/rectifier test details – XRV750-P models onward (1993-on)

∞ Infinity   Ω Ohms   kΩ K-ohms

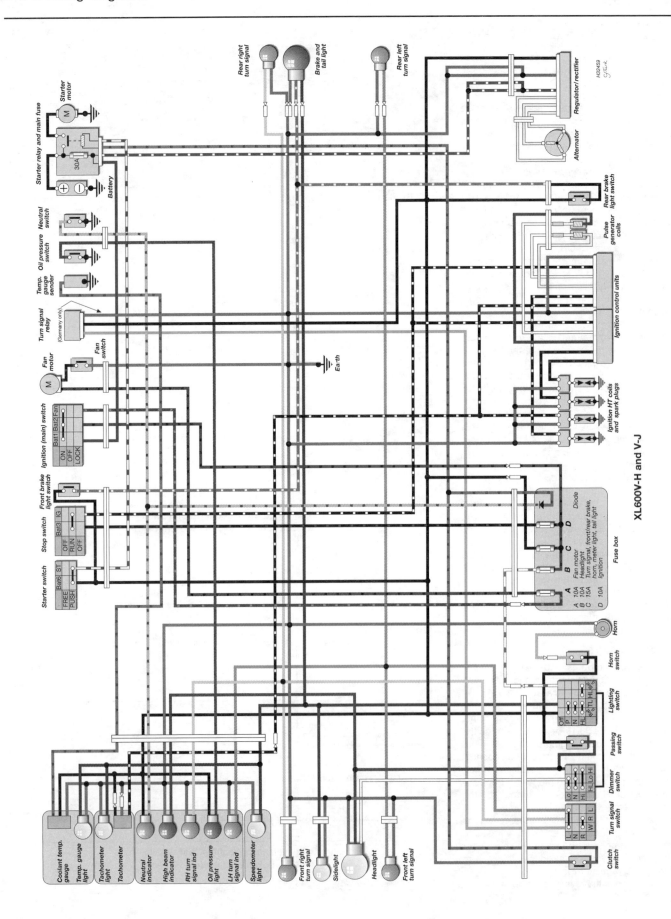

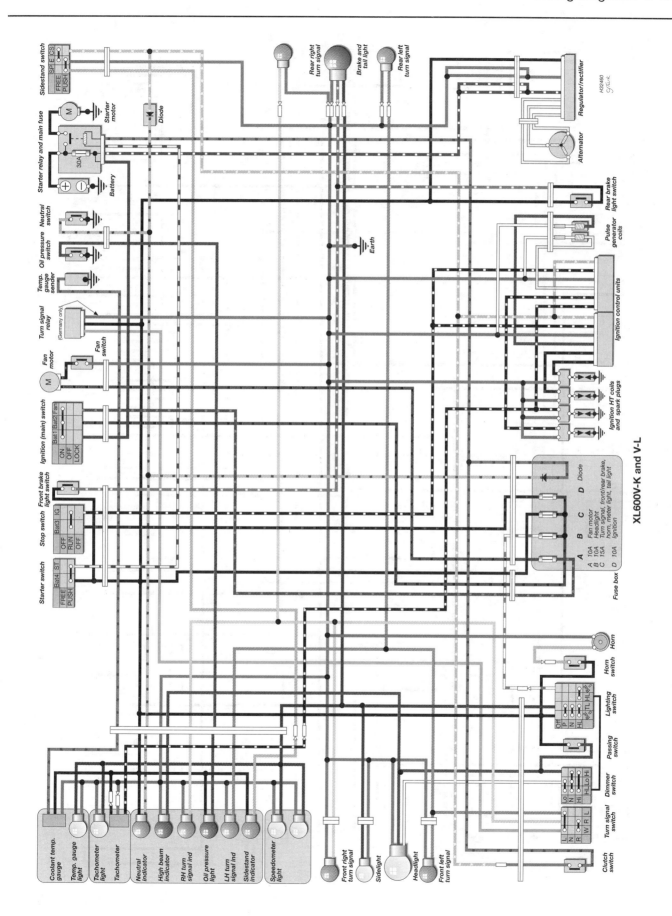

XL600V-K and V-L

9

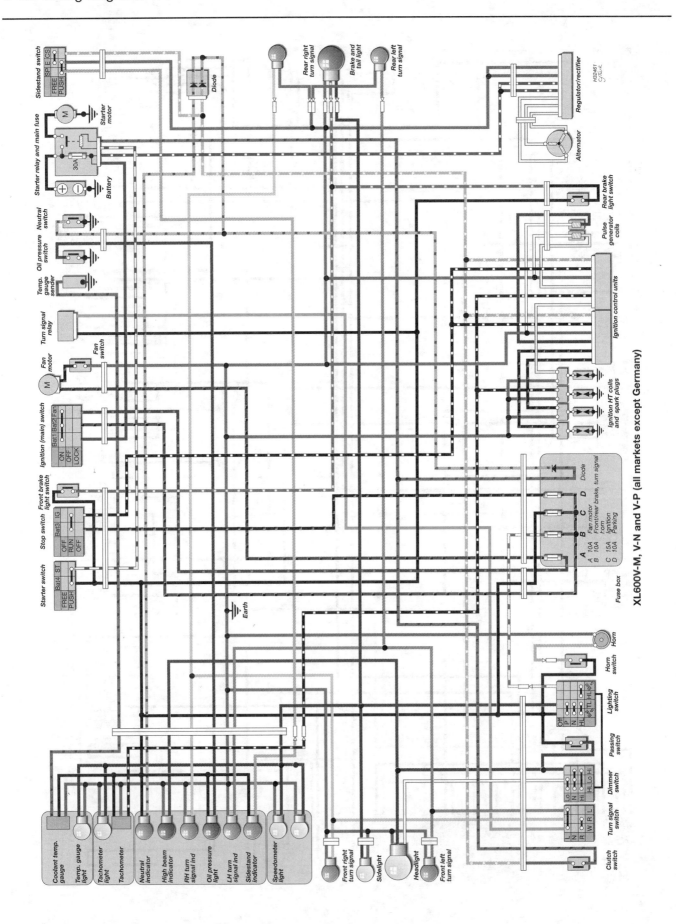

XL600V-M, V-N and V-P (all markets except Germany)

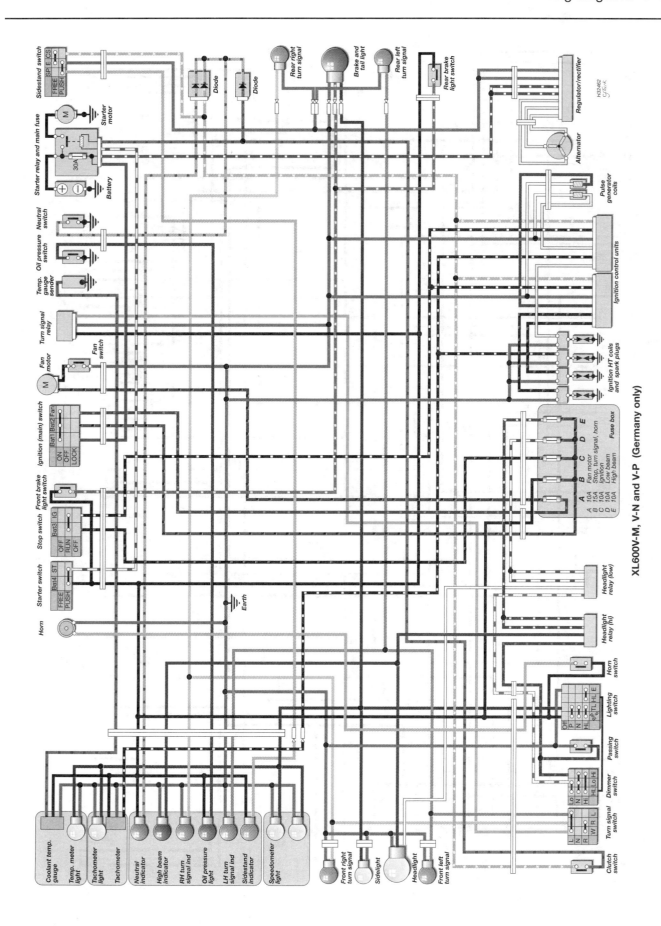

XL600V-M, V-N and V-P (Germany only)

9

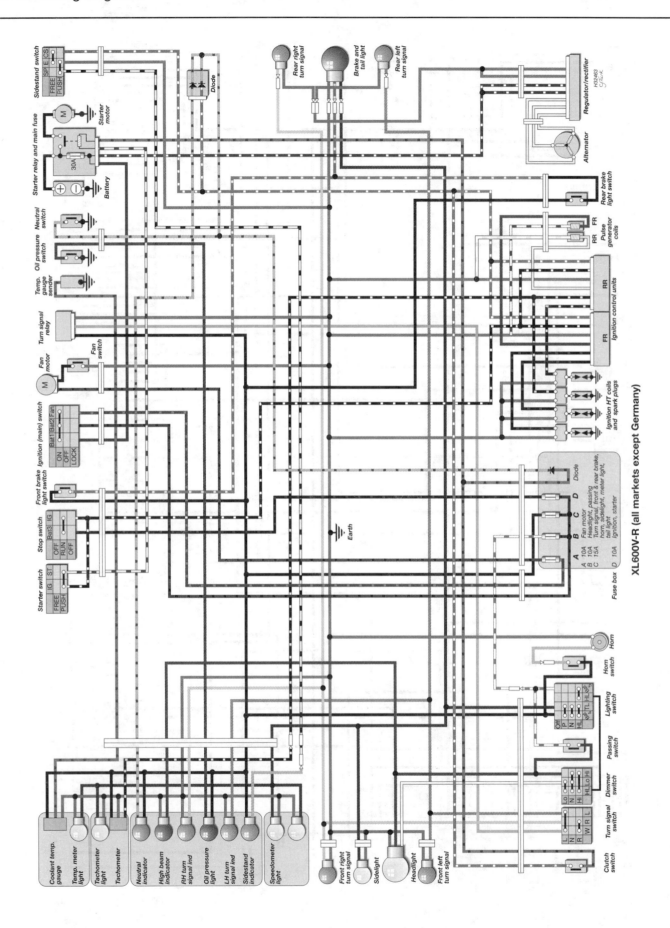

XL600V-R (all markets except Germany)

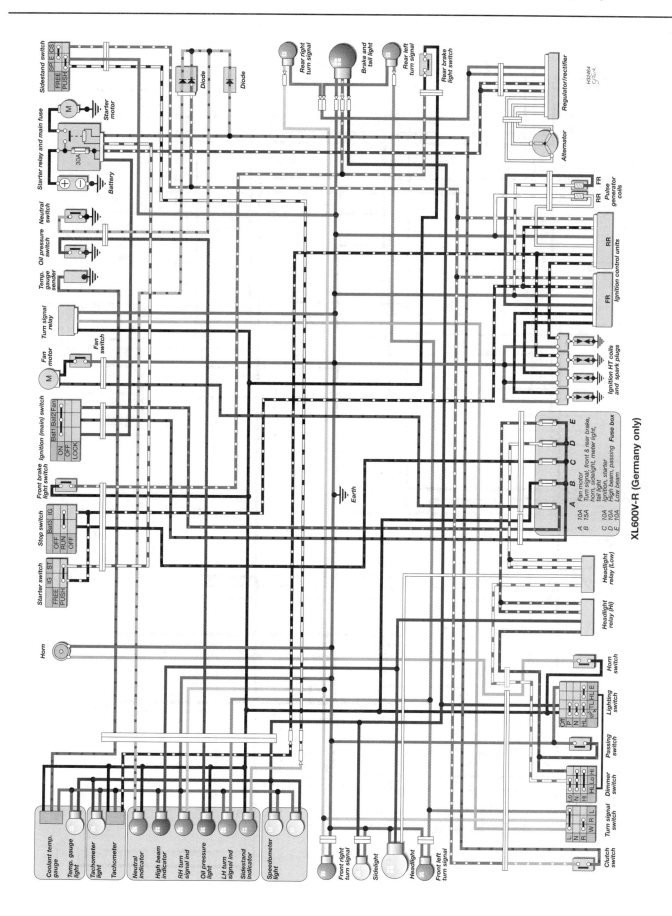

XL600V-R (Germany only)

9

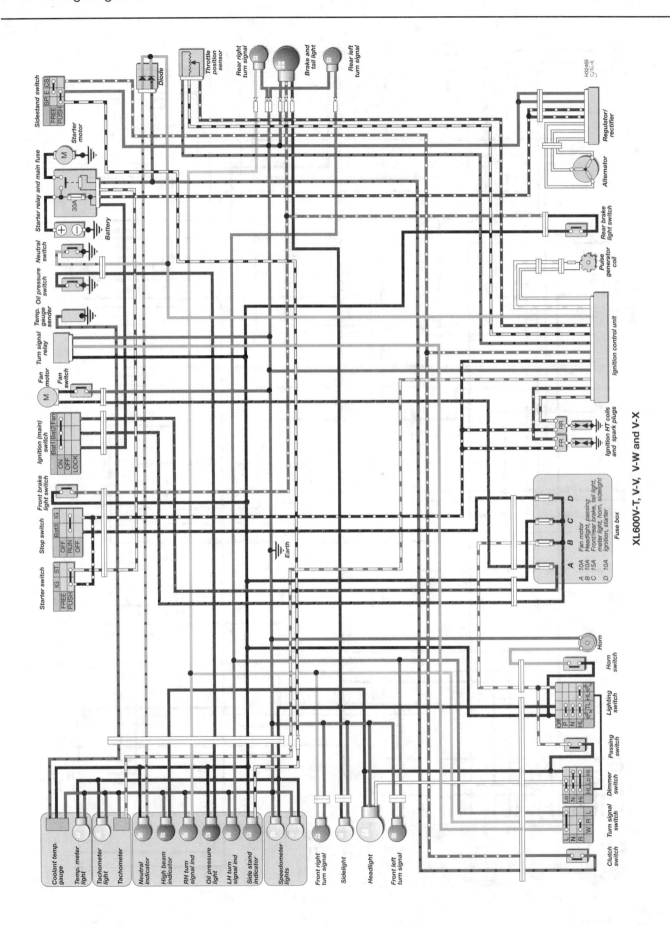

XL600V-T, V-V, V-W and V-X

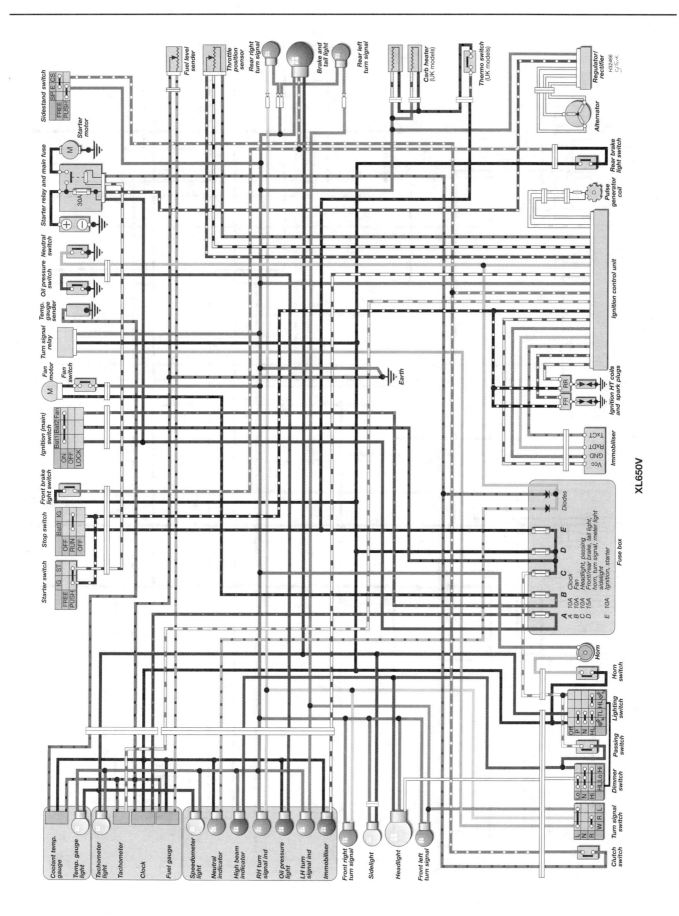

XL650V

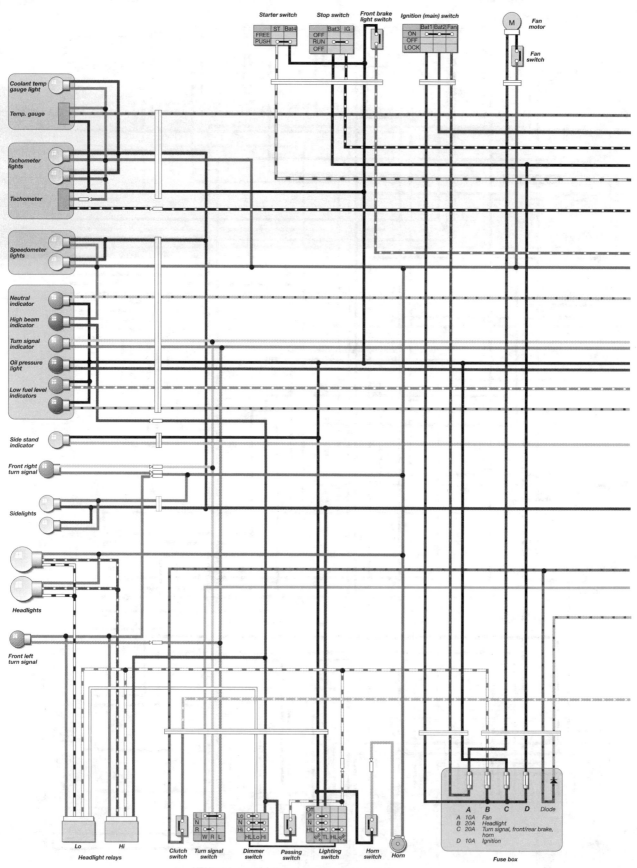

XRV750-L and M (all markets except Germany)

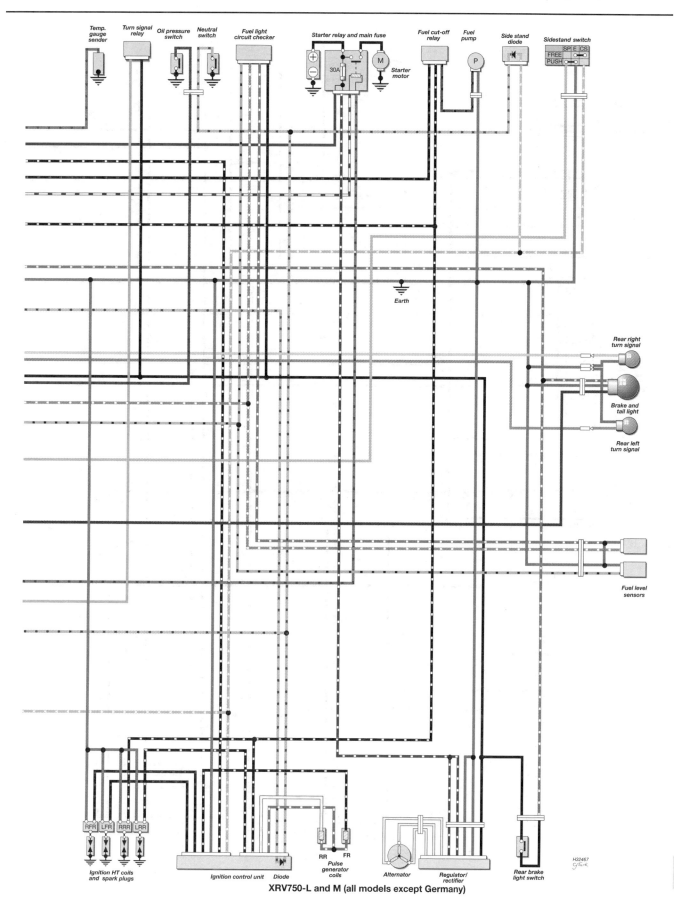

XRV750-L and M (all models except Germany)

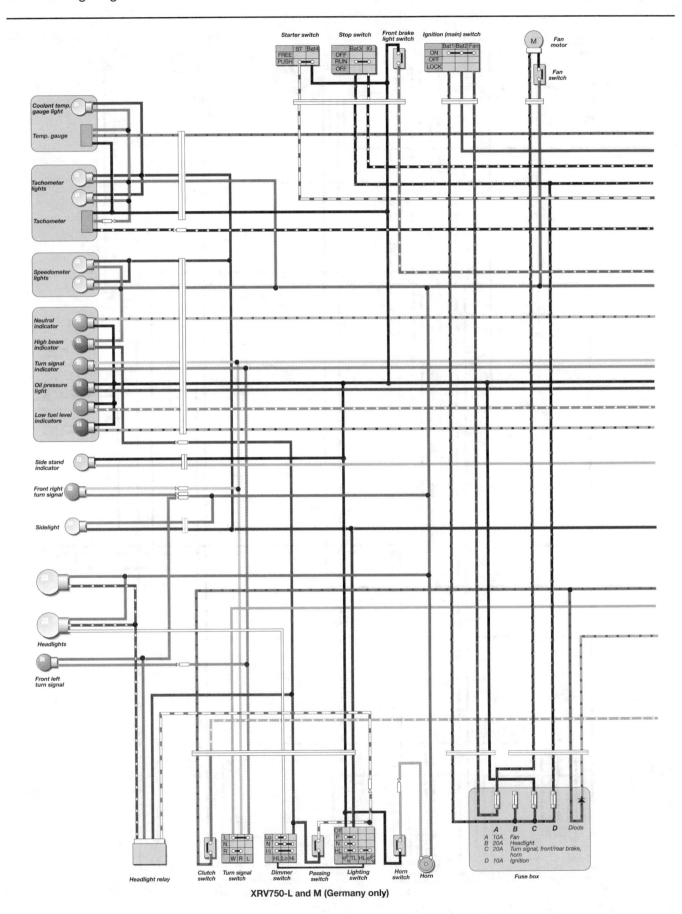

Starter switch
Stop switch
Front brake light switch
Ignition (main) switch
Fan motor
Fan switch

Coolant temp. gauge light
Temp. gauge

Tachometer lights
Tachometer

Speedometer lights

Neutral indicator
High beam indicator
Turn signal indicator
Oil pressure light
Low fuel level indicators

Side stand indicator

Front right turn signal

Sidelight

Headlights

Front left turn signal

Headlight relay
Clutch switch
Turn signal switch
Dimmer switch
Passing switch
Lighting switch
Horn switch
Horn
Fuse box

A   10A   Fan
B   20A   Headlight
C   20A   Turn signal, front/rear brake, horn
D   10A   Ignition

Diode

XRV750-L and M (Germany only)

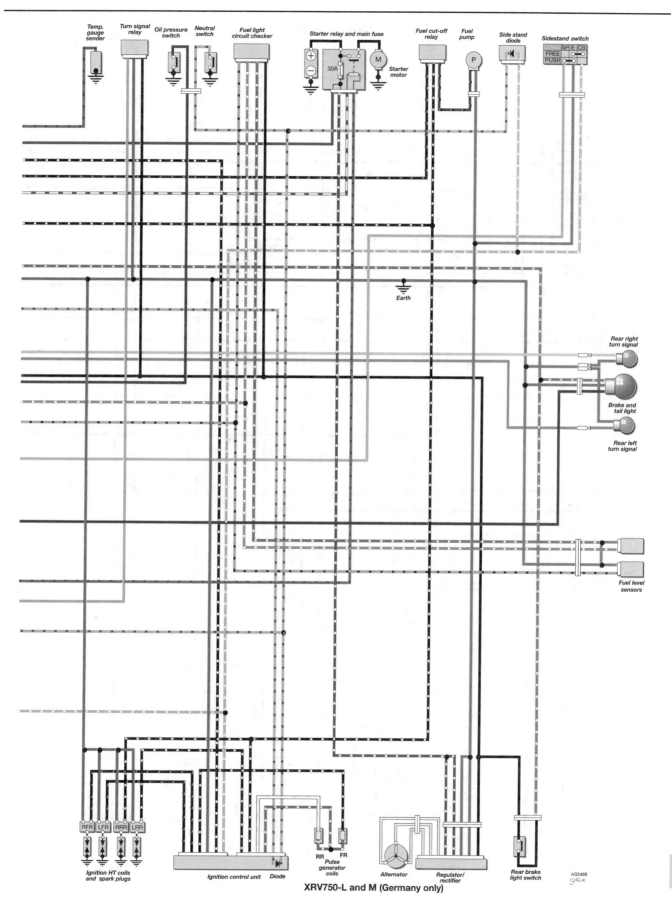

Temp. gauge sender
Turn signal relay
Oil pressure switch
Neutral switch
Fuel light circuit checker
Starter relay and main fuse
30A
M
Starter motor
Fuel cut-off relay
Fuel pump
P
Side stand diode
Sidestand switch
SP E CS
FREE
PUSH

Earth

Rear right turn signal

Brake and tail light

Rear left turn signal

Fuel level sensors

RFR LFR RRR LRR
Ignition HT coils and spark plugs
Ignition control unit
Diode
RR Pulse generator coils FR
Alternator
Regulator/ rectifier
Rear brake light switch

H32468

XRV750-L and M (Germany only)

9

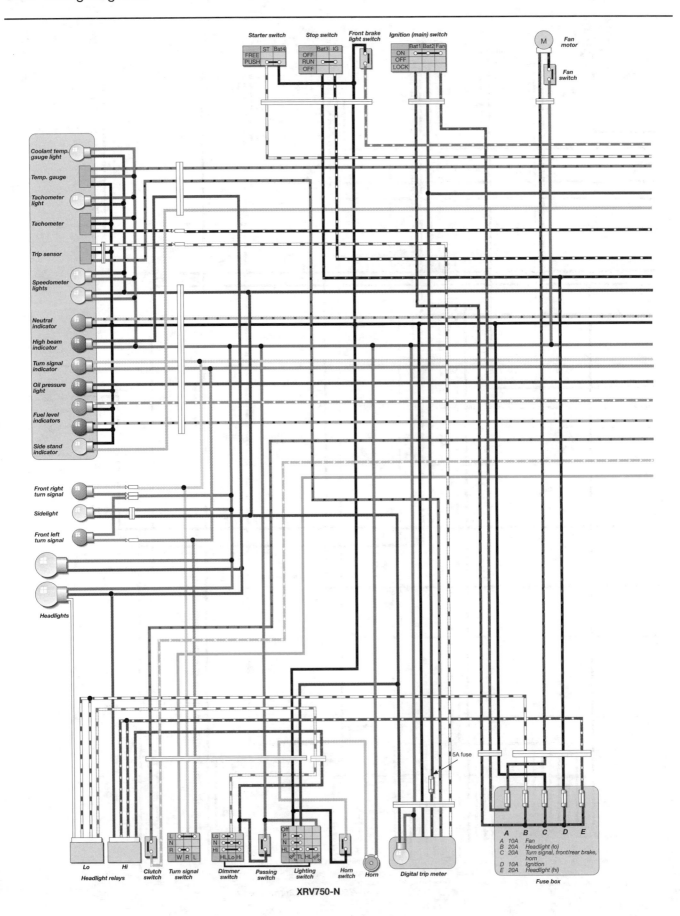

XRV750-N

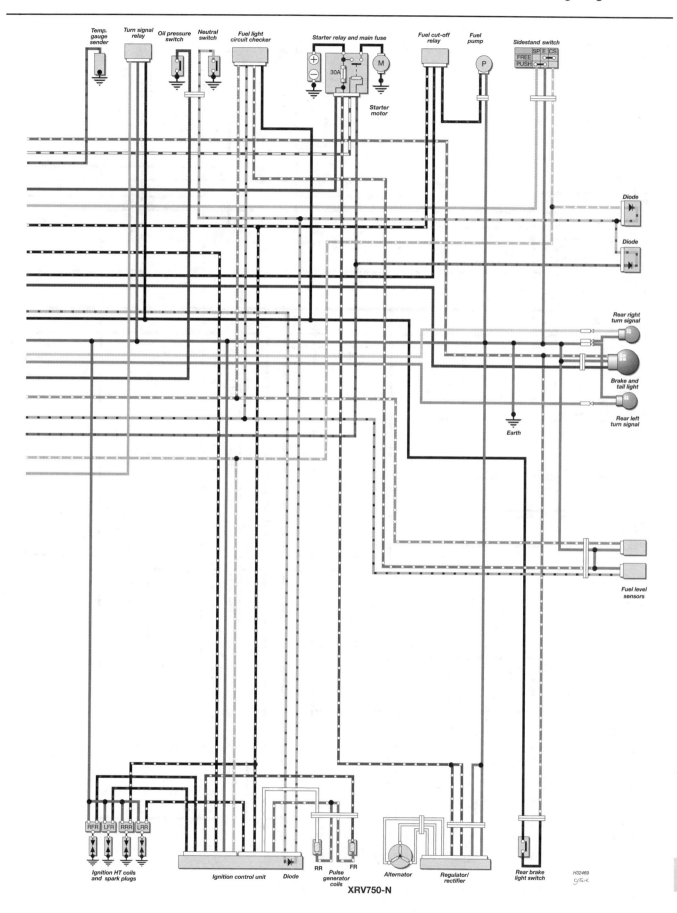

XRV750-N

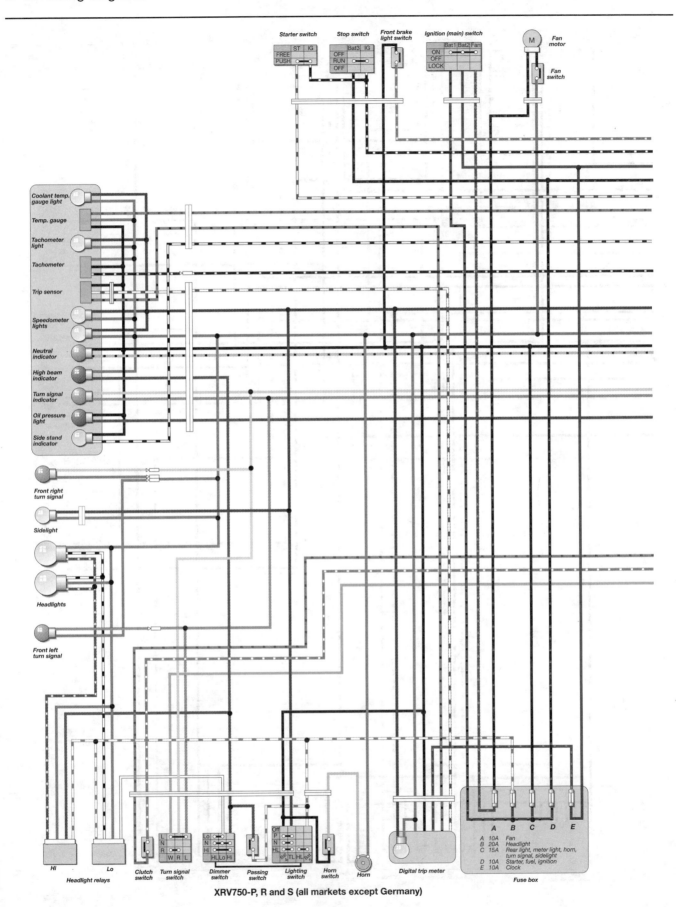

XRV750-P, R and S (all markets except Germany)

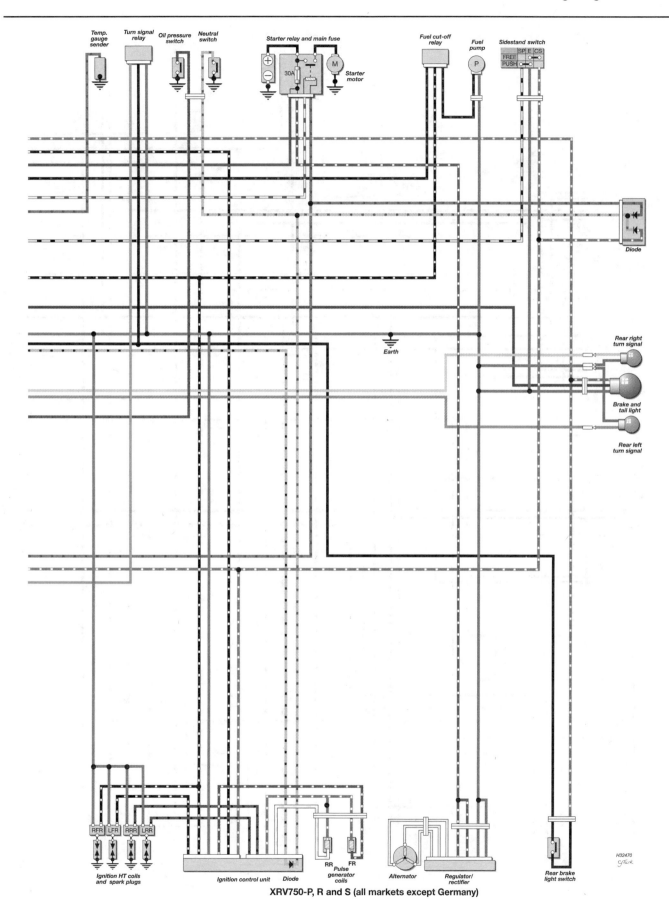

XRV750-P, R and S (all markets except Germany)

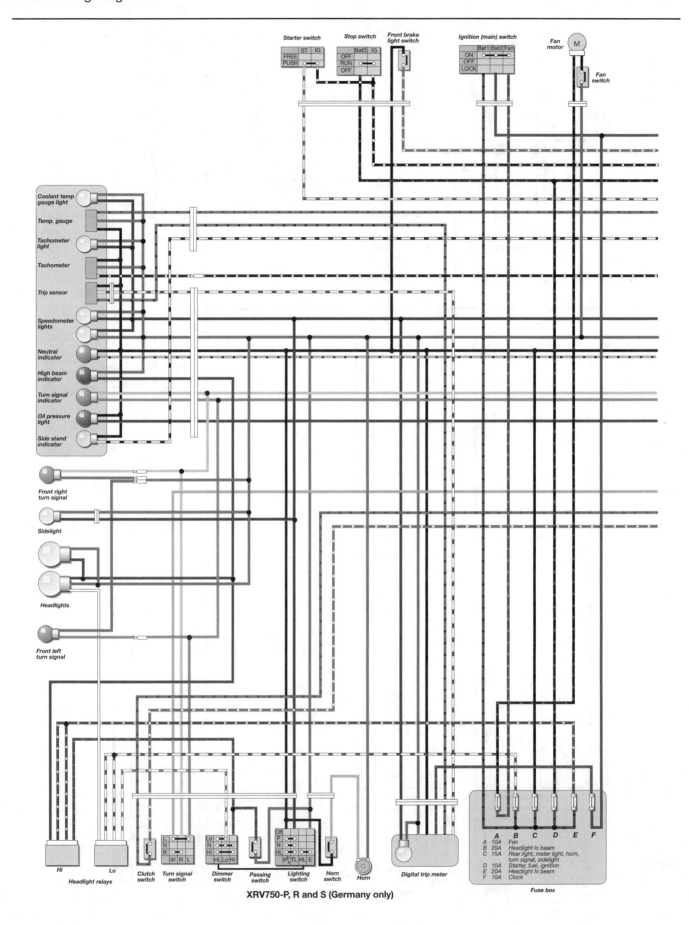

XRV750-P, R and S (Germany only)

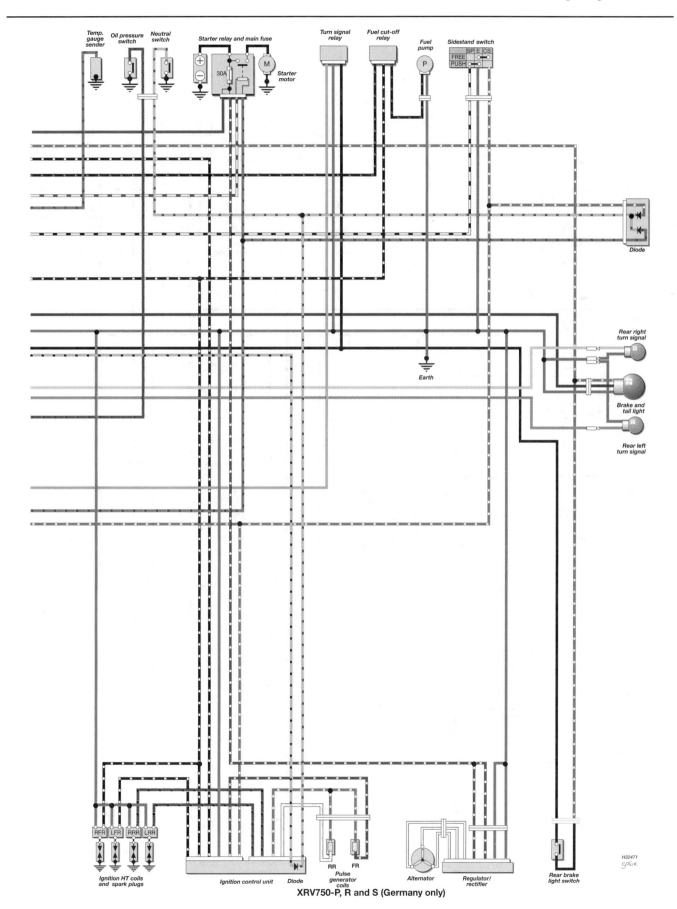

Temp. gauge sender

Oil pressure switch

Neutral switch

Starter relay and main fuse

Starter motor

Turn signal relay

Fuel cut-off relay

Fuel pump

Sidestand switch

30A

Diode

Earth

Rear right turn signal

Brake and tail light

Rear left turn signal

RFR LFR RRR LRR

Ignition HT coils and spark plugs

Ignition control unit

Diode

RR FR

Pulse generator coils

Alternator

Regulator/ rectifier

Rear brake light switch

XRV750-P, R and S (Germany only)

H32471

9

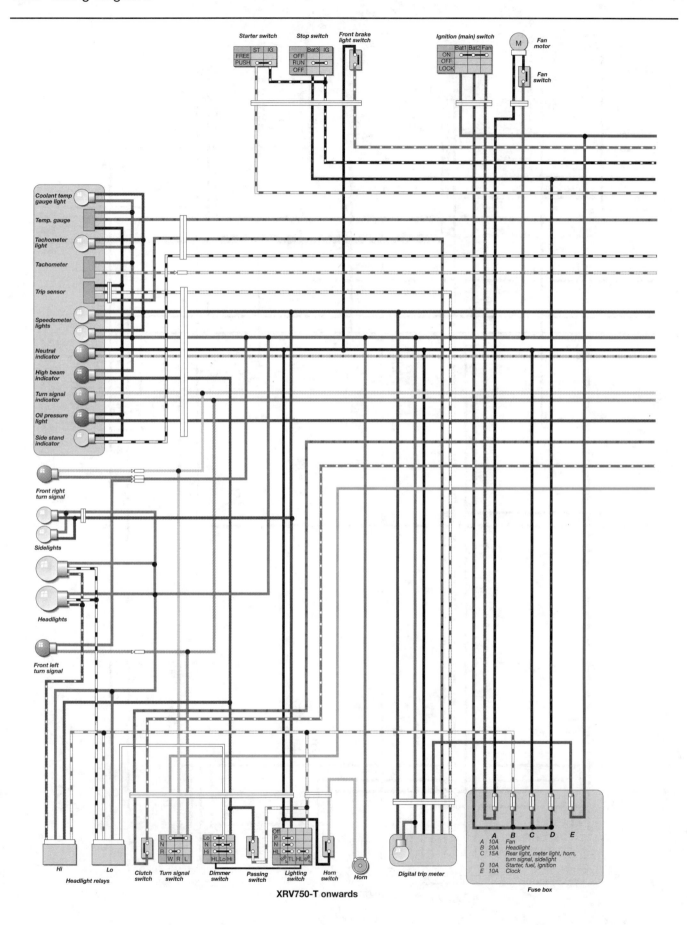

XRV750-T onwards

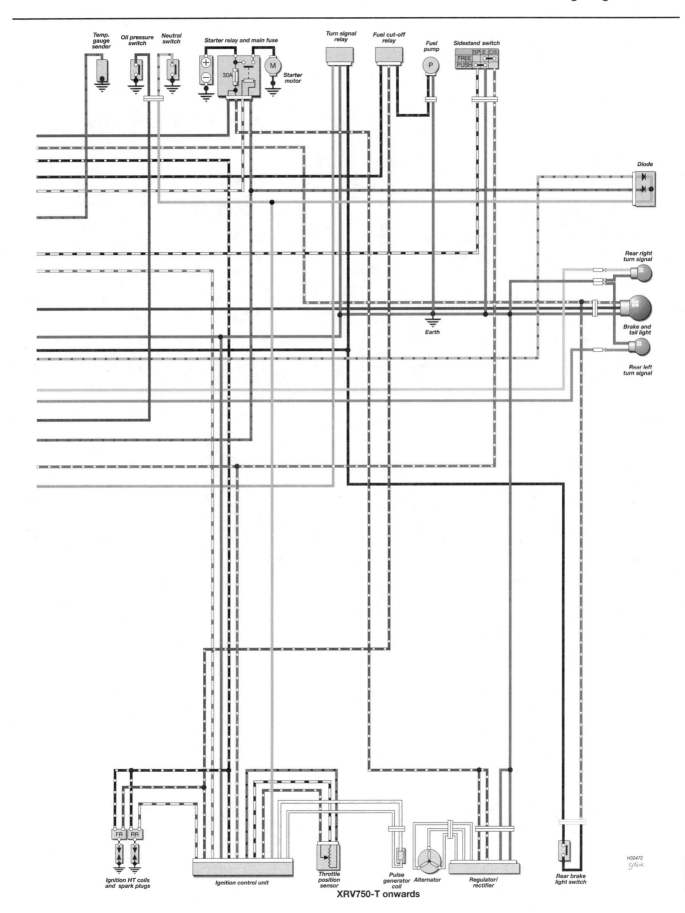

XRV750-T onwards

Notes

Reference

Tools and Workshop Tips

● Building up a tool kit and equipping your workshop ● Using tools ● Understanding bearing, seal, fastener and chain sizes and markings ● Repair techniques

Security

● Locks and chains ● U-locks ● Disc locks ● Alarms and immobilisers ● Security marking systems ● Tips on how to prevent bike theft

Lubricants and fluids

● Engine oils ● Transmission (gear) oils ● Coolant/anti-freeze ● Fork oils and suspension fluids ● Brake/clutch fluids ● Spray lubes, degreasers and solvents

Conversion Factors

34 Nm × 0.738
= 25 lbf ft

● Formulae for conversion of the metric (SI) units used throughout the manual into Imperial measures

MOT Test Checks

● A guide to the UK MOT test ● Which items are tested ● How to prepare your motorcycle for the test and perform a pre-test check

Storage

● How to prepare your motorcycle for going into storage and protect essential systems ● How to get the motorcycle back on the road

Fault Finding

● Common faults and their likely causes ● How to check engine cylinder compression ● How to make electrical tests and use test meters

Technical Terms Explained

● Component names, technical terms and common abbreviations explained

Index

Buying tools

A toolkit is a fundamental requirement for servicing and repairing a motorcycle. Although there will be an initial expense in building up enough tools for servicing, this will soon be offset by the savings made by doing the job yourself. As experience and confidence grow, additional tools can be added to enable the repair and overhaul of the motorcycle. Many of the specialist tools are expensive and not often used so it may be preferable to hire them, or for a group of friends or motorcycle club to join in the purchase.

As a rule, it is better to buy more expensive, good quality tools. Cheaper tools are likely to wear out faster and need to be renewed more often, nullifying the original saving.

> ⚠️ **Warning: To avoid the risk of a poor quality tool breaking in use, causing injury or damage to the component being worked on, always aim to purchase tools which meet the relevant national safety standards.**

The following lists of tools do not represent the manufacturer's service tools, but serve as a guide to help the owner decide which tools are needed for this level of work. In addition, items such as an electric drill, hacksaw, files, soldering iron and a workbench equipped with a vice, may be needed. Although not classed as tools, a selection of bolts, screws, nuts, washers and pieces of tubing always come in useful.

For more information about tools, refer to the Haynes *Motorcycle Workshop Practice TechBook* (Bk. No. 3470).

Manufacturer's service tools

Inevitably certain tasks require the use of a service tool. Where possible an alternative tool or method of approach is recommended, but sometimes there is no option if personal injury or damage to the component is to be avoided. Where required, service tools are referred to in the relevant procedure.

Service tools can usually only be purchased from a motorcycle dealer and are identified by a part number. Some of the commonly-used tools, such as rotor pullers, are available in aftermarket form from mail-order motorcycle tool and accessory suppliers.

Maintenance and minor repair tools

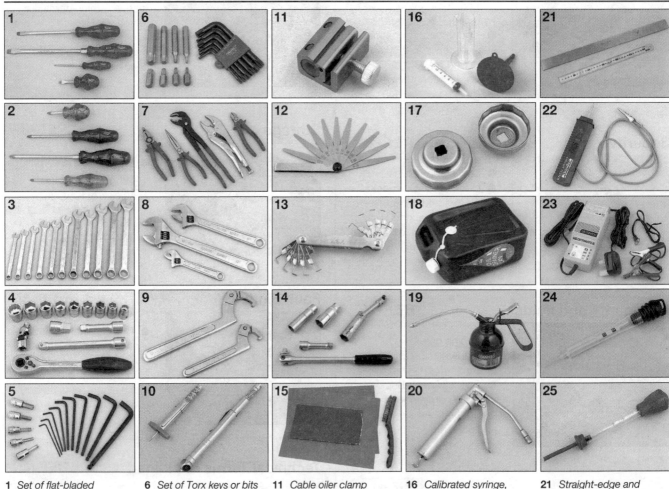

1. Set of flat-bladed screwdrivers
2. Set of Phillips head screwdrivers
3. Combination open-end and ring spanners
4. Socket set (3/8 inch or 1/2 inch drive)
5. Set of Allen keys or bits
6. Set of Torx keys or bits
7. Pliers, cutters and self-locking grips (Mole grips)
8. Adjustable spanners
9. C-spanners
10. Tread depth gauge and tyre pressure gauge
11. Cable oiler clamp
12. Feeler gauges
13. Spark plug gap measuring tool
14. Spark plug spanner or deep plug sockets
15. Wire brush and emery paper
16. Calibrated syringe, measuring vessel and funnel
17. Oil filter adapters
18. Oil drainer can or tray
19. Pump type oil can
20. Grease gun
21. Straight-edge and steel rule
22. Continuity tester
23. Battery charger
24. Hydrometer (for battery specific gravity check)
25. Anti-freeze tester (for liquid-cooled engines)

Repair and overhaul tools

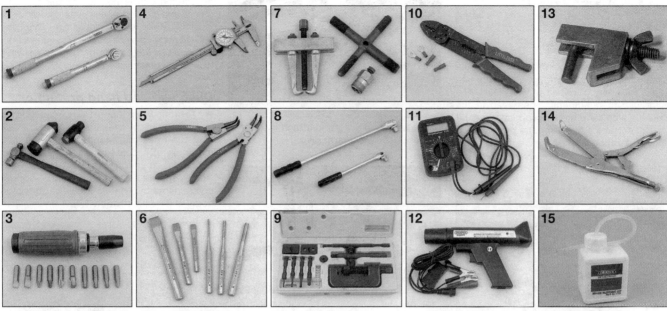

1 Torque wrench
   (small and mid-ranges)
2 Conventional, plastic or
   soft-faced hammers
3 Impact driver set

4 Vernier gauge
5 Circlip pliers (internal and
   external, or combination)
6 Set of cold chisels
   and punches

7 Selection of pullers
8 Breaker bars
9 Chain breaking/
   riveting tool set

10 Wire stripper and
    crimper tool
11 Multimeter (measures
    amps, volts and ohms)
12 Stroboscope (for
    dynamic timing checks)

13 Hose clamp
    (wingnut type shown)
14 Clutch holding tool
15 One-man brake/clutch
    bleeder kit

Specialist tools

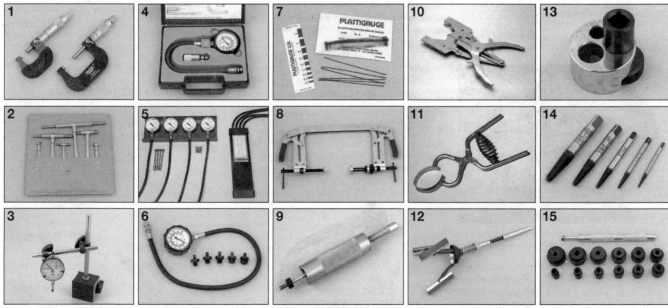

1 Micrometers
   (external type)
2 Telescoping gauges
3 Dial gauge

4 Cylinder
   compression gauge
5 Vacuum gauges (left) or
   manometer (right)
6 Oil pressure gauge

7 Plastigauge kit
8 Valve spring compressor
   (4-stroke engines)
9 Piston pin drawbolt tool

10 Piston ring removal and
    installation tool
11 Piston ring clamp
12 Cylinder bore hone
    (stone type shown)

13 Stud extractor
14 Screw extractor set
15 Bearing driver set

1 Workshop equipment and facilities

The workbench

● Work is made much easier by raising the bike up on a ramp - components are much more accessible if raised to waist level. The hydraulic or pneumatic types seen in the dealer's workshop are a sound investment if you undertake a lot of repairs or overhauls (see illustration 1.1).

1.1 Hydraulic motorcycle ramp

● If raised off ground level, the bike must be supported on the ramp to avoid it falling. Most ramps incorporate a front wheel locating clamp which can be adjusted to suit different diameter wheels. When tightening the clamp, take care not to mark the wheel rim or damage the tyre - use wood blocks on each side to prevent this.
● Secure the bike to the ramp using tie-downs (see illustration 1.2). If the bike has only a sidestand, and hence leans at a dangerous angle when raised, support the bike on an auxiliary stand.

1.2 Tie-downs are used around the passenger footrests to secure the bike

● Auxiliary (paddock) stands are widely available from mail order companies or motorcycle dealers and attach either to the wheel axle or swingarm pivot (see illustration 1.3). If the motorcycle has a centrestand, you can support it under the crankcase to prevent it toppling whilst either wheel is removed (see illustration 1.4).

1.3 This auxiliary stand attaches to the swingarm pivot

1.4 Always use a block of wood between the engine and jack head when supporting the engine in this way

Fumes and fire

● Refer to the Safety first! page at the beginning of the manual for full details. Make sure your workshop is equipped with a fire extinguisher suitable for fuel-related fires (Class B fire - flammable liquids) - it is not sufficient to have a water-filled extinguisher.
● Always ensure adequate ventilation is available. Unless an exhaust gas extraction system is available for use, ensure that the engine is run outside of the workshop.
● If working on the fuel system, make sure the workshop is ventilated to avoid a build-up of fumes. This applies equally to fume build-up when charging a battery. Do not smoke or allow anyone else to smoke in the workshop.

Fluids

● If you need to drain fuel from the tank, store it in an approved container marked as suitable for the storage of petrol (gasoline) (see illustration 1.5). Do not store fuel in glass jars or bottles.

1.5 Use an approved can only for storing petrol (gasoline)

● Use proprietary engine degreasers or solvents which have a high flash-point, such as paraffin (kerosene), for cleaning off oil, grease and dirt - never use petrol (gasoline) for cleaning. Wear rubber gloves when handling solvent and engine degreaser. The fumes from certain solvents can be dangerous - always work in a well-ventilated area.

Dust, eye and hand protection

● Protect your lungs from inhalation of dust particles by wearing a filtering mask over the nose and mouth. Many frictional materials still contain asbestos which is dangerous to your health. Protect your eyes from spouts of liquid and sprung components by wearing a pair of protective goggles (see illustration 1.6).

1.6 A fire extinguisher, goggles, mask and protective gloves should be at hand in the workshop

● Protect your hands from contact with solvents, fuel and oils by wearing rubber gloves. Alternatively apply a barrier cream to your hands before starting work. If handling hot components or fluids, wear suitable gloves to protect your hands from scalding and burns.

What to do with old fluids

● Old cleaning solvent, fuel, coolant and oils should not be poured down domestic drains or onto the ground. Package the fluid up in old oil containers, label it accordingly, and take it to a garage or disposal facility. Contact your local authority for location of such sites or ring the oil care hotline.

OIL CARE
FOLLOW THE CODE
OIL BANK LINE
0800 66 33 66
www.oilbankline.org.uk

Note: It is antisocial and illegal to dump oil down the drain. To find the location of your local oil recycling bank, call this number free.

In the USA, note that any oil supplier must accept used oil for recycling.

2 Fasteners -
screws, bolts and nuts

Fastener types and applications

Bolts and screws

● Fastener head types are either of hexagonal, Torx or splined design, with internal and external versions of each type **(see illustrations 2.1 and 2.2)**; splined head fasteners are not in common use on motorcycles. The conventional slotted or Phillips head design is used for certain screws. Bolt or screw length is always measured from the underside of the head to the end of the item **(see illustration 2.11)**.

2.1 Internal hexagon/Allen (A), Torx (B) and splined (C) fasteners, with corresponding bits

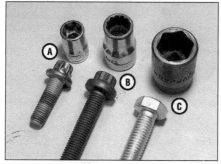

2.2 External Torx (A), splined (B) and hexagon (C) fasteners, with corresponding sockets

● Certain fasteners on the motorcycle have a tensile marking on their heads, the higher the marking the stronger the fastener. High tensile fasteners generally carry a 10 or higher marking. Never replace a high tensile fastener with one of a lower tensile strength.

Washers (see illustration 2.3)

● Plain washers are used between a fastener head and a component to prevent damage to the component or to spread the load when torque is applied. Plain washers can also be used as spacers or shims in certain assemblies. Copper or aluminium plain washers are often used as sealing washers on drain plugs.

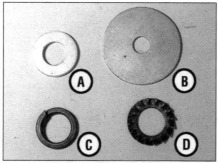

2.3 Plain washer (A), penny washer (B), spring washer (C) and serrated washer (D)

● The split-ring spring washer works by applying axial tension between the fastener head and component. If flattened, it is fatigued and must be renewed. If a plain (flat) washer is used on the fastener, position the spring washer between the fastener and the plain washer.

● Serrated star type washers dig into the fastener and component faces, preventing loosening. They are often used on electrical earth (ground) connections to the frame.

● Cone type washers (sometimes called Belleville) are conical and when tightened apply axial tension between the fastener head and component. They must be installed with the dished side against the component and often carry an OUTSIDE marking on their outer face. If flattened, they are fatigued and must be renewed.

● Tab washers are used to lock plain nuts or bolts on a shaft. A portion of the tab washer is bent up hard against one flat of the nut or bolt to prevent it loosening. Due to the tab washer being deformed in use, a new tab washer should be used every time it is disturbed.

● Wave washers are used to take up endfloat on a shaft. They provide light springing and prevent excessive side-to-side play of a component. Can be found on rocker arm shafts.

Nuts and split pins

● Conventional plain nuts are usually six-sided **(see illustration 2.4)**. They are sized by thread diameter and pitch. High tensile nuts carry a number on one end to denote their tensile strength.

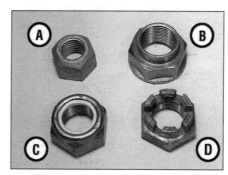

2.4 Plain nut (A), shouldered locknut (B), nylon insert nut (C) and castellated nut (D)

● Self-locking nuts either have a nylon insert, or two spring metal tabs, or a shoulder which is staked into a groove in the shaft - their advantage over conventional plain nuts is a resistance to loosening due to vibration. The nylon insert type can be used a number of times, but must be renewed when the friction of the nylon insert is reduced, ie when the nut spins freely on the shaft. The spring tab type can be reused unless the tabs are damaged. The shouldered type must be renewed every time it is disturbed.

● Split pins (cotter pins) are used to lock a castellated nut to a shaft or to prevent slackening of a plain nut. Common applications are wheel axles and brake torque arms. Because the split pin arms are deformed to lock around the nut a new split pin must always be used on installation - always fit the correct size split pin which will fit snugly in the shaft hole. Make sure the split pin arms are correctly located around the nut **(see illustrations 2.5 and 2.6)**.

2.5 Bend split pin (cotter pin) arms as shown (arrows) to secure a castellated nut

2.6 Bend split pin (cotter pin) arms as shown to secure a plain nut

Caution: If the castellated nut slots do not align with the shaft hole after tightening to the torque setting, tighten the nut until the next slot aligns with the hole - never slacken the nut to align its slot.

● R-pins (shaped like the letter R), or slip pins as they are sometimes called, are sprung and can be reused if they are otherwise in good condition. Always install R-pins with their closed end facing forwards **(see illustration 2.7)**.

2.7 Correct fitting of R-pin. Arrow indicates forward direction

Circlips (see illustration 2.8)

● Circlips (sometimes called snap-rings) are used to retain components on a shaft or in a housing and have corresponding external or internal ears to permit removal. Parallel-sided (machined) circlips can be installed either way round in their groove, whereas stamped circlips (which have a chamfered edge on one face) must be installed with the chamfer facing away from the direction of thrust load **(see illustration 2.9)**.

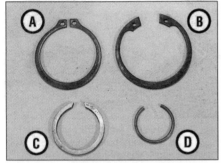

2.8 External stamped circlip (A), internal stamped circlip (B), machined circlip (C) and wire circlip (D)

● Always use circlip pliers to remove and install circlips; expand or compress them just enough to remove them. After installation, rotate the circlip in its groove to ensure it is securely seated. If installing a circlip on a splined shaft, always align its opening with a shaft channel to ensure the circlip ends are well supported and unlikely to catch **(see illustration 2.10)**.

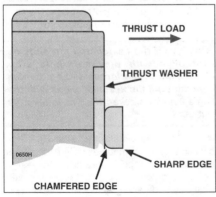

2.9 Correct fitting of a stamped circlip

THRUST LOAD

THRUST WASHER

SHARP EDGE

CHAMFERED EDGE

0650H

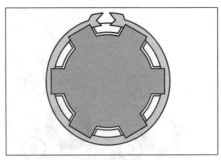

2.10 Align circlip opening with shaft channel

● Circlips can wear due to the thrust of components and become loose in their grooves, with the subsequent danger of becoming dislodged in operation. For this reason, renewal is advised every time a circlip is disturbed.

● Wire circlips are commonly used as piston pin retaining clips. If a removal tang is provided, long-nosed pliers can be used to dislodge them, otherwise careful use of a small flat-bladed screwdriver is necessary. Wire circlips should be renewed every time they are disturbed.

Thread diameter and pitch

● Diameter of a male thread (screw, bolt or stud) is the outside diameter of the threaded portion **(see illustration 2.11)**. Most motorcycle manufacturers use the ISO (International Standards Organisation) metric system expressed in millimetres, eg M6 refers to a 6 mm diameter thread. Sizing is the same for nuts, except that the thread diameter is measured across the valleys of the nut.

● Pitch is the distance between the peaks of the thread **(see illustration 2.11)**. It is expressed in millimetres, thus a common bolt size may be expressed as 6.0 x 1.0 mm (6 mm thread diameter and 1 mm pitch). Generally pitch increases in proportion to thread diameter, although there are always exceptions.

● Thread diameter and pitch are related for conventional fastener applications and the accompanying table can be used as a guide. Additionally, the AF (Across Flats), spanner or socket size dimension of the bolt or nut **(see illustration 2.11)** is linked to thread and pitch specification. Thread pitch can be measured with a thread gauge **(see illustration 2.12)**.

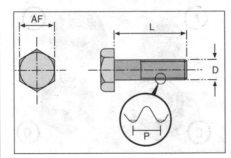

AF

L

D

P

2.11 Fastener length (L), thread diameter (D), thread pitch (P) and head size (AF)

2.12 Using a thread gauge to measure pitch

AF size	Thread diameter x pitch (mm)
8 mm	M5 x 0.8
8 mm	M6 x 1.0
10 mm	M6 x 1.0
12 mm	M8 x 1.25
14 mm	M10 x 1.25
17 mm	M12 x 1.25

● The threads of most fasteners are of the right-hand type, ie they are turned clockwise to tighten and anti-clockwise to loosen. The reverse situation applies to left-hand thread fasteners, which are turned anti-clockwise to tighten and clockwise to loosen. Left-hand threads are used where rotation of a component might loosen a conventional right-hand thread fastener.

Seized fasteners

● Corrosion of external fasteners due to water or reaction between two dissimilar metals can occur over a period of time. It will build up sooner in wet conditions or in countries where salt is used on the roads during the winter. If a fastener is severely corroded it is likely that normal methods of removal will fail and result in its head being ruined. When you attempt removal, the fastener thread should be heard to crack free and unscrew easily - if it doesn't, stop there before damaging something.

● A smart tap on the head of the fastener will often succeed in breaking free corrosion which has occurred in the threads **(see illustration 2.13)**.

● An aerosol penetrating fluid (such as WD-40) applied the night beforehand may work its way down into the thread and ease removal. Depending on the location, you may be able to make up a Plasticine well around the fastener head and fill it with penetrating fluid.

2.13 A sharp tap on the head of a fastener will often break free a corroded thread

● If you are working on an engine internal component, corrosion will most likely not be a problem due to the well lubricated environment. However, components can be very tight and an impact driver is a useful tool in freeing them **(see illustration 2.14)**.

2.14 Using an impact driver to free a fastener

● Where corrosion has occurred between dissimilar metals (eg steel and aluminium alloy), the application of heat to the fastener head will create a disproportionate expansion rate between the two metals and break the seizure caused by the corrosion. Whether heat can be applied depends on the location of the fastener - any surrounding components likely to be damaged must first be removed **(see illustration 2.15)**. Heat can be applied using a paint stripper heat gun or clothes iron, or by immersing the component in boiling water - wear protective gloves to prevent scalding or burns to the hands.

2.15 Using heat to free a seized fastener

● As a last resort, it is possible to use a hammer and cold chisel to work the fastener head unscrewed **(see illustration 2.16)**. This will damage the fastener, but more importantly extreme care must be taken not to damage the surrounding component.

> **Caution: Remember that the component being secured is generally of more value than the bolt, nut or screw - when the fastener is freed, do not unscrew it with force, instead work the fastener back and forth when resistance is felt to prevent thread damage.**

2.16 Using a hammer and chisel to free a seized fastener

Broken fasteners and damaged heads

● If the shank of a broken bolt or screw is accessible you can grip it with self-locking grips. The knurled wheel type stud extractor tool or self-gripping stud puller tool is particularly useful for removing the long studs which screw into the cylinder mouth surface of the crankcase or bolts and screws from which the head has broken off **(see illustration 2.17)**. Studs can also be removed by locking two nuts together on the threaded end of the stud and using a spanner on the lower nut **(see illustration 2.18)**.

2.17 Using a stud extractor tool to remove a broken crankcase stud

2.18 Two nuts can be locked together to unscrew a stud from a component

● A bolt or screw which has broken off below or level with the casing must be extracted using a screw extractor set. Centre punch the fastener to centralise the drill bit, then drill a hole in the fastener **(see illustration 2.19)**. Select a drill bit which is approximately half to three-quarters the

2.19 When using a screw extractor, first drill a hole in the fastener . . .

diameter of the fastener and drill to a depth which will accommodate the extractor. Use the largest size extractor possible, but avoid leaving too small a wall thickness otherwise the extractor will merely force the fastener walls outwards wedging it in the casing thread.

● If a spiral type extractor is used, thread it anti-clockwise into the fastener. As it is screwed in, it will grip the fastener and unscrew it from the casing **(see illustration 2.20)**.

2.20 . . . then thread the extractor anti-clockwise into the fastener

● If a taper type extractor is used, tap it into the fastener so that it is firmly wedged in place. Unscrew the extractor (anti-clockwise) to draw the fastener out.

> ⚠ **Warning: Stud extractors are very hard and may break off in the fastener if care is not taken - ask an engineer about spark erosion if this happens.**

● Alternatively, the broken bolt/screw can be drilled out and the hole retapped for an oversize bolt/screw or a diamond-section thread insert. It is essential that the drilling is carried out squarely and to the correct depth, otherwise the casing may be ruined - if in doubt, entrust the work to an engineer.

● Bolts and nuts with rounded corners cause the correct size spanner or socket to slip when force is applied. Of the types of spanner/socket available always use a six-point type rather than an eight or twelve-point type - better grip

2.21 Comparison of surface drive ring spanner (left) with 12-point type (right)

is obtained. Surface drive spanners grip the middle of the hex flats, rather than the corners, and are thus good in cases of damaged heads **(see illustration 2.21).**

● Slotted-head or Phillips-head screws are often damaged by the use of the wrong size screwdriver. Allen-head and Torx-head screws are much less likely to sustain damage. If enough of the screw head is exposed you can use a hacksaw to cut a slot in its head and then use a conventional flat-bladed screwdriver to remove it. Alternatively use a hammer and cold chisel to tap the head of the fastener around to slacken it. Always replace damaged fasteners with new ones, preferably Torx or Allen-head type.

A dab of valve grinding compound between the screw head and screw-driver tip will often give a good grip.

Thread repair

● Threads (particularly those in aluminium alloy components) can be damaged by overtightening, being assembled with dirt in the threads, or from a component working loose and vibrating. Eventually the thread will fail completely, and it will be impossible to tighten the fastener.

● If a thread is damaged or clogged with old locking compound it can be renovated with a thread repair tool (thread chaser) **(see illustrations 2.22 and 2.23)**; special thread

2.22 A thread repair tool being used to correct an internal thread

2.23 A thread repair tool being used to correct an external thread

chasers are available for spark plug hole threads. The tool will not cut a new thread, but clean and true the original thread. Make sure that you use the correct diameter and pitch tool. Similarly, external threads can be cleaned up with a die or a thread restorer file **(see illustration 2.24).**

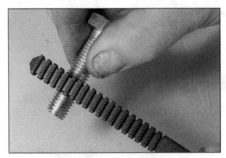

2.24 Using a thread restorer file

● It is possible to drill out the old thread and retap the component to the next thread size. This will work where there is enough surrounding material and a new bolt or screw can be obtained. Sometimes, however, this is not possible - such as where the bolt/screw passes through another component which must also be suitably modified, also in cases where a spark plug or oil drain plug cannot be obtained in a larger diameter thread size.

● The diamond-section thread insert (often known by its popular trade name of Heli-Coil) is a simple and effective method of renewing the thread and retaining the original size. A kit can be purchased which contains the tap, insert and installing tool **(see illustration 2.25)**. Drill out the damaged thread with the size drill specified **(see illustration 2.26)**. Carefully retap the thread **(see illustration 2.27)**. Install the

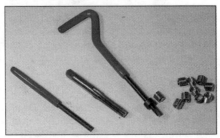

2.25 Obtain a thread insert kit to suit the thread diameter and pitch required

2.26 To install a thread insert, first drill out the original thread . . .

2.27 . . . tap a new thread . . .

2.28 . . . fit insert on the installing tool . . .

2.29 . . . and thread into the component . . .

2.30 . . . break off the tang when complete

insert on the installing tool and thread it slowly into place using a light downward pressure **(see illustrations 2.28 and 2.29)**. When positioned between a 1/4 and 1/2 turn below the surface withdraw the installing tool and use the break-off tool to press down on the tang, breaking it off **(see illustration 2.30)**.

● There are epoxy thread repair kits on the market which can rebuild stripped internal threads, although this repair should not be used on high load-bearing components.

Thread locking and sealing compounds

● Locking compounds are used in locations where the fastener is prone to loosening due to vibration or on important safety-related items which might cause loss of control of the motorcycle if they fail. It is also used where important fasteners cannot be secured by other means such as lockwashers or split pins.

● Before applying locking compound, make sure that the threads (internal and external) are clean and dry with all old compound removed. Select a compound to suit the component being secured - a non-permanent general locking and sealing type is suitable for most applications, but a high strength type is needed for permanent fixing of studs in castings. Apply a drop or two of the compound to the first few threads of the fastener, then thread it into place and tighten to the specified torque. Do not apply excessive thread locking compound otherwise the thread may be damaged on subsequent removal.

● Certain fasteners are impregnated with a dry film type coating of locking compound on their threads. Always renew this type of fastener if disturbed.

● Anti-seize compounds, such as copper-based greases, can be applied to protect threads from seizure due to extreme heat and corrosion. A common instance is spark plug threads and exhaust system fasteners.

3 Measuring tools and gauges

Feeler gauges

● Feeler gauges (or blades) are used for measuring small gaps and clearances (see illustration 3.1). They can also be used to measure endfloat (sideplay) of a component on a shaft where access is not possible with a dial gauge.

● Feeler gauge sets should be treated with care and not bent or damaged. They are etched with their size on one face. Keep them clean and very lightly oiled to prevent corrosion build-up.

3.1 Feeler gauges are used for measuring small gaps and clearances - thickness is marked on one face of gauge

● When measuring a clearance, select a gauge which is a light sliding fit between the two components. You may need to use two gauges together to measure the clearance accurately.

Micrometers

● A micrometer is a precision tool capable of measuring to 0.01 or 0.001 of a millimetre. It should always be stored in its case and not in the general toolbox. It must be kept clean and never dropped, otherwise its frame or measuring anvils could be distorted resulting in inaccurate readings.

● External micrometers are used for measuring outside diameters of components and have many more applications than internal micrometers. Micrometers are available in different size ranges, eg 0 to 25 mm, 25 to 50 mm, and upwards in 25 mm steps; some large micrometers have interchangeable anvils to allow a range of measurements to be taken. Generally the largest precision measurement you are likely to take on a motorcycle is the piston diameter.

● Internal micrometers (or bore micrometers) are used for measuring inside diameters, such as valve guides and cylinder bores. Telescoping gauges and small hole gauges are used in conjunction with an external micrometer, whereas the more expensive internal micrometers have their own measuring device.

External micrometer

Note: *The conventional analogue type instrument is described. Although much easier to read, digital micrometers are considerably more expensive.*

● Always check the calibration of the micrometer before use. With the anvils closed (0 to 25 mm type) or set over a test gauge (for

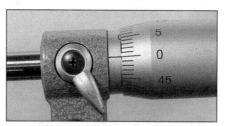

3.2 Check micrometer calibration before use

the larger types) the scale should read zero **(see illustration 3.2)**; make sure that the anvils (and test piece) are clean first. Any discrepancy can be adjusted by referring to the instructions supplied with the tool. Remember that the micrometer is a precision measuring tool - don't force the anvils closed, use the ratchet (4) on the end of the micrometer to close it. In this way, a measured force is always applied.

● To use, first make sure that the item being measured is clean. Place the anvil of the micrometer (1) against the item and use the thimble (2) to bring the spindle (3) lightly into contact with the other side of the item **(see illustration 3.3)**. Don't tighten the thimble down because this will damage the micrometer - instead use the ratchet (4) on the end of the micrometer. The ratchet mechanism applies a measured force preventing damage to the instrument.

● The micrometer is read by referring to the linear scale on the sleeve and the annular scale on the thimble. Read off the sleeve first to obtain the base measurement, then add the fine measurement from the thimble to obtain the overall reading. The linear scale on the sleeve represents the measuring range of the micrometer (eg 0 to 25 mm). The annular scale

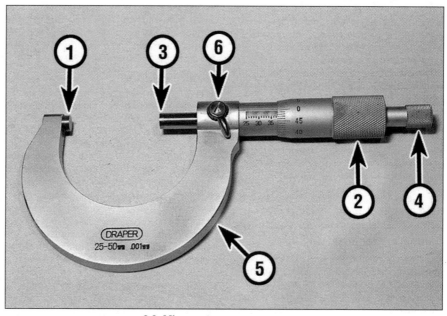

3.3 Micrometer component parts

1	Anvil	3	Spindle	5	Frame
2	Thimble	4	Ratchet	6	Locking lever

on the thimble will be in graduations of 0.01 mm (or as marked on the frame) - one full revolution of the thimble will move 0.5 mm on the linear scale. Take the reading where the datum line on the sleeve intersects the thimble's scale. Always position the eye directly above the scale otherwise an inaccurate reading will result.

In the example shown the item measures 2.95 mm **(see illustration 3.4)**:

Linear scale	2.00 mm
Linear scale	0.50 mm
Annular scale	0.45 mm
Total figure	**2.95 mm**

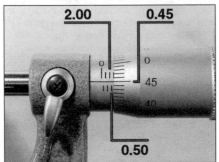

3.4 Micrometer reading of 2.95 mm

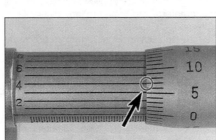

3.5 Micrometer reading of 46.99 mm on linear and annular scales . . .

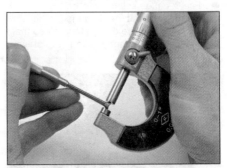

3.6 . . . and 0.004 mm on vernier scale

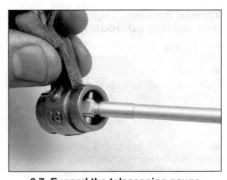

3.7 Expand the telescoping gauge in the bore, lock its position . . .

3.8 . . . then measure the gauge with a micrometer

3.9 Expand the small hole gauge in the bore, lock its position . . .

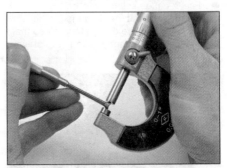

3.10 . . . then measure the gauge with a micrometer

Most micrometers have a locking lever (6) on the frame to hold the setting in place, allowing the item to be removed from the micrometer.
● Some micrometers have a vernier scale on their sleeve, providing an even finer measurement to be taken, in 0.001 increments of a millimetre. Take the sleeve and thimble measurement as described above, then check which graduation on the vernier scale aligns with that of the annular scale on the thimble **Note:** *The eye must be perpendicular to the scale when taking the vernier reading - if necessary rotate the body of the micrometer to ensure this.* Multiply the vernier scale figure by 0.001 and add it to the base and fine measurement figures.

In the example shown the item measures 46.994 mm **(see illustrations 3.5 and 3.6)**:

Linear scale (base)	46.000 mm
Linear scale (base)	00.500 mm
Annular scale (fine)	00.490 mm
Vernier scale	00.004 mm
Total figure	**46.994 mm**

Internal micrometer

● Internal micrometers are available for measuring bore diameters, but are expensive and unlikely to be available for home use. It is suggested that a set of telescoping gauges and small hole gauges, both of which must be used with an external micrometer, will suffice for taking internal measurements on a motorcycle.
● Telescoping gauges can be used to measure internal diameters of components. Select a gauge with the correct size range, make sure its ends are clean and insert it into the bore. Expand the gauge, then lock its position and withdraw it from the bore **(see illustration 3.7)**. Measure across the gauge ends with a micrometer **(see illustration 3.8)**.
● Very small diameter bores (such as valve guides) are measured with a small hole gauge. Once adjusted to a slip-fit inside the component, its position is locked and the gauge withdrawn for measurement with a micrometer **(see illustrations 3.9 and 3.10)**.

Vernier caliper

Note: *The conventional linear and dial gauge type instruments are described. Digital types are easier to read, but are far more expensive.*
● The vernier caliper does not provide the precision of a micrometer, but is versatile in being able to measure internal and external diameters. Some types also incorporate a depth gauge. It is ideal for measuring clutch plate friction material and spring free lengths.
● To use the conventional linear scale vernier, slacken off the vernier clamp screws (1) and set its jaws over (2), or inside (3), the item to be measured **(see illustration 3.11)**. Slide the jaw into contact, using the thumb-wheel (4) for fine movement of the sliding scale (5) then tighten the clamp screws (1). Read off the main scale (6) where the zero on the sliding scale (5) intersects it, taking the whole number to the left of the zero; this provides the base measurement. View along the sliding scale and select the division which lines up exactly with any of the divisions on the main scale, noting that the divisions usually represents 0.02 of a millimetre. Add this fine measurement to the base measurement to obtain the total reading.

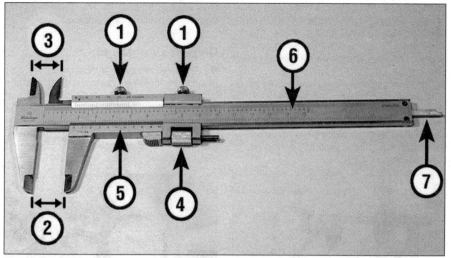

3.11 Vernier component parts (linear gauge)

1 Clamp screws	3 Internal jaws	5 Sliding scale	7 Depth gauge
2 External jaws	4 Thumbwheel	6 Main scale	

In the example shown the item measures 55.92 mm **(see illustration 3.12)**:

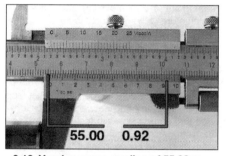

3.12 Vernier gauge reading of 55.92 mm

Base measurement	55.00 mm
Fine measurement	00.92 mm
Total figure	**55.92 mm**

● Some vernier calipers are equipped with a dial gauge for fine measurement. Before use, check that the jaws are clean, then close them fully and check that the dial gauge reads zero. If necessary adjust the gauge ring accordingly. Slacken the vernier clamp screw (1) and set its jaws over (2), or inside (3), the item to be measured **(see illustration 3.13)**. Slide the jaws into contact, using the thumbwheel (4) for fine movement. Read off the main scale (5) where the edge of the sliding scale (6) intersects it, taking the whole number to the left of the zero; this provides the base measurement. Read off the needle position on the dial gauge (7) scale to provide the fine measurement; each division represents 0.05 of a millimetre. Add this fine measurement to the base measurement to obtain the total reading.

In the example shown the item measures 55.95 mm **(see illustration 3.14)**:

Base measurement	55.00 mm
Fine measurement	00.95 mm
Total figure	**55.95 mm**

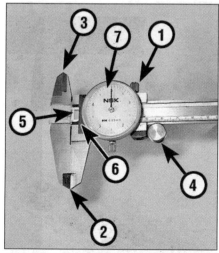

3.13 Vernier component parts (dial gauge)

1 Clamp screw	5 Main scale
2 External jaws	6 Sliding scale
3 Internal jaws	7 Dial gauge
4 Thumbwheel	

3.14 Vernier gauge reading of 55.95 mm

Plastigauge

● Plastigauge is a plastic material which can be compressed between two surfaces to measure the oil clearance between them. The width of the compressed Plastigauge is measured against a calibrated scale to determine the clearance.
● Common uses of Plastigauge are for measuring the clearance between crankshaft journal and main bearing inserts, between crankshaft journal and big-end bearing inserts, and between camshaft and bearing surfaces. The following example describes big-end oil clearance measurement.
● Handle the Plastigauge material carefully to prevent distortion. Using a sharp knife, cut a length which corresponds with the width of the bearing being measured and place it carefully across the journal so that it is parallel with the shaft **(see illustration 3.15)**. Carefully install both bearing shells and the connecting rod. Without rotating the rod on the journal tighten its bolts or nuts (as applicable) to the specified torque. The connecting rod and bearings are then disassembled and the crushed Plastigauge examined.

3.15 Plastigauge placed across shaft journal

● Using the scale provided in the Plastigauge kit, measure the width of the material to determine the oil clearance **(see illustration 3.16)**. Always remove all traces of Plastigauge after use using your fingernails.

Caution: Arriving at the correct clearance demands that the assembly is torqued correctly, according to the settings and sequence (where applicable) provided by the motorcycle manufacturer.

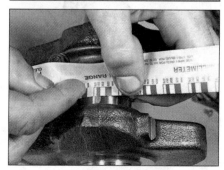

3.16 Measuring the width of the crushed Plastigauge

Dial gauge or DTI (Dial Test Indicator)

● A dial gauge can be used to accurately measure small amounts of movement. Typical uses are measuring shaft runout or shaft endfloat (sideplay) and setting piston position for ignition timing on two-strokes. A dial gauge set usually comes with a range of different probes and adapters and mounting equipment.

● The gauge needle must point to zero when at rest. Rotate the ring around its periphery to zero the gauge.

● Check that the gauge is capable of reading the extent of movement in the work. Most gauges have a small dial set in the face which records whole millimetres of movement as well as the fine scale around the face periphery which is calibrated in 0.01 mm divisions. Read off the small dial first to obtain the base measurement, then add the measurement from the fine scale to obtain the total reading.

In the example shown the gauge reads 1.48 mm (see illustration 3.17):

Base measurement	1.00 mm
Fine measurement	0.48 mm
Total figure	**1.48 mm**

3.17 Dial gauge reading of 1.48 mm

● If measuring shaft runout, the shaft must be supported in vee-blocks and the gauge mounted on a stand perpendicular to the shaft. Rest the tip of the gauge against the centre of the shaft and rotate the shaft slowly whilst watching the gauge reading (see illustration 3.18). Take several measurements along the length of the shaft and record the

3.18 Using a dial gauge to measure shaft runout

maximum gauge reading as the amount of runout in the shaft. **Note:** *The reading obtained will be total runout at that point - some manufacturers specify that the runout figure is halved to compare with their specified runout limit.*

● Endfloat (sideplay) measurement requires that the gauge is mounted securely to the surrounding component with its probe touching the end of the shaft. Using hand pressure, push and pull on the shaft noting the maximum endfloat recorded on the gauge (see illustration 3.19).

3.19 Using a dial gauge to measure shaft endfloat

● A dial gauge with suitable adapters can be used to determine piston position BTDC on two-stroke engines for the purposes of ignition timing. The gauge, adapter and suitable length probe are installed in the place of the spark plug and the gauge zeroed at TDC. If the piston position is specified as 1.14 mm BTDC, rotate the engine back to 2.00 mm BTDC, then slowly forwards to 1.14 mm BTDC.

Cylinder compression gauges

● A compression gauge is used for measuring cylinder compression. Either the rubber-cone type or the threaded adapter type can be used. The latter is preferred to ensure a perfect seal against the cylinder head. A 0 to 300 psi (0 to 20 Bar) type gauge (for petrol/gasoline engines) will be suitable for motorcycles.

● The spark plug is removed and the gauge either held hard against the cylinder head (cone type) or the gauge adapter screwed into the cylinder head (threaded type) (see illustration 3.20). Cylinder compression is measured with the engine turning over, but not running - carry out the compression test as described in

3.20 Using a rubber-cone type cylinder compression gauge

Fault Finding Equipment. The gauge will hold the reading until manually released.

Oil pressure gauge

● An oil pressure gauge is used for measuring engine oil pressure. Most gauges come with a set of adapters to fit the thread of the take-off point (see illustration 3.21). If the take-off point specified by the motorcycle manufacturer is an external oil pipe union, make sure that the specified replacement union is used to prevent oil starvation.

3.21 Oil pressure gauge and take-off point adapter (arrow)

● Oil pressure is measured with the engine running (at a specific rpm) and often the manufacturer will specify pressure limits for a cold and hot engine.

Straight-edge and surface plate

● If checking the gasket face of a component for warpage, place a steel rule or precision straight-edge across the gasket face and measure any gap between the straight-edge and component with feeler gauges (see illustration 3.22). Check diagonally across the component and between mounting holes (see illustration 3.23).

3.22 Use a straight-edge and feeler gauges to check for warpage

3.23 Check for warpage in these directions

● Checking individual components for warpage, such as clutch plain (metal) plates, requires a perfectly flat plate or piece or plate glass and feeler gauges.

4 Torque and leverage

What is torque?

● Torque describes the twisting force about a shaft. The amount of torque applied is determined by the distance from the centre of the shaft to the end of the lever and the amount of force being applied to the end of the lever; distance multiplied by force equals torque.

● The manufacturer applies a measured torque to a bolt or nut to ensure that it will not slacken in use and to hold two components securely together without movement in the joint. The actual torque setting depends on the thread size, bolt or nut material and the composition of the components being held.

● Too little torque may cause the fastener to loosen due to vibration, whereas too much torque will distort the joint faces of the component or cause the fastener to shear off. Always stick to the specified torque setting.

Using a torque wrench

● Check the calibration of the torque wrench and make sure it has a suitable range for the job. Torque wrenches are available in Nm (Newton-metres), kgf m (kilograms-force metre), lbf ft (pounds-feet), lbf in (inch-pounds). Do not confuse lbf ft with lbf in.

● Adjust the tool to the desired torque on the scale (see illustration 4.1). If your torque wrench is not calibrated in the units specified, carefully convert the figure (see *Conversion Factors*). A manufacturer sometimes gives a torque setting as a range (8 to 10 Nm) rather than a single figure - in this case set the tool midway between the two settings. The same torque may be expressed as 9 Nm ± 1 Nm. Some torque wrenches have a method of locking the setting so that it isn't inadvertently altered during use.

● Install the bolts/nuts in their correct location and secure them lightly. Their threads must be clean and free of any old locking compound. Unless specified the threads and flange should be dry - oiled threads are necessary in certain circumstances and the manufacturer will take this into account in the specified torque figure. Similarly, the manufacturer may also specify the application of thread-locking compound.

● Tighten the fasteners in the specified sequence until the torque wrench clicks, indicating that the torque setting has been reached. Apply the torque again to double-check the setting. Where different thread diameter fasteners secure the component, as a rule tighten the larger diameter ones first.

● When the torque wrench has been finished with, release the lock (where applicable) and fully back off its setting to zero - do not leave the torque wrench tensioned. Also, do not use a torque wrench for slackening a fastener.

Angle-tightening

● Manufacturers often specify a figure in degrees for final tightening of a fastener. This usually follows tightening to a specific torque setting.

● A degree disc can be set and attached to the socket (see illustration 4.2) or a protractor can be used to mark the angle of movement on the bolt/nut head and the surrounding casting (see illustration 4.3).

4.2 Angle tightening can be accomplished with a torque-angle gauge . . .

4.1 Set the torque wrench index mark to the setting required, in this case 12 Nm

4.3 . . . or by marking the angle on the surrounding component

Loosening sequences

● Where more than one bolt/nut secures a component, loosen each fastener evenly a little at a time. In this way, not all the stress of the joint is held by one fastener and the components are not likely to distort.

● If a tightening sequence is provided, work in the REVERSE of this, but if not, work from the outside in, in a criss-cross sequence (see illustration 4.4).

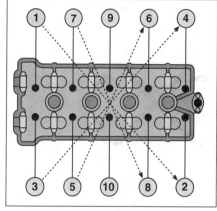

4.4 When slackening, work from the outside inwards

Tightening sequences

● If a component is held by more than one fastener it is important that the retaining bolts/nuts are tightened evenly to prevent uneven stress build-up and distortion of sealing faces. This is especially important on high-compression joints such as the cylinder head.

● A sequence is usually provided by the manufacturer, either in a diagram or actually marked in the casting. If not, always start in the centre and work outwards in a criss-cross pattern (see illustration 4.5). Start off by securing all bolts/nuts finger-tight, then set the torque wrench and tighten each fastener by a small amount in sequence until the final torque is reached. By following this practice,

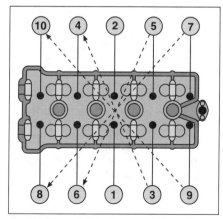

4.5 When tightening, work from the inside outwards

the joint will be held evenly and will not be distorted. Important joints, such as the cylinder head and big-end fasteners often have two- or three-stage torque settings.

Applying leverage

● Use tools at the correct angle. Position a socket wrench or spanner on the bolt/nut so that you pull it towards you when loosening. If this can't be done, push the spanner without curling your fingers around it **(see illustration 4.6)** - the spanner may slip or the fastener loosen suddenly, resulting in your fingers being crushed against a component.

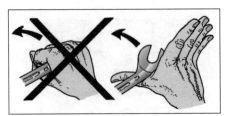

4.6 If you can't pull on the spanner to loosen a fastener, push with your hand open

● Additional leverage is gained by extending the length of the lever. The best way to do this is to use a breaker bar instead of the regular length tool, or to slip a length of tubing over the end of the spanner or socket wrench.
● If additional leverage will not work, the fastener head is either damaged or firmly corroded in place (see *Fasteners*).

5 Bearings

Bearing removal and installation

Drivers and sockets

● Before removing a bearing, always inspect the casing to see which way it must be driven out - some casings will have retaining plates or a cast step. Also check for any identifying markings on the bearing and if installed to a certain depth, measure this at this stage. Some roller bearings are sealed on one side - take note of the original fitted position.
● Bearings can be driven out of a casing using a bearing driver tool (with the correct size head) or a socket of the correct diameter. Select the driver head or socket so that it contacts the outer race of the bearing, not the balls/rollers or inner race. Always support the casing around the bearing housing with wood blocks, otherwise there is a risk of fracture. The bearing is driven out with a few blows on the driver or socket from a heavy mallet. Unless access is severely restricted (as with wheel bearings), a pin-punch is not recommended unless it is moved around the bearing to keep it square in its housing.

● The same equipment can be used to install bearings. Make sure the bearing housing is supported on wood blocks and line up the bearing in its housing. Fit the bearing as noted on removal - generally they are installed with their marked side facing outwards. Tap the bearing squarely into its housing using a driver or socket which bears only on the bearing's outer race - contact with the bearing balls/rollers or inner race will destroy it **(see illustrations 5.1 and 5.2)**.
● Check that the bearing inner race and balls/rollers rotate freely.

5.1 Using a bearing driver against the bearing's outer race

5.2 Using a large socket against the bearing's outer race

Pullers and slide-hammers

● Where a bearing is pressed on a shaft a puller will be required to extract it **(see illustration 5.3)**. Make sure that the puller clamp or legs fit securely behind the bearing and are unlikely to slip out. If pulling a bearing

5.3 This bearing puller clamps behind the bearing and pressure is applied to the shaft end to draw the bearing off

off a gear shaft for example, you may have to locate the puller behind a gear pinion if there is no access to the race and draw the gear pinion off the shaft as well **(see illustration 5.4)**.

> *Caution: Ensure that the puller's centre bolt locates securely against the end of the shaft and will not slip when pressure is applied. Also ensure that puller does not damage the shaft end.*

5.4 Where no access is available to the rear of the bearing, it is sometimes possible to draw off the adjacent component

● Operate the puller so that its centre bolt exerts pressure on the shaft end and draws the bearing off the shaft.
● When installing the bearing on the shaft, tap only on the bearing's inner race - contact with the balls/rollers or outer race with destroy the bearing. Use a socket or length of tubing as a drift which fits over the shaft end **(see illustration 5.5)**.

5.5 When installing a bearing on a shaft use a piece of tubing which bears only on the bearing's inner race

● Where a bearing locates in a blind hole in a casing, it cannot be driven or pulled out as described above. A slide-hammer with knife-edged bearing puller attachment will be required. The puller attachment passes through the bearing and when tightened expands to fit firmly behind the bearing **(see illustration 5.6)**. By operating the slide-hammer part of the tool the bearing is jarred out of its housing **(see illustration 5.7)**.
● It is possible, if the bearing is of reasonable weight, for it to drop out of its housing if the casing is heated as described opposite. If this

5.6 Expand the bearing puller so that it locks behind the bearing . . .

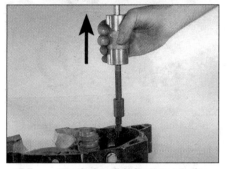

5.7 . . . attach the slide hammer to the bearing puller

method is attempted, first prepare a work surface which will enable the casing to be tapped face down to help dislodge the bearing - a wood surface is ideal since it will not damage the casing's gasket surface. Wearing protective gloves, tap the heated casing several times against the work surface to dislodge the bearing under its own weight **(see illustration 5.8)**.

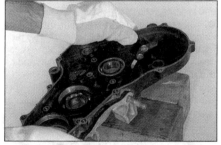

5.8 Tapping a casing face down on wood blocks can often dislodge a bearing

● Bearings can be installed in blind holes using the driver or socket method described above.

Drawbolts

● Where a bearing or bush is set in the eye of a component, such as a suspension linkage arm or connecting rod small-end, removal by drift may damage the component. Furthermore, a rubber bushing in a shock absorber eye cannot successfully be driven out of position. If access is available to a engineering press, the task is straightforward. If not, a drawbolt can be fabricated to extract the bearing or bush.

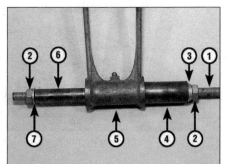

5.9 Drawbolt component parts assembled on a suspension arm

1 Bolt or length of threaded bar
2 Nuts
3 Washer (external diameter greater than tubing internal diameter)
4 Tubing (internal diameter sufficient to accommodate bearing)
5 Suspension arm with bearing
6 Tubing (external diameter slightly smaller than bearing)
7 Washer (external diameter slightly smaller than bearing)

5.10 Drawing the bearing out of the suspension arm

● To extract the bearing/bush you will need a long bolt with nut (or piece of threaded bar with two nuts), a piece of tubing which has an internal diameter larger than the bearing/bush, another piece of tubing which has an external diameter slightly smaller than the bearing/ bush, and a selection of washers **(see illustrations 5.9 and 5.10)**. Note that the pieces of tubing must be of the same length, or longer, than the bearing/bush.
● The same kit (without the pieces of tubing) can be used to draw the new bearing/bush back into place **(see illustration 5.11)**.

5.11 Installing a new bearing (1) in the suspension arm

Temperature change

● If the bearing's outer race is a tight fit in the casing, the aluminium casing can be heated to release its grip on the bearing. Aluminium will expand at a greater rate than the steel bearing outer race. There are several ways to do this, but avoid any localised extreme heat (such as a blow torch) - aluminium alloy has a low melting point.
● Approved methods of heating a casing are using a domestic oven (heated to 100°C) or immersing the casing in boiling water **(see illustration 5.12)**. Low temperature range localised heat sources such as a paint stripper heat gun or clothes iron can also be used **(see illustration 5.13)**. Alternatively, soak a rag in boiling water, wring it out and wrap it around the bearing housing.

> ⚠ **Warning: All of these methods require care in use to prevent scalding and burns to the hands. Wear protective gloves when handling hot components.**

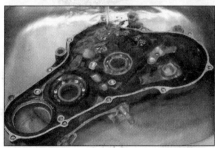

5.12 A casing can be immersed in a sink of boiling water to aid bearing removal

5.13 Using a localised heat source to aid bearing removal

● If heating the whole casing note that plastic components, such as the neutral switch, may suffer - remove them beforehand.
● After heating, remove the bearing as described above. You may find that the expansion is sufficient for the bearing to fall out of the casing under its own weight or with a light tap on the driver or socket.
● If necessary, the casing can be heated to aid bearing installation, and this is sometimes the recommended procedure if the motorcycle manufacturer has designed the housing and bearing fit with this intention.

● Installation of bearings can be eased by placing them in a freezer the night before installation. The steel bearing will contract slightly, allowing easy insertion in its housing. This is often useful when installing steering head outer races in the frame.

Bearing types and markings

● Plain shell bearings, ball bearings, needle roller bearings and tapered roller bearings will all be found on motorcycles **(see illustrations 5.14 and 5.15)**. The ball and roller types are usually caged between an inner and outer race, but uncaged variations may be found.

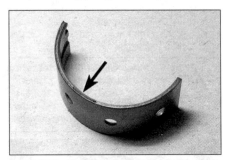

5.14 Shell bearings are either plain or grooved. They are usually identified by colour code (arrow)

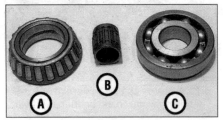

5.15 Tapered roller bearing (A), needle roller bearing (B) and ball journal bearing (C)

● Shell bearings (often called inserts) are usually found at the crankshaft main and connecting rod big-end where they are good at coping with high loads. They are made of a phosphor-bronze material and are impregnated with self-lubricating properties.

● Ball bearings and needle roller bearings consist of a steel inner and outer race with the balls or rollers between the races. They require constant lubrication by oil or grease and are good at coping with axial loads. Taper roller bearings consist of rollers set in a tapered cage set on the inner race; the outer race is separate. They are good at coping with axial loads and prevent movement along the shaft - a typical application is in the steering head.

● Bearing manufacturers produce bearings to ISO size standards and stamp one face of the bearing to indicate its internal and external diameter, load capacity and type **(see illustration 5.16)**.

● Metal bushes are usually of phosphor-bronze material. Rubber bushes are used in suspension mounting eyes. Fibre bushes have also been used in suspension pivots.

5.16 Typical bearing marking

Bearing fault finding

● If a bearing outer race has spun in its housing, the housing material will be damaged. You can use a bearing locking compound to bond the outer race in place if damage is not too severe.

● Shell bearings will fail due to damage of their working surface, as a result of lack of lubrication, corrosion or abrasive particles in the oil **(see illustration 5.17)**. Small particles of dirt in the oil may embed in the bearing material whereas larger particles will score the bearing and shaft journal. If a number of short journeys are made, insufficient heat will be generated to drive off condensation which has built up on the bearings.

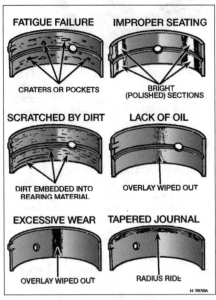

5.17 Typical bearing failures

● Ball and roller bearings will fail due to lack of lubrication or damage to the balls or rollers. Tapered-roller bearings can be damaged by overloading them. Unless the bearing is sealed on both sides, wash it in paraffin (kerosene) to remove all old grease then allow it to dry. Make a visual inspection looking to dented balls or rollers, damaged cages and worn or pitted races **(see illustration 5.18)**.

● A ball bearing can be checked for wear by listening to it when spun. Apply a film of light oil to the bearing and hold it close to the ear - hold the outer race with one hand and spin the inner

5.18 Example of ball journal bearing with damaged balls and cages

5.19 Hold outer race and listen to inner race when spun

race with the other hand **(see illustration 5.19)**. The bearing should be almost silent when spun; if it grates or rattles it is worn.

6 Oil seals

Oil seal removal and installation

● Oil seals should be renewed every time a component is dismantled. This is because the seal lips will become set to the sealing surface and will not necessarily reseal.

● Oil seals can be prised out of position using a large flat-bladed screwdriver **(see illustration 6.1)**. In the case of crankcase seals, check first that the seal is not lipped on the inside, preventing its removal with the crankcases joined.

6.1 Prise out oil seals with a large flat-bladed screwdriver

● New seals are usually installed with their marked face (containing the seal reference code) outwards and the spring side towards the fluid being retained. In certain cases, such as a two-stroke engine crankshaft seal, a double lipped seal may be used due to there being fluid or gas on each side of the joint.

● Use a bearing driver or socket which bears only on the outer hard edge of the seal to install it in the casing - tapping on the inner edge will damage the sealing lip.

Oil seal types and markings

● Oil seals are usually of the single-lipped type. Double-lipped seals are found where a liquid or gas is on both sides of the joint.
● Oil seals can harden and lose their sealing ability if the motorcycle has been in storage for a long period - renewal is the only solution.
● Oil seal manufacturers also conform to the ISO markings for seal size - these are moulded into the outer face of the seal (see illustration 6.2).

6.2 These oil seal markings indicate inside diameter, outside diameter and seal thickness

7 Gaskets and sealants

Types of gasket and sealant

● Gaskets are used to seal the mating surfaces between components and keep lubricants, fluids, vacuum or pressure contained within the assembly. Aluminium gaskets are sometimes found at the cylinder joints, but most gaskets are paper-based. If the mating surfaces of the components being joined are undamaged the gasket can be installed dry, although a dab of sealant or grease will be useful to hold it in place during assembly.
● RTV (Room Temperature Vulcanising) silicone rubber sealants cure when exposed to moisture in the atmosphere. These sealants are good at filling pits or irregular gasket faces, but will tend to be forced out of the joint under very high torque. They can be used to replace a paper gasket, but first make sure that the width of the paper gasket is not essential to the shimming of internal components. RTV sealants should not be used on components containing petrol (gasoline).
● Non-hardening, semi-hardening and hard setting liquid gasket compounds can be used with a gasket or between a metal-to-metal joint. Select the sealant to suit the application: universal non-hardening sealant can be used on virtually all joints; semi-hardening on joint faces which are rough or damaged; hard setting sealant on joints which require a permanent bond and are subjected to high temperature and pressure. **Note:** *Check first if the paper gasket has a bead of sealant*

impregnated in its surface before applying additional sealant.
● When choosing a sealant, make sure it is suitable for the application, particularly if being applied in a high-temperature area or in the vicinity of fuel. Certain manufacturers produce sealants in either clear, silver or black colours to match the finish of the engine. This has a particular application on motorcycles where much of the engine is exposed.
● Do not over-apply sealant. That which is squeezed out on the outside of the joint can be wiped off, whereas an excess of sealant on the inside can break off and clog oilways.

Breaking a sealed joint

● Age, heat, pressure and the use of hard setting sealant can cause two components to stick together so tightly that they are difficult to separate using finger pressure alone. Do not resort to using levers unless there is a pry point provided for this purpose (see illustration 7.1) or else the gasket surfaces will be damaged.
● Use a soft-faced hammer (see illustration 7.2) or a wood block and conventional hammer to strike the component near the mating surface. Avoid hammering against cast extremities since they may break off. If this method fails, try using a wood wedge between the two components.

Caution: If the joint will not separate, double-check that you have removed all the fasteners.

7.1 If a pry point is provided, apply gently pressure with a flat-bladed screwdriver

7.2 Tap around the joint with a soft-faced mallet if necessary - don't strike cooling fins

Removal of old gasket and sealant

● Paper gaskets will most likely come away complete, leaving only a few traces stuck on

Most components have one or two hollow locating dowels between the two gasket faces. If a dowel cannot be removed, do not resort to gripping it with pliers - it will almost certainly be distorted. Install a close-fitting socket or Phillips screwdriver into the dowel and then grip the outer edge of the dowel to free it.

the sealing faces of the components. It is imperative that all traces are removed to ensure correct sealing of the new gasket.
● Very carefully scrape all traces of gasket away making sure that the sealing surfaces are not gouged or scored by the scraper (see illustrations 7.3, 7.4 and 7.5). Stubborn deposits can be removed by spraying with an aerosol gasket remover. Final preparation of

7.3 Paper gaskets can be scraped off with a gasket scraper tool . . .

7.4 . . . a knife blade . . .

7.5 . . . or a household scraper

7.6 Fine abrasive paper is wrapped around a flat file to clean up the gasket face

7.7 A kitchen scourer can be used on stubborn deposits

the gasket surface can be made with very fine abrasive paper or a plastic kitchen scourer **(see illustrations 7.6 and 7.7)**.

● Old sealant can be scraped or peeled off components, depending on the type originally used. Note that gasket removal compounds are available to avoid scraping the components clean; make sure the gasket remover suits the type of sealant used.

8 Chains

Breaking and joining final drive chains

● Drive chains for all but small bikes are continuous and do not have a clip-type connecting link. The chain must be broken using a chain breaker tool and the new chain securely riveted together using a new soft rivet-type link. Never use a clip-type connecting link instead of a rivet-type link, except in an emergency. Various chain breaking and riveting tools are available, either as separate tools or combined as illustrated in the accompanying photographs - read the instructions supplied with the tool carefully.

⚠ **Warning: The need to rivet the new link pins correctly cannot be overstressed - loss of control of the motorcycle is very likely to result if the chain breaks in use.**

● Rotate the chain and look for the soft link. The soft link pins look like they have been

8.1 Tighten the chain breaker to push the pin out of the link . . .

8.2 . . . withdraw the pin, remove the tool . . .

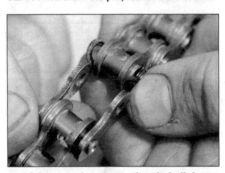

8.3 . . . and separate the chain link

deeply centre-punched instead of peened over like all the other pins **(see illustration 8.9)** and its sideplate may be a different colour. Position the soft link midway between the sprockets and assemble the chain breaker tool over one of the soft link pins **(see illustration 8.1)**. Operate the tool to push the pin out through the chain **(see illustration 8.2)**. On an O-ring chain, remove the O-rings **(see illustration 8.3)**. Carry out the same procedure on the other soft link pin.

Caution: Certain soft link pins (particularly on the larger chains) may require their ends to be filed or ground off before they can be pressed out using the tool.

● Check that you have the correct size and strength (standard or heavy duty) new soft link - do not reuse the old link. Look for the size marking on the chain sideplates **(see illustration 8.10)**.

● Position the chain ends so that they are engaged over the rear sprocket. On an O-ring

8.4 Insert the new soft link, with O-rings, through the chain ends . . .

8.5 . . . install the O-rings over the pin ends . . .

8.6 . . . followed by the sideplate

chain, install a new O-ring over each pin of the link and insert the link through the two chain ends **(see illustration 8.4)**. Install a new O-ring over the end of each pin, followed by the sideplate (with the chain manufacturer's marking facing outwards) **(see illustrations 8.5 and 8.6)**. On an unsealed chain, insert the link through the two chain ends, then install the sideplate with the chain manufacturer's marking facing outwards.

● Note that it may not be possible to install the sideplate using finger pressure alone. If using a joining tool, assemble it so that the plates of the tool clamp the link and press the sideplate over the pins **(see illustration 8.7)**. Otherwise, use two small sockets placed over

8.7 Push the sideplate into position using a clamp

8.8 Assemble the chain riveting tool over one pin at a time and tighten it fully

8.9 Pin end correctly riveted (A), pin end unriveted (B)

the rivet ends and two pieces of the wood between a G-clamp. Operate the clamp to press the sideplate over the pins.

● Assemble the joining tool over one pin (following the maker's instructions) and tighten the tool down to spread the pin end securely **(see illustrations 8.8 and 8.9)**. Do the same on the other pin.

 Warning: Check that the pin ends are secure and that there is no danger of the sideplate coming loose. If the pin ends are cracked the soft link must be renewed.

Final drive chain sizing

● Chains are sized using a three digit number, followed by a suffix to denote the chain type **(see illustration 8.10)**. Chain type is either standard or heavy duty (thicker sideplates), and also unsealed or O-ring/X-ring type.

● The first digit of the number relates to the pitch of the chain, ie the distance from the centre of one pin to the centre of the next pin **(see illustration 8.11)**. Pitch is expressed in eighths of an inch, as follows:

8.10 Typical chain size and type marking

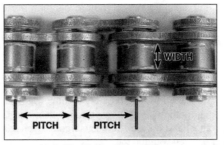

8.11 Chain dimensions

| Sizes commencing with a 4 (eg 428) have a pitch of 1/2 inch (12.7 mm) |
| Sizes commencing with a 5 (eg 520) have a pitch of 5/8 inch (15.9 mm) |
| Sizes commencing with a 6 (eg 630) have a pitch of 3/4 inch (19.1 mm) |

● The second and third digits of the chain size relate to the width of the rollers, again in imperial units, eg the 525 shown has 5/16 inch (7.94 mm) rollers **(see illustration 8.11)**.

9 Hoses

Clamping to prevent flow

● Small-bore flexible hoses can be clamped to prevent fluid flow whilst a component is worked on. Whichever method is used, ensure that the hose material is not permanently distorted or damaged by the clamp.

a) A brake hose clamp available from auto accessory shops **(see illustration 9.1)**.
b) A wingnut type hose clamp **(see illustration 9.2)**.

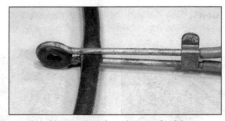

9.1 Hoses can be clamped with an automotive brake hose clamp . . .

9.2 . . . a wingnut type hose clamp . . .

c) Two sockets placed each side of the hose and held with straight-jawed self-locking grips **(see illustration 9.3)**.
d) Thick card each side of the hose held between straight-jawed self-locking grips **(see illustration 9.4)**.

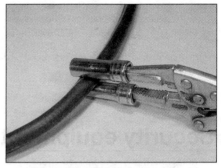

9.3 . . . two sockets and a pair of self-locking grips . . .

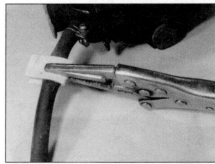

9.4 . . . or thick card and self-locking grips

Freeing and fitting hoses

● Always make sure the hose clamp is moved well clear of the hose end. Grip the hose with your hand and rotate it whilst pulling it off the union. If the hose has hardened due to age and will not move, slit it with a sharp knife and peel its ends off the union **(see illustration 9.5)**.

● Resist the temptation to use grease or soap on the unions to aid installation; although it helps the hose slip over the union it will equally aid the escape of fluid from the joint. It is preferable to soften the hose ends in hot water and wet the inside surface of the hose with water or a fluid which will evaporate.

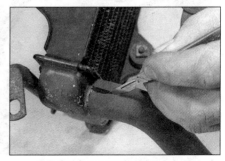

9.5 Cutting a coolant hose free with a sharp knife

Introduction

In less time than it takes to read this introduction, a thief could steal your motorcycle. Returning only to find your bike has gone is one of the worst feelings in the world. Even if the motorcycle is insured against theft, once you've got over the initial shock, you will have the inconvenience of dealing with the police and your insurance company.

The motorcycle is an easy target for the professional thief and the joyrider alike and the official figures on motorcycle theft make for depressing reading; on average a motorcycle is stolen every 16 minutes in the UK!

Motorcycle thefts fall into two categories, those stolen 'to order' and those taken by opportunists. The thief stealing to order will be on the look out for a specific make and model and will go to extraordinary lengths to obtain that motorcycle. The opportunist thief on the other hand will look for easy targets which can be stolen with the minimum of effort and risk.

Whilst it is never going to be possible to make your machine 100% secure, it is estimated that around half of all stolen motorcycles are taken by opportunist thieves. Remember that the opportunist thief is always on the look out for the easy option: if there are two similar motorcycles parked side-by-side, they will target the one with the lowest level of security. By taking a few precautions, you can reduce the chances of your motorcycle being stolen.

Security equipment

There are many specialised motorcycle security devices available and the following text summarises their applications and their good and bad points.

Once you have decided on the type of security equipment which best suits your needs, we recommended that you read one of the many equipment tests regularly carried out by the motorcycle press. These tests compare the products from all the major manufacturers and give impartial ratings on their effectiveness, value-for-money and ease of use.

No one item of security equipment can provide complete protection. It is highly recommended that two or more of the items described below are combined to increase the security of your motorcycle (a lock and chain plus an alarm system is just about ideal). The more security measures fitted to the bike, the less likely it is to be stolen.

will be supplied with a carry bag which can be strapped to the pillion seat.

● Heavy-duty chains and locks are an excellent security measure (see illustration 1). Whenever the motorcycle is parked, use the lock and chain to secure the machine to a solid, immovable object such as a post or railings. This will prevent the machine from being ridden away or being lifted into the back of a van.

● When fitting the chain, always ensure the chain is routed around the motorcycle frame or swingarm (see illustrations 2 and 3). Never merely pass the chain around one of the wheel rims; a thief may unbolt the wheel and lift the rest of the machine into a van, leaving you with just the wheel! Try to avoid having excess chain free, thus making it difficult to use cutting tools, and keep the chain and lock off the ground to prevent thieves attacking it with a cold chisel. Position the lock so that its lock barrel is facing downwards; this will make it harder for the thief to attack the lock mechanism.

Ensure the lock and chain you buy is of good quality and long enough to shackle your bike to a solid object

Lock and chain

Pros: *Very flexible to use; can be used to secure the motorcycle to almost any immovable object. On some locks and chains, the lock can be used on its own as a disc lock (see below).*

Cons: *Can be very heavy and awkward to carry on the motorcycle, although some types*

Pass the chain through the bike's frame, rather than just through a wheel . . .

. . . and loop it around a solid object

U-locks

Pros: *Highly effective deterrent which can be used to secure the bike to a post or railings. Most U-locks come with a carrier which allows the lock to be easily carried on the bike.*

Cons: *Not as flexible to use as a lock and chain.*

● These are solid locks which are similar in use to a lock and chain. U-locks are lighter than a lock and chain but not so flexible to use. The length and shape of the lock shackle limit the objects to which the bike can be secured **(see illustration 4)**.

Disc locks

Pros: *Small, light and very easy to carry; most can be stored underneath the seat.*

Cons: *Does not prevent the motorcycle being lifted into a van. Can be very embarrassing if you*

U-locks can be used to secure the bike to a solid object – ensure you purchase one which is long enough

forget to remove the lock before attempting to ride off!

● Disc locks are designed to be attached to the front brake disc. The lock passes through one of the holes in the disc and prevents the wheel rotating by jamming against the fork/brake caliper **(see illustration 5)**. Some are equipped with an alarm siren which sounds if the disc lock is moved; this not only acts as a theft deterrent but also as a handy reminder if you try to move the bike with the lock still fitted.

● Combining the disc lock with a length of cable which can be looped around a post or railings provides an additional measure of security **(see illustration 6)**.

Alarms and immobilisers

Pros: *Once installed it is completely hassle-free to use. If the system is 'Thatcham' or 'Sold Secure-approved', insurance companies may give you a discount.*

Cons: *Can be expensive to buy and complex to install. No system will prevent the motorcycle from being lifted into a van and taken away.*

● Electronic alarms and immobilisers are available to suit a variety of budgets. There are three different types of system available: pure alarms, pure immobilisers, and the more expensive systems which are combined alarm/immobilisers **(see illustration 7)**.
● An alarm system is designed to emit an audible warning if the motorcycle is being tampered with.
● An immobiliser prevents the motorcycle being started and ridden away by disabling its electrical systems.
● When purchasing an alarm/immobiliser system, check the cost of installing the system unless you are able to do it yourself. If the motorcycle is not used regularly, another consideration is the current drain of the system. All alarm/immobiliser systems are powered by the motorcycle's battery; purchasing a system with a very low current drain could prevent the battery losing its charge whilst the motorcycle is not being used.

A typical disc lock attached through one of the holes in the disc

A disc lock combined with a security cable provides additional protection

A typical alarm/immobiliser system

Indelible markings can be applied to most areas of the bike – always apply the manufacturer's sticker to warn off thieves

Security marking kits

Pros: *Very cheap and effective deterrent. Many insurance companies will give you a discount on your insurance premium if a recognised security marking kit is used on your motorcycle.*

Cons: *Does not prevent the motorcycle being stolen by joyriders.*

● There are many different types of security marking kits available. The idea is to mark as many parts of the motorcycle as possible with a unique security number **(see illustrations 8, 9 and 10)**. A form will be included with the kit to register your personal details and those of the motorcycle with the kit manufacturer. This register is made available to the police to help them trace the rightful owner of any motorcycle or components which they recover should all other forms of identification have been removed. Always apply the warning stickers provided with the kit to deter thieves.

Chemically-etched code numbers can be applied to main body panels . . .

Ground anchors, wheel clamps and security posts

Pros: *An excellent form of security which will deter all but the most determined of thieves.*

Cons: *Awkward to install and can be expensive.*

. . . again, always ensure that the kit manufacturer's sticker is applied in a prominent position

● Whilst the motorcycle is at home, it is a good idea to attach it securely to the floor or a solid wall, even if it is kept in a securely locked garage. Various types of ground anchors, security posts and wheel clamps are available for this purpose **(see illustration 11)**. These security devices are either bolted to a solid concrete or brick structure or can be cemented into the ground.

Permanent ground anchors provide an excellent level of security when the bike is at home

Security at home

A high percentage of motorcycle thefts are from the owner's home. Here are some things to consider whenever your motorcycle is at home:

✔ Where possible, always keep the motorcycle in a securely locked garage. Never rely solely on the standard lock on the garage door, these are usual hopelessly inadequate. Fit an additional locking mechanism to the door and consider having the garage alarmed. A security light, activated by a movement sensor, is also a good investment.

✔ Always secure the motorcycle to the ground or a wall, even if it is inside a securely locked garage.
✔ Do not regularly leave the motorcycle outside your home, try to keep it out of sight wherever possible. If a garage is not available, fit a motorcycle cover over the bike to disguise its true identity.
✔ It is not uncommon for thieves to follow a motorcyclist home to find out where the bike is kept. They will then return at a later date. Be aware of this whenever you are returning

home on your motorcycle. If you suspect you are being followed, do not return home, instead ride to a garage or shop and stop as a precaution.
✔ When selling a motorcycle, do not provide your home address or the location where the bike is normally kept. Arrange to meet the buyer at a location away from your home. Thieves have been known to pose as potential buyers to find out where motorcycles are kept and then return later to steal them.

Security away from the home

As well as fitting security equipment to your motorcycle here are a few general rules to follow whenever you park your motorcycle.
✔ Park in a busy, public place.
✔ Use car parks which incorporate security features, such as CCTV.

✔ At night, park in a well-lit area, preferably directly underneath a street light.
✔ Engage the steering lock.
✔ Secure the motorcycle to a solid, immovable object such as a post or railings with an additional lock. If this is not possible,

secure the bike to a friend's motorcycle. Some public parking places provide security loops for motorcycles.
✔ Never leave your helmet or luggage attached to the motorcycle. Take them with you at all times.

Lubricants and fluids

A wide range of lubricants, fluids and cleaning agents is available for motor-cycles. This is a guide as to what is available, its applications and properties.

Four-stroke engine oil

● Engine oil is without doubt the most important component of any four-stroke engine. Modern motorcycle engines place a lot of demands on their oil and choosing the right type is essential. Using an unsuitable oil will lead to an increased rate of engine wear and could result in serious engine damage. Before purchasing oil, always check the recommended oil specification given by the manufacturer. The manufacturer will state a recommended 'type or classification' and also a specific 'viscosity' range for engine oil.

● The oil 'type or classification' is identified by its API (American Petroleum Institute) rating. The API rating will be in the form of two letters, e.g. SG. The S identifies the oil as being suitable for use in a petrol (gasoline) engine (S stands for spark ignition) and the second letter, ranging from A to J, identifies the oil's performance rating. The later this letter, the higher the specification of the oil; for example API SG oil exceeds the requirements of API SF oil. **Note:** *On some oils there may also be a second rating consisting of another two letters, the first letter being C, e.g. API SF/CD. This rating indicates the oil is also suitable for use in a diesel engines (the C stands for compression ignition) and is thus of no relevance for motorcycle use.*

● The 'viscosity' of the oil is identified by its SAE (Society of Automotive Engineers) rating. All modern engines require multigrade oils and the SAE rating will consist of two numbers, the first followed by a W, e.g.

10W/40. The first number indicates the viscosity rating of the oil at low temperatures (W stands for winter – tested at –20°C) and the second number represents the viscosity of the oil at high temperatures (tested at 100°C). The lower the number, the thinner the oil. For example an oil with an SAE 10W/40 rating will give better cold starting and running than an SAE 15W/40 oil.

● As well as ensuring the 'type' and 'viscosity' of the oil match the recommendations, another consideration to make when buying engine oil is whether to purchase a standard mineral-based oil, a semi-synthetic oil (also known as a synthetic blend or synthetic-based oil) or a fully-synthetic oil. Although all oils will have a similar rating and viscosity, their cost will vary considerably; mineral-based oils are the cheapest, the fully-synthetic oils the most expensive with the semi-synthetic oils falling somewhere in-between. This decision is very much up to the owner, but it should be noted that modern synthetic oils have far better lubricating and cleaning qualities than traditional mineral-based oils and tend to retain these properties for far longer. Bearing in mind the operating conditions inside a modern, high-revving motorcycle engine it is highly recommended that a fully synthetic oil is used. The extra expense at each service could save you money in the long term by preventing premature engine wear.

● As a final note always ensure that the oil is specifically designed for use in motorcycle engines. Engine oils designed primarily for use in car engines sometimes contain additives or friction modifiers which could cause clutch slip on a motorcycle fitted with a wet-clutch.

Two-stroke engine oil

● Modern two-stroke engines, with their high power outputs, place high demands on their oil. If engine seizure is to be avoided it is essential that a high-quality oil is used. Two-stroke oils differ hugely from four-stroke oils. The oil lubricates only the crankshaft and piston(s) (the transmission has its own lubricating oil) and is used on a total-loss basis where it is burnt completely during the combustion process.

● The Japanese have recently introduced a classification system for two-stroke oils, the JASO rating. This rating is in the form of two letters, either FA, FB or FC – FA is the lowest classification and FC the highest. Ensure the oil being used meets or exceeds the recommended rating specified by the manufacturer.

● As well as ensuring the oil rating matches the recommendation, another consideration to make when buying engine oil is whether to purchase a standard mineral-based oil, a semi-synthetic oil (also known as a synthetic blend or synthetic-based oil) or a fully-synthetic oil. The cost of each type of oil varies considerably; mineral-based oils are the cheapest, the fully-synthetic oils the most expensive with the semi-synthetic oils falling somewhere in-between. This decision is very much up to the owner, but it should be noted that modern synthetic oils have far better lubricating properties and burn cleaner than traditional mineral-based oils. It is therefore recommended that a fully synthetic oil is used. The extra expense could save you money in the long term by preventing premature engine wear, engine performance will be improved, carbon deposits and exhaust smoke will be reduced.

● Always ensure that the oil is specifically designed for use in an injector system. Many high quality two-stroke oils are designed for competition use and need to be pre-mixed with fuel. These oils are of a much higher viscosity and are not designed to flow through the injector pumps used on road-going two-stroke motorcycles.

Transmission (gear) oil

● On a two-stroke engine, the transmission and clutch are lubricated by their own separate oil bath which must be changed in accordance with the Maintenance Schedule.

● Although the engine and transmission units of most four-strokes use a common lubrication supply, there are some exceptions where the engine and gearbox have separate oil reservoirs and a dry clutch is used.

● Motorcycle manufacturers will either recommend a monograde transmission oil or a four-stroke multigrade engine oil to lubricate the transmission.

● Transmission oils, or gear oils as they are often called, are designed specifically for use in transmission systems. The viscosity of these oils is represented by an SAE number, but the scale of measurement applied is different to that used to grade engine oils. As a rough guide a SAE90 gear oil will be of the same viscosity as an SAE50 engine oil.

Shaft drive oil

● On models equipped with shaft final drive, the shaft drive gears are will have their own oil supply. The manufacturer will state a recommended 'type or classification' and also a specific 'viscosity' range in the same manner as for four-stroke engine oil.

● Gear oil classification is given by the number which follows the API GL (GL standing for gear lubricant) rating, the higher the number, the higher the specification of the oil, e.g. API GL5 oil is a higher specification than API GL4 oil. Ensure the oil meets or

exceeds the classification specified and is of the correct viscosity. The viscosity of gear oils is also represented by an SAE number but the scale of measurement used is different to that used to grade engine oils. As a rough guide an SAE90 gear oil will be of the same viscosity as an SAE50 engine oil.

● If the use of an EP (Extreme Pressure) gear oil is specified, ensure the oil purchased is suitable.

Fork oil and suspension fluid

● Conventional telescopic front forks are hydraulic and require fork oil to work. To ensure the forks function correctly, the fork oil must be changed in accordance with the Maintenance Schedule.

● Fork oil is available in a variety of viscosities, identified by their SAE rating; fork oil ratings vary from light (SAE 5) to heavy (SAE 30). When purchasing fork oil, ensure the viscosity rating matches that specified by the manufacturer.

● Some lubricant manufacturers also produce a range of high-quality suspension fluids which are very similar to fork oil but are designed mainly for competition use. These fluids may have a different viscosity rating system which is not to be confused with the SAE rating of normal fork oil. Refer to the manufacturer's instructions if in any doubt.

Brake and clutch fluid

● All disc brake systems and some clutch systems are hydraulically operated. To ensure correct operation, the hydraulic fluid must be changed in accordance with the Maintenance Schedule.

● Brake and clutch fluid is classified by its DOT rating with most motorcycle manufacturers specifying DOT 3 or 4 fluid. Both fluid types are glycol-based and can be mixed together without adverse effect; DOT 4 fluid exceeds the requirements of DOT 3

fluid. Although it is safe to use DOT 4 fluid in a system designed for use with DOT 3 fluid, never use DOT 3 fluid in a system which specifies the use of DOT 4 as this will adversely affect the system's performance. The type required for the system will be marked on the fluid reservoir cap.

● Some manufacturers also produce a DOT 5 hydraulic fluid. DOT 5 hydraulic fluid is silicone-based and is not compatible with the glycol-based DOT 3 and 4 fluids. Never mix DOT 5 fluid with DOT 3 or 4 fluid as this will seriously affect the performance of the hydraulic system.

Coolant/antifreeze

● When purchasing coolant/antifreeze, always ensure it is suitable for use in an aluminium engine and contains corrosion inhibitors to prevent possible blockages of the internal coolant passages of the system. As a general rule, most coolants are designed to be used neat and should not be diluted whereas antifreeze can be mixed with distilled water to provide a coolant solution of the required strength. Refer to the manufacturer's instructions on the bottle.

● Ensure the coolant is changed in accordance with the Maintenance Schedule.

Chain lube

● Chain lube is an aerosol-type spray lubricant specifically designed for use on motorcycle final drive chains. Chain lube has two functions, to minimise friction between the final drive chain and sprockets and to prevent corrosion of the chain. Regular use of a good-quality chain lube will extend the life of the drive chain and sprockets and thus maximise the power being transmitted from the transmission to the rear wheel.

● When using chain lube, always allow some time for the solvents in the lube to evaporate before riding the motorcycle. This will minimise the amount of lube which will 'fling' off from the chain when the motorcycle is used. If the motorcycle is equipped with an 'O-ring' chain, ensure the chain lube is labelled as being suitable for use on 'O-ring' chains.

Degreasers and solvents

● There are many different types of solvents and degreasers available to remove the grime and grease which accumulate around the motorcycle during normal use. Degreasers and solvents are usually available as an aerosol-type spray or as a liquid which you apply with a brush. Always closely follow the manufacturer's instructions and wear eye protection during use. Be aware that many solvents are flammable and may give off noxious fumes; take adequate precautions when using them (see Safety First!).

● For general cleaning, use one of the many solvents or degreasers available from most motorcycle accessory shops. These solvents are usually applied then left for a certain time before being washed off with water.

Brake cleaner is a solvent specifically designed to remove all traces of oil, grease and dust from braking system components. Brake cleaner is designed to evaporate quickly and leaves behind no residue.

Carburettor cleaner is an aerosol-type solvent specifically designed to clear carburettor blockages and break down the hard deposits and gum often found inside carburettors during overhaul.

Contact cleaner is an aerosol-type solvent designed for cleaning electrical components. The cleaner will remove all traces of oil and dirt from components such as switch contacts or fouled spark plugs and then dry, leaving behind no residue.

Gasket remover is an aerosol-type solvent designed for removing stubborn gaskets from engine components during overhaul. Gasket remover will minimise the amount of scraping required to remove the gasket and therefore reduce the risk of damage to the mating surface.

Spray lubricants

● Aerosol-based spray lubricants are widely available and are excellent for lubricating lever pivots and exposed cables and switches. Try to use a lubricant which is of the dry-film type as the fluid evaporates, leaving behind a dry-film of lubricant. Lubricants which leave behind an oily residue will attract dust and dirt which will increase the rate of wear of the cable/lever.

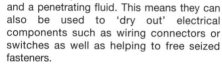

● Most lubricants also act as a moisture dispersant and a penetrating fluid. This means they can also be used to 'dry out' electrical components such as wiring connectors or switches as well as helping to free seized fasteners.

Greases

● Grease is used to lubricate many of the pivot-points. A good-quality multi-purpose grease is suitable for most applications but some manufacturers will specify the use of specialist greases for use on components such as swingarm and suspension linkage bushes. These specialist greases can be purchased from most motorcycle (or car) accessory shops; commonly specified types include molybdenum disulphide grease, lithium-based grease, graphite-based grease, silicone-based grease and high-temperature copper-based grease.

Gasket sealing compounds

● Gasket sealing compounds can be used in conjunction with gaskets, to improve their sealing capabilities, or on their own to seal metal-to-metal joints. Depending on their type, sealing compounds either set hard or stay relatively soft and pliable.

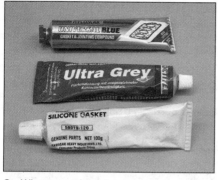

● When purchasing a gasket sealing compound, ensure that it is designed specifically for use on an internal combustion engine. General multi-purpose sealants available from DIY stores may appear visibly similar but they are not designed to withstand the extreme heat or contact with fuel and oil encountered when used on an engine (see 'Tools and Workshop Tips' for further information).

Thread locking compound

● Thread locking compounds are used to secure certain threaded fasteners in position to prevent them from loosening due to vibration. Thread locking compounds can be purchased from most motorcycle (and car) accessory shops. Ensure the threads of the both components are completely clean and dry before sparingly applying the locking compound (see 'Tools and Workshop Tips' for further information).

Fuel additives

● Fuel additives which protect and clean the fuel system components are widely available. These additives are designed to remove all traces of deposits that build up on the carburettors/injectors and prevent wear, helping the fuel system to operate more efficiently. If a fuel additive is being used, check that it is suitable for use with your motorcycle, especially if your motorcycle is equipped with a catalytic converter.

● Octane boosters are also available. These additives are designed to improve the performance of highly-tuned engines being run on normal pump-fuel and are of no real use on standard motorcycles.

Conversion Factors

Length (distance)

Inches (in)	x 25.4	= Millimetres (mm)	x 0.0394	= Inches (in)
Feet (ft)	x 0.305	= Metres (m)	x 3.281	= Feet (ft)
Miles	x 1.609	= Kilometres (km)	x 0.621	= Miles

Volume (capacity)

Cubic inches (cu in; in³)	x 16.387	= Cubic centimetres (cc; cm³)	x 0.061	= Cubic inches (cu in; in³)
Imperial pints (Imp pt)	x 0.568	= Litres (l)	x 1.76	= Imperial pints (Imp pt)
Imperial quarts (Imp qt)	x 1.137	= Litres (l)	x 0.88	= Imperial quarts (Imp qt)
Imperial quarts (Imp qt)	x 1.201	= US quarts (US qt)	x 0.833	= Imperial quarts (Imp qt)
US quarts (US qt)	x 0.946	= Litres (l)	x 1.057	= US quarts (US qt)
Imperial gallons (Imp gal)	x 4.546	= Litres (l)	x 0.22	= Imperial gallons (Imp gal)
Imperial gallons (Imp gal)	x 1.201	= US gallons (US gal)	x 0.833	= Imperial gallons (Imp gal)
US gallons (US gal)	x 3.785	= Litres (l)	x 0.264	= US gallons (US gal)

Mass (weight)

Ounces (oz)	x 28.35	= Grams (g)	x 0.035	= Ounces (oz)
Pounds (lb)	x 0.454	= Kilograms (kg)	x 2.205	= Pounds (lb)

Force

Ounces-force (ozf; oz)	x 0.278	= Newtons (N)	x 3.6	= Ounces-force (ozf; oz)
Pounds-force (lbf; lb)	x 4.448	= Newtons (N)	x 0.225	= Pounds-force (lbf; lb)
Newtons (N)	x 0.1	= Kilograms-force (kgf; kg)	x 9.81	= Newtons (N)

Pressure

Pounds-force per square inch (psi; lbf/in²; lb/in²)	x 0.070	= Kilograms-force per square centimetre (kgf/cm²; kg/cm²)	x 14.223	= Pounds-force per square inch (psi; lbf/in²; lb/in²)
Pounds-force per square inch (psi; lbf/in²; lb/in²)	x 0.068	= Atmospheres (atm)	x 14.696	= Pounds-force per square inch (psi; lbf/in²; lb/in²)
Pounds-force per square inch (psi; lbf/in²; lb/in²)	x 0.069	= Bars	x 14.5	= Pounds-force per square inch (psi; lbf/in²; lb/in²)
Pounds-force per square inch (psi; lbf/in²; lb/in²)	x 6.895	= Kilopascals (kPa)	x 0.145	= Pounds-force per square inch (psi; lbf/in²; lb/in²)
Kilopascals (kPa)	x 0.01	= Kilograms-force per square centimetre (kgf/cm²; kg/cm²)	x 98.1	= Kilopascals (kPa)
Millibar (mbar)	x 100	= Pascals (Pa)	x 0.01	= Millibar (mbar)
Millibar (mbar)	x 0.0145	= Pounds-force per square inch (psi; lbf/in²; lb/in²)	x 68.947	= Millibar (mbar)
Millibar (mbar)	x 0.75	= Millimetres of mercury (mmHg)	x 1.333	= Millibar (mbar)
Millibar (mbar)	x 0.401	= Inches of water (inH₂O)	x 2.491	= Millibar (mbar)
Millimetres of mercury (mmHg)	x 0.535	= Inches of water (inH₂O)	x 1.868	= Millimetres of mercury (mmHg)
Inches of water (inH₂O)	x 0.036	= Pounds-force per square inch (psi; lbf/in²; lb/in²)	x 27.68	= Inches of water (inH₂O)

Torque (moment of force)

Pounds-force inches (lbf in; lb in)	x 1.152	= Kilograms-force centimetre (kgf cm; kg cm)	x 0.868	= Pounds-force inches (lbf in; lb in)
Pounds-force inches (lbf in; lb in)	x 0.113	= Newton metres (Nm)	x 8.85	= Pounds-force inches (lbf in; lb in)
Pounds-force inches (lbf in; lb in)	x 0.083	= Pounds-force feet (lbf ft; lb ft)	x 12	= Pounds-force inches (lbf in; lb in)
Pounds-force feet (lbf ft; lb ft)	x 0.138	= Kilograms-force metres (kgf m; kg m)	x 7.233	= Pounds-force feet (lbf ft; lb ft)
Pounds-force feet (lbf ft; lb ft)	x 1.356	= Newton metres (Nm)	x 0.738	= Pounds-force feet (lbf ft; lb ft)
Newton metres (Nm)	x 0.102	= Kilograms-force metres (kgf m; kg m)	x 9.804	= Newton metres (Nm)

Power

Horsepower (hp)	x 745.7	= Watts (W)	x 0.0013	= Horsepower (hp)

Velocity (speed)

Miles per hour (miles/hr; mph)	x 1.609	= Kilometres per hour (km/hr; kph)	x 0.621	= Miles per hour (miles/hr; mph)

Fuel consumption*

Miles per gallon (mpg)	x 0.354	= Kilometres per litre (km/l)	x 2.825	= Miles per gallon (mpg)

Temperature

Degrees Fahrenheit = (°C x 1.8) + 32   Degrees Celsius (Degrees Centigrade; °C) = (°F - 32) x 0.56

It is common practice to convert from miles per gallon (mpg) to litres/100 kilometres (l/100km), where mpg x l/100 km = 282

About the MOT Test

In the UK, all vehicles more than three years old are subject to an annual test to ensure that they meet minimum safety requirements. A current test certificate must be issued before a machine can be used on public roads, and is required before a road fund licence can be issued. Riding without a current test certificate will also invalidate your insurance.

For most owners, the MOT test is an annual cause for anxiety, and this is largely due to owners not being sure what needs to be checked prior to submitting the motorcycle for testing. The simple answer is that a fully roadworthy motorcycle will have no difficulty in passing the test.

This is a guide to getting your motorcycle through the MOT test. Obviously it will not be possible to examine the motorcycle to the same standard as the professional MOT tester, particularly in view of the equipment required for some of the checks. However, working through the following procedures will enable you to identify any problem areas before submitting the motorcycle for the test.

It has only been possible to summarise the test requirements here, based on the regulations in force at the time of printing. Test standards are becoming increasingly stringent, although there are some exemptions for older vehicles. More information about the MOT test can be obtained from the TSO publications, *How Safe is your Motorcycle* and *The MOT Inspection Manual for Motorcycle Testing*.

Many of the checks require that one of the wheels is raised off the ground. If the motorcycle doesn't have a centre stand, note that an auxiliary stand will be required. Additionally, the help of an assistant may prove useful.

Certain exceptions apply to machines under 50 cc, machines without a lighting system, and Classic bikes - if in doubt about any of the requirements listed below seek confirmation from an MOT tester prior to submitting the motorcycle for the test.

Check that the frame number is clearly visible.

HAYNES HINT *If a component is in borderline condition, the tester has discretion in deciding whether to pass or fail it. If the motorcycle presented is clean and evidently well cared for, the tester may be more inclined to pass a borderline component than if the motorcycle is scruffy and apparently neglected.*

Electrical System

Lights, turn signals, horn and reflector

✔ With the ignition on, check the operation of the following electrical components. **Note:** *The electrical components on certain small-capacity machines are powered by the generator, requiring that the engine is run for this check.*

a) *Headlight and tail light. Check that both illuminate in the low and high beam switch positions.*
b) *Position lights. Check that the front position light (or sidelight) and tail light illuminate in this switch position.*
c) *Turn signals. Check that all flash at the correct rate, and that the warning light(s) function correctly. Check that the turn signal switch works correctly.*
d) *Hazard warning system (where fitted). Check that all four turn signals flash in this switch position.*
e) *Brake stop light. Check that the light comes on when the front and rear brakes are independently applied. Models first used on or after 1st April 1986 must have a brake light switch on each brake.*
f) *Horn. Check that the sound is continuous and of reasonable volume.*

✔ Check that there is a red reflector on the rear of the machine, either mounted separately or as part of the tail light lens.
✔ Check the condition of the headlight, tail light and turn signal lenses.

Headlight beam height

✔ The MOT tester will perform a headlight beam height check using specialised beam setting equipment **(see illustration 1)**. This equipment will not be available to the home mechanic, but if you suspect that the headlight is incorrectly set or may have been maladjusted in the past, you can perform a rough test as follows.
✔ Position the bike in a straight line facing a brick wall. The bike must be off its stand, upright and with a rider seated. Measure the height from the ground to the centre of the headlight and mark a horizontal line on the wall at this height. Position the motorcycle 3.8 metres from the wall and draw a vertical

Headlight beam height checking equipment

line up the wall central to the centreline of the motorcycle. Switch to dipped beam and check that the beam pattern falls slightly lower than the horizontal line and to the left of the vertical line **(see illustration 2)**.

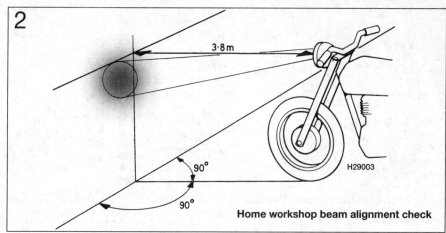

Home workshop beam alignment check

Exhaust System and Final Drive

Exhaust

✔ Check that the exhaust mountings are secure and that the system does not foul any of the rear suspension components.
✔ Start the motorcycle. When the revs are increased, check that the exhaust is neither holed nor leaking from any of its joints. On a linked system, check that the collector box is not leaking due to corrosion.

✔ Note that the exhaust decibel level ("loudness" of the exhaust) is assessed at the discretion of the tester. If the motorcycle was first used on or after 1st January 1985 the silencer must carry the BSAU 193 stamp, or a marking relating to its make and model, or be of OE (original equipment) manufacture. If the silencer is marked NOT FOR ROAD USE, RACING USE ONLY or similar, it will fail the MOT.

Final drive

✔ On chain or belt drive machines, check that the chain/belt is in good condition and does not have excessive slack. Also check that the sprocket is securely mounted on the rear wheel hub. Check that the chain/belt guard is in place.
✔ On shaft drive bikes, check for oil leaking from the drive unit and fouling the rear tyre.

Steering and Suspension

Steering

✔ With the front wheel raised off the ground, rotate the steering from lock to lock. The handlebar or switches must not contact the fuel tank or be close enough to trap the rider's hand. Problems can be caused by damaged lock stops on the lower yoke and frame, or by the fitting of non-standard handlebars.
✔ When performing the lock to lock check, also ensure that the steering moves freely without drag or notchiness. Steering movement can be impaired by poorly routed cables, or by overtight head bearings or worn bearings. The tester will perform a check of the steering head bearing lower race by mounting the front wheel on a surface plate, then performing a lock to

lock check with the weight of the machine on the lower bearing (see illustration 3).
✔ Grasp the fork sliders (lower legs) and attempt to push and pull on the forks (see

Front wheel mounted on a surface plate for steering head bearing lower race check

illustration 4). Any play in the steering head bearings will be felt. Note that in extreme cases, wear of the front fork bushes can be misinterpreted for head bearing play.
✔ Check that the handlebars are securely mounted.
✔ Check that the handlebar grip rubbers are secure. They should by bonded to the bar left end and to the throttle cable pulley on the right end.

Front suspension

✔ With the motorcycle off the stand, hold the front brake on and pump the front forks up and down (see illustration 5). Check that they are adequately damped.

Checking the steering head bearings for freeplay

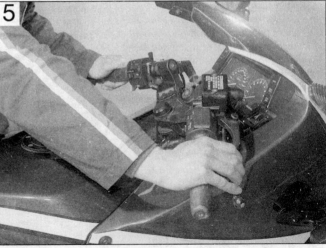

Hold the front brake on and pump the front forks up and down to check operation

Inspect the area around the fork dust seal for oil leakage (arrow)

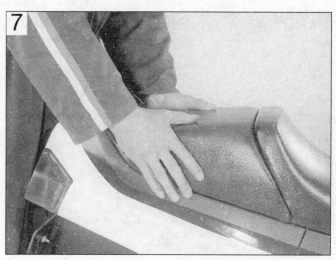

Bounce the rear of the motorcycle to check rear suspension operation

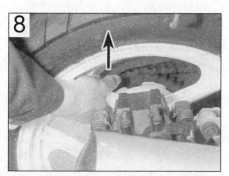

Checking for rear suspension linkage play

✔ Inspect the area above and around the front fork oil seals (see illustration 6). There should be no sign of oil on the fork tube (stanchion) nor leaking down the slider (lower leg). On models so equipped, check that there is no oil leaking from the anti-dive units.
✔ On models with swingarm front suspension, check that there is no freeplay in the linkage when moved from side to side.

Rear suspension

✔ With the motorcycle off the stand and an assistant supporting the motorcycle by its handlebars, bounce the rear suspension (see illustration 7). Check that the suspension components do not foul on any of the cycle parts and check that the shock absorber(s) provide adequate damping.
✔ Visually inspect the shock absorber(s) and check that there is no sign of oil leakage from its damper. This is somewhat restricted on certain single shock models due to the location of the shock absorber.
✔ With the rear wheel raised off the ground, grasp the wheel at the highest point and attempt to pull it up (see illustration 8). Any play in the swingarm pivot or suspension linkage bearings will be felt as movement. Note: *Do not confuse play with actual suspension movement.* Failure to lubricate suspension linkage bearings can lead to bearing failure (see illustration 9).
✔ With the rear wheel raised off the ground, grasp the swingarm ends and attempt to move the swingarm from side to side and forwards and backwards - any play indicates wear of the swingarm pivot bearings (see illustration 10).

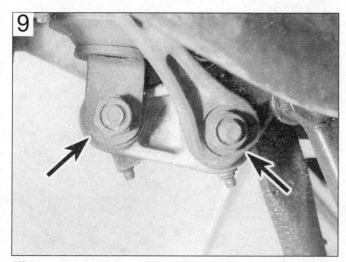

Worn suspension linkage pivots (arrows) are usually the cause of play in the rear suspension

Grasp the swingarm at the ends to check for play in its pivot bearings

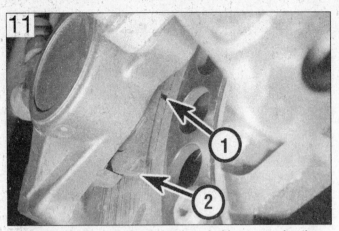

Brake pad wear can usually be viewed without removing the caliper. Most pads have wear indicator grooves (1) and some also have indicator tangs (2)

On drum brakes, check the angle of the operating lever with the brake fully applied. Most drum brakes have a wear indicator pointer and scale.

Brakes, Wheels and Tyres

Brakes

✔ With the wheel raised off the ground, apply the brake then free it off, and check that the wheel is about to revolve freely without brake drag.

✔ On disc brakes, examine the disc itself. Check that it is securely mounted and not cracked.

✔ On disc brakes, view the pad material through the caliper mouth and check that the pads are not worn down beyond the limit (see illustration 11).

✔ On drum brakes, check that when the brake is applied the angle between the operating lever and cable or rod is not too great (see illustration 12). Check also that the operating lever doesn't foul any other components.

✔ On disc brakes, examine the flexible hoses from top to bottom. Have an assistant hold the brake on so that the fluid in the hose is under pressure, and check that there is no sign of fluid leakage, bulges or cracking. If there are any metal brake pipes or unions, check that these are free from corrosion and damage. Where a brake-linked anti-dive system is fitted, check the hoses to the anti-dive in a similar manner.

✔ Check that the rear brake torque arm is secure and that its fasteners are secured by self-locking nuts or castellated nuts with split-pins or R-pins (see illustration 13).

✔ On models with ABS, check that the self-check warning light in the instrument panel works.

✔ The MOT tester will perform a test of the motorcycle's braking efficiency based on a calculation of rider and motorcycle weight. Although this cannot be carried out at home, you can at least ensure that the braking systems are properly maintained. For hydraulic disc brakes, check the fluid level, lever/pedal feel (bleed of air if its spongy) and pad material. For drum brakes, check adjustment, cable or rod operation and shoe lining thickness.

Wheels and tyres

✔ Check the wheel condition. Cast wheels should be free from cracks and if of the built-up design, all fasteners should be secure. Spoked wheels should be checked for broken, corroded, loose or bent spokes.

✔ With the wheel raised off the ground, spin the wheel and visually check that the tyre and wheel run true. Check that the tyre does not foul the suspension or mudguards.

✔ With the wheel raised off the ground, grasp the wheel and attempt to move it about the axle (spindle) (see illustration 14). Any play felt here indicates wheel bearing failure.

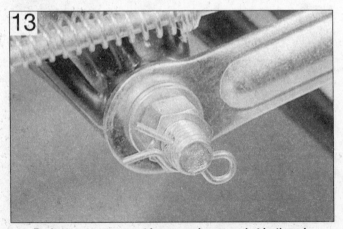

Brake torque arm must be properly secured at both ends

Check for wheel bearing play by trying to move the wheel about the axle (spindle)

Checking the tyre tread depth

Tyre direction of rotation arrow can be found on tyre sidewall

Castellated type wheel axle (spindle) nut must be secured by a split pin or R-pin

Two straightedges are used to check wheel alignment

✔ Check the tyre tread depth, tread condition and sidewall condition **(see illustration 15)**.

✔ Check the tyre type. Front and rear tyre types must be compatible and be suitable for road use. Tyres marked NOT FOR ROAD USE, COMPETITION USE ONLY or similar, will fail the MOT.

✔ If the tyre sidewall carries a direction of rotation arrow, this must be pointing in the direction of normal wheel rotation **(see illustration 16)**.

✔ Check that the wheel axle (spindle) nuts (where applicable) are properly secured. A self-locking nut or castellated nut with a split-pin or R-pin can be used **(see illustration 17)**.

✔ Wheel alignment is checked with the motorcycle off the stand and a rider seated. With the front wheel pointing straight ahead, two perfectly straight lengths of metal or wood and placed against the sidewalls of both tyres **(see illustration 18)**. The gap each side of the front tyre must be equidistant on both sides. Incorrect wheel alignment may be due to a cocked rear wheel (often as the result of poor chain adjustment) or in extreme cases, a bent frame.

General checks and condition

✔ Check the security of all major fasteners, bodypanels, seat, fairings (where fitted) and mudguards.

✔ Check that the rider and pillion footrests, handlebar levers and brake pedal are securely mounted.

✔ Check for corrosion on the frame or any load-bearing components. If severe, this may affect the structure, particularly under stress.

Sidecars

A motorcycle fitted with a sidecar requires additional checks relating to the stability of the machine and security of attachment and swivel joints, plus specific wheel alignment (toe-in) requirements. Additionally, tyre and lighting requirements differ from conventional motorcycle use. Owners are advised to check MOT test requirements with an official test centre.

Preparing for storage

Before you start

If repairs or an overhaul is needed, see that this is carried out now rather than left until you want to ride the bike again.

Give the bike a good wash and scrub all dirt from its underside. Make sure the bike dries completely before preparing for storage.

Engine

● Remove the spark plug(s) and lubricate the cylinder bores with approximately a teaspoon of motor oil using a spout-type oil can **(see illustration 1)**. Reinstall the spark plug(s). Crank the engine over a couple of times to coat the piston rings and bores with oil. If the bike has a kickstart, use this to turn the engine over. If not, flick the kill switch to the OFF position and crank the engine over on the starter **(see illustration 2)**. If the nature on the ignition system prevents the starter operating with the kill switch in the OFF position,

remove the spark plugs and fit them back in their caps; ensure that the plugs are earthed (grounded) against the cylinder head when the starter is operated **(see illustration 3)**.

⚠️ *Warning: It is important that the plugs are earthed (grounded) away from the spark plug holes otherwise there is a risk of atomised fuel from the cylinders igniting.*

HAYNES HiNT *On a single cylinder four-stroke engine, you can seal the combustion chamber completely by positioning the piston at TDC on the compression stroke.*

● Drain the carburettor(s) otherwise there is a risk of jets becoming blocked by gum deposits from the fuel **(see illustration 4)**.

● If the bike is going into long-term storage, consider adding a fuel stabiliser to the fuel in the tank. If the tank is drained completely, corrosion of its internal surfaces may occur if left unprotected for a long period. The tank can be treated with a rust preventative especially for this purpose. Alternatively, remove the tank and pour half a litre of motor oil into it, install the filler cap and shake the tank to coat its internals with oil before draining off the excess. The same effect can also be achieved by spraying WD40 or a similar water-dispersant around the inside of the tank via its flexible nozzle.

● Make sure the cooling system contains the correct mix of antifreeze. Antifreeze also contains important corrosion inhibitors.

● The air intakes and exhaust can be sealed off by covering or plugging the openings. Ensure that you do not seal in any condensation; run the engine until it is hot,

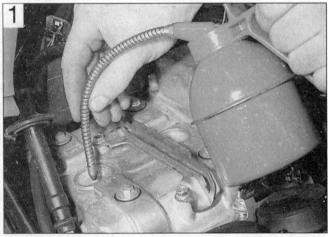

Squirt a drop of motor oil into each cylinder

Flick the kill switch to OFF . . .

. . . and ensure that the metal bodies of the plugs (arrows) are earthed against the cylinder head

Connect a hose to the carburettor float chamber drain stub (arrow) and unscrew the drain screw

Exhausts can be sealed off with a plastic bag

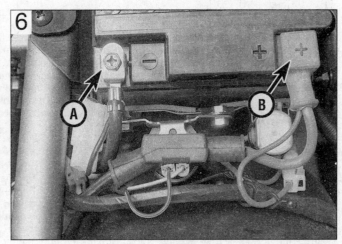

Disconnect the negative lead (A) first, followed by the positive lead (B)

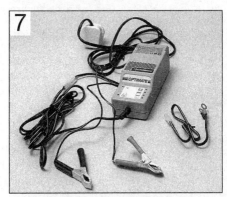

Use a suitable battery charger - this kit also assess battery condition

then switch off and allow to cool. Tape a piece of thick plastic over the silencer end(s) **(see illustration 5)**. Note that some advocate pouring a tablespoon of motor oil into the silencer(s) before sealing them off.

Battery

● Remove it from the bike - in extreme cases of cold the battery may freeze and crack its case **(see illustration 6)**.

● Check the electrolyte level and top up if necessary (conventional refillable batteries). Clean the terminals.
● Store the battery off the motorcycle and away from any sources of fire. Position a wooden block under the battery if it is to sit on the ground.
● Give the battery a trickle charge for a few hours every month **(see illustration 7)**.

Tyres

● Place the bike on its centrestand or an auxiliary stand which will support the motorcycle in an upright position. Position wood blocks under the tyres to keep them off the ground and to provide insulation from damp. If the bike is being put into long-term storage, ideally both tyres should be off the ground; not only will this protect the tyres, but will also ensure that no load is placed on the steering head or wheel bearings.
● Deflate each tyre by 5 to 10 psi, no more or the beads may unseat from the rim, making subsequent inflation difficult on tubeless tyres.

Pivots and controls

● Lubricate all lever, pedal, stand and

footrest pivot points. If grease nipples are fitted to the rear suspension components, apply lubricant to the pivots.
● Lubricate all control cables.

Cycle components

● Apply a wax protectant to all painted and plastic components. Wipe off any excess, but don't polish to a shine. Where fitted, clean the screen with soap and water.
● Coat metal parts with Vaseline (petroleum jelly). When applying this to the fork tubes, do not compress the forks otherwise the seals will rot from contact with the Vaseline.
● Apply a vinyl cleaner to the seat.

Storage conditions

● Aim to store the bike in a shed or garage which does not leak and is free from damp.
● Drape an old blanket or bedspread over the bike to protect it from dust and direct contact with sunlight (which will fade paint). This also hides the bike from prying eyes. Beware of tight-fitting plastic covers which may allow condensation to form and settle on the bike.

Getting back on the road

Engine and transmission

● Change the oil and replace the oil filter. If this was done prior to storage, check that the oil hasn't emulsified - a thick whitish substance which occurs through condensation.
● Remove the spark plugs. Using a spout-type oil can, squirt a few drops of oil into the cylinder(s). This will provide initial lubrication as the piston rings and bores comes back into contact. Service the spark plugs, or fit new ones, and install them in the engine.

● Check that the clutch isn't stuck on. The plates can stick together if left standing for some time, preventing clutch operation. Engage a gear and try rocking the bike back and forth with the clutch lever held against the handlebar. If this doesn't work on cable-operated clutches, hold the clutch lever back against the handlebar with a strong elastic band or cable tie for a couple of hours **(see illustration 8)**.
● If the air intakes or silencer end(s) were blocked off, remove the bung or cover used.
● If the fuel tank was coated with a rust

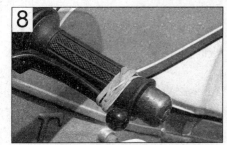

Hold clutch lever back against the handlebar with elastic bands or a cable tie

preventative, oil or a stabiliser added to the fuel, drain and flush the tank and dispose of the fuel sensibly. If no action was taken with the fuel tank prior to storage, it is advised that the old fuel is disposed of since it will go off over a period of time. Refill the fuel tank with fresh fuel.

Frame and running gear

● Oil all pivot points and cables.

● Check the tyre pressures. They will definitely need inflating if pressures were reduced for storage.

● Lubricate the final drive chain (where applicable).

● Remove any protective coating applied to the fork tubes (stanchions) since this may well destroy the fork seals. If the fork tubes weren't protected and have picked up rust spots, remove them with very fine abrasive paper and refinish with metal polish.

● Check that both brakes operate correctly. Apply each brake hard and check that it's not possible to move the motorcycle forwards, then check that the brake frees off again once released. Brake caliper pistons can stick due to corrosion around the piston head, or on the sliding caliper types, due to corrosion of the slider pins. If the brake doesn't free after repeated operation, take the caliper off for examination. Similarly drum brakes can stick due to a seized operating cam, cable or rod linkage.

● If the motorcycle has been in long-term storage, renew the brake fluid and clutch fluid (where applicable).

● Depending on where the bike has been stored, the wiring, cables and hoses may have been nibbled by rodents. Make a visual check and investigate disturbed wiring loom tape.

Battery

● If the battery has been previously removal and given top up charges it can simply be reconnected. Remember to connect the positive cable first and the negative cable last.

● On conventional refillable batteries, if the battery has not received any attention, remove it from the motorcycle and check its electrolyte level. Top up if necessary then charge the battery. If the battery fails to hold a charge and a visual checks show heavy white sulphation of the plates, the battery is probably defective and must be renewed. This is particularly likely if the battery is old. Confirm battery condition with a specific gravity check.

● On sealed (MF) batteries, if the battery has not received any attention, remove it from the motorcycle and charge it according to the information on the battery case - if the battery fails to hold a charge it must be renewed.

Starting procedure

● If a kickstart is fitted, turn the engine over a couple of times with the ignition OFF to distribute oil around the engine. If no kickstart is fitted, flick the engine kill switch OFF and the ignition ON and crank the engine over a couple of times to work oil around the upper cylinder components. If the nature of the ignition system is such that the starter won't work with the kill switch OFF, remove the spark plugs, fit them back into their caps and earth (ground) their bodies on the cylinder head. Reinstall the spark plugs afterwards.

● Switch the kill switch to RUN, operate the choke and start the engine. If the engine won't start don't continue cranking the engine - not only will this flatten the battery, but the starter motor will overheat. Switch the ignition off and try again later. If the engine refuses to start, go through the fault finding procedures in this manual. **Note:** *If the bike has been in storage for a long time, old fuel or a carburettor blockage may be the problem. Gum deposits in carburettors can block jets - if a carburettor cleaner doesn't prove successful the carburettors must be dismantled for cleaning.*

● Once the engine has started, check that the lights, turn signals and horn work properly.

● Treat the bike gently for the first ride and check all fluid levels on completion. Settle the bike back into the maintenance schedule.

This Section provides an easy reference-guide to the more common faults that are likely to afflict your machine. Obviously, the opportunities are almost limitless for faults to occur as a result of obscure failures, and to try and cover all eventualities would require a book. Indeed, a number have been written on the subject.

Successful troubleshooting is not a mysterious 'black art' but the application of a bit of knowledge combined with a systematic and logical approach to the problem. Approach any troubleshooting by first accurately identifying the symptom and then checking through the list of possible causes, starting with the simplest or most obvious and progressing in stages to the most complex.

Take nothing for granted, but above all apply liberal quantities of common sense.

The main symptom of a fault is given in the text as a major heading below which are listed the various systems or areas which may contain the fault. Details of each possible cause for a fault and the remedial action to be taken are given, in brief, in the paragraphs below each heading. Further information should be sought in the relevant Chapter.

1 Engine doesn't start or is difficult to start

- [ ] Starter motor doesn't rotate
- [ ] Starter motor rotates but engine does not turn over
- [ ] Starter works but engine won't turn over (seized)
- [ ] No fuel flow
- [ ] Engine flooded
- [ ] No spark or weak spark
- [ ] Compression low
- [ ] Stalls after starting
- [ ] Rough idle

2 Poor running at low speed

- [ ] Spark weak
- [ ] Fuel/air mixture incorrect
- [ ] Compression low
- [ ] Poor acceleration

3 Poor running or no power at high speed

- [ ] Firing incorrect
- [ ] Fuel/air mixture incorrect
- [ ] Compression low
- [ ] Knocking or pinking
- [ ] Miscellaneous causes

4 Overheating

- [ ] Engine overheats
- [ ] Firing incorrect
- [ ] Fuel/air mixture incorrect
- [ ] Compression too high
- [ ] Engine load excessive
- [ ] Lubrication inadequate
- [ ] Miscellaneous causes

5 Clutch problems

- [ ] Clutch slipping
- [ ] Clutch not disengaging completely

6 Gear changing problems

- [ ] Doesn't go into gear, or lever doesn't return
- [ ] Jumps out of gear
- [ ] Overselects

7 Abnormal engine noise

- [ ] Knocking or pinking
- [ ] Piston slap or rattling
- [ ] Valve noise
- [ ] Other noise

8 Abnormal driveline noise

- [ ] Clutch noise
- [ ] Transmission noise
- [ ] Final drive noise

9 Oil pressure low

- [ ] Engine lubrication system

10 Abnormal frame and suspension noise

- [ ] Front end noise
- [ ] Shock absorber noise
- [ ] Brake noise

11 Excessive exhaust smoke

- [ ] White smoke
- [ ] Black smoke
- [ ] Brown smoke

12 Poor handling or stability

- [ ] Handlebar hard to turn
- [ ] Handlebar shakes or vibrates excessively
- [ ] Handlebar pulls to one side
- [ ] Poor shock absorbing qualities

13 Braking problems

- [ ] Brakes are spongy, don't hold
- [ ] Brake lever or pedal pulsates
- [ ] Brakes drag

14 Electrical problems

- [ ] Battery dead or weak
- [ ] Battery overcharged

1 Engine doesn't start or is difficult to start

Starter motor doesn't rotate

☐ Engine kill switch OFF.
☐ Fuse blown. Check main fuse and starter circuit fuse (Chapter 9).
☐ Battery voltage low. Check and recharge battery (Chapter 9).
☐ Starter motor defective. Make sure the wiring to the starter is secure. Make sure the starter relay clicks when the start button is pushed. If the relay clicks, then the fault is in the wiring or motor.
☐ Starter relay faulty. Check it according to the procedure in Chapter 9.
☐ Starter button not contacting. The contacts could be wet, corroded or dirty. Disassemble and clean the switch (Chapter 9).
☐ Wiring open or shorted. Check all wiring connections and harnesses to make sure that they are dry, tight and not corroded. Also check for broken or frayed wires that can cause a short to ground (earth) (see wiring diagram, Chapter 9).
☐ Ignition (main) switch defective. Check the switch according to the procedure in Chapter 9. Replace the switch with a new one if it is defective.
☐ Engine kill switch defective. Check for wet, dirty or corroded contacts. Clean or replace the switch as necessary (Chapter 9).
☐ Faulty neutral, side stand (where fitted) or clutch switch. Check the wiring to each switch and the switch itself according to the procedures in Chapter 9.

Starter motor rotates but engine does not turn over

☐ Starter clutch defective. Inspect and repair or renew (Chapter 2).
☐ Damaged idle or starter gears. Inspect and renew the damaged parts (Chapter 2).

Starter works but engine won't turn over (seized)

☐ Seized engine caused by one or more internally damaged components. Failure due to wear, abuse or lack of lubrication. Damage can include seized valves, rockers, camshafts, pistons, crankshaft, connecting rod bearings, or transmission gears or bearings. Refer to Chapter 2 for engine disassembly.

No fuel flow

☐ No fuel in tank.
☐ Fuel tank breather hose obstructed.
☐ Fuel tap strainer, or in-line filter (XRV models), clogged. Remove the tap and clean it and the filter (Chapter 4).
☐ Fuel tap vacuum hose split or detached (XL models). Check the hose.
☐ Fuel tap diaphragm split (XL models). Remove the tap and check the diaphragm (Chapter 4).
☐ Fuel line clogged. Pull the fuel line loose and carefully blow through it.
☐ Float needle valve clogged. For both of the valves to be clogged, either a very bad batch of fuel with an unusual additive has been used, or some other foreign material has entered the tank. Many times after a machine has been stored for many months without running, the fuel turns to a varnish-like liquid and forms deposits on the inlet needle valves and jets. The carburettors should be removed and overhauled if draining the float chambers doesn't solve the problem.
☐ Fuel pump faulty (XRV models). Check the fuel pump flow and renew the pump if necessary (Chapter 4).

Engine flooded

☐ Float height too high. Check as described in Chapter 4.
☐ Float needle valve worn or stuck open. A piece of dirt, rust or other debris can cause the valve to seat improperly, causing excess fuel to be admitted to the float chamber. In this case, the float chamber should be cleaned and the needle valve and seat inspected. If the needle and seat are worn, then the leaking will persist and the parts should be replaced with new ones (Chapter 4).
☐ Starting technique incorrect. Under normal circumstances (i.e., if all the carburettor functions are sound) the machine should start with little or no throttle. When the engine is cold, the choke should be operated and the engine started without opening the throttle. When the engine is at operating temperature, only a very slight amount of throttle should be necessary. If the engine is flooded, turn the fuel tap OFF or disconnect the vacuum hose (according to model – see Chapter 4) and hold the throttle open while cranking the engine. This will allow additional air to reach the cylinders. Remember to turn the fuel tap back ON or attach the vacuum hose.

No spark or weak spark

☐ Ignition switch OFF.
☐ Engine kill switch turned to the OFF position.
☐ Battery voltage low. Check and recharge the battery as necessary (Chapter 9).
☐ Spark plugs dirty, defective or worn out. Locate reason for fouled plugs using spark plug condition chart and follow the plug maintenance procedures (Chapter 1).
☐ Spark plug caps or secondary (HT) wiring faulty. Check condition. Renew either or both components if cracks or deterioration are evident (Chapter 5).
☐ Spark plug caps not making good contact. Make sure that the plug caps fit snugly over the plug ends.
☐ Ignition control unit defective. Check the unit (Chapter 5).
☐ Pulse generator coil defective. Check the unit (Chapter 5).
☐ Ignition HT coils defective. Check the coils (Chapter 5).
☐ Ignition or kill switch shorted. This is usually caused by water, corrosion, damage or excessive wear. The switches can be disassembled and cleaned with electrical contact cleaner. If cleaning does not help, renew the switches (Chapter 9).
☐ Wiring shorted or broken between:
   a)   *Ignition (main) switch and engine kill switch (or blown fuse)*
   b)   *Ignition control unit and engine kill switch*
   c)   *Ignition control unit and ignition HT coils*
   d)   *Ignition HT coils and spark plugs*
   e)   *Ignition control unit and pulse generator coil*
☐ Make sure that all wiring connections are clean, dry and tight. Look for chafed and broken wires (Chapters 5 and 9).

1 Engine doesn't start or is difficult to start (continued)

Compression low

☐ Spark plugs loose. Remove the plugs and inspect their threads. Reinstall and tighten to the specified torque (Chapter 1).

☐ Cylinder head(s) not sufficiently tightened down. If a cylinder head is suspected of being loose, then there's a chance that the gasket or head is damaged if the problem has persisted for any length of time. The head nuts/bolts should be tightened to the proper torque in the correct sequence (Chapter 2).

☐ Improper valve clearance. This means that the valve is not closing completely and compression pressure is leaking past the valve. Check and adjust the valve clearances (Chapter 1).

☐ Cylinder and/or piston worn. Excessive wear will cause compression pressure to leak past the rings. This is usually accompanied by worn rings as well. A top-end overhaul is necessary (Chapter 2).

☐ Piston rings worn, weak, broken, or sticking. Broken or sticking piston rings usually indicate a lubrication or carburation problem that causes excess carbon deposits or seizures to form on the pistons and rings. Top-end overhaul is necessary (Chapter 2).

☐ Piston ring-to-groove clearance excessive. This is caused by excessive wear of the piston ring lands. Piston replacement is necessary (Chapter 2).

☐ Cylinder head gasket(s) damaged. If a head is allowed to become loose, or if excessive carbon build-up on the piston crown and combustion chamber causes extremely high compression, the head gasket may leak. Retorquing the head is not always sufficient to restore the seal, so gasket replacement is necessary (Chapter 2).

☐ Cylinder head(s) warped. This is caused by overheating or improperly tightened head nuts/bolts. Machine shop resurfacing or head replacement is necessary (Chapter 2).

☐ Valve spring broken or weak. Caused by component failure or wear; the springs must be renewed (Chapter 2).

☐ Valve not seating properly. This is caused by a bent valve (from over-revving or improper valve adjustment), burned valve or seat (improper carburation) or an accumulation of carbon deposits on the seat (from carburation or lubrication problems). The valves must be cleaned and/or replaced and the seats serviced if possible (Chapter 2).

Stalls after starting

☐ Improper choke action. Make sure the choke plungers are staying in the out position (Chapter 4).

☐ Ignition malfunction (Chapter 5).

☐ Carburettor malfunction (Chapter 4).

☐ Fuel contaminated. The fuel can be contaminated with either dirt or water, or can change chemically if the machine is allowed to sit for several months or more. Drain the tank and float chambers (Chapter 4).

☐ Intake air leak. Check for loose carburettor-to-intake manifold connections, loose vacuum gauge adapter screws or hoses (as applicable), or loose carburettor tops (Chapter 4).

☐ Engine idle speed incorrect. Turn idle adjusting screw until the engine idles at the specified rpm (Chapter 1).

Rough idle

☐ Ignition malfunction (Chapter 5).

☐ Idle speed incorrect (Chapter 1).

☐ Carburettors not synchronised. Adjust carburettors with vacuum gauge or manometer set as described in Chapter 1.

☐ Pilot jet or air passage clogged. Remove and overhaul the carburettors, and check jet sizes (Chapter 4).

☐ Fuel contaminated. The fuel can be contaminated with either dirt or water, or can change chemically if the machine is allowed to sit for several months or more. Drain the tank and float chambers (Chapter 4).

☐ Intake air leak. Check for loose carburettor-to-intake manifold connections, loose vacuum gauge adapter screws or hoses (as applicable), or loose carburettor tops (Chapter 4).

☐ Air filter clogged. Replace the air filter element (Chapter 1).

2 Poor running at low speeds

Spark weak

- ☐ Battery voltage low. Check and recharge battery (Chapter 9).
- ☐ Spark plugs fouled, defective or worn out. Refer to Chapter 1 for spark plug maintenance.
- ☐ Spark plug cap or HT wiring defective. Refer to Chapters 1 and 5 for details on the ignition system.
- ☐ Spark plug caps not making contact. Make sure they are securely pushed on to the plugs.
- ☐ Incorrect spark plugs. Wrong type, heat range or cap configuration. Check and install correct plugs listed in Chapter 1.
- ☐ Ignition control unit defective (Chapter 5).
- ☐ Pulse generator coil defective (Chapter 5).
- ☐ Ignition HT coils defective (Chapter 5).

Fuel/air mixture incorrect

- ☐ Pilot screws out of adjustment (Chapter 4).
- ☐ Pilot jet or air passage clogged. Remove and overhaul the carburettors (Chapter 4).
- ☐ Air bleed holes clogged. Remove carburettor and blow out all passages (Chapter 4).
- ☐ Air filter clogged, poorly sealed or missing (Chapter 1).
- ☐ Air filter housing poorly sealed. Look for cracks, holes or loose clamps and replace or repair defective parts.
- ☐ Fuel level too high or too low. Check the level (Chapter 4).
- ☐ Fuel tank breather hose obstructed.
- ☐ Carburettor intake manifolds loose. Check for cracks, breaks, tears or loose clamps. Replace the rubber intake manifold joints if split or perished.
- ☐ Incorrect carburettor jet sizes. Check according to the Specifications in Chapter 4.

Compression low

- ☐ Spark plugs loose. Remove the plugs and inspect their threads. Reinstall and tighten to the specified torque (Chapter 1).
- ☐ Cylinder head(s) not sufficiently tightened down. If a cylinder head is suspected of being loose, then there's a chance that the gasket and head are damaged if the problem has persisted for any length of time. The head nuts/bolts should be tightened to the proper torque in the correct sequence (Chapter 2).
- ☐ Improper valve clearance. This means that the valve is not closing completely and compression pressure is leaking past the valve. Check and adjust the valve clearances (Chapter 1).
- ☐ Cylinder and/or piston worn. Excessive wear will cause compression pressure to leak past the rings. This is usually accompanied by worn rings as well. A top end overhaul is necessary (Chapter 2).
- ☐ Piston rings worn, weak, broken, or sticking. Broken or sticking piston rings usually indicate a lubrication or carburation problem that causes excess carbon deposits or seizures to form on the pistons and rings. Top-end overhaul is necessary (Chapter 2).

- ☐ Piston ring-to-groove clearance excessive. This is caused by excessive wear of the piston ring lands. Piston replacement is necessary (Chapter 2).
- ☐ Cylinder head gasket(s) damaged. If a head is allowed to become loose, or if excessive carbon build-up on the piston crown and combustion chamber causes extremely high compression, the head gasket may leak. Retorquing the head is not always sufficient to restore the seal, so gasket replacement is necessary (Chapter 2).
- ☐ Cylinder head(s) warped. This is caused by overheating or improperly tightened head nuts/bolts. Machine shop resurfacing or head replacement is necessary (Chapter 2).
- ☐ Valve spring broken or weak. Caused by component failure or wear; the springs must be renewed (Chapter 2).
- ☐ Valve not seating properly. This is caused by a bent valve (from over-revving or improper valve adjustment), burned valve or seat (improper carburation) or an accumulation of carbon deposits on the seat (from carburation, lubrication problems). The valves must be cleaned and/or replaced and the seats serviced if possible (Chapter 2).

Poor acceleration

- ☐ Carburettors leaking or dirty. Overhaul the carburettors (Chapter 4).
- ☐ Timing not advancing. The pulse generator coil or the ignition control unit may be defective. If so, they must be replaced with new ones, as they can't be repaired.
- ☐ Carburettors not synchronised. Adjust them with a vacuum gauge set or manometer (Chapter 1).
- ☐ Engine oil viscosity too high. Using a heavier oil than that recommended in Chapter 1 can damage the oil pump or lubrication system and cause drag on the engine.
- ☐ Brakes dragging. Usually caused by debris which has entered the brake piston seals, or from a warped disc or bent axle. Repair as necessary (Chapter 7).
- ☐ Fuel flow restricted. Check the tap and its filter, and all the hoses from the tank; on XRV models also check the in-line fuel filter. If the breather hose is blocked a vacuum can form in the tank which will restrict flow.
- ☐ Fuel pump flow rate insufficient (XRV models). Check the pump (Chapter 4).

Miscellaneous causes

- ☐ Modification to exhaust system. Most aftermarket exhaust systems cause the engine to run leaner, which make them run hotter. When installing an accessory exhaust system, always check whether different carburettor jet sizes are needed and rejet the carburettors accordingly, if necessary (see Chapter 4). Often the best way to determine this is by running the bike on a Dyno.

3 Poor running or no power at high speed

Firing incorrect

☐ Air filter restricted. Clean or replace filter (Chapter 1).
☐ Spark plugs fouled, defective or worn out. See Chapter 1 for spark plug maintenance.
☐ Spark plug caps or HT wiring defective. See Chapters 1 and 5 for details of the ignition system.
☐ Spark plug caps not in good contact (Chapter 5).
☐ Incorrect spark plugs. Wrong type, heat range or cap configuration. Check and install correct plugs listed in Chapter 1.
☐ Ignition control unit defective (Chapter 5).
☐ Ignition HT coils defective (Chapter 5).

Fuel/air mixture incorrect

☐ Main jet clogged. Dirt, water or other contaminants can clog the main jets. Clean the fuel tap filter, the in-line filter (XRV models), the float chamber area, and the jets and carburettor orifices (Chapter 4).
☐ Main jet wrong size. Check the jet sizes according to the Specifications in Chapter 4. The standard jetting is for sea level atmospheric pressure and oxygen content – if you are constantly running at high altitude (where the oxygen content of the air is reduced), the mixture will be affected.
☐ Throttle shaft-to-carburettor body clearance excessive. Refer to Chapter 4 for inspection and part replacement procedures.
☐ Air bleed holes clogged. Remove and overhaul carburettors (Chapter 4).
☐ Air filter clogged, poorly sealed, or missing (Chapter 1).
☐ Air filter housing poorly sealed. Look for cracks, holes or loose clamps, and replace or repair defective parts.
☐ Fuel level too high or too low. Check the float height (Chapter 4).
☐ Fuel tank breather hose obstructed. If the breather hose is blocked a vacuum can form in the tank which will restrict flow.
☐ Carburettor intake manifolds loose. Check for cracks, breaks, tears or loose clamps. Replace the rubber intake manifolds if they are split or perished (Chapter 4).

Compression low

☐ Spark plugs loose. Remove the plugs and inspect their threads. Reinstall and tighten to the specified torque (Chapter 1).
☐ Cylinder head(s) not sufficiently tightened down. If a cylinder head is suspected of being loose, then there's a chance that the gasket and head are damaged if the problem has persisted for any length of time. The head nuts/bolts should be tightened to the proper torque in the correct sequence (Chapter 2).
☐ Improper valve clearance. This means that the valve is not closing completely and compression pressure is leaking past the valve. Check and adjust the valve clearances (Chapter 1).
☐ Cylinder and/or piston worn. Excessive wear will cause compression pressure to leak past the rings. This is usually accompanied by worn rings as well. A top end overhaul is necessary (Chapter 2).
☐ Piston rings worn, weak, broken, or sticking. Broken or sticking piston rings usually indicate a lubrication or carburation problem that causes excess carbon deposits or seizures to form on the pistons and rings. Top-end overhaul is necessary (Chapter 2).
☐ Piston ring-to-groove clearance excessive. This is caused by excessive wear of the piston ring lands. Piston replacement is necessary (Chapter 2).

☐ Cylinder head gasket(s) damaged. If a head is allowed to become loose, or if excessive carbon build-up on the piston crown and combustion chamber causes extremely high compression, the head gasket may leak. Retorquing the head is not always sufficient to restore the seal, so gasket replacement is necessary (Chapter 2).
☐ Cylinder head(s) warped. This is caused by overheating or improperly tightened head nuts/bolts. Machine shop resurfacing or head replacement is necessary (Chapter 2).
☐ Valve spring broken or weak. Caused by component failure or wear; the springs must be renewed (Chapter 2).
☐ Valve not seating properly. This is caused by a bent valve (from over-revving or improper valve adjustment), burned valve or seat (improper carburation) or an accumulation of carbon deposits on the seat (from carburation, lubrication problems). The valves must be cleaned and/or replaced and the seats serviced if possible (Chapter 2).

Knocking or pinking

☐ Carbon build-up in combustion chamber. Use of a fuel additive that will dissolve the adhesive bonding the carbon particles to the crown and chamber is the easiest way to remove the build-up. Otherwise, the cylinder heads will have to be removed and decarbonised (Chapter 2).
☐ Incorrect or poor quality fuel. Old or improper grades of fuel can cause detonation. This causes the knocking or pinking sound. Drain old fuel and always use the recommended fuel grade.
☐ Spark plug heat range incorrect. Uncontrolled detonation indicates the plug heat range is too hot. The plug in effect becomes a glow plug, raising cylinder temperatures. Install the proper heat range plug (Chapter 1).
☐ Improper air/fuel mixture. This will cause the cylinders to run hot, which leads to detonation. Clogged jets or an air leak can cause this imbalance. See Chapter 4.

Miscellaneous causes

☐ Throttle valve doesn't open fully. Adjust the throttle grip freeplay (Chapter 1).
☐ Clutch slipping. May be caused by an incorrectly adjusted cable (see Chapter 1), or loose or worn clutch components. Refer to Chapter 2 for clutch overhaul procedures.
☐ Timing not advancing. Check as described in Chapter 5.
☐ Engine oil viscosity too high. Using a heavier oil than the one recommended in Chapter 1 can damage the oil pump or lubrication system and cause drag on the engine.
☐ Brakes dragging. Usually caused by debris which has entered the brake piston seals, or from a warped disc or bent axle. Repair as necessary.
☐ Fuel flow restricted. Check the tap and its filter, and all the hoses from the tank; on XRV models check the in-line fuel filter. If the breather hose is blocked a vacuum can form in the tank which will restrict flow.
☐ Fuel pump flow rate insufficient (XRV models). Check the pump (Chapter 4).
☐ Modification to exhaust system. Most aftermarket exhaust systems cause the engine to run leaner, which make them run hotter. When installing an accessory exhaust system, always check whether different carburettor jet sizes are needed and rejet the carburettors accordingly, if necessary (see Chapter 4). Often the best way to determine this is by running the bike on a Dyno.

4 Overheating

Engine overheats

- ☐ Coolant level low. Check and add coolant (Chapter 1).
- ☐ Leak in cooling system. Check cooling system hoses and radiator for leaks and other damage. Repair or replace parts as necessary (Chapter 3).
- ☐ Thermostat sticking closed. Check and replace as described in Chapter 3.
- ☐ Faulty radiator cap. Remove the cap and have it pressure tested.
- ☐ Coolant passages clogged. Have the entire system drained and flushed, then refill with fresh coolant.
- ☐ Water pump defective. Remove the pump and check the components (Chapter 3).
- ☐ Clogged radiator fins. Clean them by blowing compressed air through the fins from the backside, and straighten any bent fins that restrict air flow.
- ☐ Cooling fan or fan switch fault (Chapter 3).

Firing incorrect

- ☐ Spark plugs fouled, defective or worn out. See Chapter 1 for spark plug maintenance.
- ☐ Incorrect spark plugs.
- ☐ Ignition control unit defective (Chapter 5).
- ☐ Faulty ignition HT coils (Chapter 5).

Fuel/air mixture incorrect

- ☐ Main jet clogged. Dirt, water or other contaminants can clog the main jets. Clean the fuel tap filter, the in-line filter (XRV models), the float chamber area, and the jets and carburettor orifices (Chapter 4).
- ☐ Main jet wrong size. Check the jet sizes according to the Specifications in Chapter 4. The standard jetting is for sea level atmospheric pressure and oxygen content – if you are constantly running at high altitude (where the oxygen content of the air is reduced), the mixture will be affected.
- ☐ Throttle shaft-to-carburettor body clearance excessive. Refer to Chapter 4 for inspection and part replacement procedures.
- ☐ Air bleed holes clogged. Remove and overhaul carburettors (Chapter 4).
- ☐ Air filter clogged, poorly sealed, or missing (Chapter 1).
- ☐ Air filter housing poorly sealed. Look for cracks, holes or loose clamps, and replace or repair defective parts.
- ☐ Fuel level too high or too low. Check the float height (Chapter 4).
- ☐ Fuel tank breather hose obstructed. If the breather hose is blocked a vacuum can form in the tank which will restrict flow.
- ☐ Carburettor intake manifolds loose. Check for cracks, breaks, tears or loose clamps. Replace the rubber intake manifolds if they are split or perished (Chapter 4).

Compression too high

- ☐ Carbon build-up in combustion chamber. Use of a fuel additive that will dissolve the adhesive bonding the carbon particles to the piston crown and chamber is the easiest way to remove the build-up. Otherwise, the cylinder heads will have to be removed and decarbonised (Chapter 2).
- ☐ Improperly machined head surface or installation of incorrect gasket during engine assembly.

Engine load excessive

- ☐ Clutch slipping. Can be caused by damaged, loose or worn clutch components. Refer to Chapter 2 for overhaul procedures.
- ☐ Engine oil level too high. The addition of too much oil will cause pressurisation of the crankcase and inefficient engine operation. Check Specifications and drain to proper level (Chapter 1).
- ☐ Engine oil viscosity too high. Using a heavier oil than the one recommended in Chapter 1 can damage the oil pump or lubrication system as well as cause drag on the engine.
- ☐ Brakes dragging. On disc brakes this is usually caused by debris which has entered the brake piston seals, or from a warped disc or bent axle. On a drum brake this is usually caused by a seized brake operating mechanism.

Lubrication inadequate

- ☐ Engine oil level too low. Friction caused by intermittent lack of lubrication or from oil that is overworked can cause overheating. The oil provides a definite cooling function in the engine. Check the oil level (Chapter 1).
- ☐ Poor quality engine oil or incorrect viscosity or type. Oil is rated not only according to viscosity but also according to type. Some oils are not rated high enough for use in this engine. Check the Specifications section and change to the correct oil (Chapter 1).
- ☐ Faulty oil pump causing reduced pressure in system. Check the pump for wear (see Chapter 2).

Miscellaneous causes

- ☐ Modification to exhaust system. Most aftermarket exhaust systems cause the engine to run leaner, which make them run hotter. When installing an accessory exhaust system, always check whether different carburettor jet sizes are needed and rejet the carburettors accordingly, if necessary (see Chapter 4). Often the best way to determine this is by running the bike on a Dyno.

5 Clutch problems

Clutch slipping

- ☐ Clutch cable incorrectly adjusted (see Chapter 1).
- ☐ Friction plates worn or warped. Overhaul the clutch assembly (Chapter 2).
- ☐ Plain plates warped (Chapter 2).
- ☐ Clutch springs broken or weak. Old or heat-damaged (from slipping clutch) springs should be replaced with new ones (Chapter 2).
- ☐ Clutch release mechanism defective. Replace any defective parts (Chapter 2).
- ☐ Clutch centre or housing unevenly worn. This causes improper engagement of the plates. Replace the damaged or worn parts (Chapter 2).

Clutch not disengaging completely

- ☐ Clutch cable incorrectly adjusted (see Chapter 1) or faulty. The inner cable could be seizing in outer cable, caused by dirt, kinks or incorrect routing. Check the cable and renew if necessary (see Chapter 2).
- ☐ Clutch plates warped or damaged. This will cause clutch drag, which in turn will cause the machine to creep. Overhaul the clutch assembly (Chapter 2).

- ☐ Clutch spring tension uneven. Usually caused by a sagged or broken spring. Check and replace the springs as a set (Chapter 2).
- ☐ Engine oil deteriorated. Old, thin, worn out oil will not provide proper lubrication for the plates, causing the clutch to drag. Replace the oil and filter (Chapter 1).
- ☐ Engine oil viscosity too high. Using a heavier oil than recommended in Chapter 1 can cause the plates to stick together, putting a drag on the engine. Change to the correct weight oil (Chapter 1).
- ☐ Clutch housing guide seized on input shaft. Lack of lubrication, severe wear or damage can cause the guide to seize on the shaft. Overhaul of the clutch, and perhaps transmission, may be necessary to repair the damage (Chapter 2).
- ☐ Clutch release mechanism defective. Overhaul the components in the clutch cover (Chapter 2).
- ☐ Loose clutch centre nut. Causes housing and centre misalignment putting a drag on the engine. Engagement adjustment continually varies. Overhaul the clutch assembly (Chapter 2).

6 Gear changing problems

Doesn't go into gear or lever doesn't return

- ☐ Clutch not disengaging. See above.
- ☐ Selector fork(s) bent, worn or seized. Overhaul the transmission (Chapter 2).
- ☐ Gearchange shaft bent. Remove the gearchange mechanism and check the shaft and all components (see Chapter 2).
- ☐ Gear(s) stuck on shaft. Most often caused by a lack of lubrication or excessive wear in transmission bearings and bushings. Overhaul the transmission (Chapter 2).
- ☐ Selector drum binding. Caused by lubrication failure or excessive wear. Replace the drum and bearing (Chapter 2).
- ☐ Gearchange lever return spring weak or broken (Chapter 2).
- ☐ Gearchange lever broken. Splines stripped out of lever or shaft, caused by allowing the lever to get loose. Replace necessary parts (Chapter 2).
- ☐ Gearchange mechanism stopper arm broken or worn. Full engagement and rotary movement of selector drum results. Replace the arm (Chapter 2).

- ☐ Stopper arm spring broken. Allows arm to float, causing sporadic gearchange operation. Replace spring (Chapter 2).
- ☐ Gearchange mechanism selector arm broken or worn, or missing pins on selector drum. Remove the gearchange mechanism and check the arm and all components (see Chapter 2).

Jumps out of gear

- ☐ Selector fork(s) or selector drum tracks worn or damaged. Overhaul the transmission (Chapter 2).
- ☐ Gear groove(s) worn. Overhaul the transmission (Chapter 2).
- ☐ Gear dogs or dog slots worn or damaged. The gears should be inspected and replaced. No attempt should be made to service the worn parts.

Overselects

- ☐ Stopper arm spring weak or broken (Chapter 2).
- ☐ Gearchange shaft return spring post broken or distorted (Chapter 2).

7 Abnormal engine noise

Knocking or pinking

☐ Carbon build-up in combustion chamber. Use of a fuel additive that will dissolve the adhesive bonding the carbon particles to the piston crown and chamber is the easiest way to remove the build-up. Otherwise, the cylinder heads will have to be removed and decarbonised (Chapter 2).

☐ Incorrect or poor quality fuel. Old or improper fuel can cause detonation. This causes the knocking or pinking sound. Drain the old fuel and always use the recommended grade fuel (Chapter 4).

☐ Spark plug heat range incorrect. Uncontrolled detonation indicates that the plug heat range is too hot. The plug in effect becomes a glow plug, raising cylinder temperatures. Install the proper heat range plug (Chapter 1).

☐ Improper air/fuel mixture. This will cause the cylinders to run hot and lead to detonation. Clogged jets or an air leak can cause this imbalance. See Chapter 4.

Piston slap or rattling

☐ Cylinder-to-piston clearance excessive. Caused by improper assembly. Inspect and overhaul top-end parts (Chapter 2).

☐ Connecting rod bent. Caused by over-revving, trying to start a badly flooded engine or from ingesting a foreign object into the combustion chamber. Replace the damaged parts (Chapter 2).

☐ Piston pin or piston pin bore worn or seized from wear or lack of lubrication. Replace damaged parts (Chapter 2).

☐ Piston ring(s) worn, broken or sticking. Overhaul the top-end (Chapter 2).

☐ Piston seizure damage. Usually from lack of lubrication or overheating. Replace the pistons and cylinder block with new ones, as necessary (Chapter 2).

☐ Connecting rod upper or lower end clearance excessive. Caused by excessive wear or lack of lubrication. Replace worn parts with new ones.

Valve noise

☐ Incorrect valve clearances. Adjust the clearances by referring to Chapter 1.

☐ Valve spring broken or weak. Check and replace weak valve springs (Chapter 2).

☐ Camshaft(s) or cylinder head(s) worn or damaged. Lack of lubrication at high rpm is usually the cause of damage. Insufficient oil or failure to change the oil at the recommended intervals are the chief causes. Since there are no replaceable bearings in the head, the head itself and/or the camshaft will have to be replaced if there is excessive wear or damage (Chapter 2).

Other noise

☐ Cylinder head gasket(s) leaking.

☐ Exhaust pipe leaking at cylinder head connection. Caused by improper fit of pipe or loose exhaust flange. All exhaust fasteners should be tightened evenly and carefully. Failure to do this will lead to a leak.

☐ Crankshaft runout excessive. Caused by a bent crankshaft (from over-revving) or damage from an upper cylinder component failure. Can also be attributed to dropping the machine on either of the crankshaft ends.

☐ Engine mounting bolts loose. Tighten all engine mount bolts (Chapter 2).

☐ Crankshaft bearings worn (Chapter 2).

☐ Camchains, guide blades or tensioner blades worn. Replace according to the procedure in Chapter 2.

☐ Camchain tensioner failure (Chapter 2).

8 Abnormal driveline noise

Clutch noise

☐ Clutch outer drum/friction plate clearance excessive (Chapter 2).

☐ Loose or damaged clutch pressure plate and/or bolts (Chapter 2).

Transmission noise

☐ Bearings worn. Also includes the possibility that the shafts are worn. Overhaul the transmission (Chapter 2).

☐ Gears worn or chipped (Chapter 2).

☐ Metal chips jammed in gear teeth. Probably pieces from a broken clutch, gear or selector mechanism that were picked up by the gears. This will cause early bearing failure (Chapter 2).

☐ Engine oil level too low. Causes a whine or howl from transmission. Also affects engine power and clutch operation (Chapter 1).

Final drive noise

☐ Chain not adjusted properly (Chapter 1).

☐ Front or rear sprocket loose. Tighten fasteners (Chapter 6).

☐ Sprockets worn. Renew sprockets (Chapter 6).

☐ Rear sprocket warped. Renew sprockets (Chapter 6).

☐ Loose or worn rear wheel or sprocket coupling bearings. Check and replace as needed (Chapter 7).

9 Oil pressure low

Engine lubrication system

☐ Engine oil level low. Inspect for leak or other problem causing low oil level and add recommended oil (Daily (pre-ride) checks).

☐ Engine oil viscosity too low. Very old, thin oil or an improper weight of oil used in the engine. Change to correct oil (Chapter 1).

☐ Engine oil pump defective, blocked oil strainer gauze or failed relief valve. Carry out oil pressure check (Chapter 1).

☐ Camshaft or journals worn. Excessive wear causing drop in oil pressure. Renew camshaft and/or cylinder head. Abnormal wear could be caused by oil starvation at high rpm from low oil level or improper weight or type of oil (Chapter 1).

☐ Crankshaft and/or bearings worn. Same problems as above. Check and renew crankshaft and/or bearings (Chapter 2).

10 Abnormal frame and suspension noise

Front end noise

☐ Low fluid level or improper viscosity oil in forks. This can sound like spurting and is usually accompanied by irregular fork action (Chapter 6).

☐ Spring(s) weak or broken. Makes a clicking or scraping sound. Fork oil, when drained, will have a lot of metal particles in it (Chapter 6).

☐ Steering head bearings loose or damaged. Clicks when braking. Check and adjust or replace as necessary (Chapters 1 and 6).

☐ Fork yokes loose. Make sure all clamp pinch bolts are tightened to the specified torque (Chapter 6).

☐ Fork tube bent. A possibility if machine has been in an accident. Replace tube(s) with new one(s) (Chapter 6).

☐ Front axle or axle clamp nuts loose. Tighten them to the specified torque (Chapter 7).

☐ Loose or worn wheel bearings. Check and renew as needed (Chapter 7).

Shock absorber noise

☐ Fluid level incorrect. Indicates a leak caused by defective seal. Shock will be covered with oil. Replacement parts are available for some of the models covered – seek advice on repair from a Honda dealer or suspension specialist (Chapter 6).

☐ Defective shock absorber with internal damage. This is in the body of the shock and can't be remedied. The shock must be replaced with a new one (Chapter 6).

☐ Bent or damaged shock body. Replace the shock with a new one (Chapter 6).

☐ Loose or worn suspension linkage components. Check and replace as necessary (Chapter 6).

☐ Loose bolts in suspension assembly. Check all bolts and tighten to the specified torque settings (Chapter 6).

Brake noise – disc brake

☐ Worn brake pads – if there is no friction material left there will be a metal-on-metal grinding sound, and the brake disc will be damaged.

☐ Squeal caused by pad shim not installed or positioned correctly (where fitted) (Chapter 7).

☐ Squeal caused by dust on brake pads. Usually found in combination with glazed pads. Clean using brake cleaning solvent (Chapter 7).

☐ Contamination of brake pads. Oil, brake fluid or dirt causing brake to chatter or squeal. Renew the pads (Chapter 7).

☐ Pads glazed. Caused by excessive heat from prolonged use or from contamination. Do not use sandpaper, emery cloth, carborundum cloth or any other abrasive to roughen the pad surfaces as abrasives will stay in the pad material and damage the disc. A very fine flat file or wire brush can be used, but pad renewal is recommended as a cure (Chapter 7).

☐ Disc warped. Can cause a chattering, clicking or intermittent squeal. Usually accompanied by a pulsating lever and uneven braking. Renew the disc (Chapter 7).

☐ Loose or worn wheel bearings. Check and renew as needed (Chapter 7).

Brake noise – drum rear brake

☐ Worn brake shoes – if there is no friction material left there will be a metal-on-metal grinding sound, and the brake drum will be damaged.

☐ Squeal caused by dust on brake shoes. Usually found in combination with glazed shoes. Clean using brake cleaning solvent (Chapter 7).

☐ Contamination of brake shoes. Oil or dirt causing brake to chatter or squeal. Renew the shoes (Chapter 7).

☐ Shoes glazed. Caused by excessive heat from prolonged use or from contamination. Do not use sandpaper, emery cloth, carborundum cloth or any other abrasive to roughen the friction material surface as abrasives will stay in the material and damage the drum. A very fine flat file or wire brush can be used, but shoe renewal is recommended as a cure (Chapter 7).

11 Excessive exhaust smoke

White smoke

☐ Piston oil ring worn. The ring may be broken or damaged, causing oil from the crankcase to be pulled past the piston into the combustion chamber. Replace the rings with new ones (Chapter 2).

☐ Cylinders worn, cracked, or scored. Caused by overheating or oil starvation. Check the cylinder bores, lubrication system and cooling system (see Chapters 2 and 3).

☐ Valve stem oil seal damaged or worn. Replace oil seals with new ones (Chapter 2).

☐ Valve guide worn. Perform a complete valve job (Chapter 2).

☐ Engine oil level too high, which causes the oil to be forced past the rings. Drain oil to the proper level (Chapter 1).

☐ Head gasket broken between oil return and cylinder. Causes oil to be pulled into the combustion chamber. Replace the head gasket and check the head for warpage (Chapter 2).

☐ Abnormal crankcase pressurisation, which forces oil past the rings. Clogged breather is usually the cause.

Black smoke

☐ Air filter clogged. Clean or replace the element (Chapter 1).

☐ Main jet too large or loose. Compare the jet size to the Specifications (Chapter 4).

☐ Choke cable or plungers stuck, causing fuel to be pulled through choke circuit (Chapter 4).

☐ Fuel level too high. Check and adjust the float height(s) as necessary (Chapter 4).

☐ Float needle valve held off needle seat. Clean the float chambers and fuel line and replace the needles and seats if necessary (Chapter 4).

Brown smoke

☐ Main jet too small or clogged. Lean condition caused by wrong size main jet or by a restricted orifice. Clean float chambers and jets and compare jet size to Specifications (Chapter 4).

☐ Fuel flow insufficient – float needle valve stuck closed due to chemical reaction with old fuel; fuel level incorrect; restricted fuel line; faulty fuel pump (Chapter 4).

☐ Carburettor intake manifold clamps loose (Chapter 4).

☐ Air filter poorly sealed or not installed (Chapter 1).

12 Poor handling or stability

Handlebars hard to turn

- [ ] Steering head bearing adjuster nut too tight. Check adjustment as described in Chapter 1.
- [ ] Bearings damaged. Roughness can be felt as the bars are turned from side-to-side. Renew bearings and races (Chapter 6).
- [ ] Races dented or worn. Denting results from wear in only one position (e.g., straight ahead), from a collision or hitting a pothole or from dropping the machine. Renew races and bearings (Chapter 6
- [ ] Steering stem lubrication inadequate. Causes are grease getting hard from age or being washed out by high pressure car washes. Disassemble steering head and repack bearings (Chapter 6).
- [ ] Steering stem bent. Caused by a collision, hitting a pothole or by dropping the machine. Replace damaged part. Don't try to straighten the steering stem (Chapter 6).
- [ ] Front tyre air pressure too low (Chapter 1).

Handlebars shake or vibrates excessively

- [ ] Tyres worn or out of balance (Chapter 7).
- [ ] Swingarm bearings worn. Renew worn bearings (Chapter 6).
- [ ] Wheel rim(s) warped or damaged. Inspect wheels for runout (Chapter 7).
- [ ] Wheel bearings worn. Worn front or rear wheel bearings can cause poor tracking. Worn front bearings will cause wobble (Chapter 7).
- [ ] Handlebar clamp bolts loose (Chapter 6).
- [ ] Fork yoke bolts loose. Tighten them to the specified torque (Chapter 6).
- [ ] Engine mounting bolts loose. Will cause excessive vibration with increased engine rpm (Chapter 2).

Handlebar pulls to one side

- [ ] Frame bent. Definitely suspect this if the machine has been dropped. May or may not be accompanied by cracking near the bend. Renew the frame (Chapter 6).
- [ ] Wheels out of alignment. Caused by improper location of axle spacers or from bent steering stem or frame (Chapter 6).
- [ ] Swingarm bent or twisted. Caused by age (metal fatigue) or impact damage. Renew the swingarm (Chapter 6).
- [ ] Steering stem bent. Caused by impact damage or by dropping the motorcycle. Renew the steering stem (Chapter 6).
- [ ] Fork tube bent. Disassemble the forks and replace the damaged parts (Chapter 6).
- [ ] Fork oil level uneven. Check and add or drain as necessary (Chapter 6).

Poor shock absorbing qualities

- [ ] Too hard:
    - a) Fork oil level excessive (Chapter 6).
    - b) Fork oil viscosity too high. Use a lighter oil (see the Specifications in Chapter 6).
    - c) Fork tube bent. Causes a harsh, sticking feeling (Chapter 6).
    - d) Fork internal damage (Chapter 6).
    - e) Shock shaft or body bent or damaged (Chapter 6).
    - f) Shock internal damage.
    - g) Tyre pressure too high (Chapter 1).
- [ ] Too soft:
    - a) Fork or shock oil insufficient and/or leaking (Chapter 6).
    - b) Fork oil level too low (Chapter 6).
    - c) Fork oil viscosity too light (Chapter 6).
    - d) Fork springs weak or broken (Chapter 6).
    - e) Shock internal damage or leakage (Chapter 6).

13 Braking problems

Brakes are spongy, don't hold – disc brakes

- [ ] Air in brake line. Caused by inattention to master cylinder fluid level or by leakage. Locate problem and bleed brakes (Chapter 7).
- [ ] Brake pads or disc worn (Chapters 1 and 7).
- [ ] Brake fluid leak. See paragraph 1.
- [ ] Contaminated pads. Caused by contamination with oil, grease, brake fluid, etc. Renew the pads. Clean disc thoroughly with brake cleaner (Chapter 7).
- [ ] Brake fluid deteriorated. Fluid is old or contaminated. Drain system, replenish with new fluid and bleed the system (Chapter 7).
- [ ] Master cylinder internal parts worn or damaged causing fluid to bypass (Chapter 7).
- [ ] Master cylinder bore scratched by foreign material or broken spring. Repair or renew master cylinder (Chapter 7).
- [ ] Disc warped. Renew the disc (Chapter 7).

Brake lever or pedal pulsates – disc brakes

- [ ] Disc warped. Renew disc (Chapter 7).
- [ ] Axle bent. Renew axle (Chapter 7).

- [ ] Brake caliper bolts loose (Chapter 7).
- [ ] Brake caliper slider pins sticking, causing caliper to bind. Lubricate the slider pins and renew the dust boots if they have cracked (Chapter 7).
- [ ] Wheel warped or otherwise damaged (Chapter 7).
- [ ] Wheel bearings damaged or worn (Chapter 7).

Brakes drag – disc brakes

- [ ] Master cylinder piston seized. Caused by wear or damage to piston or cylinder bore (Chapter 7).
- [ ] Lever balky or stuck. Check pivot and lubricate (Chapter 7).
- [ ] Brake caliper binds. Caused by inadequate lubrication of slider pins (Chapter 7).
- [ ] Brake caliper piston seized in bore. Caused by wear or ingestion of dirt past deteriorated seal (Chapter 7).
- [ ] Brake pad damaged. Pad material separated from backing plate. Usually caused by faulty manufacturing process or from contact with chemicals. Renew pads (Chapter 7).
- [ ] Pads improperly installed (Chapter 7).

14 Electrical problems

Battery dead or weak

- [ ] Battery faulty. Caused by sulphated plates which are shorted through sedimentation. Also, broken battery terminal making only occasional contact (Chapter 9). On non MF batteries, make sure the electrolyte level is correct (Chapter 1).
- [ ] Battery cables making poor contact (Chapter 9).
- [ ] Load excessive. Caused by addition of high wattage lights or other electrical accessories.
- [ ] Ignition (main) switch defective. Switch either grounds (earths) internally or fails to shut off system. Renew the switch (Chapter 9).
- [ ] Regulator/rectifier defective (Chapter 9).

- [ ] Alternator stator coil open or shorted (Chapter 9).
- [ ] Wiring faulty. Wiring grounded (earthed) or connections loose in ignition, charging or lighting circuits (Chapter 9).

Battery overcharged

- [ ] Regulator/rectifier defective. Overcharging is noticed when battery gets excessively warm (Chapter 9).
- [ ] Battery defective. Replace battery with a new one (Chapter 9).
- [ ] Battery amperage too low, wrong type or size. Install manufacturer's specified amp-hour battery to handle charging load (Chapter 9).

Checking engine compression

● Low compression will result in exhaust smoke, heavy oil consumption, poor starting and poor performance. A compression test will provide useful information about an engine's condition and if performed regularly, can give warning of trouble before any other symptoms become apparent.
● A compression gauge will be required, along with an adapter to suit the spark plug hole thread size. Note that the screw-in type gauge/adapter set up is preferable to the rubber cone type.
● Before carrying out the test, first check the valve clearances as described in Chapter 1.
1 Run the engine until it reaches normal operating temperature, then stop it and remove the spark plug(s), taking care not to scald your hands on the hot components.
2 Install the gauge adapter and compression gauge in No. 1 cylinder spark plug hole (see illustration 1).

Screw the compression gauge adapter into the spark plug hole, then screw the gauge into the adapter

3 On kickstart-equipped motorcycles, make sure the ignition switch is OFF, then open the throttle fully and kick the engine over a couple of times until the gauge reading stabilises.
4 On motorcycles with electric start only, the procedure will differ depending on the nature of the ignition system. Flick the engine kill switch (engine stop switch) to OFF and turn the ignition switch ON; open the throttle fully and crank the engine over on the starter motor for a couple of revolutions until the gauge reading stabilises. If the starter will not operate with the kill switch OFF, turn the ignition switch OFF and refer to the next paragraph.
5 Install the plugs back in their caps and arrange the plug electrodes so that their metal bodies are earthed (grounded) against the cylinder heads; this is essential to prevent damage to the ignition system (see illustration 2). Position the plugs well away from the plug holes otherwise there is a risk of atomised fuel

All spark plugs must be earthed (grounded) against the cylinder head

escaping from the plug holes and igniting. As a safety precaution, cover the valve covers with rag and disconnect the fuel pump wiring connector on XRV750 models (see Chapter 4). On XL600V and XRV750 models, turn the fuel tap(s) OFF. Turn the ignition switch and kill switch ON, open the throttle fully and crank the engine over on the starter motor for a couple of revolutions until the gauge reading stabilises.
6 After one or two revolutions the pressure should build up to a maximum figure and then stabilise. Take a note of this reading and on multi-cylinder engines repeat the test on the remaining cylinders.
7 The correct pressures are given in Chapter 2 Specifications. If the results fall within the specified range and on multi-cylinder engines all are relatively equal, the engine is in good condition. If there is a marked difference between the readings, or if the readings are lower than specified, inspection of the top-end components will be required.
8 Low compression pressure may be due to worn cylinder bores, pistons or rings, failure of the cylinder head gasket, worn valve seals, or poor valve seating.
9 To distinguish between cylinder/piston wear and valve leakage, pour a small quantity of oil into the bore to temporarily seal the piston rings, then repeat the compression tests (see illustration 3). If the readings show

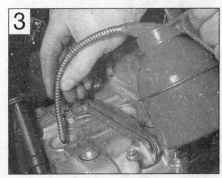

Bores can be temporarily sealed with a squirt of motor oil

a noticeable increase in pressure this confirms that the cylinder bore, piston, or rings are worn. If, however, no change is indicated, the cylinder head gasket or valves should be examined.
10 High compression pressure indicates excessive carbon build-up in the combustion chamber and on the piston crown. If this is the case the cylinder head should be removed and the deposits removed. Note that excessive carbon build-up is less likely with the used on modern fuels.

Checking battery open-circuit voltage

 Warning: The gases produced by the battery are explosive - never smoke or create any sparks in the vicinity of the battery. Never allow the electrolyte to contact your skin or clothing - if it does, wash it off and seek immediate medical attention.

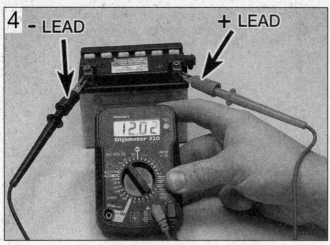

Measuring open-circuit battery voltage

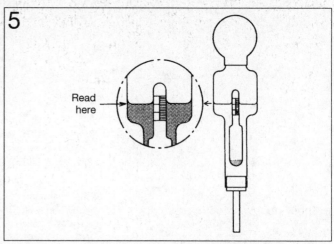

Float-type hydrometer for measuring battery specific gravity

● Before any electrical fault is investigated the battery should be checked.

● You'll need a dc voltmeter or multimeter to check battery voltage. Check that the leads are inserted in the correct terminals on the meter, red lead to positive (+ve), black lead to negative (-ve). Incorrect connections can damage the meter.

● A sound fully-charged 12 volt battery should produce between 12.3 and 12.6 volts across its terminals (12.8 volts for a maintenance-free battery). On machines with a 6 volt battery, voltage should be between 6.1 and 6.3 volts.

1 Set a multimeter to the 0 to 20 volts dc range and connect its probes across the battery terminals. Connect the meter's positive (+ve) probe, usually red, to the battery positive (+ve) terminal, followed by the meter's negative (-ve) probe, usually black, to the battery negative terminal (-ve) **(see illustration 4)**.

2 If battery voltage is low (below 10 volts on a 12 volt battery or below 4 volts on a six volt battery), charge the battery and test the voltage again. If the battery repeatedly goes flat, investigate the motorcycle's charging system.

Checking battery specific gravity (SG)

⚠️ **Warning: The gases produced by the battery are explosive - never smoke or create any sparks in the vicinity of the battery. Never allow the electrolyte to contact your skin or clothing - if it does, wash it off and seek immediate medical attention.**

● The specific gravity check gives an indication of a battery's state of charge.

● A hydrometer is used for measuring specific gravity. Make sure you purchase one

which has a small enough hose to insert in the aperture of a motorcycle battery.

● Specific gravity is simply a measure of the electrolyte's density compared with that of water. Water has an SG of 1.000 and fully-charged battery electrolyte is about 26% heavier, at 1.260.

● Specific gravity checks are not possible on maintenance-free batteries. Testing the open-circuit voltage is the only means of determining their state of charge.

1 To measure SG, remove the battery from the motorcycle and remove the first cell cap. Draw

Digital multimeter can be used for all electrical tests

some electrolyte into the hydrometer and note the reading **(see illustration 5)**. Return the electrolyte to the cell and install the cap.

2 The reading should be in the region of 1.260 to 1.280. If SG is below 1.200 the battery needs charging. Note that SG will vary with temperature; it should be measured at 20°C (68°F). Add 0.007 to the reading for every 10°C above 20°C, and subtract 0.007 from the reading for every 10°C below 20°C. Add 0.004 to the reading for every 10°F above 68°F, and subtract 0.004 from the reading for every 10°F below 68°F.

3 When the check is complete, rinse the hydrometer thoroughly with clean water.

Checking for continuity

● The term continuity describes the uninterrupted flow of electricity through an electrical circuit. A continuity check will determine whether an **open-circuit** situation exists.

● Continuity can be checked with an ohmmeter, multimeter, continuity tester or battery and bulb test circuit **(see illustrations 6, 7 and 8)**.

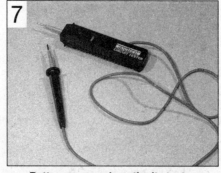

Battery-powered continuity tester

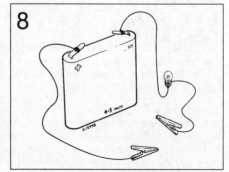

Battery and bulb test circuit

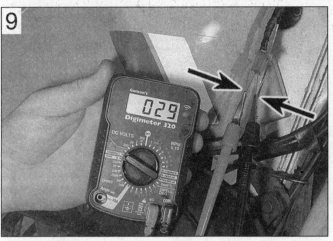

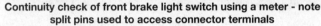

Continuity check of front brake light switch using a meter - note split pins used to access connector terminals

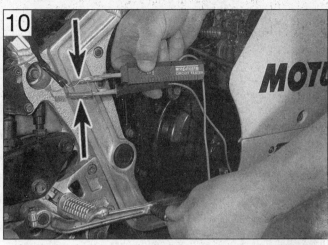

Continuity check of rear brake light switch using a continuity tester

● All of these instruments are self-powered by a battery, therefore the checks are made with the ignition OFF.

● As a safety precaution, always disconnect the battery negative (-ve) lead before making checks, particularly if ignition switch checks are being made.

● If using a meter, select the appropriate ohms scale and check that the meter reads infinity (∞). Touch the meter probes together and check that meter reads zero; where necessary adjust the meter so that it reads zero.

● After using a meter, always switch it OFF to conserve its battery.

Switch checks

1 If a switch is at fault, trace its wiring up to the wiring connectors. Separate the wire connectors and inspect them for security and condition. A build-up of dirt or corrosion here will most likely be the cause of the problem - clean up and apply a water dispersant such as WD40.

2 If using a test meter, set the meter to the ohms x 10 scale and connect its probes across the wires from the switch **(see illustration 9)**. Simple ON/OFF type switches, such as brake light switches, only have two wires whereas combination switches, like the ignition switch, have many internal links. Study the wiring diagram to ensure that you are connecting across the correct pair of wires. Continuity (low or no measurable resistance - 0 ohms) should be indicated with the switch ON and no continuity (high resistance) with it OFF.

3 Note that the polarity of the test probes doesn't matter for continuity checks, although care should be taken to follow specific test procedures if a diode or solid-state component is being checked.

4 A continuity tester or battery and bulb circuit can be used in the same way. Connect its probes as described above **(see illustration 10)**. The light should come on to indicate continuity in the ON switch position, but should extinguish in the OFF position.

Wiring checks

● Many electrical faults are caused by damaged wiring, often due to incorrect routing or chaffing on frame components.

● Loose, wet or corroded wire connectors can also be the cause of electrical problems, especially in exposed locations.

1 A continuity check can be made on a single length of wire by disconnecting it at each end and connecting a meter or continuity tester across both ends of the wire **(see illustration 11)**.

2 Continuity (low or no resistance - 0 ohms) should be indicated if the wire is good. If no continuity (high resistance) is shown, suspect a broken wire.

Checking for voltage

● A voltage check can determine whether current is reaching a component.

● Voltage can be checked with a dc voltmeter, multimeter set on the dc volts scale, test light or buzzer **(see illustrations 12 and 13)**. A meter has the advantage of being able to measure actual voltage.

● When using a meter, check that its leads are inserted in the correct terminals on the meter, red to positive (+ve), black to negative (-ve). Incorrect connections can damage the meter.

● A voltmeter (or multimeter set to the dc volts scale) should always be connected in parallel (across the load). Connecting it in series will destroy the meter.

● Voltage checks are made with the ignition ON.

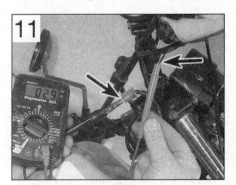

Continuity check of front brake light switch sub-harness

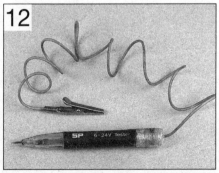

A simple test light can be used for voltage checks

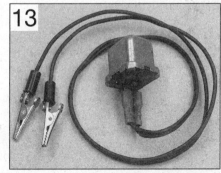

A buzzer is useful for voltage checks

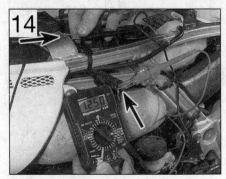

Checking for voltage at the rear brake light power supply wire using a meter . . .

1 First identify the relevant wiring circuit by referring to the wiring diagram at the end of this manual. If other electrical components share the same power supply (ie are fed from the same fuse), take note whether they are working correctly - this is useful information in deciding where to start checking the circuit.
2 If using a meter, check first that the meter leads are plugged into the correct terminals on the meter (see above). Set the meter to the dc volts function, at a range suitable for the battery voltage. Connect the meter red probe (+ve) to the power supply wire and the black probe to a good metal earth (ground) on the motorcycle's frame or directly to the battery negative (-ve) terminal **(see illustration 14)**. Battery voltage should be shown on the meter

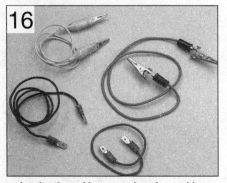

A selection of jumper wires for making earth (ground) checks

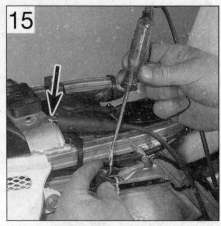

. . . or a test light - note the earth connection to the frame (arrow)

with the ignition switched ON.
3 If using a test light or buzzer, connect its positive (+ve) probe to the power supply terminal and its negative (-ve) probe to a good earth (ground) on the motorcycle's frame or directly to the battery negative (-ve) terminal **(see illustration 15)**. With the ignition ON, the test light should illuminate or the buzzer sound.
4 If no voltage is indicated, work back towards the fuse continuing to check for voltage. When you reach a point where there is voltage, you know the problem lies between that point and your last check point.

Checking the earth (ground)

● Earth connections are made either directly to the engine or frame (such as sensors, neutral switch etc. which only have a positive feed) or by a separate wire into the earth circuit of the wiring harness. Alternatively a short earth wire is sometimes run directly from the component to the motorcycle's frame.
● Corrosion is often the cause of a poor earth connection.
● If total failure is experienced, check the security of the main earth lead from the

negative (-ve) terminal of the battery and also the main earth (ground) point on the wiring harness. If corroded, dismantle the connection and clean all surfaces back to bare metal.
1 To check the earth on a component, use an insulated jumper wire to temporarily bypass its earth connection **(see illustration 16)**. Connect one end of the jumper wire between the earth terminal or metal body of the component and the other end to the motorcycle's frame.
2 If the circuit works with the jumper wire installed, the original earth circuit is faulty. Check the wiring for open-circuits or poor connections. Clean up direct earth connections, removing all traces of corrosion and remake the joint. Apply petroleum jelly to the joint to prevent future corrosion.

Tracing a short-circuit

● A short-circuit occurs where current shorts to earth (ground) bypassing the circuit components. This usually results in a blown fuse.

● A short-circuit is most likely to occur where the insulation has worn through due to wiring chafing on a component, allowing a direct path to earth (ground) on the frame.

1 Remove any bodypanels necessary to access the circuit wiring.
2 Check that all electrical switches in the circuit are OFF, then remove the circuit fuse and connect a test light, buzzer or voltmeter (set to the dc scale) across the fuse terminals. No voltage should be shown.
3 Move the wiring from side to side whilst observing the test light or meter. When the test light comes on, buzzer sounds or meter shows voltage, you have found the cause of the short. It will usually shown up as damaged or burned insulation.
4 Note that the same test can be performed on each component in the circuit, even the switch.

A

ABS (Anti-lock braking system) A system, usually electronically controlled, that senses incipient wheel lockup during braking and relieves hydraulic pressure at wheel which is about to skid.
Aftermarket Components suitable for the motorcycle, but not produced by the motorcycle manufacturer.
Allen key A hexagonal wrench which fits into a recessed hexagonal hole.
Alternating current (ac) Current produced by an alternator. Requires converting to direct current by a rectifier for charging purposes.
Alternator Converts mechanical energy from the engine into electrical energy to charge the battery and power the electrical system.
Ampere (amp) A unit of measurement for the flow of electrical current. Current = Volts ÷ Ohms.
Ampere-hour (Ah) Measure of battery capacity.
Angle-tightening A torque expressed in degrees. Often follows a conventional tightening torque for cylinder head or main bearing fasteners **(see illustration)**.

Angle-tightening cylinder head bolts

Antifreeze A substance (usually ethylene glycol) mixed with water, and added to the cooling system, to prevent freezing of the coolant in winter. Antifreeze also contains chemicals to inhibit corrosion and the formation of rust and other deposits that would tend to clog the radiator and coolant passages and reduce cooling efficiency.
Anti-dive System attached to the fork lower leg (slider) to prevent fork dive when braking hard.
Anti-seize compound A coating that reduces the risk of seizing on fasteners that are subjected to high temperatures, such as exhaust clamp bolts and nuts.
API American Petroleum Institute. A quality standard for 4-stroke motor oils.
Asbestos A natural fibrous mineral with great heat resistance, commonly used in the composition of brake friction materials. Asbestos is a health hazard and the dust created by brake systems should never be inhaled or ingested.
ATF Automatic Transmission Fluid. Often used in front forks.
ATU Automatic Timing Unit. Mechanical device for advancing the ignition timing on early engines.
ATV All Terrain Vehicle. Often called a Quad.
Axial play Side-to-side movement.
Axle A shaft on which a wheel revolves. Also known as a spindle.

B

Backlash The amount of movement between meshed components when one component is held still. Usually applies to gear teeth.
Ball bearing A bearing consisting of a hardened inner and outer race with hardened steel balls between the two races.
Bearings Used between two working surfaces to prevent wear of the components and a build-up of heat. Four types of bearing are commonly used on motorcycles: plain shell bearings, ball bearings, tapered roller bearings and needle roller bearings.
Bevel gears Used to turn the drive through 90°. Typical applications are shaft final drive and camshaft drive **(see illustration)**.

Bevel gears are used to turn the drive through 90°

BHP Brake Horsepower. The British measurement for engine power output. Power output is now usually expressed in kilowatts (kW).
Bias-belted tyre Similar construction to radial tyre, but with outer belt running at an angle to the wheel rim.
Big-end bearing The bearing in the end of the connecting rod that's attached to the crankshaft.
Bleeding The process of removing air from an hydraulic system via a bleed nipple or bleed screw.
Bottom-end A description of an engine's crankcase components and all components contained there-in.
BTDC Before Top Dead Centre in terms of piston position. Ignition timing is often expressed in terms of degrees or millimetres BTDC.
Bush A cylindrical metal or rubber component used between two moving parts.
Burr Rough edge left on a component after machining or as a result of excessive wear.

C

Cam chain The chain which takes drive from the crankshaft to the camshaft(s).
Canister The main component in an evaporative emission control system (California market only); contains activated charcoal granules to trap vapours from the fuel system rather than allowing them to vent to the atmosphere.
Castellated Resembling the parapets along the top of a castle wall. For example, a castellated wheel axle or spindle nut.
Catalytic converter A device in the exhaust system of some machines which converts certain pollutants in the exhaust gases into less harmful substances.
Charging system Description of the components which charge the battery, ie the alternator, rectifier and regulator.
Circlip A ring-shaped clip used to prevent endwise movement of cylindrical parts and shafts. An internal circlip is installed in a groove in a housing; an external circlip fits into a groove on the outside of a cylindrical piece such as a shaft. Also known as a snap-ring.
Clearance The amount of space between two parts. For example, between a piston and a cylinder, between a bearing and a journal, etc.
Coil spring A spiral of elastic steel found in various sizes throughout a vehicle, for example as a springing medium in the suspension and in the valve train.
Compression Reduction in volume, and increase in pressure and temperature, of a gas, caused by squeezing it into a smaller space.
Compression damping Controls the speed the suspension compresses when hitting a bump.
Compression ratio The relationship between cylinder volume when the piston is at top dead centre and cylinder volume when the piston is at bottom dead centre.
Continuity The uninterrupted path in the flow of electricity. Little or no measurable resistance.
Continuity tester Self-powered bleeper or test light which indicates continuity.
Cp Candlepower. Bulb rating commonly found on US motorcycles.
Crossply tyre Tyre plies arranged in a criss-cross pattern. Usually four or six plies used, hence 4PR or 6PR in tyre size codes.
Cush drive Rubber damper segments fitted between the rear wheel and final drive sprocket to absorb transmission shocks **(see illustration)**.

Cush drive rubbers dampen out transmission shocks

D

Degree disc Calibrated disc for measuring piston position. Expressed in degrees.
Dial gauge Clock-type gauge with adapters for measuring runout and piston position. Expressed in mm or inches.
Diaphragm The rubber membrane in a master cylinder or carburettor which seals the upper chamber.
Diaphragm spring A single sprung plate often used in clutches.
Direct current (dc) Current produced by a dc generator.

Decarbonisation The process of removing carbon deposits - typically from the combustion chamber, valves and exhaust port/system.

Detonation Destructive and damaging explosion of fuel/air mixture in combustion chamber instead of controlled burning.

Diode An electrical valve which only allows current to flow in one direction. Commonly used in rectifiers and starter interlock systems.

Disc valve (or rotary valve) A induction system used on some two-stroke engines.

Double-overhead camshaft (DOHC) An engine that uses two overhead camshafts, one for the intake valves and one for the exhaust valves.

Drivebelt A toothed belt used to transmit drive to the rear wheel on some motorcycles. A drivebelt has also been used to drive the camshafts. Drivebelts are usually made of Kevlar.

Driveshaft Any shaft used to transmit motion. Commonly used when referring to the final driveshaft on shaft drive motorcycles.

E

Earth return The return path of an electrical circuit, utilising the motorcycle's frame.

ECU (Electronic Control Unit) A computer which controls (for instance) an ignition system, or an anti-lock braking system.

EGO Exhaust Gas Oxygen sensor. Sometimes called a Lambda sensor.

Electrolyte The fluid in a lead-acid battery.

EMS (Engine Management System) A computer controlled system which manages the fuel injection and the ignition systems in an integrated fashion.

Endfloat The amount of lengthways movement between two parts. As applied to a crankshaft, the distance that the crankshaft can move side-to-side in the crankcase.

Endless chain A chain having no joining link. Common use for cam chains and final drive chains.

EP (Extreme Pressure) Oil type used in locations where high loads are applied, such as between gear teeth.

Evaporative emission control system Describes a charcoal filled canister which stores fuel vapours from the tank rather than allowing them to vent to the atmosphere. Usually only fitted to California models and referred to as an EVAP system.

Expansion chamber Section of two-stroke engine exhaust system so designed to improve engine efficiency and boost power.

F

Feeler blade or gauge A thin strip or blade of hardened steel, ground to an exact thickness, used to check or measure clearances between parts.

Final drive Description of the drive from the transmission to the rear wheel. Usually by chain or shaft, but sometimes by belt.

Firing order The order in which the engine cylinders fire, or deliver their power strokes, beginning with the number one cylinder.

Flooding Term used to describe a high fuel level in the carburettor float chambers, leading to fuel overflow. Also refers to excess fuel in the combustion chamber due to incorrect starting technique.

Free length The no-load state of a component when measured. Clutch, valve and fork spring lengths are measured at rest, without any preload.

Freeplay The amount of travel before any action takes place. The looseness in a linkage, or an assembly of parts, between the initial application of force and actual movement. For example, the distance the rear brake pedal moves before the rear brake is actuated.

Fuel injection The fuel/air mixture is metered electronically and directed into the engine intake ports (indirect injection) or into the cylinders (direct injection). Sensors supply information on engine speed and conditions.

Fuel/air mixture The charge of fuel and air going into the engine. See **Stoichiometric ratio**.

Fuse An electrical device which protects a circuit against accidental overload. The typical fuse contains a soft piece of metal which is calibrated to melt at a predetermined current flow (expressed as amps) and break the circuit.

G

Gap The distance the spark must travel in jumping from the centre electrode to the side electrode in a spark plug. Also refers to the distance between the ignition rotor and the pickup coil in an electronic ignition system.

Gasket Any thin, soft material - usually cork, cardboard, asbestos or soft metal - installed between two metal surfaces to ensure a good seal. For instance, the cylinder head gasket seals the joint between the block and the cylinder head.

Gauge An instrument panel display used to monitor engine conditions. A gauge with a movable pointer on a dial or a fixed scale is an analogue gauge. A gauge with a numerical readout is called a digital gauge.

Gear ratios The drive ratio of a pair of gears in a gearbox, calculated on their number of teeth.

Glaze-busting see **Honing**

Grinding Process for renovating the valve face and valve seat contact area in the cylinder head.

Gudgeon pin The shaft which connects the connecting rod small-end with the piston. Often called a piston pin or wrist pin.

H

Helical gears Gear teeth are slightly curved and produce less gear noise that straight-cut gears. Often used for primary drives.

Installing a Helicoil thread insert in a cylinder head

Helicoil A thread insert repair system. Commonly used as a repair for stripped spark plug threads (**see illustration**).

Honing A process used to break down the glaze on a cylinder bore (also called glaze-busting). Can also be carried out to roughen a rebored cylinder to aid ring bedding-in.

HT (High Tension) Description of the electrical circuit from the secondary winding of the ignition coil to the spark plug.

Hydraulic A liquid filled system used to transmit pressure from one component to another. Common uses on motorcycles are brakes and clutches.

Hydrometer An instrument for measuring the specific gravity of a lead-acid battery.

Hygroscopic Water absorbing. In motorcycle applications, braking efficiency will be reduced if DOT 3 or 4 hydraulic fluid absorbs water from the air - care must be taken to keep new brake fluid in tightly sealed containers.

I

lbf ft Pounds-force feet. An imperial unit of torque. Sometimes written as ft-lbs.

lbf in Pound-force inch. An imperial unit of torque, applied to components where a very low torque is required. Sometimes written as in-lbs.

IC Abbreviation for Integrated Circuit.

Ignition advance Means of increasing the timing of the spark at higher engine speeds. Done by mechanical means (ATU) on early engines or electronically by the ignition control unit on later engines.

Ignition timing The moment at which the spark plug fires, expressed in the number of crankshaft degrees before the piston reaches the top of its stroke, or in the number of millimetres before the piston reaches the top of its stroke.

Infinity (∞) Description of an open-circuit electrical state, where no continuity exists.

Inverted forks (upside down forks) The sliders or lower legs are held in the yokes and the fork tubes or stanchions are connected to the wheel axle (spindle). Less unsprung weight and stiffer construction than conventional forks.

J

JASO Quality standard for 2-stroke oils.

Joule The unit of electrical energy.

Journal The bearing surface of a shaft.

K

Kickstart Mechanical means of turning the engine over for starting purposes. Only usually fitted to mopeds, small capacity motorcycles and off-road motorcycles.

Kill switch Handebar-mounted switch for emergency ignition cut-out. Cuts the ignition circuit on all models, and additionally prevent starter motor operation on others.

km Symbol for kilometre.

kmh Abbreviation for kilometres per hour.

L

Lambda (λ) sensor A sensor fitted in the exhaust system to measure the exhaust gas oxygen content (excess air factor).

Lapping see **Grinding**.
LCD Abbreviation for Liquid Crystal Display.
LED Abbreviation for Light Emitting Diode.
Liner A steel cylinder liner inserted in a aluminium alloy cylinder block.
Locknut A nut used to lock an adjustment nut, or other threaded component, in place.
Lockstops The lugs on the lower triple clamp (yoke) which abut those on the frame, preventing handlebar-to-fuel tank contact.
Lockwasher A form of washer designed to prevent an attaching nut from working loose.
LT Low Tension Description of the electrical circuit from the power supply to the primary winding of the ignition coil.

M

Main bearings The bearings between the crankshaft and crankcase.
Maintenance-free (MF) battery A sealed battery which cannot be topped up.
Manometer Mercury-filled calibrated tubes used to measure intake tract vacuum. Used to synchronise carburettors on multi-cylinder engines.
Micrometer A precision measuring instrument that measures component outside diameters **(see illustration)**.

Tappet shims are measured with a micrometer

MON (Motor Octane Number) A measure of a fuel's resistance to knock.
Monograde oil An oil with a single viscosity, eg SAE80W.
Monoshock A single suspension unit linking the swingarm or suspension linkage to the frame.
mph Abbreviation for miles per hour.
Multigrade oil Having a wide viscosity range (eg 10W40). The W stands for Winter, thus the viscosity ranges from SAE10 when cold to SAE40 when hot.
Multimeter An electrical test instrument with the capability to measure voltage, current and resistance. Some meters also incorporate a continuity tester and buzzer.

N

Needle roller bearing Inner race of caged needle rollers and hardened outer race. Examples of uncaged needle rollers can be found on some engines. Commonly used in rear suspension applications and in two-stroke engines.
Nm Newton metres.
NOx Oxides of Nitrogen. A common toxic pollutant emitted by petrol engines at higher temperatures.

O

Octane The measure of a fuel's resistance to knock.
OE (Original Equipment) Relates to components fitted to a motorcycle as standard or replacement parts supplied by the motorcycle manufacturer.
Ohm The unit of electrical resistance. Ohms = Volts ÷ Current.
Ohmmeter An instrument for measuring electrical resistance.
Oil cooler System for diverting engine oil outside of the engine to a radiator for cooling purposes.
Oil injection A system of two-stroke engine lubrication where oil is pump-fed to the engine in accordance with throttle position.
Open-circuit An electrical condition where there is a break in the flow of electricity - no continuity (high resistance).
O-ring A type of sealing ring made of a special rubber-like material; in use, the O-ring is compressed into a groove to provide the sealing action.
Oversize (OS) Term used for piston and ring size options fitted to a rebored cylinder.
Overhead cam (sohc) engine An engine with single camshaft located on top of the cylinder head.
Overhead valve (ohv) engine An engine with the valves located in the cylinder head, but with the camshaft located in the engine block or crankcase.
Oxygen sensor A device installed in the exhaust system which senses the oxygen content in the exhaust and converts this information into an electric current. Also called a Lambda sensor.

P

Plastigauge A thin strip of plastic thread, available in different sizes, used for measuring clearances. For example, a strip of Plastigauge is laid across a bearing journal. The parts are assembled and dismantled; the width of the crushed strip indicates the clearance between journal and bearing.
Polarity Either negative or positive earth (ground), determined by which battery lead is connected to the frame (earth return). Modern motorcycles are usually negative earth.
Pre-ignition A situation where the fuel/air mixture ignites before the spark plug fires. Often due to a hot spot in the combustion chamber caused by carbon build-up. Engine has a tendency to 'run-on'.
Pre-load (suspension) The amount a spring is compressed when in the unloaded state. Preload can be applied by gas, spacer or mechanical adjuster.
Premix The method of engine lubrication on older two-stroke engines. Engine oil is mixed with the petrol in the fuel tank in a specific ratio. The fuel/oil mix is sometimes referred to as "petroil".
Primary drive Description of the drive from the crankshaft to the clutch. Usually by gear or chain.
PS Pfedestärke - a German interpretation of BHP.
PSI Pounds-force per square inch. Imperial measurement of tyre pressure and cylinder pressure measurement.
PTFE Polytetrafluroethylene. A low friction substance.

Pulse secondary air injection system A process of promoting the burning of excess fuel present in the exhaust gases by routing fresh air into the exhaust ports.

Q

Quartz halogen bulb Tungsten filament surrounded by a halogen gas. Typically used for the headlight **(see illustration)**.

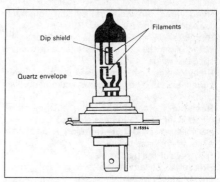

Quartz halogen headlight bulb construction

R

Rack-and-pinion A pinion gear on the end of a shaft that mates with a rack (think of a geared wheel opened up and laid flat). Sometimes used in clutch operating systems.
Radial play Up and down movement about a shaft.
Radial ply tyres Tyre plies run across the tyre (from bead to bead) and around the circumference of the tyre. Less resistant to tread distortion than other tyre types.
Radiator A liquid-to-air heat transfer device designed to reduce the temperature of the coolant in a liquid cooled engine.
Rake A feature of steering geometry - the angle of the steering head in relation to the vertical **(see illustration)**.

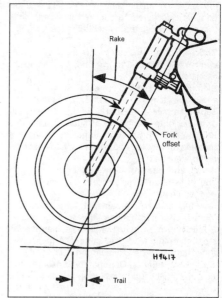

Steering geometry

Rebore Providing a new working surface to the cylinder bore by boring out the old surface. Necessitates the use of oversize piston and rings.

Rebound damping A means of controlling the oscillation of a suspension unit spring after it has been compressed. Resists the spring's natural tendency to bounce back after being compressed.

Rectifier Device for converting the ac output of an alternator into dc for battery charging.

Reed valve An induction system commonly used on two-stroke engines.

Regulator Device for maintaining the charging voltage from the generator or alternator within a specified range.

Relay A electrical device used to switch heavy current on and off by using a low current auxiliary circuit.

Resistance Measured in ohms. An electrical component's ability to pass electrical current.

RON (Research Octane Number) A measure of a fuel's resistance to knock.

rpm revolutions per minute.

Runout The amount of wobble (in-and-out movement) of a wheel or shaft as it's rotated. The amount a shaft rotates 'out-of-true'. The out-of-round condition of a rotating part.

S

SAE (Society of Automotive Engineers) A standard for the viscosity of a fluid.

Sealant A liquid or paste used to prevent leakage at a joint. Sometimes used in conjunction with a gasket.

Service limit Term for the point where a component is no longer useable and must be renewed.

Shaft drive A method of transmitting drive from the transmission to the rear wheel.

Shell bearings Plain bearings consisting of two shell halves. Most often used as big-end and main bearings in a four-stroke engine. Often called bearing inserts.

Shim Thin spacer, commonly used to adjust the clearance or relative positions between two parts. For example, shims inserted into or under tappets or followers to control valve clearances. Clearance is adjusted by changing the thickness of the shim.

Short-circuit An electrical condition where current shorts to earth (ground) bypassing the circuit components.

Skimming Process to correct warpage or repair a damaged surface, eg on brake discs or drums.

Slide-hammer A special puller that screws into or hooks onto a component such as a shaft or bearing; a heavy sliding handle on the shaft bottoms against the end of the shaft to knock the component free.

Small-end bearing The bearing in the upper end of the connecting rod at its joint with the gudgeon pin.

Spalling Damage to camshaft lobes or bearing journals shown as pitting of the working surface.

Specific gravity (SG) The state of charge of the electrolyte in a lead-acid battery. A measure of the electrolyte's density compared with water.

Straight-cut gears Common type gear used on gearbox shafts and for oil pump and water pump drives.

Stanchion The inner sliding part of the front forks, held by the yokes. Often called a fork tube.

Stoichiometric ratio The optimum chemical air/fuel ratio for a petrol engine, said to be 14.7 parts of air to 1 part of fuel.

Sulphuric acid The liquid (electrolyte) used in a lead-acid battery. Poisonous and extremely corrosive.

Surface grinding (lapping) Process to correct a warped gasket face, commonly used on cylinder heads.

T

Tapered-roller bearing Tapered inner race of caged needle rollers and separate tapered outer race. Examples of taper roller bearings can be found on steering heads.

Tappet A cylindrical component which transmits motion from the cam to the valve stem, either directly or via a pushrod and rocker arm. Also called a cam follower.

TCS Traction Control System. An electronically-controlled system which senses wheel spin and reduces engine speed accordingly.

TDC Top Dead Centre denotes that the piston is at its highest point in the cylinder.

Thread-locking compound Solution applied to fastener threads to prevent slackening. Select type to suit application.

Thrust washer A washer positioned between two moving components on a shaft. For example, between gear pinions on gearshaft.

Timing chain See **Cam Chain**.

Timing light Stroboscopic lamp for carrying out ignition timing checks with the engine running.

Top-end A description of an engine's cylinder block, head and valve gear components.

Torque Turning or twisting force about a shaft.

Torque setting A prescribed tightness specified by the motorcycle manufacturer to ensure that the bolt or nut is secured correctly. Undertightening can result in the bolt or nut coming loose or a surface not being sealed. Overtightening can result in stripped threads, distortion or damage to the component being retained.

Torx key A six-point wrench.

Tracer A stripe of a second colour applied to a wire insulator to distinguish that wire from another one with the same colour insulator. For example, Br/W is often used to denote a brown insulator with a white tracer.

Trail A feature of steering geometry. Distance from the steering head axis to the tyre's central contact point.

Triple clamps The cast components which extend from the steering head and support the fork stanchions or tubes. Often called fork yokes.

Turbocharger A centrifugal device, driven by exhaust gases, that pressurises the intake air. Normally used to increase the power output from a given engine displacement.

TWI Abbreviation for Tyre Wear Indicator. Indicates the location of the tread depth indicator bars on tyres.

U

Universal joint or U-joint (UJ) A double-pivoted connection for transmitting power from a driving to a driven shaft through an angle. Typically found in shaft drive assemblies.

Unsprung weight Anything not supported by the bike's suspension (ie the wheel, tyres, brakes, final drive and bottom (moving) part of the suspension).

V

Vacuum gauges Clock-type gauges for measuring intake tract vacuum. Used for carburettor synchronisation on multi-cylinder engines.

Valve A device through which the flow of liquid, gas or vacuum may be stopped, started or regulated by a moveable part that opens, shuts or partially obstructs one or more ports or passageways. The intake and exhaust valves in the cylinder head are of the poppet type.

Valve clearance The clearance between the valve tip (the end of the valve stem) and the rocker arm or tappet/follower. The valve clearance is measured when the valve is closed. The correct clearance is important - if too small the valve won't close fully and will burn out, whereas if too large noisy operation will result.

Valve lift The amount a valve is lifted off its seat by the camshaft lobe.

Valve timing The exact setting for the opening and closing of the valves in relation to piston position.

Vernier caliper A precision measuring instrument that measures inside and outside dimensions. Not quite as accurate as a micrometer, but more convenient.

VIN Vehicle Identification Number. Term for the bike's engine and frame numbers.

Viscosity The thickness of a liquid or its resistance to flow.

Volt A unit for expressing electrical "pressure" in a circuit. Volts = current x ohms.

W

Water pump A mechanically-driven device for moving coolant around the engine.

Watt A unit for expressing electrical power. Watts = volts x current.

Wear limit see **Service limit**

Wet liner A liquid-cooled engine design where the pistons run in liners which are directly surrounded by coolant **(see illustration)**.

Wet liner arrangement

Wheelbase Distance from the centre of the front wheel to the centre of the rear wheel.

Wiring harness or loom Describes the electrical wires running the length of the motorcycle and enclosed in tape or plastic sheathing. Wiring coming off the main harness is usually referred to as a sub harness.

Woodruff key A key of semi-circular or square section used to locate a gear to a shaft. Often used to locate the alternator rotor on the crankshaft.

Wrist pin Another name for gudgeon or piston pin.

Note: *References throughout this index are in the form - "Chapter number" • "Page number"*

Haynes Motorcycle Manuals – The Complete List

Title	Book No
APRILIA RSV1000 Mille (98 - 03)	♦ 4255
BMW 2-valve Twins (70 - 96)	♦ 0249
BMW K100 & 75 2-valve Models (83 - 96)	♦ 1373
BMW R850, 1100 & 1150 4-valve Twins (93 - 04)	♦ 3466
BSA Bantam (48 - 71)	0117
BSA Unit Singles (58 - 72)	0127
BSA Pre-unit Singles (54 - 61)	0326
BSA A7 & A10 Twins (47 - 62)	0121
BSA A50 & A65 Twins (62 - 73)	0155
DUCATI MK III & Desmo Singles (69 - 76)	◊ 0445
Ducati 600, 620, 750 and 900 2-valve V-Twins (91 - 05)	♦ 3290
Ducati 748, 916 & 996 4-valve V-Twins (94 - 01)	♦ 3756
GILERA Runner, DNA, Ice & SKP/Stalker (97 - 04)	4163
HARLEY-DAVIDSON Sportsters (70 - 03)	♦ 2534
Harley-Davidson Shovelhead and Evolution Big Twins (70 - 99)	2536
Harley-Davidson Twin Cam 88 (99 - 03)	♦ 2478
HONDA NB, ND, NP & NS50 Melody (81 - 85)	◊ 0622
Honda NE/NB50 Vision & SA50 Vision Met-in (85 - 95)	◊ 1278
Honda MB, MBX, MT & MTX50 (80 - 93)	0731
Honda C50, C70 & C90 (67 - 99)	0324
Honda XR80/100R & CRF80/100F (85 - 04)	2218
Honda XL/XR 80, 100, 125, 185 & 200 2-valve Models (78 - 87)	0566
Honda H100 & H100S Singles (80 - 92)	◊ 0734
Honda CB/CD125T & CM125C Twins (77 - 88)	◊ 0571
Honda CG125 (76 - 05)	◊ 0433
Honda NS125 (86 - 93)	◊ 3056
Honda MBX/MTX125 & MTX200 (83 - 93)	◊ 1132
Honda CD/CM185 200T & CM250C 2-valve Twins (77 - 85)	◊ 0572
Honda XL/XR 250 & 500 (78 - 84)	0567
Honda XR250L, XR250R & XR400R (86 - 03)	2219
Honda CB250 & CB400N Super Dreams (78 - 84)	◊ 0540
Honda CR Motocross Bikes (86 - 01)	2222
Honda CBR400RR Fours (88 - 99)	◊ ♦ 3552
Honda VFR400 (NC30) & RVF400 (NC35) V-Fours (89 - 98)	◊ ♦ 3496
Honda CB500 (93 - 01)	◊ ♦ 3753
Honda CB400 & CB550 Fours (73 - 77)	0262
Honda CX/GL500 & 650 V-Twins (78 - 86)	0442
Honda CBX550 Four (82 - 86)	◊ 0940
Honda XL600R & XR600R (83 - 00)	2183
Honda XL600/650V Transalp & XRV750 Africa Twin (87 - 02)	♦ 3919
Honda CBR600F1 & 1000F Fours (87 - 96)	♦ 1730
Honda CBR600F2 & F3 Fours (91 - 98)	♦ 2070
Honda CBR600F4 (99 - 02)	♦ 3911
Honda CB600F Hornet (98 - 02)	◊ ♦ 3915
Honda CB650 sohc Fours (78 - 84)	0665
Honda NTV600 Revere, NTV650 and NT650V Deauville (88 - 01)	◊ ♦ 3243
Honda Shadow VT600 & 750 (USA) (88 - 03)	2312
Honda CB750 sohc Four (69 - 79)	0131
Honda V45/65 Sabre & Magna (82 - 88)	0820
Honda VFR750 & 700 V-Fours (86 - 97)	♦ 2101
Honda VFR800 V-Fours (97 - 01)	♦ 3703
Honda VFR800 V-Tec V-Fours (02 - 05)	♦ 4196
Honda CB750 & CB900 dohc Fours (78 - 84)	0535
Honda VTR1000 (FireStorm, Super Hawk) & XL1000V (Varadero) (97 - 00)	♦ 3744
Honda CBR900RR FireBlade (92 - 99)	♦ 2161
Honda CBR900RR FireBlade (00 - 03)	♦ 4060
Honda CBR1100XX Super Blackbird (97 - 02)	♦ 3901
Honda ST1100 Pan European V-Fours (90 - 01)	♦ 3384
Honda Shadow VT1100 (USA) (85 - 98)	2313
Honda GL1000 Gold Wing (75 - 79)	0309
Honda GL1100 Gold Wing (79 - 81)	0669

Title	Book No
Honda Gold Wing 1200 (USA) (84 - 87)	2199
Honda Gold Wing 1500 (USA) (88 - 00)	2225
KAWASAKI AE/AR 50 & 80 (81 - 95)	1007
Kawasaki KC, KE & KH100 (75 - 99)	1371
Kawasaki KMX125 & 200 (86 - 02)	◊ 3046
Kawasaki 250, 350 & 400 Triples (72 - 79)	0134
Kawasaki 400 & 440 Twins (74 - 81)	0281
Kawasaki 400, 500 & 550 Fours (79 - 91)	0910
Kawasaki EN450 & 500 Twins (Ltd/Vulcan) (85 - 04)	2053
Kawasaki EX & ER500 (GPZ500S & ER-5) Twins (87 - 99)	♦ 2052
Kawasaki ZX600 (Ninja ZX-6, ZZ-R600) Fours (90 - 00)	♦ 2146
Kawasaki ZX-6R Ninja Fours (95 - 02)	♦ 3541
Kawasaki ZX600 (GPZ600R, GPX600R, Ninja 600R & RX) & ZX750 (GPX750R, Ninja 750R)	♦ 1780
Kawasaki 650 Four (76 - 78)	0373
Kawasaki Vulcan 700/750 & 800 (85 - 04)	♦ 2457
Kawasaki 750 Air-cooled Fours (80 - 91)	0574
Kawasaki ZR550 & 750 Zephyr Fours (90 - 97)	♦ 3382
Kawasaki ZX750 (Ninja ZX-7 & ZXR750) Fours (89 - 96)	♦ 2054
Kawasaki Ninja ZX-7R & ZX-9R (94 - 04)	♦ 3721
Kawasaki 900 & 1000 Fours (73 - 77)	0222
Kawasaki ZX900, 1000 & 1100 Liquid-cooled Fours (83 - 97)	♦ 1681
MOTO GUZZI 750, 850 & 1000 V-Twins (74 - 78)	0339
MZ ETZ Models (81 - 95)	◊ 1680
NORTON 500, 600, 650 & 750 Twins (57 - 70)	0187
Norton Commando (68 - 77)	0125
PEUGEOT Speedfight, Trekker & Vivacity Scooters (96 - 05)	◊ 3920
PIAGGIO (Vespa) Scooters (91 - 03)	◊ 3492
SUZUKI GT, ZR & TS50 (77 - 90)	◊ 0799
Suzuki TS50X (84 - 00)	◊ 1599
Suzuki 100, 125, 185 & 250 Air-cooled Trail bikes (79 - 89)	◊ 0797
Suzuki GP100 & 125 Singles (78 - 93)	◊ 0576
Suzuki GS, GN, GZ & DR125 Singles (82 - 05)	◊ 0888
Suzuki 250 & 350 Twins (68 - 78)	0120
Suzuki GT250X7, GT200X5 & SB200 Twins (78 - 83)	◊ 0469
Suzuki GS/GSX250, 400 & 450 Twins (79 - 85)	0736
Suzuki GS500 Twin (89 - 02)	♦ 3238
Suzuki GS550 (77 - 82) & GS750 Fours (76 - 79)	0363
Suzuki GS/GSX550 4-valve Fours (83 - 88)	1133
Suzuki SV650 (99 - 02)	♦ 3912
Suzuki GSX-R600 & 750 (96 - 00)	♦ 3553
Suzuki GSX-R600 (01 - 02), GSX-R750 (00 - 02) & GSX-R1000 (01 - 02)	♦ 3986
Suzuki GSF600 & 1200 Bandit Fours (95 - 04)	♦ 3367
Suzuki GS850 Fours (78 - 88)	0536
Suzuki GS1000 Four (77 - 79)	0484
Suzuki GSX-R750, GSX-R1100 (85 - 92), GSX600F, GSX750F, GSX1100F (Katana) Fours	♦ 2055
Suzuki GSX600/750F & GSX750 (98 - 02)	♦ 3987
Suzuki GS/GSX1000, 1100 & 1150 4-valve Fours (79 - 88)	0737
Suzuki TL1000S/R & DL1000 V-Strom (97 - 04)	♦ 4083
Suzuki GSX1300R Hayabusa (99 - 04)	♦ 4184
TRIUMPH Bonneville (01 - 05)	♦ 4364
Triumph Tiger Cub & Terrier (52 - 68)	0414
Triumph 350 & 500 Unit Twins (58 - 73)	0137
Triumph Pre-Unit Twins (47 - 62)	0251
Triumph 650 & 750 2-valve Unit Twins (63 - 83)	0122
Triumph Trident & BSA Rocket 3 (69 - 75)	0136
Triumph Fuel Injected Triples (97 - 00)	♦ 3755
Triumph Triples & Fours (carburettor engines) (91 - 99)	♦ 2162
VESPA P/PX125, 150 & 200 Scooters (78 - 03)	0707
Vespa Scooters (59 - 78)	0126
YAMAHA DT50 & 80 Trail Bikes (78 - 95)	◊ 0800
Yamaha T50 & 80 Townmate (83 - 95)	◊ 1247
Yamaha YB100 Singles (73 - 91)	◊ 0474

Title	Book No
Yamaha RS/RXS100 & 125 Singles (74 - 95)	0331
Yamaha RD & DT125LC (82 - 87)	◊ 0887
Yamaha TZR125 (87 - 93) & DT125R (88 - 02)	◊ 1655
Yamaha TY50, 80, 125 & 175 (74 - 84)	◊ 0464
Yamaha XT & SR125 (82 - 02)	◊ 1021
Yamaha Trail Bikes (81 - 00)	2350
Yamaha 250 & 350 Twins (70 - 79)	0040
Yamaha XS250, 360 & 400 sohc Twins (75 - 84)	0378
Yamaha RD250 & 350LC Twins (80 - 82)	0803
Yamaha RD350 YPVS Twins (83 - 95)	1158
Yamaha RD400 Twin (75 - 79)	0333
Yamaha XT, TT & SR500 Singles (75 - 83)	0342
Yamaha XZ550 Vision V-Twins (82 - 85)	0821
Yamaha FJ, FZ, XJ & YX600 Radian (84 - 92)	2100
Yamaha XJ600S (Diversion, Seca II) & XJ600N Fours (92 - 03)	♦ 2145
Yamaha YZF600R Thundercat & FZS600 Fazer (96 - 03)	♦ 3702
Yamaha YZF-R6 (98 - 02)	♦ 3900
Yamaha 650 Twins (70 - 83)	0341
Yamaha XJ650 & 750 Fours (80 - 84)	0738
Yamaha XS750 & 850 Triples (76 - 85)	0340
Yamaha TDM850, TRX850 & XTZ750 (89 - 99)	◊ ♦ 3540
Yamaha YZF750R & YZF1000R Thunderace (93 - 00)	♦ 3720
Yamaha FZR600, 750 & 1000 Fours (87 - 96)	♦ 2056
Yamaha XV (Virago) V-Twins (81 - 03)	♦ 0802
Yamaha XVS650 & 1100 Drag Star/V-Star (97 - 05)	♦ 4195
Yamaha XJ900F Fours (83 - 94)	♦ 3239
Yamaha XJ900S Diversion (94 - 01)	♦ 3739
Yamaha YZF-R1 (98 - 03)	♦ 3754
Yamaha FZS1000 Fazer (01 - 05)	4287
Yamaha FJ1100 & 1200 Fours (84 - 96)	♦ 2057
Yamaha XJR1200 & 1300 (95 - 03)	♦ 3981
Yamaha V-Max (85 - 03)	♦ 4072
Yamaha Kodiak & Grizzly ATVs (93 - 05)	♦ 2567

ATVs

Title	Book No
HONDA ATC70, 90, 110, 185 & 200 (71 - 85)	0565
Honda Rancher, Recon & TRX250EX ATVs	2553
Honda TRX300 Shaft Drive ATVs (88 - 00)	2125
Honda TRX300EX & TRX400EX ATVs (93 - 04)	2318
Honda Foreman 400 and 450 ATVs (95 - 02)	2465
KAWASAKI Bayou 220/250/300 & Prairie 300 ATVs (86 - 03)	2351
POLARIS ATVs (85 - 97)	2302
Polaris ATVs (98 - 03)	2508
YAMAHA YFS200 Blaster ATV (88 - 02)	2317
Yamaha YFB250 Timberwolf ATVs (92 - 00)	2217
Yamaha YFM350 & YFM400 (ER and Big Bear) ATVs (87 - 03)	2126
Yamaha Banshee and Warrior ATVs (87 - 03)	2314

TECHBOOK SERIES

Title	Book No
ATV Basics	10450
Motorcycle Basics TechBook (2nd Edition)	3515
Motorcycle Electrical TechBook (3rd Edition)	3471
Motorcycle Fuel Systems TechBook	3514
Motorcycle Maintenance TechBook	4071
Motorcycle Modifying	4272
Motorcycle Workshop Practice TechBook (2nd Edition)	3470

GENERAL MANUALS

Title	Book No
Twist and Go (automatic transmission) Scooters Service and Repair Manual	4082

◊ = not available in the USA   ♦ = Superbike

The manuals on this page are available through good motorcycle dealers and accessory shops.
In case of difficulty, contact: **Haynes Publishing**
(UK) +44 1963 442030   (USA) +1 805 498 6703
(FR) +33 1 47 17 66 29   (SV) +46 18 124016
(Australia/New Zealand) +61 3 9763 8100